Immigration Worldwide

Immigration Worldwide

Policies, Practices, and Trends

Edited by

Uma A. Segal

Doreen Elliott

Nazneen S. Mayadas

OXFORD

UNIVERSITY PRESS

2010

OXFORD

UNIVERSITY PRESS

Oxford University Press, Inc., publishes works that further
Oxford University's objective of excellence
in research, scholarship, and education.

Oxford   New York
Auckland   Cape Town   Dar es Salaam   Hong Kong   Karachi
Kuala Lumpur   Madrid   Melbourne   Mexico City   Nairobi
New Delhi   Shanghai   Taipei   Toronto

With offices in
Argentina   Austria   Brazil   Chile   Czech Republic   France   Greece
Guatemala   Hungary   Italy   Japan   Poland   Portugal   Singapore
South Korea   Switzerland   Thailand   Turkey   Ukraine   Vietnam

Published by Oxford University Press, Inc.
198 Madison Avenue, New York, New York 10016

www.oup.com

Oxford is a registered trademark of Oxford University Press

Library of Congress Cataloging-in-Publication Data
Immigration worldwide : policies, practices, and trends / edited by
Uma A. Segal, Doreen Elliott, Nazneen S. Mayadas.
    p. cm
Includes bibliographical references and index.
ISBN 978-0-19-538813-8 (cloth : alk. paper)
1. Emigration and immigration—Government policy—Case studies.
2. Human beings—Migrations—Case studies.   3. Migrations of nations—Case studies.
4. Human capital—Case studies.   I. Segal, Uma Anand.
II. Elliott, Doreen.   III. Mayadas, Nazneen S. (Nazneen Sada)
JV6035.I465 2010
304.8—dc22
2009016952

9   8   7   6   5   4   3   2

Printed in the United States of America
on acid-free paper

To all who migrate from their homeland and to all who welcome them.

Civilization is the encouragement of differences.
Mohandas Karamchand Gandhi (1869–1948)

A man's homeland is wherever he prospers.
Aristophanes (450 BC–388 BC), *Plutus, 388 B.C.*

Preface

The focus of this volume is on the immigration experience of the world's approximately 200 million international migrants; this figure is equivalent to the population of Brazil, the fifth-largest country in the world. International migrants comprise one in 35 people or 3 percent of the world's population (GCIM, 2005:83). This book is organized around the exploration of the immigration process and takes an analytical look at the policies that determine a country's attitude toward immigrants, that is, their reception, settlement and progress toward economic self-sustainability within the host economy.

While this book is set in the context of human migration, it is specifically about immigration policies and practices of selected host countries, and offers two models for their study. The first is a model developed by Segal (2002), which forms the basis for country case studies. "The purpose of the case studies is to illustrate and clarify many theoretical mechanisms and to advance understanding of the impact of different migration policies" (Ozden & Schiff, 2007:2). The second is a model of policy analysis, which is used to analyze the case studies.

Model one is based on the rationale that the immigration experience begins long before the immigrant enters the host country, including reasons for emigration from the country of birth, through to settlement in the adopted country. The book is focused on immigration set in the broader context of human migration. Authors were invited to develop their chapters using this holistic view of the immigrant experience. Hence chapters consider broader issues of human migration as immigration policies are best understood against the backdrop of the total process of migration. The second model, set out in Chapter Two, follows the tradition of social policy analysis and provides an analytic system for each country study.

This book is primarily designed for practitioners, educators, and social policy analysts in the field of migration studies. Since the study of human migration is based on applied social science, the chapter authors represent the disciplines of social work, sociology, human geography, and political science, all of which contribute a particular perspective. The authors are scholars distinguished in their own disciplines and countries and are selected on the basis of previous publications in the field of immigration.

It is not an easy task to select countries for a specialized project such as this. The challenge is to make a determination of country inclusion, for all nations do, indeed, see immigrant flows.

The countries represented in this study reflect a coherent and well-defined rationale based on the following factors:

- **Representation of geographic regions**: The chapters consider selected countries representing all geographic regions at various levels of socioeconomic development.

- **Size of immigration flow** (Table P-1): Countries selected for inclusion represent countries with high, increasing, or low immigration inflows.
- **Trends in regional movements:** The African Union and the European Union present unique and changing patterns of immigration.

Clearly, the list of receiving countries included is not exhaustive. Table P-1 identifies countries that are included in one of three categories: (1) countries with large immigrant populations that are adapting policies and programs to either accommodate or curtail the flows, (2) nations beginning to see increases in immigration, or (3) countries with low immigration (United Nations, 2006).

Additional chapters on Africa and the European Union serve to provide overviews of migration in these areas: In the latter, country borders are easily and legally crossed, resulting in changes in the way in which human migration is perceived. In the former, political and cultural boundaries may not coincide and movements across them may not be readily regulated. Therefore, both of these areas are regarded as deserving special consideration because of the issues raised. To give an understanding of some of these issues in Africa, Nigeria, Ghana, and South Africa have been selected.

Historically, South America has experienced several immigration waves. Brazil has been included to illustrate this pattern, portraying a land that once had a large migration movement and is still exploring ways to integrate successive generations.

Political and economic conditions in Asian countries have led to the flight of both political and economic refugees into neighboring Asian countries. As such, included are developing countries, such as Thailand, India, Pakistan, and Taiwan, that continue to attract labor migrants and refugees from countries that are in an even less privileged position or are in poverty and political turmoil.

Developed countries such as the United States, the United Kingdom, Australia, New Zealand, Germany, and Canada, which have long had consistent immigrant flows, continue to maintain this pattern. However, because of support received from the European Union for the infrastructure of several developing countries and the opening of borders across Europe, nations such as Greece, Portugal, Ireland, Italy, Spain, and Poland are now also reporting substantial immigration movements, particularly of cross-national labor migrants and undocumented immigrants.

Israel, a major immigration country to Jewish persons from around the world as well as to non-Jewish migrants who enter for economic reasons, is included, as is Egypt, which has long been a country of immigration in the Middle East and currently receives refugees both from the Middle East and Africa. Some countries, such as China, Sweden, and Russia are included as these seek to attract professional and/or labor migrants to strengthen the political economy of the nation or to combat a declining population and a shortage in the labor force. Nations that are primarily emigrant or transit countries are not included in these chapters.

While acknowledging the importance of all migration movements experienced by nations

Table P-1. Countries Included in Studies

Highest immigrant populations	Increasing immigrant populations	Low or declining immigrant populations	Regional movements
United States	Greece	Egypt	African Union
Russian Federation	Ireland		European Union
Germany	Israel	Taiwan	
France	Poland	China	
Canada	New Zealand	South Africa	
India	Portugal	Ghana	
United Kingdom	Sweden	Nigeria	
Spain	Thailand	Brazil	
Australia			
Pakistan			

around the world, the editors have selected to specifically focus on immigration and the entry and settlement of people in countries other than those in which they were born. This volume is not a *compendium* but a *perspective* focused specifically on immigration in the broader context of human migration. The outcome is a rich and varied account of the state of the art of immigration issues and policies worldwide that includes consideration of some countries and policies not normally considered in a collection of such studies.

References

GCIM (2005) Migration in an interconnected world: New directions for action. Switzerland. Global Commission on International Migration available at http://www.gcim.org/attachements/gcim-complete-report-2005.pdf.

Özden, Ç. & M. Schiff, eds. (2007). *International Migration, Economic Development, and Policy.* New York: Palgrave Macmillan.

Segal, U.A. (2002). *A Framework for Immigration: Asians in the United States.* New York: Columbia University Press.

Acknowledgments

The editors most sincerely thank each of the distinguished authors of the chapters in this volume: their scholarship has added significantly to the interdisciplinary knowledge base on global immigration. We thank them for their patience and graciousness during the editorial process and their responsiveness and timely delivery of manuscripts. We are also grateful to all who have provided support services in the development of this book. Graduate research assistants at the University of Missouri–St Louis were instrumental at several critical stages. Maurita Mendelson undertook research to assist in identifying outstanding scholars who have made important contributions to the literature and research on immigration in their respective countries. Mary Ford's assistance in diligently reviewing manuscripts was superb, as was Jo Ellen La Rue's attention to detail regarding the formatting of the introductory materials. Tamara Peterson ensured that the final copy was consistent with Oxford University Press guidelines. Maria Bailey at the University of Texas at Arlington provided outstanding secretarial assistance whenever needed and her skilful work on the indexing is greatly appreciated. Their collective contributions have assisted considerably in the completion of this complex project. Thanks are due also to Mallory Jensen and to Nicholas Liu of Oxford University Press for their assistance at different stages in the manuscript review and publication preparation process. We are grateful to Padmapriya Ramalingam who coordinated the copy editing process with great patience and professionalism. Finally, we would like to acknowledge. Oxford University Press and especially Maura Roessner, for her faith in the value of this project: her tenacity in pursuit of academic rigor earned our thanks and respect, and her support and encouragement have been invaluable.

Contents

Contributors

Adejumoke Alice Afolayan, Ph.D.
Professor of Geography
University of Ibadan, Ibadan, Nigeria

Kylie Agllias
Lecturer in Social Work
University of Newcastle, New South Wales,
    Australia

Richard Bedford, Ph.D.
Professor of Population Geography
Director of the Population Studies Centre
University of Waikato, New Zealand

Pieter Bevelander, Ph.D.
Associate Professor at MIM, Malmö Institute of
    Migration, Diversity and Welfare
Senior Lecturer at the Department of IMER
Malmö University, Sweden

João Casqueira Cardoso, Ph.D., J.D.
Associate Professor
Coordinator of the Centre for Studies on Minorities
    (CENMIN)
University Fernando Pessoa and Ponte de Lima
    College, Portugal

Supang Chantavanich, Ph.D.
Professor of Sociology
Director, Asian Research Center for Migration,
Institute of Asian Studies
Chulalongkorn University, Thailand

Kim-wah Chung, Ph.D.
Assistant Professor
Department of Applied Social Sciences
Hong Kong Polytechnic University, Hong Kong

Betsy Cooper, M.S.
D.Phil. Candidate in Politics
Oxford University, UK

David Corkill, Ph.D.
Professor of Iberian Studies
Manchester Metropolitan University, UK

Zeila de Brito Fabri Demartini, Ph.D.
Research Director, Centro de Estudos Rurais e
    Urbanos (CERU/USP)
Professor, Methodist University of São Paulo
    (UMESP)
São Paulo, Brazil

Gail Desmond, M.S.W.
Ph.D. Student
Howard University, Washington, DC, USA

Doreen Elliott, Ph.D.
Professor of Social Work and Distinguished
    Teaching Professor
School of Social Work
The University of Texas at Arlington, USA

A. Essuman-Johnson, Ph.D.
Senior Lecturer in Political Science
University of Ghana, Ghana

Treasa Galvin, D. Phil
Senior lecturer in Sociology, University of Botswana
Research Associate, Sociology Department, Trinity
    College, Dublin, Ireland

Usha George, Ph.D.
Dean at the Faculty of Community Services
Ryerson University, Toronto, Canada

Mel Gray, Ph.D.
Professor of Social Work
Researcher in the Institute of Advanced Study for
    Humanity (IASH)
University of Newcastle, New South Wales,
    Australia

Aleksandra Grzymała-Kazłowska, Ph.D.
Assistant Professor
Insititue of Sociology, Warsaw University, Poland

Wenruo Hou, M.A.
Professor of Social Security at the School of
    Labor & Personnel
Renmin University, Beijing, China

Nathalie Huegler, M.A.
Ph.D. Student
London Metropolitan University, UK

Vladimir Iontsev, Ph.D.
Head of the Department of Population
Faculty of Economics
Moscow State "Lomonosov" University, Russia

Shireen S. Issa, M.S.
Program Manager
Aga Khan Development Network (AKDN), Pakistan

Irina Ivakhnyuk, Ph.D.
Senior Researcher and Deputy Director of the
    Department of Population
Faculty of Economics
Moscow State "Lomonosov" University, Russia

Ratchada Jayagupta, Ph.D.
National Project Coordinator (NPC)
Thailand Office for United Nations Inter-Agency
    Project on Human Trafficking in the Greater
    Mekong Sub-Region, Thailand

Adriana Kemp, Ph.D.
Associate Professor
Department of Sociology and Anthropology
Tel Aviv University, Israel

Joseph S. Lee, Ph.D.
Wen Say-ling Professor of Management
Vice President of National Central University,
    Taiwan

Karen Lyons, Ph.D.
Emeritus Professor of International Social Work
London Metropolitan University, UK

Brij Maharaj, Ph.D.
Professor and Discipline Chair (Geography)
University of KwaZulu-Natal
School of Environmental Studies, South Africa

Nazneen Sada Mayadas, D.S.W.
Professor Emerita
School of Social Work
The University of Texas at Arlington, USA

Ines Michalowski, Ph.D.
Senior Researcher
Social Science Research Center Berlin (WZB),
    Germany

Andrew Joseph Novak, J.D.
Law Clerk
U.S. Department of Labor, Washington,
    DC, USA

Marek Okólski, Ph.D.
Professor and Chair of Demography, Faculty of
    Economic Sciences, Warsaw University Professor
    at the Institute of Sociology, Warsaw School of
    Social Psychology, Poland

Jacques Poot, Ph.D.
Professor of Population Economics
University of Waikato, Hamilton,
    New Zealand

Ji Qi
Graduate Student
Department of Applied Social Sciences
Hong Kong Polytechnic University, Hong Kong

Rebeca Raijman, Ph.D.
Associate Professor
Department of Sociology and Anthropology
University of Haifa, Israel

Fariyal Ross-Sheriff, Ph.D.
Graduate Professor and the Director of Ph.D.
    Program in Social Work
Howard University, Washington, DC, USA

Ranabir Samaddar, Ph.D.
Director, Calcutta Research Group
Kolkata, India

Andrea Schmelz, Ph.D.
Researcher, Network Migration in Europe, Berlin
Instructor, Catholic University of Applied Sciences
Berlin, Germany

Uma A. Segal, Ph.D.
Professor and Director of the Baccalaureate Social
    Work program
School of Social Work
University of Missouri–St. Louis, USA

Svetlana Soboleva, Ph.D.
Chief Researcher and Deputy Head of the Social
    Problems Department

Institute of Economics and Industrial Engineering
Siberian Branch of the Russian Academy of
  Sciences, Novosibirsk, Russia

Will Somerville, M.Sc.
Senior Policy Analyst, Migration Policy Institute
  (MPI), Washington DC, USA
Senior Consultant at the Equality and Human
  Rights Commission (EHRC) and at the Prime
  Minister's Strategy Unit, London, UK

Anna Triandafyllidou, Ph.D.
Assistant Professor, Democritus University of
  Thrace, Greece
Senior Research Fellow, Hellenic Foundation
  for European and Foreign Policy
Athens, Greece

Ayman Zohry, Ph.D.
President, Egyptian Society for Migration Studies
Cairo, Egypt

PART I

Introduction

1

The Immigration Process

Uma A. Segal, Nazneen S. Mayadas, and Doreen Elliott

The phenomenon of immigration is neither novel nor recent, having been part of the human experience since time immemorial, with economics, politics, and religion, as well as a yen for exploration and adventure, fueling such movements. While migration may occur as a response to crises, it is also a concomitant search for opportunity, and the immigration experience begins not when immigrants arrive at a host country's borders, but long before, while they are still in their homelands. It is here that the impetus to leave the homeland arises, and it is from here that immigrants draw their resources—economic, social, and emotional—to undertake the greatest challenge of their lives. The process, starting with migration from the native place through adjustment to life in the country of adoption, is lengthy and complex, with the success of the immigrant dependent on the interplay of personal and environmental factors. Not all people of a country have both the desire and the wherewithal to migrate to a new land. Even in the presence of a wish to leave the country of birth and sufficient resources, the opportunity must be ripe.

The process of leaving the homeland is precipitated by a number of factors; likewise, *immigration*, the process of entering and settling

into a new country, is also influenced by several variables. Figure 1-1 presents a framework of the salient ingredients in immigration, regardless of the country of origin or destination, and presents a framework of these dimensions.

Salient Factors in Home Country

Conditions in Home Country

When conditions in a home country are satisfactory and meet physical, social, and emotional needs, the likelihood of leaving is minimal. Economic, political, or religious turbulence can cause dissatisfaction and result in mass migrations. For example, poor economic conditions, low income, and overcrowding in the home country often force individuals to seek opportunities elsewhere. As an illustration, from 1996 and well into 2003, Indonesia evidenced a prolonged economic crisis that continued to deepen, while news reports indicated that political corruption precluded any possibility of rapid recovery. Employment options for many Indonesians were increasingly limited, and legal and illegal migration out were high. International migration is driven by imbalances in supply and demand for labor that promotes

3

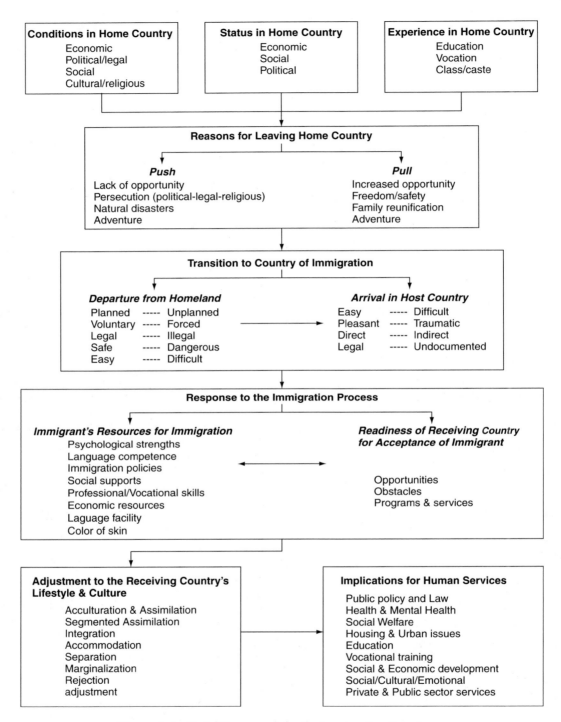

Figure 1-1. Model/Framework for the Immigration Experience.

low wages in countries where labor is plentiful and higher wages where it is scarce. Economic conditions may be dire and affect basic subsistence, or such that individuals are unable to fulfill their aspirations, leading them to voluntarily explore alternatives. While the world economy appears to be sound in 2007, the Worldwatch Institute (2006) released a report that suggests that the economic gains in 2006–2007 mask underlying crises related to violation of the Earth's ecosystems. Furthermore, although, overall, countries may be in better economic situations than they were in the 1990s, clearly, none has eradicated poverty, hence the impetus to seek better opportunities continues to exist even in the face of improved country conditions. Poor economic conditions may be exacerbated by weather conditions. In 2006 and 2007, several crises associated with weather conditions affected poor farmers dramatically: Syria was afflicted by drought in the winter and floods in the summer (IRIN, 2007a); Pakistan and Afghanistan reported floods in July 2007 that devastated several areas, killing numbers of people already in poverty (IRIN, 2007b, 2007c); across the Sahel, the monsoon season began, but not in the traditional areas where it is expected, thus causing homelessness and devastation (IRIN, 2007d). Since most of these nations lack contingency plans, citizens must seek their livelihoods elsewhere

Political upheavals can be instrumental in increasing dissatisfaction. When nations change in political power, when power structures alter, or individuals disagree with political ideologies, the climate is ripe for migration out of the nation. War, coupled with political and religious persecution, has fueled several movements such as the migrations of Southeast Asians during the Vietnamese War (1959–1975, the Bosnians during the civil conflicts in Bosnia-Herzegovina (1992–1995), and the Afghanis and Iraqis after the U.S. invasions of Afghanistan (2001–present) and Iraq (2003–present), the Sudanese in the province of Darfur (2003–present) as individuals flee unbearable and oppressive forces and seek political or religious asylum in other countries. Present-day wars target civilians with torture and abuse. International, civil, and religious strife, as well as cultural conflicts, often result in the violation of human rights. Amnesty

International,[1] an organization committed to the preservation of human rights, consistently identifies ongoing human rights violations across the globe. In a survey of 195 countries between 1997 and mid-2000, Amnesty International (2000) found reports of torture or ill-treatment by state officials in more than 150 of these nations. These included occurrences such as the rape of women, the execution of prisoners, the persecution of those who contradict the government, and the maltreatment and victimization of anyone disagreeing with the ruling elite. Its most recent 2005 report on 149 countries reveals that national governments fail to address human rights violations (http://web.amnesty.org/report 2005/index-eng).

Precipitating circumstances that increase the probability of persecution or forced migration of groups result in involuntary migration and the search for refugee status in the country of asylum. The United Nations High Commissioner for Refugees reports refugee movements daily.[2] In mid-2007, Somali boat people were continuing to cross the Gulf of Aden into Yemen (United Nations, 2007a); Iraqi refugees were flowing into neighboring Syria and Jordan, with Syria reporting their entry at the rate of 30,000 a month (United Nations, 2007b); growing numbers of Colombian refugees were arriving in Venezuela (United Nations, 2007c).

Finally, gender plays a significant part in immigration opportunities and outcomes. Especially for women, in many cultures restrictive traditions and social conditions have encouraged adventure and migration with anticipation of freedom from total dependence and confining customs and expectations (Espiritu, 1997; Pedraza, 1996). The UNHCR increasingly recognizes that the forms of persecution women experience differ substantially from those facing men (Haines, 2001). Female victims of domestic violence have been offered asylum by countries such as the United States. because their own governments have been unwilling or unable to protect them (Associated Press, 2001, DataTimes, 2001). Women fearing female genital mutilation (FGM) in their homelands have, at various times, sought and been granted asylum in such countries as Australia, Canada, Sweden, and the United States. (Amnesty International, 2002). Although less likely to migrate than men, due to restricted opportunities and greater constraints at home, when possibilities do arise, either in the form of asylum from gender-related violence[3] or to study or work in highly skilled occupations (i.e., nursing, computer software industry), they frequently migrate in numbers greater than would be expected based on familial and societal norms. The tremendous changes produced by the process of migrating out of the country allow women to break from traditional roles and patterns of dependence to assert unenvisioned freedoms.

Status & Experience in Home Country

The socioeconomic backgrounds of those who migrate away from their homes vary widely. Contrary to popular belief, it is not the poorest or the most oppressed who leave their countries. Voluntary immigrants must have the resources—physical, economic, educational, social, and emotional—to make the transition, and unlike escapees, they tend to be governed from the start by socioeconomic variables (Portes & Rumbaut, 2006). Both legal and undocumented immigrants are generally self-selected, prompted by ambition, energy, fortitude, and adaptability (Fukuyama, 1994). In fact, since the very poor and the unemployed seldom migrate, either legally or illegally, the primary cause of voluntary migration is an awareness of individuals while they are still in sending countries that host countries have the means to help them fulfill their aspirations (Portes & Rumbaut, 2006).

Voluntary Immigrants. Portes and Rumbaut (2006) identify three types of voluntary immigrants: laborers, entrepreneurs, and professionals.

Labor migrants. Labor migrants are able to scrape together the financial resources to leave their countries of origin. With low levels of education and few skills applicable in the industrial world, labor migrants, such as Mexicans to the United States, move in search of unskilled, low-paying occupations in fruit picking, domestic work, and the food industry, where the wages, though substandard, nevertheless increase their

earning capacity. Most frequently, labor migrants are not isolated individuals seeking to improve their lot, but family representatives sent to support those remaining behind. Although families must invest income and suffer the absence of some members, such representative migration is perceived as an investment against sudden declines in economic opportunities. By sending earning members to other countries, families can diversify their economic risks. The longer a migration flow exists between specific countries, the greater is the likelihood that increasingly poor individuals, a larger proportion of women and children, and a smaller percentage of undocumented immigrants will move between those countries (Massey, 1990).

Entrepreneurial migrants. Entrepreneurial immigrants are those with substantial business acumen and expertise who recognize the opportunity for growth and development through leaving the country. With business skills and access to sources of capital and labor in their own countries, they bring with them the makings of success. Furthermore, in carving an avenue for economic mobility for themselves, they enable others, often from the extended family or from the same region in the country of origin, to follow. Their sociopolitical standing in their home countries is substantially higher than that of the migrant workers, and they generally have networks through which they can explore resources and opportunities in other countries.

Professional migrants. Considered the "brain drain" of their homelands, professional migrants are educated individuals with high levels of professional competence, often in areas such as engineering, medicine, and technology. They move to another country to enhance their careers, leaving countries where the infrastructure is insufficient to accommodate their level of expertise. Although they rarely accept menial jobs, regardless of the extent and depth of their training, experience, and expertise, they usually enter at the bottom of their occupational ladders and progress based on merit. These individuals, in addition to high academic and professional achievement, usually have the financial, familial, and social supports for exodus from the homeland and may have had political influence had they selected to remain in their countries of origin.

Refugees & Involuntary Immigrants

Refugees and displaced persons, as involuntary immigrants, have a very different home-country status from voluntary immigrants. While voluntary immigrants plan their move based on the resources they possess and the networks they have established, the refugees' departure from their countries of birth is often sudden, uprooting, and traumatic. Most frequently identified are political or religious refugees who belong to minority groups and find themselves targeted for heightened persecution and oppression. Bosnian Muslims, targeted for elimination, were forced to flee their homes in record numbers; Tutsis were brutally attacked, and of those who were not killed during the 1994 genocide in Rwanda, many escaped the country; Sudanese in the Darfur region continue to seek refuge.

While a higher socioeconomic status does not greatly affect refugees' ability to escape persecution if they remain in their homelands, it does provide them greater opportunities to avoid the potential terrors before they are victimized. Those of higher socioeconomic status are also more cognizant of environmental factors and the personal dangers lurking in the political shadows. Hence, they often flee before the fullfledged eruption of hazards. For example, the refugees from Vietnam began arriving in the United States in 1975, soon after the fall of Saigon and the end of the Vietnam War and constituted those individuals who had the human resources to adapt rapidly to the West. These were individuals who constituted the first wave of refugees. Most frequently the first wave of refugees from a country torn by international or civil war or oppression, include the highly educated, affluent, and well connected, who rapidly adjust to other societies. Second and third wave refugees out of Vietnam and other Southeast Asian countries left in the 1980s and 1990s, and came with less human capital. This was consistent with refugee flight patterns, for unlike the elite of the first cohort, the second and subsequent groups of refugees are usually farmers, peasants, and laborers, who leave after

experiencing persecution, and who often do not have the skills that can be easily adapted to less agrarian economies.

Reasons for Leaving the Home Country

While the configuration of events leading to migration may differ among individuals, there appears to be an interplay of two phenomena that is the catalyst for migration: A push from the country of origin, and a pull to the country of immigration, identified by immigration scholars as the "push" and "pull" of immigration. The "push" out of the country of origin often emerges from its internal conditions and intensifies with the personal circumstances of individuals. The "pull" to another country or region works in tandem with the "push" from the home country. In the absence of all dissatisfaction in the country of origin, the likelihood that individuals will move is practically nonexistent. Moving from the familiar to the unfamiliar may occur because something elsewhere is more attractive (even if it is the search for adventure) than what an individual or group currently possesses, and the prospect of acquiring or achieving that "something" is impossible or difficult without the move.

Neoclassical economic approaches suggest that potential migrants are rational income maximizers who move to new environments whenever the anticipated gains of moving are sufficiently high (Massey, 2004; Massey et al., 1993). Economic incentives, however, may not be the sole motivators in this cost-benefit analysis. Such a balance is weighed not only as economic achievement, but also in terms of social and emotional gains and in view of economic investment and social losses. While economic opportunity is often a significant underlying, and even a primary, reason for emigrating, it is certainly not the only one.

Many individuals migrate to attain the dream of a lifestyle that they are unable to achieve in their home countries or to enter an accessible labor market. Increased educational and social opportunities, the relaxation of immigration laws and policies, postcolonial access and the presence of international connections, and the desire for exploration may all be instrumental in spurring immigration. Attraction may include freedom from religious and political persecution, as well as freedom from restrictive societal and traditional expectations. Significant among these may be the desire and opportunity for reunification with family members who had left earlier.

Once established in a country, an immigrant group forms a network that links its members with each other and also with relatives in the home country (Bashi, 2007). This provides a channel through which contacts can be recruited from the home country for employers of the immigrants. Although traditional societies voluntarily send few emigrants, the disruption of traditional lifestyles (i.e., changes from agrarian to industrial economies), can serve as "pull" factors with offers of employment drawing individuals away from their homes. Ethnic networks, particularly formal ones such as "Chinatowns" and "Little Indias" can promote and support individuals, making the process of exodus less fearsome and more attractive. Incentives may also be provided by the host country either by directly inviting immigrants to serve specialized labor markets or by broadening immigration policies (Portes & Rumbaut, 2006).

The configurations of reasons people leave a particular country and the reasons they immigrate to another are myriad, the two occur in tandem. While the strength of each may vary, they work in concert to provide the immigrant with the incentive to move.

Transition to the Country of Immigration

Immigration to another country occurs for a variety of reasons, and the process varies for individuals. If entry into the country of immigration is direct, or if the country of immigration is the country of choice, the experience may not be traumatic. Furthermore, much is dependent on the receiving country's immigration policies and the perception of immigrants by the receiving agents at the first port of call. When these are unequivocally welcoming, the experience of immigration is not likely to traumatize those who have left their homelands. Immigration, itself, is a contentious issue about which numerous people in host countries are ambivalent. Any review of newspaper accounts across the world will reveal continuing discussions and debates

about the merits of newcomers. Segments of society perceive immigrants as assets to the receiving country, while others view them as threats that deplete it of resources and endanger the opportunities of the natives. These perceptions are reflected in the treatment of immigrants by border authorities (see recent and ongoing news reports by Amnesty International).

For legal immigrants, ease of entry into a country involves a number of processes, including the acquisition of an immigrant visa, which is often based on receiving countries' perceptions of the immigrants' potential to contribute to their own and the receiving country's well-being. Furthermore, virtually every industrialized nation, as well as several developing ones, now house populations of immigrants who are undocumented and who cross borders without the requisite official authorization. While, for them, there is no question of seeking an entry visa, the likelihood of being apprehended and imprisoned or returned to their country of origin increases exponentially.

While legal migration out of the home country is often, although not always, based on personal decisions, immigration is contingent on the host country's receptiveness. Refugee movement out of a country, and undocumented immigration into a country, on the other hand, are unendorsed by authorities. Movements that are not legally sanctioned significantly multiply the difficulties, dangers, and traumas of people in passage, while those that are legally approved allow greater access to the comfort and ease of transit.

Response to the Immigration Process

The complexity of reactions to immigration must be viewed from both the perspective of the immigrant and of the receiving country. Immigration frequently poses a dilemma, with benefits and costs associated for both immigrants and receiving countries. It would be simplistic to suggest that when benefits outweigh the costs, the response is positive. Much is dependent on current political, economic, and social conditions in the receiving country as well as the human capital immigrants bring. These two sets of factors, the immigrants' resources for immigration and the receptiveness of the receiving country are highly interactive, with each substantially influencing the other.

Immigrants' Resources for Immigration

"Give me your tired, your poor, your huddled masses yearning to breathe free..." reads the Emma Lazarus poem inscribed on the Statue of Liberty in the New York harbor. While a laudable sentiment, it hardly reflects the face of all immigrants, either to the United States or elsewhere. Even under the most deplorable circumstances, it is not the most needy, weak, and oppressed who leave but those who have, at the very least, physical, emotional, and psychological fortitude. Without personal strengths, individuals are less likely to leave their homelands, and if they do, they are less likely to survive. It is essential to view immigrants through Saleebey's (2002) "strengths perspective," identifying their human capital, namely their assets and capabilities, to understand their responses to the process of migration.

Education and vocation are the two primary factors that positively affect transition. Literacy not only provides individuals with knowledge, but also opens a world of opportunity by equipping them with the tools to be lifelong learners. With the skills of literacy, they are able to read and better comprehend explanations of situations that are initially alien. While knowledge of the language of the country into which individuals are entering greatly enhances the process of adjustment, being literate in one's native language reinforces self-efficacy and strengthens prospects of pursuing learning in other languages and environments. Therefore, in general, the higher the level of education possessed by individuals, the greater is their ability to adjust outside the home country.

Along with education, a significant element in the adjustment process is occupation. The extent to which professions are transportable certainly depends on whether they are useful to the economy of the country of adoption. When individuals have spent their lives in agrarian communities, developing their competence in farming, transitions to fast-paced computerized and industrialized societies make their farming skills obsolete. On the other hand, practice in computer software enhances the likelihood of finding a congruous niche in a technological environment.

While the importance of education and vocation cannot be overemphasized, they do not always ensure the same level of success outside one's home country. In addition to other factors that must be taken into account, and that are discussed later, language competence may not only be a mediating variable but the principal initial barrier confronting all immigrants, from the least educated peasants to the most literate professionals. For example, it is not unusual for a practicing physician—an individual with a high level of education and a cross-nationally valued profession—to lack the language skills to pass licensing examinations. Sophisticated scientific jargon is difficult for those with only conversational knowledge of a foreign language, and experienced practitioners may be forced into fields that are not commensurate with their knowledge, skills, or expertise.

Another barrier to the unconditional acceptance of persons is stratification by class and caste, which determines the social hierarchy of societies. In many nations, privileges are bestowed by birth, and while movement from one class to another is difficult, changing caste is impossible. Bound by the threads of tradition, regardless of skill, values, or hopes, certain opportunities elude those of the lower classes and castes (Lucas, 2005). Caste and class often dictate the professions which people follow, the style of life they lead, and the areas in which they reside. Furthermore, social norms may also preclude any interaction across levels of class and caste. Expectations of behavior and relationships may hinder growth and development in people of the lower strata, while, at the same time, put in the path of the higher echelons opportunities and experiences that they may neither merit nor have the capability to fully utilize.

A large proportion of immigrants, both legal and undocumented, leave their homes in search of improved economic opportunities. The distribution of these economic migrants is bimodal: One group consists of the educated and skilled, with substantial financial resources in their home countries, the other consists of those with minimal education, skills, or material resources

(Tsay & Hayase, 2001). The former seeks to enhance its career opportunities and lifestyles, while the latter migrates to accept relatively menial jobs that, nevertheless, provide economic improvement. Furthermore, those who leave their homelands without planning, such as second wave refugees, may lack skills that are transferable to the host country, but when ambition and desire to improve personal circumstances are strong, transition can be eased.

The availability of economic resources enhances rapid independence and adjustment in new countries. Immigrants with sufficient finances will find housing and meet their other needs more readily than those who have little, or who have had to leave their material wealth in their homelands. However, financial assistance may be available from other sources. The presence of family or other members of the immigrant community in the host country who are willing to pool funds can speed adjustment.

Many new immigrants to a country arrive with little facility in the language of the host country, which is often the primary obstacle. Without language ability, seeking housing or employment, accessing health care or other services, or learning a vocation become impossible. Language competence increases ability to negotiate through a nation's bureaucracies, and literacy, or the ability to read and write in the host language further improves opportunities.

The stresses on immigrants and refugees in translocation are enormous and well documented.[4] Many are associated with the traumas of dramatic migration processes. However, other stresses result from culture-shock in an alien environment, where language, social structures, norms, expectations, and values substantially differ from those that have been elemental to the immigrants' understanding of themselves. Here, well-understood role relationships change and established patterns of interaction are questioned. When immigrants have the psychological capability of coping, they are more likely to be able to control the direction of their lives. On the other hand, they may experience post-traumatic stress disorder, as do many refugees. Without sufficient and appropriate social and emotional support, and perhaps therapy, many fail to find the immigration experience satisfactory, remaining unhappy, resenting their lives in the new land, and pining for their homelands (Ahearn, 2000).

An unchangeable characteristic of immigrants is the color of their skin, as is the global hierarchy of races and preferences for fairer skin tones (Espiritu, 1996). The immigrants' skin color and ethnicity may serve as an asset if they are similar to those of the majority group in the host country. Conversely, where there is dissimilarity of skin color and ethnicity from that of the majority group, then the process of adjustment can be arduous. To balance the "wrong" ethnicity and skin color, immigrants must possess other assets. Particularly useful are professional skills, language competence, and psychosocial strengths and supports. When immigrants fill a need in the society, skin color may not constitute a major obstacle. Furthermore, while indications are that skin color universally defines "foreignness," regardless of specific culture, identity, behaviors, or network affiliation, even the "appropriate" skin color may not preclude prejudice and racism (Hickman & Walter, 1995; Reitz & Sklar, 1997).

Economic, professional, and educational resources and language capability are the most helpful in easing an individual into a new society. However, other areas can also make the transition less formidable. Social supports through a network, both in the receiving country and those that come with immigrants, ensure some familiarity in the new environment. More importantly, perhaps, is the psychological efficacy of individuals. This may include the ability to weather stressful and dangerous experiences, flexibility and adjustment to unknown circumstances, faith in their own capabilities and strengths, and hope for the future.

Readiness of Receiving Country for Immigrants

The readiness of a receiving country to accept immigrants in general, or an immigrant group in particular is, itself, a complex matter. When immigration is viewed as inextricably bound to a nation's political, economic, and social well-being as well as its future security interests, it is likely to be welcomed. Nevertheless, immigration policies of many countries are temporal, reflecting what is believed to be of benefit at a particular moment. Nations also fulfill international agreements in the resettlement or provision of asylum to large numbers of refugees, to facilitate government action, and for humanitarian reasons. Policies that allow immigration are coupled with those that permit the expulsion or deportation of foreign nationals.

Although opportunities may be available to immigrants, they may be rife with obstacles, mirroring the nation's ambivalence toward a particular immigrant group. Thus, the country's receptiveness is also reflected in the services accessible to immigrants. These include programs addressing the basic health, education, and welfare needs of the immigrant community, as well as those that provide psychosocial and emotional support. Acceptance of a group is also highly influenced by the receiving country's openness to diversity and ethnic-specific factors such as language facility, skin color, and other sociocultural characteristics (Mayadas & Elliott, 1992). The identities of immigrants are shaped not only by the social location of their group within the host society, but also by the position of their country of origin within the global racial order in which the more occidental features increases the value of the group (Espiritu, 1996).

Refugee migration, which is usually chaotic, requires substantial adjustments by receiving countries. Many renegotiate their policies regarding short- and long-term asylum and struggle to bear the burden of pressures associated with such movements. On the other hand, voluntary economic movement is a chain that links the world and is a significant part of the trend toward a global system of economics and communications propelling the international community toward change (Parfit, 1998). Foreigners who specialize in skills not readily available in the host country may fill needs of the business community, yet political concerns may limit newcomers, regardless of shortages (Bruner, 1997). Thus, quantitative immigration policy restrictions may heighten illegal immigration, or groups may enter under nonimmigrant trainee or exchange agreements. On the other hand, immigration policy may be relatively open and natives may perceive a threat of lost employment opportunities.

Adjustment to Receiving Country

The range of material focusing on the adjustment of immigrants to a new country is vast. Economic, psychosocial, and cultural adjustment and the assimilation of foreigners in the cultures of indigenous people are of continuing interest as global migration increases. Individuals adapt to new circumstances in a variety of ways, which are affected by their personal resources, their desire, and the receiving country's acceptance. Literature suggests a continuum along which individuals adjust to the host country, and positions on the continuum may change over time (Figure 1-2). At one end lies total acculturation and assimilation, while at the other end lies rejection.

Early assimilation theorists believed total assimilation into a "melting pot" was the ideal, with the preferred goal for all immigrants being to become similar to the dominant group in the place of destination (Rumbaut, 1997). This perspective was based on the assumption that in order to have equal access to the resources in a receiving country, diverse groups gradually shed their traditions (Zhou, 1997). The assimilationists postulated that migration resulted in the emergence of the "marginal man," who was at the same time attempting to assimilate into the host culture and being drawn back into the traditional one (Park, 1928, 1950). However, Warner and Srole (1945), suggested that the external factors of the society, such as natives' response to immigrants' skin color, language of origin, and religion, also played a significant part in the assimilation of particular groups. Gordon (1964), on the other hand, argued that the assimilation process begins with cultural assimilation, and then progresses through structural, marital, identificational, attitudinal, behavioral, and civic assimilation, but it does not necessarily result in total assimilation since this depends on acceptance by the dominant group. The classical assimilation theorists viewed distinctive ethnic traits as disadvantageous to immigrants (Zhou, 1997) and held that until and unless they relinquished their traditions they would remain "marginal." Underpinning these classical theories is the belief that the goal of immigrants is, and

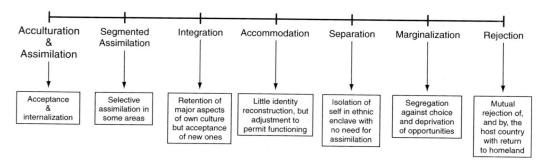

Figure 1-2. The Continuum of Adjustment.[5]

should be, complete internalization of the receiving country's values, attitudes, and behaviors.

However, such internalization may not be preferred by immigrants, allowed by indigenous peoples, or possible because of personal or environmental circumstances. The acculturation of individuals assumes acclimatization to a new culture and society, often converting ways of thought and behavior. The effects of acculturation on the life satisfaction of immigrants are mixed. Three aspects of acculturation—perception of acceptance by natives, change in cultural orientation, and language use—have been found to be associated with better mental health (Mehta, 1998). Complete acculturation can result in such conformity that one blends in with another group. The original culture is determined to be inconsequential and contact with the majority is considered very important (Van Oudenhoven, Prins & Buunk, 1998). The more immigrants affirm values of the receiving country through assimilation, the greater is the likelihood of acceptance by natives. Likewise, the more positive the indigenous reactions, the greater is the life satisfaction and sense of competence among immigrants (Vanselm, Sam & Van Oudenhoven, 1997).

The traditional pattern of acculturation presented in most literature suggests assimilation into the dominant society, yet the research of Portes & Zhou (1993) found a second direction that leads to permanent poverty and assimilation into the underclass. Moreover, though generally positively associated with life in a new country, assimilation appears also to adversely affect

family life and organization (Faragallah, Schumm & Webb, 1997). Increased assimilation may contradict traditional expectations among members of an immigrant group, may expose underlying ethnocentrism, and may result in discontent (Rumbaut, 1997). Hence, rather than assimilating, immigrants are more likely to fall along the continuum of adjustment (Figure 1-2), accepting certain new norms while maintaining some traditional ones.

Implications for Policy and Services—A Focus on Social Capital

Across the globe, people are migrating—across continents and nations, and in record numbers. With the ease of transportation and changes in immigration and refugee policies, increasing numbers of people leave their places of birth to escape unacceptable conditions or to explore opportunities. Receiving countries have felt their impact and must modify, expand, or develop policies, programs, and services that include them. When immigrants arrive with strong human capital, substantial changes in host nations may not be as necessary as when they do not have adequate assets. Nevertheless, the influx of people of differing traditions, values, expectations, and skills bears implications for services, ranging in breadth from public policy and law to individual psychosocial adjustment.

As new arrivals enter a nation, its policies and laws must be addressed to ensure that the formal structures of society are in place for the diversifying population. These might revolve around the nation's foreign policies, international relationships with sending countries, immigration itself, and the extent to which the immigration laws will be inclusive or restrictive. They must also address economic, health care, social welfare, and education policies and must ensure that immigrants have the protection of the nation's legal system. Policy that addresses business functions and practices, including hiring, wages, and equal access must enable immigrants to become familiar with relevant economic policy, exercise their rights, and be protected from exploitation. Health care policy may revolve around the diverse issues of public health and community needs, including primary care. Health promotion and protection issues may focus on education and prevention for immigrants, and especially for new arrivals. Issues surrounding health expenditures and health coverage for the immigrant must be resolved as must those around the actual delivery of services, access and utilization opportunities, and mechanisms to assess the satisfaction of immigrants with the quality of health care. Policies should ensure that opportunities are available for immigrants and the nature of the barriers to adequate health care is addressed.

Serageldin (1999) indicates that social capital, "the internal social and cultural coherence of society, the norms and values that govern interactions among people and the institutions in which they are embedded" (p. i), is essential in ensuring that opportunities within a nation are strong and viable. By definition, social capital requires some cooperation among individuals and groups and is a form of public "good" or benefit (Grootaert, 1997). Social capital is a necessity in the creation of human capital (Coleman, 1988), and immigrants' adjustment is often linked to the social capital available to them.

In 1997, Japan's Ministry of Education, the *Monbush*, stated that education constitutes the foundation of all social systems. Immigrants may, or may not, have come with an adequate education. The educational system and education policy of the host country must allow access to levels and types of education and institutions that are appropriate to their needs. Adult education programs to improve literacy will ensure better adjustment to the new environment. Furthermore, appropriate education for immigrant children must take into account difficulties that can occur as they enter a school system without a working knowledge of the medium of instruction. Variations in cultural patterns and behavior ought to be accommodated by schools, with an awareness that, even in the best of circumstances, immigration is traumatic.

The nation's welfare policies must guarantee that all immigrants have admittance to appropriate public welfare services and subsidies and are connected to private welfare programs as necessary. Hence, public policy and law must be reviewed frequently to assess their adequacy for all the nations' residents and should be so modified as to remove barriers to the administration and utilization of the services they govern.

The availability and accessibility to social capital are paramount in the successful settlement of immigrants in their country of adoption. The implementation of sustainable development projects ensuring that immigrants receive the social and economic tools to succeed in their new countries is essential. In addition to providing new arrivals with economic subsidies, housing and health care, community based educational programs and training ought to provide the components for new immigrants to move away from dependency on society's support programs (Lobo & Mayadas, 1997). Hence, knowledge about prevention of disease, ability to function through society's institutional structures, and earning capacity in the legitimate economy of the country will enhance the likelihood of self-sufficiency. Social and mental health services need to recognize the difficulties associated with the immigration experience and assist immigrants in their adjustment to the receiving country. This may include helping immigrants understand the norms and expectations of the country as well as implications for their own traditions and family and community relationships.

It is safe to say that the flow of immigrants strains the receiving country's support service systems. It behooves policy makers and service providers to be cognizant of the experience of immigrants so that they can appropriately meet the needs and the demands of this group and ensure that the nation's social capital is available to this population in enhancing its human capital. Receiving countries must recognize that migration across their borders will persist with improvements in transportation and as reasons for moving further emerge.

In admitting immigrants, a nation makes a commitment to them. Unless it is willing to help them through the transitional period of adjustment, their unmet economic, social, health, and mental health needs can, in both the short and the long term, drain substantial resources. On the other hand, early attention to these very immigrants may accelerate their entry as contributors to society (Mayadas & Elliott, 2002). While some experiences are unique to a particular immigrant group and to a specific individual, much in the immigrant experience is shared—from exodus to immigration, including reactions to and of the receiving country. The framework presented here can help develop an understanding of the immigration experience and may provide a foundation for the interpretation of the experience of particular groups within the context of the receiving country's readiness to accept them. As immigration accelerates, it will be imperative for policy makers and service providers to become more sensitive to the unique needs of new arrivals and assess the degree to which programs and services are inclusive and supportive or xenophobic and discriminatory. Such assessments may ensure that programs are modified to manage a mutually satisfactory adjustment between both the immigrant group and the host country.

Notes

1. See Amnesty International's website: http://www.amnesty.org. Retrieved July 12, 2007.
2. See United Nations High Commissioner for Refugees' website: http://www.unhcr.ch.
3. See Amnesty International's website: http://www.amnesty.org.
4. See United Nations High Commissioner for Refugees' website: http://www.unhcr.ch.
5. From Segal, U. (2002). *A framework for immigration: Asians in the United States.* New York, NY: Columbia University Press.

References

Ahearn, F.L. (ed). (2000). *Psychosocial wellness of refugees: Issues in qualitative and quantitative research.* New York, NY: Berghahn Books.

Alba, R.D. & Nee, V. (1997). Rethinking Assimilation Theory for a new era of immigration. *International Migration Review*, 31(4), 826–975.

Amnesty International. (2000). *Torture worldwide: An affront to human dignity.* New York, NY: Amnesty International.

Amnesty International. (2002). Female Genital Mutilation. Website: www.amnesty.org//ailib/intcam/femgen/fgm1.htm.

Associated Press. (2001, March 22). Court grants Mexican girl asylum on grounds of father's abuse. Associated Press Leased Line via NewsEdge Corporation: BC-CA—Persecution Asylum, 0340.

Bashi, V.F. (2007). *Survival of the knitted: immigrant social networks in a stratified world.* Stanford, CA: Stanford University Press.

Bruner, R.W. (1997, November 3). Execs burn over proposed limits on foreign hires. *Electronic News*, 43(2192), 30–31.

Coleman, J.S. (1988). Social capital in the creation of human capital. *American Journal of Sociology*, 94 (supplement), S95–S120.

DataTimes. (2001, October 24). Battered Mexican woman granted new asylum hearing. DataTimes via NewsEdge Corporation, *The San Francisco Chronicle*.

Espenshade, T.J. (1995). Unauthorized immigration to the United States. *Annual Review of Sociology*, 21, 195–216.

Espiritu, Y.L. (1996). Colonial oppression, labour importation, and group formation: Filipinos in the United States. *Ethnic and Racial Studies*, 19(1), 29–48.

Espiritu, Y.L. (1997). *Asian American Women and Men.* Thousand Oaks, CA: Sage.

Faragallah, M.H., Schumm, W.R. & Webb, F.J. (1997). Acculturation of Arab-American immigrants: An exploratory study. *Journal of Comparative Family Studies*, 28(3), 182.

Fukuyama, F. (1994). Immigrants and family values. In Mills, N. (ed). *Arguing immigration: Are new immigrants a wealth of diversity . . . or a crushing burden?* New York: Simon & Schuster, 151–168.

Gordon, M.M. (1964). *Assimilation in American life*, New York: Oxford University Press.

Grootaert, C. (1997). Social Capital: The missing link? In *Expanding the measure of wealth: Indicators of environmentally sustainable development.* Environmentally Sustainable Development Studies and Monographs Series No. 7. Washington, DC: The World Bank.

Haines, R. (2001). Gender-related persecution. Paper commissioned by the UNHCR as a background paper for an expert round-table discussion on gender-related persecution organized as part of the Global Consultations on International Protections in the context of the 50th anniversary of the 1951 Convention relating to the Status of Refugees. Website: www.unhcr.ch/cgi-bin/lexis/vbi/home?page=search.

Hickman, M.J. & Walter, B. (1995). Deconstructing whiteness-Irish women in Britain. *Feminist Review*, 50, 5–19.

IRIN. (2007a). Syria: Harvest hit by poor weather, inefficient farming practices. Website: www.irinnews.org/Report.aspx?ReportID=73088. Retrieved July 12, 2007.

IRIN. (2007b). Pakistan: Top official compares storm to 2005 earthquake. Website: www.irinnews.org/Report.aspx?ReportID=730869. Retrieved July 12, 2007.

IRIN. (2007c). Afghanistan: Hundreds of families displaced by floods, livelihoods lost. Website: www.irinnews.org/Report.aspx?ReportID=73075. Retrieved July 12, 2007.

IRIN. (2007d). Sahel: Flood season starts but not where it shouldwww.irinnews.org/Report.aspx?ReportID=72869. Retrieved July 12, 2007.

Lee, K.K. (1998). *Huddled masses, muddled laws: Why contemporary immigration policy fails to reflect public opinion*, Westport, CT: Praeger.

Lobo, M. & Mayadas, N.S. (1997) International social work practice: A refugee perspective. In Mayadas, N.S., Watts, T.D. & Elliott, D. (Eds.) International Handbook on Social Work Theory and Practice. Westport, CT. Greenwood Press.

Lucas, R.E. (2005). *International migration and economic development: Lesons from low-income countries*. Northhampton, MA: Edward Elgar Publishing.

Massey, D.S. (1990). Social structure, household strategies, and the cumulative causation of migration. *Population Index*, 56(1), 3–26.

Massey, D.S. (2004). Social and economic aspects of migration. *Annals of the New York Academy of Sciences*, 1038(1), 206–212.

Massey, D.S., Arango, J., Hugo, G., Kouaouci, A., Pellerino A. & Taylor, J.E. (1993). Theories of international migration: A review and appraisal. *Population Development Review*, 19(3), 431–466.

Mayadas, N. S., & Elliott, D. (1992). Integration and xenophobia: An inherent conflict in international migration. *Journal of Multicultural Social Work*, 2(1), 47–62. Also published in Shen Ryan, A. (ed.) *Social work with immigrants and refugees*. Binghampton, NY: Haworth Press, 1992, 47–67.

Mayadas, N.S. & Elliott, D. (2002). Social work's response to refugee issues: a global perspective. In K.N. George (ed). *Social Work Today: Present realities future prospects*. The Madras School of Social Work Golden Jubilee Commemorative Volume. Madras School of social work, 107–119.

Mehta, S. (1998). Relationship between acculturation and mental health for Asian Indian immigrants in the United States. *Genetic, Social, & General Psychology Monographs*, 124(1), 61–78.

Monbusho. (1997). Program for Educational Reform. Website: http://www.mext.go.jp/english/news/1997/01/970102.htm, Accessed: July 16, 2007.

National Research Council. (1998). *The immigration debate: Studies on the economic, demographic and fiscal effects of immigration*, Washington, DC: National Academy Press.

Nayyar, D. (1998). Pressures and structural change: Case study of Indonesia. International Labor Organization, International migration papers #20 (web site: http://www.ilo.org/public/english/protection/mig rant/papers/emindo/index.htm).

Parfit, M. (1998, October). Human migration. *National Geographic*, 6–35.

Park, R. E. (1928). Human migration and the marginal man. *American Journal of Sociology*, 33(6), 881–893.

Park, R.E. (1950). *Race and culture*. Glencoe, IL: Free Press.

Pedraza, S. (1996). Origins and destinies: Immigration, race, and ethnicity in American history. In Pedraza, S. & Rumbaut, R. G. (eds.). *Origins and destinies: Immigration, race and ethnicity in America*, New York: Wadsworth Publishing Company, 1–20.

Portes, A. & Rumbaut, R.G. (2006). *Immigrant America: A portrait*. 3rd edition. Berkeley: University of California Press.

Portes, A. & Zhou, M. (1993). The new second generation: Segmented assimilation and its variants among post-1965 immigrant youth. *Annals of the American Academy of Political and Social Sciences*, 530, 74–96.

Redmond, R. (2002, October 22). Tanzania / Eastern D.R. Congo / Burundi. Summary of statement by UNHCR spokesperson at the press briefing, Palais des Nations in Geneva. UNHCR News Stories.

Reed, J.D., Kraft, B. & Rudulph, E. (1985, July 8). Now America is the thing to do. *Time*, 87.

Reitz, J.G. & Sklar, S.M. (1997). Race, culture, and the economic assimilation of immigrants. *Sociological Forum*, 12(2), 233–277.

Rothstein, R. (1994). Immigration dilemmas. In Mills, N. (ed). *Arguing immigration: Are new immigrants a wealth of diversity . . . or a crushing burden?* New York: Simon & Schuster, 48–63.

Rumbaut, R. (1997). Assimilation and its discontents: Between rhetoric and reality. *International Migration Review*, 31(4), 923–960.

Saleebey, D. (2002). Introduction: Power in the people. In Saleebey, D. (ed). *The Strengths Perspective in social work practice.* 3rd edition. Boston, MA: Allyn & Bacon.

Segal, U. (2002). *A framework for immigration: Asians in the United States.* New York, NY: Columbia University Press.

Serageldin, I. (1999). Foreword. In Feldman, T.R. & Assaf, S. *Social capital: Conceptual frameworks and empirical evidence.* Social Capital Initiative, working paper #5. Washington, DC: World Bank.

Tinker, H. (1995). The British colonies of settlement. In Cohen, R. (ed). *The Cambridge survey of world migration.* Cambridge, UK: Cambridge University Press, 14–20.

Tsay, C-l. & Hayase, Y. (eds). (2001). Special issue: International migration and structural change in the APEC member economies. *Asian and Pacific Migration Journal*, 10 (3/4).

United Nations. (2007a). Plight of refugees crossing Gulf of Aden draws call to action from UN agency. Website: www.unlorg/apps/news/story.asp?News ID=23193&Cr1= somali&Cr1=yemen. Retrieved July 12, 2007.

United Nations. (2007b). UN agency appeals for urgent aid to support countries hosting Iraqi Refugees. Website: www.unlorg/apps/news/story.asp? NewsID=23153&Cr=iraq&Cr1=.Retrieved July 12, 2007.

United Nations. (2007c). UN refugee agency steps us activities along Colombian-Venezuelan border. Website: www.unlorg/apps/news/story.asp?News ID=23094&Cr1=venezuela. Retrieved July 12, 2007.

Van Oudenhoven, J.P., Prins, K.S. & Buunk, P.B. (1998). Attitudes of minority and majority members towards adaptation of immigrants. *European Journal of Social Psychology*, 28(6), 995–1013.

Vanselm, K., Sam, D.L. & Van Oudenhoven, J.P. (1997). Life satisfaction and competence of Bosnian refugees in Norway. *Scandinavian Journal of Psychology*, 38(2), 143–149.

Warner & Srole (1945). *The Social Systems of American Ethnic Groups,* New Haven, CT: Yale University Press.

Worldwatch Institute. (2006, July 12). Vital signs 2006–2007: Economic gains mask underlying crisis. Website: www.worldwatch.org/node/4345. Retrieved July 12, 2007.

Zhou, M. (1997). Segmented assimilation-issues, controversies, and recent research on the new second generation. *International Migration Review*, 31(4), 975–1880.

2

Immigration Worldwide: Trends and Analysis

Doreen Elliott, Nazneen S. Mayadas, and Uma A. Segal

While chapter one provides a comprehensive model to explicate the immigrant experience, chapter two presents theories of immigration, historical trends, and a model of policy analysis. The chapter is organized in three sections. The first section discusses briefly a historical perspective; the second section summarizes current immigration trends and statistics, a brief overview of explanatory theories of immigration, and consideration of the costs and benefits of immigration worldwide. The third section of this chapter discusses issues related to international comparative analysis and offers a model to assist analysis which may be applied across the various country chapters represented here.

A Historical Perspective on Immigration

Migration has been part of human experience since before recorded history. Humankind was essentially nomadic before agricultural methods were established. Based on archeological evidence the seat of migration is assessed to be in East Africa. From there the earliest migration, approximately 60,000 years ago, was through Asia and Indonesia to Australia and New Guinea. About 46,000 years later a second wave of migration took a more northerly route through Eurasia and across the Bering Strait into the Americas. An offshoot of this route was west toward present-day Europe. The central Mediterranean area was populated about 8,000 years ago. Stories of human migration have been perpetuated in writings such as the Bible, which documents Moses leading his followers to the "promised land," and in Homer's *Odyssey*, which tells the story of the wanderings of Odysseus (Cohen, 1995).

However, to understand modern population movements, it is important to review the time span starting in sixteenth century in Europe and ending with the close of the twentieth century (Cohen, 1995). Massey (1999) proposes that there have been four significant periods.

The Mercantile Period (1500–1800)

This period is associated with European colonization and trade, which gave Europe control over an appreciable part of the world. This is also the time when the slave trade from Africa to the Americas resulted in an estimated population shift of ten million Africans to the Americas with major social and demographic consequences. After the abolition of slavery, cheap labor was supplied by migrations of indentured laborers from Asia, including India and China, who worked on the plantations for the export of raw materials for Europe's economic expansion.

The Industrial Period (1800–1925)

This was a consequence of the first period's economic growth and of industrialization. There was a considerable exodus of European migrants from countries such as Britain, Italy, Norway, Spain, and Sweden, to America to gain from the New World's growing economy. The majority of migrants went to the Americas, but others went to Australia and New Zealand also.

Limited Migration (1930–1960)

World War I, the Great Depression and the break-up of the British Empire were some of the factors leading to this period of limited migration.

Postindustrial Migration (1960s to 1990s)

This period saw the expansion of human migration to a global phenomenon. Emigration from Asia, Africa, and South America increased at this time, and as the century progressed, patterns of migration became more complex, with traditionally sending countries becoming receiving countries also. During this period, the characteristics of immigrants changed from being predominantly European to include Asians, as immigration policies in America and Australasia changed according to the needs of the economy for more labor. The growth of industrialization in Asian countries such as Japan, Korea, Taiwan, and Hong Kong led to population movements also responding to labor needs of the new industrial and technological economies. Thus with persons from varying economic backgrounds and status now moving around the world in a way unprecedented in modern times, one could witness the consolidation of the age of global immigration (Massey, 1999; Hayter, 2004; Cohen, 1995).

Although the twentieth century saw migration movements of unprecedented proportions,

nations' ease of international migration varied by nation and time period. For example, Australia severely restricted non-White migration, and in 1901 passed its Immigration Restriction Act, which effectively controlled migration until 1973. From 1882 to 1965, most Asians and several European groups were restricted from migrating to the United States. Japan's Immigration Control and Refugee-Recognition Act (ICRRA) was passed in 1951 and amended subsequently twice in the 1980s, and while Japan places no quotas on immigration, applicants must satisfy 28 statutes of residence to enter, work, and stay in Japan.

Rights and Restrictions in the Twenty-First Century

There is evidence toward the end of the twentieth century and the beginning of the twenty-first century of a new fifth period to add to Massey's four periods, that is, immigration policies that were loosening may now be returning to increasing restrictiveness, especially in the developed world. In the postindustrial age, economic globalization means that economies are increasingly interdependent, and at the same time the gap between rich and poor countries has increased. Goods and capital assets flow freely in this global market, while labor movement is severely restricted. Rich countries have a per capita GDP 66 times greater than poor countries (GCIM, 2005). Irregular migration and human trafficking are the price that people from poor countries will pay to enter the richer nations and gain more than twenty times their income in the developing world even while being paid low wages in the host country. Irregular migrants are a needed supplement to the labor force in many developed countries, yet their rights remain unrecognized and their working conditions and low wages when viewed historically will be the shame of the developed world. It is possible that this new period will see new categories of labor migration recognized and institutionalized, such as temporary labor migrants and transnationals, and will also see the relaxing of immigration restrictions. The European Community has paved the way to a certain extent, though the patterns of labor migration are not yet without problems there.

Current Immigration Trends Worldwide

According to the Global Commission on International Migration (GCIM), an estimated 200 million people have lived outside the country in which they were born for more than one year (GCIM, 2005). In absolute numbers, 200 million is a significant number of people, however, it is important to note that it represents only three percent of the world's population and indicates that an overwhelming majority does not leave the homeland, because of lack of either interest or opportunity. Nevertheless, migration has provided many challenges and opportunities to countries receiving new populations and has resulted in changes to both their migration and internal policies. Sixty percent of the world's migrants live in developed countries: Almost one in 10 persons in developed countries is an immigrant (United Nations, 2006). Of these, the United Nations estimates that 158 million are voluntary international migrants (United Nations, 2004:vii). Additionally, at the start of 2007, there were 32.9 million people "of concern" to UNHCR (up from 2006 by 56% when there were 20.8 million "of concern"; UNHCR, 2008). Of these 9.9 were recognized refugees, fleeing political persecution and life threatening conditions; 740,000 were asylum seekers; 5.8 million were stateless people; 2.6 million were returned refugees and internally displaced people; and one million were "others of concern" to the UNHCR (UNHCR, 2007). Of 158 million international migrants in 2005, approximately 49 percent were women and girls (United Nations, 2005). These figures are in the context of a world population of approximately 6.5 billion (United Nations 2006). The *New York Times* (June 22, 2007) provides a snapshot of global migration, including for each nation the net flow of migrants, the share of total migrants, the share of the local population, the remittances sent to the home country, and the remittances sent based on the GDP.[1]

The major movement of immigrants is toward the developed world, where gradually the flow increased by 3 percent during the 1990s, with no increase in immigrants to the developing world (United Nations, 2004). A parallel increase is in the proportion of women and girl migrants to developed countries where they reached 51 percent of the total immigrant population by 2000 (United Nations, 2005:iv). This trend in migration to the developed countries has advantages for those countries, where because of the demographic consequences of declining fertility rates and longer life expectancy, populations are declining without immigration. The ratio of migrants to native born peoples worldwide is 1 in 35. However, for developing countries, the ratio is 1 in 70 (United Nations, 2006). Table 2-1 below shows clearly the trend for migration to be to the developed world with North America, Oceania, and Europe being the major areas of net gain in population. The less developed areas of Latin America, Africa, and Asia show a net loss of population through migration.

Table 2-1. Global Migration: Patterns and Trends 2000–2005

Region	Net Migration rate per 1,000 population
North America	+4.2
Oceania	+3.2
Europe	+1.5
Latin America and the Caribbean	−1.5
Africa	−0.5
Asia	−0.3

Source: Adapted from United Nations (2006). http://www.un.org/esa/population/publications/2006 Migration_Chart/International_Migration_2006_files/Migration2006.pdf

While regions of the Global South, overall, indicate a loss of population, migration across borders does occur, with movements of people within the region, and this is not reflected in the table (See *New York Times*, June 22, 2007: http://www.nytimes.com/ref/world/20070622_CAPE VERDE_GRAPHIC.html)

The Pros and Cons of Immigration

Immigration has an important and often unrecognized impact on demographics in developed economies. During the first half of this century, the populations of most developed countries are projected to become smaller and older as a result of below-replacement fertility and increased longevity. In the absence of migration, the declines in population size will be even greater than those projected, and population aging will be more rapid (United Nations, 2000). Other advantages of immigration may be considered to be the provision of new opportunities for individuals and families, easing the effect of unemployment in economies that send migrants, the receipts of remittances, technology transfer, and investments from the Diasporas, along with increased trade (United Nations, 2004). In considering the costs and benefits of worldwide immigration patterns, remittances to the home country are an important consideration. For some countries, (e.g., El Salvador, Eritrea, Jamaica, Jordan, Nicaragua, and Yemen), the remittances from émigrés exceeds 10 percent of the national budget. These remittances are important in the microeconomics of the family, where they may buy luxury items, and help to establish and grow family assets (United Nations, 2003).

Despite these advantages, by the turn of the century, in 2001, approximately 25 percent of all countries reported immigration as being too high. This view is shared alike by both developed and developing nations and both groups have aimed to lower numbers of immigrants and develop more restrictive policies: 44 percent of developed countries and 39 percent of developing countries (United Nations, 2003). Clearly the disadvantages of immigration currently seem to be in the forefront. These include the loss of highly skilled workers, commonly referred to as "the brain drain" resulting in reduced quality in some services and industries, reduced growth and productivity, lower return from investment in education, loss of tax revenues, and the fact that remittances from overseas diminish over time (United Nations, 2004).

Explanatory Theories of Immigration

The study of immigration is interdisciplinary, and the nature of theories is inevitably dependent on the academic discipline of the proponent. Human geographers, economists, demographers, anthropologists, political scientists, and social workers are just some of the disciplines from which scholars of immigration may propose theories. Portes (1999) has proposed that a grand theory of immigration would be of little value because of the

degree of high level generalization necessary. Instead, he proposes that the best explanations come from mid-level theories. However, mid-level theories tend to become discipline dependent, and draw from a limited range of knowledge, focusing on the knowledge base of the particular academic discipline. Massey, in his 1999 review of explanatory theories of human migration, puts forward six theory groups. In these groups the influence of a disciplinary frame of reference can be seen. However, he also presents and discusses a synthesis approach to these theories as a seventh possible group, which assists in transcending some of the academic discipline restrictions, while stopping short of grand theory. Massey's review includes neoclassical economics, the new economics of migration, segmented labor market theory, world systems theory, social capital theory, cumulative causation, and the above mentioned synthesis approach.

Labor supply and demand is the focus of the *neoclassical economics* approaches. It is argued at the macroeconomic level that labor will move from a country with a plentiful labor supply and therefore low wages, to a country with a low labor supply and high wages. A parallel microeconomic process also occurs in this case, argues Massey (1999), where individuals and families make a cost benefit analysis of migration that informs and motivates their decision to migrate or not. The *new economics approach* moves away from income as a measure of success or satisfaction and focuses more on relative deprivation (Kubursi, 2006). This involves comparing with others in the full range of the socioeconomic structure of a society. As countries get richer, the sense of relative deprivation increases, and the more likely the individual or representatives of the family are to migrate, it is argued. Remittances support the family in the homeland (Nyame & Grant, 2007). The neoclassical economics model and the new economics model both involve individual decision making in the immigration process. *Segmented labor market* theory (Vilalta-Bufi, 2007) moves to a more structural explanation of human migration. The need for a class of low wage earners in an advanced industrial economy, and the inability or unwillingness of the economic system to provide a higher level of minimum wage because of the need to preserve status and hierarchy in the social structure, offers opportunity to immigrants who see the low wages as an improvement on their condition in their native country and also offers the opportunity for increased status because of the remittances that can be returned to the family in the home country. Like the segmented labor market theory, *world systems theory*, which recognizes the economic interdependence (and inequality) of nations (Goldfrank, Goodman & Szasz, 1999) provides yet another predominantly structural explanation of migration as opposed to individual and family decisions proposed by the neoclassical and new economics models. World systems theory suggests that in the process of becoming involved in a developing country, capitalist countries dislodge the equilibrium through new economic, social, cultural, and political influences and create motivation for migration through contact with capitalist products and lifestyle. This theory it may be argued, is evidenced by the fact that migrants do not come from the poorest countries that have had no contact with capitalism, but from the countries that have had contact with global capital systems. Furthermore, this system perpetuates the poverty of the poorer countries, because the system is so arranged to be in favor of the rich countries. *Social capital theory* accepts the individual nature of the migration decision, but proposes that as a result of successive migrations, institutions, social welfare agencies, and entrepreneurs, all form social capital and make following migrant journeys much less of a risk. Thus others are likely to be motivated to migrate (Akcapar, 2007; Cheong, Edwards, Goulbourne & Solomos, 2007). The final explanation Massey (1999) reviews is *cumulative causation theory*, developed by Myrdal (1957) and further applied by Massey (1990; Heer, 2002). Similar to social capital theory, cumulative causation theory argues that successive immigrations make the process easier for those who follow, but in this case in a broader context than the single variable of social capital. Variables considered by cumulative causation theorists include: "the expansion of networks, the distribution of income, the distribution of land, the organization of agriculture, culture, the regional distribution of human capital, the social meaning of work, and the structure of production" (Massey, 1999:45).

It is not impossible, argues Massey, in presenting his empirically based synthesis of these models, that all of these factors can be operating and they are certainly not mutually exclusive. He further suggests:

a satisfactory theoretical account of international migration must contain at least four elements: a treatment of the structural forces that promote emigration from developing countries; a characterization of the structural forces that attract immigrants into developed nations; a consideration of the motives, goals and aspirations of the people who respond to these structural forces by becoming international migrants; and a treatment of the social and economic structures that arise to connect areas of out- and in- migration. (Massey, 1999:50)

The first chapter of this volume, based on the model proposed by Segal (2002), includes all these factors. Zolberg (1999, 2006) focuses on an additional set of theories around the role of the state in migration theory. He proposes a mid-range theory concerned with the role of the state, discussing the interaction of global capitalism with the formation of nation state identity and political boundaries. Other recent approaches consider a gender based analysis and social network theories including transnational communities (Pessar, 1999; Schiller, 1999).

Issues in Comparative Analysis

This volume consists of country case studies from around the world. It may be said of this approach that the variance in the data presented makes it difficult to do comparative studies, since programs, policies, and cultures differ so much that comparisons are never equal. On the pro side, the chapters offer rich data for students and scholars to analyze according to their particular purpose and interest. The case study has been a long established method in social science research since J. S. Mill wrote *System of Logic* in 1843, establishing the principles of inductive generalization from different cases. Social science research methodologists continue to debate the effectiveness of the case study as a method of social research, although scholars still use the method (Sanderson, 1995; Tilly, 1998). Readers should be aware therefore of some of the advantages and disadvantages of this

Table 2-2. Five Common Misunderstandings and Corrections Concerning Case Study Research

	Misunderstanding	Flyvbjerg's Correction
Misunderstanding no. 1.	General, theoretical (context-independent) knowledge is more valuable than concrete, practical (context-dependent) knowledge	Predictive theories and universals cannot be found in the study of human affairs. Concrete, context-dependent knowledge is therefore more valuable than the vain search for predictive theories and universals.
Misunderstanding no. 2.	One cannot generalize on the basis of an individual case; therefore, the case study cannot contribute to scientific development.	One can often generalize on the basis of a single case, and the case study may be central to scientific development via generalization as supplement or alternative to other methods. But formal generalization is overvalued as a source of scientific development, whereas "the force of example" is underestimated.
Misunderstanding no. 3.	The case study is most useful for generating hypotheses, that is, in the first stage of a total research process, while other methods are more suitable for hypotheses testing and theory building.	The case study is useful for both generating and testing of hypotheses but is not limited to these research activities alone.
Misunderstanding no. 4.	The case study contains a bias toward verification, that is, a tendency to confirm the researcher's preconceived notions.	The case study contains no greater bias toward verification of the researcher's preconceived notions than other methods of inquiry. On the contrary, experience indicates that the case study contains a greater bias toward falsification of preconceived notions than toward verification.
Misunderstanding no. 5.	It is often difficult to summarize and develop general propositions and theories on the basis of specific case studies.	It is correct that summarizing case studies is often difficult, especially as concerns case process. It is less correct as regards case outcomes. The problems in summarizing case studies, however, are due more often to the properties of the reality studied than to the case study as a research method. Often it is not desirable to summarize and generalize case studies. Good studies should be read as narratives in their entirety.

Source: Bent, Flyvbjerg, "Five Misunderstandings About Case-Study Research." In Clive Seale, Giampietro Gobo, Jaber F. Gubrium, and David Silverman, eds., *Qualitative Research Practice*. London and Thousand Oaks, CA: Sage, 2004, pp. 420–434. PDF format, Quoted in Levi-Faur (2005). http://poli.haifa.ac.il/~levi/casem.html#b.

approach to social science information. Critiques have usually been proposed from the perspective of a positivist approach, and a major area of concern has been the issues around establishing causal inferences derived from inductive logic (Rose, 1991). A related concern is the inability to control for all variables in a comparison, especially given considerations of equifinality, leading to spurious

inferences. Other criticisms are that there are too many variables and too few cases and that case selection may bias results. Additionally, Goldthorpe (1997) argues that comparative research has further problems. The "Galton problem," derived from a critique of an earlier sociological study, suggests that the treatment of nations as independent are untenable in an increasingly global world.

On the pro side of the argument for a case study approach, it is argued that case studies can indeed be used both for theory building, and also for explaining, illustrating, analyzing, and testing existing theories. The rise of postmodernism has deemphasized positivism and given new credibility to constructionist approaches such as the case study. Case studies rich in variables can discuss how different combinations of independent variables can interact to produce different levels and types of dependent variables. This assists in hypothesis forming. With regard to theory building, Leeming (2005) argues that there are three essential components: first there must be a conceptual scheme, second there is an examination of the relationships between variables or properties, and third there is a means of evaluating and verifying. Özden and Schiff (2007:2) propose that studies on migration fall into three categories, dependent on the methodology of the study. Macroeconometric studies of cross-country comparisons forms their first category: they argue that these give an overview, but are limited in their ability to provide explanations for migration at the nation-state level. Their second category consists of microeconometric studies that focus on the nation-state level, and so complement the first category of studies. The third group of studies proposed by Özden and Schiff are "policy *centric*" case studies that "illustrate and clarify many theoretical mechanisms and to advance the understanding of the impact of different migration policies" (2). This volume is in the tradition of the third category of studies: the case study approach in this volume sets the background for theory building. The framework for understanding immigration along with the questions for analysis provide a means of examining and comparing the data, and the bibliographic information provided along with each chapter offers resources to enable scholars to follow up further more detailed specific country information to provide the means for evaluation. Comparisons of similar information based on the framework for immigration often can highlight issues that may be "writ large" in another society, thus allowing scholars to review their own society and policies from a new perspective. Further advantages of case comparison research is that it contributes to intercultural understanding in a global world and thus ultimately contributing to world peace and it extends knowledge of social systems, allowing for the implementation of more effective programs. Levi-Faur (2005) offers a concise, at-a-glance summary of some of the pros and cons of case study research.

One of the ways in which a comparative analysis may be carried out is to borrow a format from the well-established model and method of policy analysis in order to assist in the extrapolation of themes and trends from the case studies.

The study of social policy offers various models of analysis, and examples of these may found in the following texts: Dobelstein (1990), Gil (1992), Segal and Brzuzy (1998), Karger and Stoesz (2006). These models of policy analysis usually include identifying the social issue and its history; including a consideration of causes; identifying the main stakeholders; identifying the norms, values, and ideologies that lie behind the policy; and an evaluation of the costs, benefits, effectiveness, and intended and unintended outcomes of the policy. The series of questions below are based on this approach to guide the analysis of the case studies based on the framework for immigration described in Chapter One.

Model for the Analysis of Immigration Trends, Issues, and Policies

Economic. Identify and analyze the main economic trends that impact a country's migration policies:

1. What is the country's history of migration trends as a receiving and/or sending country? Is it predominantly a migrant receiving or sending country?
2. What level of labor (skilled, unskilled) and what industries and services are maintained by immigrant labor?
3. How does immigrant workers' pay compare with the general population?
4. Does the government encourage or discourage immigrant labor?
5. Are there plans to "liberalize" labor movement across the country's borders?

Political. *Identify and analyze political issues, historical and current, that may be either major influences, or contextual issues in framing a country's response to immigration.*

1. Do current policies restrict or encourage immigration?
2. Are current policies selective about who may or may not enter, with regard to nation of origin, ethnicity, socioeconomic status, education, profession, and so on?
3. How effective are these policies?
4. What is the current policy regarding asylees?
5. Are undocumented or irregular migrants a significant political consideration?
6. Is human trafficking a problem? If so what policies address this issue?
7. Was there an appreciable impact linking immigration with terrorism after 2001?
8. Has significant "brain drain" effect produced return migration incentives and policies?
9. How significant is xenophobia and public concern about immigration a factor in policy making on immigrant populations?
10. How do immigration policies deal with the different classes of foreigners entering the country, for example, immigrants, migrants, migrant labor, refugees, economic refugees, asylees, internally displaced persons?
11. What human rights guarantees are evident in the county's policies? Is there evidence of racial, gender, or other oppression?
12. Who are the major players and stakeholders who influence policies relating to immigration and immigrants?

Sociocultural. *What sociocultural patterns and trends influence the quality of life of immigrants in the country(ies) studied?*

1. What demographic trends in both the sending and receiving countries influence immigration and migrant labor policies?
2. How does migration affect demographic trends including population growth?
3. What policies are in place relating to family reunification of immigrants?
4. What access to welfare and other benefits do immigrants have (e.g., health care, housing, education, employment)? Are

they com-parable to those of the general population?
5. How far are national or religious customs of immigrants restricted? (e.g., headwear).
6. How far are immigrant populations acculturated, assimilated, marginalized, or excluded?
7. Is the treatment of migrants consistent with the United Nations' Convention on Human Rights?
8. How significant a factor is xenophobia and public concern about immigration in policy making on immigrant populations?
9. Are there special issues relating to women and children who are immigrants?
10. Are there special issues regarding race and ethnicity in immigrant populations?
11. Are immigrants marginalized economically and socially?
12. Where do immigrants tend to live, for example, areas of country, neighborhoods?
13. What is the status of children born to immigrants? Does it compare with the native born population?
14. Is there due consideration of the trauma experienced by refugees, asylees, and some migrant laborers in their attempts to enter a country of settlement?
15. Are immigrants eligible to eventually attain citizenship?

Outcomes and Evaluation. *What are the outcomes and costs/benefits?*

1. What are the goals of immigration policies?
2. What are the costs of immigration to the country, for example, depletion of resources, challenges to established norms, diversification of population?
3. What are the benefits of immigration to the country, for example, increased labor force, additional resources, diversification of population?
4. What are the costs to individual migrants, for example, loss of natural supports, challenge to tradition, dilution of culture?
5. What are the benefits to individual migrants, for example, increased economic and professional opportunities, personal growth and development?

6. What are the overall strengths and weaknesses in immigration policies?
7. Are immigration policies designed in the interests of both the receiving country and the individual immigrant?
8. What are the unintended consequences of migration policies for the country and for the individual immigrant?
9. What changes are recommended to bring about a more egalitarian opportunity structure for immigrants?

The country case studies in this volume offer a comprehensive collection of information for exploring social trends in order to examine and explicate existing theories, construct new theories, examine the similarities and differences in immigration issues around the world, and analyze the social, economic, and cultural issues arising out of human migration patterns. These are also a valuable resource for researchers in identifying themes for further study, given that the responses are based on a common framework (Segal, 2002), which emphasizes that the complexity of reactions to immigration must be viewed from both the perspective of the immigrant and of the receiving country. A great deal depends on current political, economic, and social conditions in the receiving country as well as the human capital immigrants bring. These two sets of factors, the immigrants' resources for immigration and the receptiveness of the receiving country are highly interactive, with each demonstrating substantial influence on the other.

The chapters explore the consequences of immigration for each nation and elucidate the unique experiences, opportunities, and challenges as each country develops, modifies, and adapts its policies, programs, and services in the context of its own immigration experience.

Note

1. Website: http://www.nytimes.com/ref/world/20070622_CAPEVERDE_GRAPHIC.html#, accessed February 1, 2008.

References

Akcapar, S.K. (2006). Conversion as a migration strategy in a transit country: Iranian Shiites becoming Christians in Turkey. *International Migration Review*, 50(4).

Cohen, R. (1995). Prologue, Chapter one. In Cohen, R., (ed.) *The Cambridge survey of world migration*. Cambridge, UK: Cambridge University Press.

Dobelstein, A.W. (1990). *Social Welfare: Policy and Analysis*. Chicago: Nelson Hall.

Cheong, P.H., Edwards, R., Goulbourne, H., & Solomos, J. (2007). Immigration, social cohesion and social capital: A critical review. *Critical Social Policy*, 27(1), 24–49.

Gil, D.G. (1992). *Unraveling social policy*. 5th ed. Rochester, NY: Schenkman Books.

GCIM (2005). *Migration in an interconnected world: New directions for action*. Report of the Global Commission on International Migration, Switzerland. Downloaded 8/10/2005 from: www.gcim.org.

Goldthorpe, J.H. (1997). Current issues in comparative macrosociology. A debate on methodological issues. *Comparative Social Research*, 16, 1–26.

Goldfrank, W.L., Goodman, D., & Szasz, A. (eds.) (1999). *Ecology and the world system*. Westport, CT: Greenwood Press.

Hayter, T. (2004). *Open borders: The case against immigration controls*. Sidmouth, UK: Pluto Press.

Heer, D.M. (2002). When cumulative causation conflicts with relative economic opportunity: Recent change in the Hispanic population of the United States. *Migraciones Internacionales*, 1(3), 32–53. Downloaded 2/1/2008 from: http://redalyc.uaemex.mx/redalyc/pdf/151/15101302.pdf.

Karger H.J., & Stoesz, D. (2006). *American social welfare policy. A pluralist approach*. Boston, MA: Pearson.

Kubursi, A. (2006). The economics of migration and remittances under globalization. Downloaded 2/1/2008 from: http://www.un.org/docs/ecosoc/meetings/2006/hls2006/Preparatory/Statements/Kubursi_RT6.pdf.

Leeming, M. (2005). *Sociological theory: A social science approach to the family*. Downloaded 10/14/2005 from : http://www.stolaf.edu/people/leming/soc371res/theory.html.

Levi-Faur, D. (2005). Comparative methods in political and social research. Downloaded 10/15/2005 from: http://poli.haifa.ac.il/~levi/method.html.

Massey, D.S. (1990). Social structure, household strategies, and the cumulative causation of migration. *Population Index*, 56, 3–36.

Massey, D.S. (1999). Why does immigration occur? A theoretical synthesis. Chapter 2 in: Hirschman, C., Kasinitz, P., & DeWind, J. *The handbook of international migration: The American experience*. New York: Russell Sage Foundation.

Morawska, E. (2007). International migration: Its various mechanisms and different theories that try to explain it. Malmö University/School of International Migration and Ethnic Relations: Willy Brandt Series of Working Papers in International Migration and Ethnic Relations. Downloaded 2/1/2008 from: http://dspace.mah. se:8080/dspace/bitstream/2043/5224/1/WB1%2007 %20inlaga_1.pdf.

Myrdal, G. (1957). The principle of circular and cumulative causation. In Myrdal, G. (ed), *Rich lands and poor: The road to world prosperity.* New York, NY: Harper, 11–22.

Nayame, F.K. & Grant, J.A. (2007). Implications of migration patterns associated with the mining and minerals industry in Ghana. Downloaded 2/1/ 2008 from: http://www.imi.ox.ac.uk/pdfs/Nyame% 20Grant%20Ghana%2007.pdf.

Özden., C. & Schiff, M., (2007). Preface. In Schiff, M. & Özden., C. (eds.) *International migration, economic development & policy.* Washington, DC: World Bank and Palgrave Macmillan.

Pessar, P.R. (1999). The role of gender, households, and social networks in the migration process: A review and appraisal. Chapter 3 in Hirschman, C., Kasinitz, P., & DeWind, J. *The handbook of international migration: The American experience.* New York: Russell Sage Foundation.

Portes, A. (1999). Immigration theory for a new century: Some problems and opportunities. Chapter 1 in Hirschman, C., Kasinitz, P., & DeWind, J. *The handbook of international migration: The American experience.* New York: Russell Sage Foundation.

Rose, Richard. (1991) Comparing forms of comparative analysis. *Political Studies,* 39, 446–462.

Sanderson, S.K. (1995). *Sociological worlds.* Los Angeles: Roxbury Publishing.

Schiller, N.G. (1999). Transmigrants and nation states: Something old and something new in the U.S. immigrant experience. Chapter 5 in Hirschman, C., Kasinitz, P., & DeWind, J., *The handbook of international migration: The American experience.* New York: Russell Sage Foundation.

Segal, E.A. & Brzuzy, S. (1998). *Social welfare policy, programs, and practice.* Itasca, IL: Peacock.

Segal, U.A. (2002). *A framework for immigration: Asians in the United States.* New York: Columbia University Press.

Suhrke, A. (1995). *Refugees and asylum in the Muslim world.* In Cohen, R., *The Cambridge survey of world migration.* Cambridge, UK: Cambridge University Press.

Tilly, C. (1998). *Durable inequality.* Berkeley: University of California Press.

United Nations (2000). *Replacement migration.* Population Division, Department of Economic and Social affairs, United Nations Secretariat.

Downloaded 10/15/2005 from: http://www.un.org/ esa/population/publications/migration/ presseng.htm.

United Nations (2003). *International migration 2002.* Population Division. United Nations publication (ST/ESA/SER.A/219) Downloaded 10/7/2005 from: http://www.un.org/esa/population/publications/ ittmig 2002/Migration2002.pdf.

United Nations (2004). *World economic and social survey 2004: International migration.* The Department of Economic and Social Affairs of the United Nations Secretariat, New York, United Nations publication Sales No. E.04.II.C.3. Downloaded 10/8/2005 from: http://www.un.org/ esa/policy/wess/wess2004files/part2web/preface.pdf.

United Nations (2005). *2004 world survey on the role of women in development: Women and international migration.* Department of Economic and Social Affairs of the United Nations Secretariat, Division for the Advancement of Women. New York, United Nations. United Nations publication Sales No. E.04.IV.4.

United Nations. (2006). *International migration 2006.* Department of Economic and Social Affairs, Population Division. Downloaded 2/1/2008 from: http://www.un.org/esa/population/publications/ 2006 Migration_Chart/International_Migration_ 2006_files/Migration2006.pdf.

UNHCR (2006). *Basic facts. Refugees by numbers 2006.* United Nations High Commissioner for Refugees. Downloaded 2/1/2008 from: http://www. unhcr.ch/cgi-bin/texis/vtx/basics/opendoc.htm?tbl =BASICS&id=3b028097c.

UNCHR (2007). *Protecting refugees and the role of the UNHCR.* United Nations High Commissioner for Refugees. Downloaded 2/1/2008 from http://www. unhcr.org/basics/BASICS/4034b6a34.pdf.

US Bureau of the Census (2004). *Global population at a glance, 2002 and beyond.* U.S. Department of Commerce, Economics and Statistics Administration U.S. Census Bureau. Downloaded 10/7/ 2005 from: http://www.census.gov/ipc/prod/wp02/ wp02-1.pdf.

Vilalta-Bufi, M. (2007). Labor mobility and inter-industry wage variation, DEGIT Conference Papers c012_024, DEGIT, Dynamics, Economic Growth, and International Trade.

Zolberg, A. R. (1999). Matters of State: Theorizing immigration policy. Chapter 4 in Hirschman, C., Kasinitz, P., & DeWind, J. *The handbook of international migration: The American experience.* New York. Russell Sage Foundation.

Zolberg, A. R. (2006). *A nation by design: Immigration policy in the fashioning of America.* Cambridge, MA: Harvard University Press.

PART II

Nations with Large Immigrant Populations

3

United States

The Changing Face of the United States of America

Uma A. Segal

This "land of opportunities," the United States of America, has mixed, conflicting attitudes, perceptions, and responses to the presence of immigrants in general and immigrants from specific nations in particular. It is clear that for a large proportion of immigrants, a primary impetus is economic opportunity; likewise, several deliberations in the United States surround the economic impact of migration. Ongoing immigration debates juggle arguments regarding assets these newcomers bring to the country with those about drains they place on its infrastructure, and the United States remains divided on the net worth of immigration in the twenty-first century. Since the terror attacks of September 11, 2001, on the Pentagon in Washington, DC, and the World Trade Center in New York, suspicion of foreigners, particularly those of color, has developed exponentially, and xenophobia continues to be evident. It is in this climate of cultural chauvinism that on January 20, 2009, citizens of the United States placed in their highest office, the presidency, Barack Hussein Obama II, the son of a Kenyan immigrant. Yes, it is a land of opportunity.

Individuals and families from around the globe form a continuous stream of immigrants to the United States. The backlog of visa applications and waiting lists to enter the nation stretches to several years. Undocumented immigrants, both those who arrive without legal papers and those who overstay their visits, abound. Record numbers of refugees and asylees are admitted from countries in political turmoil. Disproportionately large numbers of entrants into the United States in recent years have been people of color from Asia, Africa, and Central and South America, and despite encountering a series of barriers, an overwhelming majority remains applying for permanent residence. Reasons for this ongoing influx are readily apparent, for in spite of the problems prevalent in the United States, it continues to be one of the most attractive nations in the world. There is much in the United States that native-born Americans take for granted and that is not available in many other countries, and there are several amenities, opportunities, possibilities, lifestyles, and freedoms in the United States that are not found together in any other nation.

In theory, and often in reality, this is a land of freedom, of equality, of opportunity, of a superior quality of life, of easy access to education, and of relatively few human rights violations. It is a land that, in the twenty-first century, is struggling toward multiculturalism and pluralism in its institutions and social outlook. It is a land that, compared to several others, offers newcomers a relatively easy path through which to become integrated into its largesse. While the debate over the value of immigration persists, the fact is that it is a debate, and while immigration policies are not without discrimination and selectivity, they are more open now than ever before. Thus, despite both political and social perceptions of foreigners following the September 11, 2001, terror attacks, despite increased security measures and scrutiny of individuals, and despite some highly disturbing xenophobic backlash, new immigrants continue to arrive in the United States in record numbers. In addition, almost all of the vast numbers that entered years before value the quality of life this nation continues to allow them, for frequently, even when life in the United States is difficult, it is less so than it would have been in their countries of origin. Beginning with an overview of the impact of historical and current immigration legislation, this chapter presents the demographic profile of the country's foreign-born population, the mutual influences between immigrants and the nation's economic, social, political, and cultural environments, and implications of these phenomena.

Immigration Legislation

Immigration policy defines the parameters of those admitted into a country, identifying who may be allowed in and under what circumstances; it also specifies who should be prevented from coming. *Immigrant policy*, on the other hand, addresses issues of immigrant integration: Once they are in, how are these newcomers helped to integrate into society, and what resources may they access and with what stipulations.

The United States developed immigration legislation as early as the late nineteenth century, passing the Chinese Exclusion Act on May 6, 1882, and restricting, for the first time, the entry of people based on ethnicity. This was followed by several other regulatory measures and Acts[1] that circumscribed entry into the United States. The history of immigration to this country may be divided into seven periods during which legal measures controlled the

categories of people allowed immigration (Kim, 1994:8–9).

1. *The colonial period (1609–1775)*: most immigrants were from the British Isles and the colonies had little effective control.
2. *The American Revolutionary period (1776–1840)*: European immigration slowed because of war and general "antiforeign" feelings.
3. *The "old" immigration period (1841–1882)*: local governments recruited people from Northern Europe. Chinese could also immigrate with little difficulty.
4. *The regulation period (1882–1920)*: Chinese were excluded from immigrating, but major entry occured from Central, Eastern, and Southern Europe.
5. *The restriction and exclusion period (1921–1952)*: A quota system restricted immigration from Central, Eastern, and Southern Europe, and all Asians were excluded from admission and from eligibility for U.S. citizenship.
6. *The partial liberalization period (1952–1965)*: Asians were assigned the same quota as those from Central, Eastern, and Southern Europe, and also allowed naturalization.
7. *The liberalized policy period (1965–present)*: the quota policy was repealed to allow entry to immigrants from Third World (and all) countries.

The Immigration and Nationality Act

The October 3, 1965, amendments to the 1952 Immigration and Nationality Act had a major and permanent impact on U.S. immigration, dramatically altering the traditional immigrant origins and numbers. Prior to 1965 and the liberalization of immigration laws, the majority of entrants into the United States were from European countries. Under President Johnson's guidance, Congress moved to base immigration criteria on occupation rather than national origin. When the 1965 amendments: (1) abolished national origins quota; (2) established preferences for relatives of citizens and permanent residents; (3) exempted immediate relatives of citizens and some special groups (certain ministers of religion, former employees of U.S. government abroad, etc.); and (4) expanded limits of world coverage to a 20,000-per-country limit, the influx of newcomers from non-European countries was, and continues to be, unprecedented. While minor modifications are frequently made to the Immigration and Nationality Act of 1965, and the number of worldwide quotas occasionally changes, it remains the primary force directing immigration. Now the numbers of immigrants admitted legally are: (1) fixed by law; (2) limited only by demands for those considered eligible; and (3) restricted by processing constraints (Gordon, 2005). The 2009 fiscal year limits are for the categories below:[2]

Family Sponsored Immigrants (226,000 annual numbers)
1. Unmarried adult sons and daughters of citizens (23,400 annually)
2. Spouses and unmarried sons and unmarried daughters of permanent resident aliens (114,200)
3. Married sons and married daughters of citizens (23,400)
4. Adult brothers and sisters of citizens (65,000)

Employment-Based Immigrants (140,000 annually)
1. Priority workers (40,040)

   a. Aliens with extraordinary ability
   b. Professors and researchers
   c. Certain multinational executives and managers

2. Members of the professions holding advanced degrees (40,040)
3. Skilled workers, professionals, and other workers (40,040)
4. Special immigrants, usually refugees adjusting their status (9,940)
5. Employment creators, "investors" (9,940)

   Diversity (55,000 annually, effective 1995)
   Non-preferential immigrants ineligible under the other categories

A large number of legal immigrants are those not subject to these numerical limits—relatives of U.S. citizens, children adopted from abroad, and children born abroad to permanent residents. These can be as many as 500,000. An interesting addition to immigration quotas is the "investor program" that issues approximately 10,000 visas annually to those who are willing to invest between $500,000 and one million dollars in the United States. In reality, immigrant numbers are substantially greater as those already in the United States may "adjust" their status (i.e., from student, visitor) to immigrant. Table 3-1 provides a general view of immigrant visas issued to people outside the U.S.; these numbers include neither status adjustments during that period nor those not subject to these limits (i.e. relatives of U.S. citizens).

Several immigration-related legislation or actions, however, since the beginning of the liberalization period, have affected diverse populations in a variety of ways, from entry

Table 3-1. Immigrant Visas Issued at Foreign Service Posts (2004–2008)

	2004	2005	2006	2007	2008
Immigrant Categories					
Immediate Relatives	151,724	180,432	224,187	219,323	238,848
Special Immigrants	675	782	766	1,648	2,558
Vietnam Amerasian immigrants	37	119	96	69	77
Family Sponsored Preference	152,454	146,279	139,753	151,128	169,896
Employment-Based Preference	28,656	21,290	15,706	19,685	13,461
Armed Forces Special Immigrants	7	4	0	2	2
DV Diversity Transition	45,849	46,099	44,349	38,762	45,246
Schedule A Worker	0	7,242	24,208	3,757	0
Total	**379,402**	**402,247**	**449,065**	**434,374**	**470,088**

Source: U.S. Department of State, Report of the Visa Office. Website: http://www.travel.state.gov/pdf/FY08-AR-TableI.pdf, accessed February 12, 2009.

into the United States itself to access to fundamental rights. Some are sketched below:

1980: *The Refugee Act* removed refugees as a preference category. The President and Congress determine the annual ceiling and country distributions (ceilings have ranged from 50,000–90,000).

1986: *The Immigration Reform and Control Act (IRCA)* legalized several undocumented immigrants but made it unlawful to hire undocumented workers.

1990: *The Immigration Act of 1990* increased the annual immigrant limit to 700,000 and established the Immigrant Investor Program.

1996: *Welfare Reform* ended many cash and medical assistance programs for most legal immigrants.

1996: *The Illegal Immigration Reform and Immigrant Responsibility Act (IIRIRA)* expanded enforcement operations of the Immigration and Naturalization Service.

2001: *The USA Patriot Act*, in response to the September 11, 2001, terror attacks on New York and Washington, DC, gives federal officials greater power to intercept national and international communications.

The *Comprehensive Immigration Reform Act of 2007* was a bill that focused on managing unauthorized migration, but failed to pass the House. Its primary components were increased border security, creation of a guest worker program, a path to citizenship for undocumented workers, worksite enforcement, and criminal penalties for those continuing to reside illegally in the country. While the bill did not pass, the issues remain in the forefront of concern.

Demographic Trends

Newcomers to the United States enter under a variety of conditions. Early migrants of the nineteenth and early twentieth centuries came as volunteer immigrants, indentured laborers, or as slaves. Most however, were considered "legal immigrants," particularly in the absence of any legislation. Present-day immigrants may be categorized as voluntary immigrants (illegal or undocumented) or as refugees (and asylees). Several legal immigrants, after a minimum length of residence in the country, choose to apply for U.S. citizenship.

The U.S. Census Bureau (2008) indicates that in 2007, of the approximately 301.6 million residents of the country, 38 million (12.6%) were foreign born (Figure 3-1).

Another 16 million (22.9% of all children under age 18) were of the second generation, children with at least one immigrant parent. In 2007, 25,270 asylees[3] also were admitted as immigrants and, in the same year, 660,477 thousand individuals were naturalized, although another 89,683 were denied citizenship. Immigration trends indicate that the percentage of the foreign-born population has

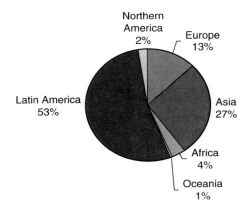

Figure 3-1. Origins of the Foreign Born — 2007
Source: U.S. Census, 2008.

been rising dramatically: In the 1980 Census, it constituted 6.2% of the population, increasing to 7.9% in 1990 and 11.1% in 2000.

It is clear from the distribution of sending countries, that although the largest number of immigrants to the United States is Mexican (Table 3-2), this is still only about 10%–15% of the total entrants; the percentage is even less if refugee numbers (Table 3-3) are included (U.S. Census Bureau, 2008). Hence, it is essential that, while recognizing the strong Mexican presence, one remain cognizant of the diversity of immigrants in the United States.

Among those who voluntarily migrate to the United States are immigrants without the requisite papers, the unauthorized/undocumented population. While there is no valid method of counting undocumented immigrants, estimates by the Pew Hispanic Center (Passel & Cohn, 2008) suggest numbers ranging from between 10.2 million in 2004 and 11.9 million in 2008, peaking at 12.4 million in 2007. They are currently estimated to be four percent of the population with regional origins believed to be as found in Figure 3-2 (Passel & Cohn, 2008).

Despite perceptions of undocumented immigrants being those who slip across borders without appropriate documentation, the Office of Homeland Security reported in 2000 that about one-third of all undocumented immigrants are

Table 3-2. Immigrants Admitted by Region and Select Country of Last Residence (2004–2007)

Region and country of birth	2004	2005	2006	2007
All countries	957,883	1,122,257	1,266,129	1,052,415
Europe	135,663	180,396	169,156	120,759
Asia	319,025	382,707	411,746	359,387
Africa	62,623	79,697	112,100	89,277
Oceania	6,954	7,432	8,000	6,639
America	408,972	432,726	548,812	434,272
Canada	22,439	29,930	23,913	20,324
Mexico	173,711	157,992	170,042	143,180
Caribbean	82,116	91,371	144,477	114,318
Cuba	15,385	20,651	44,248	25,441
Dominican Republic	30,063	27,365	37,997	27,875
Haiti	13,695	13,491	21,625	29,978
Jamaica	13,581	17,774	24,538	18,873
Other Caribbean	9,392	12,090	16,069	12,151
Central America	61,253	52,629	74,244	53,834
South America	69,452	100,803	136,134	102,616

Source: U.S. Department of Homeland Security. Office of Immigration Statistics. (2008). *2007 yearbook of immigration statistics.* Website: http://www.dhs.gov/xlibrary/assets/statistics/yearbook/2007/ois_2007_yearbook.pdf, accessed February 8, 2009.

Table 3-3. Refugee Arrivals by Region (2004–2007)

Region of birth	2004	2005	2006	2007
Total	52,837	53,738	41,150	48,217
Europe	9,254	11,316	10,456	4,561
Asia	10,896	14,977	9,245	23,195
Africa	29,110	20,746	18,185	17,485
Oceania	0	0	0	0
North America	2,998	6,368	3,145	2,922
South America	579	331	119	54

Source: U.S. Department of Homeland Security. Office of Immigration Statistics. (2008). *2007 yearbook of immigration statistics.* Website: http://www.dhs.gov/xlibrary/assets/statistics/yearbook/2007/ois_2007_yearbook.pdf, accessed February 8, 2009.

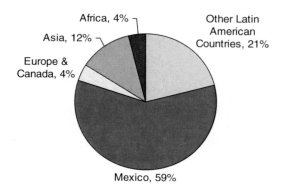

Figure 3-2. Unauthorized Immigrants by Region—2007

"overstays" who fail to return to their homelands when the period of their visas expires (GAO, 2004).

Refugees and asylees, unlike immigrants, are usually involuntary migrants. The United States has always been a refuge for those fleeing from persecution and, traditionally, has the largest number of the world's refugees (Mayadas & Segal, 2000), those people so identified by the 1951 convention and the 1967 protocol of the United Nations High Commissioner for Refugees.[4] The U.S. President, in consultation with Congress, establishes annual numbers and allocations of refugees based on current world political climate. In recent years, these annual ceilings have been as high as 91,000 in 1999 and as low as 70,000 in 2005 and 2006 (U.S. Department of State, 2005). Ceilings have risen again to 80,000 in both 2008 and 2009, but the 2008 allocations are not projected to be achieved (Table 3-4).

Asylees differ from refugees in that they usually enter the United States on their own,

and once within the United States they apply for asylum, which may or may not be granted. Frequently detained until a determination is made, they are either legally admitted into the country as refugees or are repatriated to their homelands. All refugees may apply to adjust their status to permanent resident after a year.

In throwback fashion to earlier migration periods of the early twentieth century, the nation is beginning to see three additional groups of migrants—victims of human smuggling, victims of human trafficking, and mail-order brides. Those smuggled into the country enter a consensual agreement and pay a substantial price to enter the country clandestinely, but after arriving in the United States, find they are burdened with debt and have few employment opportunities. There are criminal penalties for smuggling individuals into the United States (U.S. Department of Justice, 2005a) but it continues as a lucrative business. Victims of human trafficking,

Table 3-4. Refugee Admissions by Region (2008 and 2009)

Region	Fiscal Year (FY) Ceiling 2008	FY 2008 Projected Arrivals	Proposed FY Ceiling 2009
Africa	16,000	8,000	12,000
East Asia	20,000	18,000	19,000
Europe and Central Asia	3,000	3,000	2,500
Latin America/ Caribbean	5,000	4,500	4,500
East/South Asia	28,000	25,500	37,000
Unallocated Reserve	8,000		5,000
Total	80,000	59,000	80,000

Source: Proposed Refugee Admissions for FY 2009, Report to the Congress. Website: http://www.state.gov/documents/organization/113507.pdf, accessed February 16, 2009.

estimated to be between 14,500 to 17,500 annually, are exploited for illicit reasons and are practical slaves to those who bring them into the country; approximately 7,000 are brought from Asia, 5,000 from Europe/Eurasia, and 3,500 from Latin America (U.S. Department of Justice, 2005b). In 2000, the United States passed the Victims of Trafficking and Violence Protection Act of 2000 that provides protection to victims, regardless of nationality.

Finally, the mail-order bride market is burgeoning, and a "Google" search results in over 3 million internet websites catering to a growing clientele. Mail-order brides are usually women from developing countries who register with a catalog or website their intent to marry foreign men. Usually there is no period of courtship, and marriages take place in absentia, with the man having "shopped" for the wife who best fits his needs. These women can enter the country legally as wives of U.S. citizens.

Under continuing discussion is a guest worker program that will allow temporary workers to enter the country for a period to assume jobs for which U.S. employers are unable to find native employees. While this may appear to be a novel idea, it has long been a part of the cross-border movement for Mexican workers who have entered the United States for seasonal work and returned home at the end of the season. Known as circular migration, this pattern is evidenced regularly and increasingly both in the United States and internationally (Hugo, 2003; Zuniga, 2006). However, currently, a significant number of workers who had entered the country illegally, but traditionally followed the pattern of circular migration, are now choosing to remain in the United States, as moving across the U.S.–Mexico border is substantially more dangerous (Zuniga, 2006). Migration researchers, further, are reporting two new phenomena with immigrants choosing to either return permanently to their homelands (return migrants) several years after leaving, or dividing their time equally between their natal countries and the United States (transnationals).

Regardless of the process and reasons that immigrants enter the United States, it is clear that for a large proportion, a primary impetus is economic opportunity. Furthermore, most rarely completely sever ties with their

homelands, and a significant number sends remittances to support family members, organizations, or communities in the country of origin.

Demographic Characteristics

Table 3-5 compares aggregates of the foreign-born and native populations revealing that the percent distribution is relatively equivalent for both groups. The foreign born are more likely to be married and twice as likely to be enrolled in graduate education as are the natives. This suggests that several of the former may arrive in the country for higher education, especially since the educational difference is not as evident among those who are no longer enrolled in an academic program.

Economic Impact of Immigration

Many deliberations in the United States revolve around the economic impact of migration. The ongoing immigration debate juggles arguments regarding the assets newcomers bring to the country with those about the drains they place on the infrastructure, and the country is divided on the current net worth of immigration in the twenty-first century.

The Immigrant Workforce

Recent foci on immigration reform and the guest worker program have drawn attention to undocumented workers. One must bear in mind in all deliberations that of the 34 million documented immigrants in the United States in 2004, over 27 million were between the ages of 16 and 65 years, and the majority of them were in the workforce and across the occupational structure (Table 3-6). A significant proportion of the legitimate workforce, they have the appropriate documentation and are essential to the functioning of the country. While immigrants in 2004 constituted 11% of the population, they made up 14% of the labor force and 20% of the low-wage earners (Nightingale & Fix, 2004), and in 2007, the foreign born accounted for 15.7% of the civilian labor force (Terrazas & Batalova, 2008). Table 3-7 provides an occupation comparison between the native and foreign-born population. Ironically, immigrant unemployment rates have fallen faster than those

Table 3-5. Select Demographic Characteristics, 2007

Subject	Total	Native	Foreign born
Total population	301,621,159	263,561,465	38,059,694
Male	49.3%	49.1%	50.3%
Female	50.7%	50.9%	49.7%
Median age (years)	36.7	35.8	40.2
Population 15 years and over	240,724,018	204,762,339	35,961,679
Never married	30.8%	31.8%	24.9%
Now married, except separated	50.2%	48.5%	59.9%
Divorced or separated	12.7%	13.2%	10.1%
Widowed	6.3%	6.5%	5.2%
Population 3 years and over enrolled in school	79,329,527	73,741,332	5,588,195
Nursery school, preschool	6.2%	6.5%	1.7%
Elementary school (grades K-8)	45.6%	46.9%	29.1%
High school (grades 9-12)	22.0%	21.9%	22.8%
College or graduate school	26.2%	24.7%	46.3%
Population 25 years and over	197,892,369	166,289,255	31,603,114
Less than high school graduate	15.5%	12.4%	32.0%
High school graduate (includes equivalency)	30.1%	31.3%	24.0%
Some college or associate's degree	26.9%	28.7%	17.2%
Bachelor's degree	17.4%	17.6%	16.0%
Graduate or professional degree	10.1%	9.9%	10.9%
Population 5 years and over	280,950,438	243,190,088	37,760,350
English only	80.3%	90.3%	15.6%
Language other than English	19.7%	9.7%	84.4%
Speak English less than "very well"	8.7%	1.9%	52.4%

Source: http://factfinder.census.gov/servlet/STTable?_bm=y&-state=st&-qr_name=ACS_2007_1YR_G00_S0501&-ds_name= ACS_2007_1YR_G00_&-CONTEXT=st&-_caller=geoselect&-geo_id=01000US&-format=&-_lang=en, Accessed February 15, 2009.

of natives, yet their wages have increased half as fast. Therefore, while, in general, immigrants have a higher employment rate and are composed of two-parent families, they are more likely to live in poverty than are native born Americans (Nightingale & Fix, 2004).

Several big businesses, construction companies, agriculture, and employers in many service industries contend that the absence of immigrant workers, specifically the unauthorized workforce, would cause a major catastrophe in the U.S. economy. There is a strong, steady demand for migrant workers in agriculture, construction, manufacturing, and hospitality (Caulfield, 2006; Kochhar, 2005). About 6.3 million undocumented workers are Mexican and estimated to fill 25% of all agricultural, 17% of office and house cleaning, 14% of construction, and 12% of food preparation jobs, yet it is clear that the United States is severely divided about their presence. The *New York Times* featured numerous articles on undocumented Mexican workers reporting that, although border enforcement has heightened since 1990, and although policy makers are aware that most migrants come to work, policing the workplace has low priority. For under $50, one can buy a set of forged documents (social security card and permanent residency card) that protect employers from appearing to have violated the law (Portes, 2006). Interestingly, the country benefits, as millions of unauthorized workers are listed in company books, receiving wages that appear to be legal, and so they pay taxes—but they do not draw on the benefits.

Labor Market, Low-Wage, and Entry-Level Occupations

Ness (2006) writes of the immigrant workforce that has been essential in filling low-wage,

Table 3-6. Employment and Foreign-Born Civilian Population 16+ Years by World Region of Birth: 2004 (in thousands)

Employment Status & Occupation Group	World Region of Birth									
	Foreign Born		Europe		Asia		Latin America		Other Areas	
	Number	%	Number	%	Number	%	Number	%	Number	%
Total Civilian Labor Force	**21,168**	**100.0**	**2,424**	**100.0**	**5,470**	**100.0**	**11,641**	**100.0**	**1,633**	**100.0**
Employed	19,857	93.8	2,294	94.6	5,178	94.7	10,844	93.2	1,542	94.4
Unemployed	1,310	6.2	130	5.4	292	5.3	797	6.8	91	5.6
Total Employed	**19,857**	**100.0**	**2,294**	**100.0**	**5,178**	**100.0**	**10,844**	**100.0**	**1,542**	**100.0**
Management, Professional, and Related Occupations	5,225	26.3	953	41.6	2,332	45.0	1,340	12.4	601	39.0
Service Occupations	4,631	23.3	315	13.7	830	16.0	3,175	29.3	311	20.2
Sales and Office Occupations	3,737	18.8	556	24.2	1,221	23.6	1,666	15.4	294	19.1
Farming, Fishing, and Forestry Occupations	309	1.6	1	0.1	15	0.3	289	2.7	4	0.3
Construction, Extraction, & Maintenance Occupations	2,556	12.9	214	9.3	173	3.4	2,047	18.9	122	7.9
Production, Transportation, and Material Moving	3,398	17.1	254	11.1	606	11.7	2,327	21.5	210	13.6

Source: U.S. Census Bureau, *Current population survey, annual social and economic supplement, 2004.* Immigration Statistics Staff, Population Division, Internet Release Date: February 22, 2005.

Table 3-7. Labor Force and Poverty Rates—Native & Foreign Born (2007)

Subject	Total	Native	Foreign Born
Total population	**301,621,159**	**263,561,465**	**38,059,694**
Population 16 years and over	**236,416,572**	**200,722,532**	**35,694,040**
In labor force	64.8%	64.4%	66.9%
Not in labor force	35.2%	35.6%	33.1%
Civilian employed population 16 years and over	**142,588,118**	**120,050,146**	**22,537,972**
CLASS OF WORKER			
Private wage & salary workers	78.6%	77.6%	84.0%
Government workers	14.5%	15.6%	8.3%
Self-employed workers in own business	6.7%	6.6%	7.5%
Unpaid family workers	0.2%	0.2%	0.3%
OCCUPATION			
Management, professional, and related occupations	34.6%	36.0%	27.2%
Service occupations	16.7%	15.6%	23.1%
Sales and office occupations	25.6%	27.0%	18.0%
Farming, fishing, and forestry occupations	0.7%	0.5%	2.0%
Construction, extraction, maintenance, & repair	9.7%	9.0%	13.4%
Production, transportation, & material moving	12.7%	12.0%	16.4%
INDUSTRY			
Agriculture, forestry, fishing and hunting, and mining	1.8%	1.7%	2.4%
Construction	7.7%	7.1%	11.5%
Manufacturing	11.3%	10.9%	13.1%
Wholesale trade	3.2%	3.2%	3.2%
Retail trade	11.4%	11.8%	9.5%
Transportation and warehousing, and utilities	5.2%	5.3%	4.7%
Information	2.5%	2.6%	1.8%
Finance and insurance, and real estate	7.2%	7.5%	5.7%
Professional, scientific, management/administrative	10.3%	10.1%	11.5%
Educational services, health care, social assistance	21.2%	22.0%	16.6%
Arts, entertainment, recreation, & hospitality	8.8%	8.2%	11.7%
Other services (except public administration)	4.8%	4.5%	6.3%
Public administration	4.7%	5.2%	2.1%
Population 16 years and over with earnings (12-month)	**94,817,488**	**79,186,476**	**15,631,012**
$1 to $9,999 or loss	2.0%	1.9%	2.4%
$10,000 to $14,999	4.8%	4.1%	8.6%
$15,000 to $24,999	16.7%	15.0%	25.4%
$25,000 to $34,999	18.5%	18.4%	18.8%
$35,000 to $49,999	21.0%	21.8%	16.5%
$50,000 to $74,999	19.6%	20.7%	14.0%
$75,000 or more	17.3%	18.0%	14.2%
Male (median earnings)	**44,255**	**46,695**	**32,451**
Female (median earnings)	**34,278**	**35,138**	**29,365**
Population for whom poverty status is determined	**293,744,043**	**256,229,568**	**37,514,475**
Below 100 percent of the poverty level	13.0%	12.6%	15.6%
100 to 199 percent of the poverty level	17.7%	16.8%	24.1%
At or above 200 percent of the poverty level	69.3%	70.6%	60.4%
All families	9.5%	8.6%	14.4%
With related children under 18 years	14.9%	13.9%	18.8%
With related children under 5 years only	16.0%	15.8%	17.0%
Married-couple family	4.5%	3.4%	10.7%
With related children under 18 years	6.4%	4.6%	13.3%

Table 3-7. (*Continued*)

With related children under 5 years only	5.9%	4.5%	11.7%
Female householder, no husband present, family	28.2%	27.8%	30.6%
With related children under 18 years	36.5%	36.0%	39.7%
With related children under 5 years only	44.8%	45.2%	42.1%

Source: U.S. Census Bureau, 2007, http://factfinder.census.gov/servlet/STTable?_bm=y&-state=st&-qr_name=ACS_ 2007_1YR_G00_S0501&-ds_name=ACS_2007_1YR_G00_&-CONTEXT=st&-_caller=geoselect&-geo_id=01000US&- format=&-_lang=en. Accessed February 18, 2009.

entry-level occupations that most U.S.-born Americans seek to avoid but upon which the nation has come to depend. Furthermore, despite the tendency to believe that these occupations are filled only by unauthorized workers, both formal and informal labor market intermediaries, including educational institutions, employment agencies, and community organizations, channel new immigrants to potential employers (Theodore & Mehta, 2001). Nor are low wages for immigrants limited to blue-collar occupations. Immigrants entering the United States on the H-1B visa (issued to "high-tech" foreign workers) usually are at the bottom of the pay scale for their positions and paid $13,000 less than their American counterparts (Miano, 2005).

Some studies contradict research that immigrants are taking jobs that are not of interest to native workers. Sum, Harrington, and Khatiwada (2006) found that immigrant workers displaced young native workers, aged 16–34 years. Controversial authority George Borjas (2001) suggests that net gains to the U.S. economy are only $8 billion annually and because many immigrants work for lower wages and immigration actually shifts several billions of dollars each year to employers. He further posits that because current immigrants are less educated and skilled than their predecessors, they may be more dependent on public assistance and live in segregation and poverty.

Brain Drain, Brain Gain, and Brain Waste

Most individuals who undertake the challenge of migration to an alien land are rarely without substantial human capital. While this capital may not be in the form of tangible assets, it often is found in psychological, intellectual, and physical capabilities. The United States frequently benefits from resources that immigrants bring in their quest for opportunity. A significant number comes for education, eventually adjusting to immigrant status. Long known as the "brain drain" for the country of origin, it has now been recognized as a "brain gain" to receiving countries. As one reviews the list of U.S. Nobel Prize winners, evidence suggests that a disproportionate number were born elsewhere.

The brain drain can, nevertheless, benefit sending countries in the form of remittances. The World Bank reports that although most expatriates send money to support family members, the receiving country's economy benefits from the flow of these additional monies. Thus, the brain drain serves to provide income and help offset poverty for poorer or less-educated family members and, to some extent, counteracts the effects of the loss of educated individuals (Ozden & Schiff, 2006), helping build capacity in the country of origin (Asian Development Bank, 2005). These remittances, furthermore, can be quite substantial; in 2008, $45.9 billion were sent from the United States to Latin American countries (Inter-American Development Bank, 2008). Such remittances not only allow sending countries to develop their social capital, they also enable expatriates to firmly establish and maintain connections to their home communities (Mooney, 2004).

An even more recent and disturbing phenomenon is the "brain waste" reported by the Migration Policy Institute (Batalova, Fix, & Creticos, 2008). Over 1.3 million college educated immigrants (one in five) are working in unskilled jobs as taxi drivers, dishwashers, and security guards. Either because their credentials are not transferable, their knowledge of the professional jargon in English in not sufficient, or they are unable to find positions commensurate with their qualifications, they settle for occupations far below their capabilities. Batalova et al. (2008) lament this brain waste and the unrealized returns not only to the immigrant but to the United States and propose a closer look at integration policies, including credentialing and intensive English language and culture training programs.

Social Impact of Migration Policies

Immigrant Influences on the United States and the Native-Born

As immigrants enter the United States and adapt to life in their new homeland, they bring with them a diversity of cultures and norms. The United States prides itself at being a multicultural nation of immigrants, and as the United States influences these New Americans, the country is influenced by them. The country is substantially impacted by the multiplicity of languages that are spoken by immigrants, and from any cursory look at border towns in the Southwestern United States, or in Florida, New York, or California, it is apparent that the impact of the Spanish language is profound and permanent. Immigrants influence the U.S. culture and society through their social norms, family patterns, art, music, dance, cuisine, and businesses. They expose native-born Americans to alternative modes of behavior and social relationships, differences in perceptions and interpretations, and variations in experiences and observations. They may challenge traditional American norms and require that Americans reassess or defend them. Orum (2005) suggests that it is essential that one evaluate the impact immigrants have on host nations. Focusing only on immigrant adaptation, which is the tendency of most theoreticians, provides only a partial picture.

Impact on Health, Education, and Social Service Systems

Health Systems. U.S. health policy, which allows health coverage for many, but not for all, has particular implications for those in or near poverty and those of low socioeconomic status and income that are self-employed. The latter are the least likely to be able to afford private insurance coverage, yet they are ineligible for means-tested coverage such as Medicaid. Large segments of the immigrant population are self-employed and the exorbitant costs of private insurance may well correlate with low insurance coverage. Furthermore, new immigrants are likely to be poor and stay poor because they have higher levels of unemployment, less education, and larger families than do native-born groups (Haniffa, 1999).

Implications of health policy for immigrants are not limited to issues of coverage; several other cultural and educational concerns confound access to health care services. Health policy currently does not focus on how services are utilized, and general access to health care services is fraught with problems for many immigrant groups. Even if immigrants do have good health care coverage, they may be less knowledgeable about the availability of programs and services. They may also be more suspicious of different treatment methods, uncomfortable with interaction patterns with health care providers, and confused by governmental and other insurance programs and reimbursement procedures. Any or all of these factors discourage them from utilizing the health services that are available to them. A number of specific phenomena are often prevalent in the immigrant experience of illness and treatment; the most pervasive of these may be poor knowledge of preventative health care, the use of home remedies, and the underutilization of services.

Even with good U.S. health programs, cultural, linguistic, and economic barriers can deny the immigrant opportunities for disease prevention, early diagnosis, prompt treatment, and participation in clinical trials (Tu, Taplin, Barlow, & Boyko, 1999). Immigrants who are educated, professional, and can function in the mainstream are better equipped to meet their health needs. Recent immigrants are much less likely than either native-born individuals or those who have been in the United States longer to access medical care or have contact with physicians. Some, in fact, access care as infrequently as those who have no health insurance at all (Leclere, Jensen & Biddlecom, 1994). Thus, when a large segment of the immigrant population finally turns to health care services, it may be through the already overburdened emergency rooms or through practitioners who are unprepared to communicate with them, either because of language differences, cultural barriers, or unfamiliarity with social norms.

Educational Systems. The national policy [20 USCS, Sec. 1221–1 (1999)] states:

Recognizing that the Nation's economic, political, and social security require a well-educated citizenry, the Congress (1) reaffirms, as a matter of high priority, the Nation's goal of equal education opportunity, and (2) declares it to be the policy of the United States of America that every citizen is entitled to an education to meet his or her full potential without financial barriers. (p. 10)

Referring to federal immigration policies, Congress specified in 20 USCS, Sec. 7402–1 (1999) that the collection of language-minority Americans in the United States speak almost all the world's languages and that there are even greater numbers of children and young people of limited English proficiency. These children face numerous challenges in their efforts to received adequate education and become an integral part of U.S. society. Several decades ago, Congress recommended that elementary and secondary school education be strengthened with bilingual education, language-enhancement, and language-acquisition programs, however, recent immigrant backlash has resulted in "English only" resolutions in a number of states. Congress also proposed an emergency immigrant education policy to help the large number of immigrant children who lack English language skills to make the transition. Free public school education to the secondary school level, furthermore, is available to all residents in the United States regardless of visa status, and children under the age of 16 years are mandated to be enrolled in school. Thus, this mandate (and access) applies to all immigrant children, whether they are documented or unauthorized.

In response to the awareness that limited English language capabilities of adults also handicap their functioning in the United States, several public educational institutions, libraries, and nonprofit organizations have begun free language classes for adults. Many of these do not ask immigration status. Thus, not only have governmental policies been modified to adapt to the educational needs of immigrants, other institutions are voluntarily assuming the responsibility of providing educational access for immigrants.

Social Service Systems. Amendments to the Social Security Act of 1935 currently provide for: (1) a combination of old age and survivors' insurance (OASI) and disability insurance (DI), known as (OASDI); (2) unemployment insurance; (3) federal assistance to the elderly, the visually impaired, and those with disabilities under the Supplemental Security Income (SSI) program; (4) public assistance to families under the new Temporary Assistance to Needy Families (TANF) program; (5) federal health insurance for the elderly (Medicare); and (6) federal and state health assistance for the poor (Medicaid). While some immigrants benefit from the services delivered through the Social Security Act, their use often differs from that of the native-born population, both because of their sociodemographic characteristics and because of the changes in eligibility requirements enacted by Congress in 1996. Several of these changes that were implemented specifically limit immigrant access, particularly to cash assistance and medical benefits until they have been in the country a certain length of time.

In general, social welfare services are minimally accessed by immigrants for a number of cultural reasons, among them are shame in seeking assistance from outside the family and fear and distrust of governmental authority. Thus, although there may be a need, this population may not seek assistance, even when it is qualified or in need. Consequently, the social services are frequently under the misconception that immigrants either have few social service needs or the family and/or immigrant community is able to address them. Results are that needs are not *addressed, and immigrant families may struggle alone with dysfunction (Segal, 2002). Although the increased attention to the experience of refugees in the United States is an important step made by the social services, outreach efforts to other immigrant groups may be effective in preventing future and greater difficulties for these populations and the community at large.

Inter-Group Marriages and Families

Most societies of the world have traditionally frowned upon marriages or intimate extramarital relationships between people of different socioeconomic backgrounds. Prohibition against marriages and relationships between two people of different races or ethnic groups has been even more common. Marriage between members of different groups is both a transcendence of ethnic segregation and the forging of an American identity that is distinct from the ethnic American identity of subgroups (Rodriguez, 2000). It not only attests to a newly formed American identity but also loosens ethnic and cultural ties with the parental generation, making an even stronger statement of adaptation and commitment to the United States Both foreign-born Asians and foreign-born Latinos have higher rates of intermarriage than do U.S. European or African Americans, and intermarriage rates for second and third generations of the former two groups are extremely high (Rodriguez, 2000). The native-born, second generation is more likely than immigrants to intermarry, but even for immigrants, the prevalence of intermarriage steadily increases with the length of time spent in the United States It is apparent that while immigrants are being influenced by the host country, increasing intermarriage is modifying family relationships. Increasing societal acceptance of diverse options lowers pressure for ethnic groups to assimilate to all European American norms. Beyond the outward indices, trends show that assimilation by the White culture is also under way as it begins to embrace family values and philosophies that are basic to Asian, African, and Latino societies.

Development of Human Capital

U.S. society is increasingly aware of ethnic and cultural differences among immigrants, particularly those of color and the native-born populations. Interest in understanding attitudes, values, religions, and behaviors is reflected in the burgeoning literature on immigrants and refugees. As newcomers adapt to their new environments, the environment itself is being sensitized to their diversity.

Less focus has been placed on the systematic understanding of the socioeconomic levels of these immigrant groups and their implications for adaptation and achievement. Based on the allocation of immigration visas, there have been a variety of legal immigrant streams that have entered the United States in the last few decades. While earlier immigrants of the 1960s were, primarily of a professional stream, current streams are more likely to include large numbers entering through family reunification processes. These individuals and groups may not have the human capital and skills that are readily transferable into the fast-paced technological society. Further, refugees and undocumented immigrants may frequently find themselves on the fringes of society—the former for a significant portion of their lives, and the latter, almost for their entire stay in the United States Thus, a large segment of the immigrant group, particularly the newer immigrants of the last decade, is likely to be marginalized. Without the requisite English language competencies, education, and usable job skills, many hover at poverty levels. Many immigrants in the beginning of the twenty-first century have been highly successful, while others have continued to struggle. With the bimodal distribution of the immigrant population's level of achievement, and the rising numbers of unmet health, education, and welfare needs, this can be a social, if not an economic, drain on the country.

Many new immigrants to a country arrive with little facility in the language of the host country, which is often the primary obstacle. Without language ability, seeking housing or employment, accessing health care or other services, or learning a vocation become impossible. Language competence increases ability to negotiate through a nation's bureaucracies, and literacy, or the ability to read and write in the host language further improves opportunities.

English Language Training, Job Training, and Training in Social/Cultural and Workplace Norms

Immigrant children fairly rapidly learn the English language, even if they are denied a bilingual education, for despite laws in the mid-twentieth century that required the establishment of bilingual programs, in the last two and a half decades, increasing numbers of states are moving toward an "English only" policy in schools. However, of the 1.2 million individuals in adult education classes, over half are there to learn English and another 3 million are awaiting English language education (Murguia & Munoz, 2005). Although federally funded programs expanded during the Clinton administration, these have since declined. In a study of immigrants in New York City and Los Angeles County, where 20% of the immigrant population lived in 2000, immigrants with low English proficiency were more likely to be poor and lack sufficient food (Fix & Capps, 2002).

The Refugee Resettlement Program that has as its primary goal "self-sufficiency in the shortest time possible," provides English language education for a period of only about eight months, and within that time, refugees must find jobs that will sustain them. If their English language competence is low, they get positions in low-paying entry level occupations with little possibility for advancement. To support their families, they often work at a second job, leaving little time to gain functional literacy in English, and the development of their human capital is severely curtailed. Functional English, furthermore, is not always sufficient for workplace success; essential also is the understanding of social and cultural workplace norms. The Center for Immigrant Education and Training, at the La Guardia Community College in New York, prepares immigrants to enter the workforce with the necessary vocational and cultural skills. Other such programs around the country focus on job training for immigrants, recognizing that many may not have skills readily transferable to the U.S. economy.

Training of Native-Born Employers and Service Providers

If 12% of the population is of the immigrant generation and another 13% is second generation, most individuals will have the opportunity to work with, for, or alongside these groups. Learning about immigrants is increasingly imperative if employers and service providers are to adequately utilize their resources or have their resources utilized. At the very least, both employers and service providers must: (1) be culturally aware; (2) avoid discrimination, intimidation, and exploitation; and (3) protect workplace rights. Grey (2002) provides a practical and "culturally competent" guide for managers and supervisors in "welcoming" immigrants into Iowa. This guide recommends, in addition to learning about immigrant populations and the immigrant experience: (1) bringing on board the leadership of organizations before expecting changes in the organization; (2) undertaking an audit regarding the readiness of the organization to integrate these new groups into their functioning; (3) if the organization is not prepared, developing guidelines for becoming so and integrating communication and training programs for both long-term workers and new organizational recruits; and (4) making a commitment to maintaining a diverse workforce by making long-term cultural changes, focusing on similarities rather than differences, and generating a cross-cultural organizational attitude.

Increasing Health Care Access

The Centers for Disease Control found that foreign-born adults were uninsured at higher rates (26%) than their U.S.-born counterparts (11%), and Hispanic adults were the most likely to be without insurance (37%; Dey & Lucas, 2006). Immigrants were twice as likely as native-born adults to have no usual source of health care, less likely to have spoken to a health care practitioner in the past year, or ever, and yet they reported lower health risk factors and chronic disease than their U.S.-born counterparts. Risk factors (i.e., obesity and hypertension) tended to increase with length of time in the United States. Other publications indicate that in their early years in the United States, regardless of their immigration status, many fear deportation, lack of confidentiality, and poor communication and choose not to seek health care services. Additional issues that interfere with access for all citizens also affect immigrants, including long waiting periods, appointments set far in the future, and limited physician access. Addressing health care needs is fundamental to ensuring a sense of well-being, which, in turn, allows individuals to engage in those activities that will develop their personal resources or human capital.

Closing Remarks

Since September 11, 2001, and the terror attacks on the United States, there has been a substantial increase in xenophobia against all foreigners but particularly toward those who look as though their origins are Middle Eastern. While some segments of the country are appreciating the ever growing diversity in race, ethnicity, and culture, others are threatened by it. It is safe to say that the flow of immigrants can strain the receiving country in a variety of ways. It behooves policy makers and service providers to be cognizant of the implications of both immigration and integration policies. Receiving countries must recognize that migration across their borders will persist with improvements in transportation and with further emerging reasons for relocating.

In admitting immigrants, countries make a commitment to them. Unless a country is willing to help them through the transitional period of adjustment, their unmet economic, social, health, and mental health needs can, in both the short and the long term, drain a nation's resources. On the other hand, early attention to these very immigrants may accelerate their entry as contributors to society (Mayadas & Elliott, 2003).

This chapter has tried to discuss issues facing immigrants and refugees in the United States They share the experience of being newcomers to this land of opportunity and of having left much in their homelands. A close inspection of the 2007 census data[5] makes it abundantly clear that there is no single profile of immigrants or refugees. They range in age from infancy to well into old age. They may be single, married, divorced, or widowed; they may come with families, without families, or as part of an extended family. They may be white, black, brown, yellow, red, or any other color under which the human species is categorized. They may be living in the United States legally or illegally. They may be highly professional and skilled, or they may be unprofessional with skills not transferable to the United States economy. They may be extremely wealthy or very poor. They may be fluent in the English language and speak several other languages, or they may speak only their mother tongue, which may not be English, and they may be illiterate even in that. They may be from cultures that are highly hierarchical and autocratic, or they may be from cultures with greater equality. Clearly, barring the fact that they were born outside the United States, immigrants and refugees may share little common with others from different countries or even from their own countries.

Underlying difficulties in understanding is a far reaching xenophobia—both of the immigrants and by them. It is difficult to assess who should be responsible for crossing the divide—is it the host or is it the self-invited newcomer? For immigrants, as for all people, much is dependent on their personal resources. Even more than this, however, is the readiness of the United States to accept immigrants and their American-born descendents. Immigration policies may reflect the interests of the nation in allowing entry to certain groups of people, however, it is the opportunities and obstacles that immigrants and their offspring, particularly those of color, encounter on a daily basis that affect the ease of adjustment and mutual acceptance. Immigrants and the host nation must make a conscious level to adapt to each other—it is neither the exclusive responsibility of the host nation nor of the immigrant.

For any immigrant community, it is a long road from its country of origin. The physical distance may be great, but the social, psychological, and emotional distance of immigrant travel is always greater. Nevertheless, the human condition and its similarities bind peoples together to a much greater extent than one tends to accept, regardless of social norms, culture, religion, or language. As a land of immigrants, if the United States is to be truly multicultural, as it claims to be, it must also be pluralistic and recognize, accept, and laud the differences in peoples as a national asset. It does not have the corner on cultural diversity and immigration struggles, and in this increasingly interdependent world, it must allow effective policies, programs, and services from other nations to inform its own practices.

Notes

1. Detailed legislation is available through the U.S. Department of Homeland Security, U.S. Citizenship and Immigration Services website: http://www.uscis.gov/portal/site/uscis/menuitem.eb 1d4c2a3e5b9ac89243c6a7543f6d1a/?vgnextoid=dc 60e1df53b2f010VgnVCM1000000ecd190aRCRD& vgnextchannel=dc60e1df53b2f010VgnVCM100000 0ecd190aRCRD, accessed February 5, 2009.
2. U.S. Department of State. Retrieved February 15, 2009, from http://travel.state.gov/visa/immigrants/ types/types_1306.html.
3. Asylees seek refugee status once they have arrived in the United States, either at the port of entry or after having been in the country for a length of time.
4. UNHCR: The UN Refugee Agency. Website: http:// www.unhcr.org/protect/3c0762ea4.html, Accessed February 10, 2009.
5. www.census.gov.

References

Asian Development Bank. (2005). *Brain drain versus brain gain: The study of remittances in Southeast Asia and promoting knowledge exchange through Diasporas.* Fourth Coordination Meeting on International Migration, New York, NY: U.N. Secretariat. Retrieved October 7, 2006, from http:// www.un.org/esa/population/meetings/fourthcoord 2005/P13_ADB.pdf.

Batalova, J., Fix, M., & Creticos, P.A. (2008). *Uneven progress: The employment pathways of skilled immigrants in the United States.* Migration Policy Institute. Retrieved February 10, 2009, from http://www.migrationpolicy.org/pubs/BrainWaste Oct08.pdf.

Borjas, G. (2001). *Heaven's door.* Princeton, NJ: Princeton University Press.

Borjas, G., Grogger, J., & Hanson, G. H. (2006). *Immigration and African-American employment opportunities: The response of wages, employment, and incarceration to labor supply shocks.* Retrieved

February 10, 2009, from http://www.nber.org/ digest/may07/w12518.html.

Caulfield, J. (2006). Line in the sand. *Builder, 29*(9), 90–97. Retrieved October 7, 2006, from http:// proquest.umi.com.

Dey, A. N., & Lucas, J. W. (2006, March 1). Physical and mental health characteristics of U.S.- and foreign-born adults: United States, 1998–2003. *Advance Data.* Hyattsville, MD: U.S. Department of Health and Human Services, Centers for Disease Control, 1–19.

Fix, M. E., & Capps, R. (2002). Immigrant well-being in New York and Los Angeles. *Immigrant families and workers: Facts and perspectives.* Retrieved October 9, 2006, from http://www.urban.org/ url.cfm?ID=310566.

GAO [U.S. General Accounting Office] (2004). Overstay tracking: A key component of homeland security and a layered defense. Report to the Chairman, Committee on the Judiciary, House of Representatives. Retrieved February 10, 2009 from http://www.gao.gov/new.items/d0482.pdf.

Gordon, L.W. (2005). Trends in the gender ratio of immigrants to the United States. *International Migration Review, 39*(4), 796–818.

Grey, M. A. (2002). *Welcoming new Iowans: A guide for employers and supervisors,* Cedar Falls: University of Northern Iowa. Retrieved February 10, 2009, from http://www.bcs.uni.edu/icili/ PDFDocument/book%203-4.pdf#search=%22%22 cultural%20competence%22%20immigrants%20% 22business%20practice%22%22.

Haniffa, A. (1999, September 17). New immigrants likely to be poor and stay poor, says study. *India Abroad,* 39.

Hugo, G. (2003). Circular migration: Keeping development rolling? *Migration Information Source.* Retrieved October 5, 2006, from http://www. migrationinformation.org/Feature/display.cfm?ID=129.

Inter-American Development Bank. (2008). *The changing pattern of remittances: 2008 survey of remittances from the U.S.A. to Latin America.* Retrieved February 9, 2009, from http://idb docs.iadb.org/wsdocs/getdocument.aspx?docnum= 1418521.

Kim, H-C. (1994). *A legal history of Asian Americans, 1790–1990,* Westport, CT: Greenwood Press.

Kochhar, R. (2005). *Survey of Mexican migrants, part three.* Pew Hispanic Center, Washington, DC. Retrieved May 31, 2006, from http:// pewhispanic.org/reports/report.php?ReportID=58.

Leclere, F. B., Jensen, L., & Biddlecom, A. E. (1994). Health care utilization, family context, and adaptation among immigrants to the United States. *Journal of Health and Social Behavior, 35*(4), 370–384.

Mayadas, N. S., & Elliott, D. (2003). Social work's response to refugee issues. In *Madras School of Social Work's 50th Anniversary publication*, Tamil Nadu, India.

Mayadas, N. S., & Segal, U. (2000). A. Refugees in the 1990s: A U.S. perspective. In B. Pallassana (ed), *Social work practice with immigrants and refugees* (pp. 167–197). New York: Columbia University Press.

Miano, J. (2005). *The bottom of the pay scale: Wages for H-1B computer programmers*. Center for Migration Studies. Retrieved October 7, 2006, from http://www.cis.org/articles/2005/back1305.pdf.

Mooney, M. (2004). Migrants' social capital and investing remittances in Mexico. In J. Durand & D. S. Massey (eds), *Crossing the border: Research from the Mexican Migration Project* (pp. 45–62). New York, NY: Russell Sage Foundation.

Murguia, J., & Munoz, C. (2005, November 10). From immigrant to citizen. *The American Prospect*. Retrieved July 31, 2009, from http://www.prospect.org/web/page.ww?section=root&name=ViewPrint& articleId=10487.

Ness, I. (2006). *Immigrants, unions, and the new U.S. labor market*. Philadelphia, PA: Temple University Press.

Nightingale, D. S., & Fix, M. (2004). Economic and labor market trends. *Future of Children*, 14(2), 49–59. Retrieved October 7, 2006, from http://www.futureof children.org/usr_doc/fixnightingale.pdf.

Office of Homeland Security. (2008). *2007 yearbook of immigration statistics*. Washington, DC: Office of Homeland Security.

Orum, A. (2005). Circles of influence and chains of command: The social processes whereby ethnic communities influence host societies. *Social Forces*, 84(2), 921–939.

Ozden, C., & Schiff, M. (eds). (2006). *International migration, remittances, and the brain drain*, Washington, DC: The World Bank & Palgrave Macmillan.

Passel, J. S., & Cohn, D. (2008). *Trends in Unauthorized Immigration: Undocumented Inflow Now Trails Legal Inflow*. Washington, DC: Pew Hispanic Center. Retrieved February 10, 2009 from http://pewhispanic.org/files/reports/94.pdf.

Portes, A. (2006). *Alejandro Portes advocates enlightened programs for immigrants*. UNC School of Education: SOC News. Retrieved July 31, 2009, from http://soe.unc.edu/news_events/news/2006/portes_alejandro.php.

Rodriguez, C. E. (2000). *Changing race: Latinos, the census, and the history of ethnicity in the united states*. New York, NY: New York University Press.

Segal, U. A. (2002). *A framework for immigration: Asians in the United States*, New York: Columbia University Press.

Sum, A., Harrington, P., & Khatiwada, I. (2006). *The impact of new immigrants on young native-born workers, 2000–2005*. Center for Immigration Studies. Retrieved February 10, 2009, from http://www.cis.org/articles/2006/back806.pdf.

Terrazas, A. & Batalova, J. (2008). The Most Up-to-Date Frequently Requested Statistics on Immigrants in the United States. Migration Information Source. Retrieved February 9, 2009, from http://www.migrationinformation.org/USFocus/display.cfm?ID =714#3.

Theodore, N., & Mehta, C. (2001). *Day labor, low-wage work, and immigrant employment opportunities in Chicago*. Paper prepared for presentation to the Illinois Immigration Policy Project. Retrieved October 7, 2006, from http://www.roosevelt.edu/ima/pdfs/immigrantemployment.pdf#search=%22 %22low%20wage%22%20%22entry%20level%22% 20%22labor%20market%22%20immigrant%22.

Tu, S-P., Taplin, S. H., Barlow, W. E., & Boyko, E. J. (1999). Breast cancer screening by Asian-American women in a managed care environment. *American Journal of Preventative Medicine*, 17(1), 55–61.

U.S. Census Bureau. (2008). *American FactFinder*. Retrieved February 10, 2009, from http://fact finder.census.gov/home/saff/main.html?_lang=en.

U.S. Department of State. (2005). *Proposed refugee admissions for fiscal year 2006 report to the Congress*. Retrieved January 26, 2006, from http://www.state.gov/g/prm/refadm/rls/rpts/52366.htm# proposed.

U.S. Department of Justice. (2005a). Distinctions between Human Smuggling and Human Trafficking. Human Smuggling and Trafficking Center. Retrieved February 16, 2009, from http://www.usdoj.gov/crt/crim/smuggling_trafficking_ facts.pdf.

U.S. Department of Justice. (2005b). Human trafficking. Retrieved February 16, 2009, from http://www.ojp.usdoj.gov/ovc/ncvrw/2005/pg5l. html.

Zuniga, V. (2006, April 5). *New destinations*. Presentation at the University of Missouri-St. Louis.

4

Russia

Immigration to Russia

Vladimir Iontsev, Irina Ivakhnyuk, and Svetlana Soboleva

Historical Roots of Current Migration Trends

The migration history of contemporary Russia definitely proves that without knowledge of the past it is often very difficult to understand the present and to argue about the future. Therefore, a very brief historical overview of international migration in Russia seems appropriate in the context of this chapter. In many respects international migration trends in this region, especially their ethnic facets, are deeply rooted in Russia's history.

For centuries Russia has been facing immigration, which has exceeded emigration during certain periods of time and therefore significantly affected economic and demographic development of the country. Both in the past and in the present Russia has been lacking people to populate and develop its vast territories (17 million sq. km; average density 9 persons per 1 sq. km). In the middle of the eighteenth century, the distinguished Russian scientist Mikhail Lomonosov (1711–1765) stressed essential significance of population size and growth for Russia, and claimed that "population is the State's might and power rather than its infinite spaces useless without inhabitants" (Iontsev,

1998). At the turn of the twentieth and the twenty-first centuries this argument seems to be just as important.

In the beginning of the 1990s, Russia passed through one of the most dramatic tumbles in its history; as a result, the former administrative republic of the Soviet Union has become a separate sovereign State. The USSR[1] collapse has resulted in an upsurge of international migrations to and from Russia, and the overwhelming number of them are population movements between Russia and other post-Soviet states. Less than two decades ago these states were a part of the common country—the Soviet Union, or earlier—the Russian Empire.

Since the eighteenth century numerous migration flows to marches of the Russian Empire both in its European and Asian parts took place. During the Soviet period they were mainly population movements from the center of the country to the "sister republics." The reasons for such a prolonged centrifugal trend in population movements were primarily political and economic: they were aimed at colonization and development of the remote territories, development of cities and industries there, and consolidation of the country. During the pre-Soviet period, 1796–1916, the total outflow of population from European territories of Russia to its marches is estimated as 7 million persons; among them ethnic Russians were 80% (*Population Encyclopedia*, 1994). In the Soviet period, the opposite—centripetal—trends also existed; however, the total negative migration balance between Russia and other Soviet republics in 1917–1992 was about 4 million persons. These former population movements, which were at that time internal migrations by nature, in many respects determined causes and the structure of the current mass migration exchange between Russia and so-called new foreign states (Iontsev & Magomedova, 1999; Kabuzan, 1998).

"New Foreign States" Phenomenon

The term "new foreign states" (*blijnee zarubejie*) appeared in Russia in 1992 to define the former Soviet republics that have become the newborn sovereign states (in contrast to "old foreign states" (*dalnee zarubejie*), i.e., all other countries outside the ex-USSR territory). Strictly speaking, immigration to Russia from the "new foreign states" can be analyzed only after 1992, when new independent countries in the territory of the former Soviet Union appeared and inter-republican administrative boundaries acquired the status of international borders.

However, it should be noted that the process of return migration of the Russian population from neighboring republics had been going on since the late 1960s. Before 1992, return migration of ethnic Russians was caused primarily by economic reasons; it was a sort of reemigration of those Russian specialists who—half-voluntarily, half-forcedly—moved from Russia to Soviet republics in accordance with "Communist party calls," university graduates" assignments, or for realization of large-scale federal industrial projects, and so forth, in the 1950s through the 1960s. When they faced growing pressure at local labor markets from indigenous population, in the Caucasus and Central Asian republics in particular, some of them returned to Russia.

After 1992, the situation changed dramatically: international borders between newly independent countries have changed the nature of population movements. At the same time social policy of the State in all of these new countries

except for Russia was directed at "pushing out" the aliens. Slogans of ethnic superiority of indigenous populations popularized by new political leaders for their political self-establishment have resulted in the splash of ethnic intolerance and open nationalistic conflicts, as well as in ousting of "ethnically different" population from local labor markets, and finally in mass migration outflows to the places where these people hoped to find guaranties at least of ethnic security (Iontsev & Ivakhniouk, 2002:57). For "ethnic Russians" living in other "new foreign states," their historical motherland, Russia, seemed a safe asylum. While some researchers use the term "repatriation" for return migration of Russians in the post-Soviet period, we prefer to put this term in quotes, as in fact persons who moved from their native places to other regions of the USSR during the Soviet or pre-Soviet periods were not emigrants as they participated in *internal but not international* migrations. They did not leave their mother country (or *patria*), because the whole Soviet Union was in fact their motherland. Correspondingly, their return migration (or migration of their descendants) in the post-Soviet period cannot be defined as "repatriation" in its classical meaning, namely, "return to the *country* of citizenship, permanent residence or origin."

Over the period of 1992–2007 about 7.5 million persons arrived to Russia from ex-Soviet states for permanent residence (see Table 4-1). Among them, 70% were ethnic Russians. In fact, the scale of return migration could be even bigger. By the beginning of the 1990s, over 38 million persons originating from the Russian Federation in the current or previous generations (among them 25.3 million "ethnic Russians" and 12.7 million other Russian nationalities) lived in other former Soviet republics (*Population Encyclopedia*, 1994:414). According to some estimates, up to 50% of them had an intention to immigrate to Russia after the USSR had collapsed (Ushkalov, 1999, p. 84).

Forced Migration

Return migrations of Russians from the "new foreign states" in the early 1990s were mainly panicked, emergency ones, caused by the post-collapse shock and the political and economic

Table 4-1. Permanent Immigration to Russia, 1990–2007, Thousands

	1992	1993	1994	1995	1996	1997	1998	1999	2000	2001	2002	2003	2004	2005	2006	2007	1990–2007
Total number of immigrants	926.0	922.4	1146.7	842.1	633.6	584.6	498.0	369.6	359.3	193.4	184.6	129.1	119.1	177.2	186.4	286.9	7559.0
hereof from:																	
former Soviet states	924.3	920.0	1144.4	839.7	631.2	581.0	494.8	366.7	350.3	186.2	177.3	119.6	110.3	168.6	177.7	273.9	7466.0
other countries	1.7	2.4	2.3	2.4	2.4	3.6	3.2	2.9	9.0	7.2	7.3	9.5	8.8	8.6	8.7	13.0	93.0

Source: National Statistics Committee data.

uncertainty. Nationalist unrest and civil wars provoked flows of refugees and forced migrants.

It was a reflex reaction of population to a modified political situation, a fear of becoming an oppressed ethnic minority in new sovereign countries based on the idea of ethnic homogeneity. According to results of a survey conducted at the end of the 1990s, about 70% of immigrants to Russia claimed that they have *personally* experienced discrimination because of their ethnicity in the country of their previous residence and over 90% confirmed that their family members or friends have been discriminated against because of their ethnicity. Discrimination was usually related to career development, employment opportunities, access to social security benefits, and the right to get information in the native language (Vitkovskaya & Zayonchkovskaya, 2001:240–241).

Russians were especially rapidly leaving military conflict areas: for example, over half of the Russian population left Caucasian states (Georgia, Armenia, Azerbaijan) and Tajikistan within 7 years. From Kazakhstan, where in 1989 over 10 million Russians lived, 20% of them left for Russia (this was about 40% of the total number of Russians "repatriated" to Russia). It is worth noting that they were primarily well-educated people and skilled specialists (Vishnevsky, 2002:112).

For the first time in its history Russia was facing a massive inflow of refugees and forced migrants. It necessitated elaboration of appropriate laws, regulations, and government structures and institutions. The 1993 Federal Law "On Refugees and Forced Migrants" determined privileges for Russian citizens who were forced to leave other post-Soviet countries. In order to implement this Law, the Federal Migration Service was founded. After signing the 1951 UN Convention on the status of refugees and its 1967 Protocol in 1993, Russia experienced an inflow of forced migrants from many developing countries (mainly Afghanistan).

The Russian government, supported and inspired by international organizations that started their activities in Russia in the early 1990s (first of all, United Nations High Commissioner for Refugees and International Organization for Migration), were concerned about the social integration of refugees. Refugee status guarantees access to medical care and education, including school education for children of refugees and forced migrants. The UNHCR Office in Russia has developed a special program for female refugees aimed at facilitating their integration in the Russian society. The program includes vocational training, organization of Russian language courses for women, babysitting their children when women are absent, organization of hobby groups, and other services.

During 1993–2007, over 1.6 million persons were granted refugee and "forced migrant" status in Russia; however, with time they have lost their status in accordance with Russian legislation. The refugee status is granted for a term of three years. The "forced migrant" status, which is granted to Russian citizens or citizens of the ex-USSR countries who find themselves in refugee-like situations, is granted for a term of five years. However, termination of refugee status does not necessarily mean obtaining other legal status or a possibility to return to a country of origin. So, many former refugees are staying in Russia as illegal immigrants. In 2007, the total number of refugees and "forced migrants" was 6.8 thousand persons, of whom 6.5 were internal migrants, primarily in the North Caucasus region.

New Motives for Immigration

After 1995, the stage of panicked, reactive and largely forced migration of Russians was coming to an end. Very notably, the motivations behind migration shifted; economic factors (both push and pull ones) gained a greater role. The economic situation in Russia seemed relatively more sustainable in contrast to the even deeper economic crisis in the other CIS (Commonwealth of Independent States) states. The Commonwealth of Independent States unites countries of the former Soviet Union excluding Baltic states. In search of jobs and better living standards, the indigenous populations of "new foreign states" started to move to Russia.

According to National Statistics Committee data, the gross national product per capita in Russia in 1996 was 6,742 USD; it was twice as high as in Ukraine (3,325 USD), three times higher than in Moldova (2,100 USD), and five times higher than in Tajikistan (Vorobyeva, 2001:82). Average wages (in USD equivalent) in

Ukraine was 2.1 times less than in Russia, in Kazakhstan 1.7 times less, in Kyrgyzstan 3.8 times less, in Moldova 4.5 times less, in Armenia 6.6 times less, in Azerbaijan 9.4 times less, and in Tajikistan 30 times less. By 2007 disparities between economic situations and opportunities for population between Russia and other CIS states were the same, if not deeper. Average monthly wages in Russia were 443 USD compared to 208 USD in Ukraine, 130 USD in Moldova, 120 USD in Azerbaijan, 113 USD in Georgia, 86 USD in Kyrgyzstan, and 37 USD in Tajikistan (CISStat, 2007).

"Transparent" borders between Russia and other ex-Soviet republics and the existence of multiple familial, emotional, professional and other connections were strong motives for immigration inflow to Russia. This was true both for Russians and other ethnic groups of the former Soviet Union as life spent in a common country strongly affected their migration behavior: for many of them it was easier to decide on moving to the neighboring and "familiar" Russia than to any other foreign country outside the former USSR. This kind of socio-psychological domination of migration flows vector in the post-Soviet space is noticeable not only in permanent migration but in various types of temporary migration that are in fact prevailing in recent years.

Human Capital Characteristics

The sociodemographic structure of permanent immigrants to Russia in the 1990s proves their high human capital characteristics. Highly skilled immigrants (graduates from universities and high professional schools) were 80% of this group. It is important that often they have been educated in Russian universities and professional schools; therefore, they can more easily integrate in the Russian labor market despite rapid transitional changes. The age group 30–49 years is prevalent and they can be regarded as an efficient replenishment of labor resources. As is typical for permanent migration, 80% of immigrants come accompanied by their children (Goskomstat, 2003).

However, it is already clear that the post-Soviet political and economic crisis that provoked large-scale forced migration flows first of all encouraged the most educated and well-to-do people to move: for them, it was easier to take the risk and costs of migration as well as to integrate in the receiving society due to high human capital characteristics. Further waves of immigrants to Russia were fewer both in numbers and in qualitative characteristics. For example, in 2006 immigrants with higher education to Russia were 20% of the total number of immigrants over 14 years old (Goskomstat, 2007:129).

Migration Inflow Dynamics

In the mid-1990s immigration inflow to Russia started to decline (having peaked in 1992–1994), and by the beginning of the 2000s it was less than 200,000 persons a year (Table 4-1). The reasons were both objective and subjective. The migration potential of Russians living outside Russia is naturally declining, partly because they have already left for Russia and partly because they have adapted themselves to the existing situation in their countries of residence. At the same time impeding factors appeared. The lack of a legislative base for interrelations between newly sovereign countries, in particular the lack of guarantees of basic civic and social rights for persons who wish to move from one former Soviet state to another has presented one obstacle. The absence of a clear official position in Russia toward accepting incoming ex-Soviet citizens into Russian citizenship was another barrier for many potential would-be migrants. "Demonstration effect" is also to be taken into consideration: low State support to resettlers, bureaucratic difficulties with registration at the place of residence, and a strict connection between social security guarantees and citizenship hamper integration of migrants and cause disillusionment both in migrants and in those potential migrants who have not made a final decision about moving. As a result, the number of immigrants from former Soviet republics has dramatically declined. Table 4-1 shows that in 2007 the number of immigrants to Russian from CIS states for permanent residence (286,900 persons) increased again. This is mainly the result of radical shift in Russian migration policies toward encouragement of immigration inflow of former compatriots.

In addition, pushed by unemployment and lack of economic opportunities in their countries of residence, citizens of "new foreign states" are coming to Russia in search of jobs and earnings. Thus, earnings-oriented temporary migrations to Russia have dominated since the late 1990s. Due to translucent borders and poor immigration control, they take place in irregular forms in most cases. Between 1994 and 2007 Russia received about 4 million regular and over 15 million irregular labor migrants.

Immigration from "Old" Foreign Countries

Migration balance between Russia and "old" foreign countries (in terms of nonreturn migration) was negative for the whole period of 1990–2007. It has declined from 100,000 persons in the early 1990s to roughly -50,000 in the early 2000s and -10,000 in 2007. Annual immigration was steadily growing from 1 to 2 thousand in the early post-Soviet years to 8–10 thousand currently (see Table 4-1). The reason lies in the structure of immigration by countries: the major source countries are the United States, Israel, and Germany—the same top list of countries of destination for Russian emigrants in early 1990s. So, the growing immigration for permanent residence to Russia is in fact return migration of those Russian citizens (primarily the Germans and the Jews) who decided to leave Russia but failed to integrate in the receiving countries.

The new source country is China: Chinese migrants pushed by economic and demographic reasons and encouraged by the support of the Chinese Government come to Russia both in quest of jobs and in quest of residence. Some scholars argue that by the mid-twenty-first century the number of Chinese people in Russia will exceed 10 million, so they will be the second-largest ethnic group in Russia after Russians (Verlin, 2002; Guelbras, 2002:29). For the present, the total number of Chinese migrants who live in Russia more or less permanently is close to one million, and they are the most numerous foreign ethnic group after Ukrainians in the country. In addition, there are a large number of Chinese "tourists" who come to Russia for business or private purposes, and irregular migrants. Demographically and economically,

China "presses" Russia, especially in its Far East region. Population in the three Chinese provinces neighboring Russia's Far East exceeds 110 million persons, and population density is 130 persons per square kilometer, while in the four Russian administrative regions close to the border—Jewish Autonomous Region, Amur Region, Primorskiy Region, and Khabarovskiy Territory—population density is only 4 persons per square kilometer, that is, 30 times less, and the number of citizens is less than 6 million. Poorly populated but rich with natural resources (timber, metals, minerals), the Russian eastern territories appear a desired and promising aim for Chinese immigrants (Datsyshen, 2002).

Chinese migration to Russia is supported and guided by Chinese ethnic communities (associations). In a number of Russian cities they have developed into strong and active economic and social organisms, developing "in parallel," that is, noncrossing, with local society and industry (Guelbras, 2002:26–29). Having developed an independent community press, financial system, and various companies—hotels, hostels, warehouses, restaurants, and other businesses—the Chinese communities take complete charge of their compatriots in their migration movements and business activities. The survey of the Chinese ethnic community in Moscow has proved the appearance of Chinese firms dealing with invitations and visa support for Chinese people who would like to immigrate to Russia or to other countries using Russia as a transit stage.

Immigration and Demographic Development

The role of immigration for the future development of Russia can hardly be overvalued. Already net migration has become an essential factor of Russia's demographic development due to dramatic natural decrease of population. In 1992–2007, natural decrease of Russian population exceeded 13 million persons (over 900 thousand persons annually in the latest years). Steady negative population growth is indicated in 80 out of Russia's 88 administrative territories. Russia faces also an absolute labor force decrease: small numbers of young people born during the economic recession at the beginning of the 1990s are reaching working age, while the elder age groups (born during the postwar rise in fertility) are leaving labor-active age cohorts.

Long-term demographic perspective is even more distressing: by 2050 population in Russia will probably be less than 90 million persons (40% less than the current number) and labor age groups will decline from 60% to 47% of the total population, while population over 60 years will increase twofold: from 20% to 43% (Vishnevsky, 2002:182–193).

The present deep demographic crisis in Russia is to be evaluated more widely than merely a decline in numbers of people. The crisis is related to negative trends in all demographic indices: falling fertility, decline in number of marriages and growth of divorces, life expectancy decline, increase in mortality rates, relatively high infant mortality, high emigration rate, including "brain drain," and as a result—steady decrease of population size, deterioration of human capital characteristics, crisis of the family institution and accelerating population aging. While the 1990s economic and political reforms have played an important role as prerequisites of the demographic crisis, in the nearest future demographic trends can be an obstacle for realization of economic programs. Social security expenses related to the population aging can become a heavy burden for the budget while some regions will simply become deserted. Under such conditions migration inflow seems important for improvement of the demographic situation and may compensate, at least, partially, for the population decline. In fact, net migration to Russia from former Soviet states in 1992–2007 was 5.2 million persons; it half-compensated for natural population decrease (see Table 4-2). However, the role of migration in managing the demographic crisis should not be overestimated.

Immigration can only smooth the current demographic crisis to a certain extent; it can soften some negative consequences, and solve some regional demographic problems, but no more. The sample of developed countries shows that only in the circumstances of "mild depopulation" can migration be an effective demographic tool (for example, in Germany depopulation has gone on since the end of the 1960s, however natural decrease is measured in as a very small percentage, and labor shortages are effectively covered by migrants). In Russia, the situation is absolutely different.

In order to withstand the demographic crisis in Russia and provide its further positive development, a complex of measures is necessary; proper immigration policy can only be an effective supplement to general population policy aimed at stimulating fertility, enhancing the family institution, and regarding an individual's life as the most important value for the State.

Labor Migration to Russia

In the 1990s Russia became a destination country for labor migrants, primarily from the former USSR countries. As mentioned above, Russia looks economically more attractive than the majority of its neighboring countries. Besides, common language and culture, mutually recognized diplomas, and similar skills requirements have significance here.

Another decisive motivation for labor migration is the situation in the Russian national labor market. The labor market is in the process of being reshaped in accordance with new economic conditions. So, there is lack of balance between labor demand and supply. National labor resources for low-skilled manual labor in agriculture, construction industry, and transports do not cover high demand. Russian citizens ignore these jobs due to low salary, lack of prestige, and hard working conditions. Over 800,000 vacancies are registered annually in employment offices throughout Russia; only by 40% they are filled by local workers (Goskomstat, 2007:301).

It can be concluded that nowadays in Russia side by side with unemployment (6.8%) there exists high demand for foreign labor to take low-paid manual jobs in production industries. At the same time, in accordance with global trend of service sector growth, the share of foreign workers employed in commerce, catering, and public services in Russia is rapidly increasing. Currently 41% of migrant workers in Russia are occupied in construction, 14% in mining and manufacturing, 10% in agriculture, 35% in commerce and catering (Goskomstat, 2007).

Compared to national workers, foreign workers often seem more attractive to employers because they agree to lower wages, do not demand proper working conditions, and are

Table 4-2. Net Migration between Russia and Other Former Soviet States, 1992–2007, Thousands

	1992	1993	1994	1995	1996	1997	1998	1999	2000	2001	2002	2003	2004	2005	2006	2007	1992–2007
Ukraine	−110.0	17.3	139.0	89.0	87.1	68.7	54.6	22.4	39.1	12.5	16.2	6.7	4.6	18.1	20.8	41.0	527.1
Belarus	−21.3	−11.4	15.6	10.1	2.4	−1.5	−5.3	−7.6	−3.0	−4.7	−2.0	−1.7	0	0.8	−0.7	0.7	−29.6
Moldova	9.9	4.5	12.0	10.4	11.0	7.9	6.0	4.8	9.4	5.9	6.2	5.2	3.9	5.7	8.0	13.5	124.3
Georgia	46.2	65.0	62.2	43.7	34.5	21.7	18.1	17.1	18.4	8.3	6.2	4.6	4.2	4.8	6.2	10.0	371.2
Azerbaijan	50.7	43.1	43.4	37.8	35.4	25.5	18.3	12.0	11.7	3.4	3.9	2.5	1.3	3.4	7.6	19.7	319.7
Armenia	12.0	27.9	44.6	31.3	22.4	16.4	14.4	12.4	14.4	4.5	5.7	4.0	2.4	7.0	12.2	30.0	261.6
Uzbekistan	86.4	70.6	135.4	97.1	36.6	31.7	36.6	36.6	37.7	22.9	23.5	20.3	7.9	29.8	36.5	52.1	761.7
Kyrgyzstan	49.8	86.7	56.5	18.3	10.4	7.4	5.7	6.7	13.7	9.4	12.1	6.0	8.9	15.2	15.0	24.0	345.8
Tajikistan	66.7	62.9	41.9	38.5	29.9	20.7	16.4	10.3	9.9	5.8	5.1	4.4	2.8	4.3	6.1	16.8	342.5
Turkmenistan	12.0	6.8	17.4	17.2	21.4	15.2	9.0	6.8	6.1	4.1	4.3	6.0	2.7	4.0	4.0	4.7	141.7
Kazakhstan	96.6	126.9	304.5	191.0	134.5	207.8	183.2	113.5	107.0	50.0	41.8	15.5	27.6	39.5	26.7	30.0	1696.1
Lithuania	11.7	17.0	6.9	2.8	18	0.6	0.6	0.3	0.6	0.5	0.4	9.3	0.6	0.1	0.2	0.2	60.2
Latvia	23.2	23.7	25.0	13.7	7.4	5.1	3.0	1.5	1.4	1.0	0.7	0.6	0.6	0.5	0.5	0.6	108.5
Estonia	21.8	12.8	10.2	7.7	5.0	2.9	1.2	0.3	0.4	0.1	0.2	0.1	0.1	0.2	0	0.2	63.2
Total	**355.7**	**553.8**	**914.6**	**608.6**	**439.8**	**430.1**	**361.8**	**237.0**	**266.8**	**123.7**	**124.3**	**74.6**	**74.0**	**133.3**	**143.2**	**243.6**	**5202.5**

Source: National Statistics Committee data.

more lenient toward labor code violations. Therefore, they give employers an opportunity to benefit from lower production costs and increase their competitiveness.

In 2007, over 1717.1 thousand foreign workers were registered in Russia (see Table 4-3). When compared to the total number of national labor resources (about 67 million) it does not appear to be greatly significant. However, in some regions of Russia foreign labor is an important element of the local labor market, for example in the Central Region, in the Far East Region, and in Western Siberia. These areas accumulate about 70% of registered labor migrants in Russia. In recent years, the number of foreign labor receiving regions in Russia has been increasing. While in 1994 labor migrants were employed in 23 out of 89 of Russia's administrative territories, in 2006 they were employed in every of 88 regions (Vorobyeva, 2001:92; FMS, 2007).

Major source countries are Uzbekistan (19.5%), Tajikistan (14.6%), China (13.3%), and Ukraine (12.2%)(see Table 4-3). Until 2007 the "50:50 balance" between the totality of the ex-USSR countries and "old" foreign states that might seem surprising was mainly the result of widespread practices of unregistered employment of labor migrants from Commonwealth of Independent States (CIS) countries. Illegality is in fact one of the major characteristics of migration inflows to Russia.

Illegal Immigration

The dominant type of immigration to Russia, illegal immigration is very diversified. It consists of the following major inflows (Krasinets et al., 2000:80–82):

(1) The citizens of the ex-USSR countries who come to Russia in quest of jobs and/or residence. Visa-free regimes based on bilateral and multi-lateral agreements between most post-Soviet countries allow them to cross the boundaries legally. Russia has signed agreements on visa-free entry with all the CIS states except Georgia and Turkmenistan. However, due to bureaucratic obstacles on the way to Russian citizenship and legal employment the overwhelming majority of migrants find themselves in illegal status. They are primarily employed in the informal sector of the economy. Their number is rapidly growing, and is now estimated as 5–6 million persons.

(2) Hundreds of thousands of refugees from Afghanistan, Somalia, Ethiopia, Turkey, Sri Lanka, Angola, and other countries reached Russia after the country signed the 1951 UN Convention on Refugees and its supplementary 1967 Protocol in 1993. Only a part of them were granted refugee status, while the others did not even claim for it and preferred to move to the West for better living standards or to stay in Russia illegally. They number over 200,000 persons.

(3) Transit migrants from Asian and African countries who arrive with transit visa or by visa-free channels and head toward Western Europe, where they intend to get refugee status or join their relatives. They lose their legal transit migrants status when they overstay the transit term. They often "get lost" in the vast territories of Russia for years. Their number is around 500,000 persons. Transit migrants are attracted by relatively "transparent" borders within the post-Soviet territory. In combination with agreements on visa-free entry signed by some CIS states with third countries it provides a rather comfortable and cheap land route for transit migrants from Asia to Russia or for continuing travel to the West. For example, there are agreements on visa-free entry between China and Kyrgyzstan; between Kyrgyzstan and Kazakhstan; and between Kazakhstan and Russia.

(4) Foreign citizens who after expiry of contract work in Russia (mainly from Vietnam and Korea) or after graduating from Russian universities and professional schools (from Afghanistan, Iraq, Cuba, Congo, Guinea, Ethiopia, etc.) preferred not to return to their countries but to stay in Russia. They are about 80,000 persons.

(5) Migrants who enter the country illegally, without border control or with false documents. The purpose of their arrival can be related to illegal transit toward the West, or short-term stay in Russia for criminal reasons. Very approximately they can be estimated at 100,000 to 150,000.

In fact, the poor immigration control system along with a huge segment of shadow economy

Table 4-3. Foreign Labor Force in the Russian Federation, 1994–2007, Thousands

	1994	1995	1996	1997	1998	1999	2000	2001	2002	2003	2004	2005	2006	2007
Total, including:	**129.0**	**281.1**	**292.2**	**241.5**	**242.3**	**211.4**	**213.3**	**283.7**	**359.5**	**377.9**	**460.4**	**702.5**	**1014.0**	**1717.1**
From former Soviet states:	70.8	134.4	145.6	114.0	111.1	94.7	106.4	148.6	204.6	186.9	221.2	343.7	537.7	1,152.8
Armenia	1.7	6.1	7.2	6.9	7.5	5.2	5.5	8.5	12.6	10.0	17.0	26.2	39.8	73.4
Azerbaijan	0.4	1.3	2.2	3.2	4.0	2.8	3.3	4.4	15.0	6.0	9.8	17.3	28.3	57.6
Belarus	5.8	11.1	10.3	1.0	–	–	0.01	0.02	15.1	–	–	–	–	–
Georgia	0.9	7.0	8.1	6.7	6.3	5.2	5.2	4.9	6.8	3.2	3.8	4.3	4.9	4.7
Kazakhstan	1.0	2.1	2.2	1.8	1.8	1.7	2.9	3.6	7.6	4.0	4.2	4.1	4.9	7.6
Kyrgyzstan	0.1	0.7	1.2	1.3	0.7	0.5	0.9	1.7	6.4	4.8	8.0	16.2	33.0	109.6
Moldova	3.7	6.7	9.5	9.9	10.5	8.6	11.9	13.3	40.7	21.5	22.7	30.6	51.0	93.7
Tajikistan	0.6	1.5	2.0	3.1	3.3	4.1	6.2	10.0	16.8	13.6	23.3	52.6	98.7	250.2
Turkmenistan	–	0.1	0.3	0.4	0.3	0.3	0.2	0.1	7.0	0.2	0.3	1.5	0.7	2.1
Uzbekistan	1.5	3.5	4.1	3.2	3.0	3.4	6.1	10.1	15.5	14.6	24.1	49.0	105.1	344.6
Ukraine	55.1	94.2	98.7	76.6	73.7	62.9	64.1	91.9	61.0	102.6	108.6	141.8	171.3	209.3
From other countries	58.2	146.7	146.6	128.5	131.2	116.7	106.9	135.1	154.9	191.1	238.5	358.8	476.3	563.8
China	20.3	26.5	24.0	22.2	23.3	24.3	26.2	38.6	38.7	72.8	94.1	160.6	210.8	228.8
Turkey	12.1	36.2	39.0	33.2	35.7	26.7	17.8	20.9	15.4	37.9	48.0	73.7	101.4	131.2
Vietnam											41.8	55.6	69.1	79.8
North Korea	5.9	15.0	7.8	10.4	9.4	10.1	8.7	9.9	12.7	13.1	14.7	20.1	27.7	32.6
Former Yugoslavia	3.5	16.0	18.6	16.9	14.1	9.8	8.0	10.2	10.4	10.6	9.5	12.2	17.8	25.2
Poland	1.9	7.1	7.3	3.5	3.3	2.1	2.5	2.6	5.9	1.3	1.3	1.4	2.1	2.5
USA	0.8	2.0	2.0	1.8	2.1	2.4	1.8	2.0	1.5	1.8	1.9	2.9	3.7	4.8

Source: Federal Migration Service data.

provokes large-scale illegal immigration to Russia. Production of the shadow sector of Russia's economy is estimated as a quarter of GNP, and employment as 20% of the total labor force (Maleva, 2007:147). Even transit migrants from remote countries like China, Afghanistan, Vietnam, or Ethiopia wittingly choose Russia as an "intermediate station" on their way to the West because they know from the countrymen who have used this route before that they will be able to stay in Russia for some time to prepare for their onward travel, earn some money, purchase forged documents, or wait to be joined by other migrants.

A relatively simplified entry regime at Russia's eastern borders, on the one hand, and well-organized and technically equipped border control at the western side, on the other hand, give birth to a phenomenon of "asymmetric borders" frequently mentioned by experts. As a result, Russia faces a lot of negative effects of irregular migration that is generated by "failed" transit migration in many cases when migrants run into an obstacle of strict control at both sides of the "Russian–European" border and ever-tightening entry regulations in the majority of West European states. More and more transit migrants are compelled to stay in Russia, although they were only in transit there. Therefore, Russia becomes a sort of "reservoir" for illegal migrants (Ivakhniouk, 2004a).

When employed in the shadow economy and informal sector, illegal migrants meet a threat of violence, abuse, insult, deception, and other unfavorable treatment. Once in abusive situations, lack of papers and fear of arrest or deportation often prevent illegal migrants from seeking help from authorities. The alternative protection frame comes from informal ethnic solidarity or criminal organizations.

Generally, in the context of illegal immigration Russia is facing the full range of negative effects that usually accompany illegal immigration. For Russia, the negative effects may be even more severe than in other countries because illegal migrants disorganize the national labor market that is still on the path to market economy, increase illegal employment niches, and consequently impede the transition process (Soboleva & Tchudayeva, 2007).

Noncontrolled immigration has a negative impact on the criminal situation and damages Russia's national security; it complicates socio-economic development and provokes ethnic tension between migrants and nationals. Many migrants are employed in shadow sectors, and as a result, the budget loses yearly up to 1 billion USD because of tax payment evasion by both employers and employees (Krasinets, 2002). In addition, as illegal migration contributes to development of a noncontrolled market of goods and services, it stimulates growth of shadow economy and impedes development of "civilized" labor market in Russia.

At the same time, illegal labor migration from ex-USSR countries has invisible effects related to Russia's national security. It is a paradox but a fact that by receiving illegal migrants in its territory Russia is providing itself with "safe borders" with other former Soviet states. By earning money in Russia illegal migrants from Azerbaijan, Armenia, and Central Asian countries are supporting their families in their motherlands where the economic situation is much worse and therefore they help avoid possible social outburst. The current slackening of ethnic tension and anti-Russian views in those states can be evidence of the new value of Russia (to be more exact, the Russian labor market) for the well-being of their citizens (Ivakhniouk, 2004b).

Migration Management in Post-Soviet Russia

In the beginning of the 1990s *international* migration management was quite a new issue for Russia. For decades, migration policy in the Soviet Union has been focused on management of *internal* migration flows within the country while international migration has been regulated primarily by administrative interdictions and restrictions.

The international migration boom resulting from disintegration of the Soviet Union collided with the lack of appropriate legislation and immigration institutional structure. The laws on citizenship, refugees, and forced migrants and social guarantees for international migrants were formulated during a very short period of time following Russia's emergence as a sovereign state, when there was an urgent need for national legislation. Laws were hastily written under conditions of panicked and/or forced migration flows. However, during the following decade the international migration situation changed radically, and the laws have grown outdated.

In the early 2000s, a new cycle in national migration legislation improvement was undertaken. The 2002 Federal Law on the Legal Status of Foreign Citizens in the Russian Federation and the 2002 Federal Law on Citizenship provide a better base for immigration management, though they are also subject to criticism by the civil society, executive bodies, and migrants. For example, the Law on Citizenship practically gives equal rights to migrants from the former Soviet republics and migrants from other countries in obtaining Russian citizenship, and therefore ignores the earlier common USSR citizenship and close ethnic, consanguine, and emotional links existing in the post-Soviet territory. The inadequate national legislation on migration that is understandable but inexcusable improperly narrows the scope of legitimate migration and consequently broadens the scope of irregular immigration.

Since 2003, immigrants to Russia are distributed geographically in accordance with quotas for every administrative territory (quotas are of two types: for migrant workers and temporary residence permits). However, quotas are poorly based on the territories' employment and housing facilities and social infrastructure, and therefore, the immigration process continues regardless of quotas.

An even more important gap in the immigration legislation is its lack of bilateral intergovernmental agreements between the ex-USSR states to guarantee social and legal rights succession for persons wishing to move from one former Soviet state to another. As a result, immigrants who come to Russia face difficulties in getting pension payments and other social benefits, accounting for their seniority, and so forth. With development of labor migration, the lack of bilateral agreements on social security for labor migrants from one country working in the territory of another country has become obvious.

Russia has agreements on employment and social security for the citizens of one country working in the territory of another country with some former Soviet states—Armenia (1994); Belarus, Ukraine, Moldova (1993); Kyrgyzstan (1996); and Azerbaijan (2005); and agreements on social and legal guaranties for permanent migrants who have moved from one country to another—with Azerbaijan (1997), Armenia (1997), Georgia (1994), Kazakhstan (1995), Kyrgyzstan (1995), Tajikistan (1992), Turkmenistan (1993), and Ukraine (2001). However, even when bilateral agreements on social security are signed, they do not surely guarantee labor migrants access to social benefits. For example, the survey of Ukrainian labor migrants working in Russia (2002) demonstrated their lack of access to medical care and housing. Seventy percent of Ukrainian migrants do not have medical insurance. Every fourth migrant had to go to a doctor or to a hospital during his/her stay in Russia. Only in 30% of the cases their medical expenses were covered by the employer (Pirojkov et al., 2003:71).

The institutional structure of migration management also developed inconsistently. In 1992 the Federal Migration Service (FMS) was founded. Its activities were mainly directed at refugees and forced migrants, in accordance with migration situation of the time. Again, lack of experience in international migration management resulted in failure to distinguish international and internal migration flows. For example, there was no distinction between in-Russian forced migrants who were running away from "hot points" and ethnic conflicts, on the one hand, and international migrants who arrived to Russia from neighboring ex-USSR states, on the other hand. However, these flows were already different by nature, in terms of citizenship, access to social security system, legal rights, and so forth. The deferred effect of this misunderstanding resulted in the above-mentioned 3 million "nonstatus immigrants" staying in Russia at present. Other forms of international migration, first of all economic/labor migration, dropped from the sight of policy makers at that time.

In 2000 the FMS was abolished due to its obvious ineffectiveness, and the responsibility for migration management was transferred to the Ministry of Federation, National and Migration Policy. One year later, in October 2001, the Ministry was restructured, and since February 2002 the management of migration together with migration policy is under the Ministry of Interior. This institutional change reflected a new turn in priorities: combating illegal migration, mainly in the context of its threat to national security, has become the core principle of migration management in Russia. However, very soon it became clear that police measures in combating illegal migration have very limited success and a dominating restrictive trend in migration management is contradicting Russia's demographic and economic interests.

Practical realization of migration management in the 1990s was carried out within the frames of the Federal Migration Programs (approved by the Government for every 1–2 years between 1992 and 2001). Initially, the Federal Migration Programs (FMPs) consisted of several subprograms: legal protection of migrants; accommodation and housing; employment; social security; medical care; and meal supplies for refugees and forced migrants. However, gradually the structure of the Federal Migration Programs shifted from social to administrative priorities: improvements in migration legislation; development of immigration control system; development of effective tools to manage labor migration; international cooperation in the field of migration. Being one of the urgent priorities of the government, the FMPs were supported with appropriate material and financial resources from the budget.

In 2001, the 2002 Federal Migration Program was not approved, and since that time FMPs were excluded from the list of federal programs. The reason was mainly related to the fact of institutional reorganization of migration service that has been integrated into the Ministry of Interior. However, root causes were bound up with the shortsighted position of Russian authorities and the lack of understanding of potential benefits immigration can bring to Russia's demographics and economy.

The State activity in the field of migration management can be effective and can correspond to the nation's interests when: *first*, it is based on clear understanding of the existing migration situation; *second*, it evaluates this

situation in the context of economic and demographic trends; *third*, it is guided by general development strategy of the country; and *fourth*, it employs the whole complex of migration management tools, including legislative, administrative, economic, information, and others.

The major problem for Russia until 2007 was the lack of a clear long-term immigration strategy. The lack of understanding of the scale of Russia's need for migrants based on economic and demographic expediency has provoked uncoordinated steps of the Federal Migration Service mainly aimed at restrictions rather than reasonable managing. However, migration policy is poorly developed in Russia not because the government maliciously ignores it. On the contrary, the public debate is focused on migration issues; and the number of laws, decrees, and instructions in the field of migration management adopted in the Russian Federation during the last 15 years is more than in any other country of the world during the last 30 years. But migration policy is not isolated; normally, it is inserted in the general strategy of the development of the nation and it is in fact "the derived policy." Lack of long-term strategy of national development in Russia (for example priority industries, basic resources for competitive strength, importance of high technologies, education development strategies, labor market preferences in the context of declining population of working age) makes derived policies irrational.

This is the main reason for numerous failed attempts to formulate the State concept of migration policy in Russia. In the early post-Soviet period the government had to react urgently in response to inflows of millions of forced migrants: their admission, reception, employment, accommodation, integration, and so forth. Therefore, there was an obvious lack of opportunity to concentrate on elaboration of the general State concept of immigration policy taking into consideration all the categories of migrants who were entering Russia. Under the circumstances of deep economic crisis, lack of clear economic development strategy, and lack of skilled personnel in the field, the attempts to work out a reasonable state concept of immigration policy or at least a definite state position regarding current and future international migration trends appeared unsuccessful.

Impulsive reaction of governmental institutions to the growth of large-scale spontaneous immigration flows that "suddenly" gained international character was negative. Another reaction was unlikely to happen. Spontaneous migration flows were regarded as an additional destabilizing factor under conditions of pressing economic and political crisis. At that time in Russia there were no comprehensive studies in international migration and its interrelation with economic development, that is, fundamental works that could serve as the background for long-term reasonable governmental strategy in the sphere of migration.

In 2003, the government adopted the "Concept of Migration Flows Regulation in the Russian Federation" as an official State strategy in the field of migration. It is quite clear that *regulation of migration flows* is only one side of migration policy that is to be accompanied by protection of migrants' rights and integration of migrants in the receiving society.

In 2006–2007, Russia radically revised its immigration policy. The *2006–2012 State Program on Providing Support for Voluntary Re-settlement of Compatriots to the Russian Federation* is aimed at encouragement of former Russian and USSR citizens living in other countries and having a desire to return to Russia to realize their desire relying on the State support. The benefits for resettlers include: indemnities of travel expenses and transportation of their paraphernalia; travel allowance; monthly allowance for the period until obtaining Russian citizenship (up to 6 months); "compensation packet," including services of preschool institutions, secondary education, vocational training, social welfare, health care, and assistance in job seeking.

The program is guided by the pragmatic purpose of the Russian government to alleviate the demographic crisis Russia is facing presently. The program aims not only to encourage compatriots to come and settle in Russia but to distribute them over the territory of the Russian Federation giving preferences to those migrants who move to the areas where economic and demographic situation needs urgent human inflow or where large-scale investment projects that need labor resources are being implemented.

The Program is to be implemented within 3 stages. *The first stage* (2006): working out of legislation assigned to provide legal basement of realization of the program; assessment of demand for human resources by the administrative units (republics, provinces, and territories) of the Russian Federation; information campaign. *The second stage* (2007–2008): resettlement of the program participants; integration of compatriots; evaluation of the results; if necessary, modification of further regional projects of immigration encouragement. *The third stage* (2009–2012): further realization of resettlement regional projects; evaluation of the results of the program; if necessary, shaping of a new program.

In addition, keeping in mind the purpose to widen channels for regular migration as an alternative to irregular ones, Russia has revised its labor migration policy. In 2006 migration legislation in respect of regulation of stay and work of citizens of the CIS states was modified. In January 2007 the new migration laws were put in force. To fill in the gaps in labor market under the circumstances of rapid natural population decrease and growing economic progress, the government has staked for liberalization of migration regulations. The previous employer-driven work permits scheme, which strictly attached a migrant worker to a definite employer, is replaced by a more flexible approach in which a CIS national can easily get a work permit valid at the territory of the region where it has been issued. The quota system provides supplies of foreign labor for different regions of Russia in accordance with their labor demands

During 2007—the first year after the new legislation was put in force—over 6 million migrants were registered in migration services and number of issued work permits granted to CIS citizens was over 1.1 million that is twice higher than in 2006 and thrice higher than in 2005.

This turn in the Russian migration policy demonstrates a new approach of the government toward evaluation of immigration potential and gives a legal foundation to the de facto Russian status as the country of immigration. It can be proved by sharp increase in numbers of both permanent and temporary immigrants to Russia in 2007.

Conclusion

The case of Russia in the worldwide analysis of immigration trends proves, first of all, the role of historical factors in shaping international migration flows. In the post-Soviet territory, the present migration processes are deeply rooted in the past of the former single country. Common language, economic interdependency, transportation and communication infrastructure, and close cultural and sociopsychological ties between the new sovereign nations make intraregional migrations dominate. They are primarily centered on the Russian Federation.

Historically, Russia is the center of the Eurasian space. *Economically*, it exceeds other ex-USSR republics by economic potential, labor market size, and wage level. *Demographically*, Russia faces negative population trends that make it dependent on labor migrants" inflow. *Politically*, Russia is a leader among former "sister republics" that are its major migration partners. *Geographically*, Russia is the nearest neighbor for the most part of ex-USSR states and has easy railway, road, and air transport communications with them. These factors make Russia a country of immigration in the post-Soviet region. Integration of migrants from CIS states is objectively facilitated by the relatively small sociocultural distance between former USSR nations. Despite this fact, intolerance and ethnic-based conflicts inspired by nationalist political parties complicate the immigration issue in Russia.

Immigration policy of the Russian Federation during the post-Soviet period is characterized as contradictory, inconsistent, and nonstrategic. Emphasis on rigorous police measures to combat illegal immigration, inspired by the September 11, 2001, terrorist attacks in the United States and a number of acts of terror executed by migrants in Russia, proved ineffective to establish orderly migration as the overwhelming majority of illegal migrants are just employment-seeking migrants who are often pushed into illegality by imperfect Russian legislation.

Only since 2006 has the immigration policy in the country developed a clearer purpose—of encouraging permanent and temporary immigration based on well-realized need for migrants to face existing demographic challenges. The new immigration policy of the Russian Federation is likely to even increase international migration flows within the post-Soviet territory as it gives preferences for citizens of the CIS states that have visa-free regime with Russia in terms of staying and getting citizenship and access to the Russian labor market.

Note

1. The following is a list of abbreviations used in this chapter:

   CIS—Commonwealth of Independent States
   FMP—Federal migration Program
   FMS—Federal Migration Service
   GNP—Gross National Product
   IOM—International Organization for Migration
   UN—United Nations
   UNHCR—United Nations High Commissioner for Refugees
   USD—United States Dollar
   USSR—Union of Soviet Socialist Republics

References

CISStat. (2007). Labour Market in the Countries of the Commonwealth of Independent States. Statistical Abstract. Moscow. Interstate Statistical Committee of the Commonwealth of Independent States (CISStat).

Datsyshen, V. (2002). Chinese migration in Siberia: Past and present. In: *Migration and Regional Coordination for Ethnic and Political Stability in Eurasia*. Edited by Soboleva, S., Oktyabrskaya, I. and Chudayeva, O. Novosibirsk. ArtInfoData (pp. 33–40) (in Russian). (Problemy kitayskoy migratsiyi v Sibiri: istoriya i sovremennost. In: *Migratsiya i opyt vzaimodeystviya regionov po usileniyu etnopoliticheskoy stabilnosty v Evrazii.*)

FMS. (2007). Monitoring of Regular (Legal) Labor Migration in Russia in 2005–2006. Statistical Abstract. Moscow. Federal Migration Service (in Russian). (Monitoring legalnoy (zakonnoy) vneshney trudovoy migratsii za 2005–2006 gody).

Goskomstat. (2003). Population and Migration in the Russian Federation in 2002 (Statistical Bulletin) Moscow (in Russian). (Naseleniye i migratsiya v Rossiyskoy Federatsii v 2002 godu.)

Goskomstat. (2007). Population and Migration in the Russian Federation in 2006 (Statistical Bulletin) Moscow (in Russian). (Naseleniye i migratsiya v Rossiyskoy Federatsii v 2006 godu.)

Guelbras, V. (2002). Chinese Migration and Chinese Ethnic Communities in Russia. In: *World in the Mirror of International Migration*. Scientific series: International Migration of Population: Russia and the Contemporary World. Vol.10. (pp. 18–33). Moscow: MAX Press.

Iontsev, V. (1998). Brief Historical Review of Immigration to Russia and Emigration from Russia. In: *Population and Crises*. Vol. 4, Moscow: Dialog-MGU, pp. 54–77 (in Russian). (Kratkiy istoricheskiy obzor immigratsii v Rossiyu i emigratsii iz Rossii. In: *Naseleniye i krizisy.*)

Iontsev, V. & Ivakhniouk, I. (2002). Russia in the World Migration Flows: Trends of the Last Decade (1992–2001). In: *World in the Mirror of International Migration*. Scientific series: International Migration of Population: Russia and the Contemporary World. Vol. 10. (pp. 34–78). Moscow: MAX Press.

Iontsev, V. & Magomedova, A. (1999). "External" Migrations between Russia and Other Ex-Soviet States (Historical Overview). In: *International Migration of Population: Russia and the Contemporary World*. Vol. 2. Moscow: Dialog-MGU, pp. 6–25 (in Russian). ("Vneshnyaya" migratsiya mezhdu Rossiyey i stranami blizhnego zarubejya (istoricheskiy oszor). In: *Mezhdunarodnaya migratsiya naseleniya: Rossiya i sovremenniy mir.*)

Ivakhniouk, I. (2004a). *Analysis of Economic, Social, Demographic and Political Basis of Transit Migration in Russia—Moscow Case*. Key paper for the Council of Europe Regional Conference "Migrants in Transit Countries: Sharing Responsibility for Management and Protection" 30 September—1 October 2004, Istanbul, Turkey. Council of Europe, Strasbourg.

Ivakhniouk, I. (2004b). Illegal Migration: Russia. In: *European Security*. No: 13 (4), pp. 35–54.

Kabuzan, V. (1998). *Emigration and Re-emigration in Russia in the 18th Century—the beginning of the 20th Century*. Moscow (in Russian). (Emigratsiya i re-emigratsiya v Rossii v 18-m—nachale 20-go vekov.)

Krasinets, Y., Kubishin, E., & Tiuriukanova E. (2000). *Illegal Migration to Russia*. Moscow, Academia (in Russian). (Nelegalnaya migratsiya v Rossii.)

Krasinets, Y. (2002). Irregular Migration and Employment: Major Characteristics in Border Regions. In: *Migration and Regional Coordination for Ethnic and Political Stability in Eurasia*. Edited by Soboleva, S., Oktyabrskaya, I., and Chudayeva, O. Novosibirsk. ArtInfoData (in Russian). (Nezakonnaya migratsiya I zanyatost: vazhneyshiye harakteristiki v prigranichnyh territoriyah. In:

Migratsiya i opyt vzaimodeystviya regionov po usileniyu etnopoliticheskoy stabilnosty v Evrazii.)

Maleva, T. (2007) Labor Policy at the Stage of Economic Growth. In: *Overview of Social Policy in Russia. Beginning of the 2000s*. Ed. by T. Maleva, N. Zubarevich, D. Ibragimova. Moscow: NISP, p. 111–157 (in Russian). (Politika truda na etape ekonomicheskogo rosta. In: *Obzor sotsialnoy politiki v Rossii. Nachalo 2000-h.*)

Pirojkov, S., Malinovskaya E., & Khomra A. (2003) *External Labour Migrations in Ukraine: Socio-Economic Aspect*. Kiev, NIPMB (in Russian). (Vneshniye trudoviye migratsii v Ukraine: socialno-ekonomicheskiy aspect.)

Population Encyclopedia. (1994). Moscow: BSE (in Russian). (Encyclopedia Harodonaseleniye.)

Soboleva, S., Tchudayeva O. (2007) Human Capital of Labor Immigration. In: *Proceedings of the International Conference "Migration and Development", 13–15 September 2007, Moscow, Russia*. Vol. 2. Moscow University Press, pp. 103–118 (in Russian). (Chelovecheskiy capital trudovoy immigratsii. In: *Materialy mejdunarodnoy knferentsii "migratsiya I razvitiye" [Piatiye Valenteevskiye chteniya.]*)

United Nations. (2006). International Migration 2006. New York. UN.

Ushkalov, I. (1999). Emigration and Immigration: A Russian Phenomenon. In: Scientific Series "*International Migration of Population: Russia and the Contemporary World.*" Vol. 2 Moscow: Dialog-MGU, pp. 80–87 (in Russian). (Emigratsiya I immigratsiya: rossiyskiy fenomen. In: *Mezhdunarodnaya migratsiya naseleniya: Rossiya i sovremenniy mir.*)

Verlin, Y. (2002) "Black cash" and Yellow Danger" (in Russian). In: *"Expert,"* No: 11, March 18. Moscow. (Chernyi nal I zheltaya opasnost.)

Vishnevsky, A. (ed.) (2002). *Population of Russia in 2001*. Annual Demographic Report. Moscow: Universitet Publishing House (in Russian). (*Naseleniye Rossii v 2001 godu*. Ezhegodniy demograficheskiy doklad.)

Vitkovskaya, G. & Zayonchkovskaya Zh. (2001) *Migrations in the CIS and Baltic States: through Diversity of Problems to Common Information Society*. Moscow: Adamant (in Russian). (*Migratsia v SNG i Baltii: cherez razlichiye problem k obshemu informatsionnomu obshestvu.*)

Vorobyeva, O. (ed.) (2001). *Labor Migration in Russia*, Series: "Migration of Population." Supplement to "*Migration in Russia*" Journal. Vol. 2. Moscow (in Russian). (*Trudovaya migratsiya v Rossii*. Seriya "Migratsiya naseleniya.")

5

Germany

Immigration and Integration Policies and Practices in Germany

Andrea Schmelz

Since the number of labor migrants (*Arbeitsmigranten*) in the Federal Republic of Germany passed the one million mark in the 1960s, migration and integration of immigrants has become a permanent issue on the political agenda. Fear of "ghetto-conflicts" (*Ghetto-Konflikte*) and an overstraining of the social welfare system were emphasized in the public debate. Suburban riots in France, the extremist murder of Theo van Gogh in the Netherlands, and fear of bomb attacks by Islamic fundamentalists at the beginning of the new millenium fostered concerns about the outbreak of violent conflicts in Germany.

For a long time the federal government refused to acknowledge that Germany had become a country of immigration (*Einwanderungsland*). In his memorandum "Current situation and advancement of the integration of foreign workers and their families" Heinz Kühn, the first federal agent for foreign nationals (*Ausländerbeauftragter*) and former prime minister of North Rhine–Westphalia had already questioned the negation of Germany's status as a country of immigration ("Deutschland ist kein Einwanderungsland"). Thus, the "Kühn-Memorandum" was the first document to call for a political change in perspective: policy should shift its focus from the return of

migrants to their home countries to the integration of immigrants and their families. However, another 25 years passed before Germany was publicly recognized as a country of immigration.

Diversity of the Immigrant Population

Detailed data on immigration offer information on migration and integration processes and form the basis of the governance and management of migration and integration. Since the micro census in 2005, people with migrant background who live in Germany have been registered. The micro census is an important supplement of official statistics, which have so far registered immigrants only by keeping records of their nationality. They neither distinguish between the first and second generation of immigrants nor do they record the ethnic German repatriates' origin (*Spätaussiedler*) or naturalized citizens. As a result, these groups did not show up in official migration statistics.

On the basis of the data collected by the micro census, the Federal Statistical Office (*Statistisches Bundesamt*) makes the following differentiation of the population concerning their migration status (Table 5-1):

Table 5-1. Migration Status of the German Population According to the Micro Census in 2006, Measured Per Thousand

	in %	Absolute Numbers
Overall population	100%	82,389
Persons of German origin	81.6	67,225
Persons with migrant background	18.4	15,143
Immigrants	12.7	10,431
Of which foreign nationals	6.8	5,584
Of which naturalized persons	5.9	4,847
Children or grandchildren of immigrants	6.5	4,713
Of which foreign nationals	2.1	1,716
Of which naturalized persons	3.6	2,997

Source: Migration Report 2007, ed. Federal Office for Migration and Refugees 2008.

Thanks to the micro census it is known today that not only 6.8 million foreign nationals belong to the population in Germany but that there are in total 15.1 million men, women and children with migrant background.[1]

In Germany, less than half of the population of foreign descent came into the country as guest workers or their family members or descendants of these immigrants. Immigration of labor migrants to Germany started in 1955 with the recruitment agreement (Anwerbeverträge) between Germany and Italy. Further agreements with Spain (1960), Greece (1960), Turkey (1961), Morocco (1963), Tunisia (1965), and Yugoslavia (1968) followed.

Nowadays, more than half of the foreign-born population holds a passport of one of the six main countries of recruitment. Due to increasing immigration of ethnic German repatriates (*Aussiedler*) from Eastern Europe and Sowjetunion and asylum seekers and immigrants from other continents since the end of the 1970s, the composition of the immigrated population has strongly diversified. Forming 16.5% of the immigrant population, people of Turkish descent represent the largest ethnic group, followed by people of Russian (6.2%), Polish (5.6%) and Italian (5.0%) origin (Figure 5-1). Immigrants from the Russian Federation (about 180,000) and the Ukraine (about 130,000) are nowadays more numerous than Spanish or Portuguese immigrants.

The immigrated population in Germany comes predominantly from Europe and the Mediterranean region. It is a very heterogeneous group with respect to the cultural and social

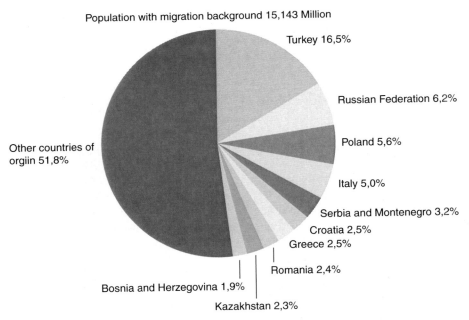

Population with migration background 15,143 Million

Turkey 16,5%

Russian Federation 6,2%

Poland 5,6%

Italy 5,0%

Serbia and Montenegro 3,2%

Croatia 2,5%

Greece 2,5%

Romania 2,4%

Kazakhstan 2,3%

Bosnia and Herzegovina 1,9%

Other countries of orgiin 51,8%

Figure 5-1. Population with Migration Background and their Countries/Regions of Origin, 2006. *Source: Migration Report 2007*, ed. by Federal Office for Migration and Refugees 2008.

Table 5-2. Influx and Emigration to and from Germany between 1991 and 2007

Year	Influx	Emigration	Net migration
1991	925,345	497,540	427,805
1992	1,211,348	614,956	596,392
1993	989,847	710,659	279,188
1994	777,516	629,275	148,241
1995	792,701	567,441	225,260
1996	707,954	559,064	148,890
1997	615,298	637,066	−21,768
1998	605,500	638,955	−33,455
1999	673,873	555,638	118,235
2000	649,249	562,794	86,455
2001	685,259	496,987	188,272
2002	658,341	505,572	152,769
2003	601,759	499,063	102,696
2004	602,182	546,965	55,217
2005	579,301	483,584	95,717
2006	558,467	483,774	74,693
2007	574,752	475,749	99,003

Source: Numbers compiled by the author on the basis of the *Migration Report 2007,* ed. Federal Office for Migration and Refugees 2008.

backgrounds as well as education and biographies of immigrants.

Compared with classical countries of immigration (*klassische Einwanderungsländer*), immigration to Germany presents a relatively recent phenomenon. Two-thirds of the people of foreign descent were born abroad; therefore, the majority of immigrants belong to the first generation of migrants. Every fifth foreign national is a second generation immigrant.

A third generation of immigrants, whose grandparents immigrated to Germany, is still relatively small in numbers, yet growing. In order to determine the state and course of immigration processes, it is important to recognize that data can only provide information on the medium-term developments since these processes have not been completed (Schönwälder 2008).

In addition, a relatively high turnover of the population of foreigners can be observed. New immigrants arrive in Germany while others leave the country or return (statistics of people moving in or out of Germany). Mobility is especially high among Poles and Turks, which statisically belong to the largest immigrant groups in Germany.

Between 1990 and 2007, 12.2 million cases of immigration were registered in Germany. In the same period, 9.4 million foreigners moved out of the country. Taking these numbers into account there was an a net migration of 2.8 million people (*Wanderungsüberschuss*).

The number of people moving into the country is defined by the following factors: (1) increased immigration of ethnic German repatriates (*Spätaussiedler*) until the mid-1990s since the 1991/92 influx of refugees from wars or civil wars in former Yugoslavia, of which the majority has already returned to their home countries; and (2) increased but temporary work migration from non-EU countries especially of contract workers (*Werkvertragsarbeiter*) or seasonal workers.

The fall of the Iron Curtain and the civil war situation in former Yugoslavia determined migration of the 1990s. At the beginning of the twenty-first century, migration has stabilized at a rather low level. (Federal Office of Migration and Refugees 2007).

The Migration Report 2007 distinguishes the following types of immigration according to entry (e.g., requirement or nonrequirement of a visa) and residence permit status:

- Migration within the boundaries of the EU (internal migration) and EU citizens
- immigration of ethnic German repatriates
- immigration for the purpose of education
- contract, seasonal, or guest worker immigration as well as further temporarily limited work migration from EU and non-EU countries
- immigration of asylum seekers and convention refugees (*Konventionsflüchtling*) as well as Jewish immigrants from the former Soviet Union
- subsequent immigration of families and spouses from non-EU countries (third-country nationals)
- immigration resulting from other reasons
- repatriations of German citizens
- irregular immigrants whose number cannot be determined[2]

The number of migrants without an official residency status, the so-called "undocumented" migrants, can only vaguely be estimated at somewhere between 100,000 and one million. Many of those who are currently working

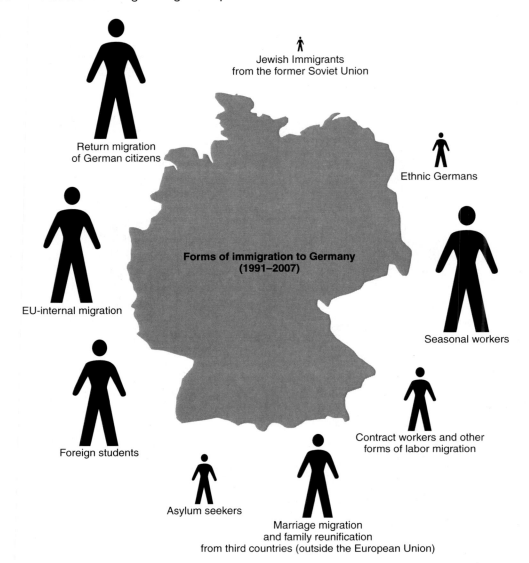

Figure 5-2. Forms of Immigration to Germany, 1991–2007.
Source: Migration Report 2007 ed. by Federal Office for Migration and Refugees 2008.

"illegally" came to Germany to earn money for themselves and their families, or came after relatives were already living here, and did not have the possibility to legally immigrate. The majority of these people entered Germany on a valid three-month tourist visa, and were submerged into illegality after their visas expired. Some of these undocumented migrants are victims of human trafficking and forced prostitution. The exact number of victims is unknown.

What all these people have in common is that they are a gladly used source of cheap labor, but have hardly any rights. "Illegal" immigrants are employed everywhere in the cleaning and child care sector in private households, and as workers in the construction and food industries. The Catholic Church's "Forum Illegalität" (Illegality Forum) has established itself as Germany's strongest political lobby for the rights of illegal migrants, above all in the area of health care, with the establishment in 2001 of the groundbreaking Maltese Migrant Services project (Alt & Bommes 2006).

East and West Germany differ extremely regarding their history of immigration before and after the reunification of Germany in 1989/ 90. Since its foundation the Federal Republic of Germany has been a country of immigration while the German Democratic Republic was marked by emigration (Schmelz 2002). While the main type of immigration in the "old" West German States was an economically inspired work migration which was originally socially agreed upon, work migration in the GDR occurred in relevant numbers only shortly before the Fall of the Wall in 1989. The largest group of contract workers came from Vietnam. Moreover, there were workers from other socialist countries that the GDR maintained close bonds with, such as Cuba, Mozambique, and Angola. In the 1980s, these workers were hired by East German companies in order to balance the labor shortage. They were sent back to their countries of origin in the context of repatriation programs shortly after the reunification in the early 1990s (Weiss 2007).

A comparison of the numbers of the foreign population of the old and new federal states shows that immigration is not as often found in the "New Laender" as it is in the "old" West German states. Table 5-3 shows the share with

migrant background by federal states. While in the three city-states Berlin, Hamburg, and Bremen, as well as in economically strong regions such as Baden-Württemberg, North Rhine–Westphalia, and Hesse, the population share of persons with migrant background is between one fifth and one fourth of the overall population, in the five "New Laender" nearly every 20th inhabitant is of foreign descent.

In Eastern Germany there are no areas of ethnic concentrations because here the number of immigrants is very low and therefore the possibility of building ethnically homogeneous networks is very limited (Weiss 2007). Since the early 1990s immigration to the "New Laender" has taken place almost entirely due to governmental assignment, it takes place in a region which offers no economic possibilities. There is hardly any labor migration because the labor market broke down in the course of the political changes after the Fall of the Wall. In the process, many workers were fired, and the economy has not recovered since. Immigration in order to find work therefore is limited to rare cases for example to those of high qualifications.

In the future, the development of immigration and emigration to and from Germany will depend upon the increasing global mobility, the continuing refugee problem, family ties, and the demand for labor. In current population

Table 5-3. Persons of Migrant Background by Federal State in 2006, Measured per Thousand

Federal State	Persons migrant background	% of the overall population	Of which foreign nationals	Share of population in %
Baden-Württemberg	2,659	24.8	1,282	11.9
Bavaria	2,362	18.9	1,182	9.5
Berlin	779	22.9	464	13.6
Bremen	163	24.5	86	12.9
Hamburg	451	25.8	248	14.2
Hesse	1,423	23.4	691	11.4
Lower Saxony	1,261	15.8	541	6.8
North Rhine–Westphalia	4,188	23.2	1,932	10.7
Rhineland-Palatinate	703	17.3	315	7.8
Saarland	192	18.3	88	8.4
Schleswig-Holstein	343	12.1	152	5.4
New Laender (except Berlin)	620	4.7	319	2.4
Total	15,143	18.4	7,300	8.9

Source: Numbers compiled by the author on the basis of the *Migration Report 2007*, ed. Federal Office for Migration and Refugees 2008.

predictions, the Federal Office for Statistics anticipates a net migration of 100,000 to 200,000 persons per year. In 2007 there were 99,003 immigrants. It is still questionable if policies of migration management succeed in attracting especially highly qualified employees from abroad (Angenendt 2008a).

Chances for the integration of immigrants are crucially defined by their residential status. The legal status of the immigrated population determines if they have access to the labor market, to political participation, and to social security, and therefore predefines the possibilities of designing future plans and opportunities in Germany. People who have been granted asylum many years ago still have to fear that they will lose this status if the political situation in their home countries improves. Many refugees and "tolerated" immigrants (*Geduldete*) have only limited possibilities of participation in the labor market because Germans and EU citizens are preferentially employed. Considering this, it is difficult for them to decide how much to invest in their children's education and their own education, especially in terms of improving German language skills. On the contrary, EU citizens who immigrated to Germany enjoy wide-reaching rights and ethnic German repatriates (*Aussiedler*) are from the outset legally on a par with Germans (Schönwälder 2008).

In order to evaluate the state of art of the immigration and integration processes in Germany and political interventions, the very heterogenous background of migrants as well as their different basic conditions in German society and the contexts of their countries of origin have to be taken into account. However, over the course of many years, scholarly research on immigrants in Germany failed to consider the different (cultural) backgrounds, the migration experiences (flight, labor migration), and the immigrants' legal status, mainly due to a lack of data on the immigrant population.

The current social situation of the immigrant population is connected with the specific migration history of Germany as well as the lack of efficient integration policy. Until the recruitment stop in 1973, the Federal Republic of Germany sought out migrant workers new federal states to fill jobs in fields such as mining and the industry, positions for which low qualifications were required. Following the structural economic change of the 1980s and 1990s, many of them found themselves unemployed and searching in vain for steady employment. Asylum seekers were often banned from the labor market for years. For many of them, this led to a downgrading of jobs in the course of the migration and immigration process and to dependency on welfare payments.

Revisited Integration Policy

In contrast to many other European immigration countries, the political debate about German immigration and integration policies in the last years has become more objective. The political climate surrounding the immigration debate of 1992/93 was very different, as the administration at the time described the high rate of immigration as a "national crisis" and a "foreigner and asylum problem." Migration was viewed as the most important domestic political issue, especially because it was accompanied by bloody acts of violence against "foreigners." Since then, the political parties have reached a widespread consensus regarding the necessity of integration and the role of the state in supporting it (Thränhardt 2008).

The legislative development from a "demonstrative reluctance to recognize" and "an avoidance of making decisions" (Bade 2007) to a commitment to integration policy took place in four stages:

A first stage comprised the reform of the alien law, which helped to facilitate naturalization and allowed for a legal claim to German citizenship. In recognition of permanent residence of foreign nationals, the Christian-Liberal coalition resolved to bring a wide-reaching revision of the alien law underway, which became effective on January 1, 1991. The main goal of the alien law reform consisted of enabling foreign nationals to be able to plan more long-term for the future through the improvement of their legal status. The most important points in the process were: reunifying families, replacing administrative discretion with legal claims, establishing the right of residence for family members, implementing the option to return and enabling the process of acquiring citizenship. The law was hotly disputed. On the one hand, the opposition parties (the Social Democrats and the Green Party), welfare organizations, and churches criticized the law as a wasted opportunity to legally recognize the reality of Germany as an immigration country. On the other hand, conservative critics argued that too little was being done to reduce the number of foreign nationals (here and following, Santel 2007).

The second stage took place in 2000 with the reform of the citizenship law under the red-green administration. It replaced the traditional, although often amended, strongly ethnonational concept of *Jus sanguinis* (inheritance of citizenship) in the Reich and Citizenship Law of 1913 with a conditional *Jus soli* (acquisition of citizenship through birth in the country). The law allowed dual-citizenship until age 23 for children born in Germany to foreign nationals with legally approved permanent residence. Before they turn 23, they have to choose one citizenship. By enabling naturalization, the reform of the law aimed to improve the integration of the foreign nationals permanently residing in Germany and their children born in the country.

The third stage constituted the revision of the immigration law. It was reformed on the basis of the report by the Independent Commission on Immigration 2001 and came into effect, after a long period of parliamentary debate, on January 1, 2005. Although the law did not incorporate all of the commission's suggestions, it established for the first time a legal framework through which immigration could be regulated. At the same time, measures promoting integration for immigrants permanently residing in Germany were legally established. The Immigration Law regulates three important core issues:

Immigration of foreign workers
Admittance of refugee asylum seekers
Integration of new immigrants

The core element of the Immigration Law is that all legal new and long-term immigrants in Germany uniformly obtain integration support as a basic offer. On the one hand, integration courses teach language skills, and on the other hand it informs immigrants about the legal system, the culture, and the history of Germany.

The Immigration Law connected migration and integration regulations in one law and declared integration to be a responsibility of the state. From the Federal Office for the Recognition of Foreign Refugees (Bundesamt für die Anerkennung ausländischer Flüchtlinge, BAFl), the new law established the Federal Office for Migration and Refugees (Bundesamt für Migration und Flüchtlinge (BAMF). This office became responsible for migration and integration on the national level, and it would be more adequately described as the "Federal Office for Migration and Integration." The Immigration Law reduced the complicated variety of immigrant resident status options and outwardly simplified the immigration administration through the "one-step government" (an institutional contact person responsible for questions concerning residence and employment rights).

The struggle to achieve a stable political compromise regarding the Immigration Law led to a conflictual political negotiation process. Political factionalism between the parties also led to conceptual losses. Most difficult proved to be the general strengthening of immigration limitations at the expense of a directed and simultaneously limited encouragement of immigration. This included the annulment of the flexible point system for the selection of qualified immigrants with the aid of variable criteria in accordance with the successful Canadian model, which first draft of the German immigration law was adopted by the Czech Republic. Furthermore, the independent expert advisory board for Immigration and Integration (Immigration Commission) was also abolished. As a result of both decisions, Germany remains behind the other European immigration countries (Bade 2007).

Since 2006, the Integration Summit, the "National Integration Plan" (2007) and the German Islam Conference (2006), have been convened by the Minister of the Interior. At the state level, which is where the primary responsibility for integration issues lies, there were simultaneously various trend-setting initiatives. Most wide-reaching was the "Action Plan Integration" developed by the state government of North Rhine–Westphalia under the direction of the first nationwide Integration Minister Laschet. A plethora of concepts and approaches to projects that have been proven successful through years of practice exist at the local level, strategically key for integration. To some extent, the projects are connected to the most diverse civil societies, while others are also initiatives funded by foundations. These efforts have been modified to adapt to the changing demands of urban immigrant communities.

With the Integration Summit and the "National Integration Plan," the federal government symbolically signaled a policy of personal commitment to integration by all members of society, bringing together the main political actors including migrant organizations. This act of symbolic policy is often criticized by welfare and immigrant organizations. The Integration Summit made two key points publicly clear: first, the recognition of immigrant organizations as partners in dialogue at the highest level enhanced their political status and probably increased the notoriety and influence of several immigrant politicians in society and collectively among immigrants. Second, the Integration Summit and "National Integration Plan" effectively publicly underlined that integration of immigrants is a central political concern and requires vigorous action. (Schönwälder 2008).

Bade, the father of German migration studies, grounds the new system of a concept-oriented integration policy on three pillars, which he describes as "preventive" (präventive), "supportive" (begleitende), and "revisited" (nachholende) integration policy, whereby the two latter pillars are closely related to one another (here and following Bade 2007).

Pillar 1: Preventive Integration Policy: The basis here is to possibly consider the professional and social qualifications of the new immigrants, which they have acquired in their countries of origin to an extent that they do not have to be further developed in a time-consuming or expensive manner. Today this is practiced in various approaches: with "Spätaussiedler" (ethnic German repatriates) in the form of language courses conducted in the region of origin and additionally with Jews from the former Soviet Union through a type of point system with criteria (especially language, occupation, age) in the context of an individual "integration prognosis." In both cases, however, the professional training and difficult access to the job market hinders the integration process.

Pillar 2: "Supportive Integration Policy": The foundation here is built upon the offers, made in the Immigration Law, to support the integration process by language and integration courses and by counseling structures for newly immigrated persons. Based on past experiences, the failures regarding German language acquisition and education both for preschool- and school-aged members of the younger generation should be avoided.

Pillar 3: "Revisited Integration Policy": This is the most important pillar of integration policy in Germany. It was only indirectly designated in the broader context of the Immigration Law—beyond a minimal allocation of courses for 50,000–60,000 people, as far as funds were available for the "first generation." In this way, the "supportive integration policy" was promoted at the cost of the "revisited" integration policy, which Bade criticizes as a legislative error. The number of foreign nationals as permanent residents who never received integration courses (language and orientation courses), viewed today as a matter of course, significantly outnumbers the ever-decreasing group of new immigrants. The concept of revisited integration policy is focused largely on second and third generation immigrants.

According to Bade, revisited integration policy can also only be conceptualized as a concomitant effort. It cannot compensate for the momentum of a delayed integration process. Instead, this policy can only seek to accompany or restimulate a discontinued or interrupted integration process.

This support through revisited integration policy is—like the supportive integration policy—oriented toward the goal of expanding the opportunities for equal participation in all branches of society. This is especially applicable for language integration, in other words, the sufficient ability to communicate in the dominant language; for social integration (which usually cannot be achieved without language ability); for cultural integration, including acceptance of the basic values of the system of laws; for economic integration, especially access to the job market and, primarily regarding young people, for the preconditions necessary for family upbringing, education, and professional training and qualification. The new state integration program brings a standardization and official planning of individual integration efforts. It thereby strives toward exercising more control over the individual integration process, increasing efficiency in integration support and thereby finally decreasing the "costs of non-integration" (Michalowski 2007). A study contracted by the Bertelsmann Foundation substantiated that the annual social costs of the inadequate integration of immigrants could be as high as 15.4 billion Euros (Fritschi & Jann 2008).

The pursuit toward defining wide-ranging concepts of integration is visible at the national level (National Integration Plan) and above all at the local level. Towns are also engaged in a process of standardization and are oriented toward monitoring the structural integration processes on the basis of determined indicators (Bommes & Krüger-Potratz 2008; Filsinger 2008). The (further) development and broad implementation of systematic continuous observation of integration and its successes and failures facilitates a "technical certainty" of the ability to regulate integration, the result of which remains open (Bommes 2008).

Indicator-based observation of integration at the national and local level as a basis for political regulation is necessary on the one hand; on the other, caution must be taken in the interpretation of the data compiled through this monitoring (Filsinger 2008). For example, the unsatisfactory integration of immigrants in the job market can be caused by discrimination, by weak integration policy, by immigrants' inadequate qualification for the particular job market or connected to a generally weak economic situation. In the current political-administrative immigration debate, the provision of further knowledge is seen as an important added value in terms of the regulation of integration (Michalowski 2007; Filsinger 2008). Integration policy is currently less oriented toward the broad concepts of integration such as multiculturalism, assimilation, or the guest worker model. Instead, it focuses pragmatically on ascertained fields of politics (Politikfeld). Integration and qualification efforts for new immigrants present one political field that state offices have increasingly regulated in past years.

In contrast to other western European countries, the formal qualification of the work force has not increased in Germany for the last several years. Younger age groups in all other Western European countries have significantly higher educational degrees than older groups. In Germany, above all the increasing lack of tertiary degrees, such as master craftsmen, technicians, and academics is problematic. In Western Europe, Germany is the only country in which younger age groups have fewer tertiary degrees than older groups. The disadvantages of immigrant populations in education and professional training contributes greatly to this. The results not only pose a burden on the future of the knowledge-based society, they also weaken—through the inadequate preconditions for productivity growth in terms of a lack of human capital—Germany's international competitiveness. Furthermore, they threaten the medium-term social peace in the immigration country itself (Bade & Bommes 2008).

According to Bade and Bommes, revisited integration policy should therefore be applied to all levels of education: for preschool- and school-aged children and for professional training and further qualification. Education for preschool- and school-aged children serves as the basis for professional training and is therefore a precondition for participation in the job market. Furthermore, revisited integration policy must also open up social constellations which comprise the families of the second and third generations. They involve above all:

a group of parents as young adults, often with broken educational careers and without professional training, in uncertain employment situations

another group as new immigrants and those belonging to the first generation in the context of intra-ethnic marriages

a group of children (of the second generation) who learn the native language of their parents as their first language

The consideration of the prior social integration processes of the second and third generations has thereby become a precondition for every effort in terms of revisited integration policy.

Integration through Education? The Long Path toward Equal Opportunity

Successful integration can, independent of a migrant background, be defined as achieving equal access to opportunities in the central sectors of society. It is especially contingent upon upbringing, education (including language ability) and professional training as a precondition for general participation in economic life and specifically in the labor market.

Integration also comprises the foundation for individuals and families to lead independent lives. From this perspective, the level of education among the population of young people of foreign descent highlights a growing gap between this group and the societal majority. This, in turn, leads to social tensions and brings about consequential costs for society.

Today the unemployment rates and the rate of poverty among the population of foreign descent greatly exceeds the corresponding numbers in the population without a migrant background (see Table 5-4). Based on the term "relative poverty," the poverty line refers to the level of income under which a person is defined as poor. In an agreement between the EU member states, the poverty threshold was delineated at 60 percent of the median income (Third Poverty and Wealth Report 2008). Children and youth of foreign origin are especially affected by the risk of poverty. More than a third of the adolescent generation of foreign descent (36.6%) belong to families who live under the poverty threshold. In families not of foreign descent, the corresponding rate is 13.7%.

As of 2006 in Germany, 6 million youths under the age of 15 are of foreign descent. This comprises more than one-quarter (27.2%) of all students at German schools. The percentage of migrant youths is especially high among children below six years (32.5%) and among those between six and ten years of age (29.2%) (Federal Office of Migration and Refugees 2007). Since the publication of the first PISA Survey (Program for International Student Assessment) in 2001, the education of young people of foreign origin has become a focus of public interest. Prior to this, research in the field of intercultural education had pointed out the deficiencies of the German school system in terms of promoting integration. The PISA results identified German schools as having a much higher rate of selectivity than schools in most of the other OECD countries. Furthermore, in comparison with other nations, success in school was found to be more dependent on the student's social and ethnic background. Several scholarly studies have shown the disadvantages that children of foreign descent face in terms of education, along with difficulties with the German, which is more or less pronounced, despite reform efforts over the last several decades (e.g., Mecheril 2004; Auernheimer 2006; Siminovskaia 2008).

Education and the German language have achieved key focus in the National Integration Plan. In the context of the development of the plan, which was proposed in July 2007 at the Second Integration Summit, two workgroups addressed topics of education. Their focuses were: "Promoting the German Language from

Table 5-4. Labor Participation, Unemployment, and Poverty Rate Based on Micro Census Data, 2006

	Labor participation rate	Unemployment rate	Poverty rate
Population without migrant background	67.6%	7.3%	11.6%
Population of migrant background	56.0%	12.3%	28.2%
Among them: ethnic German repatriates and their children	62.8%	10.9%	20.7%
Nationalized citizens and children of immigrants born as Germans	56.9%	11.4%	20.7%
Immigrants and foreign nationals born in Germany	52.5%	13.4%	34.3%
Entire population	65.4%	8.3%	14.8%

Source: Compilation of statistics from the German Government's Third Poverty and Wealth Report, 2008.

Birth" and "Ensuring Good Education and Professional Training to Increase Employment Opportunities." Under the heading "Integration through Education," the German government pledged the following in the "National Integration Plan":

The German government strives, along with federal states and communes, towards the development of day care for children under the age of three in order to accomodate on average 35 percent by 2013. The federal government will share in the costs of construction. This development

- is directed towards children with migrant background and should have positive affects on their early acquisition of the German language.
- argues for improving education through the use of budget resources that have been freed as a result of demographic change.
- will develop a plan for the general promotion of the German language in day cares and preschools
- promotes research regarding the children's progress in German language development. They should enable the development of support plans for students and further training for teachers.
- supports, along with 10 states, the development of a master plan for language education through the program "FörMig" (Language Acquisition Promotion for Children and Youth with migrant background).
- through its model program "Truancy—The Second Chance," pursues the goal to reintegrate truants in schools and improve their chances of completing a degree
- supports states' research in the field of education and in their development of plans and methods to improve integration.

(Excerpt from the Summary of the National Integration Plan 2007)

The education level of the population with migrant background has risen consistently since the mid-1990s. Since then, however, the certifiable discrepancy between the access to education in the population with and without migrant background has only changed minimally. In terms of the professional training among youth, there has even been a decline. Since 1994, when the rate of immigrant trainees reached a high point of 9.8%, the percentage has continually decreased.

Migrant Participation Based on Type of School

In the early 1980s, the compulsory education of immigrant children was widely enforced. The rate of those who left school without a degree from the elementary school was reduced from about a half to approximately one-fifth. In 2006 only 7% of German citizens left school without an elementary school degree, while the rate of dropout among immigrant youths was 18%. Today about half of all German students (45%) attend a secondary school degree (Gymnasium) in comparison to barely every fifth immigrant youth. Differences among the nationalities are clear here. Greek and Spanish students, along with those with Ukrainian and Russian heritage, are more successful in the German school system than their peers with origins from other countries (Third Poverty and Wealth Report 2008). These differences are probably related to the parents' level of education and social status along with high educational aspirations. The education of young people of foreign descent in East Germany is also more advanced than in West Germany (Weiss 2007). The migrants of the first generation in East Germany more commonly have higher educational degrees than migrants in West Germany. Youths of ethnic German orgin also seem to profit from stronger institutional support.

In terms of the transition from school to professional training and the job market, a poor secondary school degree or the lack of a degree at all has much more serious consequences for future opportunities than it did several decades ago. The level of qualification that employers expect has also risen as a result of the change in the structure of the economy (Siminovskaia 2008).

Children and youths with migrant background are doubly disadvantaged in terms of equal opportunity (Geißler & Weber-Menges 2008). As a result of the weaker economic situation of many migrant families, they often come across the same challenges as native children of families facing poverty and a lack of education.

These difficulties, compared with other European immigrant societies, are significantly pronounced in Germany. Among children who have the same level of achievement in school and belong to the same class, those whose parents are born in Germany have a higher chance of receiving a recommendation for the "Gymnasium" than children who have fathers and mothers who both do not come from Germany.

According to the results of education research, the causes of the disadvantage in educational opportunity include school-related factors such as inadequate support, more or less conscious discrimination, or the high number of migrants in schools and classes, along with familial factors like the migrant's age at emigration, the length of the children's and parents' stay in Germany, intentions of returning to the home country, and openness toward or separation from German society. It has frequently been empirically proven that immigrants of the second or third generation often tend to receive lower grades or poorer recommendations than native classmates, even if at the same level of performance. (Konsortium Bildungsberichterstattung 2006). Radtke and Gomolla (2007) show that the decisions of teachers and principals regarding significant transitions such as the start of school, transferrals to special schools for children with learning disabilities and recommendations at the end of elementary school were also influenced by criteria unrelated to school performance. This can occur at the expense of the migrant children, so that they find themselves in classes primarily with other children of foreign descent, for example. More often, language difficulties are falsely interpreted as general learning disabilities, which can have wide-reaching effects for the educational and future opportunities for migrant children.

The three-part school system in Germany and the early school career path decision regarding which further school the children will attend has even been criticized by the special correspondent for human rights as a barrier toward equal opportunity for children of foreign descent (Motakef 2006). Furthermore, the low level of expectation in terms of school achievement and success specifically targeted toward this group could be identified as a discouraging factor for these children (Schofield 2006).

Dwindling Opportunities for Professional Training and in the Job Market for Migrant Youths

The situation for professional training of youths with migrant background has developed especially dramatically over the last several years. It is increasingly difficult for them to find professional training positions, they break off their apprenticeships more frequently, and up to 40% do not receive occupational training at all (Bundesministerium für Bildung und Forschung 2007). Of those of foreign descent belonging to the age group of 25- to 35-year-olds, 41% do not have a professional degree, compared to 15% of Germans not of foreign origin.

Many young people of foreign descent have exceeded school age and can no longer be reached through schooling measures. Following school, the competition for apprenticeship positions shows—without very concrete objective reasons—that applicants from immigrant families experience a similar disadvantage as they do in school. This dynamic has intensified in the last ten years. And this does not only apply to those who could not obtain a degree from the "Hauptschule" (many of whom are native youths). As a result, explanations linked to migrants' experiences with discrimination apply here harshly.

The results of a survey of secondary school graduates conducted early 2007 by the National Institute for Occupational Training (Bundesinstituts für Berufsbildung, BIBB) showed that immigrant applicants have notably lower chances than Germans applying for apprenticeship positions even if they have achieved the same qualifications in school. A study completed by the Institute for Employment Research (Institut für Arbeitsmarkt- und Berufsforschung, IAB) in October 2008 shows that this situation has not changed (Seibert 2008). On the whole, the number of young immigrants involved in occupational training, compared to the number of young members of the majority population in such positions, has not only further decreased. The number of youth from immigrant families engaged in professional training (as a portion of the total number of young immigrants between the ages of 18 and 21 who are in these training positions) is also dropping (Bundesministerium für Bildung und Forschung 2007).

Secondary school and professional training degrees are without a doubt the most important keys for integration into the job market. At the same time, even if they have completed professional training, migrants (especially Turkish citizens) lack the same opportunities in the labor market that Germans without migration background have. Turks are more often unemployed and those who are qualified are markedly less often employed than Germans or migrants from other countries with a comparative level of education. The particular disadvantage that Turkish citizens face can therefore only partly be attributed to a low or lack of a secondary school degree. Rather, mechanisms of institutional discrimination through companies along with a lack of social networks are in turn also responsible for their disadvantage. It is becoming more common for (highly) qualified young Turks to turn their backs on Germany and find employment in reputable positions in Turkey or other countries. There they are also able to climb the social ladder, while in Germany they remain barred from these jobs despite their excellent qualifications.

Parallel Society (*Parallelgesellschaft*) and Spatial Segregation

Immigrant neighborhoods, in which a higher-than-average amount of—often generally called "foreigners"—immigrants live, are connected with deficits and problems in the perception of the majority population. Since the "guest works" began to move from their camps and homes in West German cities in the 1960s, the shabby downtown neighborhoods to which they moved have been stigmatized as "ghettos" in the frequent debates. This perception was only peripherally connected with the actual problem, namely the concept of nation, culture, and integration that has dominated the German nation state since its founding in the nineteenth century. Unlike the republican model in France, the German nation has understood itself as an ancestral and cultural community, in which national belonging required a cultural similarity. Within this concept, cultural differences are a threat to the national identity and must be domesticated. This explains the wide-spread fear in Germany of "ghettos" as quasi culturally foreign entities materializing within a city—as well as the dominant position, whereby the social integration of immigrants is only possible when perceived foreign communities dissolve in an ethnically mixed city.

This long historical thread is apparent in the regularly recurring public debates that still differentiate between "Germans" and "aliens" or "foreigners," even to the third and fourth generation, and accuse them of refusing to integrate from "parallel communities," as the "ghetto" is currently called.

The term "parallel society" (*Parallelgesellschaft*) was coined in 1996 in an interview with the sociologist Heitmeyer that was published in the German weekly newspaper *Die Zeit* (cf. Heitmeyer & Anhut 2000). In its context Heitmeyer stated that immigrants in Germany were living in a "parallel society." Over the course of the following years this term became popular in the public debate on migration though it was not based on empirical data. In the public debate the term "parallel society" is linked to the image of an ethnically homogeneous population group which separates itself spatially, socially and culturally from the mainstream society. At the same time, the term implies massive criticism of the immigrants' way of life and signals a demand for cultural assimilation. A series of scientific studies has shown that immigrant groups in Germany are less segregated than immigrant groups in Great Britain, France, the Netherlands, or Sweden. According to results from migration research, inadequate integration policy can be regarded as a main cause for voluntary or involuntary retreat from mainstream society (Thränhardt 2008).

In many cities an unequal spatial distribution of Germans and immigrants can be observed. This concentration of the immigrant population is due to the cumulation of different factors such as the cutback on industrial jobs, high unemployment rates, low salaries, a decline in purchasing power, and inadequate living infrastructure especially in peripheral areas. In comparison with the international situation spatial segregation in Germany is, however, rather low. Taking American or Canadian criteria into account leads to the conclusion that there are hardly any "ethnic residential communities" in Germany and "surely no ghettos" (Schönwälder & Söhn 2007). More typical for urban spaces are residential areas of migrants with a mixed population. According to Schönwälder and Söhn, one-fifth of the foreign population was living in residential quarters in which the share of foreign nationals was above 30%. But also in these cases German citizens still form the majority of inhabitants. Nevertheless, a tendency toward an "ethnic concentration" can be observed in Germany as well. In this context there are great differences between the various nationalities: Especially Turkish immigrants tend to settle in areas where they find themselves surrounded by their fellow countrymen. About one third of Turks live in areas in which the share of the Turkish population is about ten percent or even higher. In addition, the study shows that immigrants, more often than Germans, live in unprivileged residential quarters. One the one hand, the tendency toward a concentration of different ethnic groups in certain residential areas is relatively low in Germany. On the other, the studies mentioned above show that the concentrations in certain cities and neighborhoods are in the broadest sense relevantly linked to certain nationalities, their residential area and integration processes. Empirically this can only be substantiated through further case studies.

An ethnic and sociospatial concentration of immigrants can be regarded also in a positive light. It can help immigrants with their orientation and offers collective self-help in a foreign environment. Additionally, an ethnic concentration provides opportunities for immigrant entrepreneurs to specifically supply the demand and fulfill the expectations of the population. In societies of immigration "ethnic" concentrations in urban areas are common. They first become problematic when immigrants are excluded from education and careers in mainstream society. In this case the danger of structural segregation rises and is moreover intensified if people who have been living in this area for years decide to move somewhere else because they regard the presence of immigrants as an indicator for social downward mobility (Santel 2007).

Regardless of the empirical results, in 2004, after the attack on Theo van Gogh in the nearby Netherlands, the term "parallel society" came in second as "German negative word of the year" (*Unwort des Jahres*; word that is loaded with a negative political connotation). On the basis of spectacular individual cases a new popular academic literary genre deals with honor killings and forced marriages in particular in the largest immigrant community of Turks. Thus, in public opinion the image is created that this is a typical behavior of Turkish immigrants. Even if the debate in Germany is not as emotionally loaded as the one temporarily led in the Netherlands or in Denmark, immigrants and most of all Muslims feel Islamophobia in their daily lives (Thränhardt 2008).

Conclusion

On the one hand, the tendency toward segregation of ethnic communities in Germany is much less developed than in many other countries of immigration. On the other, there is a striking inequality concerning education of children and youth of foreign descent compared with the native population of the same age. It is alarming that immigrant youth, even with the same qualifications as their nonimmigrant counterparts, have lower chances when it comes to attending secondary school and finding a job.

To which degree a "revisited" integration policy will be able to make up for missed opportunities due to a lacking integration policy over the course of the last several decades depends on a variety of factors. These include, among others, future economic development on which politics has only a limited influence. The extent of the expansion of opportunities for migrant children is contingent upon the implementation of sound education policies that focus on the improvement of the chances early in life for future generations of immigrant children. Furthermore, such a policy has to implement effective concepts of "integrated and continuing German language promotion" in all educational institutions.

The history of migration teaches that not only immigrants but also their descendants confront social inequalities (limited professional opportunities, negative stigmatization). It takes time—sometimes up to the fourth or fifth generation—in order for these negative consequences to vanish.

However, the public debate on the introduction of affirmative action, a decidedly controversial measure aimed to create equal opportunities, is still in its infancy in Germany. The question if an implementation of such measures for certain sectors could make sense in Germany and has yet to be widely discussed. Even the antidiscrimination law that passed in 2006 does not play a decisive role in the National Integration Plan (*Nationaler Integrationsplan*).

Notes

1. According to the Federal Statistical Office all people are counted as people of foreign descent "who immigrated to the Federal Republic of Germany after 1949 as well as all foreigners born in Germany and all Germans born in Germany with at least one parent who either immigrated to Germany or is a foreigner who was born in Germany" (Federal Statistical Office, 2007) (Translation by author).
2. The Migration Report takes the following group of migrants into account: Persons, who neither have the right of asylum, hold a residence permit nor who can prove that they are being "tolerated" according to the immigration law and who are neither registered in the Central Alien Register (*Ausländerzentralregister*, AZR) nor elsewhere in official statistics.

References

Alt, J., & Bommes, M. (ed.) (2006). *Illegalität: Grenzen und Möglichkeiten der Migrationspolitik*. Wiesbaden: Verlag für Sozialwissenschaften.

Angenendt, S. (2008a). *Zukunft der europäischen Migrationspolitik: Triebkräfte, Hemnisse und Handlungsmöglichkeiten*. Ein Policy Paper im Rahmen des Projects "Governance of Migration." Berlin: Heinrich-Böll-Stiftung.

Angenendt, S. (2008b). *Die Steuerung der Arbeitsmigration in Deutschland*. Bonn: Friedrich-Ebert-Stiftung.

Auernheimer, G. (ed.) (2006). *Schieflagen im Bildungssystem: Die Benachteiligung der Migrantenkinder*. Wiesbaden: Verlag für Sozialwissenschaften.

Bade, J.K. (2007). *Versäumte Integrationschancen und nachholende Integrationspolitik*. In Bade, J.K., & Hiesserich, H.-G. (eds.), *Nachholende Integrationspolitik und Gestaltungsprspektiven der Integrationspraxis*. Göttingen V & R Unipress.

Bade, J.K., Bommes, M., & Oltmer, J. (eds.) (2008). *Nachholende Integrationspolitik: Problemfelder und Forschungsfragen*. Osnabrück: December 2008 (IMIS-Beiträge 34/2008).

Bade, J.K., & Bommes, M. (2008). *Einleitung*. In Bade, J.K., Bommes, M., & Oltmer, J. (eds.), *Nachholende Integrationspolitik: Problemfelder und Forschungsfragen*, pp. 7–13.

Bommes, M. (2008). *"Integration findet vor Ort statt" über die Neugestaltung kommunaler Integrationspolitik*. In Bommes, M. & Krüger-Potratz, M. (eds.), pp. 159–194.

Bommes, M., & Krüger-Potratz, M. (eds.) (2008). *Migrationsreport 2008: Fakten—Analysen—Perspektiven*. Frankfurt and New York: Campus-Verlag.

Bundesministerium für Bildung und Forschung (ed.) (2008). *Berufsbildungsbericht 2007*. Berlin: BMBF, Referat Öffentlichkeitsarbeit.

Federal Office of Migration and Refugees (ed.). *Migration Report 2007*. Nürnberg/Berlin: 2008 (dt.: Bundesamt für Migration und Flüchtlinge (Hg.). Migrationsbericht 2007, Dezember 2008).

Filsinger, D. (2008). *Bedingungen erfolgreicher Integration: Integrationsmonitoring und Evaluation*. Bonn: Friedrich-Ebert-Stiftung.

Fritschi, T., & Jann, B. (2008). *Gesellschaftliche Kosten unzureichender Inegration von Zuwanderinnen und Zuwandern in Deutschland: Welche Kosten entstehen, wenn Zuwanderung nicht gelingt*. Bielefeld: Bertelsmann Stiftung.

Geißler, R., & Weber-Menges, S. (2008). *Migranten im Bildungssystem: Doppelt benachteiligt*. In *Aus Politik und Zeitgeschichte* 49/2008, p. 14–22.

Halm, D., & Sauer M. *Parallelgeellschaft und Integration*. In Woyke, W. (ed.) *Integration und Einwanderung*. Schwalbach: Wochenschau Verlag, p. 59–83.

Heitmeyer, W., & Anhut, R. (Hg.) (2000). *Bedrohte.Stadtgesellschaft: Soziale Disintegrationsprozesse und ethnisch-kulturelle; Konfliktkonstellationen*. Weinheim: Juventa.

Konsortium Bildungsberichterstattung (2006). *Bildung in Deutschland: Ein indikatorengestützter Bericht mit einer Analyse zu Bildung und Migration* (im Auftrag der Kultusministerkonferenz und des Bundesministeriums für Bildung und Forschung). Bielefeld: Bertelsmann Stiftung.

Koppmans, R. (2008). *Tradeoffs between Equality and Difference: Immigration Integration, Multiculturalism, and the Welfare State in Cross-National Perspective.* Berlin: WZB.

Mecheril, P. (2004). *Einführung in die Migrationspädagogik.* Weinheim u.a.: Beltz.

Michalowski, I. (2007). *Integration als Staatsprogramm: Frankreich, Deutschland und die Niederlande im Vergleich.* Münster: LIT Verlag.

Motakef, M. (2006). *Das Menschenrecht auf Bildung und der Schutz vor Diskriminierung.* Berlin: Deutsches Institut für Menschenrechte.

Nationaler Integrationsplan. Neue Wege – Neue Chancen, ed. Bundesregierung (2006) http://www.bundesregierung.de/Content/DE/Publikation/IB/Anlagen/nationaler-integrationsplan,property=publicationFile.pdf (retrived 19 June 2009).

Radtke, F.-O., & Gomolla, M. (ed.) (2007). *Institutionelle Diskriminierung: Die Herstellung ethnischer Differenz in der Schule.* Wiesbaden: VS, Verlg für Sozialwissenschaften.

Santel, B. (2007). *In der Realität angekommen: Die Bundesrepublik als Einwanderungsland.* In Woyke, W. (ed.), *Integration und Einwanderung.* Schwalbach: WOCHENSCHAU Verlag, p. 5–33.

Seibert, H. (2008). *Junge Migranten am Arbeitsmarkt: Bildung und Einbürgerung verbessern die Chancen.* Nürnberg: Institut für Arbeitsmarkt und Berufsforschung (IAB-Kurzbericht, 17/2008).

Schierup, C.-U., Hansen, P., & Castles, S. (2006). *Migration, Citizenship, and the European Welfare State: A European Dilemma.* Oxford: Oxford University Press.

Siminovskaia, O. (2008): *Bildungs- und Berufserfolge junger Migranten: Kohortenvergleich der zweiten Gastarbeitergenerationen,* Wiesbaden: VS, Verlag für Sozialwissenschaften.

Schmelz, A. (2002). *Migration und Politik im geteilten Deutschland.* Opladen: Leske und Budrich.

Schönwälder, K. (2008). *Reformprojekt Integration.* In Kocka, J. (ed.), *Zukunftsfähigkeit Deutschlands: Sozialwissenschaftliche Essays.* Bonn: Bundeszentrale für politische Bildung, p. 315–334.

Schönwälder, K., Söhn, J. (2007). *Siedlungsstrukturen von Migrantengruppen in Deutschland: Schwerpunkte der Ansiedlung und innerstädtische Konzentrationen.* WZB Discussion Paper, Berlin.

Schofield, J.W. (2006). *Migrationshintergrund: Minderheitenzugehörigkeit und Bildungserfolg.* Forschungsergebnisse der Pädagogik und der Entwicklungs- und Sozialpsychologie. Berlin: WZB.

Strohmeyer, K.-P. (2006). *Segregation in den Städten.* Bonn: Friedrich-Ebert-Stiftung.

Third Poverty and Wealth Report of the German Government: Bundesregierung (ed.) (2008). *Lebenslagen in Deutschland. Der 3. Armuts- und Reichtumsbericht der Bundesregierung.* Berlin: Bundeszeiger.

Thränhardt, D. (ed.) (2008). *Entwicklung und Migration.* Jahrbuch Migration 2006/2007. Berlin: Lit Verlag. Introduction, pp. 5–19.

Weiss, K. (ed.) (2007). *Zuwanderung und Integration in den neuen Bundesländern.* Freiburg im Breisgau: Lambertus-Verlag.

6

France

Immigration to France: The Challenge of Immigrant Integration

Ines Michalowski

The assimilation of migrants has been a dogma in France for many years (Noiriel, 1996). In the late 1980s, the public and political debate on immigrant adjustment to the host country slowly shifted from the idea of assimilation to the idea of integration, which not only allowed for more public expression of cultural difference but was also free from any association with a colonial attitude of imposing a dominant culture. Wihtol de Wenden et al. (1999) emphasize that the French assimilation model most probably worked well during the early years, but that, at the end of the 1990s, most French experts considered it to be outmoded, even though some nostalgia for a past golden age of assimilation might be preserved in certain milieus. This shift in wording and concepts is also relevant for international comparisons of integration policies: until the end of the 1990s many works opposed a French model of Republican assimilation to either a Dutch or British multicultural or a German ethnic model (Brubaker, 1992; Schnapper, 1992; Todd, 1994; Kastoryano, 2002).

These classical comparisons of integration models have been challenged by more recent comparisons that have gone a step further by stressing that national outcomes of immigrant adaptation are neither the pure product of national models or "philosophies of integration" (Favell, 1998) nor of specific policies directed toward the reception and integration of migrants (Hagedorn, 2001). In fact, these more recent contributions argue that general social structures like the structure of the welfare state are more decisive for the position of migrants in the educational system or in the labor market than are specific measures of integration (Böcker & Thränhardt, 2003; Fleischmann & Dronkers, 2008). Thus, within the last years, research on immigrant integration has often turned away from the elaboration of different national models of integration and rather concentrated on the comparison of concrete public policies.[1] This approach was also favored by the emergence since the end of the 1990s of a large number of proactive public policies addressing immigrant integration in European Member States. The (often conservative) governments that created them presented these policies as the response to a crisis of integration. In France the notion of a crisis of integration has often been and still is linked to the children and grandchildren of former immigrants who in spite of the French model of Republican assimilation which guarantees access to full citizenship often have not attained an equal position in society.

79

Immigrant Groups in France

For the period between 2000 and 2007 the INED (National Institute for Demographic Studies) notes a positive immigration balance for metropolitan France of 711,000 migrants. Despite this positive immigration balance in the years 2000 as well as in the 1990s, the percentage of foreigners in the French population has decreased in the 1990s: while foreigners accounted for 6.5% of the population in 1982 and for 6% in 1990, they represented only 5.6% of the population in 1999 as well as in 2006 (OECD, 2008: 55). This decrease has partly been explained by growing numbers of nationality acquisitions in the 1990s, which rose from 96,000 in 1992 to 148,000 in 2000 and remained at this level in 2006. Not surprisingly, the percentage of immigrants, including both foreigners and naturalized French, which remained very stable in the years between 1975 and the end of the 1990s (namely 7.4%) rose to 8.3% in 2006 (OECD, 2008: 53–55).

The geographical origin of foreigners arriving in France has been changing (Le Moigne & Lebon, 2002). Until 1982, Europe (Italy, Spain, Portugal) was the main continent of origin for new immigrants, but it has since passed this position on to Africa. Besides migrants from the Maghreb countries (Algeria, Morocco, Tunisia) and Turkey, who taken together represent almost 46% of all new immigrants to France, the number of migrants from so-called sub-Saharan Africa, like Cameroon, Congo Kinshasa, Ivory Coast, Senegal and Mali, and now also from China make up for another 16% (OECD, 2008: 300). Furthermore, the composition of refugee flows has changed over the last years. While, in the 1990s asylum seekers from Cambodia, Laos and Vietnam, Sri Lanka, former Yugoslavia, Turkey, and Congo Kinshasa represented the majority of the (recognized) refugees, in 2006, 47% of all recognized refugees came from Serbia Montenegro, Turkey, the Russian Federation, the Democratic Republic of Congo, Sri Lanka, and Haiti (OECD, 2008: 317). Among the undocumented migrants who presented a dossier during the 1997 legalization campaign, the majority came from West Africa, followed by the Maghreb countries and Turkey. These flows seem to have changed toward the end of the 1990s, when many undocumented migrants from China and the so-called *pays de l'Est* (East and Central European countries)—particularly Romania, which had not yet accessed the European Union—arrived in France.

In 1999 the stock of immigrants from Algeria (574,000) outnumbered for the first time the stock of immigrants from Portugal (572,000). In 2005 the number of immigrants originally coming from Algeria had risen to 679,000, while the immigrant population from Portugal slightly shrank by 5,000 people, being passed in size by immigrants of Moroccan origin (625,000) (OECD, 2008: 328). Given these data, it is not astonishing that in 2006 immigrants from Algeria, Morocco, Turkey, and Tunisia also represented the four largest groups of new immigrants (OECD, 2008: 42). Among the immigrants from other countries within the European Economic Area (EEA) migrants from Portugal, Italy, Spain, Germany, Belgium, and the UK are the biggest groups in France.

Today, family reunion is the most important channel of legal immigration for third country nationals, that is, migrants from outside the EU and the European Economic Area (EEA). The number of family migrants has been steadily rising over the last years with 38,100 family migrants in 1991; 58,900 in 2000; and 88,939 in 2003. Together with the United States, France is one of the OECD countries in which family reunification represents the major channel of immigration. In 2006, the immigration of family members represented approximately 60% of all permanent immigration to France (OECD, 2008: 36). Postcolonial migrants, especially Moroccans and Algerians, form the majority of today's family migration. While in the past, their immigration and access to rights was ruled by special regimes, they are more and more treated like other immigrant groups.

This is not the case of EU citizens, who obtained many rights in the 1990s and before, such as the right to free movement, to free access to the labor market, or to participation in local elections. In addition, migrants from the EU today also profit from an image of the "good immigrant" and are much less confronted with discrimination and unemployment than are third country nationals. Since migrants from the European Economic Area (EEA) are not subject to the same restrictions on immigration as are third country nationals, the composition of their migration flow differs: while for third country nationals, who represent 79% of all immigrants (migrants from the EEA represent 21%), family migration is the most important channel of immigration to France, work is the most important reason of immigration (41%) among migrants from the EEA (Lebon, 2004: 10). In 2005 only 4% of all third country nationals legally immigrating to France were admitted on the grounds of work (cp. www.ined.fr).

The introduction of foreign labor (seasonal workers, permanent and temporary workers) to France continuously decreased between 1970 (309,301 workers) and 1998 (22,142 workers) but slowly started to rise again in the 2000s, reaching 31,204 workers in 2003. Among the permanent workers (6,500 in 2003), many immigrate as IT-specialists, technicians, managers, and skilled workers, while researchers, artists, or professional interns receive a temporary work permit (10,138 in 2003). Most of the permanent workers come from Algeria, Japan, Lebanon, Morocco, Romania, Turkey, and the United States, and most of the temporary workers are U.S.-Americans, Poles, Romanians, Chinese, Indians, and Moroccans. These permanent and temporary workers are in an advantageous position when compared with seasonal workers who depend on employer invitations in order to immigrate and are thus highly dependent on their employers. The number of migrants introduced as seasonal workers increased from 7,523 in 1998 (the lowest number since 1946) to 14,566 in 2003. Almost 95% of these migrants came from Morocco and Poland and 85% of them worked in the agricultural sector.

Other migrants admitted to France on a temporary basis are the international students whose numbers have risen from 150,000 in 1997–1998 to 250,000 in 2005[2] and reached 212,932 in 2007–2008 (www.diplomatie.gouv.fr). While the number of students from outside the EEA has risen, the percentage of students from the European Economic Area fell to only 25% in 2007–2008. The important increase of students from outside the EEA mainly results from a sharp increase of students from Africa, who represented 47% in 2007–2008. Again, the three Maghreb countries are the most important sending countries for students in France, followed by other African countries such as Senegal and the Democratic Republic of Congo. Students from Asia and Oceania represented 15% of all students in 2007–2008 (www.diplomatie.gouv.fr). As one element of a larger strategy to increase the number of skilled migrants in France, student migration is encouraged by the current government.

This is not the case for asylum seekers, but nevertheless their number rose, too (see Table 6-1). In the years 2003, 2004, and 2005, France was the leading asylum-seeker receiving country among the group of industrialized countries. After a sharp decrease in the following years, numbers have risen again in the first half of 2008, which was mainly due to an increase in claims from asylum-seekers from Mali (UNHCR, 2009: 5).

A form of subsidiary protection to the 1951 Geneva Convention, which was called "territorial asylum," was introduced in 1999 as a response to the growing conflict in Algeria. Its objective was to grant protection to persons persecuted by non-state actors. Since granting this protection was difficult from a diplomatic standpoint, recognition rates never exceeded 4%. Nonetheless, the number of applications steadily increased and almost quadrupled between 1999 and 2001, which caused waiting periods of up to 3 years. Given the fact that applicants profited from a semilegal resident status during this waiting period, filing an application for territorial asylum

Table 6-1. Number of Asylum Seekers in France

	1998	1999	2000	2001	2002	2006
Asylum seekers (Geneva Convention)	22,375	30,907	38,747	47,291	51,087	30,700

Sources: Lebon 2004: 30; OECD, 2008: 50

also paved the way toward legal residence for some migrants. In 2003, the territorial asylum was replaced by another form of subsidiary protection that conforms with the European Union Council Directive on minimum standards for qualification of third country nationals and others in need of international protection.

France's Reaction as a Host Country

Many scholars describe France's policy reaction to continued immigration and the presence of migrants as a back-and-forth between internal and external control. Externally, the migration flow is controlled through such means as visa and border controls, while the internal control focuses on migrants' access to welfare state provisions or to the labor market (Hollifield, 1994 and 1999; Lochak, 2002; Le Moigne & Lebon, 2002; Wihtol de Wenden et al., 1999). Over the past years, both categories of control instruments have been reshaped in France, not always without provoking criticism.

Migration and Integration Policymaking in the 1980s and 1990s and the Role of Party Politics

Political decisions on migration control that were taken in France in the 1990s were conceived simultaneously in opposition to and as a prolongation of the policies of the 1980s, when some major movements in the field of migration policy were made: when the Socialist Party took over in 1981, they not only introduced the 10-year resident card that dissociated the right to work and the right to reside in France (Lochak, 2002) but, as a preparation to an enforced policy against illegal immigration, they also proceeded to the regularization of some 130,000 migrants in 1981.

The 1983 municipal elections that brought the right-wing extremist *Front National* party to the fore has, at least for the following 24 years, had a strong influence on public debates about immigration in France. Especially the Socialists feared to lose votes if the *Front National* managed to present them as too lax and liberal on immigration. During a short period between 1986 and 1988, when the conservatives with Prime Minister Edouard Balladur and Interior Minister Charles Pasqua were back in power, the liberalizations undertaken beforehand by the Socialists were cut down again in the so-called first Pasqua-law of 1986. In 1988, however, the Socialists returned to government and announced the abrogation of this law. These rather liberal reforms undertaken by the Socialists at the end of the 1980s remained in place until 1993, when the second Pasqua-law and the Méhaignerie-law were published. The Méhaignerie-law stipulated a modification in French nationality law implying that children born in France of foreign parents could no longer acquire French citizenship automatically upon reaching legal adulthood but had to demonstrate their wish to obtain French nationality between the ages of 16 and 21. This change in law was supposed to send out a clear signal to the public and to immigrants in France that French nationality could not be obtained without personal effort. For the rest, the second Pasqua-law made access to permanent residence more difficult for certain categories of migrants, enforced the requirements for family reunion (especially the criteria of resources), restricted the right to residence of migrants who were close family members of French nationals, and enabled mayors to refuse a marriage if they suspected it to be of convenience. Additional restrictions were introduced with regard to the juridical and administrative detention of (illegal) immigrants and with regard to the exclusion of illegal migrants who work from the social security registers (Bernard, 1994; Lochak, 2002). This huge restrictive catalog was reviewed by the Constitutional Council, which obliged the government to reintroduce some liberal notes. In 1997, these obligatory changes were presented as the Debré law.

After the Socialist Party and new Prime Minister Lionel Jospin unexpectedly took over the government in 1997, the new Reseda law (also called Chevènement law) was introduced in May 1998. It further liberalized the existing legislation, especially with regard to nationality and stipulated that: (1) A child is French if at least one of the parents is French; (2) A child is French if it is born in France and at least one of the parents was born in France; (3) A child born in France of foreign parents and who permanently resides in France automatically acquires

French nationality upon reaching legal adulthood unless s/he declines this possibility.

Besides this reform, the Socialist government also opted for a regularization campaign in 1997/1998. It was a response to large *sans-papiers* movements that had culminated in the occupation of a church in Paris, finally evacuated by French security forces (Fassin, Morice, & Quiminal, 1997). In comparison to the 1981 regularization that was focused on the proof of stable employment (with or without working contract), the 1997 regularization campaign focused on family members who had found themselves in an irregular situation after the Pasqua legislation. Of the total amount of 150,000 cases that were presented, about 90,000 were regularized.

Migration and Integration Policymaking in the 2000s: Between European Harmonization and French Path Dependency

Since the shocking results of the first round of the presidential elections in April 2002, when the Socialist candidate Lionel Jospin was not only beaten by Jacques Chirac from the conservative party but also by the *Front National* leader Jean-Marie Le Pen, France has been ruled by the conservative party.[3] The successive governments of Raffarin, Villepin, and Fillon all introduced legislation on immigration and integration. All of these reforms are related to the name of Nicolas Sarkozy, who, first as a minister of interior under Raffarin (May 2002–March 2004) and Villepin (May 2005–March 2007), and then since 2007 as the French President, has pushed through his ideas in this field. Besides the law on asylum from 10 December 2003, which introduced a new form of subsidiary protection, the concept of "safe third countries" and other elements in line with the then-freshly voted European directives on asylum, France also adopted the law of 26 November 2003 on the control of immigration, the residence of foreigners in France and nationality matters, as well as the law of 24 July 2006 on immigration and integration (Ceseda law) and the law of 20 November 2007 on the control of immigration, on integration, and asylum (Hortefeux law).

These laws and their specific content are the result of both European developments (including

path-breaking steps also taken by neighboring countries such as Germany and the Netherlands) and of political objectives pursued by Nicolas Sarkozy and his governing party, the UMP. One of these political objectives is to clearly reduce the number of (largely unskilled) family migrants and increase the number of skilled migrants instead. Slogans such as "selected immigration, successful integration" or comparisons of a "selected" to an "endured immigration" represent this approach and provoked polemical public debates. Interestingly, these French political ambitions correspond to broader developments on the European level and reflect particularly well developments in the Netherlands and Germany—the two countries which in the 1990s still served as antimodels to the French Republican model of immigrant integration. As of early 2009, they are the only three countries in the EU that have decided to restrict family reunification procedures by introducing an integration test (and a language course in the French case) in the country of origin as a prerequisite for an immigration visa. Beyond this very special regulation on family reunification that was introduced in France by the law of 2007, the earlier law of 2003 had already regulated a broad range of issues related to entry, residence, expulsion, detention, access to the labor market, marriage, and nationality and it had introduced the notion of *intégration républicaine*, which through the law of 2006 became a condition for the attribution of a permanent residence permit. Like the integration requirement before immigration in the case of family reunification, this integration requirement for the access to permanent residence has been rendered possible by the European directives concerning the status of third country nationals who are long-term residents and concerning the right to family reunification.

Thus just like Denmark, Finland, the Netherlands, Germany, Flemish Belgium, and Austria,[4] France has introduced a series of integration measures which, given names that recall the French model of integration such as "republican integration" and "integration contract," focus on the acquisition of language skills and some basic civic knowledge. The French integration contract offers 200 to 400 hours of language training to new immigrants who do not speak French upon arrival (only 40% of the cases) as well as one day of civic education about (life in) France and it is a prerequisite for the attribution of a permanent residence permit. This contract received its present shape with the law from July 2006 but already in 1998, the Socialist government had started to set up a reception and integration measure for legal newcomers.[5] The idea then was not only to help the newcomer settle down in French society and manage the different administrative steps to be taken, but also to obtain a better view on the qualification of the migrants coming to France and to promote their integration through well-targeted measures such as language training.

The reception platforms that were created at the end of the 1990s still exist today and are organized in the local premises of the National Agency for the Reception of Foreigners and for Migrations (ANAEM), the former Office for International Migration (OMI).[6] Groups of about 20 newly arrived immigrants are invited to the platform, where they meet an ANAEM official for a personal interview, have their language skills evaluated and are asked to sign an integration contract. Until 2006, participation in the reception platform and follow-up measures such as language courses had been completely facultative but then the signature of the integration contract was rendered obligatory for obtaining a permanent residence permit. The contract focuses not on integration as a long-lasting process but on a first phase of adaptation and it defines integration as a manageable learning process. This effort for a controllable integration process is motivated by the analysis that the absence of a clear, guiding state policy of integration in the 1970s has contributed to what is currently perceived as a crisis of integration. The creation of the reception platform and the integration contract tries to break with these former policies or the lack thereof.

At the same time, the fact that individual integration trajectories are increasingly administrated and controlled gives rise to strategic ambitions that initially have not been in the center of attention, such as the protection of the national welfare state from extra costs created by low-skilled immigrants and a more skills-selective immigration policy. It can be observed that these ambitions contribute to a shift in meaning from integration programs as an integration-promoting policy measure toward integration programs as an integration-controlling policy measure, closely linked to migration control (Michalowski, 2007). Or, in other words, while integration programs started out as social policies they increasingly became law-and-order policies—a move that can also be seen in the organizational restructurings that have taken place in France over the past years: In fact, until 2005, the FASILD was in charge of funding measures in favor of integration, the Office for International Migration (OMI) was in charge, inter alia, of family reunification procedures and the reception of newly arrived immigrants in France while the ministerial Directorate for Population and Migrations (DPM) oversaw the work of both organizations and gave out the general policy directions. The DPM was placed under the auspices of the Ministry for Social Affairs. The general reform of French integration policy in the years 2005 and 2006 not only restructured the FASILD and dissolved it into the National Agency for Social Cohesion and Equal Chances (ACSE), it also merged the OMI and a social service that hitherto was commissioned by the government to work for the reception of newly arrived immigrants into the National Agency for the Reception of Foreigners and for Migrations (ANAEM). The Directorate for Population and Migrations (DPM) was taken away from the Ministry of Social Affairs and placed under the auspices of the newly created Ministry for Immigration, Integration, National Identity, and Co-Development, which closely cooperates with the Ministry of Interior on these issues. This shift of the issue of immigrant integration from Social Affairs to Justice and Home Affairs that has taken place in France in the years 2000s has also been taking place in other European Member States as well as on the level of the European institutions themselves.

Thus, on the one hand, important changes that correspond to European policies have been made in France, especially under the impulse of Nicolas Sarkozy. On the other hand, France continues to show a strong commitment to its model of Republican integration. This causes intensive discussions over the best way to tackle discrimination. While some first policies were developed in the 1970s, major discussions only started in the

1990s, partly as a response to the development of the European directives on antidiscrimination. In 1999/2000, a nationwide phone number (114) was established to receive complaints about individual cases of discrimination. These cases were then transferred to the so-called CODAC-Commissions, which were supposed to do a follow-up by speaking to the organizations or administrations that the complaints addressed. In 2000, an additional public structure, the GELD (*Groupe d'Etudes et de Lutte contre les Discriminations*), was created to support the CODAC with studies and recommendations. These early institutional structures against discrimination and racism have repeatedly been criticized for their relative ineffectiveness (Bertossi, 1999; Audebrand et al., 2001; IGAS, 2000). While many critics expected the new center-right government to abandon what is called in France "the fight against discrimination" (*la lutte contre les discriminations*) this turned out not to be the case. Instead, the center-right government set up the High Authority for the Fight against Discrimination (HALDE) as required by the European directives. In addition, Nicolas Sarkozy turned out to be open toward measures of affirmative action as well as other measures to increase diversity and repeatedly started a national debate on the issue, which many French consider to be in complete contradiction with the republican ideals.

A few years earlier, a heated academic debate between Michèle Tribalat and Hervé le Bras, the first in favor of and the latter against the introduction of ethnic categories to the French census, showed just how emotive the subject of the public recognition of ethnic difference in France really is. For about one century, the French census had been working only with the variable of nationality and the introduction of the place-of-birth variable as late as the early 1990s showed the importance of citizenship for the French model of assimilation (Simon, 1998). Michèle Tribalat (researcher at the INED, National Institute for Demographic Studies), contradicted this logic and argued that social scientists who want to analyze the situation of second generation migrants in France and deal with the question of discrimination needed more information on ethnic origins. This position was fiercely opposed by her colleague Hervé le Bras, who

talked about the "demon of origins" and argued that the publication of statistics showing ethnic categories was a clear reactionary throwback (*dérive réactionnaire*). Like others who oppose ethnic statistics, le Bras feared that they could get into the wrong hands and therefore preferred not to create them in the first place. Almost 10 years later, in November 2007, his position was indirectly confirmed by the French Constitutional Council, which declared article 63 of the 2007 Hortefeux-law which introduced the parents' place of birth into French statistics unconstitutional.

With this decision, the French Constitutional Council has once more affirmed the French republican approach to cultural difference, which instead of publicly recognizing the difference of certain groups stresses the common link among citizens through democratic representation (Schnapper, 1994). This means that the expression of ethnic, cultural, religious, or other group identities in the public sphere are deemed to be counterproductive. While discrete exceptions may be tolerated, the model generally bans expressions of cultural and religious difference in the public sphere. The democratic representation of interests is supposed to take place independently from ethnic and religious identities. This is a very idealistic, not to mention ideological, vision of the functioning of society and democracy. For this reason, republicanism has been called an illusion, especially by the children of former immigrants, who face high unemployment, low chances of social ascension, and discrimination. The riots in the suburbs (*banlieues*) of the big French cities in 2005 were considered by many the proof that the French model had failed because the official rejection of ethnic identities could not help to prevent discriminations on these grounds. Scholars who had long been in favor of the pluralistic and multicultural approaches prominent in Anglo-Saxon countries (Wieviorka, 1999; Kymlicka, 1998) joined into this criticism of the French Republican model but their voices never got as strong as those in favor of a Republican, self-chosen blindness toward ethnic and religious difference.

Thus, European integration programs for newcomers on the one hand and the prohibition against ethnic statistics on the other show that France is fluctuating between new policies that clearly correspond to developments in other European Member States and policies that respect and defend the classic French model of Republican assimilation.

Immigrant Adjustment to French Society—A Cost-Benefit Analysis?

Discussions about immigrant adjustment to a host society often are discussions about the costs and benefits of immigration. In France, such discussions were considered taboo in the 1990s because the extremist *Front National* had taken over the subject, but in the years 2000s they came up again and were even made explicit by slogans accompanying the current government policy on immigration.

Other than the often pessimistic outcomes of such cost-benefit analyses, Michèle Tribalat and others (Tribalat, 1995; Tribalat, Simon, & Riandey, 1996) have shown, based on a variety of variables such as the use of their parents' mother tongue by the children, the celebration of traditional marriages, intermarriage, the adaptation and modification of religious and social practices, as well as social mobility, that, generally speaking, assimilation is at work. Below, a couple of indicators used by Tribalat and others to evaluate the adaptation to the host country will be presented in more detail.

With regard to language skills, the studies (based on a linguistic autoevaluation of the migrant) found out that French-bilingualism is generally more frequent among the children of migrants, high in Spanish and particularly low in Turkish communities. Immigrants who already speak some French when they arrive in France are classified as francophone. In the early 1990s, this was the case of 74% of immigrants from sub-Saharan African countries, 61% of Algerians, 53% of Moroccans, and 50% of the migrants from Cambodia, Laos, or Vietnam. Only 9% of the Spanish migrants in the sample knew French before coming, while 14% of the Portuguese did so. This overall high percentage of French-speaking immigrants has been confirmed for the early years 2000 through statistics that were gathered on the reception platform. They showed that 66% of all the legal newcomers arriving in France in 2005 were francophone.[7] Related to language acquisition and use, Michèle

Tribalat and her colleagues also found out that the transmission of the parents' mother tongue to their children is usually restricted, especially if the couple is mixed or if one partner was born in France. The Turkish minority seems to be the only exception, since it often maintains Turkish as a family language even throughout several generations in France. On the other hand, the loss of the mother language is particularly high among families from Algeria. In the study, Patrick Simon argues that media consumption can be one explanation since migrants from Algeria, Morocco, and other African countries mostly consume French media, while many Turkish migrants read special European editions of their Turkish newspapers.

Concerning intermarriage rates, Tribalat et al. (1996) state that traditional forms of marriage such as polygamy and preferential marriage with a cross-cousin are clearly regressing among immigrants in France and that migrants from Turkey represent the only exception since for them preferential marriage increased during the research period. In her 1995 research, Michele Tribalat also found out that about half of the young men in families from Algeria or Morocco and about one fourth of the young women from the same families live with a partner of French origin. For the entire population, Lebon (2004: 51) shows that the percentage of marriages between French nationals decreased from 89.4% in 1997 to 83.7% in 2001. At the same time, the percentage of marriages concluded between two foreigners increased from 1.8% in 1997 to 2.5% in 2001 but the intermarriage rate also increased from 8.7% in 1997 to 13.8% in 2001. This, however, is not true for immigrants of Turkish descent, who rarely use French as a language of communication within the family and entertain social relations mainly within their community with the consequence that there is virtually no intermarriage (Tribalat, 1995; Lebon, 2004: 42). Based on her observation that many Turkish girls only go to school for a very short period and that there is no social upward mobility for the boys, Tribalat (1995) predicted important problems for the integration of immigrants of Turkish descent, an analysis that has been shared by others (Petek-Salom, 1999). The last census from 1999 also showed that Turkish immigrants in France mostly conclude endogamic marriages (79%) while immigrants of Italian very often marry a French partner (71%), including the current president. In general, according to the 1999 census, 53% of all immigrant marriages in France are intermarriages with a French citizen.

Another indicator that is used to evaluate the integration of immigrants in France is the acquisition of French nationality. In fact, citizenship is an important element of the French model of assimilation and the quick acquisition of French citizenship is considered a sign of successful integration. Most applicants ask for French nationality either after the obligatory 5 years of legal residence or after a residence period of about 15 years. In 1999, (Lebon, 2001) Portuguese showed the longest average residence period when acquiring French citizenship (about 23 years) while migrants (refugees) from Sri Lanka and Lebanon showed the lowest average residence period of only 10 years. Immigrants from the Maghreb countries mostly waited for more than 17 years while migrants and refugees from Vietnam, the Democratic Republic of Congo, Haiti, and Iran on an average waited less than 15 years before applying for French citizenship. Given the great diversity of countries of origin of the naturalized French, it might surprise that only five countries of origin, namely Morocco, Algeria, Turkey, Tunisia, and Portugal make up more than half of all acquisitions of nationality. In 2006 acquisitions of nationality in France attained a total of 147,868 acquisitions, which is an increase of more than 50% compared with 1992.

The acquisition of French nationality through naturalization is not a right but a discretionary decision taken by the administration, and at the end of the 1990s about one-fourth of all applications were refused. A "default of assimilation," as it is called by French law, can be one reason for refusal and in most cases this default either relates to insufficient knowledge of the French language or to an unstable residence in France, that is, insufficient financial resources in France (Van de Walle & Maresca, 1998). This means that the precondition of "assimilation," which sounds as if it was strongly directed toward cultural aspects, actually focuses on economic and human capital aspects. This is also confirmed by the fact that a headscarf as it is traditionally worn in Turkey or the Maghreb countries is, according

to a ministerial directive from the year 2000, not an obstacle for naturalization.[8]

With regard to political participation, it can be observed that most of the immigrants who are politically active are engaged in civic rights movements, while their official representation in the government, in parliament or in the *Sénat* is very low. Studies on the voting behavior of migrant groups with Maghrebian and Caribbean background showed that these groups have lower turnout rates, especially if they live in disadvantaged urban areas (Maxwell, 2009), while a study of the political attitudes and activities of naturalized French with Maghrebian, other African, and Turkish origin had shown very little if any difference compared to other French citizens (Brouard & Tiberj, 2005). The question of attributing voting rights to third country nationals in local elections has been brought up many times, even by center-right politician Yves Jego (UMP) but these initiatives were always blocked by the argument that in order to get voting rights, immigrants should acquire French citizenship.

Statistics from the INSEE (National Institute for Statistics and Economic Studies) showed that in 2007 the unemployment rate among the active immigrant population was about twice as high as for the active nonimmigrant population, namely 15.2% compared to 7.3%. However, if this unemployment rate is further detailed, it shows that in 2007, the unemployment rate for EU citizens was 8.1% while the unemployment rate for non-EU citizens was 22.2% (INSEE). This trend was also shown for previous years. In fact, between 1991 and 2002 when the unemployment rate of French Nationals and other EU citizens living in France has been very convergent and ranged between 7% and 14%, the unemployment rate among third country nationals has been two to three times higher and particularly high for women from third countries (Lebon, 2004: 56). In addition, the last census from 1999 showed that even immigrants with diplomas have a higher risk of unemployment (16%) than diploma-holders who do not have an immigrant family background since they only show an unemployment rate of 8%.

These high unemployment rates among migrants raise the question of ethnic discrimination, which is a phenomenon that has often been discussed over the past years, especially after the riots in the *banlieues*. The measures that have been taken in response to the riots such as the creation of the National Agency for Social Cohesion and Equal Chances (ACSE) so far have not delivered any sizable results on the labor market. A series of new initiatives launched by Nicolas Sarkozy at the end of 2008 to increase the labor market participation of people with a different ethnic background (which in France mostly are immigrants or children of immigrants) through anonymous *curricula vitae*, guaranteed access for the best students of all schools into the preparatory classes for the French elite universities, and the nomination of Yazid Sabeg as Commissioner for Diversity and Equal Chances, still has to prove its effectiveness. Through these new policies, the French government and its President Nicolas Sarkozy, who also appointed Rachida Dati as the Minister of Justice,[9] have demonstrated an increased understanding of the fact that social peace and justice in France requires enhanced efforts for the fight against discrimination.

In addition to discrimination in the labor market, many NGOs also denounced discrimination against migrants with regard to their access to social rights often made conditional upon resident status. At the end of the 1990s, however, some of these rights were extended. Since 1998, family benefits and old-age pensions can also be paid if the child or the pensioner does not reside in France and nonnationals can also profit from social aid and other noncontributory benefits if they meet certain conditions. Since 2000, legally residing foreigners who are not affiliated with any social security system are covered by the CMU (general illness insurance), while undocumented residents can receive inpatient and outpatient hospital treatment covered by the state medical aid. In 2002, however, a financial contribution was introduced for irregular migrants who receive this kind of health care, exempting only persons who are in need of a long-term treatment, minors, and pregnant women. In 2003 it was stipulated that every foreigner who wanted to benefit from the state medical aid had to prove at least 3 months of uninterrupted residence in France. Foreigners may also benefit from basic social benefits (the so-called *minimum revenue for activity*) if they have resided legally in France for at least 3 years.

A regular residence and a work permit are also required if a foreigner wants to apply for unemployment benefits. If the foreigner meets these requirements, s/he falls under the same regulations as nationals.

While the distinction between legal and illegal residence is important for the social welfare system, such discussions do not take place with regard to schooling. French schools accept children regardless of their parents' resident status. Schools also cope with the integration of students who do not speak French upon their arrival through special reception classes that are set up for these students by the CASENAV. Newly arrived students with insufficient language skills, however, are not the ones that provoke a feeling of a crisis in many French schools. This, again, is rather related to the waves of violence and the hopelessness that many schools in the *banlieues* of French cities are facing. Since the French model of integration conceives of school as the major element for social cohesion and integration into French society, the crisis these suburban schools go through is also understood as a crisis of the French system of integration.

In fact, since 1983, schools situated in poor areas where a lot of migrants live can ask to be labeled as educational priority zones (ZEP), which implies extra financing for hiring more teachers. Teachers working in such schools are not always convinced that this additional financial support outweighs the negative image that a school classified as ZEP gets. Such a bad reputation usually pushes parents who are a little better off to try to escape from the school-card obligation, allocating a child to the school in the area where s/he lives. If a complete move of the family to another part of the city is not possible, parents might try to send their child to another school by officially changing the child's residence, for example, to an uncle's house (Oberti, 1999). Once a school has acquired a negative reputation, it has great difficulties in winning back a positive image. The media report about violence, confrontations between gangs, the difficulty of applying sanctions, the lowering of educational objectives to basic skills, the early orientation toward technical or manual jobs, and the common conviction that only few students will ever make their way to university. In 2001, the renowned Institute for Political Sciences in

Paris reacted to this situation by introducing a new selection procedure for students from ZEP areas. Instead of taking the difficult entry exam these students are received for an individual interview by a large commission deciding on the admission, or they take the general exam but receive special support to prepare it. This approach has proven to be successful since it increased the share of students from low-income households who used to be virtually absent from this university beforehand.

A territorial approach comparable to the educational priority zone has been applied in urban and housing matters. In fact, one characteristic of French integration policy in the 1980s and beyond was to formulate public measures for the integration of migrants in terms of social development of certain living areas, that is, within the broader frame of urban policy instead of explicitly targeting certain populations (Behar, 2001). This policy continues to work in many urban agglomerations, where different local actors sign a common contract for the development of the urban area. Just like in the field of education, the classification as an urban priority zone (ZUP) leads to extra financing. Many *villes nouvelles*, new cities constructed in the 1960s and 1970s as an expression of a new vision of society, are today classified as ZUP. Marked by a then-very-modern form of urbanism and architecture, towns like Evry in the South of Paris were constructed as laboratories for the so-called *mixité sociale*, that is, social-class diversity. After some success in the early years, the middle-class civil servants who were supposed to live next door to people from lower social classes left the city or at least the areas with very concentrated housing and were replaced by people with lower income, including many immigrants. Despite quotas related to income, immigrants sometimes represent up to 80 percent of the population of these dwellings. Very big and dense constructions providing housing for up to 4,000 inhabitants (*la cité des 4,000 milles à la Courneuve*) were destroyed in spectacular interventions in the 1990s and 2000s to make space for a new form of urban planning.

It was in such a ZUP residential area in the city of Evry that in 2002, the local manager of a well-known French chain store stopped selling alcohol and started selling halal meat in response to his clients' demands. When the mayor of Evry, outraged about this extension of Muslim custom into the French public sphere wanted to close the store, the manager referred to other chain stores selling kosher food without causing such protest (a court ruled that the shop should remain open). This rather small incident shows that local policies are particularly sensitive to concentrations of immigrants in certain neighborhoods (Gaxie et al., 1998) and that the establishment of zones where French law and custom might not apply causes great concern. Especially after 9/11, reports such as the one presented to the Minister of Interior in June 2004 by French intelligence services have an alarming effect: based on a study of 630 French suburbs, this report concluded that approximately 300 of these suburbs (comprising 1.8 million inhabitants) are turning into ghettos where radical Islamic preachers exert a strong influence on children and youngsters. The report warned against what is known in France as the communitarian disengagement (*repli communautaire*) and against a radicalization of religious practices (such as an increasing pressure on girls to wear a headscarf). The national newspaper *Le Monde*, which published extracts of this report (July 6, 2004), however, notes that the criteria that served as a tool for classification are neither scientific nor based on incontestable statistics. In fact, the French intelligence service used a catalog of eight criteria, which were: the number of families with an immigrant background, the structure of the communitarian (ethnic) associations, the presence of ethnic business, the multiplication of Muslim places of worship, the wearing of oriental or religious clothes, anti-Semitic or anti-Western graffiti, the existence of schools with entire classes of newcomers who do not speak French, and the difficulty of retaining inhabitants of French origin. A residential area was designated as exhibiting "communitarian disengagement" if it corresponded to several of these criteria. Such reports not only recall the terrorist attacks in the United States but also the 1995 terrorist attack on the Parisian underground, which was related to France's international engagement against a radical Islamic movement (FIS) in Algeria and had been carried out by a boy of Algerian descent who had grown up in a Parisian suburb.

To counterbalance growing tension between the French Republic and its citizens and inhabitants of Muslim belief, a national consultation on Islam was organized in the 1990s (Wihtol de Wenden et al., 1999; Laurence & Vaïsse, 2006). The aim of this consultation was to create a national representation of what has been thoughtfully called Islam of France and not Islam in France. At the end of this very long process, in February 2003, the Commission for the Organization of the Consultation of Muslims in France (COMOR) agreed on the creation of the French Council on the Muslim Religion (CFCM) and of the regional representations of this council (CRCM). The CFCM is supposed to serve as an umbrella organization to the numerous existing bodies and organizations like the FNMF (National Federation of Muslims of France), the UOIF (Union of Islamic Organizations in France), or the CRMF (Representative Council of Muslims in France), which was created in 1993 by Dalil Boubakeur, head of the Great Mosque of Paris. The first national and regional elections for the CFCM (where approximately 4,000 electors representing the French mosques were allowed to vote) were won by the UOIF (Union of Islamic Organizations in France) and the FNMF (National Federation of Muslims of France), both of conservative and sometimes radical reputation. Prior to the election, however, it had been decided by former interior minister Nicolas Sarkozy that Dalil Boubakeur, the moderate rector of the Great Mosque in Paris would become the president of the CFCM (French Council of the Muslim Religion). Therefore, Mohamed Bechari (FNMF) and Fouad Alaoui (UOIF) only obtained the two vice presidencies. As can be imagined, this did not pass without criticism and was one of the reasons why Dalil Boubakeur did not represent himself at the elections in 2008, which were won by Mohammed Moussaoui. Before the elections, the different Muslim groups in France had agreed upon the sole candidacy of Moussaoui, who has the reputation of being consensual.

When Dalil Boubakeur became the president of the CFCM, he did not have an easy start, because a big public debate about students' rights to wear a headscarf at school was started. Boubakeur defended the Republican principles on the one side but on the other tried to find an acceptable solution for religious Muslims in France. As everyone realized, banning the Muslim headscarf from French classrooms was a very delicate undertaking since it meant juggling general secular (laïc) values on the one hand and specific measures against Islam on the other. Like in the earlier 1998 debate, moderate Christians, a majority of Muslims, and the liberal left rallied around arguments against the headscarf (Bernard, 1994). Different than in 1998, when three Muslim girls wearing a headscarf had been expelled from school in order to protect the secular (laïc) character of the school, however, this debate did not end by leaving up to each school how to deal with students wanting to wear a headscarf in class.[10] Instead, the Commission for a Reflection on the Application of the Laic Principle within the Republic, which was created by Jacques Chirac in 2003 and presided over by Bernard Stasi, came up with a proposal for a law.

The commission was charged with devising measures for a peaceful implementation of the laic principle and determining the place that should be accorded to the expression of religious convictions in France. The report was received positively, although the media criticized the subtleness of differentiating between ostensible and ostentatoire religious signs. While in 1989 the Conseil d'Etat (State Council) prohibited religious signs that are ostentatoire, then defined as religious signs that represent an act of pressure, provocation, proselytism, or propaganda, the Stasi report recommended the prohibition against religious signs that are ostensible, that is, signs that aim at the immediate recognition of belonging to a certain religious group. The corresponding law was passed on March 15, 2004, and entered into force in September 2004. It prohibits signs of religious belief judged ostensible within the school premises such as headscarves, yarmulkes and big crosses, but allows more discrete signs like a small cross, a star of David or a hand of Fatima. The law also stipulates that if a Muslim girl does not respect the prohibition the headmaster shall engage in a dialogue and, if the girl insists on wearing a headscarf, she may be expelled her from school (Bowen, 2007). The hostage-taking of two French journalists in Iraq in August 2004 aiming to force the French government to abolish what has been known as the law on headscarves rallied some former opponents to the law. French Muslim organizations that previously had taken a stance against the law modified their position. UOIF (Union of Islamic Organizations in France) president Allaoui, who initially called on Muslim girls to go to school dressed with the clothing they had chosen to wear, then affirmed that the law once voted would become "our law," the Republic's law and the law of all citizens.

The discussions about the accommodation of Islam and the integration of Muslims have brought cultural and religious questions back into the center of public attention. In past and present discussions, however, immigration has also been strongly associated with economic cost-benefit analyses. A salient example from the past is a report written in 1984 by students of the National School of Administration (ENA). Reporting on immigrants and social protection, the ENA students (future high functionaries) have evaluated the contribution and costs of immigrants in the social protection system. Speaking in terms of debit and credit balance, the ENA report states that over the past years (i.e., in the 1970s and 1980s), immigrants contributed more to the system than they consumed. For the 1990s and years 2000, however, the authors of the report predict a possible negative balance. The ENA report was followed by the Milloz-report, a report done for and used by the extremist right-wing *Front National* and first published in 1990 and then in 1997 as a book.[11] The book was strongly contradicted by the philosopher Pierre Taguieff and the demographer Michèle Tribalat and strongly discredited any other comparable approach in France. As early as 1986 Abdemalek Sayad criticized the discussions that were provoked by the *Front National*. According to Sayad, these discussions transformed political arguments against immigration into technical arguments about costs and benefits, which seem to have an absolute, scientifically neutral value and are easier to communicate to the public.

A couple of other studies followed since 2004, but because of this initial intervention of the extremist right FN, these studies always have to confront doubts about their underlying motifs and are not commissioned by the government as

it is the case in neighboring countries such as Germany and the Netherlands. With the arrival of the center-right administration led by Nicolas Sarkozy such analyses might return to more neutral grounds although even the government-commissioned studies in the neighboring countries have shown that cost-and-benefit analyses are more than most other studies in the field of immigration subject to the political opinion of the author. As Sayad (1986) already mentioned, calculations of the costs and benefits of immigration are by no means as obvious as they might suggest they are since the author may think of an extensive list of costs[12] and compare it to only few selected benefits. Sayad argues that the immigrants' contributions to the host country may be more difficult to evaluate because they often happened without being noticed. This is why Richard (1999) points to the fact that by the end of the 1970s, immigrants had constructed about one housing unit out of two, 90% of the nation's highways and one machine out of seven.

Another prominent example of contributions that have long passed unnoticed was the case of the so-called *tirailleurs sénégalais*, Senegalese sharp shooters who fought in the French army during World War I and engaged in *la résistance* against German occupation during World War II. For many years, the engagement of these soldiers were not honored, neither politically nor financially, until protests finally led to the 2001 decision by the *Conseil d'Etat* (State Council) declaring illegal that soldiers from the former colonies received a pension inferior to the one of their French comrades (their pension had not been augmented since 1959). In May 2004 the government paid, retroactively from January 1999 onward, a higher pension. At this point in time, however, many of the former soldiers had already passed away. Recalling the expression of a "debt of blood" that the former *tirailleurs* had used from 1918 onward, undocumented African immigrants unsuccessfully demanded their regularization during the *sans-papiers* movements at the end of the 1990s (Dewitte, 1999).

The new national Museum for the history of immigration (*Cité nationale de l'histoire de l'immigration*) that was started in 2007, however, can be interpreted as an attempt to publicly recognize the contributions that immigrants made to the French nation in the past. In addition, by choosing the former colonial palace at the Porte Dorée in Paris as a location for the museum, this museum alludes to the famous slogan of the colonized in England "we are here because you were there."

Conclusion

The 1990s have not only raised many questions about the reaction toward religious Muslims in France and provoked the idea of a crisis of the French model of assimilation. The 1990s have also contributed to the understanding that other European Member States are confronted with similar questions on migrant adaptation and integration. As part of the European integration process, French migration and asylum policies have been adjusted to converge with new European directives. The directives on the status of third country nationals who are long-term residents and on family reunion regulate the judicial aspects of integration while rather informal procedures such as the activities of the European network of national contact points on integration composed of national representatives from the competent ministries contribute to the harmonization of concrete policies directed toward the social and cultural adaptation of migrants. Under the guidance of its President Nicolas Sarkozy, France is taking a leading role in the development of a common European practice and policy for immigrant integration.

The present contribution has shown that despite the criticism that has been voiced, France also sticks to its traditional Republican model of integration. In the European sphere, however, simplified dichotomies between that are countries doing well at immigrant integration and others that are doing badly because of certain integration models have lost much of their interest. The integration policies and outcomes are instead compared according to a range of indicators. One example is the MIPEX-index, carried out by the British Council and the Migration Policy Group on behalf of the European Commission, which mainly measures how liberal or illiberal certain policies directed toward migrants are. Such comparisons do not focus on ideal models of integration but they gather a large number of facts and information

(also see Koopmans et al., 2005). In these comparisons, if they have a normative orientation, France is usually relatively well placed. Being the EU Member State with the biggest Muslim population, it repeatedly turns out to be the European country most at ease with Muslims (GMF, 2008). This shows that existing problems might be overestimated and that the French motor of integration is working better than often assumed—even if the large majority of the immigrants who live in France today have not undergone the new policies for the selection of the most cost-effective migrants.

Notes

1. Some studies, however, show that besides increasing convergence in policies, substantial differences in citizenship regimes persist (Koopmans et al., 2005).
2. Rapport d'information fait au nom de la commission des Affaires étrangères, de la défense et des forces armées sur l'accueil des étudiants étrangers en France, par Mme Monique Cerisier-ben Guiga et M. Jacques Blanc, annexe au procès-verbal de la séance du 30 juin 2005, document 446.
3. While the Front National remained strong after the elections in 2002, gaining many voices in the regional elections in 2004, it progressively lost its voters in the following years. In 2007, when Nicolas Sarkozy ran for President, the Front National only received 10.4% of all the votes in the first round of the presidential elections compared to 16.9% in 2002. Then, during the parliamentary elections that followed a few months later, the Front National was reduced to only 4% of the votes, showing how successful Nicolas Sarkozy's strategy for fishing these votes has been.
4. Like France, all these countries have created these reception and integration measures for immigrants since the end of the 1990s (Michalowski, 2007).
5. This so-called *plate-forme d'accueil* (reception platform) was of course not the first policy measure taken by a French government for the incorporation of immigrants. Since the 1970s the state-run FAS (Social Action Fund for immigrant workers and their families), later called the FASILD and today called ACSE, has selected and financed a wide range of initiatives, courses, services, and organizations working in the field of immigrant adaptation. Then, in the 1990s, this approach to integration was considered insufficient, calls for a public structure in charge of the reception of immigrants became louder, and the reception platform was created.

6. In 2005, the ANAEM was created by an integration of the former OMI and a social service for immigrants that had been largely government-funded, called the SSAE.
7. Cp. Direction de la Population et des Migrations, Bilan au 1er juin 2005, published at: www. social.gouv.fr/htm/pointsur/accueil/index_accueil. htm, last accessed in August 2007.
8. However, if a woman wears a hijab or a niqab, the official conducting the naturalization interview is instructed to ask further questions about an eventual affiliation with a radical movement.
9. Besides the fact that Rachida Dati represents French citizens whose parents migrated to France from Morocco and Algeria and who seek for upward mobility, the particularity of this appointment was that Rachida Dati has not been charged with immigrant integration and social affairs as it often happens but that she occupies the post of the Minister of Justice.
10. The Constitutional Court recommended an individual regulation for each case but claimed that in any case, proselytism should be excluded.
11. Pierre Milloz (1997). *L'immigration sans haine ni mépris. Les chiffres qu'on vous cache.* Paris: Editions nationals (Front National).
12. Jean-Paul Gourévitch for example compares the costs of immigration for the sending states, the costs for development aid, costs for security, fiscal and social costs, costs for social security and for education, costs for state policies in the field of immigration and integration (including subsidies for the newly funded ministry for the history of immigration) to only one benefit that he calls "the real contribution to the national budget" and which he considers to be particularly low because of the low wages that immigrants earn, cp. Gourévitch, J.-P. (2008).

References

Anderson, B. (1983). *Imagined communities. Reflections on the origin and spread of nationalism.* London/New York: Verso.

Audebrand, E., et al. (2001). La mise en œuvre locale du 114. *Migrations Etudes,* 99.

Behar, D. (2001). L'intégration à la française, entre rigueur et pragmatisme. Le cas des politiques de l'habitat. *Hommes & Migrations,* 1229, 77–85.

Bernard, Ph. (1994). *L'immigration.* Paris: Le Monde, Marabout Editions.

Bertossi, C. (1999). Le Code, les CODAC et la citoyenneté européenne. *Hommes & Migrations,* 1219, 18–26.

Böcker, A., & Thränhardt, D. (2003). Erfolge und Misserfolge der Integration—Deutschland und die Niederlande im Vergleich. *Aus Politik und Zeitgeschichte,* B 26, 3–11.

Bowen, J. (2007). *Why the French don't like headscarves. Islam, the state, and public space.* Princeton, NJ: Princeton University Press.

Brouard, S., & Tiberj, V. (2005). *Français comme les autres? Enquête sur les citoyens d'origine magrébine, africaine et turque.* Paris: Presses de Sciences Po.

Brubaker, R. (1992). *Citizenship and nationhood in France and Germany.* Cambridge, MA: Harvard University Press.

Dewitte, Ph. (1999). Des tirailleurs aux sans-papiers. La République oublieuse. *Hommes & Migrations,* 1221, 6–11.

Eurostat (2001). *Annual report on asylum and migration 2001.* Retrieved Sept. 1, 2004, from http://www.europa.eu.int/comm/justice_home/doc_centre/asylum/statistical/docs/2001/population_by_citizenship_en.pdf.

Fassin, D., Morice, A., & Quiminal, C. (Eds.) (1997). *Les lois de l'inhospitalité. Les politiques de l'immigration à l'épreuve des sans-papiers.* Paris: La Découverte.

Favell, A. (1998). *Philosophies of integration. Immigration and the idea of citizenship in France and Britain.* Basingstoke, UK: Macmillan.

Fleischmann, F., & Dronkers, J. (2008). De sociaaleconomische integratie van immigranten in de EU. Een analyse van de effecten van bestemmings- en herkomstlanden op de eerste en tweede generatie. *Sociologie,* 4, 2–37.

Gaxie, D., et al. (1998). *Rapport final de l'enquête sur les politiques municipales d'intégration des populations d'origine étrangère.* CRPS (Centre de Recherches Politiques de la Sorbonne) unpublished.

GMF (German Marshall Fund of the United States) (2008). Transatlantic trends. Immigration. Key findings 2008. Washington, DC.

Hagedorn, H. (2001). *Wer darf Mitglied werden? Einbürgerung in Deutschland und Frankreich im Vergleich.* Opladen: Leske + Budrich.

Haut Conseil à l'Intégration, HCI. (2002). *Les parcours d'intégration. Rapport au Premier ministre.* Paris: La Documentation française.

Hollifield, J.F. (1994). Immigration and republicanism in France. The hidden consensus. In W. Cornelius, Ph.L. Martin, J.F. Hollifield, & T. Tsuda (Eds.), *Controlling immigration. A global perspective* (pp. 179–210). Stanford, CA: Stanford University Press.

Hollifield, J.F. (1999). Ideas, institutions and civil society. On the limits of immigration control in France. In G. Brochmann & T. Hammar (Eds.), *Mechanisms of immigration control* (pp. 59–95). Oxford/New York: Berg.

IGAS. (2000). *Bilan du fonctionnement des CODAC.* Report 155. Paris: Ministère de l'Emploi et de la solidarité, unpublished.

Kastoryano, R. (2002). *Negotiating identities. States and immigrants in France and Germany.* Princeton, NJ: Princeton University Press.

Koopmans, R., Statham, P., Giugni, M., & Passy, F. (2005). *Contested citizenship. Immigration and cultural diversity in Europe.* Minneapolis/London: University of Minnesota Press.

Kymlicka, W. (1998). American multiculturalism in the international arena. *Dissent,* fall, 73–79.

Laurence, J., & Vaïsse, J. (2006). *Integrating Islam. Political and religious challenges in contemporary France.* Washington, DC: Brookings Press.

Lebon, A. (2001). *Les acquisitions de la nationalité en 2000.* Paris: Ministère de l'Emploi et de la solidarité.

Lebon, A. (2004). *Immigration et présence étrangère en France en 2002.* Paris: La Documentation Française.

Le Moigne, G., & Lebon, A. (2002). *L'immigration en France. Que sais-je?* (2nd ed.). Paris: Presses Universitaires de France.

Lochak, D. (2002). La politique d'immigration en France et l'évolution de la législation. In E. Bribosia & A. Rea (Eds.), *Les nouvelles migrations. Un enjeu européen* (pp. 113–138). Bruxelles: Editions complexes.

Maxwell, R. (2009). Political participation in France among non–European origin migrants. Segregation or integration? *Journal of Ethnic and Migration Studies,* forthcoming.

Michalowski, I. (2007). *Integration als Staatsprogramm. Deutschland, Frankreich und die Niederlande im Vergleich.* Münster/Zürich: Lit-Verlag.

Noiriel, G. (1996). *The French melting pot. Immigration, citizenship, and national identity* (2nd ed.). Minneapolis/London: University of Minnesota Press.

Oberti, M. (1999). Ségrégation dans l'école et dans la ville. *Mouvements. Sociétés, Politique, Culture,* 5, 37–45.

OECD (2008). *International Migration Outlook. Sopemi 2008.* Paris: OECD.

Office des Migrations Internationales (2004). *OMI stats. Annuaire des migrations 2003.* Paris: OMI.

Petek-Salom, G. (1999). La difficile intégration des immigrés de Turquie. In Ph. Dewitte (Ed.), *Immigration et integration. L'état des savoirs* (pp. 149–155). Paris: La Découverte.

Richard, J.-L. (1999). "Trente Glorieuses." Quand les immigrés devaient "rapporter." *Hommes & Migrations,* 1221, 12–23.

Sayad, A. (1986). "Coûts" et "profits" de l'immigration. Les présupposés politiques d'un débat économique. *Actes de la Recherche en Sciences Sociales,* 61, 79–82.

Schnapper, D. (1992). *L'Europe des Immigrés.* Paris: François Bourin.

Schnapper, D. (1994). *La communauté des citoyens. Sur l'idée moderne de nation.* Paris: Gallimard.

Simon, P. (1998). Nationalité et origine dans la statistique française. Les catégories ambiguës. *Population,* 3, 541–568.

Todd, E. (1994). *Le destin des immigrés. Assimilation et ségrégation dans les démocraties occidentales.* Paris: Seuil.

Tribalat, M. (1995). *Faire France. Enquête sur les immigrés et leurs enfants.* Paris: La Découverte.

Tribalat, M., Simon, P., & Riandey, B. (1996). *De l'immigration à l'assimilation. Enquête sur les populations d'origine étrangère en France.* Paris: La Découverte.

UNHCR (2009). Asylum levels and trends in industrialised countries. First half 2008. Statistical Overview of Asylum Applications Lodged in 38 European and 6 Non-European Countries, Geneva.

Van de Walle, I., & Maresca, B. (1998). Les naturalisés des années 90. *Migrations Etudes,* 83.

Weil, P. (1997). *Mission d'étude des législations de la nationalité et de l'immigration.* Collection des rapports officiels. Rapports au Premier ministre. Paris: La Documentation Française.

Wieviorka, M. (1999). Le multiculturalisme. Solution, ou formulation d'un problème? In Ph. Dewitte (Ed.), *Immigration et intégration. L'état des savoirs* (pp. 418–425). Paris: La Découverte.

Wihtol de Wenden, C. (1999). Post 1945 migration to France and modes of socio-political mobilisation. *IMIS Beiträge,* 13, 43–73.

7

Canada

Immigration to Canada

Usha George

Migration is presently viewed as an inevitable consequence of globalization, particularly economic globalization. Global migrations also include worldwide movements of refugees and asylum seekers, the majority of which take place within the poorer countries of the South. Canada, Australia, New Zealand, and the United States account for between 1.1 and 1.3 million permanent immigrants per year (International Organization for Migration, 2003). These countries are referred to as traditional countries of immigration (TCI).

The purpose of this chapter is to provide an overview of Canadian immigration. It begins with a historical overview of Canadian immigration policy and practice and a brief introduction of the current immigration policy. A description of the demographic changes in Canada that have resulted from changing immigration policies is followed by an examination of the theories of immigration and immigrant adaptation as they apply to Canada. Subsequently, immigrant needs and challenges, as well as services and programs available for immigrant settlement are presented. The next section reviews available evidence on the level of integration of immigrants into Canadian society and polity. The

chapter ends with an examination of the post–September 11 changes to the Canadian immigration system.

Historical Overview of Canadian Immigration Policy

Canada has a long history of immigration, although figures are available only since 1860. Over the years, the flow of immigrants into Canada has been intimately connected with Canadian immigration policy and practice, which has been the subject of a great deal of scholarly work. To cite only a few examples, Bolaria and Li (1988) have examined the experiences of Aboriginal and visible minority communities in the context of Canada's attempts to build a capitalist society, while other scholars (Abu-Laban, 1998; Christensen, 1999; Green & Green, 1996; Henry, Tator, Mattis, & Rees, 2000; Isajiw, 1999; Knowles, 2000) have studied Canadian immigration in historical stages based on changes in immigration policy.

Prior to the 1960s, Canada had a clear preference for immigrants from Europe, as concerns about the ethnic composition of the Canadian population were foremost in the minds of policy makers. In contrast, the first half of the 1960s signaled a movement toward the removal of preferences based on national origins, due to decreases in European immigration to Canada as a result of post–World War II prosperity and Canada's emerging status as an international power (Henry et al., 2000). The 1966 *White Paper on Immigration* formed the basis for the new immigration regulations of 1967. In an unprecedented move, racial discrimination was eliminated as the basis for immigration to Canada and a point system was introduced to bring fairness and justice to the immigration process. Applicants in the newly created category of "independent immigrants" were to be assessed on the basis of nine characteristics, which included education and training; personal qualities, such as adaptability, motivation and initiative, age, and knowledge of English and French; and the demand for the applicant's occupation in Canada. Beginning in 1968, the ethnic composition of Canada's population changed as a result of the nonracist immigration policy (Isajiw, 1999). In 1969, Canada endorsed the United Nations Convention Relating to the Status of Refugees (Isajiw, 1999), which led to its admission of refugees from Cambodia, Chile, Czechoslovakia, Tibet, Uganda, and Vietnam. In order to address emerging concerns over the volume of immigration, a government study of immigration was tabled in the House of Commons, which became the *Immigration Act* of 1976. The 1976 Act, implemented in 1978, was framework legislation that contained only the main provisions and left most of the details to regulations.

The Act and the accompanying regulations were changed a number of times during the following 28 years of implementation. By the end of the 1980s, immigration was subject to new criticism due to an economic recession and increased number of asylum seekers. In 1993, the Immigration Act (1976) was amended to introduce three classes of immigrants: family, refugees, and independent immigrants, consisting of business immigrants, skilled workers, and assisted relatives. Since then, most of Canada's immigration has been from non-European/traditional countries (Isajiw, 1999).

The Immigration Act of 1976 provides the context to examine immigrant flows to Canada. The Act stipulated four basic categories of individuals eligible for landed immigrant status: family class; independent class, selected on the basis of the point system; assisted relatives, who were distant relatives sponsored by a family member in Canada and who met some of the selection criteria of the independent class; and the humanitarian class, consisting of refugees as defined in the 1951 United Nations Convention on Refugees, and a designated class of displaced persons who do not qualify as refugees under the United Nations' definition. The Act required the Minister of Immigration to announce Annual Immigration Plans, which would estimate the number of immigrants that Canada could accommodate on an annual basis and were required to be presented to Parliament after mandatory consultations with provincial governments and members of the private and voluntary sectors (Knowles, 2000).

Recent Developments in Canadian Immigration Policy

Immigration and Refugee Protection Act (2001)

In 1994, the federal government held national public consultations on the future of immigration policy in order to accommodate the policy to the socioeconomic and political context at that time. A nonpartisan group, set up for the purpose, produced a report entitled *Not Just Numbers: A Canadian Framework for Future Immigration*, containing 172 recommendations. Incorporating these recommendations, Bill C-11 was presented to the House of Commons in February 2001. The House passed the Bill on June 13, 2001, to be known as The Immigration and Refugee Protection Act, which replaced the 1976 Immigration Act.

The 2001 Act is framework legislation, similar to the 1976 Immigration Act, which stipulates the broad provisions and leaves the detailed regulations to be formulated by Citizenship and Immigration Canada (CIC), the federal department responsible for immigration. The Act stipulates the principles of equality and freedom from discrimination and equality of status for both official languages (English and French).

The Act and accompanying regulations specify separate objectives for immigration and refugee admission, provisions regarding consultations with provinces, volume and selection criteria of immigrants, definition and processing of refugees, sponsorship rights, fees, and rules for appeals and deportations. The Act notes that immigration policy must fulfill Canada's international obligations, such as upholding the Convention on the Rights of the Child, Convention on the Rights of Refugees, Convention Against Torture, Convention on the Reduction of Statelessness, and the American Declaration of the Rights and Duties of Man. It also refers to the Canadian Charter of Rights and Freedoms' guarantee of the rights of immigrants and refugees in Canada.

Three categories of immigrants are recognized in the Act for permanent resident status: family class; economic class, in which immigrants are selected based on their ability to become economically self-sufficient in Canada; and Convention refugees, who can be selected inside or outside of Canada. The Act established a definition of family class that, for the first time, included parents, common-law partners, and same-sex partners. Additionally, the Act redefined dependent child to include individuals under the age of 22, whereas the previous Act only included those under age 19.

The Act reduced the length of sponsorship requirement from 10 to 3 years for spouses and common-law partners (including same-sex partners). Sponsors are now required to be only 18 years old, whereas the former Act required a minimum age of 19. It introduced provisions to address default on sponsorship and court ordered child support payments and to respond to domestic abuse cases. Furthermore, an in-Canada landing class for sponsored spouses and partners of both immigrants and refugees was created, and sponsored spouses, partners, and dependent children are exempted from inadmissibility on the basis of excessive demand on health and social services (Citizenship and Immigration Canada [CIC], 2001). However, family reunification provisions are generally left to regulations (Canadian Council for Refugees, 2001).

The Act requires permanent residents to meet the physical residency requirement of being present in Canada for a cumulative period of two years for every five working years, although exceptions are permitted for people who have to spend time outside Canada to accompany a Canadian citizen, to work for a Canadian company, or for humanitarian reasons. It requires permanent residents to have fraud-resistant permanent resident cards. Oral appeals to the Immigration and Refugee Board are available for loss-of-status cases (CIC, 2001).

Perhaps one of the most unique features of the Act is its movement away from using an occupation-based model for the purpose of selecting skilled workers in the economic class, to employing a model based on transferable skills. The proposed Human Capital Model replaces the General Occupation List and intended occupation concepts. This model gives more weight to education and knowledge of an official language, although lack of knowledge of an official language does not bar admission. An in-Canada landing class has been created for temporary workers, which includes recent graduates who have a permanent job offer and have been working in Canada. The Act also proposes to establish entrepreneur programs, criteria to assess the business experience of investors, and a net worth for entrepreneurs (CIC, 2001). Considering the high demand for some types of skilled labor, the Ministry of Citizenship and Immigration Canada recently introduced Bill C-50, which allows the fast tracking of applications of persons who have the skills for jobs available in Canada (CIC, 2008).

Convention refugees and persons in need of protection are the two classes of refugees recognized under the Act. The Act intends to strengthen refugee protection and overseas resettlement by ensuring that people in need of urgent protection are brought to Canada within days and by pursuing agreements with nongovernmental organizations to locate and prescreen refugee applications in areas where refugees are most in need of protection. The Act also provides for faster and fairer inland refugee processing through the requirement that referral to the Immigration and Refugee Board is made within three working days, with the norm being single interviewers supported by paper appeal. A single hearing is to examine all risk grounds, such as the Geneva Convention, the Convention against Torture, and the risk of cruel and unusual punishment. It also reduces the waiting period for landing in Canada for undocumented refugees who are unable to obtain documents from their country of origin, from five to three years. A security check is to be initiated when a person makes a refugee claim, the merit of which is determined by an independent adjudicator. Provisions concerning enforcement are perhaps the most controversial in the Act. The Act increases penalties for existing offences, creates a new offense for human trafficking, and introduces a life imprisonment penalty for migrant smuggling and trafficking.

Live-in Caregiver Program

Another significant component of current Canadian immigration policy and practice is the domestic worker program, presently known as the Live-in Caregiver Program. This program has undergone a number of changes since its inception during the early part of the nineteenth century (Cohen, 1994).

The point system, introduced in 1967, applied to domestics, although the criteria were different for domestics than for immigrants in the economic class. In 1973, the Employment Authorization Program was introduced for the first time. Domestic workers were not permitted to apply for landed status under the policy of this program; however, the lobbying efforts of organizations supportive of domestic workers in Canada led to the then Minister of Immigration's appointment of a task force to review the policy and the government's introduction of a new policy in 1979 called Foreign Domestic Movement. This policy's main provision was that domestics could apply from within Canada to be permanent residents after two years of continuous service if they also demonstrated self-sufficiency or the potential to achieve self-sufficiency. The new policy outlined the salaries and benefits for workers, as well as employers' responsibilities. In 1988, the government introduced new guidelines to evaluate applicants, and in 1992, further revisions resulted in the current program. Conditions apply to candidates for admission to the program and eligibility for landed status. The program has been widely criticized (e.g., Calliste, 1991; Cohen, 1994; Cunningham, 1995; Stasiulis & Bakan, 1997a, 1997b; Villasin & Phillips, 1994) for its

sexist and classist regulations, such as the "live-in" requirement.

The province of Quebec has its own immigration regulations.

Canada's Demographic Transition

Primary Sending Countries

The peak years of immigration in Canadian history were 1913, when more than 400,000 newcomers came to Canada, and 1957, when over 280,000 newcomers arrived. The periods with the least number of newcomers since 1860 are 1895–1896, when less than 20,000 immigrants entered the country, and the 1940s, when the number of immigrants decreased to less than 10,000 (CIC, 2002).

Europe and the United Kingdom accounted for 90 percent of the immigration to Canada prior to 1961; in 2006, the immigration from United Kingdom and Europe fell to 10.8 percent. There have also been significant changes in the number of immigrants entering Canada from South and Central America and Africa. Those from South and Central America have increased from less than one percent before 1961 to ten percent of the total number of permanent residents in Canada in 2006. Prior to 1961, immigrants from Africa constituted only less than one percent of the total admissions. By 2006, immigrants from Africa and the Middle East increased to 11.8 percent of the total admissions. Immigrants from United States accounted for 6.3 percent of the total immigrant population in 2006. The Asia Pacific region continues to be the source of more than half of Canada's immigrants, accounting for 61 percent of total immigration to Canada in 2006 (CIC, 2007).

China, India, the Philippines, and Pakistan have remained the top four source countries of newcomers to Canada since 2000, accounting for approximately 13 percent, 12 percent, 7 percent, and 5 percent respectively in 2006 (CIC, 2007).

According to CIC (2007), the "humanitarian population" that entered Canada in 2006 was 33,684. This population includes approximately 93 percent refugees, the remaining 7 percent of which comprises individuals who did not make refugee claims but were processed under special programs put in place to address refugee-like cases. The five primary source countries for the adult refugee claimants in the 2006 humanitarian population were Mexico (21 percent), China (7 percent), Columbia (6 percent), Sri Lanka (4 percent), and India (3 percent). Sixty-one percent of the annual flow of humanitarian population in 2006 settled in Ontario, with 20 percent residing in the Toronto census metropolitan area. Ontario is also the destination for a majority of new immigrants. In 2006, 111,312 (47 percent) of all new immigrants settled in Ontario), of which 87,136 (36 percent) settled in Toronto. Quebec, British Columbia, and Alberta were other popular destinations for all immigrants with 38,379 (15.3 percent) settling in Montreal; 36,271 (14.4 percent) in Vancouver; and 11,827 (4.7 percent) in Calgary (CIC, 2007).

Characteristics of Recent Immigrants

Among immigrants who arrived during the period 2000–2001, a high proportion had university education, most had knowledge of at least one official language, the vast majority intended to become Canadian citizens, and most were satisfied with life six months after arrival. Women immigrants made up 75% of those admitted as spouses and dependents in the economic class and 63% of those admitted under the family class. Overall, 55 percent of immigrants reported having a university education. Among the 25- to 44-year-olds in 2001, 69 percent had a university education, whereas this was the case for only 22 percent of the native-born population (Statistics Canada, 2003). Upon arrival, 82 percent of new immigrants reported the ability to converse well in either French or English, the majority of whom were also in the working-age group of 25–44 years (88 percent), and were university educated (92 percent). Those who could not speak an official language tended to be older and female (Statistics Canada). Almost all (98 percent) of these immigrants did not apply to immigrate to any other country, and 91 percent indicated their plans to settle permanently in Canada and become citizens (Statistics Canada). Six months after arrival, 73 percent expressed satisfaction with their new life in Canada, 18 percent reported neither satisfaction

nor dissatisfaction, and 9 percent indicated that they were dissatisfied (Statistics Canada).

Immigration by Class of Immigrants

As mentioned earlier, Canadian immigration policy stipulates three classes of arrivals for permanent residency in Canada: economic class, family class, and refugee class. The number of expected new arrivals is provided in the Annual Immigration Plan, presented to Parliament by the Minister of Immigration. It serves as a guide to CIC, although the actual number of arrivals may vary slightly from the plans.

The Annual Plans for 2006 and the actual numbers of persons admitted under the various classes are presented in Table 7-1.

Over the past 17 years there have been considerable changes in the number of immigrants admitted to Canada according to class. The most notable difference is in the economic class, which increased from 8 percent in 1986 to 55 percent in 2006. Those admitted in the family class decreased from 43 percent of all admittances in 1986 to 28 percent of admittances in 2006. The number of refugees admitted accounted for 19 percent of admittances in 1986, and was 20 percent in 2006 (CIC, 2002, 2007).

Immigrant Adaptation and Integration in Canada

Historically, Canada's need for skilled labor to build railways and support industries such as mining, fishing, and lumber was instrumental in establishing immigration. Recently, the need for skilled labor in Canada's industrial and high-tech fields has continued to expand, and recognition of this need has spurred immigration.

Two current characteristics of Canadian society drive its need for immigration, namely the drop in natural population growth combined with the aging population, and the lack of skilled labor. Canada's natural population growth has declined steadily in recent decades "from 3 percent in the 1950s to less than 1 percent in the late 1990s" (Knowles, 2000, p. 4).

Isajiw's (1999) account of the history of Canadian immigration provides the explicit connections between immigration and the context of

Table 7-1. Anticipated and Actual Numbers of Newcomers in 2006 (CIC, 2005, 2007)

Immigrant Category	2006 Anticipated Number of Newcomers According to Immigration Plans	2006 Actual number of Newcomers*
Economic Class		
Skilled workers	105,000–116,000	105,944
Business	9,000–11,000	12,076
Provincial/territorial nominees	9,000–11,000	13,336
Live-in caregivers	3,000–5,000	6,895
Total economic	**126,000–143,000**	**138,251**
Family Class		
Others (Spouses, partners and children)	44,000–46,000	48,486
Parents and grandparents	17,000–19,000	20,005
Others		2,016
Total family class	**61,000–65,000**	**70,507**
Protected Persons/Refugee		
Government Assisted	7,300–7,500	7,326
Privately sponsored	3,000–4,000	3,337
Refugees landed in Canada	19,500–22,000	15,892
Dependents abroad of protected persons landed in Canada	3,000–6,800	5,948
Total Protected Persons/Refugee	**32,800–40,300**	**32,503**
Humanitarian Cases	5,100–6,500	10,221
Permit Holders	100–200	136
Others		25
Total Immigrants and Refugees	**225,000–255,000**	**251,643**

* Without backlog cases.
Source: at Citizenship and Immigration Canada (2007). Facts and Figures 2006. ** Retrievedon August 5, 2009 from HYPERLINK "/exchweb/bin/redcs.asp? URL=http://www.cic.gc.ea/english/pdf/pub/facts 2007. pdf" http// www.cic.gc.ca/english/pdf/pub/facts 2007.pdf

home countries. In the recent past, apart from international and internal pressure to establish a more equitable immigration system, Canada's immigration policy was influenced by the "availability" of immigrants. After World War II, the increasing economic prosperity of European countries reduced the number of European immigrants to Canada (Henry et al., 2000). Although the distinction between push and pull factors was not clear, push factors were generally thought to operate when individuals decided to leave their country of origin due to worsening economic conditions, including high levels of unemployment, whereas pull factors were considered to be at play when people were attracted to a country due to the opportunities it offered for economic betterment and social mobility (Isajiw).

Upon examining the socioeconomic and political conditions of the main source countries of Canada's immigrants in the last 25 years, it becomes clear that immigration flows are influenced by "push" factors as well. During the early 1990s, Hong Kong was one of the top ten source countries for Canada's immigrants, with the exodus prompted by fears of the Mainland takeover of Hong Kong in 1999. Most of the current South and South-East Asian source countries of Canada's immigrants—Bangladesh, India, Pakistan, the Philippines, and Sri Lanka—have high levels of educated unemployment, as well as population displacement due to natural calamities, ethnic conflicts, and political uncertainties. Policies of economic liberalization coupled with high levels of human capital have prompted many Mainland Chinese people to immigrate to Canada. Most of Canada's recently sponsored refugees and refugee claimants have arrived from war-torn countries such as Afghanistan,

Ethiopia, Somalia, Vietnam, and the former Yugoslavia (Kosovo).

Direct immigration from home countries characterizes the migration flows to Canada, especially in the case of family and economic classes. In recent times, expatriates, mainly Asians working in Middle Eastern countries, have been entering Canada under the economic class; a phenomenon prompted by the inability of these expatriates to gain full citizenship rights in those countries. Both Hong Kong immigrants and Asian immigrants from the Middle East have introduced a novel trend in Canadian immigration—the phenomenon of astronaut families (Alaggia, Chau, & Tsang, 2001). The term astronaut families refer to those families who, after migration to Canada, leave the children in Canada and return to their home countries for mainly economic reasons. The children, referred to as satellite children, may stay with one parent, relatives, family friends, or on their own.

Theories of Immigration

As mentioned in the introduction, migration is currently explained as an inevitable consequence of economic globalization. Economic globalization leads to greater income inequality between developed and developing countries (Brah, 2002). Pressure for better employment opportunities arises as levels of human capital in developing countries increase, and the movement of skilled labor from developing countries is supported by the increasing need for skilled labor in developed countries.

Intellectual fashions in immigration studies have shifted from assimilation to softer notions of integration (Castles, as cited in Reitz, 2003). Although multiculturalism was popular in the 1980s, notions of citizenship and intergroup relations gained currency in the 1990s. The present buzzword is "transnationalism," and debates are on as to whether it is a new process or a new name for an age-old process of immigrant existence within host countries.

Canadian studies on immigrant adjustment have employed sociological, psychological, and social psychological concepts and frameworks. For example, Bolaria and Li (1988) examined immigrants in Canada in the context of Canada's quest to expand its capitalist base.

Berry's (1992) four acculturation options—assimilation, integration, separation, and marginalization—described as both strategies and outcomes—have been used in a number of studies to examine immigrant adjustment to Canada. Acculturation (Berry), originally understood as a group level phenomenon, is now recognized as an individual phenomenon. For groups, changes occur on a number of levels including physical, biological, political, economic, cultural, and social levels. For individuals, changes occur in personal and ethnic identity, attitudes, and behaviors.

More recently, research has pointed to social capital as an important factor mediating newcomers' ability to capitalize on human capital and access economic advancement. The concept of social capital refers to the benefit accrued from relations among persons (Coleman, 1988) and is understood as the network of connections, loyalties, and mutual obligations that induce people to extend favors and preferential treatment and to act in each others' best interests (Gold, 1995). Loury (1977) first introduced the term to describe the family and community resources that impact positively on a child's development.

Family support has been identified as a key element of social capital in the settlement of immigrants and refugees (Boyd, 1989; George & Fuller-Thompson, 1997; Hao & Johnston, 2000; Short & Johnston, 1997). Family networks provide the support required to establish economic security (Boyd). In Canada, studies of a number of refugee groups have demonstrated the importance of family networks in the settlement process (George & Tsang, 2000). For example, in a study of more than 500 refugees in Canada, Lamba and Krahn (2003) revealed that the participants drew on family networks to solve financial and personal problems. As the settlement process continued, social ties were not only maintained by the refugees, but also strengthened and purposefully developed into more extensive networks including neighbors, coworkers, employers, community members, and service providers.

Multiculturalism, Integration, and Settlement

The concepts of multiculturalism, integration, and settlement have acquired a great deal of currency in Canada. Established in 1971 by the federal government, the policy of multicultural-ism "was aimed at the greater integration of Canadian society by providing the diverse ethnic minority groups with a sense of belonging to Canada. Its original aim was identity incorpora-tion, giving ethnic minority groups a public recognition of their identity, but within the mainstream recognizing that ethnic diversity is part of Canadian identity" (Isajiw, 1999, p. 245). The Department of Canadian Heritage adminis-ters a number of programs in line with the pol-icy's objectives through The Multiculturalism Program. Multiculturalism has many suppor-ters, as well as critics.

A number of observations can be made from a review of the literature on immigrant adaptation and integration. The terms "acculturation," "integration," and "adaptation" are often used interchangeably. Adaptation and integration are conceptualized as processes, strategies, and outcomes. They are considered to be bidirec-tional: the immigrant undergoes change, as does the host society. Adaptation and integration are described as multidimensional, with a num-ber of levels, such as psychological, social, political, and economic. At each of these levels, adaptation and integration may occur at varying rates and intensities for groups and individuals.

Terms such as "settlement," "resettlement," "adaptation," "adjustment," and "integration" are used almost interchangeably to refer to the process by which newcomers become part of Canadian society. Generally, settlement is seen as a first step toward adaptation, which leads to integration. Settlement is treated as the immedi-ate short-term process and integration as the longer-term process. These two terms almost always appear together in discussions on immi-grant adjustment to Canada (George, 2006).

CIC (2002) describes integration as a two-way process that involves adjustment on the part of both newcomers and the receiving country. This definition forms the foundation of numerous government initiatives aimed at the incorpora-tion of immigrants into Canadian society. CIC identifies language difficulties, discrimination, and the absorptive capacity of the major urban centers as barriers to integration. Integration is described as "social participation," which refers to activities engaged in by immigrants in the overlapping social, cultural, economic, and poli-tical spheres (Valtonen, 1996). Drawing on Breton (1992, as cited in Valtonen) to describe the outcome of integration as individual and group involvement in and becoming part of the various social, institutional, and cultural arenas of the receiving society, Valtonen lists factors that facilitate immigrant integration, such as ethno-cultural affinity; social and class differ-ences between country of origin and host coun-try; social capital; liberal immigration policy; welfare and service provisions accessible to immigrants and dominant groups alike; and humanitarian features of social services.

Guest and Stamm (1993) conceptualize inte-gration as three identifiable paths related to the roles that immigrants occupy. These paths, community social integration, residential inte-gration, and personal integration, are not given equal importance; they depend mostly on the life cycle status of newcomers. Measures of age and presence of spouse and children are the strongest correlates of the paths of integration.

Various human capital factors such as lan-guage skills, occupational status, and education have been shown to have a positive impact on the integration of newcomers (Greenwood, 1985; Liang, 1994; Long, 1992); however, they do not account for the differential experience of immi-grant groups or the differences between immi-grants and natives (Bartel & Koch, 1991; Kritz & Nogle, 1994). Concepts of differential integra-tion have been suggested that describe the selec-tive adoption of host society characteristics. Education and knowledge of the language of the receiving society are viewed as important factors (Henry, 1994). Henry considers immi-grants' entry into relations outside their own groups—referred to as social integration—an important feature of newcomers' adaptation and orientation toward the new country. Immigrant adaptation has been described as a two-way process in which the ease of adaptation is a function of both the immigrant and the host society (Frideres, 1989). Ataca and Berry (2002) describe adaptation as a multifaceted concept with psychological, sociocultural, and marital dimensions. In a study of refugee adaptation in Canada, Montgomery (1996) highlighted three main aspects of adaptation: subjective adapta-tion, sociocultural adaptation, and economic adaptation. The criteria for adaptation are multi-faceted (Montgomery, 1996; Scott & Scott, 1989). "Some criteria refer to 'objective' circumstances such as home ownership, gainful employment, and satisfactory academic progress of one's children. Other criteria are mainly subjective, such as satisfaction with one's living conditions, jobs, friends and family relations" (Scott & Scott, p. 10).

Immigrant Settlement Needs and Services

Do immigrants and refugees face similar challenges in the host country? The argument is often made that refugees have to be treated differently due to the fact the refugees share the experience of forced migration. Refugees deal with traumatic experiences, such as torture and persecution, the death of close family members, and loss of social supports. Refugees often arrive without immediate families, may not have relatives or friends in Canada, and many suffer mental health problems. Upon arriving, refugees, especially those who make refugee claims, face a number of external challenges until they are able to regularize their immigration status. Therefore, the settlement process for refugees may be more difficult and lengthy than that for immigrants.

In discussing the needs of newcomers, it is often difficult to distinguish needs from the challenges and barriers newcomers face in settlement; in the experiences of all newcomers, these are intertwined. It is also important to recognize that special populations such as women, children, youth, and seniors face specific challenges in settlement. Numerous studies have been conducted on the settlement needs of newcomers, the majority of which have been carried out by community-based researchers.

Studies of different newcomer groups to Canada identify the basic settlement needs of newcomers as general orientation to Canadian life; establishing community connections; securing housing, employment, and language training; and obtaining information on available services (George, Fong, Da, & Chang, 2004; George & Michalski, 1996; George & Mwarigha, 1999; George & Tsang, 1998; Michalski, 1997). The primary needs of newcomers at the initial stage of settlement include: employment, language skills acquisition, and basic orientation. Career advancement, ethnocultural identification, and full political and social participation in the new society become of increasing importance in the later stages of adaptation and integration (George, 2002).

Lack of access to employment is a major theme in immigrant settlement studies. In the case of foreign trained professionals, the process of becoming a member in the licensed professions and trades in Canada is complex, expensive, and lengthy. Part of the complexity arises from the fact that immigration is a federal responsibility, whereas licensing is within the purview of provincial professional licensing bodies. Most of these professional licensing bodies are becoming increasingly aware of this problem and are working to improve access to membership for foreign trained professionals. This has been a difficult issue all along, but in recent times it has attracted a great deal of attention, especially in the context of increasing numbers of highly skilled newcomers entering Canada. Reitz (2005) argues that due to labor market changes, as well as changes in recruitment and hiring practices, qualified immigrants have increasing difficulty gaining access to knowledge occupations, such as science, engineering, health, and education professions.

A Government of Ontario study (2002) of the experiences of immigrants looking for employment in Ontario's regulated professions found the following factors important in facilitating the entry of foreign trained professionals into their professions: occupation-specific information about the province's labor market and licensing procedures; occupation-specific official language skills; computer, occupation, and language courses taken after arrival in Canada; and assessments of academic credentials. The study noted that the province benefits most from foreign trained professionals' human capital when their first job is in the exact profession for which they were trained or a related profession, and that Government of Canada visa offices and the Internet are critical mechanisms for disseminating information about the labor market and licensing procedures.

On the whole, immigrants and refugees are seen as underutilizing human services mainly due to lack of access to appropriate programs and services (Henry et al., 2000). Lack of information about the services, lack of services, service providers' lack of knowledge of the linguistic and cultural needs of different groups, and inappropriate service models are all factors contributing to lack of access.

Settlement Programs and Services in Canada

Settlement services are aimed at promoting the full and equal participation of those new to Canadian society (Canadian Council for Refugees, 1998). "Settlement services are a range of services that assist newcomers after arrival and in the laying of a suitable foundation for the long term goal of becoming an informed participant in Canadian society" (African Community Services of Peel, 2000, p. 13). They have also been described as a human right and, thus, it could be seen as incumbent on host societies to provide such services (Clark, 1997).

Most of Canada's settlement programs are funded by the federal government and administered through nonprofit agencies, many of which are ethnospecific and were established by newcomer communities. These agencies provide culturally and linguistically sensitive services, as well as access to much-needed social capital.

CIC's Immigrant Settlement and Adaptation Program (ISAP) Stream A program funds organizations to deliver direct services to immigrants. Eligible participants in ISAP Stream A programs include permanent residents; individuals who have been allowed to remain in Canada and to whom CIC intends to grant permanent resident status; and nonimmigrant foreign caregivers, who may subsequently apply for permanent resident status from with Canada. ISAP Stream A includes the programs Settlement Workers in Schools (SWIS), Newcomer Information Centres (NIC), and Job Search Workshop (JSW), as well as the website settlement.org. The ISAP Stream B program funds organizations to improve settlement service delivery, through activities such as workshops, research projects, and staff training programs.

SWIS is a school-based outreach program that connects newly arrived families to services and resources in the school and community. Although SWIS is only available in six Ontario communities at present, CIC plans to expand the program. The NIC program provides information centers to assist newcomers with finding the resources they need to facilitate their settlement, such as referral to community and government programs. JSW is a five-day preemployment workshop program aimed at assisting recent immigrants with developing the skills required to find employment in the shortest possible amount of time.

Other CIC-funded initiatives are the Host Program, Language Instruction for Newcomers to Canada (LINC), and the CIC website. The Host program matches new immigrants with Canadian volunteers for a six-month period. Volunteers assist new immigrants in adjusting to life in Canada, for example by helping them practice an official language. The LINC program offers free basic language training to adult permanent residents.

CIC also has initiatives that are targeted to refugees such as the Resettlement Assistance Program (RAP), Immigrant Loans Program (ILP), Interim Federal Health Program (IFHP), and Private Sponsorship of Refugees Program (PSRP). The RAP provides funding for various forms of settlement support, such as meeting the refugee at the airport or port of entry, providing temporary accommodation, and supporting income for up to one year or until the refugee becomes self-sufficient (whichever comes first). This program is available to Convention Refugees Abroad and members of the Humanitarian Protected Persons Abroad Classes admitted to Canada as government-assisted refugees. The ILP provides loans for the costs of medical examinations abroad, travel documents, transportation to Canada, and the Right of Permanent Residence fee. Assistance loans are also available to disadvantaged newcomers in order to cover expenses such as housing rental, telephone deposits, and work tools. Government assisted or privately sponsored convention refugees and members of the Humanitarian Protected Persons Abroad Classes are eligible for ILP. The IFHP provides health care services for refugee claimants and other refugees who are not covered under provincial health plans. The PSRP allows Canadian groups to assume responsibility for assisting refugee settlement by providing the required financial and emotional support. It includes the Joint Assistance Sponsorship Program (JASP), in which sponsors and the government share the responsibility to support special-needs refugees, such as women-at-risk, in cases where resettlement is urgently needed or a refugee family may require longer-term support to resettle in Canada.

Integration of Immigrant Populations in Canada

On the whole, immigrants transfer valuable human capital to Canada. Using Canadian census data from 1961 to 1986 and immigrant landing data, Akbari (1999) examined the educational attainments of new arrivals in Canada over the period of 1956–1994. Results show that since 1956 the percentage of immigrants with high school education or less has been declining when compared to the Canadian-born population, while the percentage of immigrants with university degrees has been rising and has been higher than that of the Canadian-born. Akbari maintains that this study refutes the widely held view that since 1967 Canadian immigration policy's increased focus on the family and refugee classes has resulted in the admission of immigrants who are less educated than those who arrived prior to 1967. In 2006, of the immigrants who entered the country under the family class, over 28% had a bachelors degree or higher education and in the skilled worker category, over 76% of principal applicants and over 41% of their spouses and dependents had a bachelors and higher degree (CIC, 2007). It is necessary, therefore, that other factors, such as discrimination and general economic conditions should be examined in depth to explain the recent evidence of the decline of immigrant economic performance.

Studies of economic and social outcomes for immigrants are too numerous to cite; however, recent topics include the job displacement effects of immigration (Roy, 1997); immigrant occupational mobility (Green, 1999); earnings of immigrant men (Green & Worswick, 2002);

immigrant poverty (Kazemipur & Halli, 2001); immigrant occupational status and earnings, as compared to those in Israel (Lewin-Epstein, Semyonov, Kogan, & Wanner, 2003); the earnings of self-employed immigrants (Frenette, 2004); role of immigration in income inequality in urban and rural areas (Moore & Pacey, 2003); immigrants' labor market integration (Hum & Simpson, 2003); and impact of fields of study and educational credentials on the earnings of immigrants who are visible minorities (Anisef, Sweet, & Frempong, 2003). The studies outlined below provide a more holistic picture of immigrants' relationship to the labor market and economy in Canada.

Confirming the trends in low income for recently arrived immigrants, CIC's study observes that low income rates for new immigrants have increased over the 1980–2000 period in all census metropolitan areas in Canada and that "between 1980 and the year 2000, there was a growing divergence between the incomes of immigrants and those of others" (CIC, 2004a, p. 3). This finding is disturbing considering the fact that the majority of Canada's new immigrants are highly educated foreign trained professionals.

A Statistics Canada (2004) study found that during the period 1991–2001, at least 25 percent of recent immigrants with a university education were employed in a job requiring no more than a high-school education, which was twice the percentage for nonimmigrant Canadians. This finding was attributed to a lack of professional and social networks, nonrecognition of foreign credentials, limited language ability, and discrimination.

Despite higher levels of education in comparison to native-born Canadians, foreign trained recent immigrants to Canada have a tougher time finding work, and their incomes are falling behind (Reitz, 2005). In 1980, the average newly arrived immigrant man earned about 80 percent of the average Canadian salary; however, in 2000, he is earning only 60 percent of the average Canadian's salary. In 1980, 86 percent of immigrant men were employed compared with 91 percent of native-born Canadians. By 2000, only 68 percent of newcomers had jobs, in comparison with 85 percent of the native-born (Reitz, 2005). A recent analysis of the 2006 census figures reveals that immigrants that had arrived in the country between 2000 and 2004 earned only 63 cents for every dollar earned by their Canadian counterparts, four cents less per dollar in comparison to the earnings in the year 2000. Women were affected even more, as they earned 56 cents for every dollar in 2005 compared to 65 cents in 2000 for every dollar earned by Canadian-born women (Statistics Canada, 2008) The same report noted that the gaps between the earnings of new immigrants and their Canadian born counterparts had been widening over the past quarter century even though the educational attainments of recent immigrants had risen much faster comparatively in the same period. The earning gaps were larger among Canadian immigrants and their Canadian counterparts with a university degree as compared to those who were less educated (Statistics Canada). Immigrants' entry into self-employment offers interesting insights into integration in the host country. In contrast to earlier evidence in the United States and Canada, Li's (2001) study on the economic returns of self-employment to Canadian immigrants from 1980 to 1995 demonstrated that self-employed immigrants earned less than salaried workers. Li (2002) concludes that, in the Canadian context, immigrants enter self-employment as a strategy for self-preservation because they encounter many obstacles to employment.

Through an analysis of census data of 1980 to 2000, Frenette and Morissette (2005) show that the earning gaps between immigrants and Canadian born workers have increased substantially in recent years. They conclude that "abnormal" high income growth rates for the immigrants would be required before the income levels of the two groups could converge.

Lo et al. (2000) found no evidence that Toronto's immigrants admitted between 1980 and 1995 were an economic drain on Canadian society; instead, they made positive net contributions to Canada's treasury. Although they were not able to contribute at the same level as average Canadians do, the authors anticipated that these immigrants would eventually do so, given that the majority of study participants had been in Canada for less than six years and the gap in economic contributions of immigrants and native-born Canadians tends to decrease over time. The study also demonstrated that, contrary to popular belief, immigrants admitted for family reunification were not economic burdens to Canada and that the only class of immigrants who appear to receive more benefits than the amount they pay are refugees and their dependents.

According to Grignon and Laryea (n.d.), evidence on the economic and social integration of recently arrived immigrants in the 1990s demonstrates significant declines in labor market and social outcomes as compared to those of earlier cohorts; however, it also shows that outcomes improve over time. They note that poverty is increasingly concentrated and long-term for recent immigrants and refugees. They also report that despite increasing educational levels and "self-assessed" official language knowledge, low employment rates and lower initial earnings have characterized these immigrants' experiences in the labor market, with those from sub-Saharan African countries faring worse than members of other groups. Grignon and Laryea (n.d.) summarize the barriers to economic and social integration for immigrants as the poor economy in the early to mid-1990s; lack of credentials, licensing, and experience recognition; inadequate language proficiency; discrimination; competition from increasingly educated Canadians; lack of Canadian work experience; lack of skill bridging programs; lack of Canadian networks; and lack of accessible information prior to immigration to Canada.

Political and civic participation is another important element in discussions on immigrant integration. Comparing naturalization statistics in Canada and the United States, Bloemraad (2003, as cited in Reitz, 2003) argues that institutional differences contribute to immigrant political incorporation. The findings that, in comparison to the United States, Canadian immigrants (in Toronto) are more politically active and Canadian citizenship rates are much higher are explained as a result of Canada's institutional structures, which provide a range of services and supports to immigrant communities.

Immigration's impact on the economy and society is shaped not only by the characteristics of immigrants themselves, but also by the features of the host society (Reitz, 2003).

Interest in the impact of the host society on immigrants is related to the recognition of international immigration as an ongoing global process. In a collection of essays titled *Host Societies and the Reception of Immigrants*, Reitz suggests four dimensions of the features of host societies as significant determinants in the incorporation of immigrants: preexisting ethnic or race relations within the host population; differences in labor market and related institutions; impact of government policies and programs such as immigration policy, policies for immigrant integration, and policies for the regulation of social institutions; and the changing nature of international boundaries as a result of globalization. These four dimensions are not mutually exclusive; they intersect with each other in significant ways.

Effects of Events of September 11, 2001

Despite the legal entry of the terrorists into the United States as visa students, after September 11, 2001, the U.S. media, as well as many reports in the Canadian media, propagated the view that border security on the Canadian side was not adequate to prevent prospective terrorists from entering the United States (Adelman, 2002). In a report of the Standing Committee on Citizenship and Immigration to the House of Commons, it was observed that although immigration and border security were being examined together this did not indicate that immigrants or refugees represent a risk to Canada and that the legal entry of the terrorists was not related to individuals attempting to enter Canada as refugees. Generally, the opposition parties in the House supported the report and, thereafter, the Canadian media made efforts to demonstrate the independence of refugee and security issues (Adelman, 2002).

Another impact of September 11 was the introduction of Bill C-36, which actually concerned human and economic rights, rather than immigrant and refugee issues. The Bill became law in 2001 as An Act to amend the Criminal Code, the Official Secrets Act, the Canada Evidence Act, the Proceeds of Crime (Money Laundering) Act and other Acts, and to Enact Measures Respecting the Registration

of Charities, in Order to Combat Terrorism. The first part of the Bill introduced amendments to the Criminal Code, such as those to implement international conventions related to terrorism, create terrorism-related offenses, and allow for the seizure, restraint, and forfeiting of property owned by terrorists or linked to terrorist activities. It also allowed for the deletion of hate propaganda from public websites and made damage to property associated with religious worship a new offense (Adelman, 2002). The second part changed the Official Secrets Act into the Security of Information Act in order to respond to threats of espionage by foreign powers and terrorist groups, coercive activities against émigré communities in Canada, and economic espionage, as well as to create new offenses to fight counterintelligence-gathering activities (Adelman, 2002). The third part, widely criticized by human rights advocates and civil libertarians as infringing upon rights guaranteed under the Privacy Act (1980), amended the Canada Evidence Act to require parties in legal proceedings to alert the Attorney General of Canada should they expect the disclosure of sensitive information that could have a negative effect upon international relations, national defense or security, and to permit the Attorney General to assume carriage of a prosecution and prohibit the disclosure of such information (Adelman, 2002). Part four renamed a previous act as the Proceeds of Crime (Money Laundering) and Terrorist Financing Act, which provided for assisting in the detection of terrorist activities, facilitating the investigation and prosecution of such offenses, and improving Canada's ability to cooperate in the international fight against terrorism (Adelman, 2002). The fifth part amended a number of Acts to improve the Canadian government's security apparatus. Part six amended the Income Tax Act to keep supporters of terrorist or related activities from receiving the tax privileges of registered charities and introduced the Charities Registration (Security Information) Act (Adelman, 2002).

Security was tightened at the U.S. border, in contrast to the previous stress under the North American Free Trade Agreement on making the border unobtrusive. As a result, people and goods attempting to cross over from Canada experienced long delays, which had a negative impact upon the Canadian economy (Adelman, 2002).

Canadian immigrants and citizens of visible minority and/or Muslim background have raised a number of concerns regarding the treatment they received in the hands of immigration officials and security agents after September 11. By far the most significant structural change took place on December 12, 2003, with the creation of Canadian Border Service Agency (CBSA), which was to be a part of the newly created Department of Public Safety and Emergency Preparedness. The functions of intelligence, interdiction, and enforcement were immediately transferred from CIC to the CBSA. CIC continues to work on citizenship, admissibility policies (with the exception of policies related to security, war crimes, and organized crime), settlement and integration issues, and refugee protection. The main programs within CIC's responsibility are citizenship, integration, refugee claim processing and sponsorship, settlement, permanent and temporary resident processing, nonstatus documents (student and employment authorizations), visa policy, compliance with terms and conditions, and preremoval risk assessment (CIC, 2004b).

Canada also entered a Safe Third Country Agreement with the United States, which came into force on December 29, 2004. The agreement stipulates that the first country of asylum, in this case Canada or the United States, is where the refugee asylum claim will be heard. Asylum seekers who enter Canada by crossing the land border with the United States will not be eligible to submit their claims in Canada. The agreement applies only to the land border, and the CBSA will assume primary responsibility for monitoring claims at the airports, marine ports, and inland offices. According to CIC (2004c), the objective of the Safe Third Country Agreement is to streamline the refugee determination system and strengthen public confidence in the system.

Conclusion

Immigration, particularly skilled migration, is expected to continue to supply Canada's labor market needs. It is estimated that by 2011,

almost 100 percent of labor market needs in Canada will be supplied by immigration. Castles (1997) notes, the contradiction between inclusion and exclusion is fundamental to global migration, as noted in the Canadian situation, where the economic integration of new immigrants is fraught with difficulties. The majority of Canada's immigrants are selected for their high levels of human capital; however, these skilled immigrants are excluded from participation in economic and social arenas. Resolution of this contradiction is of utmost importance in order to create a more equitable and just Canadian society.

References

Abu-Laban, Y. (1998). Welcome/STAY OUT: The contradiction of Canadian integration and immigration policies at the millennium. *Canadian Ethnic Studies, 30*(3), 190–211.

Adelman, H. (2002). Canadian borders and immigration post 9/11. *International Migration Review, 36*(1), 15–28. Retrieved February 8, 2005, from Worldwide Political Science Abstracts database.

African Community Services of Peel. (2000). *African Community Services of Peel: An enquiry into the delivery of ISAP settlement services to the Black/African community in Peel/Halton region.* Retrieved February 10, 2005, from http://atwork.settlement.org/downloads/African_Community_Services_of_Peel.pdf.

Akbari, A. H. (1999). Immigrant "quality" in Canada: More direct evidence of human capital content, 1956–1994. *International Migration Review, 33*(1), 156–175. Retrieved July 19, 2002, from ProQuest database.

Alaggia, R., Chau, S., & Tsang, K. T. (2001). Astronaut Asian families: Impact of migration on family structure from the perspective of the youth. *Journal of Social Work Research, 2*(2), 295–306.

Anisef, P., Sweet, R., & Frempong, G. (2003). Labour market outcomes of immigrant and racial minority university graduates in Canada. *Journal of International Migration and Integration, 4*(4), 299–522. Retrieved February 8, 2005, from Sociological Abstracts database.

Ataca, B., &, Berry, J. W. (2002). Psychological, sociocultural, and marital adaptation of Turkish immigrant couples in Canada. *International Journal of Psychology, 37*(1), 13–26.

Bartel, A. E., & Koch, M. J. (1991). Internal migration of U.S. immigrants. In J. M. Abowd & R. B. Freeman (Eds.), *Immigration, trade, and the labor market* (pp. 121–134). Chicago: University of Chicago Press.

Berry, J. W. (1992). Acculturation and adaptation in a new society. *International Migration, 30,* 69–85.

Bolaria, B. S., & Li, P. S. (1988). *Racial oppression in Canada* (2nd ed.). Toronto, Ontario, Canada: Garamond Press.

Boyd, M. (1989). Family and personal networks in international migration: Recent developments and new agendas. *International Migration Review, 23*(3), 638–670.

Brah, A. (2002). Global mobilities, local predicaments: Globalization and the critical imagination. *Feminist Review, 70,* 30–45.

Calliste, A. (1991). Canada's immigration policy and domestics from the Caribbean: The second domestic scheme. In J. Vorst et al., *Race, class, gender: Bonds and barriers* (pp. 136–168). Toronto, Ontario, Canada: Garamond Press.

Canadian Council for Refugees. (1998). *Best settlement practices: Settlement services for refugees and immigrants to Canada.* Ottawa, Ontario, Canada: Author.

Canadian Council for Refugees. (2001). *Bill C-11 brief.* Retrieved February 10, 2005, from http://www.web.ca/~ccr/c11brief.pdf.

Castles, S. (1997, June 16). *Globalisation and migration. Some pressing contradictions.* Keynote address presented at the UNESCO-MOST Inter-governmental Council, Paris. Retrieved February 14, 2005, from http://www.unesco.org/most/igc97cas.htm.

Christensen, C. P. (1999). Immigrant minorities in Canada. In F. Turner (Ed.), *Social work practice: A Canadian perspective* (pp. 179–211). Scarborough, Ontario, Canada: Prentice Hall.

Citizenship and Immigration Canada. (2001, 21 February). *Immigration and Refugee Protection Act introduced* (News release 2001–03). Retrieved February 10, 2005, from Citizenship and Immigration Canada website: http://www.cic.gc.ca/english/press/01/ index.html.

Citizenship and Immigration Canada. (2002). *Facts and figures 2002: Immigration overview.* Retrieved February 10, 2005, from Citizenship and Immigration Canada website: http://www.cic.gc.ca/english/pub/facts2002/index.html.

Citizenship and Immigration Canada. (2004a). Low income trends among immigrants. *The Monitor, Fall.* Retrieved January 30, 2005, from Citizenship and Immigration Canada website: http://www.cic.gc.ca/english/monitor/issue07/06-feature.html.

Citizenship and Immigration Canada. (2004b, December 13). *Transition at Citizenship and Immigration Canada.* Retrieved January 29, 2005, from Citizenship and Immigration Canada website: http://www.cic.gc.ca/english/department/cic-changes.html.

Citizenship and Immigration Canada. (2004c, December 29). *Safe Third Country Agreement comes into force today* (News release 2004–20). Retrieved January 29, 2005, from Citizenship and Immigration Canada website: http://www.cic.gc.ca/english/press/ 04/0420-pre.html.

Citizenship and Immigration Canada. (2005). Annual Report to Parliament on Immigration, 2005. Retrieved on September 17, 2008, from http://www.cic.gc.ca/English/resources/publications/annual-report2005/section1.asp.

Citizenship and Immigration Canada. (2007). Facts and Figures 2006. Retrieved on September 17, 2008, from http://www.cic.gc.ca/English/resources/statistics/facts2006/index.asp.

Citizenship and Immigration Canada (2008). Changes to improve immigration system pass; consultations next step. Retrieved on October 27, 2008, from http://www.cic.gc.ca/EnGLIsh/department/media/releases/2008/2008-06-17.asp.

Clark, T. (1997). Reconceiving resettlement services as international human rights obligations. *Refuge, 15*(6), 19–21.

Cohen, R. (1994). A brief history of racism in immigration policies for recruiting domestics. *Canadian Woman Studies, 4*(2), 83–86.

Coleman, J. S. (1988). Social capital in the creation of human capital. *American Journal of Sociology, 95,* 95–120.

Cunningham, A. N. (1995). Gender and immigration law: The recruitment of domestic workers to Canada, 1867–1940. *Indian Journal of Gender Studies, 2*(1), 25–43.

Frenette, M. (2004). Do the falling earnings of immigrants apply to self-employed immigrants? *Labour, 18*(2), 207–232. Retrieved February 8, 2005, from EconLit database.

Frenette, M., & Morissette, R. (2005). Will they ever converge? Earnings of immigrant and Canadian-born workers over the last two decades. *The International Migration Review, 39*(1), 228–258.

Frideres, J. S. (1989). Visible minority groups and second-language programs: Language adaptation. *International Journal of the Sociology of Language, 80,* 83–98.

George, U. (2002). A needs-based model for settlement service for newcomers to Canada. *International Social Work, 45*(4), 465–480.

George, U. (2006). Immigrant integration: Simple questions, complex answers. *Canadian Diversity, 5*(1), 3–6.

George, U., Fong, E., Da, W. W., & Chang, R. (2004). *Recommendations for the delivery of ISAP services to Mandarin speaking newcomers from Mainland China: Final report.* Toronto, Ontario, Canada: Joint Centre of Excellence for Research on Immigration and Settlement.

George, U., & Fuller-Thompson, E. (1997). To stay or not to stay: Characteristics associated with newcomers planning to remain in Canada. *Journal of Regional Science, 20*(1–2), 181–194.

George, U., & Michalski, J. (1996). *A snapshot of newcomers: Final report.* Toronto, Ontario, Canada: Centre for Applied Social Research.

George, U., & Mwarigha, M. S. (1999). *Consultation on settlement programming for African newcomers: Final Report.* Ontario, Canada: University of Toronto, Centre for Applied Social Research.

George, U., & Tsang, A. K. T. (2000). Newcomers to Canada from former Yugoslavia: Settlement issues. *International Social Work, 43*(3), 381–393.

George, U., & Tsang, K. T. (1998). *The settlement and adaptation of former-Yugoslavian newcomers.* Ontario, Canada: University of Toronto, Centre for Applied Social Research.

Gold, S. J. (1995). Gender and social capital among Israeli immigrants in Los Angeles. *Diaspora, 4*(3), 267–301.

Government of Ontario. (2002). *The facts are in! A study of the characteristics and experiences of immigrants seeking employment in regulated professions in Ontario.* Toronto, Ontario, Canada: Author. Retrieved February 10, 2005, from Government of Ontario, Ministry of Training, Colleges and Universities website: http://www.edu.gov.on.ca/eng/document/reports/facts02.pdf.

Green, D. A. (1999). Immigrant occupational attainment: Assimilation and mobility over time. *Journal of Labor Economics, 17*(1), 49–79.

Green, A., & Green, D. (1996). *The economic goals of Canada's immigration policy, past and present.* Retrieved February 10, 2005, from http://www.econ.ubc.ca/dp9618gr.pdf.

Green, D. A., & Worswick, C. (2002). *Earnings of immigrant men in Canada: The roles of labour market entry effects and returns to foreign experience.* Retrieved January 29, 2005, from Citizenship and Immigration Canada website: http://www.cic.gc.ca/english/research/papers/earnings/earnings-toc.html.

Greenwood, M. J. (1985). Research on internal migration in the United States: A survey. *Journal of Economic Literature, 13,* 397–433.

Grignon, L., & Laryea, S. A. (n.d.). *Economic and social performance outcomes of recent immigrants: How can we improve them?* (Metropolis Conversation Series, Conversation Five). Retrieved February 8, 2005, from http://canada.metropolis.net/research-policy/conversation/conversation_5.html.

Guest, A. M., & Stamm, K. R. (1993). Paths of community integration. *Sociological Quarterly, 34*(4), 581–595.

Hao, L., & Johnston, R. W. (2000). Economic, cultural, and social origins of emotional well-being. *Research on Aging, 22*(6), 599–629.

Henry, F. (1994). *The Caribbean diaspora in Toronto: Learning to live with racism.* Ontario, Canada: University of Toronto Press.

Henry, F., Tator, C., Mattis, W., & Rees, T. (2000). *The colour of democracy: Racism in Canadian society* (2nd ed.). Toronto, Ontario: Harcourt Canada.

Hum, D., & Simpson, W. (2003). Labour market training of new Canadians and limitations to the intersectionality framework. *Canadian Ethnic Studies, 35*(3), 56–69.

International Organization for Migration. (2003). *World migration 2003.* Available from International Organization for Migration Web site:http://www.iom.int.

Isajiw, W. W. (1999). *Understanding diversity: Ethnicity and race in the Canadian context.* Toronto, Ontario, Canada: Thompson Educational.

Kazemipur, A., & Halli, S. S. (2001). Immigrants and "new poverty": The case of Canada. *International Migration Review, 35*(4), 1129–1156. Retrieved February 8, 2005, from Applied Social Sciences Index and Abstracts database.

Knowles, V. (2000). *Forging our legacy: Canadian citizenship and immigration, 1900–1977.* Retrieved February 10, 2005, from Citizenship and Immigration Canada website: http://www.cic.gc.ca/english/department/legacy/.

Kritz, M. M., & Nogle, J. M. (1994). Nativity concentration and internal migration among the foreign-born. *Demography, 31*(3), 509–524.

Lamba, N. K., & Krahn, H. (2003). Social capital and refugee resettlement: The social networks of refugees in Canada. *Journal of International Migration and Integration, 4*(3), 335–360.

Lewin-Epstein, N., Semyonov, M., Kogan, I., & Wanner, R. A. (2003). Institutional structure and immigrant integration: A comparative study of immigrants' labor market attainment in Canada and Israel. *International Migration Review, 37*(2), 389–420. Retrieved February 8, 2005, from Sociological Abstracts database.

Li, P. S. (2001). *Economic returns of immigrants' self-employment.* Retrieved January 29, 2005, from Citizenship and Immigration Canada website:

http://www.cic.gc.ca/english/research/papers/returns/returns-toc.html.

Li, P. S. (2002). *Destination Canada: Immigration debates and issues*. Toronto, Ontario, Canada: Oxford University Press.

Liang, Z. (1994). Social contact, social capital, and the naturalization process: Evidence from six immigrant groups. *Social Science Research, 23,* 407–437.

Lo, L., Preston, V., Wang, S., Reil, K., Harvey, E., & Siu, B. (2000). *Immigrants' economic status in Toronto: Rethinking settlement and integration strategies* (CERIS Working Paper No. 15). Toronto, Ontario, Canada: Joint Centre of Excellence for Research on Immigration and Settlement.

Long, L. (1992). Changing residence: Comparative perspectives on its relationship to age, sex, and marital status. *Population Studies, 46*(1), 141–158.

Loury, G. (1977). A dynamic theory of racial income differences. In P. A. Wallace and A. Le Mund (Eds.), *Women, minorities and employment discrimination* (pp. 153–186). Lexington, MA: Lexington Books.

Michalski, J. (1997). *A study of Iraqi refugees: Final report*. Ontario, Canada: University of Toronto, Centre for Applied Social Research.

Montgomery, J. R. (1996). Components of refugee adaptation. *International Migration Review, 30*(3), 679–697.

Moore, E. G., & Pacey, M. A. (2003). Changing income inequality and immigration in Canada, 1980–1995. *Canadian Public Policy, 29*(1), 33–52. Retrieved February 8, 2005, from EconLit database.

Reitz, J. G., (Ed.) (2003). *Host societies and the reception of immigrants*. San Diego: University of California, Center for Comparative Immigration Studies.

Reitz, J. G. (2005). Tapping immigrants' skills: New directions for Canadian immigration policy in the knowledge economy. *IRPP Choices, 11*(1), 1–18. Retrieved February 4, 2005, from http://www.irpp.org/choices/archive/vol11no1.pdf.

Roy, A. S. (1997). Job displacement effects of Canadian immigrants by country of origin and occupation. *International Migration Review, 31*(1), 150–161. Retrieved February 11, 2005, from Expanded Academic ASAP database.

Scott, W. A., & Scott, R. (1989). *Adaptation of immigrants: Individual differences and determinants*. Oxford: Pergamon Press.

Short, K. H., & Johnston, C. (1997). Stress, maternal distress, and children's adjustment following immigration: The buffering role of social support. *Journal of Counselling and Clinical Psychology, 65*(3), 494–503.

Stasiulis, D. K., & Bakan, A. B. (1997a). Negotiating citizenship: The case of foreign domestic workers in Canada. *Feminist Review, 57*(autumn), 112–139.

Stasiulis, D. K., & Bakan, A. B. (1997b). Regulation and resistance: Strategies of migrant domestic workers in Canada and internationally. *Asian and Pacific Migration Journal, 6*(1), 31–57.

Statistics Canada. (2003). *Longitudinal survey of immigrants to Canada: Process, progress and prospects* (Catalogue no. 89–611-XIE). Ottawa, Ontario: Author. Retrieved February 9, 2005, from http://www.statcan.ca/cgi-bin/downpub/freepub. cgi.

Statistics Canada. (2004). Study: Immigrants settling for less? *The Daily*. Retrieved February 11, 2005, from http://www.statcan.ca/Daily/English/040623/d040623c.htm.

Statistics Canada. (2008). Earnings and incomes of Canadians over the past quarter century, 2006 census. Catalogue no 97–563-X. Ottawa.Valtonen, K. (1996). Bread and tea: A study of the integration of low-income immigrants from other Caribbean Territories into Trinidad. *International Migration Review, 30*(4), 995–1019.

Villasin, F. O., & Phillips, A. M. (1994). Falling through the cracks: Domestic workers and. Progressive Movements. *Canadian Women's Studies, 14*(2), 87–90.

8

India

Refugees and Dynamics of Hospitality: The Indian Story

Ranabir Samaddar

The Politics of Hospitality and Care

If refugee care, resettlement, and rehabilitation sit at the heart of the ethics of care and hospitality, the Indian experiences reflect on some of the relevant questions: How can one study the dynamics of hospitality? Is it a policy study? But, can there be a policy for "hospitality," a policy to be "kind"? Or, will it be a study of institutions involved in practices of care and hospitality? Does caring actually begin when the policy of self-care ends? Or, is self-care always involved in caring for others—a state of care known by the well-known phrase "calculated hospitality"? Finally, how are we to look at a State, which rules as well as cares—the two functions, though connected with each other, appear as separate and distinct activities, and actually build on each other? From which arises the broader question, wherefrom does the capacity to care grow?

In terms of a study of refugee protection by the State, these questions would mean attending to: (1) the definition of the term "refugee" and its scope; (2) the concept of *non-refoulement* (the principle of no forcible return) and its scope; (3) and, the administrative-judicial machinery to determine the status of a shelter-seeker as a refugee and once determined, the quantum of

assistance the shelter-seeker needs and gets.[1] It also means trying to understand, where the refugee features in such policy formulation. We know that easy means of physical accessibility, cultural and economic networks, and political support of host government and communities are significant elements in the determination of a policy on the refugees—these are elements that impel care; but these elements add to the power of the State to decide toward whom to extend hospitality, and whom to deny (Bhagwati, 1999, p. 21). In a subcontinental region such as India, partitioned not once but twice, the politics of nationhood is built upon experiences of how some have become citizens and some have not been able to, while some have remained familiar as strangers, while again the experiences of some whose fate has remained that of the dreaded alien throughout their existence here. State's care of our bodies and souls and its power over the same is written in these experiences—as if the function of care and power could be scripted only through events, experiences, and contingencies of alienhood. To care, therefore, is to stretch the limits of the possible. We have, in the experiences of the refugees and in the accounts of extending care and asylum facilities, always a double imperative of how the State governs—a contradictory logic of power and care, and a paradoxical injunction built on the heritage of rule.

India did not sign the Refugee Convention of 1951 nor the Additional Protocol of 1967; many have therefore termed the history of how some refugees were saved, cared, and rehabilitated in this country, while many were left out, refused, and neglected in the same period in and by the same country, in a well-known phrase from the literature from refugee studies as "calculated kindness" (Loescher & Scanlan, 1986). Refugees from Burma were welcomed at one point, ignored at another, and prevented or obstructed from entering India at yet another point. One observer has called it the "full circle" (Bhaumik, 2003). Similarly, while some groups of refugees such as the Tibetans were almost allowed to be "Indianised," some other groups such as the Sri Lankan refugees, spent (and still spend) their long years in India in strictly watched camps. An expert, after examining the logical structure of these contradictions and ambivalence in the Indian State's asylum policy, has termed it as "strategic ambiguity" (Chimni, 2003). In some cases, the refugees went back quickly in hundreds and thousands as in 1971–72 after the birth of Bangladesh (Saha, 2003); while, in other cases, they remained. The Indian State, in the latter case, did not even pursue a solution, so that the refugees could be persuaded to go back, as in the case of the Tibetan refugees. We have also another group of cases such as the CHT (Chittagong Hill Tracts) refugees in Tripura or Sri Lankan refugees in Tamil Nadu, whom, the State allegedly wanted to repatriate forcibly.

These cases of differential treatment of refugees and asylum seekers do not, however, exhaust the full story of the history of the hospitality of the Indian State. Many writers have chronicled, how, as opposed to all these vagaries, refugee care in post-Partition Punjab and Bengal became part of building the new nation of India. Writing of the post-1947 care and rehabilitation of the refugees from East Pakistan, Das (2003) has commented, "The history of relief and rehabilitation in the east is one of gradual emplacement within a national body of those who were the victims of one of the world's worst population displacements. The travails and trauma that accompanied their emplacement are only

reflective of our fledgling nationhood." The chronicler on the west wrote in similar vein, "It was the characterisation of the refugee as a *critical component of nation-building* [italics author's] that marked a significant shift in conceptualisation and, consequently, in policy formulation. Linking resettlement with development, and rehabilitation with reconstruction, was a uniquely progressive and far-sighted response to a problem of crushing proportions; in this scheme of things refugees became a valuable human resource rather than, only, an onerous liability" (Menon, 2003). Thus, "all embracing response," "national effort," and "the desire to stretch the means of caring beyond the means"—these are the metaphors of a scenario invoked again and again. Even when one takes into reckoning the views from below, most famously expressed by Chatterjee (2001), who shows that it was not all that happy hour of nationalism, but a battle between the two contending notions of right and charity, there is a fundamental agreement between all sections of the actors in that contentious scenario; namely, that *we/they are part of the nation, the nation must accept us/them.* It is in this dual context of nationalism and democracy that we find not only a reemphasizing of the role of "partition-refugees" as elements of nation-building, but also a reinforcement of the state's duty to care and the imperative on its part to mobilize all powers at its command to that end—indeed to justify its status as the repository of power the state had to rearticulate its obligation to care. Probably the most important development in this context was the emergence of the two visions of rights—one emerging from the concept of nationhood and citizenship, and other emerging from the affected population's daily negotiations with governmental authority over every tiny bit of subsistence-means and the consequential expansion of the moral universe of claims. One resulted in an expansion of citizenship, and the other resulted in expansion of social security beyond strictly legal confines, which, as I intend to show, was ultimately accepted by the judicial authority and the juridical discourse. The birth of social security was made possible by detailed governmental policies and techniques for sheltering the refugee population, the expanding universe of nation, and the daily contest between the state that appeared as the government and the refugee population that became another segment of the population being governed.

Thus neither the security explanation, nor the kindness explanation, nor even the international law and international regime explanation, will be adequate in making us understand the mysteries behind one of the most observed and least comprehended political phenomena of our time, namely the asylum and refugee care policy of a postcolonial state. I am aware that a rights-based explanation may appear as the best route, because after all the refugees of Partition viewed their own return to India as a matter of right—returning home, returning to the "natural nation." Yet, as we know, the situation was ambiguous (the nation was not so "natural," and the departure too was from a "home"), and refugee protection has not evolved purely as a matter of right of the refugees, because it has evolved to an equal degree as an ethical, humanitarian task.

Rights and the Economy of Hospitality

The irony is that a regime of rights, as often found, calls for its effectiveness, centralization of power; power, to be concentrated at one point, to make rights effective, and rarely at multiple points. Yet, several accounts of protection of refugees and asylum seekers tell us how local communities, to whom the shelter-seekers were neighbors from near abroad, provided hospitality (Bose, 2001; Samaddar, 1999). The effectiveness of a rights regime, informal or formal, will depend much on this response, often depending on prevailing sentiments of tolerance, democracy, and nationalism. One of the challenges to cosmopolitanism is to make such sentiments relevant for the host communities in response to guests from near abroad—for cosmopolitanism depends on how you behave with your neighbors, and not persons or peoples you had never seen or known. It also implies that the language of rights also faces the challenge of empowering the local/host communities in extending shelter and hospitality. The call for a democratization of the rights regime from top to bottom—the international, the nation-state, and the local

power structure—will therefore inevitably arise in any discussion on the history of hospitality in India in the last fifty years.

Several accounts of the Tibetan refugees in India have shown that refugees are not always a burden; they can be creative and productive and they can add to the wealth and colors of life (Dharamsala, 1992; Norbu, 2001; Kharat, 2003). In other instances refugees as guests can become murderers, as the history of the Taliban growth in Pakistan suggests. Therefore ethic exists beyond law on refugee rights, though one can reasonably inquire, as Derrida (2001) does in a recent lecture, can one "cultivate an ethic of hospitality? Hospitality is culture itself and not simply one ethic among others" (p. 16). Against the background of several major forced population movements across the borders into the country in the last sixty years and the differential attitude of the Indian State toward them, we must first of all summarize the ten main features of the situation.

The first refugees to arrive in independent India were not the aliens who had to be given shelter; they were part of the nation.

The first practices of refugee care and administration built up through not so much law as practices—practices of care, rehabilitation, and social security.

Institutions are the concrete results of these practices and the few laws resulting in a durable tradition of hospitality, which the State neither can fully endorse and embrace, nor can reject.

"Partition refugees" thus leave a deep mark on the subsequent pattern in which the state is to combine care with power; this is the mark of ambiguity.

The contest between the notions of charity and rights that began as soon as refugees first started pouring in has influenced the subsequent discourse of "hospitality," a term that is supposed to overcome the contradiction. The current discourse of human rights on refugee protection in India takes off from this old contest between the two notions.

The foundations of the legal discourse on the aliens, as developed in the colonial time, provided the beginnings of strategic ambiguity in this respect. Who becomes alien, when, declared by whom—became a deeply circumstantial matter, never to be finally defined by law.

Alienhood thereby became the other part of a democratic state, which had needed and created at the same time the citizens as its political foundation. Thus India got citizens, who, through several succeeding years, chose to opt out of citizenship and move to other countries as aliens, or the country found herself faced with aliens who had opted for India, and now wanted her citizenship. Similarly, some communities became part-citizens, part-aliens, and some who had been citizens became, in changed circumstances, the "stranded minorities." In all these metamorphoses, the foundations laid by colonial law and practices held ground.

Because offering shelter and protection became deeply circumstantial, including the issue of near-permanent residence much beyond temporary visitation, local communities developed their response of charity and fatigue, benign care, and ill feeling and animosity—a response that characterized the conduct of the State also. Local response and responsibility have turned out to be as important if not more in influencing the fate of the refugees and the language in which the task of protecting the rights of the refugees goes on.

Keeping the shelter-seekers in ghetto, proscribing their movement, creating ever new penal colonies, thus underwriting the nature of charity that the State has been providing to shelter-seekers, become in time a feature of the asylum and care practices of the State, though with some exceptions. What began in the Andaman Islands and Dandakaranya continues to date—protecting and penalizing have become interlinked responsibilities. The policy of having prison-like refugee camps resembles such practices in the West, for example in Sungatte in France, where nondocumented would-be refugees, actually nonidentities, are detained and from where the detainees try to escape to Great Britain.

Finally, what the Convention of 1951 was powerless about is that, the States-system would finally decide the relation between visitation and residence. Thus, refugees who thought on arrival in India in 1947 that they would go back, did not, and were in all seriousness never told by the State to go back; similarly, the Tibetan refugees have not been told to go back, or repatriated; on the other hand, hundreds and thousands of refugees from East Pakistan went back as soon as the war of 1971 was over. Some of the Chakma refugees flowing into this country in successive phases stayed, some went back, and some had to be induced to go back. In some cases, the State allowed the refugees to come in, and then inexplicably, it shut the door on them. Without a deliberate effort, the behavior of the State in this respect has been exactly according to the spirit of the Cold War, which largely influenced the drafting of the 1951 Convention regarding visitation and residence. The enigma, if there is any, is therefore not so much in India's nonaccession to the Convention, but on the way it defines and configures its responsibility. *Responsibility* is the other great history, which runs parallel to that of rights and care, still largely unwritten, but this history no doubt has defined the relation between care and power.

These inferences indicate features of the social economy of care and hospitality exhibited by communities, gentry, and the State. They show the circumstances when the State has felt the need for policy initiatives to encourage citizens to give alms and show hospitality to the outsiders seeking refuge, at times insisting on compliance by the subject population of its directives, and at times setting up massive arrangements and campaigns for general hospitality. They also show the circumstances when the State has felt the need to do no more than to leave it to local population and local governments. Yet, as a result of the episodic general campaigns launched by the State for hospitality and care, organizations spring up that, taking the mandate seriously, want to carry on with the work—their hospitality then becomes a point of disturbance for the State policy of withdrawing from a general campaign for hospitality. Notwithstanding the dramatic forms of generosity of the State, therefore, it is an overall picture of graded care; a fundamentally weak welfare system; a hierarchy of priorities of the State in giving help, shelter, and care; and a differentiated notion of charity in public welfare provision for the strangers. Possibly there was never an undifferentiated notion of charity, though at times the rich and the poor were equally moved to take the work of care and charity seriously. As we know, to remove the uncertainties in responding to the needs for care, countries gradually move into a legal obligation regarding the principle of compulsory welfare of the shelter-seeker. The price to be paid, it seems, is in the form of accepting discretion of the legal authority to define the terms of entitlement. Public welfare provisions have become in this case, as in every other field, a matter of "calculation, discrimination, and discretion" (Hindle, 2001).

Refugee flows to India in time became massive and mixed flows (it had been indeed often massive, and now became mixed), and to a large extent, the foundational history of care in the early years of independent India saved many shelter-seekers, who formed part of the mixed and massive flows. Now, the two discourses have become linked—the issue of illegal immigrants and that of refugees. One influences, predicates, and prejudices the other.

The Half-Moral, Half-Legal Universe of Care

The point therefore, as the Indian experience brings out, is that a settled discourse of rights may not be enough to understand the half-moral, half-legal universe of care and hospitality. Deeply contentious issues of political judgments are involved. Let me give two instances—again from the Indian experience.

My first instance—In what way is the issue of sheltering the asylum seeker linked with the preponderant moral issue of our time, namely reconciliation and forgiveness? Return, as we know apart from the legal resolution of the issue of "fear" (Samaddar, 2001), is linked to the issue of reconciliation. It may be significant to ask what lay behind the return of the Chakmas and other refugees from the Chittagong Hill Tracts and for example, the nonreturn of the Tibetan refugees to Tibet. What was the differentiating factor? The sure answer will be, we know, that the refugees willed in one case, and did not will "return" in another. That is what is known as voluntary repatriation. This is the ground (as opposed to forcible return) on which the human rights discourse has gathered strength. But evidently the matter does not stop there. What

causes the will? In the case of the CHT refugees, a settlement or a political accommodation was the occasion of the diminution or evaporation of fear. It shows how the politics of near abroad are so closely connected with the politics of care. Yet, strangely, neither the international human rights discourse on refugee protection nor the concerned institutions admit that return is linked to settlement and does not reflect fundamentally on the quality of protection available. There is no evidence to suggest that the human rights situation is worse in China than Bangladesh or Burma, thus discouraging return. Situated as we are in this politics of near abroad, the refugee care discourse seems to be irretrievably caught in it.

My second instance—People displaced by agencies/other people are, prima facie, wronged. They are vulnerable. But how shall we judge the issue of the hierarchy of vulnerabilities? How shall we judge the moral obligation of the State toward the wronged and potential victims? We have here the issue of the principle of responsibility. Responsibility has two implications and conveys two senses—responsibility of the state and of the international community; also responsibility of the host and that of the expelling state (Beyani, 1995). Ethically then the issues are—what is morally owed to the victims of displacement? India has been kind to refugees from Sri Lanka, but it has not performed well in protecting and resettling her own Muslim citizens repeatedly displaced in riots and state violence. How to mark the issue of responsibility then? Or, how do we place and apportion responsibility for man-made disasters, say, from a disaster due to developmental process (a dam, a highway, a famine, a flood)? What is the politics of reparation in these cases? And what will be the norm of responsibility in the more complex cases of indirect displacement and repeated displacements? What will be the method? How shall we settle for what is known as minimal justice (Samaddar, 2004)? These questions are not only matters of ethics and law; they are matters of system and a humanitarian doctrine.

In short, the graded order I speak of above tells us a few things of relevance to the Indian context. The norm of non-refoulement (of refuge), thought to be the most fundamental to the system of international hospitality and protection across a broad class of states and situations, has to be seen today in a broader perspective of rights and justice. Refugees form today part of a wider phenomenon of mass flight, mass movement, and massive displacement, so that individual determination of the status of the shelter seeker is of little relevance to the victims, and the principle of no forcible return has lost some relevance in terms of actual practices of the States. The movement of the displaced is so mixed that, while no State today claims an absolute right to return a refugee to persecution and peril, there is a greater freedom of action made available to the State by this new phenomenon, with the result that the terminology of refugee protection has become almost an anachronism with the rise of new words such as "displaced persons," "illegal immigrants," "economic migrants," "aliens," "stowaways," "interdiction," "safe third country," "visa requirements," "carrier sanctions," and finally "internally guaranteed security zones." Hospitality is now subject to rules, procedures, regimes, systems, and doctrines.

Interventions by the Judiciary

How has the justice system in India responded to this deeply equivocal relation? How has juridical reasoning shaped up in such context?

In a court decision in India, five Burmese nationals detained for entering India without any valid document and charged under relevant provisions of the Foreigners' Act of 1946 (henceforth the FA) were granted bail by the Guwahati High Court to enable them to approach the UNHCR at New Delhi for refugee status, which was subsequently granted to them, and the case was then withdrawn by the prosecution (*unreported*, State v. Khy-Htoon.and 4 others, FIR No 18 (3) 89, CJM, Manipur, 1994). Similarly, in another case involving two Burmese nationals convicted for violation of the FA, the High Court ordered that the petitioners be released on an interim bail for 2 months to enable them to approach the UNHCR for grant of refugee status to them (*unreported*, State of Manipur v U Myat Kyaw and Nayzin, Civil Rule No 516 of 1991, High Court of Guwahati, 1991). The Guwahati High Court had previously granted bail in 1989 to

another Burmese national, Shar Aung A.K. Aung Thant Mint, also to enable him to approach the UNHCR in New Delhi. In another case an Iraqi national detained for using a forged passport was authorized to stay in India, and the Court ruled that with valid certification from the UNHCR with him, he could not be convicted for the offense and took a lenient view considering that he was a refugee and sentenced him to pay just a fine (*unreported*, State v Muhammad Riza Ali, FIR No 414/93, CMM New Delhi, 1995). Similarly a Sudanese woman who had come to India escaping further torture in Sudan, where she had been gang-raped for converting from Islam to Christianity, had been granted refugee status by the UNHCR; also her application to resettle in Canada had been accepted. In this case too, though she had been charged under relevant provisions of FA, the Court gave a light punishment—a small fine and imprisonment of 10 days already served (*unreported*, State v Eva Massur Ahmed, FIR No 278/95, MM, New Delhi 1995). In a case concerning an Afghan national, the Court similarly observed that with certification of refugee status, he could not be detained simply for not producing the valid residence permit instantly on demand; he was to be given 24 hours. But, ironically by another trial court decision, a foreign national who had similar certification and valid residence stay and had not been able to produce valid document at time of his arrest was sentenced to 6 weeks of rigorous punishment (*unreported*, State v Montasir M. Gubara, CC No 427/P/1994, ACJM, Mumbai, 1996).

And, in another case concerning a Burmese national who had fled to India and had been detained under the FA, and had not been able to approach the UNHCR, the Court ordered conviction and rigorous imprisonment for 6 months and deportation back to Burma. The Court also said on completion of the sentence and in response to the convict's appeal that it was not within its jurisdiction to hand over the convicted to the UNHCR (*unreported*, State v Benjamin Zang Nang, GR case no 1253 [1994], ACJM, Sealdah, West Bengal, 1996). Another case of deportation order by the Court happened when the Court sentenced an Afghan national to imprisonment for the period he had spent in jail after he had been arrested by the Border Security

Force for entering the country without any valid document notwithstanding his plea that he had entered the country to save his life, and then ordered his deportation back to Afghanistan (*unreported*, State v Akhtar Muhammad, AF/6433, CJM, Amritsar, Punjab, 1997).

Could the refugees have freedom of movement? A Sri Lankan who had been granted refugee status and was staying in Chennai was arrested in Delhi for being unable to produce any valid travel document, and detained under relevant provisions of the FA. The Court observed that refugee status did not entitle a person to move about freely, held him guilty, and sentenced him to 6 months of rigorous imprisonment (*Unreported*, State v Hudson Vilvaraj, FIR No 583/97, MM, Delhi, 1998). This decision was in conformity with the Supreme Court judgment in State of Arunachal Pradesh v Khudiram Chakma (1994, Suppl. 1 SSC 615), where Chief Justice M.N. Venkatachaiah and Justice S. Mohan held that Chakmas were not citizens of India; they as foreigners enjoyed life and liberty only to the extent that Article 21 allowed, and this right was not extendable to Article 19. Though, in the same judgment the Court held that what was "good in terms of natural justice was hence good in law" (p. 630, paragraphs 71–72), and referred to the right to enjoy asylum in international law (paragraphs 77 and 80). And, what about refugees who forged passports or travel documents to take shelter in the country? Almost uniformly, the trial courts held that such acts constituted offenses under the FA, sentenced somewhat lightly, and wherever the government had pleaded a foreigner's stay a threat to security, had ordered expulsion/deportation, or had said that further stay depended on government permission (for example, *unreported*, State v Muhammad Yashin, FIR No 289/97, SMM, Delhi, 1997).

And then there is this strange case, a case of perfect ambiguity. A woman, arrested on the ground that she was a Burmese national and had violated the FA, produced before the Court her birth certificate, residence certificate, employment certificate, and a copy of the electoral roll which had her name on it as a voter. The Court ordered her free on the grounds of evidence, but observed in view of her inability to speak the Mizo language though she had claimed to be a permanent resident of Mizoram, as to how she could be so, and felt that it was strange that she had an original birth certificate, and she had been allotted permanent residence certificate in Mizoram, particularly when the issue of foreigners was a burning issue in the state (*unreported*, State v Sungenel, GR No 979/96, ADC/Judicial Officer, Aizwal, Mizoram, 1996).

By and large, trial court decisions seem to have relied upon no standard practice or law of asylum. There have been variations. When Courts have imposed fines, in some cases the refugee-offenders have been able to pay with help from charitable organizations or NGOs. If the refugees were fortunate to get UNHCR protection, they were let free. In some cases, though not always, courts have allowed the persons to approach the UNHCR. But in other cases, the reasons of state in the form of the FA seemed to have held sway over juridical reasoning. In several cases the High Court decisions seem to confirm the stand taken by trial courts, particularly with regard to appeals by Burmese nationals under detention and jail custody not to deport them, and allow them to approach UNHCR for protection.[1] Three examples, all unreported, are:

Zothatnsangpuii v The State of Manipur, Civil Rule No 981 of 1989, the High Court of Guwahati, 1989;

Bogyi v Union of India, Civil Rule No 1847/89, the High Court of Guwahati, 1989;

U Myat Kyaw and Nayzin v State of Manipur Civil Rule 516 of 199, Imphal Bench of Guwahati High Court.

In one case, the Manipur government withdrew prosecution against a Burmese national for violating the FA when the case came to the High Court, as meanwhile the UNHCR had granted refugee status to him and Norway was willing to resettle him and the accused was permitted to exit (*unreported*, Union of India v Maung Maung Kyo Myunt, Civil Rule No 5120/94, the High Court of Delhi, 1994). Also, in a similar situation relating to an Iranian national, the Mumbai High Court ordered (1994) that with UNHCR certification available with the petitioner, he could not be deported and was free to travel to any country he desired. But in several other cases deportation was ordered, or was stayed for a limited period to enable the concerned person to approach the UNHCR, failing which deportation was to follow. And as usual, the police have not respected certification by the UNHCR with consistency; the government too has not been easy in giving exit permits. The Courts too have remained silent about refugee camps often becoming detention places.

Thus, in sum, it can be said that in municipal juridical reasoning to date, the burden of protecting an asylum seeker lies with the UNHCR. This includes the burden of resettlement, and the conditionality that the detained foreigner would not be able to move out to any place of choice without certification and assumption of responsibility by the UNHCR (for example, Sayed Ata Mohammadi v Union of India, A.D. Cri No 48 of 1994, Mumbai High Court, and Majid Ahmad v Union of India, Crl. WP No 60 of 1997, Delhi High court).

In such reasoning, as much as possible under the circumstances, leniency should be shown by the State to the offenders who have violated the FA; it is recognized that not only persecution of a particular person, but a general atmosphere of violence and insecurity can also be grounds for asking for shelter; and if the State claims that the security of the State is in jeopardy, then expulsion or deportation has to be the norm. Granting asylum is not in such reasoning the responsibility of the State, and the duty of hospitality cannot be legally enforceable.

Indeed, the Gujarat High Court summarized the position in this way (*unreported*, Kfaer Abbas Habib Al Qutaifi and Taer Ali Mansoon, Civil Rule No 3433 of 1998) in the context of India being a nonsignatory to the 1951 Convention:

First, the relevant international treaties and convention are not binding, but there is an obligation on the government to respect them.

Second, Article 21 of the Constitution is enjoyed by also a non-citizen on Indian soil, it implies the principle of *non-refoulement*; but this does not confer on the non-citizen any right to reside and resettle, nor does it mean that if the stay of a non-national is contrary to national security, s/he can stay.

Third, in cases where the international covenants and treaties reinforce the fundamental rights in India, as facets of those rights they can be enforced.

Fourth, the power of the government to expel a foreigner is absolute.

Fifth, The work of the UNHCR in certifying refugees is humanitarian, so the government has an obligation to ensure that refugees receive international protection until their problems are solved.

Finally, in view of Article 51 that directs the State to respect international legal principles, the Courts will apply those principles in domestic law in a harmonious manner, provided such obligations are not inconsistent with domestic law.

The Supreme Court has also concurred with the judicial practice of assigning the burden of protection on the UNHCR, and has ruled that the issue of "reasonable procedure" in asking a nonnational to leave the country arises only when there is UNHCR certification of the said nonnational as refugee, and not otherwise. The Court has not laid down any standard norm in sheltering or certifying a refugee. Thus there is an unwritten division of labor: the UNHCR has exercised its mandate mainly with regard to 12,000 Afghan refugees and 1,000 refugees of other nationalities; in some other cases, it has been allowed to carry out relief and settlement work; in other cases, the Government has decided the fate of the shelter seeker. Thus in the case of some 100,000 Tibetan refugees, and some 65,000 Sri Lankan refugees, the UNHCR does not have a direct role. The mandate refugees assisted by the UNHCR are the Afghans, Burmese, and small number of Iranians, Sudanese, Iraqis, and others. The government issues through the Foreigners Regional Registration Office (FRRO) renewable residential permits to mandate refugees on the basis of certificates issued by the UNHCR. Yet cases before the courts continue involving refugees undergoing legal process for illegal entry.

In this clumsy division of labor, three things stand out as odd posers:

First, the juridical reasoning does not question even in the light of Article 51 this division of labor. It refuses to see the plain fact that the FA or the Passport Act or other relevant acts are not enough to judge a refugee situation. The Court has nothing to say on the "refugee-situation." What indeed is the refugee-situation? Briefly, the refugee is a victim of a radical discontinuity with the legal past of the state whose citizen s/he was—a legal past that is unable to protect him/her at present. The refugee has thus a spatial problem of finding place and both physical and legal protection. In this sense the UNHCR becomes a government during the "temporal rift" until a specific place is found "wherein there is a direct relationship between the place the refugee resides and the government responsible for the place and territory." Stay in a refugee camp is a state of suspended animation. It just indicates a temporary protection place until some government steps up to take responsibility. The Court by not fully acknowledging the logic of the refugee situation (it does partly, which is why the permission to approach the UNHCR is given) makes refugee-ness a permanent situation. It keeps the matter humanitarian in consonance with the logic of care and hospitality, while this is a matter where the issue is directly political, that is, the humanitarian is political.

Second, this division of labor actually strengthens a more basic divide—that between the humanitarian and the political. Juridical reasoning relating to protection of the refugees has been mainly humanitarian, and not rights based, that is to say political. Thus the same Supreme Court that in the case involving Khudiram Chakma v State of Arunachal Pradesh (1994, Supplementary, 1 SCC 615) had refused to acknowledge the rights of the Chakmas to citizenship or to settlement rights in Arunachal Pradesh, held in NHRC v State of Arunachal Pradesh (1996 (1) Supreme 295: (1996) 1 SCC 742)—in the case of Chakma refugees settled in Arunachal Pradesh and now being threatened by the All Arunachal Pradesh Students' Union to leave the state—that such threats amounted to threats to the life and liberty of the Chakmas and such threats would have to be handled by the State in accordance with law. It further held that while the application for citizenship was pending, no refugee could be evicted or removed from occupation on the ground that s/he was not a citizen of India until the competent authority had decided the matter (p. 302, paragraph 21.5). In this humanitarian

logic, the Court could invoke the judgment of 1994 (p. 299, paragraph 16) that had also said that foreigners were entitled to the protection of Article 21 of the Constitution. Led by this humanitarian logic the Court thus, while denying any basic right of a threatened foreigner to get asylum (which would have predicated on the FA and the Citizenship Act), affirms the need to protect the life of an alien who has illegally entered India. The Supreme Court thus went as far as holding that "international law and international conventions and covenants may be read into national laws, if the provisions of the same elucidate and go to effectuate the fundamental rights guaranteed by the Indian Constitution" (p. 316, paragraph 11 - JT 1997 (2) SC 311: (1997) 3 SCC 433). In this it relied on *Minister for Immigration and Ethnic Affairs v. Teoh* (1995), 69 Australian L.J. 423. In the same humanitarian spirit, the Supreme Court held (*Dr. Malavika Karlekar v Union of India*, Crl. WO No 583 of 1992), in a situation where 21 persons were to be deported from Andaman Islands to Burma, that if refugee status claimed by the petitioners was pending determination and a prima facie case had been made for the grant of refugee status and that those individuals posed no danger or threat to the security of the country, they might not be deported until the question of their status could be determined. In all these cases, the insistent refusal of juridical reasoning to comment on the possibilities of the obligation on the part of the State to grant asylum that would predicate on the FA or other relevant acts, and at the same time the readiness of the same reasoning to concede that there could be humanitarian grounds on which hospitality could be provided by the State temporarily or with UNHCR certification more durably, is part of the politics of the political/humanitarian divide (Warner, 1999).

Finally, the absence or the withering of an entire range of rights on the grounds of security and the division between humanitarian and political considerations symbolizes itself not so much through the concept and person of the refugee, but by the concept and person of the alien. That this is a fundamental question of the politics of our time is borne by the fact that the alien question is everywhere—irrespective of whether the country in question is a signatory of the Convention of 1951 or not. This situation produces legal deficit on an incessant basis. The legal deficit can be explained by the following facts. In the first place, countries such as India have not signed the Convention, and while the ground of inadequacy of the Convention is often advanced as the reason for nonaccession, that situation by itself creates inadequacy of legal standards within the country, where the judiciary even while taking note of the evolving and evolved international norms cannot persuade the government of the day to sign on to international standards. And, while this is the internal impact, on a global scale the Convention by not evolving adequately and keeping itself up to the needs of the time concedes the ground of inadequacy, giving handle to countries unwilling to sign to treat the Convention regime as weak, and thus creates its own legitimacy deficit. Finally, from a more substantive viewpoint, the nondialogic process of care management harms the mandate so much that to the skeptics it appears that in an age of massive and mixed flows of unwanted peoples round the world, and in an age of evolving demands for showing more human rights concerns for victims of forced migration, a harmonization of laws and instruments is almost impossible to achieve, and protection and care will remain of a minimal nature for ages to come.

Who is an Indian and Who is an Alien?

Making differences in the category of people who migrate under forcible circumstances has been legitimized in independent India, but this has colonial beginnings. The colonial principle of difference worked as the genealogical basis of the Passports Act, Foreigners Act, and the Citizenship Act. Independent India did not adopt a homogenizing principle and strategy for all groups in terms of conferring citizenship.

It meant that matters of emigration and immigration were issues of acute political significance to the State engaged in defining the subjects of its care. Thus, the lines dividing the subjects according to priority in terms of care that the newly independent State would confer on them also divided the region into (1) nation and near abroad, (2) into citizens and noncitizens, and (3) into Indians of Indian origin and non-Indians of Indian origin (Banerjee, 2003). Visible and invisible frontiers have been created. The feature of these *nouvelles frontieres* is that they are being produced internally also; they are not merely vertical lines separating two spaces, but concentric circles continuously dividing and then locating these to rejoin them in the universe of the nation. Law, citizenship, rights, obligation, and morality—all are caught in this universe of concentric circles.

Thus the State has to decide on a perennial basis as to who is an Indian in order to decide, who is an outsider? Are the Tamils of "Indian origin" Indians? Similarly, are the Fijians of "Indian origin," or the Burmese, or the East or South Africans of "Indian origin" Indians? Will the Indian state have any responsibility toward them if they seek shelter, as they do from time to time? In such cases will it be, particularly if they had been taken abroad as indentured labor once upon a time, now accepted as the return of the prodigal son? Will the State accept emigration as the ghost that comes to visit immigration—the flows that play on nationhood? To establish such identity in the interest of governance, the state not only sought to immobilize territory by fixing the borders and delimiting the boundaries everywhere inside and outside (a process that naturally took some time), but also to project onto this foundational space a people—a nation—who must equally be immobilized by the forces of governmentality, most notably the Acts just mentioned, and the census. Yet, the inherent contradiction in these two objectives—delimiting the cartographic space and delimiting the national space—was apparent from the beginning. The massive and mixed flows of forced migration from the beginning of independence were reminders of the incommensurability of the two tasks. The other strategy was therefore to lean back on the colonial principle of making difference the cardinal technique of governing.

If imperial territorial policy depended on boundary-making exercise and the creation of buffer zones and zones of exclusion between British Indian Territory and others, imperial citizenship policy depended on creating grades of Indians. Spread out in different places across the globe such as the Fiji islands, the Malayan peninsula, East Africa, or the West Indies, besides the areas of near abroad, the Indian Diaspora constituted by indentured labor, traders, and quasi-colonial settlers was, by 1947, a new question mark to the citizenship policy of the postcolonial state. While the new Indian government did not want the return of these people to India with their claim to rights of citizenship, it could not completely close the question that sprang from the nationalizing actions elsewhere in the world. Therefore while trying to establish coherence between a geopolitical imaginary and the national Diaspora, the independent Indian state had to work its way forward through pragmatics, now falling back on imperial administrative resources, now devising new strategies. Difference and identity—both had their place in the scheme of things.

Between 1950 and 1975, the Indian government signed treaties of peace and friendship with Bhutan, Sikkim, Nepal, Burma, Sri Lanka, Bangladesh, and an odd pact with Pakistan on minorities. These treaties bore assurances of friendship on behalf of an independent and anticolonial State; they were also tokens of an imperial nation that intended to continue relations of suzerainty with its neighbors. These agreements were based on and reproduced the geopolitical imaginary of an imperial nation engaged with issues of both territory and population (the agreement between India and Sri Lanka on the Indian Tamil plantation labor in Sri Lanka is an example). Territory was fixed; so also was the attempt to fix the population. Like combating famine, combating population instability was a task of great magnitude (though the victims of famine were treated with less care than victims of forced displacement were). Population flux was a national calamity. People of Indian origin who had settled overseas were to give up what we might now call a "right of return," just as partition refugees once nationalized by being allowed to acquire citizenship, were to give up the "right to return." Population flow in the understanding of

the modern State had queered the pitch in the latter's effort to establish a singular and unitary relation between place and identity, believed to be hallmark of the modern State's existence. But, as I showed in *The Marginal Nation*, the effort to discount the existence of people within the country whose identities bear only faint resemblance to the professed national identity of the State has proved impossible. While control of territory becomes occasionally successful, control of the national space being constantly invaded by history and migration has become an excruciating challenge. It is against this background that we find the appearance in Indian state discourse of legal ambiguity on refugee rights as a strategy. Law, politics, ethics, jurisprudence, the idea of vulnerability, and security—all are reshaped by the new cult of ambiguity practiced by a modern state. The paternalism of the Indian State (the *mai-bap sarkar*) proves an enduring feature, because it sits well with the needs of ambiguity—ambiguity not only of law, but ambiguity about the nature and extent of hospitality.

The paradoxical pertinence of such a situation is a way of looking at an issue of ethics as a game being played out among various positions. The relation between care and power, as I have indicated earlier, is not a simple causal one, namely, that by caring you amass power. The relation is complex. The arrangement of care is not simply flowing from the sovereign legal authority at the top. The world of care is as multiple, heterogeneous, and segmented as the world of power. The heterogeneity of power builds up and draws on the heterogeneity of the act of caring. The more multiple is this universe, the more complex is the game.

Note

1. In his address to the Roundtable Workshop on Refugees in the SAARC Region, the President of SAARCLAW (India Chapter), A.M. Singhvi, admitted that these questions of state obligations needed to be viewed in the context of human rights. The debate on the need for a national refugee law in India and the work on a model law has been conducted, however, often from a courtroom angle, and not from the perspective of massive and mixed flows—though it must be admitted that such debate represents a clear advance from the earlier state of affairs in policy matters. On the

address, see, "Report on Roundtable Workshop on Refugees in the SAARC Region—National Legislation on Refugees", SAARCLAW and UNHCR, New Delhi, 30 April 1999; pp. 13–18.

References

Abraham, I. (2003). *War and territory.* Unpublished essay, Social Science Research Council, South Asia Program.

Banerjee, P. (2003). "Aliens in a colonial world." In R. Samaddar (Ed.), *Refugees and the state: Practices of asylum and care in India, 1947–2000* (pp. 69–105). Delhi: Sage.

Beyani, C. (1995). "State responsibility for the prevention and resolution of forced population displacements in international law." *International Journal of Refugee Law, 7,* 131–137.

Bhagwati, P.N. (1999, April). *Report on roundtable workshop on refugees in the SAARC region: National legislation on refugees.* Report of the Roundtable Workshop on Refugees in the SAARC Region, New Delhi, India.

Bhaumik, S. (2003). "The returnees and the refugees: Migration from Burma." In R. Samaddar (Ed.), *Refugees and the state: Practices of asylum and care in India, 1947–2000* (pp. 182–210). Delhi: Sage.

Bose, P.K. (Ed.) (2001). *Refugees in West Bengal: Institutional practices and contested identities.* Calcutta: Calcutta Research Group.

Chatterjee, J. (2001). "Rights or charity? Government and refugees: The debate over relief and rehabilitation in West Bengal, 1947–1950." In S. Kaul (Ed.), *Partitions of memory.* Delhi: Permanent Black.

Chimni, B.S. (2003). "Status of refugees in India: Strategic ambiguity." In R. Samaddar (Ed.), *Refugees and the state: Practices of asylum and care in India, 1947–2000* (pp. 443–471). Delhi: Sage.

Dharamsala (1992). *Life in exile.* Department of Home Affairs, Central Tibetan Relief Committee.

Das, S.K. (2003). "State response to the refugee crisis: Relief and rehabilitation in the east." In R. Samaddar (Ed.), *Refugees and the state: Practices of asylum and care in India, 1947–2000* (p. 147). Delhi: Sage.

Derrida, J. (2001). *On cosmopolitanism and forgiveness.* London: Routledge.

Hindle, S. (2001). "Dearth, fasting and alms: The campaign for general hospitality in late Elizabethan England." *Past and Present, 172,* 44–86.

Kharat, R. (2003). "Gainers of a stalemate: The Tibetans in India." In R. Samaddar (Ed.), *Refugees and the state: Practices of asylum and care in India, 1947–2000* (pp. 281–320). Delhi: Sage.

Loescher, G., & Scanlan, J. (1986). *Calculated kindness: Refugees and America's half-open door, 1945–present.* New York: Free Press.

Menon, R. (2003). "Birth of Social Security commitments: What happened in the West." In R. Samaddar (Ed.), *Refugees and the state: Practices of asylum and care in India, 1947–2000.* Delhi: Sage.

Norbu, D. (2001). "Refugees from Tibet: Structural causes of successful settlements." In S.K. Roy (Ed.), *Refugees and human rights.* Delhi: Rawat Publications.

K. P. Saha (2003). "The Genocide of 1971 and the Refugee Influx in the East." In R. Samaddar (Ed.), *Refugees and the state: Practices of asylum and care in India, 1947–2000* (pp. 211–248). Delhi: Sage.

Samaddar, R. (1999). *The Marginal nation: Transborder migration from Bangladesh to West Bengal.* Delhi: Sage.

Samaddar, R. (2001). "Power, fear, ethics." *Refugee Watch, 14.*

Samaddar, R (Ed.) (2003). *Refugees and the state: Practices of asylum and care in India, 1947–2000.* Delhi: Sage.

Samaddar, R. (2004). *The politics of dialogue: Living under the geopolitical histories of war and peace.* Aldershot, UK: Ashgate.

Singhvi, A.M. (1999, April). *Report on roundtable workshop on refugees in the SAARC region: National legislation on refugees.* Report of the Roundtable Workshop on Refugees in the SAARC Region, New Delhi, India.

UNHCR, International Association of Refugee Law Judges, & Supreme Court Bar Association. (1999). *Report on Judicial Symposium on Refugee Protection.* New Delhi, India.

Warner, D. (1999, March). "The politics of the political/humanitarian divide." *International Review of Red Cross, 31* (333), 109–116.

9

United Kingdom

Immigration to the United Kingdom

Will Somerville and Betsy Cooper

The United Kingdom (UK), in contrast to immigrant-settled countries like the United States, has had a more ambiguous experience with immigration (Somerville, 2007). Not only did the UK historically consider itself a country of refuge for the persecuted, but for generations immigration from the British Empire was unimpeded and emigration to the British Empire encouraged. It was only in the 1960s and 1970s that serious controls were put into place (Hansen, 2000). Subsequently, however, the UK has carefully controlled migration to the island, and fostered a policy of "race relations" to incorporate newcomers. Since 1990, sustained immigration flows have diversified the ethnic, linguistic, and religious composition of the British population. In parallel, policy reforms have encouraged high-skilled migration and more active integration of immigrants while continuing to restrict asylum seeking. A pending Citizenship, Immigration, and Borders (2009) bill would reinforce these recent trends.

This chapter considers the factors driving migration to the United Kingdom since 1990, the public policy responses, and the outcomes and experiences of new arrivals. It focuses attention primarily on the most recent decade, during which Labour has been in power (they were first elected under Tony Blair in 1997, subsequently won reelection in 2001 and 2005, and are now led by Prime Minister Gordon Brown).

Immigration Trends since 1990

Increased Immigration

The United Kingdom has received immigrants for centuries. Since the 1990s, the UK has experienced high and sustained levels of net immigration, which since the mid-to-late 1990s has been unprecedented. Prior to the mid-1980s, more people emigrated each year than immigrated.

The flow of immigrants reflects growth in several streams. These include growing numbers of international students, a sudden increase and then drop in asylum applications (peaking in 2001–2002), more family reunification, and a sustained increase in economic migration.

Since the mid-1990s, net immigration has exceeded 100,000 people per year; the most recent figures indicate net immigration of 1.59 million people in the period 1996–2005.

Table 9-1. Migration to Britain, 1997–2006

	British	Non-British	Total
Gross Immigration	902,000	3,668,000	4,570,000
Gross Emigration	1,521,000	1,450,000	2,970,000
Net Immigration	−619,000	+2,217,000	+1,599,000

Notes: Numbers may not round; minus sign refers to net outflow and plus sign refers to net inflow.
Source: Total International Migration, Office for National Statistics, 2006.

The net flow of non-British nationals has been even more significant: a net addition of 2.2 million people (i.e. there has been a net loss of British nationals during this period). The Office for National Statistics assumes a net immigration level of 190,000 people per year in the next decade.[1] Forecasts have been lowered in the light of the current global recession, but analysts expect continued net immigration at high levels (Communities and Local Government [CLG], 2009b; Somerville and Sumption, 2009a). Table 9-1 identifies the gross and net flows in both directions over the last decade.

Figure 9-1 highlights these trends over a longer time-span, from 1975. The data shows the notable feature over the last fifteen years: rising inflows of non-British nationals and net emigration of British nationals, mainly to countries like Australia and Spain.

Immigrant Populations in the United Kingdom

Sustained inflows of non-British nationals have increased the stock of the foreign national population in the UK, which, as of the first quarter of 2008, now stands at some 11 percent of the population. The number of foreign nationals[2] has tripled between 1984 and the present day, from 1.55 million to around 4.16 million, comprising seven percent of the total population of 60.4 million. (In 2008, the UK had 6.6 million foreign-born people, a higher figure primarily because the foreign national population excludes those who have naturalized as British citizens (Salt, 2008.)) According to migration permit statistics for 2006, 29 percent of arrivals enter on work permits, 32 percent enter as family reunification candidates or as the immediate family of

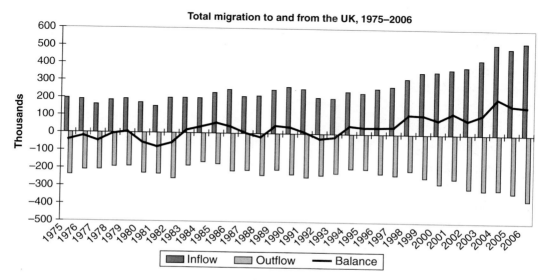

Figure 9-1. Net British and Non-British Migration to the UK
Source: Somerville, Sriskandarajah & Latorre (2009, *forthcoming*).

other permit holders, and 9 percent enter for humanitarian reasons (Organization for Economic Cooperation and Development [OECD], 2008). Most of the remainder enter through free movement from the European Union (EU).

Economic migration to the UK has increased most dramatically as a result of the enlargement of the European Union (EU) in May 2004. Most EU member state citizens do not require visas to work in the UK (although there are currently restrictions on nationals of Romania and Bulgaria) and the UK has proven an attractive destination. According to one estimate, about one million Eastern European nationals arrived in the UK between May 2004 and December 2007, though half of these people are thought to have left by the end of that period. Despite this high churn, it is estimated that nationals of these new member states have added some 500,000 people to the stock of the UK population in the space of four years.

As a result, the largest foreign-national group today in the UK is Polish, who went from being the thirteenth-biggest foreign-national group resident in the UK at the end of 2003 to the biggest by the end of 2007. According to the Labour Force Survey, in the first quarter of 2008, 521,000 Polish nationals were living in the UK, accounting for roughly one in eight of all foreign workers. The list is followed by Ireland (357,000), India (284,000), Pakistan (175,000), the United States (134,000), and France (120,000), all of which were significant sending countries to the UK before 1990.

On the other hand, flows of asylum seekers have decreased in recent years. The number of asylum applications lodged in the UK in the early and mid-1990s hovered between 20,000 and 40,000 per year. In the last decade, asylum applications have followed a parabolic curve: applications in 1997 (excluding dependants) totaled 32,500 before rising precipitously, peaking in 2002 then dropping equally fast. Applications stood at 27,900 (including dependants) in 2007 (Table 9-2).

The flow and stock figures discussed above do not, of course, include unauthorized immigrants. In 2005, the UK government released a report on the size of the illegally resident population,

Table 9-2. Asylum Applicants in the UK (1995–2006)

Year	Number of Applicants (excluding dependents)
1995	43,965
1996	29,640
1997	32,500
1998	46,015
1999	71,160
2000	80,315
2001	71,025
2002	84,130
2003	49,405
2004	33,960
2005	25,710
2006	23,520

Source: Home Office Data.

approximating the figure at 430,000 or 0.7 per cent of the UK population.[3] A more recent report estimates the figure to be higher, totaling 713,000 (Gordon *et. al,,* 2009.) In contrast to landlocked countries, which are concerned by unauthorized border crossings, the unauthorized population in the UK is likely to be characterized by those overstaying legal short-term visas or, it is thought, have at some point applied for asylum (Papademetriou and Somerville, 2008).

Ethnic Diversity

Ethnic diversity, and not immigration per se, drives the UK integration agenda. Many government social policies and most collected statistics focus primarily on ethnic minorities (i.e. not on place of birth or on parental place of birth). Immigration from the Commonwealth (notably from India, Pakistan, Bangladesh, the Caribbean, and African countries such as Ghana, Kenya, Nigeria, and Uganda) and recent inflows from other parts of the world (notably Somalia, Afghanistan, China, and Iraq) have contributed to increasing ethnic diversity in the UK over the last few decades. Even so, a significant proportion of the UK's immigrants are white, coming from European countries and other former colonies Canada, Australia, South Africa, and New Zealand. Immigrants from the United States also form a significant inflow.

Table 9-3. Percentage Breakdown of UK Population by Ethnic Group, 2001–2020

Ages 0–15	2001	2010	2020
White	88.2	85.6	82.9
Mixed	2.8	3.8	5.0
Asian	5.6	6.8	7.8
Black	2.5	2.8	2.9
Chinese & Other	0.8	1.1	1.4
Sum of groups	100.0	100.0	100.0

Source: Phil Rees, ESRC presentation, 2006.

Although finding comparable data is difficult, the absolute and relative size of the UK's ethnic minorities has grown substantially in recent decades. According to the 2001 Census, some 4.6 million people identified as nonwhite. The Labor Force Survey, a quarterly sample survey of private British households, estimates that, in early 2008, 10 percent of the UK population was nonwhite, 5 percent Asian or Asian British, 2.3 percent black or black British, and 1 percent of mixed heritage (Office for National Statistics, 2008). Table 9-3 provides an overview of ethnic diversity in the UK, projected ahead to 2020, and using a different data source (Census). By that time, close to 20 percent of the British population is expected to have a nonwhite background.

Human Capital

There is evidence of wide variation in the human capital of immigrant populations, in large part dependent on the migration class by which they were admitted (mainly family reunification; economic migrant; or asylum seeker). Some groups of recent arrivals, particularly asylum seekers, often face significant challenges with settlement, particularly in terms of English-language acquisition and overseas qualification recognition. Indians and Chinese often outperform whites in schools and in the labor market, while other groups, such as Pakistanis, Bangladeshis, and black Caribbeans, experience, on average, significantly higher unemployment and lower earnings than whites (Bloch, 2004; Prime Minister's Strategy Unit, 2003; Somerville and Wintour, 2006). In overall terms, the skills profile of immigrants to the UK represents an hourglass shape

in that immigrants are concentrated at both the high- and the low-skill ends of the spectrum.

In short, immigration has increased significantly over the last two decades. The United Nations now places the UK in its top ten of countries hosting significant numbers of migrants. Alongside Spain, the UK is new to the "top ten club." Furthermore, immigration has led to increasing ethnic diversity (within flows and more broadly in UK society) and a wide variety of human capital levels in the UK population.

Drivers of Migration to the United Kingdom

Immigrants have come to the UK for many reasons, but we can identify some general trends from data and surveys of migrant intentions. However, before suggesting some key drivers, it is important to acknowledge the role of the UK's immigration "policy model" in driving immigration. This model (discussed in more detail below) can be summarized as the liberalization or "opening up" of certain migration streams, including for students and economic migrants, and a shutting down of, in particular, the asylum route. Policy has undoubtedly had an impact on why and how immigrants have come to the UK over the last decade.

The main driver for economic migration (and undoubtedly part of the decision-making calculus for other migrants) has been the strength of the UK economy. The UK has enjoyed high growth, low unemployment, and high levels of unfilled vacancies (Somerville, 2007). (Indeed, the UK economy enjoyed uninterrupted quarterly growth from the mid-1990s until the credit crunch, entering recession officially only at the end of 2008).

Both employers and government have recruited economic migrants in order to address labor market needs.[4] According to the Labor Force Survey, in 2008 there were an estimated 2.3 million foreign nationals working in the UK. Many UK labor migration schemes are designed to fill gaps in the domestic labor market. There have been more than 500,000 unfilled vacancies since 2000, especially due to skills shortages in sectors such as education, health and public administration, financial services, and hospitality. The number of available work permits[5] tripled between 1997 and 2007, mostly in areas of high labor demand. The majority of work permits between 2000 and 2006 were issued in health and medical services (25 percent), computer services (17 percent), and administration, business, and management services (12 percent) (Somerville and Sriskandarajah, 2009). For European workers (who do not need work permits), migration has been, primarily, an economic phenomenon. Indeed, recent evidence indicates that the flow of Polish workers is diminishing in response to a more positive economic climate in Poland relative to the UK and a relative weakening of British currency (Pollard et al., 2008). The most recent evidence shows a large decrease in the inflow of Eastern European workers generally—the last quarter of 2008 shows a decline of 50 percent from one year earlier (Somerville and Sumption, 2009a, p. 25).

Strong economic opportunities may also, in part, account for strong student inflows. The UK now holds 12 percent of the global student market. However, students have many reasons for studying in the UK. These include significant outreach and marketing efforts undertaken by the Blair government; a strong global reputation for higher education; the currency of the English language; and colonial, historical ties. After graduating, students can stay on for high-skilled jobs.

Family reunion is another important stream and is self-explanatory as a driver for immigration into the UK. Much of this stream comes from former British colonies. It is also worth acknowledging that legal changes have facilitated this route, notably by dropping the "primary purpose rule" in 1997 (which had required foreign nationals to prove their marriages to British citizens were not about obtaining residency) and implementing new Human Rights legislation, which has accorded greater rights to families joining immigrants in the UK.

The reasons asylum seekers leave source countries have been contested by the UK government and some sections of society. Commentators have, for example, pointed to "magnets" such as the economy or the possibility of gaining welfare benefits, often explicitly accusing those seeking humanitarian protection of being economic migrants (i.e., claiming fraudulently). In truth, the prima facie answer that asylum seekers are seeking safety holds true. Asylum applications have and continue to correlate with conflict zones across the world and the consensus of the academic literature is that asylum seekers are not pulled by welfare systems but by concerns over personal safety. In 1996, applicants came principally from Somalia, the former Yugoslavia, former USSR, China, and Sri Lanka; in 2002, the main countries of origin were Iraq, Zimbabwe, Afghanistan, Somalia, and China; and, in 2007, they included Afghanistan, Iran, China, Iraq, and Eritrea.

Thus, in the United Kingdom pull factors—particularly the state of the economy—are generally more important than push factors in determining the direction of flows, in part because the UK's island borders and safe third country policies make it a difficult destination to reach from abroad. Asylum seekers continue to seek protection from economic and political instability in their home countries, but this represents a smaller percentage of overall migration than in the late 1990s.

The Response of United Kingdom Society to Immigration

Public Concern

Sustained net immigration over the last decade has changed the political and policy landscape in the UK. Public anxiety about immigration, fueled by media attention, has been on the rise. Monthly polling data from the IpsosMORI agency shows that, beginning in the late 1990s, people identified race and immigration as a top three most important issue facing the country in the vast majority of months. Opinion polling data from other sources shows a similarly negative attitude: between 60 and 85 percent of the public would prefer less immigration. The November 2007 Transatlantic Trends poll suggested that 62 percent of those surveyed in the United Kingdom saw immigration more as a "problem" than as an "opportunity,"[6] a far higher figure than the comparative results found in the United States and Europe.

Immigration Policies

In this context of rising numbers and anxieties UK policy makers since 1997 have drafted radical policy responses in an attempt to manage migration. To understand these changes, it is first necessary to highlight the previous "model" for the sake of comparison.

The Postwar Policy Model. The postwar policy model, created at a time when the British Empire was dismembering itself, was based on two pillars, each entrenched by three laws (Somerville, 2007). The first pillar, *limitation,* comprised three laws—enacted in 1962, 1968, and 1971—that together had the goal of "zero net immigration." The 1971 Immigration Act—the single most important immigration Act of the last 50 years—made a strong statement that Britain was a country of "zero net immigration." It repealed, with a few minor exceptions, all previous legislation and replaced them with strong control procedures for most immigrants. New legal distinctions (building on the legislation of the 1960s) between the rights of the UK-born and UK passport-holders meant that people from former British colonies—notably India, Pakistan, and the Caribbean—became subject to immigration controls (Miles & Phizacklea, 1984).

The second pillar, *integration,* involved a framework of race relations, inspired by the U.S. civil rights movement. The most potent policy measures came in the form of antidiscrimination law, in a limited form in the 1965 Race Relations Act, in an expanded form in the 1968 Race Relations Act, and most comprehensively in the 1976 Race Relations Act.

In sum, the dominant postwar policy model was a bifurcated one: emphasizing the integration of immigrants (through a "race relations" approach) and the restriction of immigration. Legislation in 1993 and 1996 changed the asylum appeals process, implemented sanctions for airlines, allowed for removals to safe third countries, and reduced benefit entitlements.[7] The essential components of this policy model were retained until Labour came to power in 1997.

Policy under New Labour: 1997–2008. Policy has shifted significantly between 1997 and December 2008, including through the liberalization of the economic migration system; increased restrictions and faster processing of asylum seekers; more strenuous control measures against unauthorized immigration; expanded internal security measures; and a reorientation of the official position on "integration," including through the expansion of antidiscrimination measures.

The major *policy change,* developed in the period 2001–2003, is the concept of "managing migration" (Somerville, 2007). This commitment to economic migration has been accepted across the political divide, and, consequently, limitation and restriction on immigration is no longer a prerequisite for UK migration policy. Accompanying programs have encouraged the migration both of high-skilled immigrants (the Highly Skilled Migrants Programme, now Tier 1 of the new Points-Based System) and low-skilled vacancies in agriculture and hospitality (the Seasonal Agricultural Workers Scheme and Sector Based Schemes).

The economic migration system in the UK is currently undergoing a further overhaul. First announced in the government's 2005 five-year plan (Home Office, 2005), and refined following a major consultation exercise in 2006, the existing labor migration schemes are being revised and consolidated into a new Points-Based System (PBS) currently being rolled out (Home Office, 2006). This new system will make the route to permanent settlement more selective and lower skilled workers will not be eligible (instead the UK will rely on European workers, who hold the right of free movement).

Measures have also been put into place to attract international students. Such efforts carried the imprimatur of former Prime Minister Tony Blair, who was personally concerned with increasing numbers (especially through two "Prime Minister's Initiatives" in 1999 and 2006). Measures included more vigorous marketing abroad, especially through British Council offices, and easing the visa processing and transition into work within the UK.

The government has also attempted to restrict particular streams, notably asylum. In response to increased numbers and public pressure, the government has introduced successive pieces of legislation which sought to curb the number of asylum applications, speed up application processing, and more effectively remove failed asylum seekers.[8] Reducing the quantity of asylum claims remains a key policy goal.

A set of measures to effectively extend UK borders abroad has also had a major impact on "undesirable" flows, including the asylum route. These include a more restrictive visa regime; a new identity management system (including the introduction of Biometric Identity Cards for all foreign nationals); increased controls at various European ports and Immigration Liaison Officers posted abroad; and financial penalties on air and truck carriers. The resulting drop in asylum claims has been hailed as a major success by the government, though these outcomes have been helped by a worldwide drop in claims (now again on the rise, according to the latest UNHCR [2008] figures).

The government has also put in place major institutional reforms, redesigning the immigration "delivery system" to reflect new priorities. The responsibilities of the Home Office were split between a new Ministry of Justice and a streamlined Home Office, while responsibilities for equality moved to the Department for Communities and Local Government (CLG). The Immigration and Nationality Directorate (IND) was also hived off into a separate agency with greater operational freedom and renamed the Borders and Immigration Agency (UKBA).

Thus, British immigration policy during the past 11 years reflects an overarching desire for greater control over migration flows while also selectively opening its borders to preferred flows. It is likely that the future policy trajectory will in large part depend on the perceived success of the new points system in managing migration.

Immigrant Incorporation Policy in the United Kingdom: From Multiculturalism to Integration

The government's approach to immigrant integration or incorporation has also shifted significantly under Labour. Traditionally the government employed a multicultural or race relations model; still the standard shorthand description of UK policy. However, since around the turn of the century, such an approach came under sustained criticism, from inside and outside government. These critiques began from the perspective that immigration and British national identity had a complicated, if not oppositional relationship. A major Runnymede Foundation report noted a number of factors—large-scale migration among them— had "shaken the unified conception of Britishness hitherto taken for granted" (Parekh, 2000). Further, new Home Secretary David Blunkett was personally invested in identity issues; he had implemented citizenship education policy while Education Minister the term before.

Three events in the year 2001 further fueled the impression that existing immigrant incorporation policy might be inadequate: riots involving minority communities in the northern towns of Bradford, Burnley, and Oldham in the summer; the peak of the Sangatte refugee crisis; and the September 11 terrorist attacks (discussed in more detail below). The July 7, 2005, terrorist attacks on London later provoked concerns about white and minority ethnic and religious groups (especially Muslims) leading segregated lives.[9] Further, throughout this period there was rising support in a limited number of areas of the UK for far-right political parties such as the British National Party (BNP). In the context of far-right popularity in other parts of Europe, this further heightened concern about popular attitudes toward diversity, immigration, and race.

The focus of immigrant integration policies has consequently shifted from multiculturalism to "integration," but its destination is still unclear. There are four semidistinct strands of policy: refugee integration policy; a new focus on "community cohesion"; active promotion of citizenship; and a strong and broad emphasis on equality.

Until recently, formal "integration" policy in the UK concerned settlement services for recognized refugees. The refugee integration strategy—first introduced in 2000 and strengthened in 2005—makes refugees eligible for orientation services and some financial assistance for integration, since 2007 in the form of interest-free loans.

Community cohesion is concerned with bringing (segregated) communities together through a variety of initiatives such as summer youth programming, school twinning projects, and mixed housing policies, mainly promulgated at a local level. Unsurprisingly, questions still remain as to whether the promotion of "cohesion" is an appropriate way to accommodate social and cultural differences in the UK.

The promotion of citizenship has involved "activating" the naturalization process through introducing citizenship tests, language tests (also for mandatory for long-term residence), and citizenship ceremonies. A proposal currently under consideration would create a year-long "probationary citizenship" stage under which migrants would not be able to access social mainstream benefits (Home Office, 2008). The right to pass from stage to stage would be based on four integration-related factors: English language ability; working and paying taxes; obeying the law; and demonstrating active citizenship (through community service).

Finally, major equal opportunity measures introduced under Labour have reinforced and extended the antidiscrimination framework. The 2000 Race Relations (Amendment) Act aimed to eradicate institutionalized racism by obligating certain public authorities, including the police and immigration services, to take action to correct ethnic inequalities in recruitment, employment, and service delivery. The 1998 Human Rights Act, which enshrined the European Convention on Human Rights (ECHR) into UK law, has further reinforced the framework. Thus, equality measures are increasingly central to public service.

Most recently, the government has begun to address immigrant incorporation more directly with the publication of a nascent national immigrant integration strategy (CLG, 2008), which complements existing strategy for incorporating refugees. However, it has decided that there is "no clear rationale for developing an integration agency" (CLG, 2009a).

In précis, the various strands of incorporation together indicate a policy shift toward *integration*. This move away from multiculturalism toward more weight on "shared values" does not indicate a wholesale regression to the acculturation overtures of a previous generation: official references to adaptation on the part of host communities are nearly always referred to as "a two-way process." Further, this is not simply

rhetorical, as the implementation of equality measures makes clear. The exception may involve the treatment of British Muslims, for whom (as we see next) the charge of assimilation has more than a kernel of truth.

The Securitization of British Immigration Policies

In many ways the September 11 terrorist attacks had little impact on British immigration policy; the seeds for certain major reforms—improving management of asylum, and encouraging citizenship and community cohesion, for example—were planted before the attacks. Further, major antiterrorism legislation had just become law in 2000. The subsequent 2001 Anti-terrorism, Crime, and Security Act (c. 24)—which allowed for the detention of certain suspected international terrorists and limited certain asylum appeals for national security reasons—contained only minor immigration provisions, and virtually all were directed toward asylum provisions.[10]

However, the direction of British immigrant incorporation policy was indeed affected by the attacks. Britain's counterterrorism strategy, Project CONTEST, acknowledged that "links between social deprivation among British Muslims and extremism is not simple cause and effect," but argued that "influencing social and economic issues" might help diminish terrorist support (Foreign and Commonwealth Office & Home Office, 2004). The suggested work program included outreach, consultation, further research, and using government resources to promote mainstream Islam. Subsequently, the Muslim Council of Britain began meeting regularly with police and intelligence agencies (Klausen, 2005, p. 34).

While the September 11 attacks did have effects on Muslim integration, the speed of these efforts picked up substantially following the 2004 Madrid and 2005 London attacks. The government paid increasing attention to the British Muslim community: it initiated a road-show of "mainstream" Islamic scholars, created regional Muslim forums against extremism and Islamophobia, and developed a Mosques and Imams National Advisory Board (HM Government, 2006, p. 14).

On the one hand, this attention led to an expansion of the equality agenda to include religious as well as race relations. The Racial and Religious Hatred Act 2006 created offenses for stirring up hatred against persons on religious grounds. On the other hand, much of the increased attention to Muslim populations falls explicitly under the heading of "Preventing Extremism." A new unit dedicated to this purpose (originally in the Home Office but now in the Department for Communities and Local Government) has undertaken extensive consultations and administers a fund mainly targeted at local authorities with large Muslim communities. Pressures have also been placed on Britain's traditionally liberal religious accommodation policies: Islamic schools, Sharia law, and religious dress have all provoked serious public debate, the last when Minister Jack Straw publicly called the headscarf "a visible statement of separation and of difference" (Straw, 2006). The reframing of Muslim integration as a security issue may have implications for incorporation outcomes in the future.

Immigrant Outcomes

To better understand immigrant "adjustment" and incorporation, one should examine how immigrants perform: culturally, politically, and economically. Evaluating the evidence on immigrant outcomes is difficult in this case, because the UK policy approach is focused on "race," "ethnicity," or "minority" status. Thus, there is little data on the long-term outcomes of immigrants who enter under particular immigrant streams, or on second generation immigrants; data and research on the experience of ethnic minority groups provides an imperfect substitute. This important caveat should be borne throughout any references to outcomes. In summary, immigrant populations have increasingly integrated into the labor market; fears of socioeconomic marginalization or separation are likely overstated. Cultural integration is a bit more ambiguous; while some acculturation has occurred, cultural accommodation policies are also thought to have encouraged ongoing cultural claims-making. The following largely focuses on the labor market experience of immigrants due to space constraints.

Broadly speaking, first generation immigrants suffer downward mobility upon arriving in the UK. (This largely conforms to international evidence.) First generation immigrants with middle and higher skills tend to have lower levels of achievement than native workers (in occupational status, employment, and other economic indicators) *relative to their education and skills*. Contributing factors include difficulties in obtaining recognition for both academic qualifications and vocational credentials and experience; a lack of knowledge of the local labor market; and above all a poor knowledge of the English language (Kempton, 2002, p. 6). Asylum seekers and refugees (the former disbarred from the labor market for the first 12 months of any claim) suffer particularly acute levels of unemployment and inactivity (Bloch, 2004).

There is also evidence of exploitation, particularly among low-skilled workers, brutally evidenced by two tragic events: the death of 58 people in the back of a truck en route to the UK in 2000 and, in 2004, the drowning of 22 Chinese cockle pickers at Morecambe Bay in northwest England. Public and political pressure after this latter tragedy led to the enactment of limited legislation regulating the behavior of employers in particularly vulnerable sectors.

This should be set against two facts: first, downward mobility of the middle and higher skilled adult first generation generally recedes over time. The balance of the evidence in the UK indicates that over 20 to 25 years, nearly all first generation adult immigrants catch up with their native-born counterparts (Dickens & McKnight, 2008), although some UK evidence indicates those from certain nonwhite, minority backgrounds do not catch up (Somerville & Wintour, 2006). The second fact is that the economic and wage returns on migration is generally significant, as migrants earn more than they could in the source country (Drinkwater, Eade, & Garapich, 2007).

For the second generation, the story can perhaps be best described as positive, but bittersweet. Platt's work (2005) finds that for Caribbeans, Black Africans, Indians, Chinese, and white migrants, children from working-class backgrounds are more likely to end up in professional/managerial class occupations than white British people from similar origins. Similarly,

Dustmann and Theodoropoulos (2006) find second generation ethnic minority immigrants attain higher educational achievements than both their parents and their native-born white counterparts, and for those that work, higher wages.

However, we should temper our view of outright success. The entrenchment of ethnic minorities in the working class suggests we might expect upward intergenerational upward mobility. In employment and wage terms, the children of immigrants have higher incomes relative to the children of natives, but given their educational achievements, the wage difference should be higher still. Moreover, there is an important exception—Pakistanis—to this overall pattern of successful upward mobility. Second generation Pakistanis have lower levels of upward mobility than their white British counterparts, even when taking education into account (Platt, 2005).

Political outcomes are difficult to measure, but some evidence is nevertheless available. While levels of ethnic voting are contested, Fieldhouse and Cutts (2008) suggest that South Asian Muslim voter turnout in the 2001 British elections (58.7 percent) was identical to the non-Asian turnout (58.4 percent). Certain ethnic groups have better outcomes on civic participation than others. According to the British Citizenship Survey, around 40 percent of mixed race, Bangladeshi, and white groups are engaged in some form of civic participation, while only about 20 percent of certain blacks and Chinese groups do so (Green, Connolly, & Farmer, 2004).

Sociocultural outcomes provoked significant debate following the 2001 disturbances and terrorist attacks, as the government feared that certain ethnic communities were leading parallel, segregated lives (Cantle, 2001). While some evidence of segregation does exist, Simpson, Ahmad, and Phillips (2007) suggest that at least in some communities this has decreased over the past decade, and that where it continues clustering may benefit migrants by encouraging social capital to develop.

Further, while migrant populations have often engaged in claims-making for equal treatment or cultural accommodation which, particularly when religion-motivated, has become a concern of policy makers, Koopmans et al. (2005) have suggested that this cultural claims-making is the product of British institutions that encourage it. There do appear to be continued inequalities as regards minority participation in certain mainstream cultural activities; despite a program to encourage participation, government research showed a decrease in the percentage of BME group attendance at arts events (Arts Council England, 2007).

Thus outcomes for first generation immigrants are mixed, but generally poorer than levels of education would predict. This applies in many areas of social policy (immigrants are overly represented in poorer quality housing for example) but aligns with findings on immigrant outcomes in other developed countries. For second generation migrants, the generally upward mobility in employment, wages, and occupations is tempered by the existence of penalties (particularly associated with ethnicity). Some groups, particularly Pakistanis, have not performed as well as expected. Political and sociocultural outcomes remain distinguishable by ethnic group.

Up until now, we have not discussed causality. Suffice it to say there are myriad reasons—inherited characteristics, human capital on arrival, heritage, luck, and so on—that play a role in labor market incorporation. Broader societal incorporation can similarly result from personal choices, societal factors (such as discrimination), or both. But we should not overlook the importance of policy, which can both inhibit and encourage settlement.

Immigrant Contributions to the United Kingdom

The literature covering immigrant contributions to the United Kingdom remains sparse outside of the field of economic impact. Cultural contributions of immigrants and their influences on the UK are nevertheless likely to be significant. At least 18 UK Nobel Laureates were former refugees, for example, and few would question immense contributions to the arts, science, music, and cuisine. On the other hand, migrants are more often portrayed in public discourse as social drains rather than social contributors, again based on anecdotal evidence of segregation and overcrowded housing in particular communities.

Turning to political contributions, we again run into the caveat that the UK generally looks at issues through a lens of ethnicity. Of the 646 seats in British Parliament, only 14 are filled by ethnic minority MPs. However, while the UK party political system and powerful executive of the "Westminster model" of government may act against immigrant involvement, immigrants can influence the political system in ways different from in other countries. For example, all Commonwealth citizens (which vitally include those from South Asia) have permission to vote in local *and national* elections.

The evidence related to the contributions of immigrants to the economy is framed within a debate on the economic costs and benefits of large immigration flows. A reading of the literature reveals migration to the UK has had negligible effects on employment levels and a small positive impact on wage levels (Haque, 2002). The macroeconomic gains include greater labor market flexibility, fewer skill shortages, and lower inflation. For example, migrants are more likely to be employed in sectors of the economy with skill shortages (Loizillon, 2004). There has also been a clear fiscal gain, estimated in the region of £2.5bn (Home Office, 2002), or as high as £5.4bn by the Centre for Economic and Business Research. Some estimates suggest that from 1999 to 2004 the foreign born contributed more than the UK born (Sriskandarajah et al., 2005, pp. 10–11). Finally, the impact of the Eastern European accession states has been viewed as particularly positive (Ernst and Young, 2006; Portes and French, 2006). Immigrants are now considered a mainstay for particular sectors of the economy, including certain low-skill sectors (agriculture, for instance) and public services (the Health Service in London).

However, there are likely to be negative as well as positive effects, particularly for those at the bottom of the labor market and for previous waves of immigrants (for a full discussion see Sumption and Somerville, 2009b). In short, little account has been taken of distributional impacts. Migration's positive wage and employment effects depend at least in part on the substitutability of migrant workers; new migrants likely have small adverse impacts on low-skilled workers who came in previous waves of immigration.

Further, some estimates suggest that migrants are a drain on social benefits, despite the fact that noncitizens are limited from accessing many such benefits in the UK. A major House of Lords report found that immigration had neutral or no overall benefits, and called for a cap on the number of immigrants coming to the country (House of Lords, 2008). Thus far, the report has failed to gain traction within the government.

Conclusion

The United Kingdom has in many ways been transformed by immigration over the last two decades. The UK now receives greater numbers from a greater number of source countries, and several large and largely unpredicted waves (along the asylum track, 1999–2002, and from Eastern Europe 2004–2007) have fundamentally changed the UK population.

Immigration has continued at sustained and high net levels against a backdrop of deep public disquiet. Partly as a result of this, and partly as a result of broader pressures—including globalization, the opening up of the European space, and interested groups within the political sphere—the UK policy "model" has been radically restructured from its previous position of "zero (net) migration" and "race relations" to a more liberal system that welcomes particular streams (workers, students) while pressing down on the humanitarian stream. The immigrant incorporation model has similarly been transformed away from race relations and toward "integration." The threat of terrorism has renewed interest in the integration of the UK's Muslim population; more funding and programming is available for this cause, generally under the auspices of "preventing violent extremism."

Evidence on the outcomes of immigrants is mixed. First generation immigrants have downward social mobility, whereas most groups in the second generation are upwardly mobile (with the important exception of Pakistanis). The contribution of immigrants to the country is also contested, particularly in the economic sphere. Immigration has a small, positive impact on the macroeconomy, with some negative distributional effects. There is far less consideration of its impacts on public services or on the long-term dynamics (both economically and socially) but it is widely recognized that immigrants underpin certain economic sectors. Policymakers have included immigrants in forward-looking calculations on demography (immigrant flows are seen as important in supporting an aging population) and on international competitiveness (as evidenced by the enthusiasm to attract and select the highly skilled).

Thus, the UK is at a crossroads: increasingly acknowledging the central role immigration will play in its economic future, while remaining ambivalent about immigration's political and sociocultural effects. The future policy direction will likely depend, among other things, on the health of the (increasingly shaky) economy, the strength of anti-immigrant political pressures, and the ability of migrants to mobilize and assert themselves in the UK context. Though the world is increasingly mobile, then, the UK experience suggests that the effects of immigration are still country-specific.

Notes

1. www.gad.gov.uk/Demography_Data/Population/2006/methodology/migrass.asp.
2. Foreign nationals includes all residents who do not have British nationality.
3. The calculation was based on figures from 2001.
4. While the number of labor migrants to the UK has grown, foreign nationals are still a relatively small percentage—less than 9 percent—of the overall UK workforce.
5. In 2006, the UK issued around 141,000 work permits. More than half were for managerial, professional, associate professional, and technical occupations.
6. This project was funded by the German Marshall Fund and the Barrow Cadbury Trust in the UK.
7. Asylum and Immigration Appeals Act 1993 (c. 23); Asylum and Immigration Act 1996 (c. 49).
8. Immigration and Asylum Act 1999 (c. 33); Nationality, Immigration and Asylum Act 2002 (c. 41); Immigration, Asylum and Nationality Act 2006 (c. 13).
9. The 9/11 attacks, and the degree that policy has subsequently undergone a "securitization," is discussed in more detail below.
10. The detention provisions were later declared unlawful under British human rights legislation.

References

Arts Council England. (2007). *Final report on PSA target 2 on the take-up of cultural opportunities by people aged 20 and over from priority groups.* London: Arts Council England. Retrieved December 15, 2008, at http://www.culture.gov.uk/images/publications/ACE_FinalPSA2Target.pdf.

Bloch, A. (2004) *Making it work.* Asylum and Migration Working Paper II. London: ippr.

Cantle, T. (2001). *Community cohesion: A report of the independent review team.* London: Home Office.

Communities and Local Government (CLG). (2008). *Managing the impacts of migration: A cross-government approach.* London: Communities and Local Government.

Communities and Local Government (CLG). (2009a). *Managing the impacts of migration: improvements and innovations.* London: Communities and Local Government.

Communities and Local Government (CLG). (2009b). *Projections of migration inflows under alternative scenarios for the UK and world economies.* Economics Paper 3. London: Communities and Local Government.

Dickens, R., & McKnight, A. (2008). *The changing pattern of earnings: Employees, migrants and low-paid families.* London: Joseph Rowntree Foundation. Retrieved December 15, 2008, from http://www.jrf.org.uk/knowledge/findings/socialpolicy/2323.asp.

Drinkwater, S., Eade, J., & Garapich, M. (2007). *Earnings and migration strategies of Polish and other post-enlargement migrants to the UK.* Presented at the European Economics and Finance Society Annual Conference, Sofia, May 31–June 3. Retrieved December 15, 2008, from http://www.eefs.eu/conf/Sofia/Papers/N734_%20Drinkwater_%20Eade_Garapich.doc.

Dustmann, C., & Theodoropoulos, N. (2006). *Ethnic minority immigrants and their children in Britain.* Cream Discussion Paper No. 10. London: CREAM.

Ernst and Young. (2006). *ITEM Club spring 2006 forecast.* London: Ernst and Young.

Fieldhouse, E., & Cutts, D. (2008). Mobilisation or marginalisation? Neighbourhood effects on Muslim electoral registration in Britain in 2001. *Political Studies,* 56, 333–354.

Foreign and Commonwealth Office & Home Office. (2004). *Young Muslims and extremism.* London: UK Foreign and Commonwealth Office and Home Office. Retrieved August 5, 2008, from http://www.globalsecurity.org/security/library/report/ 2004/muslimext-uk.htm.

Gordon, I., Scanlon, K., Travers, T., & Whitehead, C. (2009). *Economic impact on London and the UK of an earned regularisation of irregular migrants in the UK.* (Interim Report from LSE London. London: Greater London Authority (GLA).

Green, H., Connolly, H., & Farmer, C. (2004). *2003 Home Office citizenship survey: People, families, and communities.* Home Office Research Study No. 289. London: Home Office. Retrieved November 10, 2008, at http://www.homeoffice.gov.uk/rds/pdfs04/hors289.pdf.

Hansen, R. (2000). *Citizenship and immigration in postwar Britain.* Oxford: Oxford University Press.

Haque, R. (2002). *Migrants in the UK: A descriptive analysis of their characteristics and labour market performance.* London: Dept. for Work and Pensions.

HM Government. (2006). *Countering international terrorism: The United Kingdom's strategy.* London: HMSO.

Home Office. (Various years). *Asylum statistics.* London: Home Office.

Home Office. (Various years). *Control of immigration statistics.* London: Home Office.

Home Office. (2002). *The migrant population in the UK: Fiscal effects.* RDS occasional paper 77. London: Home Office.

Home Office. (2005). *Controlling our borders: Making migration work for Britain.* London: HMSO.

Home Office. (2006). *A points based system: Making migration work for Britain.* London: HMSO.

Home Office. (2008). *The path to citizenship: Next steps in reforming the immigration system.* London: HMSO.

Home Office, Department for Work and Pensions, HM Revenue and Customs, and Communities and Local Government. (Various years). *Accession monitoring reports.* London: HMSO.

House of Lords. (2008). *The economic impact of immigration.* HL82. London: HMSO.

IpsosMORI. (2008). *Long-term trends: The most important issues facing Britain today.* London: IpsosMORI.

Kempton, J. (2002). *Migrants in the UK: Their characteristics and labour market outcomes and impacts.* RDS Occasional Paper 82. London: Home Office.

Klausen, J. (2005). *The Islamic challenge: Politics and religion in Western Europe.* Oxford: Oxford University Press.

Koopmans, R., Statham, P., Giugni, M., & Passy, P. (2005). *Contested citizenship: Immigration and cultural diversity in Europe.* Minneapolis and London: University of Minnesota Press.

Loizillon, A. (2004). Principle labour migration schemes in the United Kingdom. In OECD, *Migration for employment: Bilateral agreements at a crossroads.* Paris: OECD.

Miles, R., & Phizacklea, A. (1984). *White man's country: Racism in British politics.* London and Sydney: Pluto Press.

Office for National Statistics. (2008). *Labour market statistics: July 2008.* Retrieved December 10, 2008, from http://www.statistics.gov.uk/pdfdir/lmsuk0708.pdf.

Organization for Economic Cooperation and Development (OECD). (Various years). *Trends in international migration.* Paris: OECD Publications.

Papademetriou, D., & Somerville, W. (2008) *Earned amnesty: Bringing illegal workers out of the shadows.* London: CentreForum.

Prime Minister's Strategy Unit. (2003). *Ethnic minorities and the labour market.* London: Prime Minister's Strategy Unit.

Parekh, B. (2000). *The future of multi-ethnic Britain: Report of the Commission on the Future of Multi-Ethnic Britain.* London: Profile Books Ltd.

Platt, L. (2005). *Migration and social mobility: The life chances of Britain's ethnic communities.* Bristol and York: The Policy Press and Joseph Rowntree Foundation.

Pollard, N., Latorre, M., & Sriskandarajah, D. (2008) *Floodgates or turnstiles? Post EU enlargement migration flows to (and from) the UK.* London: ippr.

Portes, J., & French, S. (2006). *The impact of free movement of workers from central and eastern Europe on the UK labour market: Early evidence.* Working Paper 18. London: Department for Work and Pensions.

Rees, P., & Butt, F. (2004). Ethnic change and diversity in England, 1981–2001. *Area, 36,* 174–186.

Salt, J. (2008). International Migration and the United Kingdom (Report of the United Kingdom SOPEMI Correspondent to the OECD, 2008), Paris: OECD. http://www.geog.ucl.ac.uk/research/mobility-identity-and-security/migration-research-unit/pdfs/Sop08_fin.pdf.

Simpson, L., Ahmad, S., & Phillips, D. (2007). *Oldham and Rochdale: Race, housing, and community cohesion.* Manchester, UK: Cathy Marsh Centre for Census and Survey Research.

Somerville, W. and Wintour, P. (2006). Employment. In S. Spencer (ed.), *Refugees and other new migrants: A review of the evidence on successful approaches to integration* (pp. 37–51). London: Home Office.

Somerville, W. (2007). *Immigration under new labour.* Bristol: Policy Press.

Somerville, W., Sriskandarajah, D., & Latorre, M. (2009). *The United Kingdom: A reluctant immigration country*. Washington, DC: Migration Information Source.

Somerville, W., & Sumption, M. (2009a). *Immigration in the UK: the recession and beyond*. London: Equality and Human Rights Commission.

Somerville, W., & Sumption, M. (2009b). *Immigration and the labour market: Theory, evidence, and policy*. London: Equality and Human Rights Commission.

Sriskandarajah, D., Cooley, L., & Reed, L. (2005). *Paying their way: The fiscal contribution of immigrants to the UK*. London: ippr.

Straw, Jack. (2006). "I felt uneasy talking to someone I couldn't see." *Guardian*, 6 October.

United Nations High Commissioner for Refugees (UNHCR). (2008). *Asylum levels and trends in industrialized countries*. Geneva: UNHCR. Retrieved December 15, 2008, at http://www.unhcr.org/statistics/STATISTICS/48f742792.pdf.

10

Spain

A "New Immigration Center"

David Corkill

Spain was a latecomer to mass immigration. In common with other countries in Southern Europe, Spain's position in the international migration system only recently shifted from that of a sending country into a receiver society (Arango 2000; King, Fielding, & Black 1997). Moreover, this transformation was compressed into a short time-span, between the late 1980s and the early years of the new century. Indeed, it was not until 1998 that Spain ceased to be a country of net migration. Since then, Spain has received the largest annual inflows of foreigners among the European Union member states (388,600 in 2006) and came second only to the United States in global terms. At the time of writing it is still too early to say what impact the financial crisis and economic downturn will have on immigration into Spain, although clearly employment opportunities in sectors where migrant workers are heavily concentrated, such as construction, will undoubtedly contract. It may well be that the era of large-scale immigration into Spain comes to an end in late 2008. Not surprisingly, becoming a "new immigration center" generated a swathe of new social, political, economic, and diplomatic issues for Spain to confront, including exclusion and integration strategies, security, ethnic relations, and policy harmonization with the European Union, among many others.

Spain has long played an integral part in European migration movements, principally as a labor exporter. Historically, emigration has been a key factor in Spanish life and is embedded in the collective memory. Large numbers left for South America at the beginning of the twentieth century to seek a better life in the New World. Between 1850 and 1950 some 3.5 million Spaniards departed for the Americas, mostly as temporary workers (LOrtega Pérez 2003). Nor should it be forgotten that from the 1950s to 1970s countries such as Greece, Italy, Portugal, and Spain became the recruiting grounds for the economically booming but labor-starved Western European economies. During this period, three-quarters of Spanish emigrants headed for Northern Europe. These outflows were accompanied by substantial interregional mobility within the country itself as Spaniards moved from the poorer rural areas to regions with growing industrial and service sectors. These migration episodes eventually came to a halt: the South American phase following World War I and the Great Depression and the West European phase following the oil crisis in 1973, which saw the end of the mass migration of Spanish workers.

Internal migrations, so buoyant between 1960 and 1973, eventually subsided during the 1980s as high unemployment limited internal migration primarily to skilled, educated workers.

Significant changes in the patterns of migration were noticeable during the last three decades of the twentieth century. For non-Spanish migrants, Spain was initially regarded as a transit point for those moving from the south to the north. These step-migrants remained in the country for a short while, prior to moving on to France, Germany, Switzerland, or some other destination in Northern Europe. Attitudes gradually changed and by the mid-1980s the proportion of migrants who decided to settle began to rise. They were attracted by the employment opportunities generated by a decade and a half of economic growth at a rate higher than that of average for the Euro area. The second trend was the increase in return migration. Reverse flows can be traced back to the 1970s. At their height, as between 1974 and 1977, more than 300,000 returned from the pool of Spaniards working abroad. The inflows continued and it is estimated that 650,000 have returned to settle in Spain since 1975 (OECD 2000). Many returned after accepting the incentives offered by some Northern European states to immigrant workers who were willing to leave, others because they had reached retirement age. According to the Social Affairs and Employment Ministry, 48,000 people returned to Spain in 2001, the largest number since 1978, including 11,000 from crisis-hit Argentina and Venezuela. Despite substantial return migration, more than 2 million Spanish nationals were still living abroad in 2002.

Another feature of migration has been the large numbers of foreigners from developed countries who choose to settle in Spain. The country became a magnet for thousands of retired workers and pensioners from northern Europe, attracted by the climate and lifestyle on offer. However, the structure of the foreign resident population underwent a significant transformation from the mid-1980s onward. The number of retirement migrants was quickly overtaken by immigrants of working age as the migrant source countries became more varied. Traditionally, foreign immigrants came from Europe and Latin America, but during the last two decades of the twentieth century considerable diversification occurred in their countries of origin. These recent arrivals from Africa, Asia, and Eastern Europe joined the long-established and largest ethnic group, the Roma, a community that traces its origins back to the fifteenth century. The Roma remain nonintegrated today, representing around 1.4 percent of total population. This study focuses on groups that have arrived since the 1980s.

Spain's emergence as a "new immigration center" owed much to the changes occurring in the structure of the Spanish economy. Rapid service sector expansion, the deregulation of labor markets and new forms of production created jobs at the top and the bottom of labor market. Meanwhile, agriculture—for so long a declining sector with a contracting workforce—was revitalized with the establishment of hot-house production units to meet the demand for year-round fruit and vegetables in the markets of Northern Europe. The burgeoning employment opportunities attracted both highly educated and qualified workers who occupied managerial posts in the expanding high-tech industries and unskilled workers who found ample employment opportunities in the booming agricultural, construction, and tourism industries. Apart from growing numbers of legal immigrants, the scale of undocumented, "illegal" migration has become a signature feature of international migration throughout Southern Europe. For this reason the informal or "black economy" has played a crucial role in determining migratory patterns (Williams & Windebank 1995).

Demographic Information

Immigration to Spain has taken place against a background of significant demographic change. The core features of this transformation include a declining birth rate, an aging population and shrinkage in the average family size. Becoming a net recipient of immigrants has reversed the steep decline in Spain's population noted since the 1980s. The country enjoyed a baby-boom in 1970s, but by the late 1990s Spain was among the EU countries with the lowest fecundity, only marginally above Italy. The lowest levels were reached in 1996, when Spain recorded a fertility rate (number of children per mother) of 1.16.

Twenty years earlier, it had been 2.80. According to provisional INE data for 2003, the rate had risen slightly to 1.30 children per mother, still well below the replacement level for a stable population (INE 2003). Put starkly, Spain faced the prospect of having a population where 4 out of 10 people have reached the retirement age. The declining birth rate was expected to result in a population as low as 28 million by 2050.

In a remarkable turnaround, Spain's National Statistics Office (Instituto Nacional de Estadística, INE) predicted that the population would in fact top 50 million by midcentury. Credit for this reversal must go to the higher fertility among foreign-born women who contributed 12.2 per cent of total births in 2003, up from 8.2 percent in 2001 (INE 2003). As the immigrant community is predominantly comprised of young people, their fertility rate is high. If we look at the average age of the three major immigrant communities, there is a considerable variation that is directly correlated to their reproductive capacity: 44 years for those coming from the EU, 33 years for the Latin Americans, and 29 for the Africans. In 2002, 10.4 percent of all births (43,469) were to a foreign mother, up from 4.9 percent in 1999 (INE 2004b). According to Anuario Estadístico de Extranjería statistics for 2003, over 10 percent of the migrants were under 16 years of age, and 8 out of 10 were aged between 16 and 64, suggesting that they will continue to have an impact on population growth. Although their presence may imply an initial cost in terms of education and health, in the longer term the newly born will make a positive contribution, both as recruits into the labor market and to ensure the future of the pension and welfare systems.

Figures from the Ministry of Labour and Immigration indicate that in 2007 the legally resident foreign population totalled just under 4 million (see Table 10-1). Unofficial estimates for 2008 put the total number at 4.8 million, or 11 percent of the total population. When undocumented migrants (estimated at 400,000) are factored in, the figure rises above 5 million. If we look back a little bit further, we get an idea of just how dramatic the recent acceleration has been. In 1975 there were only 165,000 foreign residents in Spain. Just over a decade later, some 275,000 held a valid residency permit,

Table 10-1. Legally Resident Foreigners, 1998–2007

	Total	% increase
1998	719,647	15.26
1999	801,329	11.35
2000	895,720	11.78
2001	1,109,060	23.82
2002	1,324,001	19.38
2003	1,647,011	24.40
2004	1,977,291	20.05
2005	2,738,932	38.52
2006	3,021,808	10.33
2007	3,979,014	31.68

Source: Anuario Estadístico del Año 2007.

excluding illegal immigrants and the handful of asylum-seekers. Yet by 1995, the numbers had doubled to almost half a million. Having taken 20 years to reach that total, a surge occurred in the late 1990s and there was a four-fold increase between 1998 and 2003. Between 1990 and 2005, 4 million migrants entered Spain with arrivals (half a million per annum) heavily concentrated in the early years of the new century.

In one respect, the upsurge in immigration means that, with regard to the size of its immigrant population, Spain now resembles its EU partners with a profile matching that expected of a modern advanced economy. Even as late as the 1990s, immigrants represented a tiny proportion in relation to the total population, at less than 2 percent, much lower than countries such as Germany, France, Switzerland, and Sweden, where the proportion ranged from 10 to over 20 percent. However, as a result of the new wave of immigration the gap between Spain and its EU partners has closed substantially.

While the growth in the immigrant population has followed an upward curve, it is difficult to be precise about the exact numbers of foreigners because of the existence of a large pool of illegal immigrants living and working in the country. Official sources confess to having little idea as to the true state of affairs with regard to these undocumented migrants or *sin papeles* (OECD 2003). Irregular status is encouraged by a cluster of factors, including the rigidities in the labor market, the strong demand for labor, a thriving black economy that overlaps the formal one, and a cumbersome bureaucracy that causes delays in the processing of residency and work permits. Another reason is that while successive governments pledged to reduce the numbers of undocumented immigrants, some employers were less than vocal in their support. Apart from the blind eye turned by officialdom and the limited work inspections, employers sought to maintain the advantages that undocumented workers undoubtedly bring, including ease of dismissal, lower wages, and the avoidance of tax and social security contributions. In the highly competitive global marketplace some firms found that they could only survive by resorting to this "flexible" labor (Watts 1998). As the numbers increased, migrants without a work permit have sometimes been compelled to seek work in precarious and criminal-related employment such as street vendors and in prostitution, drug dealing, and people-trafficking.

Traditionally, the vast majority of migrants entering Spain came from Europe and Latin America and comprised white, educated Christians. Even as late as the mid-1990s, around half of the foreign residents in Spain were European, principally from the UK, Germany, and Portugal. As already mentioned, the increase in migratory flows since the 1980s transformed the composition of Spain's immigrant population significantly. As the numbers grew, the proportion from non-EU countries increased and the range of source countries diversified to include Africa, principally the Maghreb, Latin America, China, and Eastern Europe. Given their different cultural and religious backgrounds, poorer educational and skills levels, it is true to say that a "Third Worldization" of immigrant flows occurred (Solé & Parella 2003).

The migrant flows can be subdivided by continent and migrant-sending countries (see Table 10-2). From Africa, migrants came from the Maghreb, principally Morocco, Algeria, and Tunisia, accompanied by smaller numbers from sub-Saharan Africa, including Senegal, Nigeria, and the Gambia. The principal source countries in Latin America were Ecuador, Colombia, Peru, Argentina, Cuba, and the Dominican Republic. Smaller numbers originated in Asia, the leading sender countries including China, the Philippines, Pakistan, and Bangladesh. The most recent and increasingly substantial source of supply has come from Eastern Europe,

Table 10-2. Legally Resident Foreigners in Spain by Country of Origin, 2007

Country of Origin	Number
Morocco	648,735
Romania	603,889
Ecuador	395,808
Colombia	254,301
United Kingdom	198,638
Bulgaria	127,058
Italy	124,936
Peru	116,202
Portugal	101,818

Source: Ministerio de Trabajo e Inmigración 2007.

principally Romania, Bulgaria, Poland, Ukraine, and Belarus.

Geographic Concentration

In territorial terms, the resident foreign-born population is concentrated in five autonomous communities, which together accounted for more than 65 percent of the total in 2007 (Ministerio de Trabajo e Inmigración 2007). The breakdown by autonomous community revealed that in 2007 Catalonia (860, 575), Madrid (712,011), Andalusia (504,122), the Valencian Community (409,058), and Murcia (188,597) were the principal poles of attraction. In the capital, one in every ten residents is now foreign, and foreign population density is highest in the Balearic Islands. Smaller numbers settle in rural areas, where they can constitute as much as one-third of the local population in sparsely populated villages; and a tiny proportion are itinerant. Foreign workers concentrate in particular industries, notably construction, agriculture, and hotel and catering, where they constitute 8 percent, 10 percent and 11 percent of the total workforce respectively (La Caixa 2004).

Another feature has been the progressive feminization of migration into Spain. During the early stages, the typical migrant was a young male, principally when Moroccan immigration was at its peak in the late 1980s and early 1990s. However, the pattern began to change after that as the numbers of female migrants, particularly among those coming from Latin America, began to rise. By the turn of the century, women constituted just under half of the foreign worker constituency. Many are of child-bearing age and, as already noted, a growing proportion give birth in Spain, a factor that facilitates their request for residency status. Women migrants are partly responsible for the substantial rise in the female participation rate, fueled by the development of domestic employment and both child and elderly care roles.

Refugees and Asylum Seekers

Spain received a steady trickle of refugees after the end of World War II, principally from the communist countries as well as Cuba, Argentina, Chile, and Uruguay. Traditionally, refugees did not target Spain, and even today Spain receives one of the lowest numbers of applications for political asylum in the EU. The Asylum Law, which dates from 1984 (modified in 1994), guarantees the right to legal and medical assistance, but those denied asylum must leave Spain within two months.

Charting the progress of asylum applications is difficult because, prior to late 1980s, the statistics on the numbers were unreliable. According to the European Council on Refugees and Exiles (ECRE), asylum applications were running at 1,000–2,000 annually. Since then, the numbers have grown steadily. UNHCR figures put the total asylum applications at 9,219 in 2001. This constituted a very small proportion of the 384,334 applications made throughout the EU. At 0.2 per thousand inhabitants, it put Spain well behind Sweden (17.8 per thousand) and Germany (11.0). For this reason, the Spanish authorities have had only limited experience in dealing with resettlement. However, NGOs did spring up to fill the void and provide assistance to the refugees arriving in Spain. As for the composition of those seeking asylum in Spain, over half originated in Latin America, just under 30 percent from Africa and just over 10 percent from Europe, mainly the former Soviet block. In 2001, in terms of gender and country-of-origin, two thirds of the asylum applicants were male, and more than half were Colombians and Cubans. The evidence is that, since the restrictive legislation was tightened up in 1994, the number of successful asylum applications is very small,

normally less than 10 percent of the total number of requests.

Reasons for Leaving Home Country

A sizable and growing literature on international migration has identified the reasons for the emergence of Southern Europe as a "new immigration center" (Baldwin Edwards 1994; King, Fielding, & Black 1997a; King, Lazaridis, & Tsardanidis 2000). The numbers of migrants increased substantially during the latter decades of the last century as the "push" factors have multiplied. Conditions in the migrant-sending countries worsened as population growth, poverty, and unemployment were compounded by political and ethnic conflicts. Inequitable income distribution within the sender country acted as a motivation to emigrate as did the widening differential between Spain's income per capita and that pertaining in the source countries. Interestingly, acute poverty is not always the principal driver in the decision to migrate. There is ample evidence that many migrants are educated, urban dwellers who are far from being the poorest in the source country and as such suffer from relative deprivation (Reyneri 2003). Improved communications and lower travel costs helped to boost the numbers opting to migrate. The existence of labor networks allowed the rapid expansion in the volume of migrants moving from the less developed countries to the European Union. Often, mafias grabbed control of the networks to exploit the lucrative trade in humans. Indeed, the abuses associated with human trafficking are one of the unwelcome features of the new immigration.

Among the "pull" factors, the most significant attractions have been the rapid economic development of Southern Europe and its incorporation into the EU, which made the region an attractive alternative destination to Northern Europe. Strong economic growth triggered changes in labor demand, notably the expansion of "hothouse" agriculture, the success of the tourism industry, and service sector growth in general. Moreover, the rising prosperity and high growth rates achieved since joining the EU in 1986 has converted Spain into a favored destination for economic migrants (Harrison & Corkill 2004).

A number of factors specific to Spain are also relevant. There are the historic and cultural links with the sending countries. Many of the leading source countries were formally part of the Spanish empire, as was the case with Cuba, Ecuador, Morocco, Argentina, Colombia, Peru, the Philippines, and Dominican Republic. The linguistic and cultural closeness goes a long way to explaining the large migrant flows from these former colonial territories. Migrants from Ecuador have demonstrated the fastest growth in recent years, partly in response to the agreement signed between the governments in Madrid and Quito in 2001. In return for the voluntary repatriation of undocumented immigrants, Spain promised to give preferential treatment to Ecuadorians applying for work and residence permits. Geography also played its part. Spain's relatively long coastline and proximity to Africa confers a strategic position as a bridge between Europe and Africa. Another reason was the restrictive immigration policies applied elsewhere in Northern Europe, particularly France, which made Spain a more attractive alternative for North Africans in particular. It gained a reputation because of the relative ease of entry and the abundant job opportunities in either the formal or informal economy available to work-seeking migrants (Martínez Viega 1999). Meanwhile, additional obstacles to entering the United States encouraged ever greater numbers of Latin Americans to select Spain as an alternative destination. For others, like the Argentines, the pressure to emigrate was enhanced by the dire economic conditions in their country. With regard to the Africans, the most important "push" factors that can be identified were the growing poverty, unemployment, and population growth, all of which exerted pressure to leave. In addition, the increasing number of civil wars and conflicts across Africa lies behind the rise in forced migration. In other cases, cultural motives hold sway. The migrants may be seeking political freedoms, or to break free from their family in a traditional society. Then there are economic migrants, motivated by a desire to improve the quality of their lives and those of their families at home by sending back remittances (Corkill 2001b). Here, the role of the

mass media, which transmit images of life in the destination countries, acts as a catalyst in the decision to emigrate.

Since the Maastricht Treaty, migrants from EU countries can work in Spain, while noncommunity migrants require a work permit. For the latter, entry into Spain can take different forms. Some enter on a visa (tourist, temporary residence, or work permit), but overstay once it has expired. Others use false or forged papers supplied in their home country, while a few are rejected asylum seekers who stay on regardless of the state of their application. Significant numbers simply enter the country clandestinely as undocumented migrants and join the ranks of the *sin papeles* (undocumented migrants). Given the large numbers of tourists entering Spain, it is relatively easy for migrants to cross the border. Most avail themselves of existing networks, often involving family or friends already living abroad in the target country, to facilitate the move. The conclusion from most research conducted among migrants in the region is that such networks are crucial influences on destination choice and that they play a vital role during the integration process. Those unable to avail themselves of family reunification or some other connection are often forced to rely on criminal networks. People traffickers smuggle in illegal workers and often supervise their work, extracting payment for the "assistance" given.

Migrants enter Spain by air, land, and sea. Latin Americans and Asians usually arrive by plane, and East Europeans often travel overland in trains, vans, or trucks. The sea-routes are across the Straits of Gibraltar, or by boat from West Africa to the Canaries archipelago. They are transported in small and often unseaworthy craft known as *pateras* or *cayucos*. As a result, some would-be migrants who avail themselves of the clandestine transport network perish in the attempt. Others attempt to enter Spain overland via Ceuta and Melilla, Spain's enclaves in North Africa. Their increasingly desperate efforts were met with a strong response from the authorities, who increased border surveillance and cordoned off the territories by erecting security barriers and watchtowers. As it became more difficult to enter Spain from the North African coast, the migrants turned their attention to the Canary Islands. In 2006, the Islands emerged as a flashpoint for people-smuggling as it quickly became a favored entry-point for Africans from Senegal, Mauritania, and parts of sub-Saharan Africa. The numbers of illegal migrants detained soared from under 2,500 in 2000 to over 32,000 in 2006, as more and more braved the 500-mile journey from Mauritania and other points on the West African coast. With a capacity for only around 5,000, the detention centers were soon overwhelmed by the volume of migrants. In Spain, detention lasts 40 days, after which, if their nationality is not established, they are free to remain in Spain or elsewhere in the EU. This underlines that migration management is more than simply border security. Spain found that it had detained many migrants from countries with which it did not have repatriation.

Readiness to Accept Immigrants

Spain has a brief history as a host country to large-scale immigration, although it can draw on the experiences of many Spaniards who in the past lived and worked abroad in not dissimilar circumstances. The impetus to formulate coherent policies with regard to immigration was two-pronged, coming from the European Union and the government response to public concerns about the perceived impact on the host society. At the governmental level, policy formulation was often tardy and reactive. The dearth of public policies to deal with the phenomenon has meant that the EU context became crucial in determining initiatives to deal with the issue (Corkill 2001a).

As immigration has climbed to the top of the European agenda, pressure has mounted for policies to be harmonized (Geddes 2000). Since Spanish policy developed within the concept of a "Fortress Europe," the focus switched to allowing EU citizens freedom of movement under the Schengen area agreement (1999) while, at the same time, limiting entry to non-EU foreigners and tailoring those who were allowed in to the requirements of the labor market. During its two terms in office (1996–2004), the right-of-center Popular Party (PP) often justified its tighter immigration policy on the grounds that the measures were necessary as part of Spain's responsibility for guarding the EU's southern flank. It explains why the language of law and order predominated in

preference to that of cohesion and integration in official pronouncements on the phenomenon.

To a large degree, public attitudes and perceptions about immigration have been molded by reports and information transmitted in the media. Among the myths nurtured in some of the press is the threat that immigration posed to traditional identities and the threat that immigrants might displace native workers from their jobs, depress earnings, and abuse the social benefit system. Another assumed relationship aired in the media is that between illegal immigration and crime (Corkill 2000). Generally speaking, the racist attitudes that have reemerged in contemporary Europe no longer place as much stress on biological differences, preferring to warn that immigration is a threat to the nation's cultural identity. Such propaganda has influenced public opinion. In its attitude surveys, the CIS (Centro de Investigaciones Sociológicas) revealed a persistent overestimation among the public with regard to immigrant numbers. Research carried out in 2004 revealed that a growing number of Spaniards (53 percent) believe that there are too many immigrants. Yet, research indicates that immigrants do not displace native workers but take up the jobs that Spaniards are no longer prepared to do, whether because of low pay, poor working conditions, low status, or for other reasons. As for cultural identity, immigration has prompted a debate about the pros and cons of a multicultural society and the autonomous community governments often reflect this in the differing integration and social cohesion strategies they adopt.

Frequent reference in the media to an "invasion" by "floods" of immigrants bolsters the image of "the other," leading to negative perceptions of the Islamic and African communities in particular. By stirring up memories of Arab dominance in Spain, the media contributed to the simplistic notion that the battle between Christianity and Islam has been renewed. Although atypical, certain images penetrate deeply into the public consciousness. For example, the racist incidents at Terrassa near Barcelona in June 1999 and at El Ejido in Almeria province in February 2000 were given blanket coverage in the media both in Spain and abroad. The El Ejido riot became etched in the public consciousness as the incident that sparked a *caza del moro* (hunt for the Moor) when Moroccan workers, who comprised over

20 percent of the local population, were racially attacked. The attack was sparked by the murder of a local woman by a mentally disturbed Moroccan, the most recent in a series of killings attributed to immigrants. The police came in for criticism for their tardy reaction to the violence and inability to protect the immigrant community (Azurmendi 2001). Other incidents that gained international notoriety included a traffic accident near Lorca in Murcia in 2001, when twelve Ecuadorians died, and the church protests and sit-ins at Seville and Huelva in June 2002, when North African workers demanded the regularization of their status. There were diplomatic repercussions too. Immigration was one of the issues that led to rising tensions between Spain and Morocco. More oil was poured on troubled waters when an uninhabited island of the North African coast was occupied by Moroccan troops. What became known as the Perejil incident saw relations between Madrid and Rabat reach their nadir during 2002. Diplomatic tensions between the two countries rose once again in November 2007 when King Juan Carlos' visit to Ceuta and Melilla provoked an angry response from Morocco, which disputes sovereignty with Spain over ownership of the territories.

As noted, both the media and the government have nurtured the impression that immigration has become a major political and social problem. As a result, few positive images have been transmitted, and the immigrant is often stigmatized as a job-stealing, social security sponger likely to be involved in criminal activities and deviant behavior. In addition, North Africans continue to be regarded as a terrorist threat, particularly after the Madrid bombings in March 2004. On the other hand, East Europeans, who have arrived in growing numbers since 2000, are generally regarded as one of "us," while the North Africans continue to be treated as the "other." There is evidence that some employers link ethnicity to the quality of the workers they employ. Moroccans are often denigrated as "unproductive" and "conflictual," whereas Latin Americans and East Europeans are regarded more favorably as "disciplined" and "hard working" (Castellanos & Perdreño 2001). In part, employers attribute these characteristics because, as the longer established foreign community, the Moroccans are more aware of their rights, better organized

than other groups and more experienced at articulating demands and extracting concessions in the workplace (Danese 1998). Ethnic segmentation is, then, a strategy designed to deal with the growing stridency of labor demands. Employers rationalize their preferences on the grounds that North Africans do not integrate into the life of the local community, whereas the Latin Americans and East Europeans do so with relative ease (Corkill 2004).

Level of Immigrant Adjustment to the Host Country

Until the 1980s, Spain had little background in terms of policy development to deal with immigration. Initially, labor migration policy was ill-defined and the police were lax in their enforcement. What legislation existed targeted the foreign tourist rather than the migrant worker. Bereft of specialists in immigration matters capable of formulating a national policy on the issue, the Spanish government tended to adopt European objectives and strategies, which leaned strongly toward restriction and exclusion. Consequently, the overemphasis on public order tended to preclude the development of policies that were sensitive to the need for immigration.

Immigration regulation dates from 1985, shortly before Spain joined the European Community, when the first Ley de Extranjería (Foreigners' Law) was introduced. In preparation for taking responsible for the Community's common external border, the government laid down strict requirements with regard to residence and work permits as well as family regrouping. The legislation on asylum seekers was tightened up and, in keeping with Spain's new role as a southern guardian of "Fortress Europe," more resources were allocated to policing and surveillance. The law focused on security and border controls in order to counter terrorists, criminals, and both drug- and people-smugglers. Opponents of the law regarded it as discriminatory and bemoaned the absence of measures to integrate migrants into Spanish society. It did allow undocumented workers to apply for regularization, but in the initial process only 23,000 of 44,000 applications for work or residence permit were granted. This created a growing army of *sin papeles*. Along with a second initiative in 1991–1992, the aim was to uncover the many thousands of migrants who did not appear in the official statistics. Like the previous exercise, it fell well below expectations, as one in four regularized migrants did not renew their residence permit in 1994. The explanation for this failure lies partly in the informal, seasonal, and short-term nature of the jobs undertaken by migrants, particularly those employed in domestic work and agriculture. As a result, immigrants continued to be marginalized with little or no access to social services and welfare provision and with the right to family reunification still unrecognized.

Reform to the Foreigners' Law in 1996 attempted to provide stability for those immigrants who were in the country legally. It established quotas; recognized certain rights, including equality, education, and the law; while a family reunification permit was introduced. Rather than the annual visa renewal system, immigrants were allowed to obtain an extension of two years when they had completed a year's residence. A "permanent work permit" could only be issued if they were able to prove legal residence in Spain for six years. This important measure made immigrants less dependent on employers and more capable of demanding their legal rights.

The January 2000 law attempted to tackle the problem of integration for the documented and undocumented immigrants. The time-span in order to qualify for a permanent residence permit was reduced from six to two years, and the right to vote in elections was conceded. In addition, access to health, education, and legal rights was extended to any undocumented migrant who was signed up to the municipal residence register. Later in 2000, the law was tightened up considerably in order to make a much clearer distinction between the legal and illegal foreigner. In May 2000, immigration matters were taken from the Labour and Social Affairs ministries and transferred to a new Delegación de Gobierno para la Extranjería y la Inmigración (Government Foreigners and Immigration Secretariat) under the Interior ministry. A fourth amendment to the *Ley de Extranjería* reform was approved by Council of Ministers on 16 May 2003, a week prior to nationwide local elections. Not surprisingly, the timing prompted the criticism that immigration was being used for electoral purposes by the incumbent Popular Party government.

Based on the premise that the "capacity for receiving (immigrants) is not unlimited," the new measures introduced fast-track expulsion procedures for illegal immigrants and expanded the range of offenses to include people-smuggling and profiting from it. According to the immigration minister, more than 92,000 illegal foreigners, including over 32,000 Romanians, were repatriated during 2003, and 677 human trafficking networks were dismantled. The policy came under serious attack from NGOs and other organizations working on behalf of immigrants because of the clear distinction made between the documented and undocumented migrant and additional obstacles erected to integration, such as limiting access to education.

Residence and work permits were replaced by visas as part of a drive by the Spanish government to simplify its procedures and ensure that migrants can only be legally employed in Spain when they are contracted in their country of origin under the yearly quota system. The idea was that a visa obtained in Spanish consulates abroad would serve as residence and work permit, eventually eliminating applications made to the police and interior ministry. Indications were that the visa requirement had begun to have an effect. Between 2001 and June 2004, official figures show that 30,829 foreigners were denied entry into Spain, almost one third of them Ecuadorians.

In practice, the new measures meant that the authorization for migrants to work and reside in Spain was dependent on their continuous employment. To some, this left them at the mercy of their employers, deterring potential complaints about working conditions and pay. Other critics went even further, arguing that the policy converted foreigners into a disposable labor reserve and left them little better than "bonded labor." It ignored the obstacles often faced by refugees in securing an "employment contract" in their country of origin and the difficulties they confronted under hostile regimes. Moreover, there was ample evidence that the quota policy had not operated as expected. Vacancies for both long-term and seasonal jobs have remained unfilled, despite the estimated 300,000 illegal immigrants in the country.

In 2000, the Interior ministry launched the GRECO program initiative to ensure the desired "controlled immigration." It drew a sharper distinction between documented and undocumented migrants, tightening up the procedures for expulsion. To this end, repatriation agreements were signed with a number of countries, including Algeria, Morocco, and Nigeria. However, immigrant's civil rights and their access to social services were improved. In another positive development, the four-year plan tried to switch the focus to the local level in an attempt to facilitate the integration process (Ortega Pérez 2003). In order to expedite the hiring of immigrant workers and achieve symmetry between immigrant numbers and labor market requirements, a series of bilateral agreements to regulate admissions were signed with the major sender countries, including Morocco, Ecuador, Poland, Romania, Colombia, and the Dominican Republic (OECD 2003). An example was the Migration Agreement (*Convenio de Flujos Migratorios*) signed in Quito in February 2001, which set out the conditions that must be fulfilled by workers en route to Spain in search of temporary or permanent employment. Any country willing to sign the agreement was promised "preferential treatment" in the future. The "sugar on the pill" to induce employers to accept quotas based on labor requirements was to be the provision of funds for training, small business support, and social integration.

As already indicated, an annual quota had first been introduced in 1993 to regulate non-EU immigration. The aim was to offer work permits to fill jobs that were shunned by Spanish workers. Given the increase in the level of education among the Spanish workforce, many are unwilling to take on certain types of employment. The quota was recognition that high levels of unemployment among the native workforce did not guarantee that more menial and less well paid job vacancies would be filled (EIRO 2002). It was adjusted from 20,000 in 1993 to 30,000 in 1999. In 2002, reforms were made to the system requiring the government to set annual quotas for

foreign workers. Work permits could only be granted after the Instituto Nacional de Empleo (National Employment Institute) determined that no unemployed local workers are available to fill the vacancies. Despite the fact that the figure set (32,000) failed to meet labor market requirements, the government reduced the quota still further to 24,000 in 2003. While the authorities attempted to use the quota to limit further immigration, the number of migrants entering Spain continued its inexorable rise.

Periodic amnesty laws have permitted illegal immigrants to apply for legal status. Four such "regularization" processes have taken place. In the first one (1985–1986), 30,181 residence and work permits were issued; in 1991, 109,135 permits; in 1996, 21,300 people benefited; and in the extraordinary amnesty of 1999, a further 70,000 permits were approved. Much larger numbers were regularized in 2000 and 2001, when about 380,000 immigrants were granted papers. However, as the permits issued were only valid initially for one year, many immigrants soon joined the ranks of the illegal residents once again (Ortega Pérez 2003). Despite calls for more amnesties to clear the remaining illegal immigrant population, the Aznar government steadfastly stuck to its policy of tailoring immigration to labor market needs through the annual quota system. Given this rigid approach and the constant stream of new arrivals, hundreds of thousands of immigrant workers remained undocumented with little prospect of obtaining residency papers. However, there were signs of more flexibility at the regional level, where responsibility for education, health, housing, and social services rests. In a parallel development, leading migrant-receiving regions began to develop their own policies for integrating their expanding immigrant communities. Where immigrants are required to learn a second language as in Catalonia, the regional parliament, the Generalitat, adopted integration plans by which the children of immigrants are considered Catalans and receive compulsory schooling (CC.OO 2003). Madrid and Andalusia now allocate a large share of their budgets to providing services for immigrants, including the provision of social centres, family reunification, language, improving the supply of affordable housing for rent and legal support.

Immigration Amnesty

The change of government following the 2004 general election prompted a significant shift in the direction of Spain's immigration policy. The new Socialist administration led by José Luis Rodríguez Zapatero attempted to tackle the problems generated by the rising numbers of illegal immigrants, estimated by the Elcano Royal Institute to have reached 1.4 million (Chislett 2005). In what amounted to an amnesty, the new measures permitted illegal residents who have a job contract and could provide proof that they had lived in Spain for six months prior to February 2005 to regularize their status by obtaining residency papers.

The shift to a more liberal approach met with criticism from the opposition Popular Party which had been responsible for the tougher line on immigration while in office. Concern was also expressed among EU members who feared that Spain would attract even more immigrants, hoping to take advantage of the amnesty. Once having obtained their residency permits they would be free to move anywhere within the EU. Calls from Brussels for greater symmetry among member states with regard to policy and legislation on the issue were met with hollow laughter in Madrid. The government countered critics at home and abroad by arguing that they had inherited such a deteriorating and untenable situation that decisive action had been required to tackle labour market irregularities, including the large informal or shadow economy and abuses perpetrated by unscrupulous employers. Clearly, the state also expected to benefit when people work legally, not least because of the boost to tax revenues.

When the three-month amnesty period ended in early May 2005, about 700,000 illegal immigrants had taken advantage of the scheme. In practice, this meant that large numbers of foreign workers who had previously worked illegally were now fully integrated into Spain's economy and society. Ecuadorians, Moroccans, Colombians and Romanians were the largest groups among the applicants. The government declared its intention to use its labour inspection regime to take a tough line against employers who continued to use illegal workers.

Once the economic downturn began to be reflected in rising unemployment during 2008, the Socialist Party government reversed its relatively liberal policy and adopted a much tougher stance on immigration. Measures were proposed to limit the number of foreigners working or seeking employment in Spain. They included an offer of unemployment pay in a lump sum in return for a commitment to repatriate and not to return for three years. In another measure to stem the flows, changes to the family reunification law increased from one year to five the period that immigrants had to be resident before they could bring their parents and in-laws to Spain.

Resources Allocated to Policing and Exclusion

Substantial resources have been channelled into upgrading Spain's control of its maritime frontier, particularly along the Mediterranean coast. To improve surveillance, the European Union helped fund a SIVE (Integrated System for External Vigilance) to combat illegal immigration. Radars and night vision cameras enabled frontier police to track any vessel at all times. Tougher measures included the opening of detention centres opened for unauthorized workers prior to any possible deportation and a greater number of inspections at work to uncover unauthorized workers. Enhanced policing did apparently staunch some of the flow across the Straits but may have inadvertently diverted some would-be immigrants to the alternative entry-point in the Canaries. The overall conclusion must be that border controls may be less effective than the pull effect of an underground economy in determining the extent of the migrant inflows.

Immigrant Contribution and Drain

On balance, the receiver country usually benefits economically from immigration, particularly with regard to the labour supply and the social security accounts. Immigrant workers are paid lower wages, do jobs that natives shun, and are often highly motivated. A study by the trade union, Comisiones Obreras (CC.OO), estimated that immigrant workers contributed between 2.5 percent and 4 percent to Spain's GDP. They made an important contribution to regional development, helping reduce regional income disparities, notably where horticulture and tourism, which rely heavily on immigrants, act as the dynamos of economic growth. Generally speaking, the economic effects of immigration depend on the characteristics of the immigrants. Usually, there are short-term benefits because the overwhelming majority are of working age. However, as they get older, they have children and require social services and other support. In social terms, the danger is that unlimited immigration can create an underclass that is often marginalized from the rest of society and discriminated against (Colectivo IOE 1998). Although unemployment rates among non-EU immigrants are higher than among Spanish nationals, they do not represent a significant drain on unemployment benefits. This is because the majority are in temporary jobs with frequent interruptions in their employment record, which effectively disqualifies them for access to unemployment benefits (OECD 2003).

The labor market is normally the primary interface between the immigrant and the host society. In the case of Spain, immigrants play a vital role in the lower echelons of what is a highly segmented labor market. A cluster of factors influence their insertion into the labor market. The first is the employment structure. Spain's economy is notable for the large number of small businesses and the high quotient of the self-employed. This means that employment opportunities still occur predominantly in the low-skilled jobs and in small, family-run firms. It explains why employers look to foreign labor, despite the existence of a pool of educated jobless native workers. The second is the existence of a large informal economy, estimated by the European Employment Observatory to have reached around 22 percent of GNP (EEO 2004), that provides an access route into employment, albeit often of the temporary and low-paid variety. Among Spaniards, only a small number of the pool of the young unemployed are forced to accept any type of work in order to survive because they live at home, where there is already usually at least one breadwinner. As a consequence, they can afford to wait for the right sort of job to come along.

Among immigrant workers, there is clear specialization by industry according to their different countries of origin. By sector of activity, the greatest number of immigrant workers is to be found in low-skill occupations throughout the economy. Typically, they are employed as agricultural laborers, construction or manufacturing workers, or in domestic work and street selling. Those involved in domestic service congregate in the larger cities, often living in their employer's home. Later, they may try to improve their conditions by moving to a job in a hotel or restaurant, doing cleaning work, caring for children or the elderly, and so forth. For Spain's primary sector, as already noted, migrant labor has become a vital component in its revival and success. It is mainly Africans who have gradually replaced local agricultural laborers in seasonal work. Adopting the centuries-old patterns of itinerant workers, some of the migrants follow the harvesting season from one region to the next.

Integration: A Plural Spain?

Even for immigrants who do not have legal status, every incentive exists for them to register with the local authority in order to gain access to services such as education, health care, and unemployment benefit. For this reason, the numbers of immigrants affiliated to the social security system has been growing steadily. However, many still inhabit the social margins. They are found in the most insecure and lowly paid employment, live in the more deprived areas in inferior housing, and often suffer rejection by the rest of society (OECD 2003). The reluctance to take advantage of the opportunities on offer is explained in part by fear and ignorance about the rights of foreign workers, a product of the short time that many of the immigrants have been in the country. Another reason is the lack of associations to facilitate integration into the host society and the confusion derived from the frequent changes to the law. Invariably, costs in terms of health are associated with the migratory experience. Among the potential negative effects on migrant health are changes in diet, working conditions (many work more than 50 hours per week), family, and status, all of which can cause psychological and other problems.

Since the 1990s, there has been a substantial increase in the number of immigrants entering the education system. The total foreign student population from primary to university level grew from 73,510 in 1996–1997 to 555,575 in 2005–2006. Provisional figures for 2007 indicated another steep increase to over 630,000. Demand has grown because of the high incidence of women, some of them pregnant when they arrive, and the family reunion policy. When they enrol their children in junior and secondary schools, non-Spanish speaking immigrant families often confront an array of problems, including the linguistic deficiency, cultural and religious differences, and so forth. Upon entry into the education system, they place a burden on the school infrastructure, not least because of their spatial concentration. In addition, there exists a pool of foreign students with poor prior educational backgrounds who are not enrolled in the secondary school system. Their existence was confirmed by a survey conducted by the Comisiones Obreras in 2002, which found that only 18 percent of African immigrant children in the 12 to16 age group attended secondary school.

During the school year 2003–2004, some 5 percent of the children enrolled in Spain's primary and secondary education system were from foreign families. More than half of them enrolled in schools in Catalonia and Madrid. In response to the demand some schools have blocked immigrant entry, citing a lack of space and resources. Others claim that they do not have enough trained teachers to bring their level of Spanish up to scratch. The scale of the problem is indicated by the fact that national illiteracy has started to edge upward after decades of decline, principally because of the immigrant population. According to the Ministry of Education, Culture, and Sport, illiteracy has risen to 2.7 percent of the total population. Of course, the danger exists that the schools merely reproduce their version of a segmented society. In response, the government has promoted cultural awareness programs to assist the integration process, but it did not help that the debate about the appropriate models of integration (multiculturalism, segregation,

assimilation, etc.) has only just begun. Meanwhile, tensions are generated by issues such as the wearing of the hijab. In 2002 a Moroccan girl, Fátima Elidrisi, was denied access to education after insisting on wearing traditional Muslim clothing when attending school. Other faith-related conflicts have been sparked by food, timetables, the calendar, and so forth, while on occasions Spaniards have accused immigrants of bringing disease and crime into local schools and communities.

In order to alleviate the burden on schools within the immigrant catchment area, one approach has been to divide the immigrant children among the public-funded colleges in a region. Another solution has been to offer "immersion" courses to help them improve their knowledge of Spanish and overcome their linguistic disadvantage. NGOs are also on hand to help out, including among others SOS Racismo, Colectivo IOE, and the trade unions. These organizations play a key role in the battle to maintain immigrant cultural identity and to integrate them into society. In some cases, they offer evening classes in Arabic and Arab culture for the children of Maghrebi migrants.

Conclusion

In many respects, the sudden appearance of immigration on the policy agenda caught Spain unawares. This is hardly surprising when, in a few short years, a country of emigrants became a receptor society. In such a fast-moving area, the authorities struggled to develop effective plans and mechanisms to deal with the challenges and often failed to consult interested parties such as the trade unions and the autonomous communities in the process. The policies adopted failed to stem the inflows of migrants and only tentatively initiated the integration process, often leaving Spain with the worst of both worlds. Inevitably, the paradoxes began to surface as Spain's EU "gatekeeper" role clashed with the national demand for cheap, flexible imported labor to lubricate the economy. So, the ideal of integration clashed with the preference for a restrictive regime that, above all, favored temporary immigration. Nor have policies yet been synchronized across the board to facilitate immigrant integration. The authorities have been slow to implement housing and land policy reforms that would boost the rental property market and expand social housing for low-paid workers, including immigrants.

In future, a balance will have to be struck between the advantages migrants bring and the cost of providing services for them. The Spanish government needs to explain to its people that immigration can benefit the national interest, even during an economic recession, when rising unemployment suggests otherwise. The evidence from countries with longer histories of immigration is that temporary migration often converts into permanent residence. Only by recognizing this reality and making appropriate investment decisions can the process of social integration begin in earnest.

Notes

Acronyms

CIS	Centro de Investigaciones Sociologicas (Socio- logical Research Centre)
CCOO	Comisiones Obreras (Workers' Commissions)
ECRE	European Council on Refugees and Exiles
EEO	European Employment Observatory
EU	European Union
GDP	Gross Domestic Product
GRECO	Global Programme to Regulate and Coordinate Foreigners and Immigration in Spain
INE	Instituto Nacional de Estadística (National Statistics Institute)
INEM	Instituto Nacional de Empleo (National Employment Institute)
NGOs	Nongovernmental Organizations
OECD	Organization for Economic Cooperation and Development
PP	Partido Popular (Popular Party)
SIVE	Integrated System for External Vigilance

References

Arango, J. (2000), "Becoming a country of immigration at the end of the twentieth century: The case of Spain." In R. King, G. Lazaridis, & C. Tsadanidis (eds.), *Eldorado or Fortress? Migration in Southern Europe*, Basingstoke, UK: Macmillan, pp. 253–276.

Azurmendi, M. (2001), "Inmigración y conflicto en el Ejido," *Claves de Razón Práctica*, 116, pp. 8–17.

Baldwin-Edwards, M., & Arango, J. (eds.), (1999), *Immigrants and the Informal Economy in Southern Europe*, London: Frank Cass.

Castellanos, M. L., & Pedreño, A. (2001), "Desde El Ejido al accidente de Lorca," *Sociologia del Trabajo*, 42, pp. 3–31.

Chislett, W. (2005), *Inside Spain 9*. Madrid: Real Instituto Elcano.

Colectivo IOE, Angel del Prado, M., Actis, W., Pereda, C., & Pérez Molina, R. (1998), *Labour Market Discrimination against Migrant Workers in Spain*, Geneva: International Labour Organization.

Corkill, D. (2000), "Race, immigration, and multiculturalism in Spain." In B. Jordan & R. Morgan-Tamosunas (eds.), *Contemporary Spanish Cultural Studies*, London: Arnold, pp. 48–57.

Corkill, D. (2001a), "Immigration, the Ley de Extranjería and the labour market in Spain," *International Journals of Iberian Studies*, 14, 3, pp. 148–156.

Corkill, D. (2001b), "Economic migrants and the labour market in Spain and Portugal," *Ethnic & Racial Studies*, 24, 5, pp. 828–844.

Corkill, D. (2004), "Immigrants and the labour market in Spain: The Case of Murcia," unpublished paper.

Cornelius, W., (1994), "Spain: The uneasy transition from labour exporter to labor importer." In W. A. Cornelius, P. L. Martin, & J. F. Hollifield (eds.), *Controlling Immigration: A Global Perspective*, Stanford, CA: Stanford University Press.

Danese, G. (1998), "Transnational collective action in Europe: The case of migrants in Italy and Spain," *Journal of Ethnic and Migration Studies*, 24, 4, pp. 715–733.

EEO (2004, May), *Monthly Labour Market Update*.

EIRO (2002, 15 November), "Government toughens policy on labour immigration," European Industrial Relations Observatory.

Geddes, A. (2000), *Immigration and European Integration: Towards Fortress Europe?* Manchester, UK: Manchester University Press.

Harrison, R. J., & Corkill, D. (2004), *Spain: A Modern European Economy*, Aldershot, UK: Ashgate.

INE (2003), *Notas de Prensa*, Madrid: INE.

INE (2004a), *Notas de Prensa*, Madrid: INE.

INE (2004b), *Extranjeros en España*, Madrid: INE.

INE (2005), *Notas de Prensa*, Madrid: INE.

King, R., Fielding, A., & Black, R. (1997a), "The international migration turnaround in Southern Europe." In R. King and R. Black (eds.), *Southern Europe and the New Immigrations*, Brighton, UK: Sussex Academic Press, pp. 1–26.

King, R., Fielding, A., & Black, R. (eds.) (1997b), *Southern Europe and the New Migration*, Brighton: Sussex Academic Press.

King, R., Lazaridis, G., & Tsardanidas, C. (eds.) (2000), *Eldorado or Fortress? Migration in Southern Europe*, Basingstoke, UK: Macmillan.

La Caixa (2004, May), *Informe Mensual.*

Martinez Viega, U. (1999), "Immigrants in the spanish labour market." In : M. Baldwin Edwards, & J. Arango (eds.), *Immigrants and the Informal Economy in Southern Europe,* London: Frank Cass, pp. 105–128.

OECD (2000), *Trends in International Migration*, Paris: OECD.

OECD (2003), *Economic Surveys: Spain*, Paris: OECD.

Ortega Pérez, N. (2003), "Spain: Forging an immigration policy," Migration Information Source (migrationinformation.org).

Reyneri, E. (2003), "Illegal immigration and the underground economy," *National Europe Centre Paper*, No. 18.

Solé, C., & Parella, S. (2003), "The labour market and racial discrimination in Spain," *Journal of Ethnic and Migration Studies*, 29, 1, pp. 121–140.

Watts, J. R. (1998) "Strange bedfellows: How Spanish labor union leaders and employers find common ground on immigration," *Policy Studies Journal*, 26, 4, pp. 657–675.

Williams, C. C., & Windebank, J. (1995), "Black market work within the European Community: Peripheral work for peripheral localities?" *International Journal of Urban & Regional Research* 19, 1, pp. 22–39.

11

Australia

The World in One Place

Mel Gray and Kylie Agllias

I—Mel—came to Australia nine years ago when I left South Africa where I was born. My parents were part of South Africa's colonial history, my mother being English and my father French. Thus transition to life in Australia was relatively smooth given the European connection across the Pacific between Africa and Australia. Prior to leaving South Africa, "the healing work of the Truth and Reconciliation Commission (TRC) as it uncovered the nature, extent and causes of gross violations of human rights during the apartheid years [had just ended. It was] . . . a critical event in South Africa's peaceful transition to democracy [which] . . . facilitated reconciliation . . . laying the foundations for the reconstruction of [a new nonracial] society" (Gray and Mazibuko 2002: 1). In Australia the Stolen Generations Inquiry had attempted to do the same but fell short of the then Prime Minister John Howard's saying "sorry" to the Aboriginal people. This was Australia as I found it, a country with an ambivalent relationship with its Indigenous Peoples and an even more contentious one with new immigrants, especially those attempting to enter as refugees or asylum seekers. So in my first years in Australia, I witnessed the arrival of the boat people, the sensational and erroneous children overboard story, the Tampa

crisis, the controversy of mandatory detention, riots and hunger strikes in detention centers, and so on.

When I was first asked to write this chapter on immigration in Australia, my first reaction was "what do I know about this?" Then it struck me that I knew a lot since I officially became an Australian citizen on Australia Day, January 26, 2003. Elsewhere I have described citizenship as "a kind of mutual acceptance marking the point at which people settle and are accepted in new environments" (Gray and Aga Askeland 2002). My colleague and cowriter, when reflecting on my question as to "where she came from," said she has a British heritage. Bearing in mind her name was Agllias, she also replied that her husband, Jim, was "Greek." She wondered why she always replies "he is Greek" when he was born in Australia. Anyway, she and her husband discussed this and it is something that he says he and others with his background have always done because it is expected of them. As a child he said he would remark that he was Greek simply because others wouldn't believe that he was Australian and the migrant kids' appearance did stand out. He says this has changed as an adult. Now people aren't asking because they think he was born elsewhere but because they are

153

interested in his background. People want to know about his ancestry and the things that he knows. He has never thought of this question as offensive (as an adult), rather he is made to feel as if he has something "unique" to offer. This makes one wonder whether this is how other immigrant groups feel in Australia and whether "assimilation" or "adaptation" is something all Australians, and not just immigrants, experience.

This is the human side to immigration. What really interests me as an immigrant, however, is that people find it easier to articulate Greek, Asian, or Italian culture, and often food provides a vehicle for this, yet they do not find it as easy to articulate what Australian culture is. Is it backyards and barbies, utes and mates, a vegemite sandwich, a "gidday mate" greeting, "fair dinkum," or giving everyone "a fair go"? Unfortunately, the media paint Australia as unfriendly when good "neighborliness" is afforded to most new arrivals. It is not by accident that Australia's favourite soap opera is called *Neighbours* for this was surely my introduction to Australian hospitality. We have great neighbors. They connect you and make you street smart. They give you the name of a good plumber and the best electrician. They tell you the good places to go and how to get the best out of your dollar. These daily experiences for new arrivals are a far cry from the images of Australia conveyed in the media.

Like many countries in the West, then, as a consequence first of colonization and later of planned immigration, the vast majority of Australia's population comprises immigrants, and immigration in Australia has always been subject to strict legal and administrative control, which, according to Richmond and Lakshmana (1976), is designed to preserve ideological purity and maintain security, an issue which has gained increasing prominence post 9/11. As we shall see, immigration has proved extremely difficult to control, first with maintaining Australia's Anglo-Celtic heritage, then with pursuing nondiscriminatory practices while, at the same time, trying to balance the ethnic composition of the population with economic needs, and most recently trying to protect the country from a perceived terror threat.

These broad periods in Australia's immigration history parallel those in most Western, predominantly English-speaking countries. First came the period of nation-building, which led to an undisputed preference for the selection of immigrants in terms of "their proximity to the predominant ethnic character of the receiving society" (Joppke 2005: 20). As we shall see, in Australia this was the period of the assimilationist white Australia policy from the beginning of Federation in 1901 until its abolition in 1973. There followed a period of nondiscriminatory immigration policy under the protective umbrella of multiculturalism, which persists today though the thorny question of asylum seekers, complicated by the events of 9/11 looked set to threaten Australia's image of itself as a country in which diverse cultures live together harmoniously. Two key events marked significant changes to Australian immigration policy since Federation, one was the threat of the so-called Asian invasion brought about by the relaxation of discriminatory assimilationist policies and the second was the rise of Islamophobia in the aftermath of 9/11. But there are signs of hope that Australians are coming to their senses despite pockets of racialism and persistent media negativity in relation to asylum seekers (Dunn et al. 2007).

Chronology of Immigration to Australia

Richmond and Lakshmana (1976) classify receiving countries into passive and active recruiters of immigrants. Countries that achieve control mainly through issuing temporary visas, as is the case with most countries in Europe, fit the first category. However, countries like Australia have a large landmass relative to the size of their population and tend to actively promote immigration while retaining a high degree of selectivity. In this respect, Australia is no different from many other developed Western countries. In sum, its immigration policy is characterized by:

Progressive liberalization of admission criteria gradually removing racial and national criteria of eligibility.

Selection related more systematically to the educational, technical and professional qualifications of applicants and to occupational demand in the receiving country.

Increased opposition to immigration from professional groups and educated classes, particularly those supporting zero population growth on environmental and ecological grounds.

Government-sponsored studies to review immigration policies in the light of broader questions of population growth and future development (Richmond and Lakshmana 1976: 184–185).

Against this backdrop, we might view developments in immigration to Australia over foddur main historical periods: (1) the early years to Federation; (2) the period of the white Australia policy from 1901 to 1973; (3) the recent past from 1981 to 2001; and (4) post 9/11 to now. The main events in Australia's immigration history are summarized in Table 11-1.

Early History in Brief

Any history of immigration in Australia has to examine the relationship between the million or so Indigenous Peoples who had inhabited the continent for an estimated 132,000 years prior to colonization and the settler population. Today this pre- and postcolonial history is widely contested, and fierce debate rages between Indigenous and settler accounts of Australia's history (Bunbury 1998; Coleman and Higgins 2000; Manne 2001; Poole 1999; Reynolds 1999). It awaits resolution and reconciliation with Indigenous Australians, though Prime Minister Kevin Rudd's apology to the Indigenous Peoples of Australia on February 13, 2008, has done a

Table 11-1. Chronology of Australian Immigration

Date	Event
1788	British convicts arrive in Australia, a land the populated by Indigenous Peoples for over 32,000 years. Indigenous Peoples numbered an estimated 500,000 to one million people, comprising 500 tribes with different customs and languages prior to European colonization (De Lepervanche 1979; Earle and Fopp 1999; Poole 1999)
1848	The Australian population reaches close to a half a million people primarily through immigration
1850	The "gold-rush" brings an influx of self-funded immigrants from England, Ireland, Scotland, and North America seeking their fortune in Australia. During the gold rush, the Australian population doubles from half a million in 1852 to one million in 1858 and the gender imbalance evens out.
	Influx of Chinese immigrants leads to fears that the white race could be swamped by the "Yellow Peril" but most return with their newfound wealth to China and, ironically, are castigated for betraying the settler-pioneer spirit (Yarwood 1968)
1858	Population doubled during the gold rush to a million and early gender imbalances even out
1861	Chinese immigrants constitute the second-largest immigrant group, totaling 3.4 percent of the Australian population, and eastern states introduce legislation to restrict Chinese immigration
1863	First shipment of South Sea Islanders—known as "kanakas" or "kanaks"—is hired as indentured labor for work on Queensland cotton and sugar plantations
1868	168,000 convicts had been shipped to Australia and jailers became the first free settlers (Jupp 1998)
1884	Royal Commission investigates the recruitment of Polynesian labor. Many are found to have no clear idea of the contracts they have entered into.
1890	The importation of "kanaka" labor is declared illegal
1892	A ten-year extension is granted to "kanaks" to allow more orderly development of the sugar industry
1901	Beginning of Federation in 1901. Federal government assumes responsibility for immigration and introduces the Immigration Restriction Act (1901), later referred to as the "White Australia" Policy. Kanaks trade again banned. Overseas-born make up 22.7 percent of the Australian population, which is nearing four million. Most are from the UK (79%) with <5 percent from Germany, China, and New Zealand.
1904	"Kanaks" declared illegal and all were to be repatriated by the end of 1906 (Yarwood 1968).
1905	The population reaches four million, i.e., just under 20 percent of Australia's current population of 21 million
1945	The Australian Labour Party establishes the Federal Department of Immigration
1947	Australian population is 7.5 million, with 10% born overseas and one percent Aboriginal
1956	Token steps are taken to allow eligibility for naturalization by those who had already settled in Australia and remained for 15 years—and admission for permanent residence of non-Europeans' immediate relatives.
1964	Rules governing entry of people of mixed racial descent are eased, though assisted passage still favors immigrants from Britain and Europe (Richmond and Lakshmana 1976).

(Continued)

Table 11-1. (Continued)

Date	Event
1966	15-year waiting period for citizenship is reduced to five year's residence
1971	Australian population reaches 12.8m
1973	Repeal of White Australia Policy introduced in 1901 and abolition of ethnic discrimination
1975	Vietnam War ends and Australia opens its doors to more than 20,000 boat people. Commonwealth Parliament passes Racial Discrimination Act.
1978	Galbally report defines multiculturalism and guides postarrival migrant services and programs, including ethnic broadcasting service (Jupp 2007)
1982	Assisted passages end (after 150 years).
1984	Australia became the world's major receiving country for refugees in per capita terms, having by this year accepted almost 100,000 Indochinese refugees (Joppke 2005). In the same year Geoffery Blainey "attacks multiculturalism and criticizes level of Asian immigration" (Jupp 2007: 221)
1988	Fitzgerald report endorses a shift to an economic focus in immigration.
1989	Temporary visas issued to Chinese (mainly students) in Australia due to Tienanmen Square incident. Mandatory detention centers established for asylum seekers
1996	Humanitarian program set at 12,000. Population 17.5 million
1997	Numbers of immigrants in the skill stream surpass family stream entrants
1999	"New points system favours skilled migrants with Australian experience or qualifications" (Jupp 2007: 223)
2001	Census reveals there are 280,000 Australian Muslims, 1.5 percent of the population. "Pacific Solution" legislation removes offshore islands from Australia's protection zone. This is a response to the "Tampa" incident.
2002	Protests at detentions centers and public debate about the treatment of asylum seekers commence (Jupp 2007)
2004	By 2004, 620,000 refugees and displaced people had resettled in Australia (Taylor 2004)
2005	Antiterrorism legislation increases powers of search, arrest, and detention
2006	Australia's population is just below 20 million, with 30 percent of residents born overseas
2007	Twenty-question Australian citizenship test introduced. Department name changed to Department of Immigration and Citizenship.
2008	On July 29, 2008 the Minister for Immigration and Citizenship, Chris Evans, announced a new direction in immigration detention policy which heralds a fundamental shift in immigration detention policy, away from the requirement that all unlawful noncitizens be detained, toward a presumption that detention will occur as a last resort and for the shortest practicable period.

great deal to heal this rift. However, there can be no denying that Australia's assimilationist policies have resulted in "the suppression and disruption of Aboriginal culture and the annihilation of a large proportion of the Aboriginal population" (Seitz and Foster 1985: 416). This history has wreaked havoc in the lives of Indigenous Peoples and remains an ever-present feature of the Australian sociopolitical landscape (see Briskman 2008).

The White Australia Policy (1901–1973)

Historically, with regard to immigration, Australia has shown a strong preference for British immigrants and failing this, for immigrants from selected European countries (Richmond and Lakshmana 1976). Thus Seitz and Foster (1985: 416) note that "from its inception as a white settlement, Australia's race and ethnic relations have been based on the assumption of British racial and cultural superiority." Some argue that Australia grew into a multicultural society by default rather than by design, since the original aim of its immigration policy was to create a homogeneous society comprising mainly people of British origin. From the outset, quotas were set to achieve this goal. The white Australia policy introduced at Federation in 1901 remained in force until its repeal in 1973 and led to this period's being classified as one of assimilationism and exclusivism, which resulted in highly restrictive immigration policies and practices (Lack and Templeton 1995; Seitz and Foster 1985). Willard (1978) believes that it was fear of Asian immigration that drew the colonies together and contributed significantly to the formation of the Commonwealth of Australia. As evidence of this, the first legislation debated and passed in the new Federal Parliament was the Immigration Restriction Act of 1901.

In the immediate postwar years defense featured prominently in the immigration agenda with perceived threats from China and Japan especially (Richmond and Lakshmana 1976). Thus vigorous attempts were made to attract permanent settlers and in 1945, the Australian Labor Party, one of Australia's main political parties, established the Federal Department of Immigration to maintain a purposeful immigration program with the aim of increasing Australia's population by one percent annually. In the ten-year period between 1945 and 1955, over a million immigrants settled in Australia, including 170,000 displaced people from central and eastern Europe fleeing fascist and communist regimes who arrived between 1947–1953 (Kunz 1971). Initially, the government offered assisted passage to former servicemen from Britain and Poland, but when it could not attract enough British immigrants—so as to preserve its Anglo-Celtic core culture—the immigration net was widened to include displaced people from Eastern Europe and later from North America, the Netherlands, and Norway (Collins 1988; Richmond and Lakshmana 1976). However, the main countries of origin of immigrants arriving between 1949 and 1959 were Britain, Italy, Germany, the Netherlands, and Greece.

The settlement policies of the postwar years were characterized by a virulent pursuit of assimilation through naturalization so that immigrants would integrate into Australian society: "In the immediate post World War II period, naturalization was officially taken to be one of the key indicators of successful assimilation" (Seitz and Foster 1985: 415). This meant that new immigrants should, just as was required of Aboriginal people before them, "give up their language, behaviour, norms, loyalties and affiliations and change even everyday habits acquired in their country of origin" (Kovacs and Cropley 1975: 15).

Throughout the nineteenth and early twentieth centuries, Australia pursued its "white" Australia assimilationist policy, showing explicit discrimination against those whom it was believed would not easily integrate into Australian society, especially Asians. It was feared that nonnaturalized, unassimilated immigrants would form enclaves with un-Australian tendencies (Kunz 1988). But as Australia developed diplomatic relations with neighboring Asian countries in the British Commonwealth, this attitude toward Asians changed, to some extent. In time, Australia began to cooperate with these Asian countries in mutually beneficial defense agreements and economic development. Increasing trade, the growth of tourism, and a growing number of Asian students studying in Australia soon led to a more sympathetic attitude and relaxation of the "white Australia" policy. Still Australia remained cautious in its immigration policies, taking token steps in 1956 to allow eligibility for naturalization by those who had already settled in Australia and admission for permanent residence of non-Europeans' immediate relatives.

The 1960s saw the gradual dismantling of the white Australia policy and the easing of racial restrictions as increasing numbers of Asian immigrants left Australia and European immigrants proved difficult to attract. Immigration requirements increasingly focused on applicants' qualifications and ability to contribute to the economy and integrate into the Australian way of life. Though the rules governing entry of people of mixed racial descent were eased in 1964, assisted passage still favored immigrants from Britain and Europe (Richmond and Lakshmana 1976). In 1966, the 15-year waiting period was reduced to five years but it was still not automatic that non-Europeans admitted on temporary visas could stay permanently.

In 1973, the white Australia policy was repealed and ethnic discrimination clauses removed from immigration requirements to be replaced by uniform rules for three main categories of immigrants: (1) those coming to be reunited with immediate family; (2) those sponsored by nondependent relatives or others; and (3) those selected to meet needs for national and economic security in keeping with Australia's capacity to provide employment, housing, education, and social services (Richmond and Lakshmana 1976: 190–191).

Deteriorating economic conditions after 1970 led to a reduction in official immigration targets from 175,000 in 1969–1970 to 50,000 in 1975–1976. In 1971 Australia had a population of 12.8 million people. Nevertheless, between 1968 and 1975, it admitted approximately 1.11 million people for permanent settlement. In the first half of the decade migration contributed about one-third of Australia's population growth (Richmond and Lakshmana 1976: 187). Given the removal of ethnic restrictions in immigration requirements, the proportion of British and European immigrants fell from 81.5 percent in 1967–1968 to 61 percent in 1974–1975. Nevertheless, 53,000 Asians were admitted to Australia between 1959 and 1975, a rise from four percent of immigrants in 1968 to 12 percent at the beginning of 1975. Asian immigrants, excluding those from the Middle East, accounted for 6.7 percent of net migration in 1966–1971 and 15.3 percent in 1971–1974.

The Recent Past (1975–2000)

The first wave of asylum seekers to try to enter Australia by boat landed on the north coast of Australia in April 1976 following the end of the Vietnam War in 1975. Australia opened its doors to these 20,000 Vietnamese "boat people" heralding one of the most dramatic stories of recent times and "the most controversial chapter in the history of Australian post-war immigration" (Collins 1988: 60). On arrival in Australia, many without papers, the boat people were housed in hostels and provided "generous social welfare and settlement assistance and English-language classes" (Manne and Corlett 2004: 2). The Australian Refugee Council was established to examine the refugee issue while all were accepted, not on the basis of individual assessment as happened in more recent times, but as a "collective group" (Manne and Corlett 2004: 2) on the recommendation of the UN High Commission for Refugees. However, the influx of Vietnamese and Cambodian people did little to alter the predominantly European immigrant population, given that between 1970 and 1980 most immigrants came from the UK, Yugoslavia, New Zealand, and Lebanon (Department of Immigration and Multicultural and Indigenous Affairs [DIMIA] 2001b).

In the late 1970s and early 1980s the emphasis in immigration policy "shifted to citizenship as one of the major elements depicting integration/assimilation within the framework of multiculturalism" (Seitz and Foster 1985: 415). Following the abolition of the white Australia policy, reformist orientations filled the air and expectations of equity and equality permeated Australian society. During this period, immigration became increasingly humanitarian, giving greater priority to family reunification, and the focus of immigration policy shifted from cultural homogeneity to acceptance and even celebration of cultural diversity (Collins 2000). Australia's national identity changed from being the "most British" country in the world to the "most multicultural" (Jupp 2002: 1).

The policy of multiculturalism had bipartisan support until the mid-1980s and enjoyed a legitimate place in Australia's public life. The conservative side of government became concerned about declining Australian values and the threat of Asian immigration to Australia's national identity—ongoing and unresolved issue since the 1970s. The increase in the Asian population was a direct result of the relaxation of skill considerations—initially the focus following the abandonment of the white Australia policy—and the shift to family and humanitarian considerations (Birrell and Birrell 1987). The fact of the matter was that while there had been an increase in the intake of Asian immigrants Asians constituted only two percent of the Australian population at that time (Joppke 2005).

Other Anglo-Australians complained that the policy of multiculturalism gave preferential treatment to minority ethnic groups and disadvantaged them; many believed that "migrant welfare programs were over-funded" (Vasta 1993: 212). By the late 1980s, there were proclamations that Australia was in a postmulticulturalism phase (Foster and Stockley 1988). Nevertheless, multiculturalism remained on the political agenda during the 1980s and, through its four-pronged humanitarian program (Jupp 2002), the government remained supportive of refugees and immigrants fleeing human rights violations in their home countries. By 1984, it had become the world's largest receiving country in per capita terms for refugees, having by that year admitted 100,000 Indochinese refugees (Joppke 2005).

In 1985, a study reported by Norman and Meikle in *Economic Effects of Immigration on Australia* (1985) drew attention to the need for planned migration tailored to Australia's economic needs, as did the Fitzgerald Report of 1988, which sharply criticized Australia's multiculturalism policy, arguing for a sharper economic focus and a move from family to skill-based selection in its related immigration policy. The focus then shifted from cultural to economic concerns, with an increasing emphasis on skilled and business migration during the Hawke Labor years at the expense of "humanitarian or family categories" (Jupp 2002: 48). Hawke was adamant that a reduction in Asian immigration "would mean reducing the skill level of the migrant intake" (in Lack and Templeton 1995: 244).

Consequently, in 1989, the Hawke Labor Government revised the policy of multiculturalism, but it did so within a new framework of neoliberalism. Multiculturalism was redefined in terms of rights and obligations according to which immigrants were entitled to retain their cultural identity, which included their language and religion, and, at the same time, enjoy equality of treatment and opportunity. In return, they were required to respect the laws and liberal values of Australian society and maintain a commitment to the Australian nation (National Multicultural Advisory Council 1999). With a shift in focus to economic concerns, immigration criteria increasingly favored applicants with high-level skills and expertise and those with financial capital. Under this Hawke Labor policy, from 1980 to 1990, immigrants came mainly from the UK, New Zealand, Vietnam, and Philippines (DIMA 2001b).

The incoming Howard Coalition Government (1996–2007) continued to extol the value of this economic focus. Ruddock (1999) also affirmed cultural diversity as a major strength as Australia moved forward into the twenty-first century. The Howard Government totally reversed the pattern of immigration in the Keating Labor Government (1993–1996), where family reunion had constituted 68.7 percent and skills entries 29.2 percent of new immigrants. When Howard came into power in 1995–1996 the family stream

accounted for 70 percent. By 2000–2001, 55.5 percent entered on skills visas and 41.5 percent on family-related visas (Department of Immigration and Multicultural and Indigenous Affairs [DIMIA] 2002a: 17). This trend continued. By 2003 the quota for independent immigrants selected because of their skills and their families was 100,000 to 110,000 per annum and for humanitarian entrants it had reached 13,000 by 2004/2005 (Taylor 2004).

According to the 2006 Census, of the 20 million people living in Australia, nearly 30 percent were born overseas, which is high when compared with other countries with planned migration programs (Australian Bureau of Statistics [ABS] 2008a). Australia continued to be an Anglophone country with 80 percent of the population speaking only English at home. The most commonly spoken non-English languages were Greek, Italian, Cantonese, Arabic, and Mandarin. With regard to religious affiliation, most Australians were Christian (64%), atheist (19%), Buddhist (2%) or Muslim (1.7%). In 2005–2006, 72 percent of immigrants were younger than 35 years of age compared to 48 percent in the general population. They entered mainly through the skill stream which, in 2006–2007, accounted for 66 percent of immigrants predominantly from the UK, India and the PRC (Department of Immigration and Citizenship [DIAC] 2008).

Since 1945 Australia has admitted over 6.8 million immigrants from well over 200 countries, including 680,000 displaced persons or refugees such that by 1991, immigration accounted for 55 percent of Australia's population growth (Murphy 1993). It has received around one million immigrants each decade since 1950, over 1.8 million since 1990 (DIAC 2007a). In the last ten years (1997–2007), migrants came predominantly from the Asian region (394,101), followed by Europe (221,787) and Oceania, which includes Melanesia, Micronesia, and Polynesia (219,923). Table 11-2 shows the characteristics of immigrants from the top ten source countries over a ten-year period between 1997 and 2007.

Given the events that were to follow post 9/11, it might be wise to examine Australia's humanitarian record at a time when its refugee policy remained relatively uncontroversial (Jupp 2002)

Table 11-2. Characteristics of Immigrant Arrivals (1997–2007) by Top Ten Source Countries

	Total Australian Population	Total Overseas born	New Zealand	United Kingdom	China	India	South Africa	Philippines	Indonesia	Malaysia	Sudan	Vietnam
~Percentage Intake 1997–98	N/A	N/A	19	12	6	4	5	4	2	1	1	.05
~Percentage Intake 2006–07	N/A	N/A	17	17	9	10	3	4	1	2	2	2
#No. of arrivals 1997–2007	N/A	N/A	183 187	140 478	81 883	69 515	49 459	37 205	26 590	23 365	23 129	22 287
#Percentage intake 1997–2007	N/A	N/A	17.4	13.4	07.8	06.6	04.7	03.5	02.5	02.2	02.2	02.1
*Census count 2006	N/A	N/A	389 470	1 038 160	206 590	147 110	104 130	120 540	50 970	92 330	19 050	159 850
*Median Age in Years	37.1	46.8	39.5	53.7	39.3	35.8	38.4	40.3	32.2	39.5	24.6	41.0
*Qualifications	52.5	N/A	51.2	56.8	55.0	76.1	68.1	64.9	62.7	66.8	38.8	35.1
*Labor Force	64.6	N/A	76.3	58.8	56.3	72.3	75.1	73.1	62.1	67.3	40.3	61.9
Participation *Unemployment	5.2	N/A	04.9	03.9	11.2	07.3	4.1	05.2	09.0	05.7	28.5	11.4
Rate *Citizenship	N/A	75.6	40	70.2	73.2	74.6	80.1	92.1	47.5	59.7	70.9	95.1
*English Proficiency	N/A	N/A	94.1	E/S	64.7	94.0	97.6	95.5	89.8	92.1	67.0	56.1

Note: The characteristics cited in this section of the table represent the characteristics of all immigrants from this source country in 2007, not just the immigrants from 1997 to 2007.

~Figures taken from Department of Immigration and Citizenship (2007b) *Settler Arrivals 2006–2007.* Canberra: Commonwealth of Australia.

Figures calculated from Department of Immigration and Citizenship (2007b) *Settler Arrivals 2006–2007.* Canberra: Commonwealth of Australia.

*Department of Immigration and Citizenship (2007c), *Australian Immigration Statistics, Community Information Summaries.* Retrieved September 24, 2008. http://www.immi.gov.au/media/publications/statistics/comm-summ/summary.html.

and refugees continued to constitute a minority of the total immigration intake. As a signatory to the United Nations Refugee Convention, the humanitarian program has consistently been Australia's contribution to the global problem of asylum seekers and refugees. The humanitarian program allocates places to onshore applicants who have been granted refugee status, offshore applicants who have been defined as refugees in need of resettlement and applicants subject to human rights violations who have support from an Australian resident (DIAC 2007a). From the mid-1990s, the humanitarian intake quota remained at around 12,000 places.

Between 1947 and 1972, Australia accepted 260,000—mainly European—refugees and displaced persons (Jupp 2002). By the 1990s attitudes toward "future seekers" had changed and the government was accused of using scare tactics to ignite fear of so-called "boat people," "queue-jumpers," and "illegal immigrants" (Klocker and Dunn 2003). As a consequence stricter "border controls" were introduced along with the policy of mandatory detention to prevent "unworthy, illegitimate, illegal, threatening, dangerous, manipulative [asylum seekers] of bad character" (Silove et al. 2007: 361) from entering Australia.

However, the government was struggling to process the backlog of asylum claims with 21,000 outstanding by mid-1993, most of which comprised post-Tiananmen PRC students seeking asylum. The government decided to grant them permanent residence subject to health and character checks to resolve the backlog (Birrell 1994). However, Birrell (1994) notes that few offshore asylum claims succeeded in the early 1990s. This contrasts strongly with those currently applying offshore for humanitarian visas, 83 percent of which were granted in 2007–2008. The four countries that provided most of the humanitarian stream in that year were Burma/Myanmar, Iraq, Afghanistan, and Sudan (DIAC 2007a).

Post 9/11: The Mandatory Detention of Asylum Seekers

The post-9/11 scenario drastically changed the orderly running of Australia's humanitarian program. The global threat of terrorism created uncertainty about the legitimacy of people seeking asylum in Australia and, in the ensuing period, Australia would become unique in establishing a policy of mandatory, indefinite detention as a deterrent to asylum seekers who tried to enter the country "illegally." Mandatory detention represents the "darker side" of Australian immigration policy. It seeks to deter people overseas from entering Australia without permission (Birrell 1994; Crock and Saul 2002; Manne and Corlett 2004; Taylor 2004).

Detention centers were first established in Australia in 1989, triggered by the arrival by boat of Cambodian asylum seekers (Mares 2001). Mandatory detention policy was passed by the Labor government in 1992 and applied to all asylum seekers who arrived in this way. From 1994, indefinite detention was legalized. Detention centers were built on- and off-shore. The building of offshore detention centers on islands off Australia, such as Christmas Island, and neighboring island states such as Nauru and Papua New Guinea, became known as the "Pacific Solution." Onshore detention centers were built in hot, arid, semidesert locations far removed from urban centers, for example, at Port Hedland in Western Australia (1991), Curtin in Western Australia (1999), and Woomera in South Australia (1999). They were modeled on correctional institutions and run under government contract by a private for-profit enterprise called Australasian Correctional Management.

Mandatory detention applies to all asylum seekers who arrive without a valid visa while their applications for refugee status are being processed, including families and unaccompanied children. Processing can take many months or even years. The number of people in detention reached its peak in 1999–2000 at 4,174. However, the average stay in detention for the years between 1989 and 1996 was 12 months. Most detainees came from Iraq, Afghanistan, and Iran, with large numbers of Chinese nationals in recent years (Silove et al. 2007). According to Silove et al. (2007: 364), there were 1,923 children in detention in 2000–2001 with 170 being unaccompanied minors, though Mares et al. (2002: 91) reported much lower figures of 521 children under the age of 18 and 53 unaccompanied minors, mostly in isolated, rather than urban Immigration Detention Centres (IDCs).

In 2002–2003 there were 12,525 listed under the humanitarian program: 4,376 in the refugee category; 7,280 in the special humanitarian category, that is, those who are outside their home country who have experienced gross violation of human rights and have been proposed or sponsored by someone in Australia; and 866 in the onshore program, that is, people on temporary and permanent protection visas who have arrived in Australia before seeking asylum (Taylor 2004). Most in the onshore category on permanent protection visas came from Sri Lanka and China, and those on temporary protection visas were mainly from Iraq and Afghanistan, while the largest group of refugees was from Sudan (31%) and Iraq (25%). The majority of asylum seekers live in the community while awaiting refugee decisions; during this waiting period they face restricted access to employment, welfare, health, and education. In 2004, there were 2,400 asylum seekers living in the community (Taylor 2004).

The mandatory detention of asylum seekers has become one of the most divisive issues in Australia, reaching a crisis point in 2005. Particularly controversial was the detention of children for long periods of time in contravention of the UN Conventions of the Rights of the Child (Human Rights and Equal Opportunity Commission [HREOC] 2004). There is mounting evidence, too, that prolonged detention results in severe mental health problems for detainees and compounds the trauma experienced in their home countries (Silove et al. 2007). Independent researchers have been denied access to detention centers and most of the data available comes from the analysis of secondary sources or clinical reports from professionals who provided services to detainees and interviews with former detainees (Silove et al. 2007). Successive commissions of inquiry, like the Palmer Commission (2005), reported on the government's mismanagement of asylum seekers. Silove et al. (2007: 387) sum up the detention debacle as follows:

[It] provides a contemporary example of how a modern, pluralistic society that subscribes to multiculturalism and liberal values can, nevertheless, adopt policies that are regressive from a human rights, transcultural and mental health perspective. Once

adopted, these policies can be adhered to stubbornly, even in the face of strong evidence indicating the harm that is being done.

The Department of Immigration and Citizenship Annual Report (2007d) showed there were 5,485 asylum seekers detained between 2006 and 2007, with a maximum of 847 on any one day. Of the 4,718 taken into detention during this period, 1,797 were overstayers, 1,437 were illegal foreign fishers, 889 were placed in an "others" category, and only 595 were unauthorized arrivals. There were 65 people on community detention orders on June 30, 2007. Of the 5,044 people released from detention during this period, 4,284 were removed from Australia, 150 were granted a protection visa and 610 were released on other grounds (DIAC 2007d).

Since 2001 there has been considerable community outrage at the detention of asylum seekers, children in particular. Groups like Amnesty International, the Refugee Council of Australia, and the Refugee Action Committee staged protests and engaged community and media attention about the plight of people in immigration detention. The Human Rights and Equal Opportunity Commission conducted several investigations during this period and annually monitored and reported on conditions inside these facilities. Despite some reports of improvements in the conditions of detention centers, each report has maintained the stance that Australia's mandatory detention laws should be repealed (HREOC 1998, 2004, 2007, 2008). In good news, governmental policy started to shift with the election of the Labour government in 2007. In 2008, the "Pacific Solution" ended with the closure of the detention center in Nauru, temporary protection visas were abolished, and the government announced a new direction in immigration detention policy toward a presumption that detention would occur as a last resort and for the shortest practicable period.

Fear of Islam

Replicating sentiments in many Western countries, Australian society came to develop a fear of Islam despite the fact that, over the years, Islamic people have lived peacefully in Australia with the Muslim population doubling every ten or so years to its current 1.7 percent (Bouma 1997; Joppke 2005; Poynting and Mason 2007). Most Australian-born Muslims—presently constituting 36 percent of the Muslim population—came from countries in the Pacific and Southeast Asia. Others came between 1970 and 1990 from Lebanon and Turkey. More recent immigrants hail from countries on the Indian subcontinent, Iran and Iraq, with reestablished flows from Bosnia and Afghanistan. To paraphrase Dunn et al. (2007), the Australian Islam community, therefore, is ethnically diverse, with Muslims having come to Australia in different eras under various categories of migration—refugee, family migrant, assisted passage, and skilled immigrant. Like Muslims in other Western nations, their settlement experiences have been diverse, with varied degrees of socioeconomic well-being across and within ancestry groups. The way in which Islam is practiced also varies dramatically sustained by the local bases of mosque organization, as well as the specific socioeconomic and cultural contexts in which Australian Muslims reside. This diversity and varied experience is poorly acknowledged, especially since the threat of global terrorism and the aftermath of 9/11 have fueled anti-Islamic sentiment without just cause given the consistent presence and harmonious coexistence of Muslims in the Australian population for well over a hundred years (Dunn et al. 2007; Poynting and Mason 2007).

Dunn et al. (2007: 564) believe that "contemporary anti-Muslim sentiment in Australia is reproduced through a racialization that includes well rehearsed stereotypes of Islam, perceptions of threat and inferiority, as well as fantasies that ... Australian Muslims ... do not belong." They identify undercurrents of Islamophobia and "national cultural selectivity in the politics of responding to asylum seekers" in negative media reporting, which they see as strongly linked to an antipathetic government. This has resulted in moral panic, misinformed opposition to mosque development, ever more restrictive asylum seeker policies, arson attacks, and racist violence. It has also led to discrimination against people who are not Muslim, such as Christian Arabs, given people's ignorance of the diversity of the Islamic population.

Mason (2006) believes that hate campaigns have transferred anti-Asian prejudice to anti-Muslim sentiments, while Manne (2002) perceives Islamophobia to be the most serious threat to multiculturalism and religious and ethnic tolerance that Australia has witnessed for very many years. It is, indeed, a worrying trend (Maddox 2005). On the positive side, "Australian Islamic organizations have ... remained positive, constructive and hopeful" (Dunn et al. 2007: 583), philosophically accepting racial jibes as part of their everyday experience. So long as majority public opinion retains a healthy scepticism to media and government reporting sanity should prevail.

Life in Australia

Why do People Immigrate to Australia?

The Longitudinal Survey of Immigrants to Australia (LSIA), conducted by the Department of Immigration, provides a rich source of data for the analysis of settlement issues for new migrants to Australia. An important difference from most other data on migrants is that the LSIA provides information on the visa category under which migrants entered Australia (Mahuteau and Junankar 2008). The study, which commenced in 1993, has collected data on three cohorts totaling about 18,000 new immigrants in the periods 1993–1994, 1998–2000, and 2004–2005.

Richardson et al. (2002) reported that pull factors that were important to migrants included increased job opportunities, a better lifestyle, and family reunification. Few reported negatively on the situation in their home country, though migrants entering via the humanitarian stream were more likely to cite political turmoil and a lack of opportunity for employment than those entering via the skills and family streams. For the family stream, family reunification featured strongly while independent, self-sponsored skill and business migrants were encouraged by better employment opportunities and quality of life.

Australia's Reception of Immigrants

Australians are positive about immigration, multiculturalism, and cultural diversity; are proud of their cosmopolitanism; and believe that immigration is beneficial to Australian society (Ang et al. 2002; Forrest and Johnston 1999). The Australian Survey of Social Attitudes (2003) showed that the majority of Australians believed that multiculturalism improved "society by bringing in new ideas and cultures" (Goot and Watson 2005: 186). Most favored cultural "blending" over cultural "distinctiveness." For the most part, Australians believe that immigrants are good for the economy (Goot and Watson 2005).

The most recent 2004–2005 LSIA (DIAC 2007e) showed overwhelmingly that new immigrants from the skill and humanitarian streams felt that they had been made to feel welcome in Australia. They liked Australian people (28%), the weather (28%), and lifestyle (19.5%). Nearly a quarter of respondents could not think of anything they disliked, while a small minority complained about the climate, cost of living, and high taxes. Seven percent had experienced racial discrimination.

Services for New Arrivals

In the mid-1980s, "cost-free immigration" and "user pays" (Jupp 2002: 152) principles were introduced with consequent cuts in health, adult migrant education, and human rights services. With the influence of neoliberalism, the privatization of welfare and unemployment services and the dismantling of labor market programs have affected most immigrants, especially those from non-English speaking backgrounds (Collins 2000). Nevertheless, a wide range of services is available for new immigrants, including health care, employment services, education, and welfare, though income support is not available for the first two years after arrival, except for those entering via the humanitarian program. Cultural and linguistically diverse services are provided by migrant resource centers that offer advice, support, and referral. Ethnic community councils provide children's services, day care centers and some services to those in rural areas. The adult migrant English program provides free language tuition, and telephone interpreting services are available. The government provides specialized support through its Integrated Humanitarian Settlement Strategy, which includes assistance with initial orientation,

securing accommodation, and community support (DIMIA 2001).

Richardson et al. (2002) reported that most new immigrants required employment, financial, language, housing, and health services, and for the most part these services were provided by the Commonwealth Government. In general, the Commonwealth Government provides social and economic support while ethnic organizations cater to cultural needs and interests (Jupp 2002). The majority of immigrants were found to have family or friends in Australia who were a major source of practical, financial, and emotional support. However, this was not automatic because some families are not in a position to provide much-needed support due to difficulties with, among other things, the English language, cramped accommodation, or job commitments (Keys Young 2002). Social isolation was sometimes experienced by immigrants who did not have family or friends in Australia. This often applied to the female spouse of the migrating couple (Jamrozik 2001; Keys Young 2002). A significant obstacle to service usage was the command of the English language, with people from non-English speaking backgrounds, referred to as NESB, often experiencing problems in accessing and understanding the services available to them. However, despite these constraints, the majority of immigrants surveyed reported satisfaction with the level and nature of services available to them, with humanitarian entrants reporting high levels of satisfaction with trauma or torture counseling (Richardson et al. 2002).

Adjustment to the Australian Way of Life

Resettlement not only requires adjustment to practical considerations, such as employment, income, and housing, but also involves the renegotiation of cultural and familial values. Adjustment is made easier when there are adequate services to ease resettlement, but new arrivals also need to be given avenues for social participation. Australians from all backgrounds report high levels of intercultural contact socially and in the workplace, and seem to be enjoying the benefits of "cross-cultural consumption," reporting that they "partake in food, music and film from different cultures on a regular basis" (Ang et al. 2002: 30–33).

The social participation of immigrants is generally high, with only slight differences in levels of participation between the Australian born, migrants from mainly English-speaking countries, and migrants from other countries. In a recent survey, 97 percent of migrants from mainly English-speaking countries had engaged in some form of informal social activity three months prior to the survey, compared to 92 percent of migrants from other countries (ABS 2008b). About 90 percent of the Australian born and migrants from mainly English-speaking countries had attended a cultural or leisure venue in the previous twelve months, compared to 80 percent of migrants from other countries, who were more likely to attend a religious or spiritual group than a sport or recreation group (ABS 2008a). However, the results of research about cultural identity showed that immigrants from non-English speaking backgrounds did not identify themselves as "Australian" as readily as one might expect. While this group reported an overall satisfaction with their lives and Australian society and the majority called Australia "home," less than 10 percent called themselves "Australian" compared to 60 percent of a national sample (Ang et al. 2002: 39). So while Australia appears to be receptive and inclusive of all immigrants, it may be that adjustment and belonging remain easier for immigrants from English-speaking and Anglo-Celtic backgrounds.

Finding work is a significant factor in adjustment. While overall unemployment rates for newly arrived immigrants are higher than for the general Australian population, employment opportunities appear to be strongly influenced by skill levels and English proficiency, resulting in higher levels of unemployment for immigrants of non-English speaking backgrounds and those entering on humanitarian grounds (Forrest and Johnston 1999). Richardson et al. (2002) found that English proficiency was the greatest barrier for immigrants who had difficulty finding employment.

The LSIA (DIAC 2007e) showed a considerable improvement in employment outcomes from its first cohort in 1993 (15%) to the 2005 cohort (4%). This is consistent with ABS data that showed the unemployment rate for the Australian-born population was four percent compared to five percent for recent immigrants in 2007 (recent immigrants were defined as those who arrived after 1997). More recent migrants (68%) were employed than Australian-born residents (66%), and over half had employment prior to, or within three months of arrival (ABS 2007). Around a quarter took more than 12 months to find work.

Migrants on low incomes were more likely to live with family or rely on government housing. Murphy (1993) reported that new immigrants often preferred high density housing in urban areas, though this changed as their standard of living improved and they became more accustomed to the Australian lifestyle. Some migrant groups tend to cluster in a particular area (Dunn et al. 2007; Murphy 1993). Research indicates that residential concentrations of immigrants tends to serve as a socioeconomic "stepping stone" rather than resistance to integration (Jayasuriya and Pookong 1999: 53). The location of family and friends already residing in Australia is the main determinant of where people choose to live (Richardson et al. 2002).

Adjustment to Australian society is greatly aided by English proficiency. The majority of immigrants speak English well after ten years in Australia (ABS 2002). Yet there are some who do not adopt the English language quite so readily. For example, after ten years in Australia, less than half the immigrants from Greece and China spoke English well (ABS 2002). Generally, humanitarian entrants have little opportunity to learn English or to prepare for a new culture prior to departure. Of the humanitarian sample in the LSIA 2002 cohort, over 80 percent did not speak English well, or at all, six months after arrival. Many had experienced pre-migration trauma which, combined with low levels of English proficiency, exacerbated the stresses of adjustment to Australia.

Different streams of immigrants encounter different obstacles on arrival but, in general, immigrants experience high levels of satisfaction with their lives after six months and report that they would encourage others to immigrate to Australia (Richardson et al. 2002). Nearly three-quarters of immigrants applied for Australian citizenship and enjoy the rights and responsibilities afforded to all Australians, including the right to vote and sit on a jury, the right to stand for parliament, the right to apply for an Australian passport, and the right to Australian diplomatic protection overseas (ABS 2003; DIMIA 2002a).

The Costs and Benefits of Migration

Research suggests that in the long term the benefits of immigration outweigh the costs (Murphy 1993; Nieuwenhuysen 1990), while costs exceed benefits in the short term (Foster and Baker 1991; Mathews 1992). However, there are major geographic variations due to the way in which immigration in Australia is controlled and financed. It is controlled by the federal government with the financing of cities and states the responsibility of state governments. State and local government depend on the redistribution of Commonwealth revenues collected by the national government. The majority of immigrants settle in the major urban centers of Sydney, Melbourne, and Perth (Murphy 1993). Hence while the central government controls the intake of refugees, state and local government is responsible for services to new arrivals. For the most part, however, immigrants benefit the Australian economy. Both federal and state governments benefit from the tax revenue gained from immigrants, although the state governments receive a lesser net gain due to their additional service expenditure (Richardson, in DIMIA 2002b). Skilled and independent entrants are readily employed, tend to earn higher incomes, and contribute more to tax revenue than other migrant streams. In comparison, family stream immigrants tend to place a small cost on the federal budget that dissipates after ten years, although they do contribute a small amount of revenue to state budgets from arrival. Humanitarian entrants are the greatest economic burden to Australia, still being a cost to state and federal governments ten years after arrival.

According to Islam and Fausten (2008: S81), "there is some evidence that overall immigration may exert positive effects on wages in Australia." Immigration also raises average Australian incomes as a result of economies of scale in the provision of goods and services in the industrial, business, and government sectors (Garnaut, in

DIMIA 2002b). The way in which income is distributed is determined by the age, education, and skill composition of the immigration intake. Current intake favoring the young, educated, and skilled should increase the ratio of people who are employed, as well as the relative incomes of the unskilled population. However, the unskilled are less likely to gain economic advantages from the wider economic expansion and tend to be more disadvantaged at times of high unemployment. While the skilled and educated are less likely to gain in the labor market, this is generally offset by the effects of scale, as well as by increased market opportunities and asset prices. Also, immigration serves to raise property prices and thus benefits established Australians who possess nontradable assets, including urban land. So while immigration has a positive effect on increasing and distributing Australia's wealth, it favors those with established wealth and higher incomes (Garnaut, in DIMIA 2002b).

Government policy increasingly focuses on Australia's capacity to compete economically in the global marketplace. In this climate, immigration makes good sense because it not only encourages the skilled and educated to come to Australia, but also strengthens ties with other countries and creates business opportunities. Increasingly in Australia, the cultural knowledge of immigrants has been acknowledged as a resource in the domestic and global economy, and notions of productive diversity have emerged. *Productive diversity* is a concept that encourages Australian companies to recognize, and use, the linguistic talents, cultural knowledge, skills, and networks of their overseas-born workers to gain economic advantage in international markets (DIMIA 2001b). The Department of Immigration and Multicultural and Indigenous Affairs (DIMIA 2001a) has founded a number of initiatives to promote sound practices that incorporate these ideals both within government departments and in the wider economic community.

Immigration also offsets Australia's aging population. Australia's fertility rates continue to decrease as life expectancy continues to increase (DIMIA 2002b). An aging population reduces the ratio of employed people in the population, places a greater burden on those in the labor force, and contributes to a slowing of economic growth. For these reasons, many believe that the intake of young immigrants can be used successfully to increase labor force growth and, at the same time, offset aging. Garnaut (in DIMIA 2002b) suggests that the age of recent immigrants has already played a positive role in lowering average ages, as well as the ratios of older people in the population.

Conclusion

Thus far, in keeping with the brief for this chapter, we have examined inter alia statistical trends in Australian immigration, waves of policy change affecting immigration, current immigration policy, the countries of origin of Australia's immigrants, services provided for them on arrival, reasons why people come to Australia, and the costs and benefits of immigration. This approach takes immigration into an objective realm where it is all too easy to forget that it is something that touches most people's lives on a daily basis. As the Special Broadcasting Services (SBS) television channel constantly reminds us, "the world is an amazing place" and Australia, like many Western countries might, in some respects, be described as "the world in one place."

Unfortunately, the media has portrayed Australia as unfriendly when most new arrivals encounter a warm reception, hospitality and good neighborliness. Yet the media images reflect a side that exists and perplexes. Recently, the Human Rights and Equal Opportunity Commission (HREOC 2004) launched a National Inquiry into Children Living in Immigration Detention Centres. All the children studied had been recognized under Australian and international law as refugees and had spent an average of 140 days in immigration detention during 2000 and 2001. Consider their response to coming to Australia. They said that their departure from their home countries followed traumatic experiences where close family members had been killed or imprisoned or had disappeared. Most had no idea where they were going or what awaited them there and, for most, the journey had been difficult and dangerous. Many had never seen the sea before embarking on a long voyage in cramped conditions in "unseaworthy" vessels. Nevertheless, the children spoke positively about their first contact with Australians but not of their experiences in detention centers, where conditions were harsh, crowded, difficult, and foreign to their cultures and prior life experiences. Moreover, they violated conditions spelled out in UN human rights conventions.

The treatment of asylum seekers is Australia's Achilles heel. Fanned by world events, in particular September 11 in New York and October 12 in Bali, a climate of fear has been created and questions have been raised as to the true plight and intentions of refugees. Suspicion of Arab and Muslim populations has resulted in a "border protection" policy. The majority of asylum seekers in 2002 were from Afghanistan, Iraq, and Iran, all of which were portrayed as havens for terrorists (McMaster 2001). These events coincide with continued attacks on Australian multiculturalism by conservative parties. Australia is not alone in adopting a tougher line on refugees. There is a hardening of attitudes toward refugees and asylum seekers globally. But sending asylum seekers back to their country is a regressive step for Australia, which sees itself as part of the global village and relies on immigration for both its population growth and its economy.

Many Australians are protesting against detention centers and many were vocal about their antiwar sentiments when the Australian Prime Minister voiced his support for the United States in Iraq. Our home town, Newcastle, has been made a *Welcome City for Refugees* as a result of the success of the local refugee action group. Others, including Rural Australians for Refugees, are protesting against the image of Australia as unwelcome to and uncaring about genuine refugees and asylum seekers. Australia is proud of its multicultural heritage and sees its cultural diversity as enriching and sustaining since, when all is said and done, with the exception of some Indigenous Peoples, almost all Australians are immigrants.

References

Ang, I., Brand, J.E., Noble, G., and Wilding, D. (2002). *Living diversity Australia's multicultural future*. Artarmon: Special Broadcasting Service Corporation.
Australian Bureau of Statistics (ABS) (2008a). *2006 Census quickstats: Australia*. Canberra: Australian

Bureau of Statistics. Retrieved 10th September 2008. http://www.abs.gov.au/websitedbs/D3310114.nsf/Home/Census+Data.

Australian Bureau of Statistics (2008b). *Australian social trends, 2008.* Retrieved September 10, 2008. http://www.abs.gov.au/ausstats/abs@.nsf/mf/4102.0?OpenDocument.

Australian Bureau of Statistics (2007). *6250.0: Labour force statistics and other characteristics of recent migrants.* Canberra: Australian Bureau of Statistics.

Australian Bureau of Statistics (2003). *Year book Australia.* Canberra: Australian Bureau of Statistics. Retrieved May 1, 2003. http://www.abs.gov.au/Ausstats/abs%40.nsf/94713ad445ff1425ca25682000192af2/4f7d3cec8f06a9f5ca256cad001f1393!OpenDocument.

Australian Bureau of Statistics (2002). *Australian social trends 2002 population composition: Older overseas-born Australians.* Canberra: Australian Bureau of Statistics. Retrieved May 1, 2003. http://www.gov.au/ausstats/abs%40.nsf/0/F7C205085706BDD7CA2569BB00164F60?Open.

Birrell, R. (1994). Immigration control in Australia. *The ANNALS of the American Academy of Political and Social Science,* 534(1), 106–117.

Birrell, R., and Birrell, T. (1987). *An issue of people: Population and Australian society.* Melbourne: Longman/Cheshire.

Bouma, G.D. (1997). The settlement of Islam in Australia. *Social Compass,* 44(1), 71–82.

Bunbury, B. (1998). *Unfinished business: Reconciliation, the Republic, and the Constitution.* Sydney: ABC Books.

Briskman, L. (2008). Decolonizing social work in Australia: Prospect or illusion. In M. Gray, J. Coates, and M. Yellow Bird, *Indigenous social work around the world: Towards culturally relevant education and practice.* Hants, UK: Ashgate.

Coleman, A., and Higgins, W. (2000). Racial and cultural diversity in contemporary citizenship. In Vandenberg, A. (ed.), *Citizenship and democracy in a global era.* Melbourne: Macmillan.

Collins, J. (2000). Immigration and immigrants: Ethnic inequality and social cohesion. In P. Boreham, Stokes, G., and Hall, R. (eds.), *The politics of Australian society: Political issues for the new century.* Sydney: Longman, pp. 302–316.

Collins, J. (1988). *Migrant hands in a distant land: Australia's post-war immigration.* Sydney: Pluto Press.

Crock, M., and Saul, B. (2002). *Future seekers: Refugees and the law in Australia.* Sydney: The Federation Press.

De Lepervanche, M. (1979). Australian immigrants: 1788–1940: Desired and unwanted. In E.L.

Wheelwright, and Buckley, K. (eds.), *Essays in the political economy of Australian capitalism* (Vol. 1). Sydney: Australia and New Zealand Book Company, pp. 72–104.

Department of Immigration and Citizenship (DIAC) (2008). *Population flows: Immigration aspects.* Retrieved September 24, 2008. http://www.immi.gov.au/media/publications/statistics/popflows2006-7/index.htm.

Department of Immigration and Citizenship (2007a). *Key facts in immigration.* Canberra: DIAC. Retrieved September 10, 2008. http://www.immi.gov.au/media/fact-sheets/02key.htm.

Department of Immigration and Citizenship (2007b). *Settler arrivals 2006–2007.* Canberra: Commonwealth of Australia.

Department of Immigration and Citizenship (2007c). *Australian immigration statistics, community information summaries.* Retrieved September 10, 2008. http://www.immi.gov.au/media/publications /statistics/comm-summ/summary.htm.

Department of Immigration and Citizenship (2007d). *Department of immigration and citizenship annual report 2006–07.* Retrieved October 11, 2008. http://www.immi.gov.au/about/reports/annual/2006-07/html/index.htm.

Department of Immigration and Citizenship (2007e). *New immigrant outcomes: Results from the third longitudinal study of immigrants to Australia.* Retrieved September 24, 2008. http://www.immi.gov.au/media/research/lsia/results_from_third_LSIA_body.pdf.

Department of Immigration and Multicultural and Indigenous Affairs (DIMIA) (2002a). *Population flows immigration aspects 2001 edition.* Canberra: DIMIA. Retrieved May 1, 2003. http://www.immi.gov.au/statistics/publications/popflows2001/popflows2001.htm.

Department of Immigration and Multicultural and Indigenous Affairs (DIMIA) (2002b). *Migration Benefiting Australia Conference proceedings Sydney 7–8 May 2002.* Canberra: DIMIA. Retrieved May 1, 2003. http://www.immi.gov.au/research/publications /conference02/index.htm.

Department of Immigration and Multicultural and Indigenous Affairs (2001a). *Integrated humanitarian settlement strategy.* Canberra: DIMIA. Retrieved May 1, 2003. http://www.immi.gov.au/facts/66ihss.htm.

Department of Immigration and Multicultural and Indigenous Affairs (DIMIA) (2001b). *Immigration: Federation to century's end, 1901–2000.* Canberra: DIMIA. Retrieved May 1, 2003. http://www.immi.gov.au/statistics/publications/federation/index.htm.

Dunn, K.M., Klocker, N., and Salabay, T. (2007). Contemporary racism and Islamaphobia in Australia. *Ethnicities*, 7(4), 564–589.

Earle, L., and Fopp, R. (1999). Indigenous Australians: Aboriginal and Torres Strait Islanders; From what has been to where now! In J. Germov and Poole, M. (eds.), *Introduction to Australian society: A sociological overview* (3rd ed.). Sydney: Harcourt Brace.

Fitzgerald, S. (1988). *Immigration: A commitment to Australia*. Canberra: Australian Government Publishing Service.

Forrest, J., and Johnston, R. (1999) Disadvantage, discrimination, and the occupational differentiation of migrant groups in Australia. *International Journal of Population Geography*, 5, 277–296.

Foster, W., and Baker, L. (1991). *Immigration and the Australian economy*. Australian Bureau of Immigration Research. Canberra: Australian Government Printing Service.

Foster, L., and Stockley, D. (1988). The rise and decline of Australian multiculturalism: 1973–1988. *Politics*, 23(2), 1–10.

Goot, M., and Watson, I. (2005) Immigration, multiculturalism, and national identity. In S. Wilson, Meagher, G., Gibson, R., Denemark, D., and Western, M. (eds.), *Australian social attitudes: The first report*. Sydney: University of New South Wales Press.

Gray, M., and Aga Askeland, G. (2002). Social work as art: Counterbalancing the tick infestation in social work. Paper presented at the IASSW Conference, Montpellier, July 15–18, 2002.

Gray, M., and Mazibuko, F.N.M. (2002). Social work in South Africa at the dawn of the new millennium. *International Journal of Social Welfare*, 11(3), 191–200.

Human Rights and Equal Opportunity Commission (HREOC) (2008). *Submission of the Human Rights and Equal Opportunity Commission (HREOC) to the Joint Standing Committee on Migration Inquiry into Immigration Detention in Australia*. Sydney: HREOC.

Human Rights and Equal Opportunity Commission (HREOC) (2007). *Summary of observations following the inspection of mainland immigration detention facilities 2007*. Retrieved October 11, 2008. http://www.humanrights.gov.au/legal/submissions/2008/20080829_immigration_detention.html.

Human Rights and Equal Opportunity Commission (HREOC) (2004). *A last resort? National inquiry into children in immigration detention*. Sydney: HREOC.

Human Rights and Equal Opportunity Commission (HREOC) (1998). *Those who've come across the seas: Detention of unauthorised arrivals*. Sydney: HREOC.

Islam, A., and Fausten, D.K. (2008). Skilled immigration and wages in Australia. *Economic Record*, 84, S66-S82.

Jamrozik, A. (2001). *Social policy in the post-welfare state: Australians on the threshold of the 21st century*. Frenchs Forest: Longman.

Jayasuriya, L., and Pookong, K. (1999). *The Asianisation of Australia? Some facts about the myths*. Carlton South: Melbourne University Press.

Joppke, C. (2005). Are "nondiscriminatory" immigration policies reversible? Evidence from the United States and Australia. *Comparative Political Studies*, 38(1), 3–25.

Jupp, J. (1998). *Immigration* (2nd ed.). Melbourne: Oxford University Press.

Jupp, J. (2007). *From white Australia to Woomera: The story of Australian immigration* (2nd ed.). Cambridge, UK: Cambridge University Press.

Jupp, J. (2002). *From white Australia to Woomera: The story of Australian immigration*. Cambridge, UK: Cambridge University Press.

Keys Young (2002). *A "client survey" on the effectiveness of DIMIA-funded community settlement services: Final report*. Belconnen: DIMIA.

Klocker, N., and Dunn, K.M. (2003). Who's driving the asylum debate? Newspaper and government representations of asylum seekers. *Media International Australia*, 109, 71–92.

Kovacs, M.L., and Cropley, A.J. (1975). *Immigrants and society: Alienation and assimilation*. Sydney: McGraw-Hill.

Kunz, E.F. (1971). *A continent takes shape*. Sydney: Collins.

Kunz, E.F. (1988). *Displaced persons: Caldwell's new Australia*. Sydney: Australian National University Press.

Lack, J., and Templeton, J. (1995). *Bold experiment: A documentary history of Australian immigration since 1945*. South Melbourne: Oxford University Press.

Maddox, M. (2005). *God under Howard: The rise of the religious right in Australian politics*. Crows Nest: Allen and Unwin.

Mahuteau, S., and Junankar, P.N. (2008). Do migrants get good jobs in Australia? The role of ethnic networks in job search. *The Economic Record*, 84, S115–130.

Manne, R. (2002). Open season on Muslims in the newest phobia. *The Sydney Morning Herald*, September 16, 13.

Manne, R. (2001). In denial: The stolen generations and the right. *The Australian Quarterly Essay*, 1, 106–113.

Manne, R., and Corlett, D. (2004). Sending them home: Refugees and the new politics of indifference. *The Australian Quarterly Essay*, 13, 1–95.

Mares, P. (2001). *Borderline: Australia's treatment of refugees and asylum seekers*. Sydney: New South Wales University Press.

Mares, S., Newman, L., Dudley, M., and Gale, F. (2002). Seeking refuge, losing hope: Parents and children in immigration detention. *Australasian Psychiatry*, 10(2), 91–96.

Mason, G. (2006). Hating through the language of care. Workshop: *Free Speech, Hate Speech, and Human Rights in Australia*. Academy of Social Sciences in Australia, Australian National University, September 8–9, Canberra.

Mathews, R. (1992). *Immigration and state budgets*. Bureau of Immigration Research, Canberra: Australian Government Printing Service.

McMaster, D. (2001). *Asylum seekers: Australia's response to refugees*. Melbourne: Melbourne University Press.

Murphy, P.A. (1993). Immigration and the management of Australian cities: The case of Sydney. *Urban Studies*, 30 (9), 1501–1519.

National Multicultural Advisory Council (NMAC) (1999). *Australian multiculturalism for a new century: Towards inclusiveness*. Canberra: Australian Government Printing Service.

Nieuwenhuysen, J. (1990). *New research on Australian immigration*. Bureau of Immigration Research, Canberra: Australian Government Printing Service.

Norman, N.R., and Meikle, K.F. (1985). *The economic effects of immigration on Australia* (Vol. 1). Melbourne: CEDA.

Palmer, M.J. (2005). *Inquiry into the circumstances of the immigration detention of Cornelia Rau: Report*. Canberra: Commonwealth of Australia.

Poole, R. (1999). *Nation and identity*. London: Routledge.

Poynting, S., and Mason, V. (2007). The resistible rise of Islamophobia: Anti-Muslim racism in the UK and Australia before 11 September 2001. *Journal of Sociology*, 43(1), 61–86.

Reynolds, H. (1999). *Why weren't we told? A personal search for the truth about our history*. Melbourne: Viking.

Richardson, S., Miller-Lewis, L., Ngo, P., and Ilsley, D. (2002). *Life in a new land: The experience of migrants in Wave 1 of LSIA and LSIA 2*. Flinders University, Adelaide: The National Institute of Labour Studies.

Richmond, A.H., and Lakshmana, G.L. (1976) Recent developments in immigration to Canada and Australia: A comparative analysis. *International Journal of Comparative Sociology*, 17 (3–4), 183–205.

Ruddock, P. (1999). Population options for Australia. *People and Place*, 7(1), 1–6.

Seitz, A., and Foster, L. (1985). Dilemmas: Australian expectations, migrant responses; Germans in Melbourne. *Australian and New Zealand Journal of Sociology*, 21(3), 414–430.

Silove, D., Austin, P., and Steel, Z. (2007). No refuge from terror: The impact of detention on the mental health of trauma-affected refugees seeking asylum in Australia. *Transcultural Psychiatry*, 44(3), 359–393.

Taylor, J. (2004). Refugees and social exclusion: What the literature says. *Migrant Action*, 26(2), 16–31.

Vasta, E. (1993). Multiculturalism and ethnic identity: The relationship between racism and resistance. *Australian and New Zealand Journal of Sociology*, 29(2), 209–225.

Willard, M. (1978). *History of the white Australia policy to 1920*. Melbourne: Melbourne University Press.

Yarwood, A.T. (1968). *Attitudes to non-European immigration*. Melbourne: Cassell Australia.

12

Pakistan

Refugee History and Policies of Pakistan: An Afghan Case Study

Shireen S. Issa, Gail Desmond, and Fariyal Ross-Sheriff

Of all the immigration and refugee concerns experienced by Pakistan, three movements—postpartition, Kashmiri, and Afghani refugees—standout as major concerns in Pakistan's 60-year history owing to the scale or duration of each movement. However, all partition refugees and the majority of Kashmiri refugees have been granted special status by Pakistan, whereas, over the years, Pakistan's reception of the Afghan refugees has fluctuated substantially. This chapter provides Pakistan's immigration and refugee history and policies, with specific focus on a background of the Afghan refugee movements in and out of Pakistan primarily in four phases. The chapter draws connections between this immigration pattern, the host countries' policies and programs, and the geopolitics that influenced this policy environment.

Pakistan's Immigration and Refugee History

The Islamic Republic of Pakistan is a Muslim majority (97%) country, a feature which has had a prominent impact on the long history of migration into and out of the country. Pakistan's partition from India resulted in the mass migration of Muslim minorities from India to Pakistan and of Hindu minorities from Pakistan to India. Postpartition, approximately 11.5 million people crossed the borders. About 6.5 million Muslims came to Pakistan, and some 5 million Hindus and Sikhs went to India (Hasan, 2004). Postpartition refugees from India and successive generations in Pakistan, reside primarily in the Sindh and Punjab provinces of Pakistan and are known as *muhajirs*, people who have left their home as "a result of partition or fear of disturbances connected therewith" (Gazdar, 2003; Zolberg, Suhrke, & Aguayo, 1989).

As a result of partition and the subsequent India-Pakistan dispute over Kashmir, Pakistan has hosted large numbers of refugees from the Indian part of Kashmir (refugee numbers have fluctuated depending on the political climate between India and Pakistan). Historically, Kashmiris have been coming to Pakistan since 1947, with inflows increasing during periods of heightened political tension between India and Pakistan. While the number of Kashmiris who have fled to Pakistan since 1947 is unknown, the population of Pakistan-administered Kashmir was at about 2.5 million in 1990, which at an expected growth rate of 3% amounts to close to 4.0 million in 2008 (Contact Pakistan, 2008). Kashmiris are not considered refugees and are required to apply for Pakistani citizenship.

Approximately, 17,000 Kashmiris are known to be residing in 17 camps located in Pakistan-administered Kashmir since 1971. The number of refugees varies with new refugees replacing those who integrate into broader society. In order to move out of the camp Kashmiris are required to apply for a permit even if the move is only temporary (Immigration and Refugee Board of Canada, 1997). Camp-based Kashmiri refugee numbers increased temporarily in the 1987–1989 and 1998–2002 periods, during which time tensions between India and Pakistan escalated. Since the late 1990s, about 2,000 internally displaced Kashmiris live in two camps for displaced people, one located in Pakistan-administered Kashmir and the other in the Northern Territories. An estimated hundreds of thousands internally displaced Kashmiris reside outside camps in these areas, with friends and relatives (USCR CRP, 2004; USCR WRS, 2008). For political reasons mostly related to maximizing the visibility of Kashmiri refugees from India, the refugees continue to live in camps. Over the years, several thousands of Kashmiris (within and outside refugee camps) have relocated to other parts of Pakistan, primarily in the Punjab (Immigration and Refugee Board of Canada, 1997).

Another major refugee movement occurred in the years immediately preceding and following the independence of Bangladesh (formerly East Pakistan) in December 1971 (Gazdar, 2003). The refugees included non-Bengali Muslims who had migrated to East Pakistan prior to the conflict and returned to West Pakistan after the formation of Bangladesh, as well as East Pakistanis residing in West Pakistan at the time of the conflict who wished to remain Pakistanis. It is estimated that there are 2.0 million Bengalis in Pakistan, of whom at least 1.0 million live in Karachi (Bloch, 2000). In the 1980s, due to widespread ethnic tensions in Myanmar (formerly Burma) large numbers (in the thousands) of Muslim Burmese facing persecution in Burma also arrived in Pakistan (Wikipedia, 2005).

In addition to the above mass refugee movements into the country, Pakistan has been host to some 2,000 to 3,000 other refugees in the 1980s and 1990s, primarily from Somalia, Iran (mostly Baha'i Muslims who cannot repatriate due to religious persecution), and Iraq. Refugees from Iraq (mainly Kurdish Iraqis) have sought protection in Pakistan at varying periods including during the Gulf War in the early 1990s and the "War on Terror" in 2004. But unlike other larger groups of refugees (including Afghans and Bengalis) who were granted de facto prima facie refugee status as a group, all asylum seekers from other countries must undergo individual status determination (UNHCR, 2003b).

At the end of 2007, with the repatriation of many Iraqis and the resettlement of other refugees over the years, UNHCR-recognized non-Afghan and non-Kashmiri refugees were residing in Pakistan (210 Somalis, 130 Iraqis, and 270 others. In comparison, assisting the Iraqis, the 387 Somalis, the 145 Iranians, and the 143 refugees from other countries may seem like a small task. But, unlike most of the Afghans who entered Pakistan before 1997 and were given refugee treatment as a group, all asylum seekers from other countries have to go through an individual status determination. Pakistan does not allow refugees to work, so the UNHCR (United Nations High Commissioner of Refugees) has been assisting the most vulnerable with small monthly support payments, with more than 1,000 others (mainly from Somalia, Iran, and Iraq) seeking asylum (UNHCR, 2008b). Most of these refugees reside in Islamabad and Rawalpindi, with about 50% representing single female-headed households with children (UNHCR Pakistan website, 2005).

Apart from refugee movements into the country, Pakistan is a receiving country for other migrants, with most belonging to other developing countries in the region and some from developed countries (Wongboonsin, 2001). Those from developed countries reside primarily in the larger cities (Karachi, Lahore) or in Islamabad and, like migrants from developing countries residing in varying urban locations, are often in the country for job-related, family, or kinship reasons.

Pakistan's Policy Environment for Immigrants and Refugees

In Pakistan, the only law pertaining to immigrants is the Foreigners Order of 1951 (amended in 2000). Accordingly, foreigners without a valid passport and visa and those who have not been exempted from this requirement can be refused entry. There is no provision for refugees or asylum seekers even though the order recognizes the difference between them and other foreigners. In addition, the order allows authorities to restrict foreigners' movement and residence inside Pakistan and condones their arrest and detention (Human Rights Watch [HRW], 2002). All immigrants or refugees in Pakistan, unless otherwise determined, are therefore considered illegal immigrants and may be detained by Pakistani authorities unless they have valid travel documents and a visa for Pakistan (USCR WRS, 2007). In many cases, asylum seekers are released upon appeal by the UNHCR and by the Ministry of States and Frontier Regions (SAFRON). UNHCR-recognized refugees are regarded as illegal immigrants awaiting repatriation or resettlement (USCR CRP 1999; UNHCR 2007a). In recent years, the 2005 census of Afghan refugees in Pakistan and the issuance (by the end of January 2007) of identity (Proof of Registration, POR) cards to approximately 2.16 million Afghans registered thereafter, resulted in the long overdue legalization of this group of refugees, allowing them to legally stay in the country through December 2009 (USCR WRS, 2007). All Afghans, over the age of five, who do not possess a POR, are considered illegal immigrants (UNHCR, 2008a).

Pakistan does not have a specific refugee law and its existing laws are not sensitive to refugees or asylum seekers. By allowing border authorities to grant or refuse permission to enter the country based on valid travel documents, the applicable federal law, the Foreigners Order, contradicts international law (1951 United Nations [UN] Convention Relating to the Status of Refugees) as it pertains to refugees. Although Pakistan has hosted the world's largest refugee populations (the Afghan refugees) for almost three decades, it is not a signatory to the 1951 UN Convention, the 1967 Protocol Relating to the Status of Refugees, or the International Covenant on Civil Rights and Political Rights. Thus, Pakistani legal authorities do not subscribe to international refugee law (UNHCR, 2004).

The applicable UN conventions that have been ratified by Pakistan are the Convention on the Rights of the Child in 1990, the Convention on the Elimination of All Forms of Discrimination against Women in 1996, and the Convention on the Elimination of All Forms of Racial Discrimination also in 1966. Pakistan is also a signatory to the International Covenant of Economic, Social, and Cultural Rights since 2004 (Office of the United Nations High Commissioner for Human Rights [OHCHR], 2008). Even so, refugees in Pakistan, whether they are adults or children, male or female, are treated as illegal immigrants—unless determined otherwise. For many, their illegal status translates into an insecure existence and as a result they often face harassment from local authorities, blackmail, fear of arrest, and deportation. Vulnerable groups such as women and children bear a disproportionate burden of these abuses (Bloch, 2000; Gazdar, 2003). The organizations responsible for dealings with refugees and immigrants in Pakistan are the Ministry of Interior (MoI), which registers the legal status of persons in Pakistan and is responsible for issuing passports and other identity documents. In addition, the National Aliens Registration Authority (NARA), a subdivision of the MoI established in August 2001, which is responsible for registering foreigners in Pakistan regarded as aliens, the Ministry of States and Frontier Regions (the Commissionerate of Afghan Refugees [CAR] is a subdivision of this agency), and international organizations such as the UNHCR and the International Organization for Migration (IOM), both of which have primarily dealt with Afghan refugees (Gazdar, 2003; Afghanistan Research and Evaluation Unit [AREU], 2005; UNHCR, 2006).

The absence of policies governing immigrants and refugees, coupled with porous borders, leaves Pakistan unable to control the influx of illegal immigrants and asylum seekers. Combined with the "politics of protection," a less-than-enabling policy environment has fueled Pakistan's vacillating treatment of refugees over the years.

Pakistan's attitude toward Partition refugees was welcoming. Indians (including Kashmiris) who came to Pakistan in the years immediately following partition were recognized as refugees seeking protection and were granted the opportunity to start their life anew (Gazdar, 2003). Some Partition-refugee colonies in Pakistan were even recognized as cities in Pakistan (U.S. Library of Congress, 1994). In particular, Kashmiris who arrived in Pakistan before 1971 were offered land, assistance, and citizenship by the government of Pakistan (USCR CRP, 1999). The 17,000 Kashmiris arriving after 1971 are categorized as being internally displaced rather than refugees, because Pakistan does not recognize India's control over any part of Kashmir. These internally displaced Kashmiris are assisted by the International Committee of the Red Cross (IRC) and the Kashmir Refugees Rehabilitation Organization, a subordinate Ministry of Kashmir Affairs and Northern Areas (KANA) (Government of Pakistan, 2008; USCR CRP, 2000).

Refugees who arrived in Pakistan due to conflicts other than partition are treated as illegal immigrants. Consequently, the approximately 2 million Bengalis reside illegally in Pakistan, "working in the fishing and carpet-weaving industries and as domestic servants" (Bloch, 2000). Refugees arriving after 1971 from Burma, Iraq, Iran, and Somalia and other neighboring countries, were also not granted refugee status and therefore were afforded no formal protection by the government. After the UNHCR's establishment in Pakistan in the 1980s, in response to large Afghan inflows, refugees from these countries (not including Bangladesh) were offered assistance in the form of shelter, financial assistance, medical care, and educational assistance by the UNHCR (USCR CRP, 2003). Until 2003, refugees in Pakistan were not officially allowed to work. However under a 2003 agreement with the government, UNHCR-recognized non-Afghan refugees residing in Pakistan in 2003 were given permission to work (UNHCR Pakistan website, 2005).

The Afghanistan Crises and Afghan Refugees in Pakistan

Pakistan has played host to Afghan refugees, the largest single refugee population in the world, for the last nearly three decades (since 1979). At the peak of the influx, in the 1980s, there were 3.5 million refugees (UNHCR, 2001). On the global scale, Pakistan continues to host the highest number of Afghan refugees, with Iran in second place (USCR WRS, 2008). In 2005, about 35% of Afghans had been in Pakistan since 1980 with two other major inflows occurring in 1985, when the war was very intense, and in 1990, with the Soviet withdrawal from Afghanistan (UNHCR Census, 2005). As of October 2008, an estimated 1.8 to 2.0 million registered refugees are in Pakistan, with about one-half of them residing in refugee camps administered by the United Nations High Commission on Refugees (UNHCR, 2008a; UNHCR, 2007b). The number of unregistered Afghan refugees living in cities and towns across Pakistan is unknown but is estimated to be in the hundreds of thousands.

Until 2005, the numbers of Afghan refugees in Pakistan were estimates at best because until then, the Pakistan government did not officially register refugees. However, a UNHCR–Government of Pakistan–sponsored census of Afghans in Pakistan in 2005, the subsequent registration of the majority of this population in 2007, and UNCHR data on assisted repatriation since 2005 has provided a better understanding of the numbers and other demographics of this population. Even so, because of 25 years of nonregistration and because of the overall legal and policy framework in the country, at least half of the registered refugees and likely many unregistered others live "in the economy" rather than in the UNHCR camps.

Support for Afghan refugees in Pakistan should be viewed in light of three critical factors. First, international support for refugees in Pakistan, which was strong in the late 1970s and in the1980s, diminished in the mid-1990s following the Soviet withdrawal from Afghanistan. Second, Pakistan, already a low-income country, experienced an economic recession in the mid-1990s. These two factors resulted in Pakistan having to rely heavily on its own limited and declining resources to care for the large Afghan refugee population. The third factor comprises three parts: (1) the changing geopolitical landscape of the region that followed as a result of the September 11, 2001, attacks in the United States; (2) Pakistan's role as the U.S. ally in the "War on Terror"; and (3) the rise of terrorist attacks worldwide with Afghanistan and Pakistan viewed by many as the hub of such activity.

The Soviet Invasion (1979 to 1989)

Afghan refugees have been coming to Pakistan in large numbers since the late 1970s, crossing a very porous border. The 1978 coup that put a communist government in power in Afghanistan resulted in an "Islamic" resistance among the Afghan population. In December 1979, the Soviet Union invaded in support of the communist government (International Crisis Group [ICG], 2007). The violence in Afghanistan spread during the consequent ten-year war between the Soviets and the opposition forces, who were called the *mujahideen* or holy warriors and were supported and trained by the United States, Pakistan, and other anticommunist nations. During the ensuing ten-year period after the Soviet invasion, hundreds of thousands of Afghans died, millions were internally displaced, and millions others sought refuge in neighboring countries, primarily Pakistan and Iran.

During Afghanistan's war with the Soviet Union, Pakistan hosted over 3.5 million refugees. Afghan refugees did flee to other countries in the region such as Iran, India, Russia, Turkmenistan, and Tajikistan. However, the largest number came to Pakistan because of proximity, the ease of entry, more favorable reception compared to other countries of first asylum, and the cultural, linguistic, ethnic, and religious affinity between the *Pashtun* Afghans and *Pashtun* Pakistanis residing in the border areas. (*Pashtuns* are the majority ethnicity, both in Afghanistan and among the refugees.) The refugees entered Pakistan through two primary entry points along the open northwest and southwest border, Torkham in the North West Frontier Province (NWFP) and Chaman in the Balochistan Province. During the peak exodus, in 1981, an estimated 4,700 refugees were crossing the border to Pakistan daily; many of them remained in Pakistan for more than two decades (Blood, 1997; UNHCR, 2001).

Civil War among Mujahideen Factions (1990 to 1995)

Refugee flows to Pakistan from Afghanistan were further exacerbated during more than a decade of civil unrest following Soviet withdrawal in 1989. The withdrawal left a puppet communist regime in power that was overthrown by *mujahideen* forces in April 1992. These events led to the formation of the Islamic State of Afghanistan. In 1992, the largest voluntary refugee repatriation in history took place, with approximately 1.5 million Afghans, 1.2 million of whom were from Pakistan, returning home (UNHCR, 2001). This was the largest and fastest repatriation program on record, until the 2002 Afghan repatriation, and was assisted by the UNHCR.

While repatriation continued in 1993, it slowed down primarily because of the international community's declining interest in Afghanistan post-Soviet defeat and the continuing tensions in Afghanistan. The Soviet defeat did not bring peace to Afghanistan. Instead, *mujahideen* groups, formed along ethnoreligious lines, started fighting each other in a struggle to control the country (Amnesty International [AI], 1993). As civil war broke out, civilians suffered arbitrary arrests, raids, rape, "disappearance," and torture. Many Afghans fled their home country, some for the second time.

The Taliban, a fundamentalist Islamist group of majority Pashtun and Sunni Muslim fighters, bred in Islamic religious schools (*madrassas*) in Afghanistan and Pakistan, emerged in 1994/1995 as the lead Afghan faction in the civil war. The Taliban believed that the key to peace in Afghanistan was the imposition of strict "Islamic" codes. As they rose to power, they temporarily brought relative stability to parts of the country by outlawing the poppy production, looting, general lawlessness, rape and other crimes against women. Yet in a short time, Afghans started resenting the Taliban's strict, fundamentalist imposition of Islam and its restrictions on the majority of society, including the banning of education for women, exclusion of women from all sectors of the workforce, persecution of academics and professionals, and violence against targeted minority groups, particularly the Hazaras and the Tajiks. However, the Taliban's increasing military power enabled them to defeat *mujahideen* forces all over Afghanistan, and as they gained greater control of territory, more refugees fled their homes (Ruiz, 1996).

The Rise and Fall of the Taliban (1996 to 2001)

The increasing political power of the Taliban culminated in September 1996 with their seizure of Kabul from the Northern Alliance (a group of *mujahideen* forces that had banded together against the Taliban), and between 1996 and 1999 approximately 900,000 refugees fled to Pakistan despite UNHCR and the World Food Program's (WFP) decision to end food aid in the camps in Pakistan in 1995 (USCR WRS, 2000; Ruiz, 2002).

The United States' attacks in Afghanistan in late 2001, in the aftermath of the events of September 11, led to more Afghans seeking refuge from the ground warfare and from war injuries to civilians. They fled to Pakistan for asylum and medical relief. At this time, Pakistan continued its relatively tough stance. Refugees were not allowed official entry through the Northwest border. In the Southwest, the Pakistan Frontier Corps were stationed at check posts along the border to determine whether Afghans wanting to cross the border were "true" refugees. Refugee entry into Pakistan was, at times, determined by bribery and extortion (Ruiz, 2002; USCR CRP, 2001). With the declaration of the interim Afghan government under President Karzai in elate 2001, after almost ten years of unrest following the Soviet retreat, Afghan refugees could once again consider voluntary repatriation to their home land.

Repatriation (2002 to 2008)

Repatriation activities started after the United States claimed victory over the Taliban at the end of 2001 and the signing of the Bonn Agreement in December 2001 (United Nations Assistance Mission in Afghanistan [UNAMA], 2005). Since then, repatriation has occurred mostly through the UNHCR voluntary repatriation program operating as part of the Tripartite Agreement between the UNHCR and the governments of Afghanistan and Pakistan. The agreement was signed in 2002 and allowed for voluntary repatriation to take place until March 2006 (UNHCR, 2003b), with UNHCR-provided transport assistance and a travel allowance of USD 60 initially and then USD 100 paid as a cash grant per person upon arrival in Afghanistan (UNHCR, 2008c). This was later extended to December 2006 and then to December 2009 (USCR WRS, 2008). No policy has emerged as of yet regarding the fate of registered or unregistered Afghans remaining in Pakistan beyond 2009.

Between March 2002 and July 2008, about 3.7 million refugees in Pakistan repatriated (of which approximately 300,000 were not assisted by UNHCR) with the largest number—1.56 million—repatriating in 2002 (UNHCR OIU, 2008). The movement of Afghan refugees from Pakistan from late 2001 to 2003 was the "largest and swiftest return" worldwide since the creation of Bangladesh in 1972 (UNHCR Pakistan website, 2005). The majority (80%) of repatriating Afghans were recent arrivals residing in Pakistan's urban areas. Refugees who had resided in camps and cities for a long time are, for the most part, well established in Pakistan and are not keen to move back (USCR CRP, 2003). Movement back to Afghanistan slowed considerably in 2006 with only 130,000 returns, peaked again in 2007 with 357,000 returns, and is expected to be about 250,000 for 2008 (UNHCR OIU, 2008). Increased returns in 2007 continuing into 2008 are primarily attributed to the "introduction of an improved return package and the application of new return procedures" (UNHCR, 2007a, p. 1).

Even given the massive repatriation of Afghan refugees from Pakistan, "representing the single largest repatriation operation in UNHCR's 58-year history, Afghans still make up the largest refugee population in the world under the UNHCR's care" (Revolutionary Association of the Women of Afghanistan [RAWA], 2008). The largest group—some 1.8 to 2.0 million registered refugees—are in Pakistan; the number of unregistered refugees is unknown but expected to be in the hundreds of thousands adding up to about 2.5 million refugees. The large number of refugees still residing in Pakistan is primarily attributable to low repatriation numbers vis-à-vis the registered and unregistered refugee population size, a demographic increase with a population growth rate of slightly higher than 3% which added about 1.5 to 2.0 million refugees in two decades (calculated on the basis of the 1980 influx of 1.5 million persons), the new waves of refugees who continue to enter Pakistan, and the previous repatriates who return to Pakistan because of unsatisfactory conditions (primarily related to security and livelihood/employment options) found upon their return (UNHCR Census, 2005). These two groups, new waves of refugees since the census in 2005 and returnees who had previously repatriated are referred to as "undocumented Afghans." They do not have refugee status and are subject to forced deportation as illegal immigrants. UNHCR data for 2005 shows an annual average inflow of about 50,000 Afghan refugees (some new and some returnees) per year into Pakistan (UNHCR Census, 2005).

Many Afghans who fled to Pakistan after September 11, 2001, and those who chose not to repatriate right away cited fear of ethnic and religious persecution (Pashtuns and other Sunni groups feared for their safety as anti-Taliban forces took over Afghanistan) (Ruiz, 2001). With limited water supply, electricity, sewerage systems, and an emaciated health and education system, Afghanistan has little to offer those who have chosen to repatriate (AREU, 2005). Those who have sought refuge in Pakistan since 2002 and others who choose not to repatriate have been influenced by the violence, instability, and deteriorating security situation that persists in Afghanistan even in times of "peace." Insecurity, shelter, and unemployment are the primary concerns of those who are hesitant to return. Since 2006, increased Taliban-led insurgent activity (in Southern Afghanistan), record-high levels of illegal drug production, and a fragile government with limited control outside of Kabul have further destabilized the country (Davis, 2008).

The experience of the last several years has shown that pressure from the Government of Pakistan, the official expiration of the Tripartite Agreement in 2009, and the UNHCR-supported repatriation program have indeed facilitated repatriation. However, despite this facilitation, factors such as lack of security, inadequate development, and limited socioeconomic opportunities in Afghanistan have played a significant role in the decision to not repatriate or, in the case of those who had chosen to repatriate, to return to Pakistan. Whether or not others agree, Afghan refugees are uncertain about their home country's readiness for their return.

Who Were/Are the Refugees? In the early 1990s, many Afghans who left belonged to minority groups that were targeted by the various *mujahideen* forces primarily on the basis of their ethnicity, political affiliation, or gender (AREU, 2005). Hence, many who left then were educated women, academics, professionals, those suspected of supporting the communist regime, and ethnic minorities (AI, 1993). This pattern continued in the late 1990s as the conservative, anti-Western, predominantly Pashtun Taliban rose to power.

In 1996, with the Taliban's capture of Kabul, those who had so far been less affected by the factional fighting outside Kabul, that is the city's elite and professionals, academics, other educated people, artists and musicians, liberal or moderate Muslims (especially women, whose rights were severely curtailed by the Taliban), and even uneducated laborers, left because they faced violent treatment at the hands of the Taliban. Furthermore, with the Pashtun-dominated Taliban's defeat of other *mujahideen* forces and their movement beyond Kabul to the northern parts of Afghanistan, religious minorities (mostly Shi'a Muslims) and ethnic minorities, particularly the Tajiks (who supported the Northern Alliance) and the Hazaras (Shi'a Muslims and an ethnic minority) also poured into Pakistan (AREU, 2005).

A significant number of the refugees in the mid to late 1990s came from urban backgrounds. In 2000, with the Taliban's move north beyond Kabul and the prolonged drought, most of the new arrivals were Tajiks from the Takhar and Parwan provinces (northeastern Afghanistan), Uzbeks and Turkmens from northern Afghanistan, and some Pashtuns residing in areas north of Kabul as well (USCR CRP, 2000). Groups that arrived during and after 2000 came mostly from the rural areas of Afghanistan and had limited education and skills (McCarthy, Harding, and Lawrence, 2001).

In 2005, the vast majority of Afghan refugees in Pakistan were Pashtuns (81.5%) (UNHCR Census, 2005). The next largest group was Tajik (7%), followed by Uzbek, Hazara,

Turkmen, Baloch, and others. The 2005 census showed that 49% of the refugee population was female. The population was younger than other more stable populations with 19% under 5 years (compared to about 14.8% of Pakistan's population under 5) and only 3.5% above 60 years. Extrapolated data suggests that 55% of the population was under 18 years. The average family size was 5.6 persons. 80% of the refugees who were still in Pakistan in early 2005 had first arrived pre-1991 with an additional 8.5% arriving between 1991 and 1995.

Until 1995, the majority of the refugees who arrived in Pakistan (mostly Pashtuns) reported to UNHCR camps in NWFP and Baluchistan. At that time, there were approximately 300 camps located mainly in Peshawar and to the north of Peshawar in the NWFP along the northern border of Afghanistan, and in Quetta in Baluchistan along the southern border. The camps in NWFP (about 200) hosted approximately 70% of the camp population, those in Baluchistan hosted about 25%, and some camps in the Punjab province were host to roughly 5% (U.S. Library of Congress, 1994). Over the years, the camps came to resemble small Pakistani villages, as the refugees became more acclimated to life in Pakistan. Many camps were home to an average of 10,000 residents each, 75% of whom were women and children (U.S. Library of Congress, 1994).

With the collapse of the communist government in 1992, the international community's interest in the Afghans' problems started declining. By 1995, donor support of Afghan refugees had diminished significantly. For Pakistan, which was hosting the largest Afghan refugee population, this meant heavy reliance on its own meager resources. For the UNHCR and other international agencies, this meant reducing the amount of assistance provided. In 1995 therefore, the UNHCR and the WFP decided to end food aid to all Afghan refugees based on the assertion that Afghans had been in Pakistan long enough to achieve self-sufficiency. Another unstated reason for ending food aid was to prompt repatriation based on the idea that Afghans had perhaps become too accustomed to life in camps (Ruiz, 2001). These rationalizations proved incorrect.

Instead, a major by-product of decreased assistance was reduced incentive for new arrivals and existing camp dwellers to stay in camps. Hundreds of thousands of camp dwellers left the camps for urban centers (Peshawar, Lahore, Islamabad, Rawalpindi, Quetta, and Karachi) where they had better chances of finding jobs. Adding to those who were leaving the camps for the urban centers, many new arrivals post-1995 simply joined family members or friends already settled in the cities, without stepping foot inside a camp.

Prior to 1995, a small number of refugees chose not to live in camps and instead settled in Peshawar, Quetta, and Karachi. Most of them were ethnic and religious minorities who feared for their safety in the Pashtun-dominated camps. The professionals and academics among the refugees also did not live in camps and went directly to urban centers in search of work and better educational opportunities. Other young refugees left the camps for similar reasons. Yet, before 1995, these urban refugees were few in number. Hence, the exodus of camp dwellers to the cities post 1995, coupled with the arrival of new refugees, had a profound impact on the social and economic environments of cities, some of which were already overpopulated. In 2005, about 1.3 million Afghans were living in refugee camps, some of them dating back 25 years, while about 1.7 million registered Afghans lived in urban settlements (Lobjakas, 2005). In early 2008, there were over 80 camps in Pakistan of which 71 were in NWFP, 12 were in Baluchistan and 1 was in Punjab. The Government of Pakistan (GoP) intends to close down all camps by December 2009 (United Nations Office for the Coordination of Humanitarian Affairs-Integrated Regional Information Networks [UNOCHA-IRIN], 2008a, 2008b).

The distribution of the 3.0 million Afghans, as per the recently conducted UNHCR census, is as below (Table 12-1). As expected, the majority of refugees were concentrated in Pakistani provinces neighboring Afghanistan—NWFP and Baluchistan—constituting 7.6% and 10%, respectively of the overall population in these two areas, with higher concentrations in certain districts and thus greater visibility and impact on local populations (UNHCR Census, 2005).

Table 12-1. Distribution of Afghan Refugee
Population in Pakistan

Province/ State in Pakistan	Number of *registered* refugees (in and outside camps) in millions	Percentage of Afghan refugee population
AJK	0.01	0.4%
Islamabad	0.05	1.5%
Sindh	0.13	4.5%
Punjab	0.20	6.8%
Balochistan	0.77	25.2%
NWFP	1.80	61.6%

Playing Host

Afghan refugees in Pakistan, primarily due to their numbers and because of the prolonged and complex nature of the multiple conflicts that have caused them to flee their country, have been treated with varying degrees of tolerance over the last twenty-five years. Pakistan's stance toward Afghan refugees has ranged from a relatively liberal policy in the early years of the conflict to an increasingly toughening stance from the mid-1990s onward. Notwithstanding its own role in fueling the Taliban's growth in the 1980s and early 1990s and hence, its political interest in the refugees, this change in attitude resulted from the recognition that Afghan refugees were putting undue pressure on the country's increasingly limited resources particularly given the simultaneous donor fatigue which was reflected in a substantial reduction in the support of the international community for Afghan refugees and for the reconstruction of Afghanistan, and Pakistan's role as a U.S. ally in the war against Afghanistan which started in 2001 (Ruiz, 2001).

In the 1980s and the 1990s Saudi Arabia, the United Arab Emirates (U.A.E), and the United States made contributions to the Taliban's growth. To strengthen its geopolitical positioning in South and Central Asia, Pakistan, with support from the United States, supplied weapons, training, and transport to the Taliban and facilitated their rise to power in the early 1990s. These countries had in common their opposition to Iran for various reasons and to its growing influence in Afghanistan and Central Asia (Peimani, 2003). An additional objective for the United States and Pakistan was the exportation

of Central Asia's oil and gas (Rashid, 2002). Many in Pakistan also hoped that a Taliban victory would bring stability to Afghanistan and Central Asia and provide some military support in addressing the Kashmir issue with India (Peimani, 2003). The alliance came to an end in 1998, when the United States ceased supporting the Taliban because of their alleged role in the bombing of two American embassies in Africa and their harboring of anti-American terrorist groups (Crystal, 2001). Later, Pakistan was also a key player in the U.S.-led bombing campaign against the Taliban starting in 2001 (Peimani, 2003), and continuing into 2008.

Even considering the role that Pakistan itself played in exacerbating the Afghan refugee crisis, the conflict in Afghanistan, which has impacted other countries, has had the most significant impact on Pakistan. For more than two decades, the influx of between 2.5 and 3.5 million refugees, some of whom brought along with them a militant culture characterized by weapons and drugs trade, and a few others who resorted to undesirable social habits such as drug and alcohol abuse and petty crimes to cope with their extreme poverty and stress, had a negative effect on life in towns and cities in close proximity to the camps and in areas surrounding those where noncamp refugees resided (USCR CRP, 2003; Hilali, 2002). Even in the absence of undesirable activities, the sheer numbers of Afghans pouring into Pakistan and struggling to gain access to education, health, and other social services placed a tremendous burden on the already limited public service system. Pakistan's receptivity and general attitude toward Afghan refugees over the years has been framed by this context.

The Impact of Legal Status or Lack Thereof

In most cases, the receptivity of the host country is reflected primarily in its laws and policies affecting refugees. Refugee policies have a major bearing on refugees' access to protection and aid, and on their quality of life in a country of first asylum or resettlement. In accordance with the 1951 UN Convention Relating to the Status of Refugees, people fleeing insecure and violence-ridden situations are frequently recognized as prima facie refugees (i.e., granted refugee status as a group without individual assessments), and are offered protection in accordance with this status (HRW, 2002). This is especially applicable in the case of mass population movements to developing countries, which lack the resources (both human and financial) to carry out "individual status determinations" (UNHCR, 1997, p. 53). However, while refugee registration is a means of encouraging legal protection, enabling refugees to receive assistance, and facilitating accurate data collection regarding refugee numbers and whereabouts thereby facilitating the determination of the population's assistance and protection needs, it is not always possible.

Although not a signatory to the UN Convention Relating to the Status of Refugees, the Government of Pakistan accepted Afghans seeking protection during the Soviet invasion era prima facie as refugees. The government's 1981 Handbook of Afghan Refugees Management stated that Afghan refugees would be granted temporary asylum for humanitarian reasons, and because of the "cultural, religious, and ethnic affinity between the two countries," would be allowed freedom of movement and access to employment opportunities (United Nations Economic and Social Council [UN-ECOSOC], 2000; Farr, 1995). Consistent with this attitude, in the early years of the refugee influx, the Government of Pakistan did attempt to register refugees. In the 1970s, registration of refugees occurred sporadically with many new arrivals simply becoming "invisible" by integrating into the mainstream of society. In the early 1980s, the government issued passbooks (*Shanakti* or identity cards) to refugee families, which served as identity documents and entitled them to receive assistance. Periodically, over the next few years, the government also registered new arrivals and issued them passbooks for receiving assistance only, not to be used for identification/legal protection purposes. Since the late 1980s however, no attempts were made by the government to register refugees, issue identification documents, or grant them legal status, and UNHCR was also not permitted to register Afghans as refugees (Malik, 2004). This changed in 2005 following the GoP/UNHCR sponsored census survey of Afghan camp and noncamp refugees and subsequent registration of these refugees by early 2007.

While in violation of international law, the refugees' lack of legal status was taken in stride by the UNHCR and the international community because throughout much of the 1980s and early 1990s, refugees did not face many protection-related problems in Pakistan. Despite the lack of legal status, Pakistan had adopted a relatively liberal policy strengthened by the host population's general sympathy toward the refugees, many of whom had managed to somewhat integrate socially and economically in accordance with their education and skills, into mainstream Pakistani society. In some cases, lack of legal status did not allow educated Afghans to access more lucrative economic opportunities, which resulted in many (much like their uneducated counterparts) joining the nonformal sector and working as domestic servants or as laborers in construction, carpet weaving, and brick making (Gazdar, 2003; Oxfam, 2003).

In the mid to late 1990s however, the reduction in international donor support led to the discontinuation of food aid and other assistance offered by UNHCR and contributed to a change in the Pakistani government's attitude toward the refugees. At the same time as donor fatigue was setting in, Pakistan's economy was taking a downturn, which led to competition among the local and refugee populations for limited jobs, health and education services, and housing with respect to those refugees who had moved out of refugee camps and were living in urban centers.

No longer were Pakistanis inclined to be tolerant of Afghan refugees. In 1999, the government stopped recognizing new arrivals as prima facie refugees (USCR CRP, 1999). Afghan refugees entering Pakistan after 1999 lived as undocumented immigrants unless they had a valid passport and visa. In the late 1990s, the government also became more reluctant to allocate land for refugee camps,* and the existing camps became overcrowded, while the security and hygiene situation deteriorated due to limited assistance (USCR CRP, 2001). Lack of legal status and consequent protection became an issue at this time as more and more refugees started leaving camps in search of economic and educational opportunities. In November 2000, the government instituted a policy to detain and deport new arrivals and Afghans who were already residing in Pakistan without official documentation. Between October 2000 and May 2001, according to the government, it forcibly returned some 7,633 Afghans, mostly men and boys (HRW, 2002). Pakistan's border closure in 2000 also meant that new arrivals who managed to cross the border were often so fearful of detention and deportation that they did not report to the UNHCR and instead tried to integrate into mainstream Pakistani population, thus increasing the number of "invisible" urban refugees (Ruiz, 2001).

Outside the camps, refugees found that they could often afford to live only in far-out areas or slums characterized by dilapidated and unhygienic living quarters, unsafe environments, high incidence of illegal activities, and other social problems. Under these circumstances, urban Afghan refugees faced increasing hostility from poor locals. The refugees' demand for housing and supply of cheap labor resulted in increased rents and reduced economic opportunities for locals. With the increasing hostility of the locals and harassment by local authorities, urban refugees found themselves in vulnerable and sometimes dangerous situations. The refugees' vulnerability was compounded by their lack of legal status and the Pakistan government's official stance that they were not allowed to work in the country. (This officially changed in May 2004 when the government granted UNHCR-recognized Afghan refugees the right to work (USCR CRP, 2004). As such, refugees often found themselves working in the lowest paid jobs in formal and nonformal sectors that were characterized by abuse and harassment (Gazdar, 2003; Ruiz, 2001). In many families, all family members, including young children, worked at minimal wages to eke out a living (Khattak, 2003).

This situation continued during and after the U.S.-led bombing campaign, with Pakistan maintaining its closed border policy even though hundreds of thousands of refugees fled Afghanistan in late 2001. After the Taliban defeat, the international community finally started considering the feasibility of Afghan refugee repatriation for the first time in many years. Subsequently, the Government of Pakistan signed the Tripartite Agreement with UNHCR and the Government of Afghanistan providing

refugees an opportunity to repatriate with assistance from UNHCR until March 2006 extended to December 2006 and then December 2009 (USCRWRS, 2008).

Since the beginning of the U.S.-led military operation in Afghanistan, regional and global geopolitics have taken a turn for the worse with respect to dealing with countries known or suspected to harbor and indeed, facilitate terrorists. With enormous international pressure on Pakistan to quell terrorism in its "backyard" and, since 2006, with Pakistan's internal instability coupled with rising insurgent activity along the Pakistan-Afghanistan border and in the tribal areas of Pakistan, Pakistan's tolerance of remaining or (re)entering Afghan refugees is at its lowest. There is no doubt, the Pakistani government has quite definitively "closed its door." At the same time, the precarious law and order situation in Afghanistan has further deteriorated and Afghans, it seems, are caught once again in a difficult position—one where they are displaced in both their native and adopted homeland.

Assistance for the Afghans

The already low socioeconomic indicators in Pakistan as well as the economic recession of the 1990s meant that the government was not much involved in the provision of social services to the refugees. The UNHCR and the Pakistan Commissionerate of Afghan Refugees (CAR) coordinated assistance in camps, including security and protection (Women's Commission for Refugee Women and Children [WCRWC], 2003). Other international organizations such as the World Food Program (WFP) and the International Organization for Migration (IOM) provided assistance, in coordination with UNHCR and CAR, to the extent that dwindling resources allowed. The Pakistan Directorate for Health (PDH), which is part of the Ministry of Health, provided most of the health services in camps, in collaboration with the UNHCR (WCRWC, 2001).

The massive attention to the Afghan refugee crisis in its early days resulted in the establishment of many international and national NGOs, including many Afghan-initiated and especially Afghan women–initiated NGOs, as well as aid agencies (WCRWC, 2001). Some of these organizations have a continued presence in Pakistan, and many Afghan refugees have been able to access beneficial programs and services (these were curtailed due to cuts in funding over the years but were nevertheless helpful). Incidentally, the limited data on refugee numbers before 2005 (caused primarily by the restrictions on refugee registration) did not allow for accurate assessments of refugee needs, and programs and services were rarely adequate to meet the basic needs of the entire refugee population (HRW, 2002).

Over the last 25 years, programs have included a wide range of services from a focus on providing emergency services (food, shelter, blankets, emergency health care, etc.) to addressing the educational needs of the children and adults (literacy and language classes), general orientation to life in Pakistan, basic and primary health care emphasizing health education, micro-enterprise and income generation projects (quilt-making, Afghan embroidery, shawl-making), vocational training to enhance refugees' chances of finding jobs in Pakistan, and basic welfare programs (WCRWC, 2001). Despite the high incidence of mental health problems among the refugee population, programs addressing psychosocial or mental health issues of refugees have been few and far between (WCRWC, 2001; Grinfeld, 2002). During the period of repatriation, many assistance programs are emphasizing vocational and skills-training programs to prepare refugees for their return so that they may contribute to the rebuilding of Afghanistan. There still exists a need for basic health, water and sanitation, and education services in camps (UNHCR, 2007a).

The Refugees' Experience in Pakistan

Challenges to Adjustment

In general, Afghan refugees coming to Pakistan faced many adjustment problems stemming primarily from the constant stress and anxiety that they endured as a result of life in war-torn Afghanistan and the harsh physical conditions under which they crossed the dangerous mountainous terrain into Pakistan. Many arrived in Pakistan suffering from mental and physical

illnesses as a result of their daily stress, the conditions of travel, or simply because they were living in a war-torn country deplete of infrastructure for providing appropriate health care services (WFMH, 2002). Apart from war injuries, some of the most common illnesses experienced by Afghans were skin infections and diarrhea (from polluted water and environments), respiratory infections, measles, and malnutrition (Medecins sans Frontieres [MSF], 2002; WCRWC, 2001).

While limited attention was paid to the mental health status of the refugees, it was difficult to ignore that many refugees exhibited psychosomatic symptoms of extreme stress such as aches and pains, gastrointestinal problems, and cramps. Many were suffering from posttraumatic stress disorder (PTSD) from their experiences of violence (including sexual violence), loss of family, and living in situations of prolonged fear, danger, and insecurity (Park, 2002; Grinfeld, 2002). Refugees also exhibited symptoms of depression and anxiety, which were manifested for some in substance abuse (drugs and alcohol) by both men and women. Visitors to camp sites were often struck by the vacant and dejected look in the eyes of many older refugees. High levels of aggression and violence were also prevalent among some younger refugees, particularly young males and little boys (Robson & Lipson, 2002).

As refugees began to adjust, because of the economic situation in Pakistan coupled with the refugees' lack of legal status and war injuries suffered by some men, it was often easier for women to find jobs (as domestic helpers, amateur tailors, and salon workers) than it was for men. In such cases, families who allowed women to work had to adjust to an economic role reversal with the women becoming the primary income earners in the household (Afghan Women's Network [AWN], 2005). Many instances of domestic abuse targeting women and arising from depression among unemployed or injured men occurred but were never publicized because of cultural taboos around discussing such issues publicly. Employed women also faced extreme stress and hardship in adjusting to the conflicting demands of their traditional homemaking responsibilities and the demands of their new income-earning opportunities. Widows especially faced many challenges in adjusting to life in a similarly male-dominated culture without the traditional protection offered by male family members. For women who were not allowed to work and whose movement was confined to the refugee camps, life in Pakistan proved just as restrictive as it had been in Afghanistan, if not more so (Minallah, 2001).

Traditional age-defined roles also underwent a change in many Afghan communities and families. Coming from a tribal culture where the authority of older male members of the community was paramount in addressing social issues and providing guidance for daily living, life in Pakistan, with its change in family roles (as younger and more educated persons took on leadership roles) and dependence on the local authority structure, somewhat undermined the position of older community members (Farr, 1995). As discussed later in this section, the physical, mental, and emotional stressors experienced by many Afghan refugees were exacerbated for those who came to Pakistan post-1995 because of the increased hardship endured during the journey to Pakistan, and the local population's and government's increasing hostility.

Apart from physical, mental, and emotional adjustment challenges, the overall human development situation of the refugee population, especially among the rural populations, was very low as a result of years of conflict (AI, 1993). The majority of the refugees struggled with limited educational levels, language barriers, interpopulation ethnic and religious rivalries, and few transferable skills, particularly among those from rural backgrounds.

Factors Influencing Coping Mechanisms

The reactions of specific groups of Afghan refugees to their move to Pakistan have been varied and dependent on many factors including age, ethnic background, gender, language competence in both Urdu (Pakistan's national language) and English, urban/rural status in Afghanistan, education levels, location in Pakistan, and the timing of their arrival in Pakistan. As with many refugee populations,

age, gender, and economic potential have been critical determinants. The older generation of refugees tended to separate themselves from the host population, whereas younger generations integrated more easily and, in some cases, assimilated into Pakistani society as they pursued educational and economic opportunities. Younger males and females who were able to access educational opportunities in Afghanistan and/or Pakistan perhaps made the most effort to assimilate into Pakistani society, continuing to access the education and vocational training system, and securing professional or academic jobs (Samim, 2002). Many young Afghans enrolled in language training and vocational training courses offered by NGOs and government institutions and excelled. As a result, many younger and/or more educated Afghan refugees have assimilated well into Pakistani society forming an important part of the business and service community as prominent business owners and supporters/founders of schools and training centers (Yaqub, 2002; AREU, 2005). Similarly, second generation Afghan refugees in Pakistan, that is, Afghan children born in Pakistan to less traditional refugee parents who emphasized their education, are also, for the most part, well integrated into Pakistani society (AREU, 2005).

As in many refugee settings, young children were perhaps the most vulnerable and also the most resilient group. Many children, like their adult counterparts, had witnessed firsthand the horrors of war prior to their arrival in Pakistan, including the torture and death of their family members. Others were victims of war-related injuries, particularly landmine injuries. Not surprisingly, then, many Afghan refugee children suffered from posttraumatic stress disorders (PTSD), manifested in nightmares, anxiety attacks, and truant behavior (Grinfeld, 2002). Still others belonged to families where at least one parent suffered from depression, anxiety, and/or PTSD, which in turn impacted children's mental health. The attitude of refugee parents toward their children's education and the economic status of the refugee family were critical determinants of children's survival and resilience. Children who had the support of their families (educated or uneducated) in accessing educational opportunities were able to integrate and assimilate into Pakistani society. Yet, even when parents were committed to the children's future, the economic conditions of certain families simply did not allow parents to afford school, forcing them instead to make their children work (as carpet-makers, domestic servants, and street beggars) and earn an income that would help the family survive (WCRWC, 2002). In other cases, cultural beliefs forced children to work in families where women were not allowed to work and where men were unable to find jobs due to economic realities in Pakistan and/or war disabilities (Grinfeld, 2002). Afghan refugee children who work in Pakistan are at significant risk in terms of their survival and physical and emotional well-being (Global Movement for Children Afghanistan Working Group, 2001; WCRWC, 2002).

Widowed and single women, as well as orphans, tended to be marginalized in Pakistani society much as they were marginalized in Afghanistan and without the help of NGOs specifically working on refugee women's and children's issues in Pakistan and those that worked to resettle them in developed countries, many faced extreme danger (Ward, 2002). In addition to those young children who had been orphaned, some young children (often young boys because young girls were rarely separated from their families) may have been sent to Pakistan with distant family members while parents stayed behind to protect property. However, often during times of economic hardship, some of these children were left to fend for themselves (WCRWC, 2002). With respect to women refugees, working women consciously accommodated, integrated, and many also accomplished segmented assimilation because of their enhanced exposure to Pakistani society through their jobs (AWN, 2005). On the other hand, nonworking women, whose movements were restricted by their male family members, remained marginalized.

Many Afghans from rural backgrounds who faced language constraints and lacked education and vocational skills also tended to separate themselves from mainstream society and remained confined to camps, whereas refugees who were from the urban areas and had a higher degree of education desired and worked toward integration. Afghan society has long been organized along tribal lines (ethnic and religious), with tribal leaders (male elders) defining and upholding social structures and systems. Those from the rural areas also tended to adhere strictly to these tribal structures and were less keen to integrate into Pakistani society. Urban Afghans, who had moved away from tribal life even in Afghanistan, were eager to make a new life for themselves in Pakistan. Modern and educated Afghans, professionals and academics with greater economic potential who were able to contribute to their selected professions in Pakistan, were able to effectively integrate. Afghan refugees in these categories were also among the first groups to be considered for resettlement in the West (United States, Canada, parts of Europe, Australia), and their stay in Pakistan was often shortened due to the success of their asylum claims. Other enterprising Afghan refugees, who picked up a trade or vocational skill through advanced training and opportunities offered by NGOs and locals, also successfully integrated into local society because of their enhanced exposure to and dealings with locals. These Afghans contributed to the local economy through their successful and creative small business ventures (AREU, 2005; UNOCHA-IRIN, 2005).

Location in Pakistan (whether in camps or in independent dwellings, and geographical location) and the period of arrival into the country also proved critical in influencing refugee survival, coping, and adjustment in Pakistan. Afghan refugees who arrived in the 1970s and 1980s had an easier time settling in Pakistan because of the government's relatively liberal policies. Many families belonging to the first and second waves of refugees, including those who experienced brief stays in the camps, were able to somewhat integrate into Pakistani society. Despite residing mostly in camps in the early days, refugees were able to integrate into the mainstream economy because of the government's liberal policies that allowed free movement and access to jobs. A majority of the pre-1996 refugees have been in Pakistan long enough to have selectively assimilated or acculturated, and even though many of them belong to the lower middle class in Pakistan, they are comfortable enough to not want to return to Afghanistan. Acculturation and assimilation into the upper classes have been rare phenomena because most Afghans in these social strata have moved out of Pakistan to Western countries.

Ethnic diversity and consequent interethnic and sectarian rivalries have been a long-standing feature of Afghanistan's history and continued to be a part of the refugees' lives in Pakistan. Ethnic divisions among Afghan refugees (mostly Pashtuns vs. northern minorities: Tajiks, Hazaras, and Uzbeks) resulted in refugee groups settling along ethnic lines both within and outside refugee camps to avoid conflict. Among the various groups of refugees, Pashtun Afghans, because of their cultural, religious, linguistic, and physical similarity to their neighbors in the Pashtun areas of Pakistan (Peshawar and parts of Balochistan) had a much easier time integrating with the local population in these areas. As a result, a majority of non-Pashtun Afghans settled in the urban areas of Pakistan, away from NWFP (Martin, 2000).

As discussed in previous sections, refugees arriving post 1995 faced major protection and security issues and adjustment challenges due to negative national policies coupled with Pakistan's relatively reduced socioeconomic absorptive capacity and the increasing hostility of locals who viewed Afghans as competition. As a result, refugees were exposed to extortion, harassment, and imprisonment by local authorities, with the threat of deportation (Ruiz, 2001). The imminence of such threats resulted in restricting the refugees' movement outside the camps or their homes, thereby limiting access to better-paying economic opportunities, health and education, and local society and culture. The fear of deportation or harassment (especially for male refugees), which became a constant feature in the lives of the new refugees, severely limited their capacity to adjust to their new environment (AREU, 2005; HRW, 2002). Additional adjustment problems arose from the government's decision to stop allotting land in 1999 for refugee camps, which resulted in "invisible" refugees living in destitute conditions in ghettos and slums. Those who arrived after 1999 and particularly, after September 11, 2001, stayed primarily within the confines of increasingly crowded refugee camps or in predominantly refugee populated areas, removed from

the local population and, as such, many of these refugees remained separated from the local culture. The challenges faced by the later waves of refugees were compounded for refugees residing in urban centers because of the limited tolerance of the local population with whom they were competing for jobs and services.

Looking Ahead — The Role of Resilience

Humanitarian aid has been called for and provided by Pakistan, UNHCR, and NGOs. The fact that many Afghan refugees consider Pakistan their "second home" and want to stay on is testimony to Pakistan's support. However, it cannot be denied that the Afghan refugees in Pakistan faced several obstacles that sometimes seemed insurmountable to outside observers. In spite of this, the courage, resilience, and tenacity of the refugees is evident not only in their stories of survival of the conflict in Afghanistan, but in their ability to recuperate from their multiple losses to survive under the difficult and sometimes hostile conditions in Pakistan and to thrive under these conditions and resettle themselves successfully in Pakistan.

The Afghans' resilience, a widely attributed trait, is well captured in the now famous photograph by Steve McCurry of Sharbat Gula, a young Pashtun Afghan woman, who was a 12-year old refugee in Nasir Bagh camp in Pakistan when her face first appeared on the cover of the National Geographic Magazine in 1984. The photograph, which was selected as one of National Geographic's 100 Best Pictures, grabbed the attention of readers all over the world "because her face, particularly her eyes, expressed pain and resilience as well as strength and beauty" (Braun, 2003). Upon meeting her again in 2002 after an extensive search, McCurry informed Sharbat that her image had become a famous symbol of the Afghan people. McCurry reported that "she was [not] particularly interested in her personal fame . . . But she was pleased when we said she had come to be a symbol of the dignity and resilience of her people" (Braun, 2003). Significantly, in her first-ever official interview, Sharbat Gula, a Pashtun Afghan, expressed a strong desire for her story to be known as a story of survival—survival during the war and survival as a refugee.

Overwhelmingly, the story of many Afghan refugees moving from Afghanistan to Pakistan, living in Pakistan, and now repatriating to Afghanistan while some continue to stay on, is a story of survival and strength. As refugees begin to return to Afghanistan from Pakistan and other countries, in the midst of tremendous insecurity and continued instability, their courage and determination is once again reflected in their desire to help rebuild their country, undeterred by the multiple challenges of restarting their lives. This time, their story is one of surviving in times of a fragile peace.

While Pakistan has been severely stressed by the Afghan refugee crisis, the story of survival told by the refugee experience is also a remarkable one. Since 1979, Afghanistan has experienced a cycle of violence, political instability, repression, persecution, insecurity, and war. Even the advent of peaceful times has been rife with suffering and insecurity. Yet both the refugees and those still living in Afghanistan have survived and rebuilt their lives against all odds, proving themselves to be remarkably resilient. As the world watches Afghanistan emerging from war, and Afghans returning to their country in large numbers, it is important that the story of struggle and survival told by Afghan refugees not be forgotten. The world is counting on their resilience for the successful rebuilding of Afghanistan.

References

Afghanistan Research and Evaluation Unit (AREU) (2005). *Afghans in Karachi: Migration, settlement, and social networks.* Case Study Series. Kabul, Afghanistan: AREU.

Afghan Women's Network (AWN) (2005). *Afghan refugees.* Retrieved April 19, 2005, from http://www.afghanwomensnetwork.org.

Amnesty International (AI) (1993). *Afghanistan: Political crisis and the refugees.* AI Index: Asia (ASA) 11/01/1993. London: Amnesty International.

Bloch, H. (2000, September 25). You cannot get there from here: Bengali immigrants in Pakistan now wish they had never left Bangladesh. *Time Magazine, Asia, 156*(12).

Blood, P. (Ed.) (1997). *Afghanistan country study.* Washington, DC: Federal Research Division, United States Library of Congress.

Braun, D. (2003). How they found *National Geographic's* "Afghan girl" [Electronic version]. *National Geographic News.*

Contact Pakistan (2008). Fact sheet Kashmir. Retrieved October 31, 2008, from http://www.contactpakistan.com.

Crystal, L. (Executive Producer) (2001, May 30). *Jim Lehrer Online News Hour Special Report: African embassy bombings; Guilty on all counts.* Retrieved from http://www.pbs.org/newshour/bb/africa/embassy_bombing/.

Davis, D. (2008, October 20). "The regime we are defending is corrupt from top to bottom." *The Independent.* Retrieved from http://www.rawa.org/temp/runews/2008/10/20/david-davis-the-regime-we-are-defending-is-corrupt-from-top-to-bottom.html.

Farr, G. (1995). Afghan refugees in Pakistan. In *The Encyclopedia Iranica* (Vol. 4, pp. 383–385) New York: Columbia University Press.

Gazdar, H. (2003, June). *A review of migration issues in Pakistan.* Paper presented at the meeting of the Regional Conference on Migration, Development, and Pro-Poor Policy Choices in Asia, Dhaka, Bangladesh.

Global Movement for Children Afghanistan Working Group (2001, June). Lost chances: The changing situation of children in Afghanistan 1990–2000. Retrieved April 19, 2005, from http://www. reliefweb.int/library/documents/2001/gmc-afg-30jun.pdf.

Government of Pakistan (2008). Retrieved from http://www.pakistan.gov.pk/ministries.

Grinfeld, M. (2002, April). Mental health consequences of conflict neglected [Electronic version]. *Psychiatric Times, 19*, 23–25.

Hasan, A. (2004, November). *The process of socioeconomic change in Pakistan.* Paper presented at The Nitze School of Advanced International Studies (SAIS), Johns Hopkins University, Washington, DC.

Hilali, A. (2002). The cost and benefits of the Afghan War for Pakistan. *Contemporary South Asia, 11*(3), 291–310.

Human Rights Watch (HRW) (2002). Closed door policy: Afghan refugees in Pakistan and Iran. In *World report 2002.* New York City: HRW.

Immigration and Refugee Board of Canada (1997). Issues paper: Pakistan; Azad Kashmir and the Northern Areas. Canada: Research Directorate. Retrieved October 31, 2008, from http://www.irb-cisr.gc.ca/en/research

International Crisis Group (ICG) (2007, December). Conflict history: Afghanistan. Retrieved October 31, 2008, from http://www.crisisgroup.org.

Khattak, S. (2003). In/Security: Afghan refugees and politics in Pakistan. *Critical Asian Studies, 35*, 195–208.

Lobjakas, A. (2005, February). *Afghanistan: UN says most of country safe for refugees' return.* Radio Free Europe/Radio Liberty. Retrieved from http://www.rferl.org.

Malik, S. (2004). Impact of international jurisdiction on Afghan refugee rights. *Refugee Watch, 22.* Mahanirban Calcutta Research Group. Retrieved from http://www.mcrg.ac.in/RW%2022.htm.

Martin, R. (2000, November 1). Regional dynamics and the security of Afghan refugees in Pakistan. *UNHCR Refugee Survey Quarterly, 19*(1), 71–78.

McCarthy, R., Harding, L., & Lawrence, F. (2001, September 28). Closed borders fuel refugee crisis: Fleeing Afghans face catastrophe, UN warns. *The Guardian* (London), 3. Retrieved April 19, 2005, from http://search.guardian.co.uk.

Medecins Sans Frontiers (MSF) (2002, February). Infamous refugee camp at Jalozai shuts down: Refugees moved to more remote, less secure areas. *MSF Field News Update.* Retrieved from http://www.doctorswithoutborders.org/news/2002/afghanistan_02.shtml.

Minallah, S. (2001, May). Behind the veil. *Newsline.* Retrieved April 17, 2005, from http://www.newsline.com.pk.

Office of the United Nations High Commissioner for Human Rights (OHCHR) (2008). *International Covenant on Economic, Social and Cultural Rights New York 16 December 1966 Signatories.* Retrieved December 15, 2008, from http://www2.ohchr.org/english/bodies/ratification/3.htm.

Oxfam (2003, November 23). *International development committee inquiry on migration and development.* Retrieved April 18, 2005, from http://www.oxfam.org.uk.

Park, K. (2002). The mental health dimension: Afghan refugees [electronic version]. *UN Chronicle, 39*(1), 14.

Peimani, H. (2003). Afghanistan and regional and non-regional powers. In *Falling terrorism and rising conflicts: The Afghan "contribution to" polarization and confrontation in West and South Asia.* (pp. 7–46). Westport, CT: Praeger.

Rashid, A. (2002). *Taliban: Islam, oil, and the new great game in Central Asia.* London: Tauris.

Revolutionary Association of the Women of Afghanistan (RAWA) (2008, June 20). Afghanistan: Returnees may become refugees again. Retrieved October 31, 2008, from http://www.rawa.org/temp/runews/category/refugees.

Robson, B., and Lipson, J. (2002). Afghans: Their history and culture. The Cultural Orientation Project. Washington, DC: The Center for Applied Linguistics.

Ruiz, H. (1996). In Focus: Afghanistan. In *World refugee survey 1996.* Washington, DC: U.S. Committee for Refugees and Immigrants (USCR).

Ruiz, H. (2001). Pakistan: Afghan refugees shunned and scorned. Washington, DC: U.S. Committee for Refugees and Immigrants (USCR).

Ruiz, H. (2002). Afghanistan: Conflict and displacement 1978 to 2001. *Forced Migration Review, 13*, 8–10.

Samim, S. (2002, November 22). Reconstruction: Educated Afghans stay away. *Institute for War and Peace Reporting, 37.*

United Nations Assistance Mission in Afghanistan (UNAMA) (2005). General backgrounder: From the Bonn Agreement to the 2005 *Wolesi Jirga* and provincial council elections. Retrieved October 31, 2008, from http://www.unama-afg.org/news/_parelection/_factsheets/_english/JEMBS%20PO%20BG%20General%20BG%20final%202005-4-1%20eng.pdf

United Nations Economic and Social Council (UN-ECOSOC) (2000). *Report of the Special Rapporteur on violence against women, its causes, and consequences.* Mission to Pakistan and Afghanistan September 1–13, 1999. Geneva: Author.

United Nations High Commissioner of Refugees (UNHCR) (1997). *The state of the world's refugees.* Geneva: Author.

UNHCR (2001). *Afghan refugee statistics.* Pakistan: Author.

UNHCR (2003a, March 17). Iraqi refugees in Pakistan, histories as complex as Iraq. Pakistan: Author. Retrieved from http://www.unhcr.org/news/NEWS/3e75d9014.html.

UNHCR (2003b, October 28). Afghan repatriation from Pakistan passes 1.9 million [Press Release]. Retrieved from http://www.globalsecurity.org/military/library/news/2003/10/mil-031028-irna06.htm.

UNHCR (2004, December). *Boosting refugee protection in Pakistan.* Geneva: Author.

UNHCR (2005). *Global refugee trends 2004.* Geneva: Author.

UNHCR (2006). *Global appeal 2006.* Retrieved from http://www.unhcr.org/home/PUBL/4371 d1a00.pdf.

UNHCR (2007a). *Global appeal 2008–2009: Pakistan.* Retrieved from http://www.unhcr.org/publ/PUBL/474ac8e10.pdf.

UNHCR (2007b, November). *Global appeal 2008–2009*. Retrieved from http://www.unhcr.org/publ/3b7b87e14.html.

UNHCR (2008a). *Country operational plan*. Pakistan: Author. Retrieved from http://www.reliefweb.int/rw/rwb.nsf/db900SID/MYAI-7K79U8?OpenDocument.

UNHCR (2008b, June). *Global report 2007*. Retrieved from http://www.unhcr.org/publ/PUBL/48490bc52.pdf.

UNHCR (2008c, October 7). Afghan returns in 2008 pass quarter million marks. Retrieved October 31, 2008, from www.reliefweb.int.

UNHCR Census (2005). *Afghan refugee survey: Census 2005*. Pakistan: Author.

UNHCR OIU (2008, July). Monthly summary report. Kabul: Operational Information Unit.

UNHCR Pakistan website (2005). Pakistan: Solving the Afghan refugee problem. Pakistan: Author. Retrieved from http://www.un.org.pk/unhcr/about.htm.

United Nations Office for the Coordination of Humanitarian Affairs-Integrated Regional Information Networks (UNOCHA-IRIN) (2005, February 21). *Integrated Afghan refugees want to stay on*. Retrieved April 17, 2005, from www.irinnews.org.

UNOCHA-IRIN. (2008a, January 31). Government aims to close more Afghan refugee camps in 2008. Retrieved October 31, 2008, from http://www.globalsecurity.org/military/library/news/2008/01/mil-080131-irin04.htm.

UNOCHA-IRIN. (2008b, March 20). Afghans reluctant to leave Jalozai refugee camp. Retrieved on October 31, 2008, from http://www.irinnews.org/report.aspx?ReportID=77380.

USCR CRP. (1999, 2000, 2001, 2002, 2003, 2004). U.S. Committee for Refugees and Immigrants. *Country report: Pakistan*. Retrieved April 17, 2005, from www.uscr.org/countryreports.

USCR WRS. (2000, 2001, 2001, 2003, 2004, 2005, 2006, 2007, 2008). U.S. Committee for Refugees and Immigrants. *World refugee survey*. Washington, DC: Author.

U.S. Library of Congress (1994). *Pakistan: A country study*. Peter Blood (Ed.). Retrieved from http://countrystudies.us/pakistan/.

Ward, J. (2002, April). *If not now, when? Addressing gender-based violence in refugee, internally displaced and post-conflict settings: A global overview*. Paper presented at the Reproductive Health Response in Conflict (RHRC) Consortium, New York.

Wikipedia (2005). Soviet invasion of Afghanistan. Retrieved April 7, 2005, from http://en.wikipedia.org/wiki/Soviet_invasion_of_Afghanistan.

Women's Commission for Refugee Women and Children (WCRWC) (2001, October 15). *Watch list on children in armed conflict: Afghanistan*. Retrieved April 7, 2005, from http://www.watchlist.org/reports/afghanistan.report.pdf.

Women's Commission for Refugee Women and Children(WCRWC) (2002, January). *Fending for themselves: Afghan refugee children and adolescents working in urban Pakistan; Mission to Pakistan*. Retrieved April 22, 2005, from http://www.womenscommission.org/pdf/af_chil.pdf.

Women's Commission for Refugee Women and Children(WCRWC) (2003, October). *Still in need: Reproductive health care for Afghan refugees in Pakistan*. Retrieved April 17, 2005, from http://www.womenscommission.org/pdf/Pk_RH.pdf.

Wongboonsin, P. (2001). *Comparative migration policies in the ESCAP region*. Paper presented at the ESCAP Meeting on Migration and Development: Opportunities and Challenges for Poverty Reduction in the ESCAP Region. Retrieved April 7, 2005, from http://www.unescap.org/esid/psis/population/popseries/apss160/apss160chap3.pdf.

World Federation for Mental Health (WFMH) (2002, First Quarter). *The plight of Afghan refugees* [Newsletter]. Alexandria, VA: Author.

Yaqub, N. (2002, March 31). Afghan repatriation starts after bitter winter. Retrieved April 11, 2005, from http://www.atimes.com/ind-pak/BC31Df.

Zolberg, A., Suhrke, A., and Aguayo, S. (1989). *Escape from violence: Conflict and the refugee crisis in the developing world*. New York: Oxford University Press.

PART III

Nations with Increasing Immigrant Populations

13

Greece

Immigration to Greece: Problems and Prospects

Anna Triandafyllidou

Understanding Migration Toward Greece

Until recently, Greece was migration sender rather than host. Emigration however came nearly to a halt in the mid to late 1970s after the tightening up of migration regimes in northern Europe. After the geopolitical changes of 1989, the country was quickly converted into a host of mainly undocumented immigrants from eastern and central Europe, as well as the Third World. Major population inflows since the late 1980s include co-ethnic returnees, the Pontic Greeks, arriving from the former Soviet Republics (Georgia, Kazakshtan, Russia, and Armenia); immigrants of Greek descent, notably ethnic Greek Albanian citizens (*Vorioepirotes*); immigrants from non-EU countries (other than the categories mentioned previously); and a smaller number of returning Greek migrants from northern Europe, the United States, Canada, and Australia.

The investigation of the factors that attract immigrants to Greece reveals interesting combinations of economic motivations with historical ties. Contrary to the argument that post-1980 migratory movements have been largely independent of geographical and historical ties

between origin and destination (King et al., 1997), in the case of Greece, ethnic ties and labor market conditions have had an equal share in determining incoming flows (Veikou, 2001). A large part of the migration patterns toward Greece correspond to preexistant ethnic ties. A number of immigrants coming from former communist states claim Greek ethnicity and choose Greece as their resettlement destination on the assumption that a presumed common cultural past should allow an easier integration. Another important reason that attracts "co-ethnics" to Greece is that according to the Greek Constitution, people from the Greek Diaspora are entitled to a favorable legal status in Greece.

The dramatic and sudden increase of immigrant influx since the early 1990s was a new and unexpected phenomenon for both the government and the population. The new situation has been characterized by administrative and political confusion with regard to migration policy, and also by a shift in popular attitudes toward foreigners. An increase in xenophobic behavior and racism has been registered since the mid-1990s. In the last few years, hesitant steps have been taken to address the integration of legal migrants. At the same time, stricter border controls remain a priority for Greek governments.

Although NGOs and to a lesser extent governmental agencies have mobilized in recent years advocating immigrant social and economic rights, recognizing that Greece has become a multicultural society, political participation of immigrants remains a taboo. Even progressive state policies are sometimes met with the citizenry's reluctance to accept foreigners as equal members of Greek society.

In this chapter, my aim is to provide a comprehensive even if short account of immigration to Greece during the past 15–20 years. In the first part of the chapter, I will review the main demographic features of the immigrant population. I will also discuss critically the main developments in Greek immigration policy since 1990. In the second part of the chapter, I will consider the Greek model of immigrant adjustment, discussing the ideal types proposed by Segal in this volume. In this respect, I will review the discriminatory policies regarding immigrants of Greek ethnic origin and others, the insertion of immigrants in the Greek labor market, and their participation in public life.

The Size of the Immigrant Population

According to the last census of the National Statistical Service of Greece (ESYE), which took place in 2001, there were 797,091 foreign residents in Greece at that time. Of those, 750,000 were citizens from outside the EU–15 countries. If we also include the population of repatriated Greeks from the former Soviet Union who migrated to Greece predominantly during the 1990s, which, according to a census carried out by the General Secretariat of Repatriated Co-Ethnics in 2000, numbered 155,319 people, the actual number of migrants in Greece in 2001 reaches approximately 900,000.

According to data of the Ministry of Interior there were 432,000 stay permits in force for non-EU25 citizens on April 30, 2008. At a conference in Athens, on November 22, 2007, the president of the Migration Policy Institute (IMEPO), a government-controlled think tank, estimated that there were 250,000 permits in process at that time. In Table 13-1 below we use this conservative estimate to calculate the total immigrant stock in Greece today.

Permits that are being processed do not appear in the Ministry of Interior records or indeed in any records as valid permits. Nonetheless, applicants for issuing/renewing a stay permit who have received a blue receipt proving that they submitted a complete application for issuing/renewing a stay permit are treated generally by local and state authorities as regular migrants. In effect they can live their lives *almost* as if they held valid permits. If checked during a random internal control they are not charged and during the Christmas, Easter, or summer breaks they can travel back to their countries of origin on the basis of special press releases of the Ministry of Interior (formerly Ministry of Public Order) issued before each holiday period. This happens because Greek authorities are aware of the long delays (that last in the best of cases three months and in the worse of cases over a year) that many migrants experience in the issuing/renewing of their stay permits by the relevant municipal, regional, and Ministry of Interior offices. Migrants holding the "blue receipts" though cannot travel to other countries nor can they travel to their country of origin at any time they wish. They are also unable to sign legal documents or address requests to public agencies as they are not fully "legal." In effect, they are held "hostage" by the inefficiency of the Greek administration.

Greek co-ethnics who are Albanian citizens (*Voreioepirotes*) hold Special Identity Cards for *Omogeneis* (co-ethnics) (EDTO) issued by the Greek police. EDTO holders are not included in the Ministry of Interior data on aliens. After repeated requests, the Ministry of Interior has released data on the actual number of valid EDTO to this date. The total number is 185,000.

Alongside the non-EU citizens and the Voreioepirotes, we should consider as immigrants in substance even if not in form, the co-ethnic returnees from the former Soviet Republics, generally referred to as *Pontic Greeks* who arrived in Greece in the late 1980s and early 1990s as economic migrants. According to the special census administered by the General Secretariat for Repatriated Co-Ethnics in the year 2000, 155,319 Pontic Greeks had settled in the country. More than half of them (about 80,000) came from Georgia, 31,000 came from Kazakhstan, 23,000 from Russia, and about 9,000 from Armenia.

Table 13-1. Estimate of Total Immigrant Stock in Greece, April 2008

	Stocks*	% of total population	Source of data
Valid stay permits	432,000	3.93	Ministry of Interior, valid permits on April 30, 2008
EU citizens with valid stay permits	54,000	0.49	Ministry of Interior, April 30, 2008
Estimate of stay permits in process	250,000	2.27	Ministry of Interior, November 07
Co-ethnics holding Special Identity Cards (EDTO)	185,000	1.72	Ministry of Interior, April 2008
Co-ethnics from former Soviet Union (Greek citizens)	155,000	1.40	Census of General Secretariat for Repatriated Co-ethnics, 2000
Irregular migrants	179,000	1.6	Maroukis (2008)
Total (including co-ethnics)	1,255,000	11.45	
Total (excluding co-ethnics)	935,000	8.53	
Total of legal migrants	1,071,000	9.77	Including those whose permits are in process
Total Population of Greece	432,000	3.93	Census 2001, rounded to the nearest million

* Rounded to the nearest thousand.

Thus, in line with our calculations there are currently about 900,000 immigrants in Greece excluding those of Greek ethnic origin (Pontic Greeks who have received citizenship and *Voreioipirotes* who hold EDTO cards) of whom at least 680,000 hold legal status (or are in the process of renewing their legal status). Including co-ethnics, the number of people of immigrant origin residing in Greece rises to 1.24 million that is about 11% of the total population.

Migrants in Greece come mostly from neighboring countries. More than half of Greece's foreign population comes from Albania, while the second largest group is Bulgarians, but their percentage on the total migrant population is considerably smaller. Table 13-2 contains data from the last census (2001), data from the Ministry of Interior concerning the number of stay permits that were valid in April 2008, and also data from the Headquarters of the Greek Police concerning the number of valid EDTO cards and valid stay permits for EU citizens for the same month, but do not include data on valid permits of refugees and asylum seekers or the number of applications that are being processed.

It is difficult to compare the data for 2001 with those of 2008 (Table 13-2 above) because the census data (2001) include undocumented migrants since the census services made an explicit effort to register all aliens residing in the country. It remains however unknown what percentage of the undocumented population was eventually registered in the census. The data for

2008 on the other hand, include only migrants who hold valid permits and exclude those who are undocumented, those whose permits are under process but also those who are in Greece as refugees or asylum seekers. Table 13-2 does give us some valuable information regarding the larger national groups present within the immigrant stock in Greece. While Albanian citizens represent approximately 60% of the total immigrant population in 2001, in 2008 they represent almost 70% of the legal foreign population that resides in the country. The percentages of Moldovan, Ukrainian, and Pakistani citizens over the total legal foreign population in April 2008 are higher than the corresponding percentages in the 2001 census. This increase shows most likely an increase in the actual numbers but also an emergence of the respective national groups from undocumented status.

Major Developments in Greek Immigration Policy since 1990

At the eve of the 1990s when immigrant flows started, Greece lacked a legislative frame for the control and management of immigration.[1] The increasing migratory pressures of the late 1980s led to the design of law 1975/1991, which was enacted by the Greek Parliament in October 1991, formally applied in June 1992, and remained in force until 2001. This law was exclusively concerned with restricting migration— its title actually was: "Entry-exit, sojourn,

Table 13-2 National Composition of the Migration Stock in 2001 and 2008

Country of Origin	Census 2001		Valid Permits April 2008		EU Citizens' Valid Permits April 2008		All foreigners EU and non-EU 39,539	
	Number	%	Number	%	Number	%	Number	%
Albania	438,036	57.49	274,390	63.51			459,390*	68.47
Bulgaria	35,104	4.60	18,154	4.2	11,805	21.90	29,959	4.47
Georgia	22,875	3.00	12,825	2.96			12,825	1.91
Romania	21,994	2.88	10,574	2.44	8,775	16.28	19,349	2.88
USA	18,140	2.38	1,893				1,893	
Russia	17,535	2.30	10,564	2.44			10,564	1.57
Cyprus	17,426	2.28			5,592	10.37	5,592	0.83
Ukraine	13,616	1.78	17,456	4.04			17,456	2.60
UK	13,196	1.73			6,715	12.45	6,715	1.00
Poland	12,831	1.68	876	0.20	6,922	12.84	7,798	1.16
Germany	11,806	1.54			4,063	7.53	4,063	0.61
Pakistan	11,130	1.46	11,084	2.56			11,084	1.65
Australia	8,767	1.15						
Turkey	7,881	1.03	1,069	0.24			1,069	0.16
Egypt	7,448	0.97	10,090	2.33			10,090	1.50
India	7,216	0.94	8,688	2.01			8,688	1.29
Philippines	6,478	0.85	6,790	1.57			6,790	1.01
Italy	5,825	0.76			2,218	4.11	2,218	0.33
Moldavia	5,718	0.75	8,767	2.02			8,767	1.31
Syria	5,552	0.72	5,586	1.29			5,586	0.83
Bangladesh	4,854	0.63	3,761	0.87			3,761	0.56
OTHER	68,385	8.97	29,455	6.81	7,810	18.60	37,265	5.55
TOTAL	**761,813**	**100.00**	**432,022**	**100.00**	**53,900**	**100.00**	670,922	100.00

* This is the total number of Albanian citizens residing in Greece, including 185,000 co-ethnics holding special identity cards (EDTO).

Source: National Statistical Service of Greece, Census 2001, and Ministry of Interior. Data for 2001 include both regular and undocumented migrants and exclude citizens from the EU 15. Data for 2008 include only legal non-EU immigrants with valid stay permits and EU citizens registered with police authorities (holders of stay permits).

employment, deportation of aliens, procedure for the recognition of alien refugees, and other provisions." Its main objectives were to prevent the entrance of undocumented immigrants and facilitate the expulsion of those already present in Greek territory, by means of simplifying the expulsion procedures, giving a certain degree of autonomy to local police and judiciary authorities and also penalizing illegal alien stay in the country. The law aimed to bring Greece into line with its European partners, cosignatories of the 1990 Dublin convention (ratified by Greece by law 1996/1991) and members of the 1990 Schengen treaty, to which Greece was accorded observer status at the time.

More specifically, a maximum time-period was set for residence and work permits regarding certain types of employment, granted by the authorities (article 23), along with a list naming categories of "unwanted aliens" (article 11). A special police force was established to maintain effective border control and regulate deportations (article 5). The conditions for recognition of refugee status were made stricter (article 24), and sanctions were imposed on those who employed foreign workers without permission or helped them in any way to cross the border (article 23). Moreover, the law defined as a *criminal* action the entrance and stay of any alien in Greece without documents and residence permits, and legalized, in this manner, deportations and expulsions even in the transit zones (article 27). According to that law, undocumented immigrants, in order to obtain residence and work permit, had to demonstrate to the police authorities within one month of entering the country, that they had a potential work contract with a specific employer for a given period of time (article 23). Additionally, the law required that the employment of nonnationals was allowed only when the job vacancy cannot be filled by Greek citizens or EU nationals, in which case the Ministry of Labor would grant work permits for the specific employment in question, only before the arrival of the foreign employees in Greece (article 22). The law allowed for a certain degree of discretion to administrative authorities in the enforcement of its provisions. For example, the specific police unit set up to patrol the borders was given the power to decide ad hoc who would or would not get permission for entry (article 4, § 2, 7).

Nongovernmental organizations and scholars criticized heavily law 1975/1991 for, among other things, its lack of touch with reality: it ignored the de facto presence of several tens of thousands of foreigners in Greece. Indeed, the aim of that law was mainly to curb migration, to facilitate removals of undocumented migrants apprehended near the borders and, if that were possible, to remove all illegal aliens sojourning in Greece. The law made nearly impracticable the entry and stay of economic migrants, seeking for jobs.

In the years that followed, hundreds of thousands of immigrants came to Greece without documents, or permits. They crossed the northern mountainous borders between Albania or Bulgaria and Greece on foot at night, or landed with small dinghies on the Greek islands of the Aegean or Crete (usually with the "help" of human smuggling networks). Some arrived at Greek airports with tourist visas, which they overstayed, and others crossed the northern Greek borders by bus, pretending that they were traveling for leisure. It took more than five years for the Greek government to realize that immigrants were there to stay and the new phenomenon could not only be managed through stricter border control and massive removal operations.

The presidential decrees 358/1997 and 359/1997 inaugurated the first immigrant regularization program, which took place in spring 1998. In total, 371,641 immigrants applied for the white card (limited duration permit) which was the first step in applying for the temporary stay permit or green card (of 1, 2, or 5 years' duration). Only 212,860 undocumented foreigners managed to submit an application for a green card. The main reason for this was that while this first regularization program was ambitious in its conception and rather open in its conditions, it met with insurmountable organizational and practical difficulties. For one, the state services responsible for managing the program were hardly prepared to receive and process the hundreds of thousands of applications.[2] In addition, proof of legal employment for a minimum number of days was an important prerequisite; the reluctance of many employers to pay social insurance contributions made it very difficult for many applicants to meet this requirement. As a result, a significant number of applications were unsuccessful in passing to the second but necessary phase of the green card application phase and despite the repeated extensions of the deadlines, presumably fell back into undocumented status. Nonetheless, this program laid the first foundations in Greece for an institutional framework able to deal with immigration. In addition, the data collected through the regularization procedure offered some first insights to the socioeconomic and demographic features of the immigrant population (see Cavounidis, 2002, Lianos, 2001).

In 2001, and before the first regularization program had come to a close, the government issued a new law (law 2910/2001) entitled "Entry and sojourn of foreigners in the Greek territory, naturalization and other measures." This law had a twofold aim. First, it included a second regularization program that aimed at attracting all the applicants who had not been able to benefit from the 1998 "amnesty" as well as the thousands of new immigrants who had, in the meantime, arrived in Greece. Second, the new law created the necessary policy framework to deal with immigration in the medium to long term. Thus, it provided not only for issues relating to border control but also for channels of legal entry to Greece for employment, family reunion, return to their country of origin (for ethnic Greeks abroad), and also studies or asylum seeking. It also laid down the conditions for naturalization of aliens residing in the country.

Another 362,000 immigrants applied to acquire legal status within the framework of the new program. Even though the implementation phase had been more carefully planned, organizational issues arose quickly. In the Athens metropolitan area in particular, the four special immigration offices set up by the regional government to receive and process the applications were completely unable to deal with the huge workload they were faced with. Following repeated recommendations by trade unions, NGOs, and the Greek Ombudsman[3] the law was revised and the relevant deadlines extended. Nonetheless, resources were still insufficient, as work and stay permits continued to be issued for one-year periods only. Hence, by the time one immigrant was done with the issuing of her/his papers, s/he had to start all over again to renew it. In addition to the cumbersome nature of the procedure, the costs (in money but also in time spent queuing) associated with this renewal process that are incurred by the migrants constituted a further hindrance. Only in January 2004 (Act 3202/2003) did the government decide to issue permits of a two-year duration, thereby facilitating the task of both the administration and the immigrant applicants.

Law 2910/2001 established a complex administrative procedure for the issuing of stay permits with the purpose of employment or studies. During the last trimester of each year, stated the law (article 19), the Organization for the Employment of the Labor Force (OAED) would issue a plan outlining the domestic labor market needs. OAED would verify the need for workers in specific sectors and areas and would forward the relevant data to the Greek consular authorities. Interested foreign citizens would then be able to apply at their local consulates and register for the advertised types of work. At the same time Greek employers who were interested in hiring a foreign worker would apply to their local prefecture (nomarchia). Subsequently the employer would choose by name people from the lists that in the meanwhile would have been sent by the consular authorities to prefectures. A prefecture would then issue and send, under certain conditions, the work invitation to a specific foreign citizen at his/her country of origin and the foreign citizen would then be able to obtain a visa for work purposes. The new migrant would have to produce a new series of documents upon arriving in Greece so as to obtain a work permit (that would replace his/her work visa) and a stay permit, conditional upon the former.

The procedure for acquiring a residence permit with the purpose of studying was similar to that. Every year, the Ministry of National Education and Religious Affairs determined the number of foreign students who could enter Greece in order to study, by department and sector. Based on the relevant report of the ministry, those who were interested applied for a visa to their local consulates and followed a procedure similar to the one described above.

The logic of the two cases discussed above was the same, despite the fact that the procedures differed as to the specific documents that needed to be submitted. It is obvious that, although the above procedure is completely logical, it was based on a series of time-consuming and costly (for the Greek state, the consulate authorities, the Greek employers, and the foreign workers) administrative actions. Moreover, the coordination of the whole procedure is, in our opinion, unfeasible because it assumes a series of acceptances (that all the steps are going to be accomplished correctly and in a short period of time) that are not realistic. The law emphasized on the lawful character of the procedure and neglected the essence: the needs of the local labor market, the importance of filling vacant places in due time in order to maintain the viability and the competition of the businesses, and finally the fact that many immigrants, pressed by poverty or political oppression, will try to migrate illegally.

Indeed, although the situation has progressively improved since 2001, in practice immigrants often receive their permit after it has expired. Therefore, they end up applying for renewal when they obtain it or sometimes even before they even receive it. This situation leads to a condition of ambiguous "legality" for migrants who are de facto obliged to have as their only documentation the receipt of the application for issuing or renewing their residence permit, but not the permit itself. This situation runs counter to the principles of a fair public administration since the foreigners have to pay a high fee (145 Euros) for the issuing/ renewal of their permit, which they never actually get to benefit from due to the enormous delays.

This type of economic migration management policies is completely inefficient in the Greek environment. In economies like Greece, where immigrants are occupied in small and medium enterprises, small family businesses, and house-holds, the demand meets the offer through social networks and personal acquaintances. It is therefore nearly impossible for the immigrants and their prospective employers to follow the legal procedure described above. As a result, the informal networks keep functioning,[4] immigrants keep coming to Greece, in many cases illegally, those who already reside in the country stay and work there with or without renewed permits and finally the responsible state authorities do not know where to end migration control and where to start managing migration.

Nonetheless, 2001 may be considered a turning point for the development of Greek migration policy. Not only was the first comprehensive migration law voted in Parliament, but it was also the first time that the government carried out a three-year action plan for immigrant integration (2002–2005), supported by the European Social Fund and the European Commission. This plan included measures for improving and facilitating migrants' insertion in the labur market, looked at issues of health care and introduced measures combating racism and xenophobia in Greek society (see http://www. ypergka.gr/index_gr.html). Unfortunately most of these measures remained only on paper.

On 23 August 2005 the government voted a new law (law 3386/2005) that regulates migratory matters and incorporates the EU Directives 2003/86 (on the right to family reunification) and 2003/109 (on the status of long-term residents) to the national legal order. This law has been in force since the January 1, 2006, but was modified in February 2007 by law 3536/2007.

Both acts (3386/2005 and 3536/2007) include new regularization programs. Article 91 of law 3386/2005 introduced a regularization program for undocumented migrants who had entered Greece before December 31, 2004. Law 3536/2007, article 18 introduced a new, smaller regularization program enabling those who had not been able to renew their permits in time, according to 3386, and those who were not able to collect the necessary insurance stamps, to remain legally. Thus the aim of these two programs (the second one ended on 30 September 2007) has been to incorporate to the legal status certain specific categories of immigrants who have lived in Greece for several years (the date

by which the foreigner had to have come to Greece remained December 31, 2004) but who, for various reasons, had not been able to legitimize their residence and employment in the country.

Act 3386/2005 regulates matters of entry, stay, and social integration of third country nationals in Greece. EU citizens, refugees, and asylum seekers are excluded from its field of effect. The new law abolishes the existence of separate work and stay permits and introduces a stay permit for different purposes (e.g., for work, study, family reunification, as well as a variety of special reasons, article 9 of the law). The application fee of 150 euros for a residence permit with a one-year duration remains, but the fee rose to 300 euros and 450 euros for permits with two- and three-years' duration correspondingly. As a result of protests by immigrant organizations and other institutions this provision was amended so that dependent family members did not have to pay the fee.

It is worth noting that for the Greek administration the work load of issuing a permit is the same (or almost the same) regardless of the duration of the permit. Therefore the application fee of 150 euros per year resembles an "additional tax" for the applying foreign citizens. The increase of the fee is all the more provocative if one considers the huge delays in issuing/renewing residence permits when the law 2910/2001 was in effect, which, to a point, continue today. According to sources in the Ministry of Interior Affairs (Int. 2) the delays have been reduced in certain municipalities but despite that, issuing or renewing a permit in three months is considered a record!

Law 3386/2005 introduces a stay permit for financial investment activities (articles 26–27), which refers to people who are willing to invest a capital of at least 300,000 euros in Greece. The permit for independent financial activity is defined separately (articles 24–25, and requires a minimum investment of 60,000 euros) and so is the residence permit for employees of companies of another EU member or a third country who are moved to Greece for a limited period of time in order to offer specific services within the frameworks of their employment for their company. Moreover the law determines the condition for issuing residence permits for a series of other categories (such as athletes and trainers, intellectuals and artists, financially independent people, practitioners of known religions, scientific researchers, tour guides, students at the Athoniada school in Athos, etc.). It is also very important that the new law has special provisions for the protection of human trafficking victims (articles 46–52).

Stay permits issued for study purposes (article 28–29) include a time limitation: the total duration of the study increased by its half plus one year for learning the language. The law indirectly emphasizes on the development of the sector of education and vocational training in Greece because it recognizes all the relevant public and private institutions of higher and professional education. In addition, it does not set a maximum yearly limit of residence permits to be issued for this reason. It also establishes the possibility for foreign students to work part-time (article 35).

Articles 53–60 of law 3386/2005 determine the right and the procedure to family reunification by incorporating the relevant EU directive to the Greek legal order. Law 3536/2007 waives the application fee for the stay permits of underage children. Articles 67–69 incorporate the EU directive for the status of long-term residents into the Greek legal order. A basic knowledge of Greek language and of Greek history and culture are among the conditions for acquiring this status. The original presidential decree that determined the details for the certification of Greek language knowledge was particularly restrictive (it only accepted high-school diplomas or the certificate of special courses that the ministry would found specifically for the status of long-term residents but did not recognize for example the degrees from Greek Universities and Technological Education Institutes or other state language departments) and was heavily criticized by NGOs and immigrant associations. Finally, a new ministerial decree was issued in November 2007 that simplified the procedure of proving one's fluency in Greek and one's knowledge of Greek history and culture.

Finally, articles 65 and 66 introduce a Complete Action Plan for the social integration of immigrants based on the respect of their fundamental rights and with the purpose of their successful integration into the Greek society,

emphasizing the following sectors: certified knowledge of the Greek language; taking introductory courses of history, culture, and way of life of the Greek society; integration to the Greek labor market; and active social participation (article 66, paragraph 4). This program has, so far, remained on paper apart from some actions funded by the community program EQUAL. Our research interview with the Ministry of Interior, Social Integration Directorate (Int. 12) in December 2007 however suggests that there is now a renewed interest and political will on the part of the relevant ministry to put into action a wide national program (called ESTIA, which literally in ancient Greek means *home*) that will bring together state and nonstate actors in a variety of actions aiming at promoting the social, cultural, and economic integration of migrants in Greek society. However, it is likely that the reorganization of the relevant Social Integration department into a Social Integration Directorate was affected by the voting of the European Fund for the Integration of Third Country Nationals in the summer of 2007.[5]

Act 3386/2005 also regulates reasons for revoking a residence permit and the procedure of administrative deportation (see particularly article 76). It is worth noting that unfortunately this law continues to prohibit (article 84) the Greek public services, legal entities, organizations of local government, organizations of public utility, and organizations of social security to offer services to foreigners who are "unable to prove that they have entered and are residing the country legally." The only exception to this prohibition is hospitals in emergency cases and in cases of offering health care to minors (under 18 years of age). Children's access to the public education system is regulated by law 2910/2001 regardless of their parents' legal status.

Models of Immigrant Adjustment

Segal in this volume proposes seven ideal types of immigrant adjustment to the host country. In my view these models should be considered as points on a continuum rather than watertight boxes of a rigid typology. The actual model of immigrant adjustment adopted in a host country may lie somewhere in between these ideal types. Also different models may be applied with

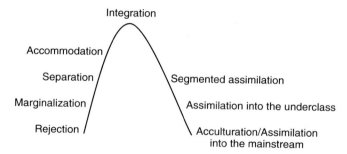

Figure 13-1. The Integration Curb

reference to specific groups of migrants (e.g., co-ethnics or citizens of former colonies).

We could imagine this typology as a curb (see Figure 13-1 below) where the two extremes (full assimilation and outright rejection) are socially and normatively less desirable than the middle points (integration or accommodation). A rejection or marginalization option and an acculturation or assimilation one imply an important loss of social and human capital for both the receiving society and the immigrant groups (and by consequence for their countries of origin). In my understanding, acculturation or assimilation may increase social cohesion but they often involve a waste of the cultural and social capital that immigrants bring with them in the form of customs, traditions, and special skills, but also ideas, intellectual products, and informal or formal networks of solidarity and assistance. On the other hand, rejection or marginalization is not only a waste of the human capital of the immigrant population but also a violation of their human dignity and basic individual rights. Separation is also a less desirable option as it usually includes political inequality and may easily slide into marginalization.

Even though scholars may be in favor of models of immigrant adjustment that are considered to be ethically just, politically acceptable, and socially viable, such as for instance the ideal types of segmented assimilation, integration, and accommodation (see chapter two, this volume, also Kontis, 2001), national governments tend to be pragmatic and are often event-driven in their policy decisions.

Greece is a typical case in this respect of a host country that reacted to developments and tried

to deal with migration flows a posteriori, applying fragmented measures rather than adopting a comprehensive approach to migration. For the past ten to fifteen years, Greek migration policy has had as its main objective to limit immigration, considering that the latter was a liability for the country's economic prosperity and for its presumed cultural and ethnic "purity." Without proper analysis of the economic or demographic effects of immigration flows, Greek governments sought mainly to stop migration at the national borders. Greek authorities, until recently, viewed international population flows as external developments from which the country could be shielded through effective policing and enforcement measures. The results of this policy were costly. Public expenditure for border control skyrocketed while an immigrant population of several hundred thousands people was left to "survive" without papers and without rights. The undocumented migration had large indirect costs related to social exclusion and social pathologies that affected not only the migrant but also the native population (see also Lymperaki and Pelagidis, 2000).

Following the above, I shall classify the Greek migration-management model as one of rejection and marginalization for most of the 1990s. Since 1997, when the first "amnesty" for undocumented migrants was approved by the Greek parliament, Greece has started to make hesitant steps up our imagined curb from rejection and marginalization to separation, and has more recently segmented assimilation of foreigners and co-ethnics.

A segmented assimilation approach has characterized the settlement of citizens from the former Soviet Republics and Albania who could claim Greek ethnicity. As I shall argue in the following sections, these two groups enjoyed preferential treatment, but the outcome of the relevant state policies was rather poor. Immigrants who could not claim a connection to Greek genealogy or culture, were marginalized and/or rejected.

During the last few years, Greek policy and public discourse have oscillated between a tolerated separation of Greek citizens and "others" to a more progressive viewpoint of assimilating cultural and ethnic diversity into the national *Leitkultur*, which is seen as cohesive and homogeneous. Albeit this assimilation comes at a price, immigrants have to assimilate culturally while socioeconomically integrating into specific niches of the labor market. They remain excluded from the political system, and even their civic involvement in public life is severely limited.

Ethnic Hierarchies

An important feature of Greek migration policy has been the distinction between immigrants of Greek descent, namely ethnic Greek Albanians and co-ethnics from the former Soviet Republics (Pontic Greeks), and "others" (Triandafyllidou and Veikou, 2002). The official policy of the Greek government was somewhat differentiated toward each of these groups. The right of Pontic Greeks to return to their "homeland" (Greece) was conceded by presidential decree in 1983. Pontic Greeks are defined by the Greek state as members of the diaspora community who "return"—even though most of them had never lived in Greece before—to their "homeland" and are, therefore, given full citizen status and benefits aiming to facilitate their integration into Greek society. Their naturalization was subject to proof of Greek origins at the Greek embassy in their previous country or residence. Because many of these people, or their ancestors, suffered oppression and persecution by the Soviet regime because of their nationality, it was relatively easy for them to prove their Greek identity. Besides, a number of alternative documents were (and still are) accepted as proof of Greek ethnicity (membership in cultural associations, religious

membership, place of residence, earlier correspondence, just to give a few examples).

In December 1990, the Greek government set up the National Institute for the Reception and Rehabilitation of Emigrant and Repatriate Co-Ethnic Greeks (E.I.Y.A.Π.O.E.E.) (on the basis of art. 8, law 1893/1990) to manage the conditions of entrance, residence, and work of Pontic Greek returnees. Accommodation, food, education for children and for adults, specialized courses of Greek language, and professional training were provided within the context of this institute's program aiming at a successful integration of Pontic Greeks into Greek society (Kassimati, 1993). Although living and working conditions of Pontic Greeks may still be of low standards and highly problematic (Mavreas, 1998; Diamanti-Karanou, 2003), there is no doubt that the policies of the Greek state toward them have been radically different from its general migration policy, affecting aliens.

As regards Greek Albanians, law 1975/1991, on the basis of article 108 of the Greek Constitution, provides them with a preferable legal status as people without Greek citizenship but with Greek nationality (article 17). Because of their ethnic minority status in southern Albania, they were perceived as refugees who suffered persecution and discrimination because of their Greek nationality and Christian Orthodox religion. Immigrants from Albania with "Greek nationality" written in their passports could register at the Aliens' Department of the Greek Ministry of Interior and Public Order and get a Temporary Residence Permit more easily than other immigrants, while their refoulement was prohibited. The legal provisions in issues of social security, retirement coverage, and medical care were of an equally discretionary positive character as opposed to those concerning other categories of foreign immigrants (article 24 of law 1975/1991).

Even though the law provided for the preferential treatment of Greek Albanians, in practice the situation has been somewhat different. First and foremost, proof of Greek origin was not always straightforward. Greek public officials reported (Triandafyllidou, 2001; Triandafyllidou and Veikou, 2002) severe difficulties in certifying the authenticity of documents presented by immigrants from Albania to prove their Greek origins. Language could not be a valid criterion because some of them spoke very poor Greek while others had learned fluent Greek during their undocumented stay in the country. Furthermore, the massive crossing of the Greek-Albanian borders by both Albanians and Greek Albanians and the practice of massive deportations adopted in the early 1990s by the Greek state made it even more difficult to apply the distinction. Meanwhile, a number of administrative circulars were issued distinguishing *Vorioepirotes* from foreign immigrants, on some occasions exempting them from the need to obtain a work permit and advising the police not to arrest them for illegal stay.

The legal status of ethnic Greek Albanians was clarified by Presidential Decree 395/1998. Ethnic Greek Albanians could thus register directly at local police stations, which issued Special Identity Cards of a three-year validity that provide for full residence and work rights and are valid travel documents throughout the Schengen area. These identity cards are issued to ethnic Greek Albanians and to the members of their families (spouses and children) regardless of the ethnic origin of the latter.

The preferential treatment of immigrants of Greek ethnic origin by the Greek state has created a lot of uncertainty and confusion among the immigrant population (ECRI, 2004). It was often unclear who was entitled to preferential treatment, and hence often people misunderstood their rights and generally mistrusted Greek authorities. At the same time such positive ethnic discrimination created feelings of resentment among other immigrants settled in the country. The rights of these latter were unclear and even when clear were not respected as they were delegated into third- or second-class individuals in the ethnic hierarchy that the Greek government applied (Triandafyllidou and Veikou, 2002). It was only in November 2006 that the Ministers of Interior and External Affairs issued a joint statement encouraging co-ethnics from Albania to naturalize and stating that the high naturalization fee would be waived for them. About 8,000 *Voriepirotes* applied for naturalization during 2007 according to data released from the Minstry of Interior in spring 2008.

Immigrant Workers in the Greek Labor Market

Greece is characterized by high unemployment rates especially among the youth, women, and people with secondary education. OECD data for 2007[6] show that the unemployment rate was 8.3%, while in 2006 there were more than 400,000 people registered as unemployed. However, there is an important imbalance in the unemployment rates of the two genders. The female rate of unemployment is nearly 13%, while for men it is 5.2%. Unemployment particularly affects youth between 15 and 29 years of age reaching 17.3% for both genders and 22% for women in this age group (data from the National Statistical Service of Greece (ESYE), referring to May 2008, obtained on June 20, 2008). Also women's participation in the labor force is rather low: 47.3% (data from OECD for 2006).

At first glance, it may come as a surprise that in the mid-1990s there were half a million migrants employed mainly in the Greek informal economy. The explanation is relatively simple and unfortunately a common pattern among southern European countries; the Greek labor market is characterized by high segmentation with special employment niches occupied by migrant workers. The native population's living standards have increased in the last decades and there is widespread participation in the tertiary and higher education. Thus, young Greeks prefer to wait for employment that conforms to their skills, meanwhile financially supported by their families, rather than take up a low-prestige, low-skill, and low-pay job.

OECD comparative statistical data[7] on participation and unemployment rates of foreigners and natives in southern European countries in the early 2000s (www.sourceoecd.org data for 2001, Table 5.3) revealed a distinctive combination of higher immigrant participation rates and similar or lower unemployment rates than natives. Having a look at the OECD data (www.sourceoecd.org, data for 2001, Table 5.4) by type of economic activity, in Greece, about one-fourth of all migrants worked in construction, 20% in mining and manufacturing, 20% in retail and wholesale services, and another 20% in households. Even if these data covered only a small part of the immigrant population in Greece, they clearly indicated the segmented nature of the Greek job market and the fact that immigrant employment was concentrated on specific economic sectors.

Empirical research on the insertion of immigrants in the Greek economy showed high levels of employment in the agricultural sector and in unskilled work (about 30% and 12% respectively, in four regions of northern Greece) (Lianos et al., 1996). This research, conducted in the mid-1990s, showed also that the salary of migrant workers was on average 40% lower than that of natives. As nearly all workers at the time were undocumented, they did not benefit from insurance coverage, and their employers "saved" that cost too. This study concluded that natives and foreigners were only partly in competition for jobs, as the latter mostly took up work that the former would not perform.

Similar patterns of limited competition were shown by a study concentrating on the agricultural sector (Vaiou and Hatzimihali, 1997). The authors pointed to the seasonal character of migration in northern Greece where immigrants from neighboring (Bulgaria and later Albania) and even more distant (Poland) countries were employed in seasonal agricultural work. Such work had long been turned down by natives and even before the massive arrival of immigrant workers, such jobs were usually taken up by members of the Muslim minority in western Thrace.

Studies concentrating on the late 1990s paint a more complete picture of immigrant contribution in the Greek economy and in particular of their insertion in the labor market. Sarris and Zografakis (1999) have argued that immigration overall has a beneficial impact on the Gross National Product (1.5% increase), on private investments (0.9% increase), and on the cost of living (contained). Immigrants also contribute to an increase in the national production. As in two-thirds of the cases they take up jobs that natives reject, immigrants also contribute to creating new jobs (or maintaining existing ones). As their work makes some small and medium enterprises economically viable, it revitalizes some economic sectors (such as agriculture and construction); and overall while it depresses low-skill wages it comparatively increases skilled wages (see also Baldwin-Edwards and Safilios-Rothschild, 1999). These findings are similar to those of a study on the effects of immigrant labor on the Italian economy and job market (Reyneri, 1998).

Sarris and Zografakis (1999) showed already in the late 1990s that immigrants contributed by a 1.5% growth to the Gross National Product (GNP) and that they had contributed to lowering prices by 2%, which meant that Greek products were becoming more competitive for exports. They calculated that about 50,000 natives had lost their jobs because of the incoming immigrant labor and that wages had been lowered by 6% in total. They also showed that two categories of Greek households, those with unskilled native workers and people with average or low incomes in urban areas (accounting for 37% of the total population) had been in competition or might have suffered from the impact of immigrants on the economy and the labor market. All other categories of the native population, both in urban regions but also in rural ones (where all categories benefit from the immigrant employment), had benefited from immigrant work. Immigrants had contributed to creating 20,000 high-skill jobs in the service sector in urban areas and 5,000 self-employed jobs in the rural areas. In sum, about two-thirds of the Greek population had experienced a positive impact while one-third a negative impact of the presence of immigrant workers.

During the years 1999–2000 there was an increased demand for unskilled male workers for the construction sector and for women to be employed in cleaning and domestic care in the Athens area (Lianos, 2001). The demand for unskilled laborers was high in the years before the 2004 Olympic Games, as many major public works were under development during that time. Indeed, in the construction sector, immigrants account for a large share of all workers. Among those, 82,922 men (72%) of the total number of immigrant construction workers are Albanians (National Insurance Service, IKA, data for 2005).

Recent data on immigrant insertion in the labor market (Zografakis, Kontis, and Mitrakos, 2007: 74) show that nearly 40% of foreign workers are employed as unskilled laborers, mainly in manual jobs, and another 35% are employed as skilled workers (craftsmen). An important part of the immigrant population though (15%) is now employed in the service sector and as sales-people at shops or open air markets. Other employees and technicians or drivers account for 2% and 3% respectively of the immigrant labor force. It is also worth noting that only 2% of immigrants are currently employed in agri-culture, compared to 7% registered in that sector at the census of 2001 (see Figure 13-2 below).

The study by Zografakis, Kontis, and Mitrakos (2007) shows also that immigrants (both regular and undocumented) contribute between 2.3% and 2.8% of the Gross National Product. Zografakis and his co-authors (2007) apply a social accounting method to calculate the con-tribution of immigrants to the GNP and to explore three different scenarios regarding the evolution of the migration phenomenon and its impact on the Greek economy and labor market. In the first scenario, they hypothesize that immi-grants continue to work but stop consuming, in the second scenario immigrant stocks increase by 200,000, and in the third scenario immigrants leave within a few years. In the first scenario, there is a negative impact on the economy because of the reduction in consumption levels, in the second scenario there is overall a positive impact because of the increased consumption and production and because the newcomers cre-ate new jobs too; however, the earlier migrants suffer from increased competition, and wages

become overall lower. In the third scenario, assuming that migrants leave the country in three progressive waves and assuming that there is an increased flexibility of native workers, at least half of the 400,000 jobs that migrants leave vacant remain vacant, creating substantial nega-tive pressures on Greek businesses and on the Greek economy as a whole. Overall consumption falls, GNP falls, the level of wages rises for unskilled workers, and the income of poorer families rises, but the income for middle and upper social class families remains the same or decreases. The deficit in the national balance of payments also increases.

The findings of Zografakis, Kontis, and Mitrakos in their recent study appear similar to those of the 1999 study by Sarris and Zografakis. In other words, immigrants compete with unskilled and low-/medium-low-income natives for jobs but overall create new jobs for natives, increase consumption, decrease prices, make Greek products and businesses more competi-tive, and contribute thus positively to the national balance of payments. Moreover in a number of sectors immigrants take up jobs that Greeks are not willing to do. If immigrants were not there to take these jobs, there would be serious negative repercussions for Greek busi-nesses, products, and exports.

A clearer, even if partial, picture (because it refers to waged labor, registered with welfare

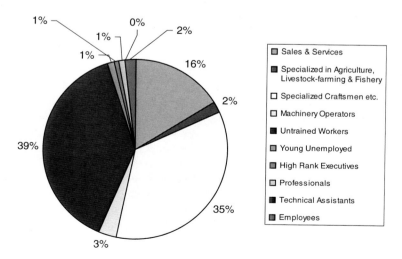

Figure 13-2. Immigrant Insertion in the Greek Labor Market (Per Sector of Employment)
Source: Zografakis, Kontis, and Mitrakos, 2007.

services) is given by the National Welfare Institute (IKA) most recent available data for May 2006. In May 2006, foreign citizens accounted for 13.55% of all insured workers at IKA, albeit men accounted for nearly 17%, while women for nearly 10% only. Albanian citizens accounted for nearly half of all foreigners registered with IKA. Among men, Albanians actually account for 60% of all foreign workers. The second largest nationality among men registered with IKA were, quite surprisingly, Pakistani citizens (6%), Russians (slightly over 5%), and Romanians (5%). Among foreign women, Albanian citizens account for nearly 40% of all foreign women workers registered with IKA, Russian citizens for 17%, and Bulgarians for 12%. These data suggest an overrepresentation of Pakistani men among IKA-insured male workers and of Russian and Bulgarian women among IKA-insured female workers. At the same time we note an under-representation of Albanian women in waged labor registered with IKA.

Regarding the sector employment, the data from IKA show that Greek and foreign workers have a significantly different pattern of distribution among sectors. Among Greek workers registered with IKA about 20% are employed in sales, 20% in manufacturing, 10% in construction, 7% in transport and communications, and 7% in the management of real estate. Among Albanian citizens this distribution is different: about half work in construction, 15% in manufacturing, 13% in tourism and catering, and 12% in sales. Among other foreigners (i.e., excluding Albanians and EU25 citizens), 22% work in construction (a percentage significantly lower than that registered for Albanian citizens), 24% in sales (double the percentage of Albanians), and another 24% in manufacturing (again a significantly higher percentage than that of Albanians). About 16% of other foreigners work in catering and tourism (a slightly higher percentage than that registered for Albanian citizens). Another 12.15% of other foreigners are employed in private homes, a sector that is nearly absent from data on Greek (only 0.34%) and Albanian (only 1.84%) citizens. It is worth noting that Albanian workers account for nearly one-third of all workers employed in the construction sector, while Greeks account for just under two-thirds of the workers in this sector.

Looking at the data of the National Welfare Institute (IKA) regarding the declared profession of insured workers we note again a significant difference in the pattern of distribution between Greek, Albanian, and other foreign citizens (non–EU25). About one quarter of Greek workers (24%) do clerical jobs, and 17% are salespersons (including both shops and open air markets). Only 18% of Greek workers are employed as unskilled manual workers and skilled crafts' workers. Among Albanians the rate for unskilled and semiskilled manual jobs is 70%, and among other foreigners it is 60% approximately. About 8% of Albanians and 10% of other foreigners are employed as skilled craftsmen, while 13% of Albanians and 15% of other foreigners are employed as salespersons (including both shops and open air markets). In other words, in the sales' professions the participation of foreign workers approximates that of Greek citizens.

Immigrant Rights and Their Participation in Public Life

In Greece, immigrant participation in public life, even in its most trivial aspects, has been seriously hampered by the undocumented status of most immigrants for nearly all of the 1990s. Even legal migrants' status was insecure because of the annual applications necessary for them to renew their stay and work permits.

The lack of high visibility movements does not mean immigrant associations have not been active in Greece, or in Athens in particular, where most immigrants concentrate. Petronoti (1998) has, for instance, documented the activities of the association of Eritreans in Athens, a tiny immigrant community, as well as the activities of the Sudanese and Filipino associations in Athens (Petronoti, 2001). Albanians, on the other hand, by far the largest immigrant group in Greece, have displayed very low levels of self-organization and civic activism.

Turning to the types of activities of these immigrant associations, the main objectives consist of providing information for the regularization procedure; contributing to the social inclusion of their members; material and psychological support in cases of emergency (for instance in case of medical assistance, imprisonment, etc); establishing a network of contacts and cooperation with Greek political and administrative actors in order to promote specific interests and immigrant rights; and last but not least promoting the culture of their country of origin though participating in festivals and other cultural events.

Regardless of ethnic or national origin, what is striking to note is the small number of immigrants that actually do participate in such associations. What are the reasons for this limited participation? Representatives of immigrant organizations that were interviewed by Soubert (2004) (including Egyptians, Syrians, Albanians, Bulgarians, Bangladeshis, and Pakistanis) listed the following as the most likely reasons: The feeling of being in Greece on a temporary basis gives them the impression that participation in an association is meaningless and time-consuming. The financial contribution to the association is sometimes a discouraging factor. They tend to have very limited free-time (it is common practice for them to work double shifts or to have two jobs), and the limited free-time that is available tends to be devoted to the family, entertainment, or religious practices. Last but not least, associations are often viewed with prejudice or distrust. In addition to the lack of conviction as to the results that the collective representation of their interests can in fact bring about, there tends to be deep mistrust that associations may be politically motivated/oriented.

Recent efforts by Greek NGOs and state organizations to organize public awareness campaigns in favor of immigrant inclusion in Greek society, although increasing in number, are far from gaining prime-time visibility of the kind that presumed immigrant criminality has been receiving for several years. Intellectuals, NGOs and the Greek Ombudsman have been increasingly active in promoting and protecting immigrants' human and more general sociopolitical rights. Trade unions have to a certain extent tried to encourage immigrant workers' membership. Trade unions of specific professions, for example, the builders' union, have formally been pro-immigrant as a means to secure their native member's rights and to avoid illegitimate competition from immigrants accepting work for lower pay and without welfare benefits. During the last ten years, the National Confederation of Greek Workers (GSEE) has taken at the forefront of pro-immigrant civic or political activism. Although leading trade union positions are still held exclusively by Greeks, strategic alliances between the GSEE and other large trade unions with immigrant associations and in particular with the Hellenic Forum of Migrants (the largest federation of immirant associations) have played an important part in putting forward the social and economic problems faced by migrant workers and their families.

Conclusion

At the eve of the twenty-first century, Greek society finds itself transformed by comparison to the 1980s. Modern Greece is now fully integrated in the European Union and the Eurozone, albeit with a still very large informal economy that is difficult to combat. The country is facing the economic and cultural tensions of globalization and at the same time has become host to nearly a million immigrants in little more than a decade. The native population is rapidly aging, causing preoccupation for, among other things, the state welfare system. The relatively high internal unemployment is paradoxically coupled with severe labor shortages in some sectors. Greek authorities have made hesitant steps toward immigrant incorporation in Greek society—for example, the inclusion of immigrant families in state housing for the first time in October 2004. Nonetheless, the majority of Greek citizens still hold xenophobic and racist attitudes with regard to immigrants (Eurobarometre 1997; 2000), Albanians in particular. Immigrant participation in public life is very limited. Ethnic associations are few and relatively small. Foreigners' participation in mainstream organizations such as political parties or trade unions is formally welcome but in effect marginalized.

The contours of the immigration situation in Greece are rather disappointing. After nearly fifteen years of massive migration the country still strives to accept its role as a host society. Migration policy planning lacks a mid- to long-term perspective, and policy measures up to now have been short-term and fragmented. Immigrant integration policy needs to be reconsidered to address the social and economic challenges of migration. At the same time a proactive migration planning and a realistic migration control policy is necessary to manage migration through legal channels, avoid the proliferation of undocumented migrants and combat human trafficking in the region.

In the post-9/11 context a lot of attention has been paid to the connection between migration and security, with particular reference to international terrorism. It is worth noting that the profiles of the suspected terrorists conform more to those of skilled legal immigrants—often sought after in developed countries—than to those of the undocumented manual workers that have swelled the ranks of undocumented migrants in Greece in the past decade. Moreover, Greece is a small country with little economic or military power and with traditionally friendly relations with the Middle East. Thus, in the post-9/11 context, Greek governments have paid less attention to international terrorism threats (even if security was a top issue on the Olympic Games 2004 agenda) while giving more emphasis to regional security threats related to political instability in neighboring Balkan countries (Albania, Kosovo, FYROM) and economic or political crisis in Turkey. Thus, although security is an issue on the Greek migration policy agenda it certainly has not radically affected the opinions and views of Greek governments on the issue.

Notes

1. Law 4310 of 1929, revised in 1948, mainly dealt with issues of emigration.
2. The main weaknesses of the program had to do with the inability of the Greek hospitals to examine thousands of applicants so that these last would receive the "good health" certificates necessary for their applications. Also, the Ministry of Justice was unable to issue in such a short time criminal record certificates to the thousands of applicants. On top of this, the Employment Institute (OAED) responsible for managing the program suffered from staff shortages. The temporary personnel eventually hired did not have the necessary training to perform their tasks efficiently and transparently. The whole process suffered from severe ideological and ethnic bias (and sometimes outright corruption) that conditioned decisions on

the eligibility of applicants (Mpagavos and Papadopoulou, 2003; Psimmenos and Kassimati, 2002).

3. See special report for law 2910/2001, submitted to the Minister of Interior in December 2001, http://www.synigoros.gr/porismata.htm#
4. The function of social networks in the search of employment is also recognized by Ambrosini (2001) in the case of Italy, which is, to a point, similar to that of Greece.
5. 12.06.2007 2007/435/EC: Council Decision of 25 June 2007 establishing the European Fund for the Integration of third-country nationals for the period 2007 to 2013 as part of the General programme Solidarity and Management of Migration Flows, *Official Journal L 168*, 28.06.2007, p. 18–36.
6. See https://stats.oecd.org.
7. These data are based on the national censuses conducted in several countries in 2000 and 2001.

References

Ambrosini, M. (2001). *La fatica di integrarsi. Immigrati e lavoro in Italia*, Bologna: Il Mulino.

Baldwin-Edwards, M. (2004). Albanian emigration and the Greek labour market: Economic symbiosis and social ambiguity. *South East Europe Review*, 1, 51–66.

Baldwin-Edwards, M., and Safilios-Rothschild, C. (1999). Unemployment and immigration in Greece: Attitudes, perceptions and realities. *South European Society and Politics*, 4, 3, 206–221.

Cavounidis, J. (2002). Migration in southern Europe and the case of Greece. *International Migration*, 40, 1, 45–69.

Diamanti-Karanou, P. (2003). Migration of ethnic Greeks from the former Soviet Union to Greece, 1990–2000: Policy decisions and implications. *Southeast European and Black Sea Studies*, 3, 1, 25–45.

ECRI (European Commission against Racism and Intolerance) (2004). *Third report on Greece: Adopted on 5 December 2003*. Strasbourg: Council of Europe.

Kassimati, K. (1993). *Pontic migrants from the former Soviet republic: Their social and economic integration*, 2nd edition. Athens: General Secretariat for Greeks Abroad and KEKMOKOP, Panteion University (in Greek).

King, R., Fielding, A., and Black, R. (1997). The international migration turnaround in Southern Europe. In R. King and R. Black (eds.) *Southern Europe and the new immigrations*. Sussex: Academic Press.

Kontis, A. (2001). Economic incorporation of immigrants in the host country. In G. Lazaridis and G. Amitsis (eds.) *Legal and socio-economic dimensions of immigration in Greece.* Athens: Papazisis, pp. 177–220 (in Greek).

Lianos, T. (2001). Illegal migrants to Greece and their choice of destination. *International Migration*, 39, 2, 3–28.

Lymperaki, A., and Pelagidis, Th. (2000). *The "fear of the alien" in the labour market: Tolerations and prejudices in development.* Athens: Polis.

Lambrianidis, L., and Lymperaki, A. (2001) *Albanian immigrants in Thessaloniki.* Thessaloniki: Paratiritis (in Greek).

Lianos T. P., Sarris, A. H., and Katseli, L. T. (1996). Illegal immigration and local labour markets: The case of northern Greece. *International Migration*, 34, 3, 449–484.

Mavreas, K. (1998). Dimensions of social exclusion: Pontic Greek and ethnic Greek Albanian refugees in Greece. *Greek Review of Social Research*, 97, 9, 185–218 (in Greek).

Mpagavos, X., and Papadopoulou, D. (2003). *Μεταναστευτικές τάσεις και Ευρωπαϊκή μεταναστευτική πολιτικής* (Immigration trends and European immigration policy). Labour Institute GSEE ADEDY Study no. 15, Athens.

Papantoniou Frangouli, M., and Leventi, M. K. (1999). The legalization of aliens in Greece. *International Migration Review*, Documentation Note, 950–5.

Petronoti, M., with the collaboration of Zarkia, K. (1998). *The portrait of an intercultural relationship.* Athens: UNESCO and EKKE (in Greek).

Petronoti, M. (2001). Ethnic mobilisation in Athens: Steps and initiatives towards integration. In A. Rogers and J. Tillie (eds.) *Multicultural policies and modes of citizenship in European cities.* Aldershot, UK: Ashgate, pp. 41–60.

Psimmenos, I., and Kassimati, K. (2002). *The Greek case: Immigration control pathways; Organisational culture and work values of Greek welfare officers.* Project report. Athens. www.iue.it/RSCAS/Research/IAPASIS/Reports.shtml.

Reyneri, E. (1998). The role of the underground economy in irregular migration to Italy: Cause or effect? *Journal of Ethnic and Migration Studies*, 25, 2, 313–331.

Sarris, A., and Zografakis, S. (1999) A computable general equilibrium assessment of the impact of illegal immigration on the Greek economy. *Journal of Population Economics*, 12, 155–182.

Soubert, L. (2004). *Immigrant associations in Greece: Solidarity groups or interest groups?* Dissertation submitted for Master's Degree in International and European Studies at the University of Athens, Department of Political Science and Public Administration.

Triandafyllidou, A. (2001). *Immigrants and national identity in Europe.* London: Routledge.

Triandafyllidou, A. and Veikou, M. (2002) The Hierarchy of Greekness. Ethnic and national identity considerations in Greek immigration policy, *Ethnicities*, 2, 2, 189–208.

Vaiou, N., and Hatzimihali, K. (1997). *With the sewing machine in the kitchen and the Poles in the fields.* Athens: Exantas (in Greek).

Veikou, M. (2001). Performing ethnic identity. In A. Marvakis, D. Parsanoglou, and M. Pavlou (eds.) *Immigrants in Greece.* Athens: Ellinika Grammata (in Greek).

Zografakis, H, Kontis, A. and Mitrakos, T. (2007). Οι οικονομικές επιπτώσεις της απασχόλησης τον μεταναστών στο Ακαθάριστο Εθνικό Προϊόν (The financial consequences of migrant employment on the GNP). Athens: IMEPO (in Greek).

14

Ireland

From Emigrant to Immigrant Society: Transition and Change in the Republic of Ireland

Treasa Galvin

The causes of human migration are both complex and varied. As a result, and at the national and international levels, patterns of migration are neither static nor consistent over time. A host of factors that operate singularly or in combination influence the content and nature of migration patterns within and between countries, regions, and continents. The characteristics of migrant groups also vary over time and are determined by (among other things) the reasons for migration, international and regional agreements on migration, and the cultural and social capital of groups. The scale of forced migration together with levels of diversity in refugee populations change in response to the emergence of new conflicts, the escalation of existing ones, and the advent of new forms of discrimination. Changes in living standards, levels of poverty, and livelihood insecurity, coupled with existing and new demands for labor in specific regions are among the causes of more general migration. As migration patterns alter, the history of migration in any one country goes through processes of transition and change. Additionally, new and emerging patterns of migration have consequences for migrants, their countries of origin, and their host societies. This chapter is concerned with processes of transition and change

in migration patterns in the Republic of Ireland over the past 15 years; the legislation and policy responses to immigration; the position of immigrants in Irish society; and the response of Irish society to immigrant groups.[1]

Background

For well over a century, from the 1870s to the 1990s, emigration was a dominant feature of Irish society. As a result and though migration has long been a feature of Irish society, until relatively recently its meaning, form, and content was largely equated with emigration. In the period since 1990, the meaning attached to "migration" in Ireland has changed significantly. During this time and though emigration has continued, Ireland has undergone the transition from a country of net emigration to one of net immigration. Hence, while in the year April 1989–April 1990 emigrants outnumbered immigrants by 23,000, in the year April 2001–April 2002 this trend was reversed, when immigrants outnumbered emigrants by 41,000 people (Hughes, 2005). In the ten-year period 1996–2006, Quinn (2006b, p. 2) notes that "Every year since 1996 the number of immigrants has exceeded the number of emigrants with the result that immigration has made a significant contribution to the growth of the Irish population . . . ." But, immigration is not a new feature of Irish society. Prior to 1990 Ireland was host to a small number of refugees, labor migrants, immigrant entrepreneurs, foreign students, and foreign spouses of Irish citizens. Rather, in the period since 1990 the diversity of the immigrant population has increased, while Ireland's role as migrant host society has become more extensive and permanent. The two main groups of migrants driving this change have been refugees and labor migrants. Among the factors that have given rise to the transition in Ireland's migration patterns are: Ireland's international obligations as a signatory (since 1955) to the 1951 Geneva Convention on refuge and asylum; new and continuing conflicts, sources of persecution, and discrimination; family reunification programs; levels of economic growth in Ireland since the late 1990s and the subsequent need for an increased workforce; and increasing international migration. Additionally, Ireland together with Austria, Belgium, Denmark, Finland, France, Germany, Great Britain, Greece, Holland, Italy, Luxemburg, Portugal, Spain and Sweden is a member country of the European Union (EU). As such it is bound by the freedom of movement between member states guaranteed to EU citizens. In May 2004 this regional grouping was enlarged to include the EU accession countries of Cyprus, the Czech Republic, Estonia, Hungary, Latvia, Lithuania, Malta, Poland, Slovakia, and Slovenia. Within the enlarged EU, the citizens of accession countries are restricted from employment in the existing member states for a transitional period of seven years, from May 2004. But as Ruhr (2004, p. 2) notes, "Ireland decided in April 2003 to forgo this option of continuing to restrict the employment of nationals of EU accession countries during the transitional period." As a result, "Ireland is one of only three EU Member States to have allowed access to its labour markets to nationals of the new Accession States" (Quinn, 2006b, p. 2). Thus since May 2004, nationals of the ten accession countries have had immediate access to the Irish labor market and no longer require employment permits to work in Ireland. However, the same provisions do not apply to nationals of Bulgaria and Romania, who joined the EU in 2007. Under the Employment Permits Act (2006), nationals of the two newest EU accession countries are required to have a work permit, though there is a provision that the work permit may be waived. Finally, citizens of Iceland, Liechtenstein, and Norway do not require permits to work in Ireland, as these countries together with the member states of the EU form the European Economic Area (EEA).

The significant increase in the number of labor migrants coming to Ireland since the mid-1990s is largely the result of the demand for workers during a period of economic growth commonly known as the "Celtic Tiger." Thus Quinn (2006a, p. 5) notes that "the growth in immigration and the drop in emigration experienced in Ireland are trends that are mainly attributable to domestic economic development. It is now accepted that the boom, in what became known as the era of the "Celtic Tiger," resulted in real growth rates in excess of 8 percent per annum during the second half of the 1990s and an increase of nearly 400,000 jobs, or almost 30 percent, from 1.3 million in 1996 to 1.7 million in 2001." Quinn and O'Connell (2007, p. 4) further note, "The economic boom of the past two decades or so have, particularly in the past decade, led to a dramatic increase in employment demand. Between 1997 and 2006, total employment grew by 35 percent, from just under 1.5 million to over 2 million. Since 2000, the unemployment rate has averaged around 4 percent (Central Statistics Office, 2006)." While in the early years of the economic boom returning Irish emigrants could meet the new and increasing demand for labor, a decrease in the the number of returning emigrants after 2000 has seen labor demands being met by immigrants from EU countries and beyond (Quinn and O'Connell, 2007). In considering Ireland's approach to the 10 EU accession states, Doyle, Hughes, and Wadensjo (2006, p. 12) note that "even though the boom period of the Irish economy peaked around the turn of the century, at the time of accession the Irish economy was still in a strong position: GDP growth was the highest in Europe, at 4.5 percent, and unemployment, at 4.4 percent, was the lowest."

Ireland's immigrant populations are a heterogeneous group whose diversity lies among other things in their countries of origin, ethnic backgrounds, gender, age, and educational levels. In dealing with the complex range of factors that cause people to become refugees, Roberts (1998, p. 378) notes, "above all they include wars, especially civil wars," while Fuglerud (1997, p. 446–447) further notes, "due to changes in patterns of conflict, most refugees today are not individually persecuted but civilians fleeing from other people's violence." Refugees in Ireland can be divided into three groups, namely, individuals who fled generally dangerous situations or conflict zones; those who had experienced various forms of persecution as a consequence of their political and other activities; and those individuals who anticipated or feared that they would be persecuted if they remained in their own societies (Galvin, 2000). General levels of political and social vulnerability characterized the position of refugees in their countries of origin, along with the economic disruptions and the lack of development that result from conflict.

Migration systems theory views migratory movements as the result of a complex process of interaction between macro and micro social structures (Castles and Miller, 2003). Among the significant macro structures are regional agreements and the role of the state, in both countries of origin and host societies, in organizing and facilitating movement (Hollifield, 2000). In the Irish case, the operation of macro structures and the emergence and use of individual networks and resources at the micro level, are both evident in relation to labor migration. Individuals coming to work in Ireland can be divided into a number of groups, namely, those from other EU member states, whose movement is facilitated by EU agreements on the movement of citizens; non-EU nationals recruited into professional, semiskilled and unskilled occupations through a targeted and government-sanctioned program; and those who come for the experience of living and working in a different cultural and social setting. The largest numbers have (of late) come from countries with: emigration traditions; high rates of unemployment; weak currencies; and high levels of poverty (Table 14-4).

In the Irish case, labor migrants initially tended to be grouped into larger numbers from a smaller number of countries than refugees. This was partly the result of the state's active role in recruiting (into Ireland) particular categories of workers from specific countries in the late 1990s. Thus, for example, nurses were recruited from the Philippines and India. The opening up of the labor migration process through the implementation of a general work-permit system and the lack of visa requirements for citizens of the 10 EU accession countries has served to increase: the level of diversity among labor migrants; the numbers coming from EU accession countries; and the sectors of the economy into which migrants come to work.

Though no immigrant skills census has been conducted in Ireland, evidence from existing research suggests quite high levels of education among various groups of migrants, but with variations within groups (Zena Project, 1999, Galvin, 2000, Conlon, O' Connor, and Parsons, 2002). Barrett, Bergin, and Duffy (2006) found that in 2003 immigrant workers had higher levels of education than their local counterparts. Thus while slightly more than 54 percent of immigrants had a third-level education the figure for the local population was 27 percent.

Ireland's Changing Migrant Population

While refugee numbers have increased significantly in Ireland since 1994 (Table 14-1), the corresponding change in the number of immigrant workers came in 1997 (Tables 14-2, 14-3, 14-4, 14-5). Initially, in the period 1997–1999, the number of applications for refugee status (16,233) exceeded the number of new applications for employment permits (10,585). Since 2000 the annual number of employment permits has grown far more rapidly than the number of applicants for asylum and refugee status. In the period 2000–2002 employment permits accounted for almost 68% of all applications for employment and asylum. While the Census of Population 2002 showed that 7.1% of the population were non-Irish nationals (Hughes, 2005), the 2006 Census reveals that 10.29% (414,512) of the population living in cities, towns, and rural areas were non-Irish nationals (Central Statistics Office [CSO], 2008). Additionally, since the late 1980s two significant changes have taken place in the nature of in-migration namely, the proportion of Irish return emigrants in the total

Table 14-1. Applications for Asylum in Ireland, 1987–2008

Year	Number of asylum applications
1987	50
1988	49
1989	36
1990	60
1991	31
1992	39
1993	91
1994	362
1995	424
1996	1,179
1997	3,883
1998	4,626
1999	7,724
2000	10,938
2001	10,325
2002	11,630
2003	7,900
2004	4,770
2005	4,323
2006	4,314
2007	3,985
2008[*]	2,885

[*] Figures are for the period January 1, 2008–September 30, 2008.
Sources: Figures for 1987: Interdepartmental Committee on Non-Irish Nationals—Interim Report on Applications for Refugee Status 25-11-1993. Dublin, Government Publications Office.
Figures for 1988–2001: Department of Justice, Equality and Law Reform, Dublin.
Figures for 2002–2004: UNHCR.
Figures for 2005–2008: Office of the Refugee Applications Commissioner (ORAC) Department of Justice, Equality and Law Reform, Dublin.

immigrant population has decreased from 64.5% in 1987 to 37.9% in 2002; while the number of immigrants from outside the EU and the United States has increased from 8.7% to 34.5% of the total immigrant population (Ruhr, 2004).

Legislative and Policy Changes

Given the past emphasis on emigration and the arrival of relatively small numbers of immigrants prior to 1990, it is perhaps not surprising that Ireland has found itself poorly equipped for its new role as migrant host society. Prior to the 1990s Ireland had no specific legislation governing refugees or other groups of migrants; it had only very basic administrative structures to deal

with migrants and their needs and very little concept of the change that large-scale immigration would mean for Irish society.

The Nationality and Citizenship Act (1935), the Aliens Act (1935), Amendments to the Aliens Act in 1946 and 1975, together with a letter from the Irish Ministry for Justice to the UNHCR in 1985 setting out the procedure for establishing refugee status and granting asylum, provided the legal framework for state policy on refuge and asylum until 1996 (Shipsey, 1994). The Aliens Act (1935) and the Aliens Order (1946) provided the legal basis for state policy on labor migrants until 2003.

Beginning in the mid-1990s a host of legislative measures have been introduced in Ireland in the area of migration. Since 1996 individuals arriving as asylum seekers and wishing to claim Convention refugee status are governed by the Refugee Act (1996), which enshrined the definition of a refugee contained in the 1951 Geneva Convention into Irish law. Amendments to the Refugee Act (1996) through the Immigration Act (2003) provide for (among other things) the introduction of the concept of a Safe Country of Origin and accelerated procedures for certain categories of asylum applicants; the fingerprinting of asylum applicants; and the translation of the Dublin 11 Regulation into Irish law. On September 1, 2003, the Dublin 11 Regulation succeeded the Dublin Convention to provide the legal basis for determining which EU member state is responsible for examining an asylum application. The Immigration Act (1999) sets out the criteria and procedures that govern the detention and removal of foreign nationals from the state and makes provision for the issuing of deportation orders.

The Employment Permits Act (2003) provided a new legal framework for the administration of an employment permit system. While this legislation was introduced largely to enable the nationals of the 10 EU accession states to access the Irish labor market after May 2004, it also put employment permits for non-EEA nationals on a legal footing for the first time. Additionally, it allows the Minister to reimpose a requirement for employment permits for nationals of the 10 EU accession states (after 2004) if conditions within the Irish labor market change.

Table 14-2. Application for Work Permits, Work Visas, and Authorizations in Ireland, 1995–2008

Year	New work permits	Work visas and authorizations[*]	Total
1995	2,563	0	2,563
1996	2,137	0	2,137
1997	2,668	0	2,668
1998	3,589	0	3,589
1999	4,328	0	4,328
2000	15,434	1,383	16,817
2001	29,594	3,749	33,343
2002	23,326	2,610	25,936
2003	21,965	1,158	23,123
2004	10,020	1,317	11,337
2005	7,354	2,585	9,939
2006	7,298	—	7,298
2007	10,134	—	10,134
2008[**]	6,945	—	6,945

[*] The work visa/authorization scheme was introduced in 2000. Figures for the years 2006, 2007, and 2008 are not available.
[**] Figures are for the period January 1, 2008–September 30, 2008.
Sources: Figures for 1995–2002: Ruhr, 2004.
Figures for work permits 2003–September 30, 2008: Irish Government—Department of Enterprise, Trade, and Employment, Dublin.
Figures for work visas/authorizations 2003: Quinn, 2006a.
Figures for work visas/authorizations January–November 2004: National Economic and Social Council of Ireland, Dublin, 2006.
Figures for work visas/authorizations 2005: Quinn and O'Connell, 2007.

Table 14-3. Work Permits Issued in Ireland by Year, 1999–2008

Year	New Permits	Renewals	Group Permits	Total
1999	4,328	1,653	269	6,250
2000	15,434	2,271	301	18,006
2001	29,594	6,485	357	36,436
2002	23,326	16,562	433	40,321
2003	19,526	21,229	463	41,681[*]
2004	10,020	23,246	801	34,067
2005	7,354	18,970	812	27,136
2006	7,298	16,600	956	24,854
2007	10,134	13,457	13	23,604
2008[**]	6,945	4,401	0	11,346

[*] The figures listed by the Department of Enterprise, Trade, and Employment (Dublin) under total permits issued by year and category for 2003 is 47,551 which is considerably higher than this figure, which is listed under total permits issued by Nationality for 2003.
[**] Figures are for the period January 1, 2008–September 30, 2008.
Source: Irish Government—Department of Enterprise, Trade, and Employment, Dublin.

In addition to the above and in the period since 1996 a number of additional laws relating to immigration have been passed: the Immigration Act (1999), which sets out the grounds for deportations; the Illegal Immigrants (Trafficking) Act (2000), which creates offences offenses in relation to facilitating illegal immigration; the Immigration Act (2003), which stipulates the sanctions for carriers of illegal immigrants, and introduces an obligation on state departments to share information on nonnationals for the purpose of administering immigration law, the

Table 14-4. Work Permits Issued by Nationality. 1999–2001

Nationality	1999	2000	2001	Total
Australia	329	759	1,114	2,202
Belarus	13	170	780	963
Bangladesh	66	281	548	895
Brazil	160	630	1,005	1,795
Bulgaria	23	161	519	703
Canada	156	775	493	1,424
China	133	371	994	1,498
Czech Republic	99	955	1,481	2,535
Estonia	2	355	1,056	1,413
India	359	633	763	1,755
Latvia	250	2,160	4,403	6,813
Lithuania	18	844	2,948	3,810
Malaysia	228	769	1,116	2,113
Moldova	14	117	463	594
New Zealand	208	416	601	1,225
Pakistan	230	452	829	1,511
Philippines	149	997	2,472	3,618
Poland	179	885	2,508	3,572
Romania	77	400	1,804	2,281
Russian Fed.	191	804	1,469	2,464
South Africa	334	642	2,271	3,247
Ukraine	41	388	1,351	1,780
USA	820	1,045	979	2,844
Other	1,671	2,824	4,789	9,284
Total	5,750	17,833	36,756	60,339

Source: Ruhr, 2004.

Immigration Act (2004), which includes a wide range of provisions previously contained in the Orders made under the 1935 Act, including the conditions under which a nonnational may be refused entry to the country and the duration of a foreign national's stay in the country, the Medical Practitioners (Amendment) Act (2002), which deals with the permanent registration of foreign medical practitioners and the Employment Permits Act (2006) which seeks to protect immigrant workers from practices such as recruitment related deductions and the retention by employers of an employee's passport or other documents.

Irish citizenship is governed by the Irish Nationality and Citizenship Act (1956) as amended by the Irish Nationality and Citizenship Act(s) 1986, 1994, 2001, and 2004. The 1989 Supreme Court ruling stipulated that the Irish born child of nonnational parents, who by being born in Ireland was a citizen of the state, "had ... a right to the 'care, company and parentage' of his or her family ..." within the

country (Quinn and Hughes, 2005, p. 6). Following this ruling the practice was to grant residency in Ireland to the foreign born parents of Irish citizen children. Though no figures are available, a number of asylum seekers applied for residency in Ireland on the basis of their Irish born children. Indeed, there are cases of asylum seekers who were advised by officials in the relevant Government Department to pursue this route to residency in Ireland as opposed to pursuing their asylum claims. The Belfast Agreement (1998) gave rise to a Constitutional change whereby the right to Irish citizenship was granted to all people born on the island of Ireland, thereby further strengthening the right to citizenship for the children of nonnational parents born in Ireland. The Irish Nationality and Citizenship Act (2004) which came into effect on January 1, 2005, sets out the revised conditions under which citizenship may be granted to the child of foreign born parents who is born in Ireland. It stipulates that one of the parents must have been legally resident on

Table 14-5. Work Permits Issued by Nationality, 2002–2008[*]

Nationality	2002	2003	2004	2005	2006	2007	2008[**]	Total
Algeria	87	96	93	91	69	59	29	524
Argentina	83	90	67	68	70	70	32	480
Australia	1,116	1,040	908	927	879	808	356	6,034
Bangladesh	767	930	1,009	900	735	666	248	5,255
Belarus	870	907	760	609	481	374	120	4,121
Botswana	18	31	34	40	50	44	21	238
Brazil	1,327	1,434	1,512	1,332	1,211	1,173	520	8,509
Bulgaria	753	770	721	569	438	38	21	3,310
Canada	294	266	269	315	335	348	186	2,013
China	1,236	1,340	1,284	1,362	1,135	1,188	536	8,081
Croatia	140	183	141	165	137	112	46	924
Czech Republic	1,138	980	265	0	0	0	0	2,383
Egypt	206	221	257	212	224	171	71	1,362
Ethiopia	14	13	15	14	14	15	4	89
Ghana	20	20	19	18	8	14	5	104
Hong Kong	184	161	180	168	89	74	23	879
Hungary	379	342	72	0	0	0	0	793
India	845	868	1,253	1,724	2,166	4,069	2,721	13,646
Indonesia	41	45	56	66	61	70	26	365
Japan	197	187	235	221	214	208	55	1,317
Kenya	15	14	9	14	17	26	14	109
Lithuania	3,816	3,914	1,238	0	0	0	0	8,968
Malaysia	1,086	900	886	932	749	797	467	5,817
Mexico	44	45	39	38	43	125	25	359
Moldova	771	941	849	715	631	534	173	4,614
Morocco	122	122	136	117	111	108	46	762
New Zealand	569	589	550	526	530	484	195	3,443
Nigeria	87	76	60	77	93	138	131	662
Pakistan	840	696	846	822	769	813	320	5,106
Peru	19	15	15	22	25	19	3	118
Philippines	3,255	3,516	4,301	4,172	3,850	3,885	1,843	24,822
Poland	3,142	3,992	1,915	0	0	0	0	9,049
Romania	2,459	2,109	2,113	1,836	1,494	119	117	10,247
Russian Fed[***]	1,238	950	–	661	456	403	144	3,852
Slovakia	459	472	119	0	0	0	0	1,050
South Africa	2,273	2,184	2,031	1,833	1,719	1,461	618	12,119
Sri Lanka	109	140	144	160	164	187	72	976
Sudan	33	12	11	12	6	6	5	85
Switzerland[***]	86	–	1	0	0	0	0	87
Tanzania	22	16	14	9	9	11	0	81
Thailand	529	483	507	559	495	486	194	3,253
Tunisia	78	71	76	84	67	54	15	445
Turkey	155	426	1,191	314	187	222	91	2,586
Ukraine	2,092	2,560	2,137	1,906	1,679	1,412	388	12,174
USA	792	834	927	1,048	1,038	1,208	712	6,559
Venezuela	15	22	19	19	20	36	9	140
Vietnam	83	73	63	87	87	57	34	484
Zambia	11	10	4	12	11	17	8	73
Zimbabwe	258	228	251	219	181	216	90	1,443
Other	5,715	5,884	3,664	1,329	1,151	1,266	612	19,621
Group Permits[****]	433	463	801	812	956	13	0	3,478
Total	40,321	41,681	34,067	27,136	24,854	23,604	11,346	20,3009

[*] Figures include new permits and permit renewals.
[**] Figures are for the period January 1, 2008–September 30, 2008.
[***] Figures for the Russian Federation 2004 and for Switzerland 2003 are not available.
[****] Figures are for all countries.
Source: Irish Government—Department of Enterprise, Trade and Employment, Dublin.

the island of Ireland for three years during the four years immediately preceding the child's birth. Periods of residence in Ireland as a foreign student or while an asylum application is being processed cannot be counted as part of the three-year requirement. Given the relatively young profile of many asylum applicants and the delays in processing their asylum claims, it is not surprising that a large number of them had started their families in Ireland and had had children there prior to 2004. To cater for all those whose residency applications had not been processed, the foreign parents of children born in Ireland before January 1, 2005, were allowed to apply for residency during the period January–March of that year.

Since the 1990s the government's main concern has been to establish the legal and administrative machinery to categorize migrants into defined groups, improve the efficiency of the immigration system, increase state control over immigration, and define the rights of individual groups and the state's obligations toward them. Consequently, a number of trends have emerged in the development of laws and policies on immigration in Ireland. Firstly, the legislation and policy formulation process has been re-active rather than pro-active in nature. Secondly, it has been focused on the need to categorize immigrant groups. Thirdly, its reactive nature means that there is now considerable variation in the laws applied to different groups of immigrants with resulting differences in their status, their rights, and the manner in which their needs are met. Constant changes in legislation during this period have generated insecurity for all immigrants and difficulties in keeping abreast with the legal and policy provisions that govern them. The interchangeable use of the terms "migrant," "refugee," and "illegal immigrant" in government and media discourse, coupled with reactive legislation to enhance state control over immigration, further deepens those insecurities. At the policy level the government's main aims have been to establish the mechanisms to meet the needs of refugees; ensure that Convention refugees have access to the same services as Irish citizens; meet and balance the needs of the labor market; and set out guidelines for the integration of immigrants into Irish society.

Immigrant Groups

The Refugee Act (1996) provides for the definition of an asylum seeker and various categories of refugees. Therein a program refugee is defined as "...a person to whom leave to enter and remain in the state for temporary protection or resettlement as part of a group of persons has been given by the Government...whether or not such a person is a refugee within the meaning of the definition of 'refugee' of section 2 of the Refugee Act 1996 (Refugee Act [1996], Section 24)." Prior to 1990, Ireland had been host to a sizable number of program refugees who arrived in Ireland under an agreement between the government and the UNHCR (Table 14-6). In the period 1956–2008 these groups included Hungarians, Chileans, Vietnamese, Iranian Baha'i, and several groups of Bosnians. The last group of program refugees invited to Ireland were those who arrived from Kosovo in 1999. "In June 2005 the Government approved an increase in the State's refugee resettlement quota from 10 cases to around 50 cases, or approximately 200 persons, per annum" (Quinn, 2006b, p. 14). Program refugees have the right to reside permanently in their host society from the time of arrival and to participate in all areas of that society. As a result and from the time of arrival in Ireland, program refugees have the same rights and entitlements as Irish citizens to employment, education and training, housing, and social welfare payments. They may apply for citizenship after three years of residence in the state (O'Regan, 1998). Among the program refugees who have come to Ireland, only significant numbers of Vietnamese, Bosnians, and those from Kosovo have remained in the state.

In comparison with program refugees, asylum seekers are temporarily resident in their host society during the asylum determination process, that is, while their claim for Convention refugee status is being processed. As they have notified the relevant authorities of their intention to claim asylum they are not undocumented or illegal immigrants. The participation of asylum seekers in their host society is both restricted and limited by the legislative and policy provisions surrounding refugee reception and resettlement. In the Irish case and under the terms of

Table 14-6. Program Refugees Admitted to Ireland, 1956–1999[*]

Year	Place of Origin	Number
1956	Hungary	530
1973–1974	Chile	120
1979	Vietnam[**]	212
1985	Iran (Baha'i)	26
1992	Bosnia[***]	178
1993	Bosnia	13
1994	Bosnia	9
1995	Bosnia	80
1996	Bosnia	83
1997	Bosnia	89
1998	Bosnia	3
1999	Kosovo[****]	1,032

[*]Figures are for each "new intake" and do not include those who were admitted under the family reunification program. No "new intake" has occurred since 1999.
[**]1979–1998—a total of 382 relatives have been admitted under the family reunification program.
[***]1993–1999—a total of 833 relatives have been admitted under the family reunification program. This includes 276 in 1999.
[****]1999—a total of 21 relatives were admitted under the family reunification program.
Source: Galvin, T. (2000), p. 2,000.

the Refugee Act (1996) asylum seekers are not entitled to take up employment or engage in education or training during the lengthy asylum determination process. Once granted Convention refugee status they have the same rights and entitlements as Irish citizens in relation to employment, education, social welfare, and so forth. Individuals who fail to acquire Convention refugee status may be given Humanitarian Leave to Remain in the state (HLR). In Ireland the Minister for Justice, Equality, and Law Reform is responsible for asylum applications and has discretionary powers to grant HLR to an individual. Thus Section 3(6) of the Immigration Act (1999) stipulates that when considering an application for "leave to remain" the Minister has regard to "humanitarian considerations."

All HLR individuals have the same rights and entitlements as Convention refugees during their stay in Ireland, with the notable exception that their residence permit is renewed on a yearly basis until or unless they acquire Irish citizenship.

With the exception of those granted Convention refugee status, HLR, or postnuptial citizenship, all non-EEA nationals require an employment permit to reside in Ireland. Under the initial employment permit scheme in the late 1990s, individuals had access to specifically designated areas of the labor market where perceived shortages of staff existed. This applied to both government and private sector employers, who were allowed under this scheme to recruit staff from abroad. Non-EEA nationals could take up employment in Ireland through an employment permit system. Two types of employment permit existed namely, work permits and work visas/authorizations. Work permits covered a broad range of employment sectors and included both low- and high-skilled occupations. The work visa/authorization program was introduced in 2000 and designed to attract highly skilled workers in areas of skills shortage. Work visas are issued to nationals of countries who require a visa to travel to Ireland, while work authorizations are issued to non–visa required foreign nationals. Since January 2000 applications for employment permits (by employers) are subject to a skill-shortage test, to establish whether an applicant from within Ireland or the EU can fill the position. Since April 2003, a number of occupational sectors, where a sufficient supply of local labor exists (to fill existing vacancies), are no longer eligible for employment permits. Legally applications for employment permits must be made while the individual is outside the state. However, Ruhr (2004, p. 16) notes that "... in 2002, 4,059 new permits (17.6 percent of all new permits issued in 2002) were issued for workers already resident in Ireland." In April 2003 the Department of Enterprise Trade and Employment introduced a "fast track" list of occupations where vacancies were unlikely to be filled by nationals of EEA countries, so that work permit applications in those areas could be processed quickly. In January 2008 the same department noted that a list of occupational sectors that are not eligible for work permits would be issued on a quarterly basis. Prior to 2004 the spouses of non-EEA nationals working in Ireland did not have the automatic right to work in the state. Since 2004 the spouses of non-EEA nationals working in Ireland on work visas/work authorizations (provided their spouse was working in the sector specified on their visa) or on certain intercompany transfers may apply for a work permit through a simplified procedure and in sectors deemed ineligible for employment permits. The spouses of work permit holders were not eligible for the new scheme unless their spouse was a researcher or academic or a medical professional registered with the appropriate professional body. In 2006 the scheme was extended to cover the spouses of all those who hold employment permits.

The Immigration Process

Refugee reception refers to the short-term provision of services, such as medical care and housing, to meet the basic needs of refugees at the time of arrival in their host society. On the other hand, refugee resettlement refers to the long-term integration of refugees into all the institutions of their host society. In practice, refugee reception and resettlement are not mutually exclusive. An individual's experiences during the initial reception process can significantly affect their long-term successful resettlement. At the same time, the need to provide for the basic needs of refugees continues for varying periods within the resettlement process.

In Ireland the refugee reception program emphasizes a basic needs approach. On arrival,

asylum seekers are defined as homeless and have their basic needs met through a state-sponsored refugee reception program, within the confines of the State Welfare System. This involves the integration of refugees into existing Community Welfare Services (CWS) on the same basis as all other recipients and in accordance with existing legislation and current policy in this area. As the reception process equates the basic needs of refugees with those of the general population, the specific needs of refugee groups are not acknowledged nor are specific policies formulated to meets those needs.

As policies on refugee reception and resettlement are not static but dynamic in nature, they change considerably over time and are the direct outcome of policy and legislative changes within refugee host societies. Over the past six years Irish refugee policy has evolved within the confines of existing state welfare legislation and policy.

Two distinct time frames have emerged in the formulation of refugee policy namely, the periods before and after April 2000. Prior to December 1999 the basic needs of refugees were met through various monetary payments within the Supplementary Welfare System. In December 1999 a "dispersal and direct provision policy," to meet the basic needs of refugees during the asylum determination process, was formulated and became formal government policy in April 2000. This was accompanied by the establishment of a specific state bureaucracy, the Reception and Integration Agency (RIA), with responsibility for the dispersal and direct-provision program. This marked a fundamental change in the nature of Ireland's refugee reception program. The dispersal policy was accompanied by the introduction of reception centers in which asylum seekers would be housed (while their claims for refugee status were being assessed) and direct provision as the system through which the basic needs of asylum seekers would be met. Since the introduction of the Social Welfare (Miscellaneous Provisions) Act (2003), asylum seekers are no longer entitled to receive a rent supplement as their needs are conceptualized as being met through the State's direct provision program. Refugee reception programs and the rights and entitlements of asylum seekers may also be affected by policies and practices that are not specifically focused on the refugee reception program. Through the Social Welfare (Miscellaneous Provisions) Act (2004), a Habitual Residence Condition (HRC) was introduced for social welfare claimants in Ireland. To be deemed "Habitually Resident" an individual has to be continually resident in Ireland or the United Kingdom for a period of two years before they make a claim for social welfare payments. In effect the HRC brought to an end the policy of universal child benefit (children's allowance) and restricted access to certain social assistance payments. The HRC was largely introduced to restrict access by nationals of the 10 EU accession states to the Irish social welfare system. However, as asylum seekers were not exempted from the HRC it has meant that asylumseekers who arrived after May 1, 2004, can no longer claim child benefit and social assistance payments such as the one parent family allowance and the disability allowance. In January 2007 it was estimated that 2,200 children of asylum seekers had been denied child benefit since the introduction of HRC in 2004 (*Irish Times*, 2007). Thus welfare restrictions aimed at migrant workers have had a direct impact on the entitlements of asylum seekers and the manner in which their needs are met within the state welfare system. Hence, changes in refugee policy and more general changes in legislation have meant that date of arrival in Ireland determines the manner in which the basic needs of individual asylum seekers are catered for. To date, within the confines of the reception program, the two methods used to meet the basic needs of refugees have in common that irrespective of their educational background or skills asylum seekers "are entirely dependent on state subvention for their housing and income needs" (O'Sullivan, 1997, p. 5). For individual asylum seekers, policy changes have meant internal differentiation of the asylum seeker population, less monetary benefits, more restricted access to Irish society, increased difficulties in integrating into their host society, increased levels of marginalization, increased difficulties once refugee status is acquired, and access to the refugee determination process but not to other areas of Irish life. For Irish society, changes in asylum policy

have meant that, while prior to April 2000, refugees were largely concentrated in the Dublin area, they now live in a variety of urban and rural settings throughout the country, though the number and composition of the asylum seeker population in any one area varies and changes over time. This policy has served to introduce nonnationals as refugees to a much broader spectrum of Irish society than in the past but has also served to stigmatize them and increase their level of isolation from the local population with resulting consequences for their long-term integration into Ireland. Additionally, local communities were either not consulted or poorly consulted before the policy was implemented and no resources were provided to facilitate them in dealing with their new population groups. Where local communities complained/objected, irrespective of the nature of that complaint, it was widely interpreted as communities not wanting to accept refugee groups or outright xenophobia or racism.

Prior to 2007 four major types of employment permits existed for immigrants seeking to work in Ireland, namely, work permits, work visas and work authorizations, permits for intracompany transfers, and permits for trainees. While work permits were valid for one year, work visas and authorizations were valid for a two-year period (Department of Enterprise, Trade, and Employment, 2005). Work visas and authorizations differed from work permits in a number of ways. Work visas and authorizations were issued directly to the employee rather than the employer. They were issued for a two-year period and could be renewed for a further two years and allowed the employee to work for any employer within the specified sector and to apply for family reunification immediately. Work permits were valid for one year, and the work permit holder could only work for the employer named on the permit. To date the majority of non-EEA nationals working in Ireland have taken up employment through the work permit system (Ruhr, 2004, Quinn and O'Connell, 2007). All types of employment permits can be renewed after the expiry of the initial time period. Prior to 2004 and once resident in Ireland, the holders of employment permits could access the full range of resources available to Irish citizens.

Since the introduction of the HRC in 2004, access to state benefits is restricted for immigrant workers. Immigrant workers can use the permit renewal process to complete the obligatory five years of residence required for citizenship. It is too early yet to ascertain how many will choose to do so.

Two significant issues have arisen in relation to employment permits in Ireland. First, as it is the employer and not the individual worker who applies for, obtains, and holds the work permit, individuals cannot easily change employers during the duration of their permit. Second, a work permit is issued to an individual and does not automatically mean that their spouse has the right to work and reside in Ireland. As a result, many migrants come alone leaving spouses, children, and other family members in their home countries. In the Irish case then, policies on employment permits place workers in a highly controlled situation, with limited access to specific areas of the labor market and vulnerable to the whims of employers. Not unlike their refugee counterparts, they can be separated from family and kin group members for considerable periods of time, and find that bringing spouses to Ireland (as with family reunification for refugees) is a slow, cumbersome process whose outcome is uncertain.

In January 2007, a new employment permit scheme was introduced that consisted of a new green card system and a revised work permit scheme. The green card system applies to highly skilled occupations with incomes in excess of 60,000 euros per annum and to a lesser extent to occupations with annual incomes between

30,000 and 60,000 euros. A green card is issued for an initial period of two years, after which permanent residence will be issued. The spouse and family members of a green card holder may join them immediately. However, the system remains employer driven, as green cards will only be issued to individuals with job offers in Ireland. The revised work permit scheme has been introduced for occupations not covered by green cards with annual incomes between 30,000 and 60,000 euros and in exceptional circumstances for occupations with annual incomes below 30,000 euros. In effect the new employment permit scheme restricts labor migration for non-EEA nationals to skills that cannot be met within the EEA.

In the period between April 2000 and December 2004 all non-EEA students in Ireland could work 20 hours each week during term time and could work full-time outside of term time. Since December 2004 only students who are pursuing courses of at least one year in duration and that lead to a "recognized qualification" can take up employment during the course of their studies in Ireland.

The growth in the Irish economy over the past five years has created employment opportunities for specific groups of immigrant workers. However, significant numbers are employed within the service sector (Tables 14-7, 14-8) which is characterized by low wages, unsociable working hours, and poor conditions of service. Data from the Central Statistics Office (CSO, Dublin) "...suggests that, in the period 1998–2002, the estimated average working hours per

Table 14-7. Work Permits Issued by Economic Sector,[*] 1999–March 10, 2003

Economic sector	1999	2000	2001	2002	2003	Total
Agriculture	424	2,965	5,836	6,265	885	16,375
Industry	391	1,721	3,140	3,160	381	8,793
Services	4,935	13,147	27,780	31,079	4,702	81,643
– Catering	660	3,929	9,267	10,309	1,301	25,466
– Medical and Nursing	651	1,328	2,266	2,873	453	7,571
– Entertainment	444	638	1,015	879	145	3,121
– Education	279	358	487	592	125	1,841
– Domestic	63	194	521	793	121	1,692
– Other services	2,838	6,700	14,224	15,633	2,557	41,952
Total	5,750	17,833	36,756	40,504	5,968	106,811

[*] Classified by the Irish Government—Department of Enterprise, Trade, and Employment, Dublin.
Source: Ruhr, 2004.

Table 14-8. Work Permits Issued by Economic Sector, 2004–2008[*]

Economic sector[**]	2004	2005	2006	2007	2008[***]	Total
Agriculture & Fisheries	3,721	2,139	1,952	1,453	539	9,804
Industry	2,184	1,680	1,676	1,775	1,068	8,383
Catering	8,306	6,976	5,842	4,801	1,890	27,815
Domestic	772	684	631	572	222	2,881
Education	717	726	798	901	300	3,442
Entertainment	984	962	1,106	120	55	3,227
Medical & Nursing	2,469	2,683	2,852	4,329	2,698	15,031
Service industry	14,571	10,952	9,795	9,505	4,559	49,382
Total	33,724	26,802	24,652	23,456	11,331	119,965

[*] Figures do not include the categories sport and exchange agreements.
[**] Classified by the Department of Enterprise, Trade, and Employment, Dublin.
[***] Figures are for the period January 1, 2008–September 30, 2008.
Source: Irish Government—Department of Enterprise, Trade, and Employment, Dublin.

week for non-EU nationals employed in Ireland significantly exceeded those for all persons employed in Ireland (41.6 and 38.1 hours, respectively) (Ruhr, 2004, p. 28).

In the Irish case then, while policy and legislative provisions to date have provided program and Convention refugees with the greatest degree of security, asylum seekers together with those on employment permits are conceptualized as temporarily residing in the state and with less legal entitlements to state resources since 2004. Finally, the employment permit scheme introduced in 2007 creates a system whereby skills and annual income give some immigrant workers far more rights than others in relation to such issues as permanent residence and family reunification.

Response to the Immigration Process

Migrants arrive in their host society with set expectations. Prior to arrival in Ireland, individuals had conceptualized their host society within the context of push factors (the causes of flight and migration); the status attached to their skills; their potential contribution to their host society; and the right to protection from persecution (outside their countries of origin) enshrined in International legal instruments, most notably the 1951 Geneva Convention, the 1967 Protocol, and the 1969 Organisation of African Unity (OAU) Convention on Refugees.

In Ireland, they encounter a society in which the meanings attached to migration, exile, refuge, and labor migrant are vastly different to those they had previously experienced or conceptualized. While prior knowledge of Ireland does not provide the necessary details about Ireland as a host society, past experiences of exile, and/or migration cannot be readily transferred to the Irish context. Though they had conceptualized their host society as a country very different from their own, individuals had not associated such difference with long-term changes in their socioeconomic status, differential degrees of isolation and insecurity, constant changes in immigration legislation and policy, and changes in individual identity. For individuals, adjusting to their new environment has meant adjusting to the meaning attached to the "status" of refugee and labor migrant within a new normative order.

Within their host society, individuals seeking refuge confront bureaucratic state machinery that determines the individual's right to refugee status. "Asylum seekers not fulfilling these legal requirements tend to be perceived, and portrayed, as attempting to deceive the system, thereby exploiting the generosity of the host country" (Fuglerud, 1997, p. 459). "For individuals, adjusting to this new environment means adjusting to exile but most importantly to a process of transition to their status as asylum-seekers and refugees" (Galvin, 2000, p. 205). In the Irish context, as generous social welfare payments are portrayed as pull factors, the label asylum seeker has acquired a "selective and materialistic meaning" (Zetter, 1991, p. 39). "Additionally, the indiscriminate use of the terms refugee, asylum seeker and illegal immigrant categorises those seeking refuge as a homogenous group. As such categorisation de-emphasises push factors and the heterogeneity of the refugee population, it serves to obscure the uniqueness of the individual's past, most especially the individual causes of flight and exile" (Galvin, 2000, p. 206). In Ireland as in other countries, the long delays in acquiring refugee status and insecurity and fear concerning the outcome of an application are among the factors that characterize the asylum experience. Dependence on the state welfare system is an important determinant of the experience of asylum seekers as they become conscious of the social stigma attached to dependence on the state welfare system in Ireland and become aware of hostility from members of Irish society to their dependence on the same. Legally imposed unemployment precludes individuals from contributing to their host society as workers and taxpayers, gives rise to a deskilling process, to role redefinition, to loss of dignity and self esteem, and to significant changes in lifestyle. Irish refugee legislation and policy gives rise to resource-based restrictive inclusion in Irish society and to the loss of social and economic status and of social roles. Individuals are left with few options but to enter the labor force as undocumented workers. At the same time, the negative way in which the label "asylum seeker" is socially constructed creates barriers to the integration process and limits the individual's ability to reestablish their social world in exile.

Individuals on employment permits do not of course confront the same difficulties in a host society as those who seek refuge. But they are equally confronted with bureaucratic state machinery that determines the duration and conditions of their stay in Ireland. The legislation and policy measures governing employment permits effectively mean that, the dependence on state welfare within the refugee experience translates into dependence on an employer for the migrant worker. As a consequence, individuals feel vulnerable and insecure. The restrictions on spouses and family members, implicit in the

work permit system, create and reinforce their status as foreigners. Large scale labor migration is a relatively new feature of Irish society. As in the case of refugees, there has been no government public education or information campaign on this issue. As a result, there is much misinformation on the working conditions of migrants and the emergence of resource-based tensions around employment. Fear that foreign workers will undercut local wages or cause a reduction in wage levels are but two of the factors, which give the label migrant worker a negative meaning. At the same time, wage rates and the high cost of living in Ireland together with obligations to family and kin group members back home, mean that migrants (where possible) tend to work additional hours and longer shifts in addition to working on leave days. In so doing, they reinforce the perception that with migrant labor comes deteriorating working conditions.

For migrants the process of learning about their new environment begins immediately and involves two separate but equally important types of information. First, specific immigration knowledge, and second, broad general knowledge of the new sociocultural environment perceived as an important component of the adaptation and integration process. At different points in time and in various combinations government officials, the media, workmates, social networks, and interaction with the general public are the main sources of both types of information. Newly acquired knowledge about Ireland frequently gives rise to disappointment and frustration. A process of alienation begins when individual expectations are not matched by experience; there is a constant emphasis on pull factors; restrictions are placed on access to a broader range of the host society's resources; there is hostility from members of the public; and when refugees and migrants generally are portrayed in a negative manner within sections of the media or by politicians or other public figures. In sum, a perceived ambivalence toward immigrants (in Irish society) gives rise to frustration and alienation for migrants. That ambivalence is experienced as a lack of acceptance and a lack of urgency in response to immigrant matters.

At another level, migrants are conscious that Irish society is benefiting from them in various ways. Refugees note that it is Irish landlords who own the houses, flats, and emergency accommodation in which they live, and Irish companies who are contracted by the government to manage the reception centers established under the dispersal and direct provision policy. The payment for such accommodation represents a monetary transfer from the state to private individuals and businesses within Irish society. Labor migrants know that they are meeting skills shortages and that like all other workers they pay taxes and make social insurance contributions.

Barriers to social interaction exist for both migrants and the Irish population. In particular the social construction of the labels "asylum seeker" and "migrant worker" gives rise to a complex set of barriers to social interaction and to the creation of secondary social networks. At the same time, the establishment of primary networks within the migrant population takes place but is not unproblematic. For migrants, past negative experiences of other groups within their countries of origin, language barriers, geographical location, and the nature of work are among the factors that delay the formation of primary networks. As Dibelius (2001) notes, once established, primary networks become invaluable resources for individuals. However, and though primary social networks are important, broader secondary social networks prevent isolation and aid the integration process. The distrust generated by the meaning attached to the labels "refugee" and "migrant worker" acts as a component in a complex set of barriers to the formation of more extensive social networks within Irish society and ultimately as a barrier to integration.

Marx (1990) notes that an individual's social world consists of the individual's social relationships and the forces that shape his or her life. To satisfy the entire range of their social and economic needs individuals require a large and diverse set of social relationships. "Such matters as finding work and a home, on one hand, and of establishing a secure and supportive environment for himself and his household on the other, can only be arranged with the help of a network of social relationships that include both simplex and multiplex relationships" (Marx 1990, p. 196).

Migration removes the individual's social networks of family and friends. Nevertheless, social networks and the specific social and economic obligations of network membership do not cease because of physical distance. The duties and responsibilities of extended family membership continue to exist for individual refugees and migrants. Primary social networks consist largely of family and friends at home (with whom they retain contact) and other migrants both in their host society and in other countries. Broader secondary social networks consist of members of Irish society. For Ireland's immigrant groups there is a tension and conflict between their perceptions of their status and the perceptions of Irish society. Among the factors that define their experience of Irish society are the social construction of negative labels; resource-based restrictive inclusion; perceived hostility from some members of Irish society; an ambivalent approach to immigration from government and a failure to acknowledge their specific needs; and a perceived lack of appreciation of their role in Irish society. For respondents their primary and secondary social networks expand slowly and to a limited extent.

In the Irish case, opportunities and obstacles are very much a characteristic of immigrant status. Among the range of barriers that confront refugees are the legal prohibition on employment for asylum seekers; delays in the processing of asylum applications during which time individuals become deskilled; government policies that stipulate that language classes, education, and training should not be made available to asylum seekers; and the lack of an appropriate authority or an examination process to convert educational and professional qualifications. Though significant numbers of migrants have arrived in Ireland since the mid-1990s, it was only in 2006 that all issues relating to the recognition of foreign qualifications were centralized under the "Recognition Ireland" service provided by the National Qualifications Authority of Ireland. For migrants more generally obstacles and barriers to Irish society arise from the protectionist policies of various professional groups; lack of affordable child care facilities especially for women as lone parents; lack of information about the labor market; and the restrictive nature of the work permit system. These barriers are cumulative in nature with significant consequences for social mobility and the success of the migration process. Finally, migrants feel alienated and frustrated by a system which for them is characterized by constant legislative and policy changes that increases their vulnerability and the failure by government to implement legislative and policy changes in areas of real concern to migrants such as family reunification.

Service Provision

In the formulation of policy, the Irish government has emphasized the integration of migrants into existing services, structures, and state institutions. As a result, for example, all immigrants have access to the public health care system; the children of all immigrants are admitted into the state education system; and asylum seekers are incorporated into the social welfare system and have access to free legal aid. In reality, the emphasis within legal and policy provisions on the categorization of migrants and associated restrictions, give migrant groups and members of individual families differential access to service provision. This is the case, for example, when the date of arrival determines the entitlements of asylum seekers or when the children of asylum seekers are incorporated into the state education system, while their parents do not have access to education or training. No comprehensive government-sponsored English language training program exists for refugees or other migrants. While English language courses are available, they are largely done within the private language school sector and chiefly aimed at attracting private, fee-paying students from other EU countries and beyond. As such, these courses are expensive and well beyond the reach of many migrants as refugees or workers in low-paid employment. The failure by the state to incorporate ethnic languages into the education system reinforces feelings of inequality and ethnic difference and has consequences for cultural transmission.

The arrival of significant numbers of migrants has posed a challenge to the Irish health services. Migrants are in a position to avail of the full range of public health care services, but their incorporation into the same has put a serious burden on existing overstretched services. Though the National Health Strategy (2001–2005) stipulates the need to acknowledge the new cultural

diversity of the population now seeking health care, this policy has not been supported by the resources necessary to make the change to a multicultural health care system. Irish hospitals are poorly equipped to deal with migrants in a number of areas. For those who do not speak English there is a constant language barrier for staff and patients, while translation services are expensive and poorly organized. Inappropriate translations all too often take place, for example when children translate for their parents or Islamic husbands translate for their wives in relation to reproductive health issues. The incorporation of migrants into already overstretched services gives rise to inaccurate perceptions on the part of migrants. Not infrequently, migrants perceive long waiting periods for treatment as prejudice and discrimination, because they are refugees or black. Yet such waiting times are a characteristic feature of the Irish public health care system. Migrants arrive with specific expectations. When those expectations are not met or when they do not have adequate information/knowledge of the shortcomings of the system they, all too often, interpret their treatment in the negative. The incorporation of immigrants into the existing public health care system equates migrant health needs with those of the general population. The specific health needs of migrant groups are deemphasized in the process, for example the need for trauma counseling for the survivors of torture.

For staff and medical personnel, the arrival of migrants has meant new and increased workloads, new demands on their time, and a host of cultural and other practices to which they have to adapt and with which they are unfamiliar. Cultural misunderstandings can also arise when nurses do not have information on cultural practices for specific groups of migrants. Thus, for example childbirth practices vary widely. Such cultural misunderstandings can and do give rise to tensions between migrants and hospital staff. Medical personnel are members of their own communities and absorb much of the mythology surrounding migrants, which exist within local communities. This is especially the case when training programs to provide them with accurate information have not been put in place. The result can be hostility toward migrants and an inability to understand and appreciate their needs. Cultural concepts of health and illness vary considerably. Many of Ireland's migrants do not subscribe to Western medical concepts. As a result they feel dissatisfied with existing services and within the confines of those services will never feel completely healed or treated. For staff, their new migrant communities pose challenges within their workloads for which many are ill prepared and equipped.

Financial Costs for the State

It would seem on first inspection that the largest drain of an economic nature is the cost to the state of the refugee reception and resettlement program. Yet, much of the resources in question are simply transfers from the state to the private sector, who run and manage refugee reception centers. While the cost of the refugee reception program has increased over time and in line with changes in the cost of commodities, the weekly cash payment to asylum seekers has not been increased since it was first introduced in April 2000. On several occasions and in seeking to exercise its power to deport individuals whose claim to asylum has failed, the state has (at considerable cost) chartered flights to return such individuals to their countries of origin. When individual refugees challenge negative decisions on asylum claims, the state has shown a propensity to seek the resolution of such cases through the High Court at considerable cost in both time and money. At the same time, the state has sought to restrict asylum seeker access to free legal aid. In general the free legal aid system in Ireland is poorly resourced and funded. It is not unusual for asylum seekers to pay a private solicitor to take their case, using their meager social welfare resources to pay for such services.

Very few specialist programs or services exist in Ireland for migrants, and almost none that is state funded. One group stands out in this respect, namely, nurses who as foreign workers are provided with a six-week familiarization course when they first arrive in Ireland and before their placement in designated hospitals. But even here the service provided is connected to their professional work and not to their migration into Ireland. Over the years, state-funded programs have come and gone, been short-term in nature and not sustained by the government. This has been the case in the provision of language and training courses for program refugees. At another level, labor migrants contribute financially as consumers and tax payers. Currently, there is no information available on the nature or quantity of migrants' financial contributions to the Irish economy. Equally, there is no available information on the cost to the state of immigrant remittances to their countries of origin.

New Layers of Diversity

Increased in-migration has brought new levels of ethnic and cultural diversity to Irish society in areas such as language, dress, food, religious and cultural variation, family structures, and kinship systems, the increased number of ethnic public events such as the annual Chinese cultural festival and the wide range of artists who perform under the auspices of the African Cultural Project. Ireland is now host to a variety of restaurants and other food outlets for example Chinese, Vietnamese, and Indian, which previously did not exist. Of late, in-migration has been accompanied by the growth of ethnic shops in both Dublin and further afield. While such businesses add to the level of cultural and social diversity in the society, they equally make an economic contribution.

At a formal political level, migrants have begun to make a contribution to Irish society at a number of levels. Fears of racism and anti-immigrant sentiment gave rise to a commitment by all political parties to exclude issues of immigration from their political campaigns during the general election in 2004. Members of migrant groups have been elected to political positions at both local and national levels. The arrival of significant numbers of immigrants has given rise to much debate on a host of issues in Irish society, for example racism, xenophobia, ethnic and cultural differences, Irish identity, and the Irish Diaspora. The "anti-immigrant platform" which was founded in 1999, has attracted a small steady stream of followers but has failed to become a significant force in Irish political life. On the other hand, a number of nongovernmental organizations and support groups, for example the Irish Refugee Council, the Immigrant Council of Ireland, the Migrant Rights Centre Ireland, the Vincentian Refugee Centre, and the

Irish Immigrant Support Group, have emerged with a specific remit to represent immigrant groups and to provide services not provided on a statutory basis by government. At the most basic level, in-migration has confronted Irish people with cultural patterns and beliefs with which many were wholly unfamiliar. As a result, people have had to adapt and adjust to the emergence of a more complex form of ethnic pluralism than was previously the case.

Conclusion

In the period since the early 1990s Irish policy and legislation on immigration has been reactive in nature. As a result, immigration has been portrayed as a temporary and somewhat problematic area, while the labels associated with different groups of migrants have adopted a negative meaning. At the same time, the incorporation of immigrants into existing systems and structures does not acknowledge their specific needs and leads to resource based tensions. Additionally, policy and legislative provisions are frequently contradictory of the existing reality. Thus while there are shortages of workers within the Irish labor market, large numbers of asylum seekers are prohibited from working or using their skills. Not infrequently do they come from the same country and training background as those recruited as labor migrants. Legislation that is reactive and restrictive generates tensions within a society. Its existence defines migrants as a problem for the local population and creates for migrants the sense of being unwelcome in their host society. In this process both migrant and local population groups focus on difference, in this case ethnic difference. As a result, social interaction takes place in the context of a heightened sense of difference and of the barriers between local and migrant groups. Within this arena migrant integration is limited in scale.

At the same time and to ensure the success of the migration process, immigrants prioritize primary social networks both within their home countries and the host society. As this process unfolds, interaction with the host society becomes more limited and of less relevance to the individual. As a result, the barriers and boundaries between the immigrant and the local population are further reinforced.

Note

1. This is an updated version of a paper originally published in the *Journal of Immigrant and Refugee Studies*, 2006, Vol. 4, No. 3, pp. 73–95.

References

Barrett, A., Bergin, A., and Duffy, D. (2006). "The Labour Market Characteristics and Labour Market Impact of Immigrants in Ireland." *Economic and Social Review*, Vol. 37, No. 1, Spring.

Castles, S., and Miller, M. J. (2003). *The Age of Migration: International Population Movements in the Modern World*. Basingstoke, UK, Palgrave Macmillan (third edition).

Central Statistics Office (CSO) (2008). *Census 2006 Non-Irish Nationals Living in Ireland*. Dublin, Government Publications.

Conlon, C., O'Connor, J., and Parsons, S. (2002). *The Labour Market Needs and Experiences of Minority Ethnic Groups, Particularly Refugees, in Ireland*. Dublin, UCD, WERRC (draft report for the Equality Authority, Dublin).

Department of Enterprise, Trade, and Employment (2005). *Work Permits Information Leaflet*. Dublin, Department of Enterprise, Trade, and Employment.

Department of Health and Children (2001). *National Health Strategy 2001–05*. Dublin, Government Publications.

Department of Justice (2000). *Information Sheet: Applications for Asylum*. Dublin, Department of Justice.

Dibelius, C. (2001). *Lone but Not Alone: A Case Study of the Social Networks of African Refugee Women in Ireland*. Dublin, TCD (Unpublished MPhil thesis).

Doyle, N., Hughes, G., and Wadensjo, E. (2006). *Freedom of Movement for Workers from Central and Eastern Europe: Experiences in Ireland and Sweden*. Stockholm, SIEPS, Report No. 5.

Faughnan, P. (1999). *Refugees and Asylum Seekers in Ireland: Social Policy Dimensions*. Dublin, UCD (Social Science Research Centre).

Fuglerud, O. (1997). "Ambivalent Incorporation: Norwegian Policy towards Tamil Asylum-Seekers from Sri Lanka." *Journal of Refugee Studies*, Vol. 10, No. 4.

Galvin, T. (2000). "Refugee Status in Exile: The Case of African Asylum-Seekers in Ireland." In MacLachlan, M., and O'Connell, M. (eds.) *Cultivating Pluralism: Psychological, Social, and Cultural Pers-pectives on a Changing Ireland*. Dublin, Oak Tree Press.

Hollifield, J. F. (2000). "The Politics of International Migration: How Can We 'Bring the State Back in'?" In Brettell, C. B., and Hollifield, J. F. (eds.) *Migration Theory: Talking across Disciplines*. London, Routledge.

Hughes, G. (2005). *Annual Report on Statistics on Migration, Asylum, and Return: Ireland 2002.* Dublin, Economic and Social Research Institute.

Interdepartmental Committee on Non-Irish Nationals (1987). *Interim Report on Applications for Refugee Status 25-11-1993.* Dublin, Government Publications.

Marx, E. (1990). "The Social World of Refugees: A Conceptual Framework." *Journal of Refugee Studies,* Vol. 3, No. 3.

National Economic and Social Council of Ireland (2006). *Managing Migration in Ireland: A Social and Economic Analysis; A Report by the International Organisation for Migration for the National Economic and Social Council of Ireland.* Report Number 116, Dublin, NESC.

Neckerman, K. M., Carter, P., and Lee, J. (1999). "Segmented Assimilation and Minority Cultures of Mobility." *Ethnic and Racial Studies,* Vol. 22, No. 6 (November).

O'Regan, C. (1998). *Report of a Survey of the Vietnamese and Bosnian Refugee Communities in Ireland.* Dublin, Refugee Agency.

O'Sullivan, E. (1997). *Homelessness, Housing Need, and Asylum Seekers in Ireland: A Report for the Homeless Initiative.* Dublin, Homeless Initiative.

Quinn, E., and Hughes, G. (2005). Illegally Resident Third Country Nationals in Ireland: State Approaches Towards Their Situation. Dublin, Economic and Social Research Institute.

Quinn, E. (2006a). *Annual Report on Statistics on Migration, Asylum, and Return: Ireland, Reference Year 2003.* Dublin, Economic and Social Research Institute.

Quinn, E. (2006b). *Policy Analysis Report on Asylum and Migration: Ireland Mid-2004 to 2005.* Dublin, Economic and Social Research Institute.

Quinn, E., and O'Connell, P. J. (2007). *Conditions of Entry and Residence of Third Country Highly-Skilled Workers in Ireland, 2006.* Dublin, Economic and Social Research Institute.

Roberts, A. (1998). "More Refugees, Less Asylum: A Regime in Transformation." *Journal of Refugee Studies,* Vol. 11, No. 4.

Refugee Agency (1997). *Information Bulletin.* Dublin, Refugee Agency.

Refugee Agency (1998a). *Annual Report 1998.* Dublin, Refugee Agency.

Refugee Agency (1998b). *Bosnian Programme Refugees in Ireland.* Dublin, Refugee Agency (information sheet).

Refugee Agency (1998c). *Vietnamese Programme Refugees In Ireland.* Dublin, Refugee Agency (information sheet).

Refugee Agency (1999). *Kosovo Programme.* Dublin, Refugee Agency (information sheet).

Refugee Agency (2000). *Information on Refugees in Ireland.* Dublin, Refugee Agency (information sheet).

Ruhr, M. (2004). *Emerging Trends and Patterns in the Immigration and Employment of Non-EU Nationals in Ireland: What the Data Reveal.* Dublin, TCD Policy Institute (working paper).

Shipsey, B. (1994). "Immigration Law and Refugees." In Heffernan, L. (ed.) *Human Rights: A European Perspective.* Dublin, The Round Hall Press.

UN High Commissioner for Refugees (UNHCR) (2005). www.unhcr.ch/.

Valtonen, K. (1998). "Resettlement of Middle Eastern Refugees in Finland: The Elusiveness of Integration." *Journal of Refugee Studies,* Vol. 11, No. 1.

Zena Project (1999). *Report of a Survey: Barriers and Needs of Bosnian Refugee Women with Regard to Education, Employment, and Social Inclusion.* Dublin, Zena Project.

Zetter, R. (1988). "Refugees and Refugee Studies: A Label and an Agenda." *Journal of Refugee Studies,* Vol. 1, No. 1.

Zetter, R. (1991). "Labelling Refugees: Forming and Transforming a Bureaucratic Identity." *Journal of Refugee Studies,* Vol. 4, No. 1.

Irish Legislation

Aliens Act, 1935.
Employment Permits Act(s), 2003, 2006.
Illegal Immigrants (Trafficking) Act, 2000.
Immigration Act(s), 1999, 2003, 2004.
Irish Nationality and Citizenship Act(s) 1956, 1986, 1994, 2001, 2004.
Medical Practitioners (Amendment) Act, 2002.
Nationality and Citizenship Act, 1935.
Refugee Act, 1996.
Social Welfare (Miscellaneous Provisions) Act(s), 2003, 2004.

International Legal Instruments

Organization of African Unity (OAU), 1969 Convention Governing the Specific Aspects of Refugee Problems in Africa.
United Nations 1951 Convention Relating to the Status of Refugees.
United Nations 1967 Protocol Relating to the Status of Refugees.

Newspaper

Irish Times, January 1, 2007.

15

Israel

The New Immigration to Israel: Becoming a De Facto Immigration State in the 1990s

Rebeca Raijman and Adriana Kemp

International migration has become one of the most important features of modern Western countries in general, and of Israeli society in particular. Israel is a society of immigrants and their offspring, where at the beginning of the twenty-first century two out of three members of the Jewish majority was foreign born (40%) or of the second generation (30%) (Cohen, 2002). The high percentage of foreign-born population situates Israel at the top of the list of major traditional countries of immigration like Australia (23%), Canada (16%), and the United States (8%), and well above immigration countries in Western Europe (e.g., France, 10%, and Germany, 6%) (Della Pergola, 1998).

Between 1948 (the establishment of the state) and 1995, immigration accounted for over 40% of Israel's population growth and for about 50% of the increase in the Jewish population (Della Pergola, 1998). Migration flows had an impact on the size of the Jewish population, and they shaped the social, cultural, political, and economic structure of the society. The character and composition of immigration flows and immigration policies are a key factor for understanding patterns of social and ethnic stratification in the Israeli society (see e.g., Lewin-Epstein & Semyonov, 2000; Semyonov & Lerenthal, 1991; Semyonov & Lewin-Epstein, 2003).

The beginning of the 1990s marked a turning point in the migration history of Israel for two reasons. First, the massive flows of immigrants arriving in the country throughout the 1990s were reminiscent in their intensity and suddenness of the large and formative immigration flows of the 1950s. They involved three main groups: (1) a mass exodus from the former Soviet Union (FSU); (2) Ethiopian Jews (many of them brought to Israel through two special operations); (3) massive overseas labor migration. Second, the ethnic composition of immigrants shifted from its predominantly Jewish component to an increasing number of non-Jewish (and non-Palestinian) immigrants who for the first time began arriving in sizable numbers. Currently, the number of non-Jewish migrants is estimated at approximately half a million. Paradoxically, half of them arrived under the auspicious of the Law of Return (1970 amendment) (primarily entrants from the FSU and Ethiopia) (see e.g., Al-Haj, 2004; Cohen, 2002; Lustick, 1999; Weiss, 2002) and the other half entered the country as temporary labor migrants through active recruitment (by employers and manpower agencies) and as undocumented workers (Raijman & Kemp, 2002).

227

For the first time Israel became a de facto immigration society in spite of its own definition as a country of aliya (Jewish immigration is designated by the Hebrew word *aliya*, meaning ascent). Israel now provides a particularly illuminating setting to examine changes in the ethnic composition of migration flows at the end of the beginning of the twenty-first century. That is because non-Jews constitute a threat not only to the social and ethnic composition of the nation but also to the Jewish character of the state. As recent public debates on reforming the citizenship and immigration laws indicate, these new patterns of immigration are likely to leave their imprint on Israel's regime of incorporation and society (see e.g., Al-Haj, 2004; Lustick, 1999; Kemp & Raijman, 2008; Shafir & Peled, 2002).

In this chapter a description of Israeli society and a brief historical outline of immigration flows is followed by an account of the Israeli incorporation regime and migration policies. Next, we describe the immigration flows since the 1990s in terms of countries of origin, sociodemographic characteristics, and modes of incorporation into the Israeli society. In the conclusion we expand on three main challenges that have emerged within the Israeli context of immigration during the last decade. These challenges bear upon the modes in which new patterns of immigration—mainly non-Jewish and black immigrants—interweave with stratification processes.

The Israeli Setting

The settlement of Jews in Palestine began at the turn of the twentieth century, and since then the history of immigration in Israel is closely intertwined with the history of nation-state building and the protracted ethnonational conflict between Jews and Palestinians (for the most recent overview of immigration patterns to Israel see Cohen, 2002). Jewish immigrants arrived in Israel in a series of waves. The first arrived at the turn of the century mainly from European countries (a detailed description of immigration flows to Israel by country of birth is presented in Table 15-1). The second wave arrived shortly after statehood (1948) in the context of incremental Jewish immigration and colonization from many countries, against the will and to the detriment of the local Arab population.

The years 1948–1951 marked what Cohen (2002) has called the "demographic transformation" of Israel. It involved two migration processes of almost equal size: the forced emigration of Palestinians (circa 760,000 who fled or were expelled from their homes in cities and villages) and immigration of Middle Eastern Jews and survivors of the Holocaust (circa 678,000). This demographic transformation secured the Jewish majority in the new state with the proportion of Jews rising from 44.7% in 1947 to 89% at the end of 1951 (Cohen, 2002, p. 37).

The most meaningful ethnic split in Israel is between Jews and Arabs (Lewin-Epstein & Semyonov, 1993). Although Arabs were granted Israeli citizenship in 1948, only since the abolition of the military administration (in 1966) have they formally enjoyed civil and political rights on an individual, liberal basis, as long as these rights do not conflict with the national goals of the Jewish majority (Shafir & Peled, 2002). Currently the Arab population constitutes approximately 20% of the citizens of Israel and they are disadvantaged relative to Jews in every aspect of social stratification, including education, occupational status, earnings, and standard of living (Lewin-Epstein & Semyonov, 1993; Semyonov, Lewin-Epstein, & Spilerman, 1996). These disadvantages can be attributed largely to socioeconomic discrimination and should also be understood within the context of the Jewish-Arab conflict (e.g., Haidar, 1990; Lewin-Epstein & Semyonov, 1993).

The combination of (1) the massive and heterogeneous immigration (from Eastern European countries and Middle Eastern countries and North Africa), and (2) the scarcity of resources in the post-Independence war period (1948–1951) had a detrimental effect on the socioeconomic achievements of the Jewish immigrants arriving during this critical period, and its imprint is evident in the stratification system to this date (Cohen & Haberfeld, 1998; Semyonov & Lewin-Epstein, 2003). The Jewish majority is divided into two major groups of distinct ethnic origin, Jews of European and American origin (Ashkenazim) and Jews of Asian and African origin (Middle East and North Africa: (Mizrahim). The latter group

Table 15-1. Percent Distribution of Immigrants by Country of Birth and Period of Arrival[*]

Period of Immigration	1919–48	1948–51	1952–67	1968–88	1989–00	2001–05	1948–2005
Country							
Total Asia	**8.4**	**34.6**	**11.5**	**10.7**	**1.4**	**1.9**	**12.7**
Iran	0.7	3.2	4.9	4.4	0.2	0.6	2.6
Iraq	0.0	18.0	0.7	0.4	0.0	0.1	4.3
Turkey	1.7	5.0	2.3	2.0	0.1	0.3	2.0
Yemen	3.3	7.0	0.4	0.0	0.0	0.0	1.7
Syria	0.0	0.4	0.8	0.7	0.0	0.0	0.4
India-Pakistan	0.0	0.3	1.9	2.2	0.1	0.4	0.9
Other Asia	2.7	0.7	0.6	1.0	0.9	0.5	0.8
Total Africa	**0.8**	**13.6**	**47.4**	**13.6**	**5.2**	**14.3**	**17.4**
Morocco	0.2	4.1	35.7	4.6	0.3	0.9	8.9
Algeria	0.0	0.6	1.8	1.4	0.2	0.7	0.8
Tunisia	0.0	1.9	5.6	1.2	0.2	0.7	1.8
Libya	0.2	4.5	0.6	0.3	0.0	0.0	1.2
Ethiopia	0.0	0.0	0.0	2.7	4.0	11.4	2.4
South-Africa	0.1	0.1	0.4	2.1	0.3	0.5	0.6
Egypt-Sudan	0.0	1.3	3.3	0.4	0.0	0.1	1.0
Other Africa	0.4	1.1	0.1	1.0	0.2	0.0	0.5
Total Europe	**78.2**	**48.5**	**36.2**	**54.4**	**89.5**	**68.0**	**62.5**
USSR/FSU	10.8	1.2	4.0	32.2	85.1	59.3	39.3
Poland	35.3	15.5	8.0	2.5	0.3	0.4	5.7
France	0.3	0.4	0.6	3.8	1.1	4.8	1.5
Romania	8.5	17.2	18.5	5.8	0.7	0.5	8.9
Hungary	2.1	2.1	2.0	0.4	0.2	0.3	1.0
Bulgaria	1.5	5.4	0.4	0.1	0.4	0.2	1.5
Czechoslovakia	3.5	2.7	0.4	0.4	0.1	0.1	0.8
Germany	10.9	1.6	0.6	1.3	0.2	0.4	0.8
UK	0.3	0.3	0.6	2.7	0.5	1.0	0.9
Other Europe	5.0	2.1	1.0	5.2	0.8	1.1	1.9
Total America	**1.6**	**0.6**	**3.8**	**21.0**	**3.9**	**15.7**	**6.7**
Argentina	0.0	0.1	1.7	5.1	1.1	6.5	2.0
USA	1.4	0.2	0.9	10.5	1.7	4.9	2.9
Brazil-Uruguay-Chile	0.0	0.1	0.7	2.5	0.4	1.9	0.8
Oceania	0.0	0.0	0.1	0.6	0.1	0.2	0.2
Other America	0.1	0.1	0.4	2.3	0.5	2.2	0.8
Unknown	**11.0**	**2.8**	**0.1**	**0.3**	**0.1**	**0.1**	**0.7**
TOTAL	**100.0**	**100.0**	**100.0**	**100.0**	**100.0**	**100.0**	**100.0**

[*] These figures relate to immigrants arriving under the Law of Return (labor migrants are not included)

Source: Table 2-1. Cohen (2002), Table 2-1, p. 40. Central Bureau of Statistics (2007), Table 4-2, pp. 228–229.

were characterized by a traditional orientation, by limited education and occupational skills, and by large families. These immigrants were lower than European-American immigrants in every aspect of socioeconomic status (education, occupation, and income) (e.g., Semyonov & Lerenthal, 1991). Although over time Jews of Asian-African origin improved their socioeconomic attainment, the gaps between ethnic groups (Mizrahim and Ashkenazim) did not narrow (Semyonov & Lewin-Epstein, 2003) even in the second generation (Cohen, 1998; Haberfeld, 1993).

Immigration in the three decades after the establishment of the state (1960s to 1980s) was more sporadic and less systematic. It was characterized by a slow but constant stream of immigrants from North and South America as well as immigrants from South Africa, Eastern Europe, and the former Soviet Union, Ethiopia, and Iran. By then, a broad infrastructure of public housing and support was available for all new immigrants. Research indicates that with increasing time in the country most of the immigrants of the 1970s and the 1980s became fully integrated and achieved higher levels of socioeconomic attainment (Cohen, 2002, p. 46; Raijman & Semyonov, 1995, 1997; Semyonov & Lerenthal, 1991). As noted, since the beginning of the 1990s Israel has witnessed a renewal of massive immigration flows. These comprise migrants and family members arriving under the Law of Return, mainly from the former Soviet Union and Ethiopia, and non-Jewish labor migration.

Jewish Migration

The winter of 1989 was a turning point in the Jewish immigration flow to Israel, reversing the declining trend manifested during the previous decade. Following the downfall of the former Soviet Union a mass of immigrants had begun exiting the Soviet republics to settle in Israel. Between 1989 and 2005 Israel—a country of only 4.5 million residents at the beginning of the 1990s—took in over 960,000 immigrants from the former Soviet Union (400,000 of whom arrived between 1989 and 1991).

By virtue of the Law of Return these immigrants were granted citizenship immediately on arrival and their process of incorporation was intensively supported by the state (Lerner & Menahem, 2003; Raijman & Semyonov, 1998). Their presence was deeply felt in the social, economic, and political spheres as their proportion in the total population increased from 3.8% in 1990 to 21% in 2005 (Central Bureau of Statistics, 2006, Table 2-23). Together with substantial influx of Soviet Jews of the 1970s, the 1990s FSU immigrants—"Russians" as they are called in Israel—constitute the largest ethnic group to have immigrated to the Israeli state.

At the other end of the the the socioeconomic spectrum are Ethiopian Jewish immigrants, known as Beta Israel or "Falashas." In the 1980s, Ethiopians—a forgotten community of Jews in Africa—became a target for Israeli government and the Jewish Agency officials, who were sent to Ethiopia to prepare a massive and secret migration (Herzog, 1999). The Ethiopian immigrants arrived in Israel in three major waves. The first (1980–1990, including Operation Moses: November 1984–January 1985) numbered 8,000 immigrants. The second, including Operation Solomon in 1991, comprised about 20,000 persons. The third wave is still ongoing, amid a major public debate in Israeli society over the inclusion since the 1990s of the converted *Falas Mura*. These Ethiopians are not considered Jews according to the *halakhah* (Jewish religious law). Many of them languish in transit camps in Addis Ababa, waiting to come to Israel under the terms of the Law of Return. By 2005 the number of Ethiopians living in Israel was estimated at 102,900; one third of them were Israeli born (Central Bureau of Statistics, 2006). The transition of Ethiopians from a rural setting to a developed society like Israel caused numerous crises, on the individual and community level alike. The perception of Ethiopian immigrants as a vulnerable population justified the intensive involvement of the state in all aspects of their integration process. Nevertheless, the Ethiopian community in Israel constitutes one of the poorest populations in the country with almost half of all Ethiopian families depending on welfare support as the only source of income (Offer, 2004, 2007).

To these main groups we should add a smaller but constant flow of Jewish migrants from Western and Central Europe and from North and South America that account for some 10% of all immigrants arriving since the 1990s. These are a very selected population, displaying relatively high levels of education and socioeconomic attainment but have not been a major focus of systematic research. One plausible explanation for this notable lacuna may be the ideological assumption that these immigrants are equipped with high human capital, furnished with a strong Zionist motivation, and endowed with a value system similar in many respects to that of the Westernized veteran Israeli Jews. Accordingly, they would not display significant differences from Israeli-born groups (Kemp & Elias, 2003). As stated, to these main immigration flows entering Israel under the Law of Return we should add a significant flow of non-Jewish overseas labor migrants (documented and undocumented) arriving during the last decade.

Non-Jewish Labor Migration

The first noncitizen workers in the Israeli labor market were Palestinians from the occupied territories (in the Gaza Strip and the West Bank) who, following the 1967 Six Day War came under Israeli military rule. Noncitizen Palestinians were recruited to perform manual jobs mainly in construction, agriculture, and services. Over the years these workers—mostly daily commuters—became highly dependent on the Israeli economy for their economic needs. By the end of the 1980s they made up about 8% of the Israeli labor force. As a distinct social group they were clearly located at the bottom of the Israeli labor market and the ethnic system (Semyonov & Lewin-Epstein, 1987).

The deterioration of the political and security situation generated by the first Palestinian uprising, the *Intifada* (which began at the end of 1987), brought about a severe labor shortage in the construction and agriculture sectors of the Israeli labor market, in which Palestinian workers had been concentrated since the early 1970s. The "temporary" solution sought to overcome labor shortages was importation of overseas labor migrants. By 2006, the total number of labor migrants in the Israeli labor market was approximately 186,000. They had arrived from virtually every corner of the world; only 55% of them held work permits (Central Bureau of Statistics, 2007a). In order to understand the different modes of incorporation of the main immigrant groups arriving in Israel during the 1990s, we now present a brief overview of the Israeli regime of incorporation.

The Israeli Incorporation Regime

Migration to Israel can be characterized as a returning ethnic migration, so the Israeli state and society belong to the category of "diaspora country." Over the years, the state of Israel has been more or less unmatched in its active recruitment of Jewish immigrants (38% of the Jewish population in the world resides in Israel: *Statistical Abstract*, 2002, Table 2-3) and its

overwhelmingly accommodating policy of granting them immediate full participatory citizenship upon arrival (Semyonov & Lewin Epstein, 2003).

The country relies purely on the system of jus sanguinis (law of blood) to determine the citizenship status of immigrants and their descendants. The centrality of the idea of migration as a return from the Diaspora is expressed in the Law of Return of 1950. This law creates a legal framework that grants Israeli citizenship to Jews and their children immediately on their immigration; since the 1970 reform, the "right of return" has been extended to grandchildren of Jews too, and their nuclear families (even if not Jewish). Paradoxically, this amendment created a new oxymoronic category of "non-Jewish *olim*" (Hebrew plural [m], singular *oleh* [m], *olah* [f], designating Jewish immigrant, from the Hebrew word *aliya*, literally "ascent": Weiss, 2002). As the cornerstone of Israel's immigration policy and its citizenship regime, the Law of Return accords to Jewish immigrants a status superior to that of native-born citizens in the form of rights and benefits that the latter do not enjoy (Cohen 2002; Shuval & Leshem, 1998). For example, Weiss (2002) points out the discriminatory approach of the 1970 amendment of the Law of Return, which omits Israeli Arabs and their family members, who are excluded from the dominant ethnonational definition of the state and polity.

The current migration regime is highly exclusionary regarding non-Jews (those not covered by the amendment to the Law of Return) and also removes a priori any possibility of incorporation for non-Jewish migrants (Shafir & Peled, 2002). Unwillingness to accept non-Jewish immigrants is expressed through exclusionary immigration policies (especially limitation of family reunion and refusal to secure residence status), restrictive naturalization rules, and a double standard: exclusionary model for non-Jews as against an "acceptance-encouragement" model for Jews (Raijman, Semyonov, & Schmidt, 2003). Israel may be viewed as an immigrant settler society based on an ethnonationalist structure, defined both ideologically and institutionally (Smooha, 1990). The presence of an unprecedented number of non-Jewish migrants who are also non-Arabs elicits new questions regarding the predominantly ethnonational character of the state and of its citizenship regime. In that sense, Israel's migration policy on non-Jews reflects the state's never-ending anxiety about a changing ethnoscape that may pose a threat to its Jewish character.

Programs and Services Available to Immigrants under the Law of Return

The social and political systems of Israel, based on immigration, were constructed with the goal of bringing Jews to Israel and easing their integration in the new country. The World Zionist Organization and the Jewish Agency established branches across the world where Jews apply for immigration to Israel and receive assistance for the actual move itself (journey, luggage). But beyond this, as a self-defined Jewish state Israel is committed to the successful integration of its (Jewish) immigrants. They not only have privileged access to citizenship and the societal goods that this formal status provides, they also benefit from social policies such as welfare and a wide variety of integration programs.

Throughout most of its history, the centralized state of Israel was intensively involved in shaping the opportunity structure and immigration policies, playing a central role in the incorporation of co-ethnic immigrants. In effect, Israel established a "social contract" that committed the state to provide settlement assistance to new immigrants during their first years after arrival. In fact, since the 1970s immigrants were given the opportunity to spend five or six months in absorption centers, where they received intensive free Hebrew instruction, health insurance, and assistance in finding employment and grants for university students. The immigrants also enjoyed interim subsistence loans, tax exemptions for cars, electrical appliances, and other household goods. In addition, the government provided a wide variety of retraining courses for immigrants whose previous training and experience were not suited to the needs of the economy; incentives and financial support were given to employers to hire immigrants (Lerner & Menahem, 2003; Shuval & Leshem, 1998). In sum, Jewish immigrants during the first years in Israel were given substantial state support to adjust to the new country.

While the active involvement of the state was evident in all spheres of the immigrants' lives, aiming to facilitate the transition to the host society, it also created dependency which in the long run may have had detrimental effects on the immigrants' socioeconomic status. The degree of state involvement in immigrant incorporation policies and the amount of resources allocated to that purpose largely shaped the system of ethnic stratification in Israel over the years (see e.g., Semyonov & Lewin-Epstein, 2003).

Recently, because of the huge size of the immigration flows, but also as part of larger liberalization processes taking place in Israel, causing a retreat in state involvement, we have witnessed a shift to a far less centralized incorporation policy, called "direct absorption" (Leshem & Lissak, 1999). Nowadays, upon arrival immigrants receive an "absorption basket"—cash and services—and they can use it as they please (Doron & Kagar, 1993; Shuval & Leshem, 1998). The value of the absorption basket was calculated as the average of the financial support previously provided to each individual. Upon arrival, a nuclear family (parents and two children) received close to $10,000 for the first year (the minimal annual wage rate is around $5,000. This new policy was applied mainly to immigrants from the FSU (and other Western countries) who arrived in the 1990s. By contrast, the integration of Ethiopian immigrants was still highly controlled by the state. While almost all Ethiopian immigrants were sent to absorption centers to "facilitate" the integration process, nearly all immigrants from the FSU (92%) were integrated through the direct absorption policy.

Since Ethiopians were considered a vulnerable population, an "immigration of distress" an intensive state intervention in all aspects of integration was quite evident (Ben-Eliezer, 2004). Ethiopian immigrants were sent to absorption centers, mostly in the periphery, where they were totally dependent on the centers' officials and employees (Herzog, 1999). Although these centers were conceived as transit points from which immigrants were supposed to move after six months, many Ethiopians were reluctant to go.

They had got used to a situation where all needs were attended to; also, many of them did not have the economic means to move to permanent housing.

The Ethiopian immigrants were granted many more resources than any other group of immigrants (e.g., the absorption basket was offered for two years, rights to *Ulpan* (Hebrew language school) were also doubled, and mortgages were offered at much lower interest rates). Nevertheless, their lack of suitable human, social, and financial capital to integrate into the new society left them segregated in poor neighborhoods (where cheap housing was affordable to those depending on the state mortgage system) with little prospects of socioeconomic mobility (Offer, 2004, 2007; Swirski & Swirski, 2002). Furthermore, the discriminatory attitude of some of the mainstream religious institutions to these immigrants, not considering them Jews, generated a state of segregation in several socioeconomic dimensions (Ben-Eliezer, 2004).

Next we set out a socioeconomic and demographic profile of immigrants entering Israel during the 1990s. Specifically, we outline the immigrants' socioeconomic characteristics and modes of incorporation into Israeli society. Because the conditions and the legal arrangements through which Jewish immigrants enter Israel and those under which overseas labor migrants are recruited are strikingly different we present each of these immigration flows (Jewish and non-Jewish) separately.

Immigration to Israel since the 1990s

Jewish Migration: A Demographic Profile

According to the Central Bureau of Statistics the total number of immigrants arriving under the Law of Return between 1989–2005 is estimated in 1,182,841. Data in Table 15-1 reveal that two groups constituted the bulk of the Jewish migration flows during these years: immigrants from the FSU, especially the European republics (85% of the total immigration), and from Ethiopia (4.5%). The remaining 10% came from Western Europe (3.4%), Central Europe (1.3%), North America (2.5%), and South

America (1.8%). The immigration flows peaked during the first years of the decade (1990–1992), and declined thereafter reaching the low figure of 19,269 in 2006 (Central Bureau of Statistics, 2007b, Table 4-2, 229).

In Table 15-2 we present basic sociodemographic characteristics of immigrants from the FSU and Ethiopia, and compare them with those of the general population of Israel in 2000. Immigrants from FSU and from Ethiopia stand in a mirror-like relationship, and point to the contrasting challenges facing Israeli society and new immigrants. The Ethiopian community displays a very young age composition compared with both FSU immigrants and the overall population of Israel. Over 40% of the Ethiopian population in Israel was aged 19 or younger, and only 7% were aged 65 and older, compared to 30% and 36% respectively among their FSU counterparts. In marked contrast to immigrants from the FSU, Ethiopians' fertility rate is higher (4.3) than the average of the FSU immigrants (1.6) and the Israeli rate (2.7). But note that fertility rates among Ethiopian women decline with time in the country, and are expected to match the rates of the veteran Jewish society in the future. The data also reveal that FSU immigrants are characterized by a high percentage of women (55%), many of whom came as heads of households (divorced and widowed). This is not a surprising finding; Israel has long attracted more female than male immigrants, perhaps, due to the supportive social policies pursued by the state (Raijman & Semyonov, 1997).

In addition, the 1990s waves included for the first time an increasing number of immigrants who were not Jewish according to *halakhah* (Jewish religious law). The percentage of non-Jews among the FSU immigrants entering under the Law of Return has risen over time. It rose from 6% in 1989 to 56.4% in 2001. This new status of non-Jewish *oleh* is likely to have substantial stratifying effects in access to the labor market and in the materialization of various social and civil rights in the context of an ethno-national state like Israel (Shafir & Peled, 2002, pp. 315–316).

The differences between the groups are most evident and pronounced with regard to educational and occupational attainment. Immigrants from the FSU display higher levels of education

Table 15-2. Select Socioeconomic Characteristics, 2000

	Immigrants from the FSU and Ethiopia, and Israeli Population		
	Former Soviet Union	Ethiopians	Israeli Population
Age Distribution	100.0	100.0	100.0
Less than 20	28.2	42.5	37.0
20–44	38.3	38.5	35.0
45–64	20.6	12.0	18.0
65+	12.9	7.0	10.0
Median Age	36.3	22.8	
Fertility Rate	1.6	4.3	2.7 [a]
% Women	55.0	51.0	50.6
% Non-Jewish (non-Palestinian)	20.5	14.0	3.5
Years of schooling [b]	13.9	4.1	12.4
	(3.0)	(5.3)	(4.3)
Percent with academic degree [b]	43.0	5.8	21.7
Percent that never studied	0.4	50.8	4.4
Percent in the labor force [b]	85.9	46.3	74.0
Occupational distribution [b]	100.0	100.0	100.0
Academic and professional	11.3	0.0	14.1
Technical	14.8	4.7	16.5
Managers	1.6	0.8	9.3
Clerical and sales	25.0	24.2	35.0
Skilled occupations in industry, construction and agriculture	31.0	32.0	19.0
Unskilled occupations in industry, construction, and agriculture	16.0	38.0	5.7

[a] Jewish women only.

[b] Individuals aged 25–55.

Sources: Demographic data are based on Central Bureau of Statistics. *Statistical Abstract, 2002*; Central Bureau of Statistics, 2003, 2004. Socioeconomic data were obtained from special analyses of *Labor Force Survey 2000* done by the authors.

than the average population of Israel. By contrast, the Ethiopians have very low educational levels (less than primary schooling). A comparison of proportions of people with academic degrees indicates that in 2000 about 50% of the FSU immigrants had completed academic education, as against about 30% of Israeli-born citizens. But only 5% of the Ethiopian immigrants had done so (over 50% of them reported that they never studied, compared with less than 4% in the general Israeli population). While other immigrant societies (e.g., the United States and countries in Western Europe) are faced with flows of low-skilled immigrants, Israel has had to deal with the massive flow of high-skill immigrants.

Consequently, Israel direly needs to generate jobs for an immigrant population characterized by specific (high) human capital endowments. At the same time the challenge is to integrate the population of Ethiopians. A large part of the Jewish community in Ethiopia lived in isolated and remote districts of the country. The great majority were peasants and artisans who used traditional technologies. Their illiteracy rate was very high and most of them brought skills that were not relevant to the Israeli labor market.

Being massive, the flows of immigrants from the FSU during the first years of the 1990s resulted in unemployment among the newly arrived. The labor market was unable to offer appropriate and adequate jobs to the large supply of highly educated immigrants. Many had to compromise with low-paying jobs below their qualifications and credentials (see e.g., Flug,

Kasir, & Ofer, 1997; Raijman & Semyonov, 1998). For example, in 1991 there were 30,000 engineers in the Israeli labor market. A flow of 200,000 immigrants brought an addition of about 22,500 engineers. Similarly, 16,000 physicians and dentists were active in Israel in 1991, and the Russian immigration brought 6,500 more physicians per year, doubling the size of this occupational group. Most of these newly arrived professionals were unable to find jobs similar to those they left behind.

However, recent indications and assessments suggest that with the passage of time in the new country many of the immigrants do experience upward occupational and economic mobility. They are closing the economic gaps with the Israeli-born populations (Semyonov, Raijman & Kotsubinski, 2002). The group of young immigrants has been relatively most successful in their integration into the Israeli labor market whereas the more mature group of immigrants is the most disadvantaged. It is still unclear whether and to what extent this trend and process of integration and mobility will continue in light of the current political and economic situation of Israel.

The data in Table 15-2 reveal that FSU immigrants have succeeded in joining the labor market, and are overrepresented in the high skilled occupations, but that the lucrative and high status managerial category remains unattained by them. The immigrants are also underrepresented in sales-type occupations (where language skills are needed) and in skilled occupations as compared with other populations. As for the Ethiopian immigrants, the data indicate that only half of this group was employed, mostly in unskilled jobs in industry and construction. Their low socioeconomic achievement is the direct result of low human capital endowments. Although younger Ethiopians and more veteran immigrants have achieved higher levels of education, participate more in the labor market, and have improve their wages over time the gaps between them and the rest of Israeli society are still very wide (Offer, 2004; Swirski & Swirski, 2002).

Non-Jewish Labor Migration

As noted, overseas labor migration is a new phenomenon but it has been a contested issue in Israeli society from the start. Documented and undocumented labor migrants comprised 9.6% of the total labor force, and together with Palestinian daily commuters they made up to 13% of the total labor force in Israel in 2000. These figures place Israel at the top of the industrialized Western countries most heavily dependent on noncitizen workers (Kemp & Raijman, 2008).

The deterioration of the political and security situation generated by the first Palestinian uprising in the occupied territories (1987) brought about a severe labor shortage in the construction and agriculture sectors, in which noncitizen Palestinian workers had been concentrated (Bartram, 1998; Semyonov & Lewin-Epstein, 1987). Periodic strikes organized by the Palestinian leadership and the systematic closure of the borders imposed by the Israeli government as a reaction to terrorist attacks impeded the entry of Palestinians to work in Israel. Employers (especially in the construction and agriculture sectors) had growing demands for cheap labor, which could not be satisfied through the supply of a native labor force given that Israelis were not willing to assume the low-status and low-paying jobs in which Palestinians had been engaged. The government's unwillingness to introduce major social and economic measures of restructuration (e.g., technological changes in construction and agriculture and raising wage levels in these sectors), the increasing demand for housing due to the massive flow of immigration at the beginning of the 1990s, and the rising level of violence between Palestinians and Israelis all set the stage for the government's decision at the end of 1993 to grant permits for massive recruitment of overseas labor migrants.

The recruitment of overseas workers was consistent with the interests of both the state and the employers, as it was considered a temporary, low-cost solution to a temporary problem. But, the transformation of overseas labor migration from a negligible matter—as it was until the beginning of the 1990s—into an institutionalized and full-fledged process at the beginning of the twenty-first century has become a feature of Israeli society.

As Figure 15-1 clearly shows, a dramatic process of de-Palestinization of the Israeli labor

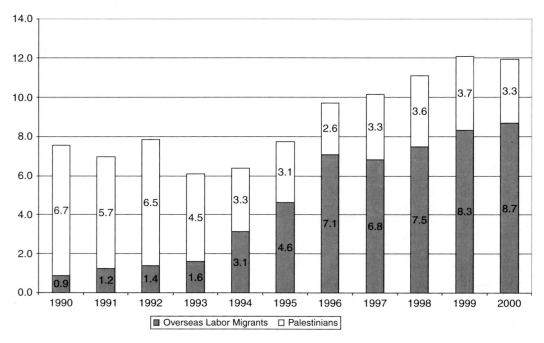

Figure 15-1. Percent of Labor Migrants and Palestinians in the Israeli Labor Force, 1990–2000

force was evinced by the decreasing number of noncitizen Palestinians, which was concomitant with the increasing number of overseas labor migrants during the 1990s. The increase in the number of labor migrants was due to a constant rise in the number of permits granted to employers, but also to a constant rise in the numbers of undocumented migrants residing in Israel (Kemp & Raijman, 2008). According to Central Bureau of Statistics, by 2007 undocumented labor migrants comprise 55% of all foreign workers in the country (Central Bureau of Statistics, 2007a).

Labor Migration Policy

Overall, Israel's labor migration policy reflects the state's continuous anxiety about a changing ethnoscape that may pose a threat to its Jewish character. State action on labor migrants is expressed as a policy of control manifested through two main pillars: indenture of legally recruited migrants, and deportation of undocumented or irregular migrants. By indenture, the state allocates and grants work permits to employers and not to employees, thus documented labor

migrants become a de facto "captive labor force," with all the flagrant violations of individual and civil liberties this entails (see Workers Hotline Reports: www.kavlaoved.org.il). By this means the state seeks not only to prevent turnover of migrant workers but also to "privatize," namely delegate its regulatory functions to the hands of employers (Raijman & Kemp, 2002). As stated above, one of the main outcomes of the "binding" system, as it is called in Israel, is that legally recruited migrant workers who wish to leave their employers become automatically "illegal." Those in the latter category are dubbed "runners" in the local employers' jargon. A paradoxical situation is thus created whereby the state directly creates what it allegedly seeks to repress. The second pillar of state policy, deportation of undocumented migrant workers, has been the pursued by the Israeli authorities since the end of 1996 (Raijman & Kemp, 2002). The overall target set by the Minister of Labor was to reduce the proportion of migrant workers from 10% of the Israeli workforce to just 1%. The deportation policy emerged as a patchwork affair and entailed the violation of basic human rights (see annual reports: http://www. kavlaoved.org.il). Many migrants were deported when they tried to demand their rights from their employers or from the National Insurance Institute (social security); hundreds were held in detention for lengthy periods under harsh conditions and without being brought to trial; families fell apart after the father was apprehended, often before the eyes of the children (for further analysis of the deportation policy, see Kemp & Raijman, 2008). Since September 2002, and upon the creation of the new Immigration Police, a quota of 50,000 undocumented migrants earmarked for deportation has been set as a target and has been by and large fulfilled (see http://www.hagira.gov.il). In 2003 the Immigration Police launched a new campaign known as "Operation Voluntary Repatriation" designed to encourage undocumented migrants to leave Israel voluntarily.

From a juridical point of view, Israel is signatory to international conventions such as that of the International Labor Organization on labor migration (1949), which the Knesset ratified in 1953, and the international convention for the protection of children. Moreover, Israel has enacted highly progressive laws on workers' rights—including a minimum wage and work hours and conditions—and on health (a patients' rights law). The territorial definition of these laws enables them to be applied without discrimination to all residents in Israel, whether they are citizens or not, and irrespective of their legal status in the country.

In practice, an immense gap exists between the provisions of these laws, which are supposed to serve migrant workers, and their implementation (see e.g., Borowoski & Yanay, 1997). What in fact underlies the violation of migrant workers' social and civil rights in Israel is not the absence of appropriate legislation but the lack of an infrastructure, compounded by the state's lack of will to enforce the laws (for a thorough analysis of the role of other state and nonstate actors in labor migration policy in Israel see: Kemp & Raijman, 2004; Raijman & Kemp, 2002).

Labor Migrants in Israel

Demographic Profile

In Table 15-3 we present information regarding countries of origin of labor migrants entering Israel with work permits by country of citizenship in 1995 and 2000. The data show that most of the migrants are young men in their mid-thirties (median age 35) coming from East Europe and Southeast Asia. The ethnic composition of the flows has changed over time, with migrants from Asia increasing their share by the end of the beginning of the twenty-first century. This is explained by the changing composition of work permits, which has reduced the number of workers in the construction and agriculture sectors (from East Europe and Thailand, respectively) and increased the number employed in nursing and geriatric care (mainly from the Philippines). Given that the majority of work permits in the latter are granted to women, the changing composition of permits by sector explains the relative increase in the share of women arriving in Israel with work permits over the last decade. Whereas the government sets quotas for foreign employment in the construction and agricultural sectors, no limits are set in the case of nursing and elder care, as it is understood that native workers would not be ready to work round the clock and for a salary well below the minimum wage.

The industrial distribution of migrant workers with permits residing in Israel in 2002 is presented in Table 15-4. Three main sectors concentrate the bulk of legally recruited migrant workers: about 28% of them work in the construction sector (mainly from Romania, China, Turkey, and the FSU), 27% in agriculture (mainly from Thailand); and 41% in nursing and elder care (mainly from the Philippines and to a lesser extent from Sri-Lanka, India, and Bulgaria). In addition, another 4.5% work in light industry (Romania, FSU, and South America), almost 3% in restaurants (Philippines, China, and Thailand), and 1% in hotels, especially in the tourist city of Eilat (Africa and FSU) (see www.kavlaoved.org.il). Legally recruited workers come alone, without their families, and for the most part they live and work in the same location (construction site, agricultural land, or private household) with their work conditions resembling a kind of "total institution" (Kemp et al., 2000). While the state permits provide a formal infrastructure of incorporation into the labor market, the "binding" system leaves little or no margin for migrant

Table 15-3. Arrival with Work Permits by Country of Citizenship & Gender

Country of Citizenship	1995		2000	
	%	% Men	%	% Men
Asia-total	33.1	81.0	44.1	63.0
India		86.0	1.3	78.0
Turkey	7.7	94.0	3.4	98.0
Lebanon	5.9	74.0	1.7	56.0
China	2.4	97.0	5.6	96.0
Philippines	2.9	18.0	14.6	17.0
Thailand	13.3	90.0	15.3	91.0
Other	0.5	79.0	2.1	66.0
Africa-total	0.4	75.0	1.1	51.0
Europe-total	62.3	87.0	51.1	78.0
Bulgaria	2.6	96.0	4.4	69.0
USSR (former)	3.2	85.0	8.2	66.0
Romania	52.7	89.0	31.8	86.0
Other	3.8	59.0	6.8	61.0
America-Oceania	3.0	70.0	3.3	63.0
USA	2.2	69.0	2.1	67.0
Other	0.8	71.0	1.1	55.0
Not Known	2.9	81.0	0.2	78.0
TOTAL	100.0	85.0	100.0	71.0
	(78,300)		(52,200)	
Mean Age	35.0		35.4	

Sources: Central Bureau of Statistics, 2004, Table 4-10.

Table 15-4. Industrial Distribution of Country of Origin

Workers with Permits—2002			
Main Countries of origin	Numbers and Percentage		Industry
Thailand, China	27.0	30,000	Agriculture
Romania, Former Soviet Union, China, Turkey	28.0	32,000	Construction
Romania, Former Soviet Union, South America	4.5	5,000	Industry
Philippines, Sri Lanka, India, Bulgaria	36.0	40,000	Health and elder care
Philippines, China, Thailand	2.7	3,000	Restaurants
Africa, Former Soviet Union	0.9	1,000	Hotels (in the city of Eilat)
	100%	110,000	TOTAL

Sources: Workers Hotline. www.kavlaoved.org.il/

associational initiatives. Moreover, the development of illegal norms such as the confiscation of passports by employers further accentuates the migrants' lack of autonomy and their dependence on employers.

As for undocumented labor migrants, they arrive from almost every corner of the world—though mainly from East Europe (primarily from the former Soviet Union and Romania), South Asia (primarily from the Philippines), Africa (primarily from Ghana and Nigeria), and South America (primarily from Colombia and Ecuador) and are employed primarily in construction and services sector (see Bar-Zuri, 2001). In contrast to their documented counterparts, undocumented migrant workers arrive haphazardly and many of them come with their families. They enter the country on a tourist visa, which forbids them to work, and become undocumented by overstaying it. Others enter the country by crossing the desert beyond Israel's border with Egypt and being smuggled across the frontier. These methods are not the only paths to illegality. An extremely common way for a worker to become undocumented is to leave the employer to whom the worker is "attached" through the "bondage" system. According to estimates, some 53% of undocumented labor migrants have become "illegal" as a direct result of the binding system (Bar-Zuri, 2001).

As noted, most undocumented labor migrants reside in the southern neighborhoods of the city of Tel Aviv. Within just a few years certain neighborhoods there, such as Neve Sha'anan, HaTikva, Shapira, and the Yemenite Quarter, became new ethnic enclaves where families of undocumented migrant workers made their homes (Kemp & Raijman, 2004; Raijman et al., 2003). As labor migrants and their families climbed to 16% of the Tel Aviv's population, it was clear that they were not only changing the composition of the labor market but reweaving the ethnic fabric of Israel's major metropolitan area (Kemp & Raijman, 2004; Schnell, 1999).

Paradoxically, the lack of state regimentation of the working and living conditions of undocumented migrant workers leaves room for the emergence of new ethnic communities and a wide array of migrants' associations. During the last decade three ethnic communities have developed in Israel among migrant workers: Black African, Latin American, and Filipino. The Latin American and African communities of migrant workers in Israel originate from all parts of the South American and African continents. Latin American labor migrants come mainly from Colombia, Ecuador, Peru, Chile, Peru, and Bolivia. African migrant workers come predominantly from Nigeria, Ghana, the Democratic Republic of Congo (formerly Zaire), the Republic of Congo, the Central

African Republic, Ethiopia, Ivory Coast, Sierra Leone, Mauritius and South Africa.

Research conducted among the undocumented communities of Latin American and African workers shows that both communities are rather young, the majority aged between 22 and 45 years, with a mean age of 37 years for Africans and 34 years for Latinos. One-fifth of the Latino migrants and almost one-third of the African respondents were living in Israel with their nuclear family, whereas a third of both Latinos and Africans left their families (spouse and/or children) in their countries of origin and sent money to support them (more women than men belonged to this category). Because the latter fear that leaving the country precluded the possibility of return, the majority of Latino and African migrant workers had not seen their families for a long time. The great majority of these two communities had neither residence nor work permits.

Labor migrants in both groups display relatively high levels of human capital acquired in their countries of origin (about 12 years of study on average, with a relatively high percent holding an academic degree). About half of the migrant workers held high-status white-collar positions before moving to Israel (15% of Latin Americans and 34% of African migrants). Their skills notwithstanding, most of them (men or women) are employed in domestic service and cleaning jobs in Israel. A unique feature is that a high percentage of men (41 and 73% for Latinos and Africans respectively) work as cleaners in private homes, thus subverting traditional definitions of gender roles in both societies (African and Latin American).

The migrants' willingness to pay the price of downward occupational mobility is due to the large salary differentials that exist between Israel and their home countries. Back home, the average monthly salary earned by migrants was $326 for Latin Americans and $212 for Africans (with women earning only about 60% of what the men made). These low wage levels—compared with an expected average wage of $1,000–$1,500 a month for cleaning homes (based on pay of $7 an hour and according to the number of hours worked)—account for people's readiness to pay the cost, not only in type of employment, but also the social and emotional price entailed in migration. This price includes being "illegal" and living on the margins of Israeli society (for a detailed analysis of the Latin American and African communities of labor migrants in Israel see: Kemp et al., 2000; Raijman et al., 2003; Raijman & Kemp, 2002). Although living on the fringe of Israeli society, undocumented labor migrants have created their own social spaces through the establishment of migrants' associations (e.g., social clubs, migrant churches, and sport clubs, among others). These serve as vehicles by which labor migrants become mobilized and open new platforms for participation in a highly exclusionary social environment (e.g., Kemp et al., 2000; Raijman et al. 2003; Kemp & Raijman, 2003). However, with the launching of the harsh deportation policy and the establishment of the new Immigration Police in Israel, the future of these communities is uncertain as many of the community leaders and members have been arrested and deported.

Conclusion

The new immigration to Israel is not without challenges. On the contrary, the 1990s brought new kinds of immigrants hitherto unknown in the Israel context. Due to space constraints, we shall only mention briefly the challenges posed by the new migration flows. Each one of these challenges—which in certain ways contribute to the "normalization" of the Israeli state as a de facto immigration state (as opposed to an exclusively Jewish immigration state)—is likely to become an intrinsic part of the stratification processes that will impinge upon next generations' socioeconomic mobility and cultural incorporation (Kemp & Elias, 2003).

Jewish and Non-Jewish FSU Immigrants: Assimilation or Segregation?

Immigrants entering Israel from the FSU during the 1990s were admittedly motivated much more by "push" than by "pull" factors, and arrived in massive numbers. So the question that looms large in both the academic and public debate is whether they may yet form an ethnic enclave within the larger society (Al-Haj, 2004). Researchers consistently pointed to

the persistence of cultural traits of the Russian immigrants that were not compatible with streamlined notions of assimilation. The immigrants' Russian cultural orientation has not weakened, but in fact has become markedly reinforced in Israel. They enjoy a high level of cultural pride, as well as a sense of lofty cultural superiority to Israeli society (Al-Haj, 2004; Remennick, 2007). They are strongly committed to cultural continuity and have developed a rich and dense institutional organization (see e.g., Al-Haj, 2004; Leshem & Lissak, 1999). We agree with Shafir and Peled that "the integration of the FSU immigrants into the society is still very much an ongoing process . . . . It is difficult to predict, therefore, whether Israel's Russian-speaking population will crystallize into a distinct ethnic group, or will disperse and join existing groups along the axes of class, ethnicity, gender, religiosity, and ideology" (2002, p. 317). The question is thus pending for the second generation.

"Black Jews"

The immigration of Ethiopians and their incorporation in Israeli society is affected by three main features that position them on the margins of society (Kemp and Elias, 2003): (1) Race: Ethiopian immigration has for the first time caused the articulation of race cleavages in Israeli society, adding to existing ethnonational, class, and religious cleavages (on the main cleavages in Israeli society see Smooha, 1978). (2) Their Jewishness is questioned and only reluctantly recognized by Israel's rabbinic authorities (Ben-Eliezer, 2004). (3) Their human capital is poor in Western terms (Offer, 2004). Although the state declared a policy of assimilation toward Ethiopian Jews in practice the new arrivals were relegated to a status of marginality (Swirski and Swriski, 2002). Some have even argued that the low socioeconomic position of Ethiopian Jews in Israel is deep-rooted in new racist discourses currently evolving in the country (Ben-Eliezer, 2004, p. 246). To what extent the second generation will succeed in achieving socioeconomic mobility despite low resources and discrimination is still difficult to assess.

However, we suggest that the ethnic mosaic of the new immigration is far more complex than it may appear at first glance, and it posits new and unforeseen challenges to the transformation of collective identities in Israel as well as to patterns of social inequality. A case in point is the non-Jewish immigrants and their family members who arrive under the Law of Return. However, many were not registered as citizens because the Ministry of Interior (under the control of Shas, the ultra-Orthodox Religious Party for most of the 1990s) refused to register them as citizens. Furthermore, even those registered as citizens had greater difficulties than usual in exercising some of their civil rights (e.g., marriage, divorce, burial, and family unification) because most issues of family law are under the jurisdiction of religious courts, which make it difficult for non-Jews to exercise some of these basic rights (see Shafir & Peled, 2002, pp. 315–316). As the possibility of a future separation between state and religion seems more or less unachievable in the near future, the chances of full legal and political equality for the new (non-Jewish) immigrant population seem slight.

Non-Jewish and Non-Palestinian Labor Migrants

Overseas labor migrants have become de facto "permanent temporary residents." The emergence of migrant workers' communities in Israel is of special interest since it challenges the basic definition of Israeli society as an ethnonational polity that encourages permanent settlement of Jewish immigrants and discourages settlement of non-Jewish migrants. In contrast to the experiences of most Jewish immigrants, foreign workers are likely to be confined at the margins of the Israeli economy and society, becoming its new "hewers of wood and drawers of water."

The manifestly Jewish ethnonational character of the nation-state renders the Israeli case especially interesting for studying the modes of incorporation of non-Jewish migrant workers and the challenges to the limits of participation posed by migrant workers for the Israeli state and society. As the number of non-Jewish migrants has continued to grow, questions about the rights of citizenship, the nature of nationality, and the viability of a multicultural society are becoming more crucial than ever before. Research conducted in Israel shows that Israelis (Jews or Arabs) are willing to benefit from the cheap labor noncitizens provide, but are reluctant to grant them equal access to social rights (Raijman & Semyonov, 2004). These exclusionary attitudes should be understood within the general context of an ethnonational state like Israel. In fact, despite similarities with European countries, the Israeli case seems more complex. The ethnic-religious nature of nationalism in Israel (and of its incorporation regime), the absence of an egalitarian notion and practice of citizenship for non-Jews, and the highly restrictive character of its naturalization policy all make Israel a de facto multicultural society with few prospects for multiculturalism.

References

Al-Haj, M. (2004). *Immigration and ethnic formation in a deeply divided society: The case of the 1990s immigrants from the Former Soviet Union in Israel.* Leiden, The Netherlands: Brill.

Bartram, D. (1998). Foreign workers in Israel: History and theory. *International Migration Review, 32,* 303–325.

Bar-Zuri, R. (2001). Foreign workers without permit in Israel, 1999. Discussion paper 5.01. Jerusalem: Ministry of Labor and Welfare Affairs, Manpower Programming Authority.

Ben-Eliezer, U. (2004). Becoming a black Jew: Cultural racism and anti-racism in contemporary Israel. *Social Identities, 10* (2), 245–266.

Borowoski, A., & U. Yanay. (1997). Temporary and illegal labour migration: The Israeli experience. *International Migration, 35* (4), 495–509.

Central Bureau of Statistics (2004). *Former Soviet Union immigrants: Selected characteristics.* Jerusalem: CBS.

Central Bureau of Statistics (2006). Statistical abstract. Jerusalem: CBS Central

Central Bureau of Statistics (2007a, July 30). Report to the newspapers, 139.

Central Bureau of Statistics (2007b). Statistical abstract. Jerusalem: CBS.

Cohen, Y. (1998). Socio-economic gaps among Jews, 1975–1995. *Israeli Sociology, 1,* 115–134 (Hebrew).

Cohen, Y. (2002). From haven to heaven: Changing patterns of immigration to Israel. In D. Levy and Y. Weiss (Eds.), *Challenging ethnic citizenship: German and Israeli perspectives on immigration* (pp. 36–56). New York and Oxford: Berghahn Books.

Cohen, Y., & Y. Haberfeld (1998). Second generation immigrants in Israel: Have the ethnic gaps in schooling and earnings declined? *Ethnic and Racial Studies*, 21, 507–528.

Della Pergola, S. (1998). The global context of migration to Israel. In E. Leshem and J. Shuval (Eds.), *Immigration to Israel: Sociological perspectives* (pp. 51–92). New Brunswick: Transaction Publishers.

Doron, A., & H. Kargar (1993). The politics of immigration policy in Israel. *International Migration*, 31, 497–512.

Flug, K., N. Kasir, & G. Ofer (1997). The absorption of Soviet immigrants into the labour market: Aspects of occupational substitution and retention. In N. Lewin-Epstein, Y. Ro'i, & P. Ritterband (Eds.), *Russian Jews on three continents: Migration and resettlement* (pp. 433–470). London: Frank Cass.

Gitelman, Z. (1995). *Immigration and identity: The resettlement and impact of Soviet immigrants on Israeli politics and society*. Los Angeles: Wilstein Institute of Jewish Policy Studies.

Haberfeld, Y. (1993). Immigration and ethnic origin: The effect of demographic attributes on earnings of Israeli men and women. *International Migration Review*, 29, 286–305.

Haberfeld, Y., M. Semyonov, & Y. Cohen (2000). Ethnicity and labour market performance among recent immigrants from the former Soviet Union to Israel. *European Sociological Review*, 16, 287–299.

Haidar, A. (1990). *The Arab population in the Israeli economy*. Tel Aviv: International Center for Peace in the Middle East.

Herzog, E. (1999). *Immigrants and bureaucrats*. New York: Berghahn Books.

Kemp, A., & N. Elias (2003). The new second generation in Israel: Key issues and main challenges. Paper presented at the Conference on The Second Generation, June 18–23, 2003, Bellagio Center, Italy.

Kemp, A., & R. Raijman (2003). Christian Zionists in the Holy Land: Evangelical churches, labor migrants, and the Jewish state. *Identities, Global Studies in Culture and Power*, 10, 295–318.

Kemp, A., & R. Raijman (2004). Tel Aviv is not foreign to you: Urban incorporation policy towards labor migrants in Israel. *International Migration Review*, 38 (1), 1–26.

Kemp, A., & R. Raijman (2008). Foreigners in a Jewish State: The new politics of labor migration in Israel. *Israeli Sociology*, 3 (1), 79–110 (Hebrew).

Kemp, A., R. Raijman, J. Resnik, & S. Schammah-Gesser (2000). Contesting the limits of political participation: Latinos and black African migrant workers in Israel. *Ethnic and Racial Studies*, 23 (1), 94–119.

Leshem, E., & M. Lissak (1999). Development and consolidation of the Russian community in Israel. In S. Weil (Ed.) *Roots and route: Ethnicity and migration in global perspective*. Jerusalem: Hebrew University Magnes Press.

Lewin-Epstein, N., & M. Semyonov (1993). *Arabs in Israel's economy: Patterns of ethnic inequality*. Boulder, CO: Westview Press.

Lewin-Epstein, N., & M. Semyonov (2000). Migration, ethnicity, and inequality: Homeownership in Israel. *Social Problems*, 47 (3), 425–444.

Lerner, M., & G. Menahem (2003). Decredentialization and recredentialization: The role of governmental intervention in enhancing occupational status of Russian immigrants in Israel in the 1990s. *Work and Occupations*, 30 (1), 3–29.

Leshem, E., & M. Sicron (1999). The absorption of Soviet immigrants in Israel. In D. Singer & R. Seldin (Eds.), *American Jewish Yearbook 1999* (pp. 448–522). New York: American Jewish Committee.

Lustick, I. (1999). Israel as a non-Arab State: The political implications of mass immigration of non-Jews. *Middle East Journal*, 53, 417–433.

Offer, S. (2004). The socio-economic integration of the Ethiopian community in Israel. *International Migration*, 42 (3), 29–55.

Offer, S. (2007). The Ethiopian community in Israel: Segregation and the creation of a racial cleavage. *Ethnic and Racial Studies*, 30 (3), 461–480.

Raijman, R., & A. Kemp (2002). State and non-state actors: A multi-layered analysis of labor migration policy in Israel. In D. Korn (Ed.), *Public policy in Israel* (pp. 155–173). New York: Lexington Books.

Raijman, R., & M. Semyonov (1995). Models of labor market incorporation and occupational cost among immigrants to Israel. *International Migration Review*, 29 (2), 375–393.

Raijman, R., & M. Semyonov (1997). Gender, ethnicity, and immigration: Double disadvantage and triple disadvantage among recent immigrant women in the Israeli labor market. *Gender & Society*, 11 (1), 108–125.

Raijman, R., & M. Semyonov (1998). Best of times, worst of times, and occupational mobility: The case of Soviet immigrants in Israel. *International Migration*, 36 (3), 291–312.

Raijman, R., & M. Semyonov (2004). Perceived threat and exclusionary attitudes toward foreign workers in Israel. *Ethnic and Racial Studies*, 27 (5), 780–799.

Raijman, R., M. Semyonov, & P. Shmidt (2003). Do foreigners deserve rights? Public views towards labor migrants in Germany and Israel. *European Sociological Review*, 19, 379–392.

Raijman, R., S. Schammah-Gesser, & A. Kemp (2003). International migration, domestic work, and care work: Undocumented Latina migrants in Israel. *Gender & Society,* 17 (5), 727–749.

Remennick, L. I. (2007). *Russian Jews in three continents: Identity, integration, and conflict.* New Brunswick and London: Transaction Publishers.

Rozenhek, Z. (2000). Migration regimes, intra-state conflicts, and the politics of exclusion and inclusion: Migrant workers in the Israeli welfare state. *Social Problems,* 47 (1), 49–67.

Schnell, Y. (1999). *Foreign workers in south Tel-Aviv-Jaffa.* Jerusalem: Florsheimer Institute for Policy Research (Hebrew).

Semyonov, M., & T. Lerenthal (1991). Country of origin, gender, and the attainment of socioeconomic status: A study of the Jewish population in Israel. *Research in Social Stratification and Mobility,* 10, 325–343.

Semyonov, M., & N. Lewin-Epstein (1987). *Hewers of wood and drawers of water: Noncitizen Arabs in the Israeli labor market.* New York: ILR Press.

Semyonov, M., & N. Lewin-Epstein (2003). Immigration and ethnicity in Israel: Returning diasporas and nation building. In R. Muenz & R. Ohliger (Eds.), *Diasporas and ethnic migrants: Germany, Israel, and post-Soviet successor states in comparative perspective* (pp. 327–337). London: Frank Cass.

Semyonov, M., N. Lewin-Epstein, & S. Spilerman (1996). The material possessions of Israeli ethnic groups. *European Sociological Review,* 3, 289–301.

Semyonov, M., R. Raijman, & E. Kotsubinski (2002). *Soviet immigrants in the Israeli labor market: A study of the first decade.* Final report to the Freiderich Ebert Foundation. (Unpublished).

Shafir, G., & Y. Peled (2002). *Being Israeli: The dynamics of multiple citizenship.* Cambridge, UK: Cambridge University Press.

Shuval, J. T., & E. Leshem (1998). The sociology of migration in Israel: A critical view. In E. Leshem and J. Shuval (Eds.), *Immigration to Israel: Sociological perspectives* (pp. 3–50). New Brunswick and London: Transaction Publishers.

Smooha, S. (1990). Minority status in an ethnic democracy: The status of the Arab minority in Israel. *Ethnic and Racial Studies,* 13, 389–413.

Swirski, S., & B. Swirski (2002). *Ethiopian Jews in Israel.* Report 11. Tel-Aviv: Adva Center. (Hebrew).

Weiss, Y. (2002). The Golem and its creator, or how the Jewish nation-state became multiethnic. In D. Levy and Y. Weiss (Eds.) *Challenging ethnic citizenship: German and Israeli perspectives on immigration* (pp. 82–104). New York and Oxford: Berghahn Books.

16

Poland

Amorphous Population Movements into Poland and Ensuing Policy Challenges

Aleksandra Grzymala-Kazlowska and Marek Okólski

Since 1989 Poland has been changing its ethnic profile. Between 1945 and 1989 Poland officially claimed it was homogeneous country concealing any differences; that presented a glaring contradiction to Poland's history as a multidenominational and multicultural state, and home for various persecuted minorities from abroad. With the restoration of democracy, Poland witnessed a revival of ethnic consciousness and differentiation. The "resurrected" old ethnic minorities were joined by new ethnic groups composed of newly arriving migrants. The majority of the native population has been increasingly challenged as it daily encounters alien cultures, triggering a series of unfamiliar social phenomena.

In Poland, immigration is still a novelty after a dozen or so years of the influx of mainly irregular and temporary migrants (see e.g., Okólski, 1998a; Iglicka & Sword, 1999; Okólski, 2000a; Iglicka, 2001; Kaczmarczyk & Okólski, 2002). Before 1990, Poland had a limited, mostly quasi-permanent migratory inflow of foreign migrants from other communist countries. During that period, Polish law did not allow for the inflow of foreign labor or the protection of refugees. Mixed marriages of Polish citizens led to the eventual emigration of a Pole rather than

the immigration of a foreigner. Not surprisingly, for example, in 1985 only 1,600 immigrants arrived, of which approximately 1,000 were returning Polish citizens. Population movements into Poland were negligible as a consequence of membership in the Soviet-led Communist bloc and a closed door policy that resulted in international semi-isolation.

Repressed movements prior to the pre-1990 period become clear with migration trends between 1989 and 1991, when major obstacles to border crossing and residence in Poland were gradually removed. By 1991, foreign entries into Poland were 36.8 million, ten times the 1985 figure, and continued to rise sharply until 1994, when they stabilized at 80–85 million annually. The numerical increase has been accompanied by a strong growth in the geographical diversity of visitors. A large percentage of those persons visited Poland for a few days or weeks but for other reasons than tourism, brief family reunion, or company business. They came to raise money by engaging in petty trade, occasional jobs, or "whatever profitable" venture (i.e., beggary, theft, prostitution, etc.), many becoming clandestine. Approximately 7,000 to 8,000 foreigners arrived yearly to settle as permanent residents, and additional tens of thousands entered because the labor market had become liberalized and work permits became available to non-Polish nationals. Rapidly, the number of legally employed foreigners approached 40,000, half of whom were temporary workers. Furthermore, by the end of 1990s, the inflow of asylum-seekers had grown to approximately 4,000 a year, and Poland had become a transit territory for massive flows of people from Eastern Europe and Asia to the West. At that time the Polish government had also launched a program of repatriation of ethnic Poles who lived in former Polish territories captured in 1939 by the Soviet Union, or remote areas of USSR to which they (or their ancestors) were deported (notably in Kazakhstan). However, a large majority of the immigrants, who took part in the ongoing program of the repatriation of Poles from the former Soviet Union, automatically become citizens of Poland on entering Poland, and do not appear in the statistics of foreigners' stock. Some of these developments are presented in Figure 16-1.

Prominent Categories of Migrants and their Structural Characteristics

Immigrant Stock and Inflow of Migrants in 2000 by Country of Origin

Table 16-1 focuses on the country of a migrant's origin in the year 2006. These data do not include information on the irregular inflow of migrants nor foreigners who illegally live in Poland. However, they may be reliable indicators of recent major sources of immigration into Poland. According to the census in 2002 the number of foreign citizens legally living in Poland was 74,257, that is 0.2% of the total population.

Ukraine, together with other neighboring countries such as Russia, Belarus, and Germany, accounted for 45.6% of the total stock of foreign residents (Table 16-1, column 1). This pattern of intensive flows of people between Poland and its neighbors, was common in Poland's history and it has been continued.

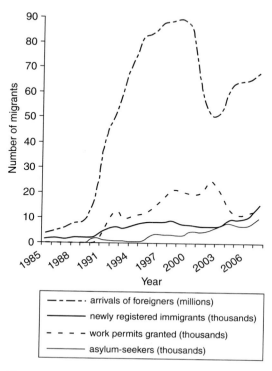

Figure 16-1. Various Types of Documented Incoming Migrants in Poland; Annual Data for 1985–2007 (arriving foreign citizens in millions; otherwise in thousands).

Table 16-1. Inflows/stocks of Migrants to/in Poland, 2006

Country	Stock of migrants (foreign citizens) staying more than 3 months (2002 cens.)	Immigration (by country of previous residence), including returning Polish citizens	New permissions for settlements	New permissions for a fixed-time residence	New permission for residence (for EU citizens)	Newly arrived foreigners registered for temporary residence (more than 3 months)	Employment consents issued to temporary residents	New refugee applications	New permissions for tolerated stay	Stock of foreign students (2006/2007)
1	2	3	4	5	6	7	8	9	10	11
Total	74 257	10 802	3 255	22 376	7 350	40 695	12 063	7 093	2 133	11 752
Ukraine	12 683	682	1 438	7 733	(b)	10 879	3 533	60	2	2 224
Russia	5 244	171	286	1 393	(b)	1 910	543	6 405	2 077	427
Belarus	3 607	248	602	1 647	(b)	3 154	1 070	51	8	1 544
Germany	12 293	3 227	(b)	(b)	4 415	4 211	398	0	0	376
Vietnam	2 363	50	138	1 496	(b)	1 641	999	27	3	180
USA	3 354	1 470	46	875	(b)	1 366	445	0	0	804
France	1 718	356	(b)	(b)	495	1 252	294	0	0	84
UnitedKingdom	1 698	1 592	(b)	(b)	404	953	(a)	0	0	72
Armenia	1 933	59	110	1 199	(b)	1 222	277	48	6	89
Bulgaria	3 321	(a)	42	497	(b)	706	175	2	0	88
Kazakhstan	1 252	87	85	277	(b)	352	17	18	0	431
China	701	(a)	13	383	(b)	590	413	5	3	110
Other most prominent countries	Italy (1 405)	Italy (377) Canada (341)	Turkey (53) Moldova (43)	Turkey (590) India (588) Japan (471) South Korea (488)	Italy (301) Netherlands (215)	Netherlands (816) Turkey (762) Italy (735) India (664) South Korea (545) Japan (489) Austria 452	Moldova (630) Turkey (507) India (430) South Korea (381) Japan (341)	Pakistan (66)		Norway (911) Sweden (511) Czech Republic (362) Lithuania (350) Canada (314) Taiwan (300)

(a) no data

(b) not applicable

Source: Central Statistical Office.

Other countries of significant migrant origin include Vietnam and the United States. A relatively high proportion of immigrants from the United States might be perceived as an effect of counterflow because of a large and longstanding emigration of Poles to that country and extensive interpersonal links established between Polish migrants and Americans. Quite different reasons underlying the presence of Vietnamese will be explored later.

The list of major countries of immigrants in 2006 (Table 16-1, column 2) differs from the list of top citizenships found in the stock of residents. Here a positive correlation between the volume of emigration to a given country and immigration from that country is even more striking, and this is due to the fact that a high proportion among the immigrants constitute reemigrants, or returning Polish citizens. This phenomenon is particularly evident among immigrants from Germany, the United Kingdom, and the United States, who accounted for 58% of the all immigrants. In general an overwhelming majority of immigrant flow to Poland originates from Europe and North America, with the evident leading role of migrants from Germany, who constitute 60% of EU citizens getting permission for residence in Poland in 2006 (Table 16-1, column 6)

The data about new permissions for settlement and permissions for a fixed-time residence (Table 16-1, columns 3 and 4) reveal a quite new (but apparently enduring) phenomenon—the coming of Vietnamese and Armenians (followed by Chinese). While immigration and remigration from Europe and North America might be considered the continuation of a long existing trend, the sizable settlement of Vietnamese and Armenians (and Chinese) began only in the 1990s, and by and large was not expected.

An intensifying foreign drive into Poland and its increasing diversity (in terms of the origin of immigrants) can be mainly observed in temporary movements. As seen in Table 16-1 (columns 6 and 7), in 2006, around 22,000 foreigners were registered as fixed-time residents, and almost 41,000 as new temporary residents. Ukrainians constituted more than one-third (almost one-half, when combined with Russians and Belarussians) of the foreigners granted fixed-time residence, however, the next largest group

was from Vietnam (6.7%) and Armenia (5.4%). Other significant non-Western nationalities included Turkish, Indian, Bulgarian, Japanese, South Korean, and Chinese.

In the 1990s, asylum-seekers became a separate category of documented migrants. Apart from a few episodes during the communist past, when the Communist regime in Poland occasionally granted political asylum to endangered leftist rebels from noncommunist countries, like Greece (in the 1940s), Chile (in the 1970s), and certain Middle East countries (since the 1960s), until 1990 Poland did not receive refugees. Even more remarkable is that Poland did not ratify the 1951 Geneva Convention until the year 1992. Since the early 1990s, refugee applications have been growing (Figure 16-1). Between 1990 and 2007 in total almost 70,000 migrants applied for a refugee status in Poland (in 2006 alone, 7,093; and in 2007, 10,048). However, only a tiny fraction (i.e., 3.1% in 1998–2001) of those applying was granted refugee status. Many persons applying for a refugee status (especially in the 1990s) in fact planned to go farther to the West and they even did not wait for a decision in their case. Since 2003, people seeking protection in Poland have been also granted permissions for tolerated stay. Between 2003 and 2007, 7,840 persons were issued a permission for tolerated stay, whereas in this period 1,558 were granted a refugee status.

The refugee profile reflected the locations of main ethnic and political conflicts or civil wars in Eastern Europe, Africa, and Asia, as well as major smuggling and trafficking routes in a given period. For example, in 1994, Armenians overshadowed other nationalities, and while in 1995 Armenia was still the top country of origin, a considerable number of self-declared refugees were from India, Russia, Afghanistan, and Somalia. In 1996 Sri Lanka became the main country of refugee origin, followed by Afghanistan and Iraq. Between 1996 and 1998 a massive inflow of people came from Afghanistan and the Indian subcontinent (along with Sri Lanka). Additionally, since 1996 the flux of refugees from Armenia to Poland has grown anew. Since 2000 Chechens started to dominate overwhelmingly in the refugee statistics—in 2006 they accounted for over 90% of applicants.

It should be mentioned that the number of undocumented (irregular) migrants coming to Poland peaked in the 1990s and probably significantly exceeded the number of registered migrants. The undocumented foreigners presented a widely differentiated mix of nationalities including a relatively stable "core" (citizens of Romania, Bulgaria, Armenia, Vietnam, Ukraine, Russia, Moldova, Mongolia) and a highly unstable "remainder" (composed of varying nations of origin such as Afghanistan, Azerbaijan, Bangladesh, Belarus, China, Somalia, India, Iraq, Pakistan, Sri Lanka, Turkey, and the former Yugoslavia). The geographical variety of this category of migrants to a large degree overlapped with that of asylum-seekers (refugees) (Okólski, 2000b).

Demographic Profile of Migrants and Their Economic Activity

Owing to the scarcity of accurate information and limited space, only a very broad sketch of immigrants' profile is presented. Generally males slightly outnumber females. However, as statistics from 2001 show, the sex distribution from Western and certain Asiatic countries was predominantly male, while a tremendous female majority entered from the former USSR. In agreement with a relatively universal tendency, immigrants were rather young. Family migration was rather uncommon, and a majority of married migrants came alone (Iglicka et al., 1997). However, the majority of migrants were married (in 2001, 56.6% of males and 58.9% of females), although over the 1990s the numbers of bachelors and spinsters increased quite considerably (Kępińska & Okólski, 2003). Educational attainment of immigrants has always been relatively high, much higher than that of emigrating Poles. In the second half of the 1990s, for instance, the absolute number of university graduates among immigrants was four times higher than among the emigrants, although the total number of emigrants exceeded that of immigrants by a factor of four (Kępińska & Okólski, 2003).

Before 1990 migrant labor was a rarity in Poland. Foreigners visiting Poland abstained from any economic activity, and a small number of foreigners who became residents were either inactive (e.g., housewives) or dispersed across professions and sectors. Although the situation changed substantially after 1989, the number of migrants regularly employed in Poland remained in the 1990s low, lower than in some much smaller Central and Eastern European (CEE) countries, such as the Czech Republic and Hungary (Okólski, 2002).

Foreign citizens, once in Poland, resort to a wide variety of economic activities, which either require advanced and highly specialized skills or do not require any skills at all. On the one hand, financial services, insurance or real estate agencies, investment or commercial banks, large industrial plants, and supermarkets employed several thousand foreigners, usually at managerial or expert positions. On the other hand, migrants occupied a number of small labor market niches (certain segments of retail and wholesale trade and fast food, seasonal work in agriculture) and are engaged in street-corner or bazaar petty trade, night-bar entertainment, household services (child or elderly care, cleaning, etc), and building or refurbishing odd jobs. They were often self-employed, and the duration of their employment was very short.

The largest groups of foreigners in the official labor market are currently Ukrainians and Belarussians, followed by the Vietnamese, Moldavians, Russians, and Turks (Table 16-1). Migrants from Ukraine work in tiny trading firms, education, or health. In contrast, migrants from the European Union remain mainly employed by medium-sized or large companies in manufacturing (German, French, Italian, & Dutch), supermarket trade (French & German), real estate (British, German, & French), education (British), and construction (French & German). The most numerous group among immigrants from Asia, the Vietnamese, usually work in two sectors: textiles and fast food restaurants. Their activity gravitates around a particular ethnic enclave, relying on close relatives or friends.

The scale of foreigner illegal economic activity is likely to be much larger than that permitted by law. Certain areas of Poland offer a great number of jobs in agriculture and in individual households. A majority of irregular migrants come from neighboring countries, Ukraine and Belarus. These migrants regularly circulate between the two countries, and their stay in

Poland is usually very short, usually under a couple of months. In the early 1990s many citizens of the former USSR were engaged in petty trade all over Poland, and the visits of those persons were even shorter. Over time, this mobility was diminishing and limited to peripheral border areas.

Reasons for the Inflow to Poland

Geopolitics and a Global Political Change

Until 1990, the population of the former Soviet block countries suffered from very limited freedom to travel abroad. While formally, there existed various bilateral agreements concerning visa-free travel, in reality only highly selected persons were allowed to leave their home countries. This radically changed between 1989 and 1991, and the movements of to and from Poland exploded. Initially, curiosity and enjoyment in the new civil rights were major motives for those travel, but, when travelers learned how to economize or even profit on international excursions, a new phenomenon of commercially oriented mobility developed (Ardittis, 1995).

Poland, along with a few other postcommunist countries, has rapidly become a destination for growing numbers (tens of millions a year) of travelers from both neighboring countries (including East Germany) and the more remote regions of the former USSR, Romania, Bulgaria, China, Mongolia, and (especially) Vietnam (Figure 16-1). For a great proportion of migrants from Eastern Europe, Poland was their first foreign country of travel (Frejka, Okólski, & Sword, 1999). A primary reason for Poland as the destination of choice seems to be her pioneering role in pursuing democratic reforms in the region and a perception of Poland (especially in the former Soviet Union) as a "Western country" or, at least, a vestibule to the West. An IOM (1993) study found that the youth in Ukraine pointed to Poland as the fifth-most attractive country, following the United States, Germany, Australia, and Canada.

A unique circumstance that stimulated a substantial inflow into Poland from northern Vietnam resulted from student exchange programs that allowed thousands of the Vietnamese

to come to communist Poland. Some of them settled in Poland, others after moving back to Vietnam, came to Poland again after the Vietnamese reforms in 1986, which led to toleration for migration and stimulated the entrepreneurship of Vietnamese society. The Vietnamese who settled in Poland were joined by other former students, their relatives, and some Vietnamese from other Eastern European countries.

Poland as a Migrant Attracting Center in the New "Migration Space"

Among the transition countries of CEE, Poland has become the first to introduce a shock therapy in the economy and to restore consumer market equilibrium. Since 1990 the deregulated and deeply liberalized Polish economy has offered good opportunities for small-scale entrepreneurs and, despite a fast growth of unemployment, a variety of jobs particularly in the informal sector. Moreover, in a relatively short time the Polish currency became convertible and the average wage went up sharply. Many economies in the region lagged behind in their transition, and initially some of them underwent a deep crisis if not disintegration. Poland, along with the Czech Republic and Hungary, became a magnet for foreigners from other CEE countries, especially those desperately trying to avoid impoverishment in their home countries.

Push Forces in Home Countries

Political, social, and economic developments in individual migrant-sending countries and the situation of various populations in those countries also strongly influence the flows of migrants into Poland (Wallace & Stola, 2001). Beside the remigration of Polish people because of failure in a host country and/or better opportunities in the postcommunist Poland (Iglicka, 2002), there are three broad groups of migrants. These might be distinguished by push factors, prompting them to move from their homelands: (1) persecution in home country; (2) employer in home country or stimuli from international labor market, and (3) deeply insufficient earnings in home country.

The first group comprised bona fide refugees from various countries. For many of those persons, arriving in Poland was often a transitory outcome of a precarious and long-lasting trip, and the causes for migration were severe as they were usually in danger at home because of political or ethnic conflicts. However, seeking protection in Poland could be accidental. For example, many Armenian refugees in Poland stopped longer than intended (in 1991 or 1992) on their way to the West, but following a sympathetic reception decided to stay, often illegally. Foreigners who might be included in the second group were highly skilled professionals, managers, or owners who obtained work permits in Poland. Most were cosmopolitan functionaries of transnational corporations, which established their subsidiaries or offices in Poland following either foreign capital flow to Poland or strong demand for specific qualifications. For this group of foreigners, as much as for a great number of refugees, Poland was usually an accidental stage in a relatively long chain of residences.

A large majority of foreigners who came to Poland in the 1990s belonged to the third group, those who were impoverished in their home countries, many of which were in transition from totalitarian to democratic order and from centrally planned to market economy. The group was strongly differentiated, but of the many sub-categories, three seem of particular interest: ethnic Poles from the former USSR, temporary migrants from the (former) communist countries, and illegal migrants (including mala fide refugees) on their way to the West. Only a small segment of them is made up of repatriates and temporary migrants who, where granted a work permit, had a status of legal foreigners in Poland.

Metamorphoses in the Process of Migration

The inflow to Poland continues to take a form of nonmigratory mobility, with predominant circular movements of false tourists from neighboring countries. Migration into Poland hardly displays any stable structural characteristics. That instability is reflected in a metamorphosis of in the types of mobility and migrant status. The most important change has been from a predominance of petty traders to that of odd-job seekers.

In the course of time, casual and highly flexible migrant workers, particularly from Ukraine and Belarus, become attached to specific employers, especially in seasonal agriculture. An important consequence was more personal and complex interactions with the native population (Okólski, 1998b). In addition, after rejection of their claims, many asylum seekers, merged into the shadow economy and informal labor market, and despite their undocumented status, have been accepted or at least tolerated by local communities. A typical example is of migrants from Armenia (Łukowski, 1997).

Another distinct change is a metamorphosis from a circular or temporary migrant into a settler. That process took two basic forms: one with irregular workers moving from being a false tourist to an illegal resident, and another from being a false tourist to a legal resident, the latter, among which Ukrainians prevail, through marriage to a Polish citizen (Górny & Kępińska, 2004).

Finally, a change from illegal transit migrant to an asylum-seeker might be mentioned. There is evidence of a sizable shift on the part of migrants smuggled from Asia to Germany from transit migrants to persons seeking protection from the Polish refugee administration (Okólski, 2000b).

The above picture of migratory movements into Poland and of migrants themselves suggests a number of general conclusions. After an initial rapid pace in the late 1990s, the inflow of immigrants to Poland stabilized. So far the inflow to Poland has been mainly temporary. Only a small fraction of migrants in the 1990s perceived Poland as an attractive country of destination. Therefore, metamorphoses from temporary or illegal status to permanency were relatively rare. However it looks like this situation is slowly changing (Grzymała-Kazłowska, 2008).

The Level of Acceptance of Migrants in Poland

The influx of foreigners in the 1990s into Poland was a novelty for a highly homogeneous postwar Polish society, although prior to World War II, ethnic minorities constituted about 36% of the population. In the 1930s, the most numerous groups were: 5 million Ukrainians,

3 million Jews, 2 million Belarussians, 780 thousand Germans, 200 thousand Lithuanians, and 140 thousand Russians (Łodziński, 1998). After World War II, as a result of the Nazi extermination of Jewish and Roma populations, shifts in Polish borders, forced displacement of ethnic minorities within and out of Poland, as well as the postwar emigration of citizens of different ethnic origins, Poland became an almost ethnically homogeneous nation. This was exceptional both for its history and for other countries of CEE. Moreover, the idea of a single nation was promoted regardless of the communist doctrine of internationalism. However it must be noticed that although an assimilation policy was commanded, it had never been fully and systematically implemented.

As a result, in postwar Poland minorities became marginalized in numbers and their ethnicity became frozen and vast numbers of minority members began to assimilate. According to rough estimates made immediately after the fall of the Communist regime, recognized ethnic minorities did not exceed 2%–4% of the Polish population, and they included, in order of decreasing size of the population: Germans, Ukrainians, Belarussians, Roma, Slovaks, Lithuanians, Russians, Jews, Armenians, Czechs, Tatars, and Karaims. The general estimate of the citizens of non-Polish origin was confirmed by the results of the recent census in 2003, where 96.74% of the population declared Polish nationality, 1.23% of the cases declared different nationalities, and the remaining 2% did not submit an answer that would allow an ethnic group rating (Główny Urząd Statystyczny, 2003).

Social Attitudes toward Immigrants

The transition to a democratic political system and free market economy was greeted in Poland with enthusiasm if not euphoria. Borders in Eastern Europe opened up and enabled extensive population movements within the region. Along with the inflow of foreigners, Poland has been witnessing the revival of suppressed ethnicities. During the first years of the political transformation, there was an aura of excitement and curiosity about the novelty of diversity. In those days, Polish citizens were also particularly

sensitive to the issue of the abuse of individual rights and interested in the fate of minorities and refugees. Poles perceived assistance to refugees as a moral duty that stemmed from a debt to pay, which was incurred by Polish political emigrants during the Communist regime. Newly arriving Westerners were seen as potential investors promoting the progress of the country. Economic migrants from Eastern Europe and less developed regions of the world were viewed as contributors to development. The inflow of labor migrants and refugees was also fuel for the national pride of Poles who felt that they began to be comparable to the West. Thus, in the 1990s tolerance toward immigrants and ethnic minorities was relatively high in Poland, the leader in the political and economic transition (Jasińska-Kania, 1999; Grzymała-Kazłowska, 2004).

In the 1990s, foreigners began to be steadily visible both in the media and on the streets, particularly in the capital and other major cities as well as in border areas. Many Poles began to have daily contact with petty traders, undocumented laborers, refugees, and Western specialists. The dynamic process of the concretization of "the other" was observed (Nowicka & Łodziński, 2001). Migrants ceased to be perceived as an intriguing, ephemeral, or temporary phenomenon and progressively were seen as a commonplace. Attitudes toward foreigners became increasingly crystallized and polarized. By the end of the 1990s, the Polish became less willing to admit foreigners into the country or to assist refugees. They also placed stronger pressure on migrants to assimilate.

By the end of the 1990s distrust, anxiety, and competition gradually replaced the previous hospitality, excitement, and interest in newcomers. In 1999, in comparison to 1990, social distance to ethnic minorities and migrants noticeably increased in Poland, as in many other European countries due to unfavorable economic and political conditions (Grzymała-Kazłowska, 2004).

According to social surveys, such as one undertaken in 1999 by the Center for Public Opinion Research (CBOS), the presence of migrants in Poland was evaluated in relation to the perception of its economic consequences. In the end of the 1990s the recession in the economy, a high unemployment rate, many unsolved social problems, and a quite unstable political situation resulted in a less favorable social climate for immigrants, who began to be viewed more as rivals in the labor market. On the other hand, in the impoverished society some groups of people appreciated the inexpensive goods and services offered by foreigners.

Besides economic threats, immigrants were strongly associated with crime. September 11, 2001, did not evoke any hysterical reactions nor deep increase in hostility toward immigrants, particularly Muslims. However, concern about migrant terrorism was aroused, and foreigners from non-European countries who were so far linked with individual criminality and ethnic gangs, began to be also linked with terrorism.

Although a substantial portion of Polish society reveals mixed feelings toward the presence of immigrants, there are not many avowed opponents to foreigners. So far there were no feelings of strong anti-immigrant hostility nor any serious organized forms of anti-immigrant protests. The examples of physical violence toward foreigners and the cases of serious racist appearances by right-wing extremists remained very infrequent and were publicly stigmatized. Strong nationalist rhetoric occurred rarely, and no party focused on the presence of migrants in Poland. However such rhetoric sometimes surfaced before the EU accession, when a major anti-EU farmers' protest party, *Samoobrona*, and a national-Catholic party, *Liga Polskich Rodzin* (currently both marginalized and outside the parliament), loudly opposed the rights of foreigners to purchase Polish land after integration with the EU.

There has been also observed a steady increase in declared toleration and reinforcement of the norm of "political correctness." After the EU accession, along with an improvement of economic situation and social optimism in Poland, pro-European attitude and the perception of immigrants have improved (CBOS, 2005).

Acceptance of migrants in Poland is closely linked with stereotypes of sending nations. In general, attitudes depend mainly on the level of modernity and prosperity of those countries, the cultural and political similarity to Polish society, previous conflicts and alliances between the nation and Poland, and the presence and image of the ethnic group in the mass media (Jasińska-Kania, 1996). Americans and Western Europeans, representing "the most advanced countries and affluent societies," are the most admired. In the social perception three categories of non-Western migrants, linked with regions of origin, are identified (Grzymała-Kazłowska & Okólski, 2003). Immigrants from Southeast Asia, particularly from Vietnam, are viewed as the most numerous and most positively received (Halik, 2000; Grzymała-Kazłowska, 2007). Migrants from the former Soviet Union, mainly Ukrainians, are perceived as physically and culturally similar to Poles, however, a complex and ambivalent attitude originates from historical experiences (Konieczna, 2002). The Roma—apart from the Polish Roma, the Roma migrants from Romania—retain long-standing negative stereotypes prevalent in Polish culture (Nowicka, 2001). However, since the mid-1990s, annual research on affinity toward other nations and ethnic groups has been showing a steady decrease in dislike toward the most rejected nations and ethnic groups, such as Roma, Romanians, Ukrainians, Russians, and Jews.

Polish Immigration Policy

The attitude of the communist country toward immigrants could be characterized by a supervisory-inspectional relationship, coupled with vague and incomplete regulations emanating from the perception of the presence of foreigners as an anomaly and ephemeral occurrence (Okólski, 1997).

With the post-1989 diversity of foreigners came a need for an institutional and legal framework, and since the end of the 1990s, there has been an intensification of regulations, growing importance of immigration management, and a coordination of activities in this field. These were reflected by the Aliens Act passed in September 1997, and its amendment passed in 2001, and the appointment of the Office for Repatriation and Foreigners, a central unit of governmental administration concerned with the coordination of all activities toward foreigners. Despite this, there is still lacking a clear general migration doctrine or a vision of immigration policy (Okólski, 1998c, Kępińska &

Stola, 2004). In general Polish immigration pol-icy has been developing under the pressure of events and international influences (such as international conventions and bilateral agree-ments). The EU integration and cooperation with the Schengen group had a major impact.

In general, the most visible Polish immigra-tion policy is connected with the control and limitation of the inflow of foreigners to Europe and issues such as regulations for the residency of foreigners, combat with various forms of illeg-ality, and migrant criminality. The Aliens Act of 1997 and its amendment revealed a catalog of repressive state activities and concentrates on the responsibilities of the migrants. The higher level of distrust toward immigrants after September 11, 2001, contributed to more restrictive and preventive admission and residence regulations specified in the act passed in 2003, amended in 2005, and 2007.

Another dimension of Polish immigration pol-icy is its focus on meeting international conven-tions pertaining to the protection of human rights and lives. Except for the Polish Constitution of 1997 including an entry on rights for asylum, general regulations regarding refugee status were introduced in the Alien Act of 1997 and amended in 2001. The next development in migration pol-icy was a separate sizable act, enacted in 2003 and amended in 2005, that introduced to the three existing forms of protection—refugee status, asy-lum, and temporary protection—a fourth possi-bility of "tolerated residence" for those who should not be expelled due to humanitarian rea-sons. In the amendment of 2008 the institution of "tolerated residence" was replaced with "supple-mentary protection," whereas "tolerated residence" become restricted only when deportation is impos-sible or unacceptable.

Two other aspects of Polish immigration pol-icy are the repatriation of foreign citizens of Polish origin and the special status of citizens of the EU, which due to its smaller relevance to the topic of the chapter and a lack of space, will not be described.

Integration of Immigrants

In general, the issue of integration is poorly pre-sent in Polish immigration policy despite its being a key concern of the EU. There are only two special categories of immigrants—acknowl-edged refugees and repatriates—who are offered special integration support.

However, the governmental organizations does not systematically and in the long term support refugees at a standard comparable to that of Western Europe. This is partly due to general socioeconomic problems occurring as a result of historical impediments and system transition in Poland, and inter alia a lack of funds, a shortage of apartments (especially coun-cil ones), and a high level unemployment (Grzymała-Kazłowska A., Stefańska R. (2008). Uchodźcy w Polsce [Refugees in Poland], Infos, nr 19(43), Warszawa: Biuro Analiz Sejmowych.).

For example, the acknowledged refugees lose their accommodation and maintenance provided by the refugee centers once they become granted refugee status. They, and since 2008 also migrants who received a right to "supplementary protec-tion," are only entitled to work without permis-sion, education, health care, and social aid, as well as a special adaptation program for a maximum of 12 months (including financial aid for rent and maintenance, Polish language courses or voca-tional trainings, the aid of social worker).

As a result refugees treat Poland as a transition country that restrains their integration process and confirm the Polish authorities' view that integration is not a salient issue.

Second, the existing program, intended to sup-port repatriates, has also a limited scope. In addition to presenting proof of Polish origin, potential repatriates must be assured by the com-mitment of local authorities or through an official invitation from a private enterprise, association, or the repatriate's family, that they will posses adequate "settlement conditions," that is, accom-modation and livelihood in Poland. Additionally, they are provided by the government with one-time financial support to resettle, Polish-language courses, and assistance with employment. Despite cultural advantages and legal status (they auto-matically acquire a Polish citizenship), many repatriates face serious problems in adaptation and the support of their process of integration seems to be inadequate (Hut, 2002).

In addition to governmental programs and services accessible to migrants, they—particu-larly refugees and repatriates—are also assisted by an increasing number of nongovernmental organizations. The integration of refugees is mainly supported by Caritas-Poland and Polish Humanitarian Action (PAH), who also help repatriates. UNHCR guides and coordintes the activities in this field, whereas the Helsinki Foundation for Human Rights (HFPC) and Amnesty International specialize in human rights watch and legal advice for immigrants, as do legal centers at Warsaw and Jagiellonian Universities. Other nongovernmental programs pertain to vocational trainings, legal guidance, and psychological counseling. Many initiatives and programs are currently financed by EU funds and programs.

In contrast, repatriation programs are not funded by the EU and international NGOs nor monitored by international institutions. The most visible organizations that assist repatriates, except the ones mentioned before) are the Polish Community, Return, Assistance for Poles in the East, and Foundation of Aid to Polish Exiles.

It has been also observed a growing number of civil initiatives aiming at creating a more tolerant society and offering programs intended to combat ethnic prejudices and promote multiculturalism (i.e., in local communities).

Conclusion

The first immigrants who appeared in Poland at the beginning of 1990s were rather a novelty for a highly homogeneous postwar Polish society. After an initially warm welcome, attitudes toward foreigners in the second half of the 1990s became more reluctant, due to the increasing perception of foreigners as rivals and individuals involved in illegal and criminal activities. The EU accession and its positive consequences increased the level of tolerance toward immigrants.

Except for some specific groups such as the Vietnamese dealing with trade and fast-food sector and Chechens applying for refugee status, the majority of immigrants in Poland come from neighboring, in cultural and spatial terms, European societies. So far the migration to Poland had mainly a transit, short-term, or illegal character, and migrants were usually only found in the biggest cities and in the border areas.

Poland still lacks an immigration doctrine and a long-term immigration policy, which can be partly explained by the relative recency of immigration; problems resulting from political, economic, and social transition; as well as transformations aligned with the EU integration. In short, Polish migration policy since 1989 has developed from an almost unregulated state with open borders and a "soft" attitude toward foreigners, through more restrictive regulations at the end of the 1990s, to the latest more differentiated and pragmatic regulations. However, the most visible dimensions of Polish immigration policy remain: the control and limitation of foreigners from less developed countries (especially non-European), the limitation of migrant criminality (i.e., illegal border crossing, smuggling and trafficking), and the control of administrative aspects of residence of foreigners in Poland. The protection of refugees, the repatriation of ethnic Poles from the former USSR, and the rights of EU citizens are other significant aspects of immigration policy. With few exceptions, Polish immigration policy in practice does not include issues of immigrant integration.

Generally speaking, in addition to governmental institutions that have been involved in assistance for immigrants, there are a variety of nonprofit organizations that provide services to some categories of migrants. However, the institutional support from both the public institutions and NGOs is limited. In this situation, a quite low level (although increasing) of acceptance of ethnocultural diversity in the Polish society makes adjustment to life in Poland particularly difficult. Migrant adaptation strategies depend on the cultural distance between immigrants and Polish society, as well as their numbers, their legal status, and the length and character of their residence in Poland, migrants' culture, and social networks. Different modes of migrant adjustment can be exemplified by such groups as the Ukrainians, the Vietnamese, and westerners (Grzymała-Kazłowska & Okólski 2003).

Thus far, the impact of immigrant populations on Polish society is rather minor since immigration to Poland is still in an embryonic stage. Although migrants have become visible in public discourse and awareness, their impact on the sociocultural sphere seems to be rather minor and dependent on the region of the country in which they settle. The most powerful migration pole is Warsaw, where clusters of migrants are becoming evident. Migrants are also concentrated in other major cities as well as the eastern, and to a lesser extent western and southern, border areas.

The economy and the labor market represent fields in which the impact of migrants is the most significant as migrants who arrive in Poland are predominantly motivated by market opportunities. Refugees do not constitute a large group as do voluntary migrants who are attracted by noneconomic factors. In addition, the largest proportion of migrants in Poland is still believed to be short-term or transit migrants and persons whose legal status is unclear or illegal. Social services pertaining to immigrants are generally weakly developed, and the issue of migrant integration is not salient in public policy.

In general, immigration to Poland can be still described by its amorphous nature characteristic of the period of transition between the first and second stages of immigration processes. The first stage was characterized by a high dynamic and irregular inflow, a lack of state immigration policy, and a novelty in immigration for the host society. Currently, Poland is approaching the second stage, during which immigration is stabilizing, becoming more permanent and controlled. A coherent immigration policy is being slowly elaborated, attitudes toward the foreign populations are being shaped, and immigrant communities are slowly emerging.

References

Ardittis, S. (1995). *The Politics of East-West Migration.* New York: St. Martin's Press.

CBOS (1999). *Stosunek do obcokrajowców przebywających w Polsce* [Attitudes toward foreigners in Poland], research announcement online at www.cbos.com.pl.

CBOS (2005). *Opinie ludności z krajów Europy Środkowej o imigrantach i uchodźcach* [Opinions of inhabitants from Central-European countries on immigrants and refugees], research announcement online at www.cbos.com.pl.

Frejka, T., M. Okólski, & K. Sword (eds.) (1999). *In-Depth Studies on Migration in Central and Eastern Europe: The Case of Ukraine.* New York and Geneva: United Nations.

Główny Urząd Statystyczny (2003). Raport z wyników narodowego spisu powszechnego ludności i mieszkań 2002 [Report on the results of national census of 2002]. Warszawa.

Górny, A., & E. Kępińska (2004). "Mixed Marriages in Migration from Ukraine to Poland." *Journal of Ethnic and Migration Studies*, 30 (2), pp. 353–372.

Grzymała-Kazłowska, A. (2004). "Three Dimensions of Tolerance." In Jasińska-Kania, A., & Marody, M. (eds.) *Poles among Europeans.* Warszawa: Wydawnictwo Scholar, pp. 183–209.

Grzymała-Kazłowska, A. (2007). *Konstruowanie 'innego': Wizerunki imigrantów w Polsce* (The construction of "the Other": The cultural representations of immigrants in Poland). Warsaw: Wydawnictwa Uniwersytetu Warszawskiego.

Grzymała-Kazłowska, A. (2008). *Między jednością a wielością: Integracja odmiennych grup i kategorii imigrantów w Polsce* [Between unity and diversity: Integration of different groups and categories of immigrants in Poland]. Warszawa: Ośrodek Badań nad Migracjami.

Grzymała-Kazłowska, A., & M. Okólski (2003). "Influx and Integration of Migrants in Poland in the Early XXI Century." CMR Working Papers, No 50. Warsaw: ISS UW.

Halik, T. (2000). "Vietnamese in Poland." In Hamilton, F., & Iglicka, K. (eds.) *From Homogeneity to Multiculturalism: Minorities Old and New in Poland.* SSEES Occasional Papers No. 45. London: School of Slavonic and East European Studies, pp. 225–239.

Hut, P. (2002). *Warunki życia i proces adaptacji repatriantów w Polsce w latach 1992–2000* [Life conditions and the process of adaptation of repatriates in Poland in 1992–2000]. IPS UW. Warszawa: Oficyna Wydawnicza ASPRA-JR.

Iglicka, K. (2001). *Poland's Post-War Dynamic of Migration.* Aldershot, UK: Ashgate.

Iglicka, K. (ed.) (2002). *Migracje powrotne Polaków: Powroty sukcesu czy rozczarowania?* [Poles' return migration: Success or disappointment?]. Warszawa: Instytut Spraw Publicznych.

Iglicka K., E. Jaźwińska, E. Kępińska, & P. Koryś (1997). *Imigranci w Polsce w świetle badania sondażowego* [Immigrants in Poland in the light of survey research]. ISS Working Papers. Seria: Prace Migracyjne, No. 10; Warszawa: ISS UW. Available online at www.iss.uw.edu.pl/osrodki/cmr/wpapers/pdf/010.pdf.

Iglicka, K., & K. Sword (eds.) (1999). *The Challenge of East-West Migration for Poland.* Houndmills, UK: Macmillan Press.

IOM (1993). *Profiles and Motives of Potential Migrants: An IOM Study Undertaken in Four Countries; Albania, Bulgaria, Russia, and Ukraine.* Geneva: International Organization for Migration.

Jasińska-Kania, A. (1996). "Stereotypowe wyobrażenia Polaków o sobie i o innych narodach" [Poles' stereotypical images about themselves and other nations]. In Marody, M., & Gucwa-Leśny, E. (eds.) *Podstawy życia społecznego w Polsce* [The basics of social life in Poland]. Warszawa: ISS UW, pp. 218–228.

Jasińska-Kania, A. (1999). "The Impact of Education on Racism in Poland Compared with Other European Countries." In Hagendoorn, L., & Shervin, N. (eds.) *Education and Racism: A Cross National Survey of Positive Effects of Education on Ethnic Tolerance.* Aldershot, UK: Ashgate, pp. 75–93.

Konieczna, J. (2002). *Wizerunek Ukrainy, Ukraińców i stosunków polsko-ukraińskich w Polsce: Raport z badań* [The picture of Ukraine, Ukrainians, and Polish-Ukrainian relations in Poland: Research report]. Warszawa: Instytut Spraw Publicznych.

Kaczmarczyk, P., & M. Okólski (2002). "From Net Emigration to Net Immigration: Socio-economic Aspects of International Population Movements in Poland." In Rotte, R., & Stein, P. (eds.) *Migration Policy and the Economy: International Experiences.* Neuried: ars et unitas, pp. 319–348.

Kępińska, E., & D. Stola (2004). "Migration Policies and Politics." In Górny, A., & Ruspini, P. (eds.) *Migration in the New Europe: East-West Revisited.* Houndmills, UK: Palgrave Macmillan.

Kępińska, E., & M. Okólski (2003). *Recent Trends in International Migration: Poland 2002.* ISS Working Papers. Seria: Prace Migracyjne; No. 46, Warszawa: ISS UW. Available online at www.iss.uw.edu.pl/osrodki/cmr/wpapers/pdf/046.pdf.

Łodziński, S. (1998). "Przekroczyć własny cień: Prawne, instytucjonalne oraz społeczne aspekty polityki państwa polskiego wobec mniejszości narodowych w latach 1989–1997" [Transgress one's own shadow: Legal, institutional, and social aspects of Polish policy toward national minorities in 1989–1997]. In Berdychowska, B. (ed.) *Mniejszości narodowe w Polsce: Praktyka po 1989 roku* [National minorities in Poland: Practice from 1989]. Warszawa: Wydawnictwo Sejmowe, pp. 11–82.

Łukowski, W. (1997). "Czy Polska stanie się krajem imigracyjnym?" [Will Poland become an immigration country?]. ISS Working Papers. Seria: Prace Migracyjne, No. 12; Warszawa: ISS UW. Available online at www.iss.uw.edu.pl/osrodki/cmr/wpapers/pdf/012.pdf.

Nowicka, E. (2001). "Rom jako swój i jako obcy: Zbiorowość Romów w świadomości społeczności wiejskiej" [The Roma as one of us and as an other: Population of Roma in a rural consciousness]. In Jasińska-Kania, A. (ed.) *Trudne sąsiedztwa: Z socjologii konfliktów narodowościowych* [Difficult neighborhoods: The sociology of national conflicts]. Warszawa: Wydawnictwo Naukowe Scholar.

Nowicka, E., & Łodziński, S. (2001). *U progu otwartego świata* [On the verge of an open world]. Kraków: Zakład Wydawniczy Nomos.

Okólski, M. (1997). *Statystyka imigracji w Polsce* [Immigration statistics in Poland]. Prace Migracyjne. ISS Working Papers. Seria: Prace Migracyjne, No. 2; Warszawa: ISS UW. Available online at www.iss.uw.edu.pl/osrodki/cmr/wpapers/pdf/002.pdf.

Okólski, M. (1998a). "Poland." In Frejka, T. (ed.) *International Migration in Central and Eastern Europe and the Commonwealth of Independent States.* New York and Geneva: United Nations.

Okólski, M. (1998b). *Imigranci: Przyczyny napływu, cechy demograficzno-społeczne, funkcjonowanie w społeczeństwie polskim* [Immigrants: Reasons of inflow, sociodemographic characteristics, and functioning in Polish society]. ISS Working Papers. Seria: Prace Migracyjne, No. 17; Warszawa: ISS UW. Available online at www.iss.uw.edu.pl/osrodki/cmr/wpapers/pdf/017.pdf.

Okólski, M. (1998c). "Refleksje na temat kształtowania polityki migracyjnej w Polsce" [Reflections on the issue of developing migration policy in Poland]. In Glabicka, K., Okólski, M., & Stola, D. *Polityka migracyjna Polski* [Polish migration policy]. *Prace Migracyjne,* ISS Working Papers. Seria: Prace Migracyjne, No. 18; Warszawa: ISS UW. Available online at www.iss.uw.edu.pl/osrodki/cmr/wpapers/pdf/018.pdf.

Okólski, M. (2000a). "Poland: Increasing diversity of migration." In Fassmann, H., & Muenz, R. (eds.) *East-West Migration in Europe.* Wien: Böhlau, pp. 141–162.

Okólski, M. (2000b). "Illegality of International Population Movements in Poland." *International Migration,* 3, pp. 57–90.

Okólski, M. (2001). "Mobilność przestrzenna z perspektywy koncepcji migracji niepełnej" [Spatial mobility from the perspective of incomplete migration]. In Jaźwińska, E., & Okólski, M. (eds.) *Ludzie na huśtawce: Migracje miedzy peryferiami Polski i Zachodu* [People on a swing: Migration between peripheries of Poland and the West]. Warszawa: Wydawnictwo Scholar, pp. 31–61.

Okólski, M. (2002). "Cudzoziemcy na oficjalnym rynku pracy w Polsce" [Foreigners on the official labor market in Poland]. *Rynek Pracy,* 5–6, pp. 58–75.

Wallace, C., & D. Stola (eds.) (2001). *Patterns of Migration in Central Europe.* Houndmills, UK: Palgrave.

17

New Zealand

Changing Tides in the South Pacific: Immigration to Aotearoa New Zealand

Richard D. Bedford and Jacques Poot

International migration has long been a major force of population change in the island nation of New Zealand. Referred to as Aotearoa ("the land of the long white cloud") in the language of the indigenous Maori population, New Zealand's human settlement commenced between 1250 and 1300 AD with successive waves of Maori migration from eastern Polynesia, followed by primarily British migration from the early nineteenth century, with the Treaty of Waitangi of 1840 setting out the terms of formal colonialization at the time. The present chapter is not concerned with historical perspectives on international migration to and from New Zealand (but see, e.g., Farmer 1985; and Bedford et al. 2002), but the chapter addresses flows, stocks, and issues as they emerged following major changes in immigration policy in the late 1980s.

At the end of 2008, New Zealand's resident population was about 4.3 million, with close to one in four born overseas. New Zealand—a geographically isolated island nation 2,200 km to the east of Australia—is one of the countries frequently cited in the literature as a "country of immigration." Since the early 1990s New Zealand has probably had a higher rate of immigration than any other developed country. Between April 1, 1990, and March 31, 2008, the total number of permanent and long-term (PLT) arrivals (number of people entering for 12 months or more) was just under 1.3 million. This is equivalent to a rate of 17 immigrants per 1,000 of the resident population per annum. However, the net gain to New Zealand's population through international PLT migration over this period was much smaller, because there is also every year a substantial outflow from the country. Between April 1, 1990, and March 31, 2008, people leaving for 12 months or more totaled about 1 million, that is, equivalent to more than three quarters of the PLT arrivals. The PLT net gain was only 3.1 per 1,000 residents per annum over this period. New Zealand is clearly also a "country of emigration"; and there is considerable "churn" in the country's contemporary international migration system.

The cause of this churn is the extensive and fluctuating international movement of New Zealanders themselves, combined with varying numbers of controlled temporary and permanent immigration. This leads to strongly fluctuating rates of net migration, which are illustrated in Figure 17-1. Net migration is the "tip of an iceberg" of arrivals and departures of more than 4.6 million per annum each, that is, more than the size of the total population. Much of this movement consists of short-term visitors and residents on short-term trips whose arrivals and departures roughly balance over a year or longer, but the bigger the gross flow, the greater the likelihood of fairly big swings in the net flow. For example, during March year 1998/99 there was a total net outflow of population of 14,092 and a few years later (2001/02) a net inflow of 67,397.

Figure 17-1 has been drawn with respect to the estimated de facto population (equivalent to the "census night" population), as from the point of view of domestic demand for everyday goods and services the physical presence of people is more important than their residency status. With this in mind it is clear that net international migration and short-term movement can have a major impact on economic conditions in the short run. On balance, net immigration has been positive during the last quarter century and has accounted for about one-third of total population growth.

Roughly half of permanent and long-term migration from New Zealand is to Australia. Under the Trans-Tasman Travel Agreement (TTTA) citizens from both countries can freely settle in either country so that, for citizens at least, the flows resemble internal migration within national borders (e.g., Poot 1995). In recent decades, stronger long-run economic growth and job creation in Australia has tended to generate net migration to that country. Depending on how New Zealander is defined, it is estimated that between one in ten and one in eight New Zealanders now lives in Australia.

Besides trans-Tasman migration, another special feature of New Zealand's international migration is the significance of the flows from and to closely linked Pacific Islands, such as Samoa (Bedford 1992). We return to the trans-Tasman migration issue and the role of New Zealand in a South Pacific migration system in the penultimate section. Overall, the structure of the chapter follows that of the others in this book.

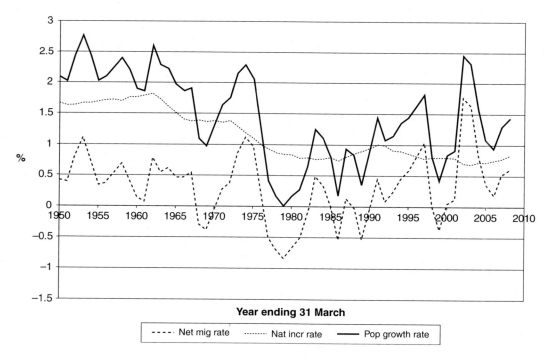

Year ending 31 March

---- Net mig rate   .... Nat incr rate   —— Pop growth rate

Figure 17-1. The Annual Rate of Net Migration, Natural Increase, and Population Growth: New Zealand 1950–2008
Source: Sweden Statistics, Population Statistics. Available: http://www.scb.se/ (2008–10–13).

The Composition of Migration Flows since 1978

In this section our focus is on migration into and out of New Zealand between April 1978 and March 2008. This is the period for which electronic data on arrivals and departures are available from Statistics New Zealand. The critical point to bear in mind relating to immigration flows is that the three decades between 1978 and 2008 coincide quite conveniently with three major periods in immigration policy. The first of these is the late 1970s to late 1980s, when there was the shift from a policy of drawing migrants from selected traditional source countries to a policy that did not discriminate on the basis of nationality of applicants for residence visas. During this decade there was a major restructuring of the New Zealand economy, initiated by a newly elected Labour Government in 1984—a restructuring that was to have some major implications for the demand for labor in different sectors of the economy, and thus the flows of migrants into and out of New Zealand. This restructuring will not be discussed in detail in this chapter—there is an extensive literature available on this subject (see for example, Evans et al. 1996; Kelsey 1995; and Le Heron and Pawson 1996). The second period is the late 1980s to the late 1990s, when a points-based selection system was introduced by a National Government elected in 1990, and further restructuring occurred, this time with reference to the

country's employment contracts legislation and welfare support system. The third period, commencing in the late 1990s, saw a change back to a Labour Government in 1999 (replaced by a National Government in November 2008) and a number of important initiatives in immigration policy that had implications for the composition of the flows into the country. The changes in immigration policy between 1986 and 2007 are summarized effectively in Merwood (2008).

The PLT arrivals, departures, and net migration gains and losses during the three decades are shown in Table 17-1. The movements of New Zealand citizens are shown separately from the movements of citizens of other countries. With regard to PLT arrivals, there were more New Zealand citizens returning in the period between April 1978 and March 1988 than there were immigrants of other nationalities coming for periods of 12 months or more. This situation changed dramatically during the second period, especially after the introduction of the points-based selection system in 1990. Between April 1988 and March 1998 the number of PLT arrivals who were not New Zealand citizens nearly doubled, while the number of New Zealand citizens returning increased very little. This trend toward significant increases in numbers of citizens of countries other than New Zealand continued through the third period (April 1998–March 2008), with a further increase of 50 percent compared with an almost static numbers of returning New Zealanders.

Table 17-1. Immigrants, Emigrants, and Net Migration, 1979–2008

Period	NZ citizens	Other citizens	Total
(Years ending March)			
a) PLT arrivals			
1979–1988	227,015	196,702	423,717
1989–1998	235,711	363,143	598,854
1999–2008	237,414	545,478	782,892
b) PLT departures			
1979–1988	457,128	127,408	584,536
1989–1998	388,816	125,241	514,057
1999–2008	497,415	184,335	681,750
c) Net migration			
1979–1988	−230,113	69,294	−160,819
1989–1998	−153,105	237,902	84,797
1999–2008	−260,001	361,143	101,142

Source: Unpublished arrival/departure data, Statistics New Zealand.

There were also major changes in the numbers of New Zealand citizens and citizens of other countries leaving New Zealand during the three decades, resulting in much smaller net gains to New Zealand's population than the growth in PLT arrivals might suggest. In addition to the major outflows of New Zealanders, which reached almost 500,000 for the decade ending March 2008, there has been some significant remigration of immigrants. During the three decades, over 400,000 citizens of countries other than New Zealand left the country after periods in residence of 12 months or more.

Until the late 1980s the great majority of New Zealand's immigrants came from a small number of "traditional" source countries—the United Kingdom (the European colonial power in the nineteenth century), Australia (the neighboring British colony that was an important source of immigrants to New Zealand in the nineteenth and the first half of the twentieth centuries), the Pacific Islands (also the original source of the Maori population), parts of northern and western Europe (especially Scandinavia in the nineteenth century and the Netherlands from the 1950s), and from Canada and the United States (but smaller flows than from Europe). These sources accounted for 82 percent of all of the PLT arrivals of citizens of countries other than New Zealand between April 1979 and March 1988 (see Table 17-2). The UK and Ireland, Australia, and the Pacific Islands accounted for 66 percent of these arrivals. "Nontraditional" sources in Asia, Africa,

Table 17-2. Immigrants by Major Source Region, 1979–2008 (Not including NZ citizens)

Nationality	Period		
	1979–1988	1989–1998	1999–2008
a) Numbers			
Traditional sources			
UK/Ireland	59,584	58,612	111,847
Australia	42,216	41,687	44,408
Pacific Islands	28,583	29,591	40,556
Others	31,126	20,489	55,917
Sub-total	161,509	163,465	252,728
Nontraditional			
Asia	27,495	160,528	237,878
Africa	2,742	14,625	29,906
Others	3,860	23,976	24,960
Subtotal	34,061	199,129	292,744
Not stated	1,132	549	6
Total	196,702	363,143	545,478
b) Percentages			
Traditional sources			
UK/Ireland	30.3	23.8	20.5
Australia	21.5	11.5	8.1
Pacific Islands	14.5	8.1	7.4
Others	15.8	9.2	10.2
Subtotal	82.1	45.0	46.3
Nontraditional			
Asia	14.0	44.2	43.6
Africa	1.4	4.0	5.5
Others	1.9	6.6	4.6
Subtotal	17.3	54.8	53.7
Not stated	0.6	0.2	0.0
Total	100.0	100.0	100.0

Source: Unpublished arrival/departure data, Statistics New Zealand.

southern and eastern Europe, the Middle East, and Latin America accounted for just over 17 percent of the PLT arrivals during this decade (Table 17-2).

During the 1990s this distribution of source countries for immigrants changed dramatically. The absolute numbers of immigrants from traditional source countries did not decline, but their share of the total PLT arrivals (excluding New Zealand citizens) fell from 82 percent to 45 percent. The biggest source now became citizens traveling on passports of countries in Asia, accounting for 44 percent. Other nontraditional sources in Africa, the Middle East, southern and eastern Europe, and Latin America accounted for just under 11 percent, giving a total of 55 percent from nontraditional sources. Since 1998 the traditional sources shown in Table 17-2 have seen increases in numbers of PLT arrivals (up by 55 percent), as have the nontraditional sources (up by 47 percent). Citizens of countries in Asia remain by far the biggest component of PLT arrivals (just under 44 percent); a very marked shift given that for the century before 1986 their entry was very strictly controlled (see McKinnon 1996; Ip 2003).

More detailed descriptions of changes in the flows of migrants from different parts of the world to and from New Zealand can be found in Bedford and Lidgard (1997) and Bedford et al. (2005).

Reasons for Leaving the Home Country

The sources of migrants entering New Zealand each year are very diverse—over 160 nationalities are recorded in the Statistics New Zealand PLT arrival flows for the 12 months ended March 31, 2008. Countries represented by 1,000 or more of their citizens arriving during 2007/08 with the intention of spending 12 months or more in New Zealand are listed and ranked in Table 17-3. For comparison, PLT arrivals from these countries in 1987/88 and 1997/98 are also provided in Table 17-3. India, China, and the Philippines are among the top five source countries in 2007/08 and barely featured at all two decades earlier.

The reasons for leaving the source countries and migrating to New Zealand vary by major source region. In the case of the Australians, the British, and the Irish, it is a case of moving to a reasonably similar social, economic, and political context. A critical reason for choosing to come to live in New Zealand by citizens from the UK and Ireland is the quality of life, especially outdoor recreation and the very diverse and picturesque physical environment. In the case of Australia, it is marriage to New Zealanders, transfers within companies that have operations in both countries, and employment in recreation industries that are

Table 17-3. Major Sources of Immigrants, Year Ending March 2008, with Corresponding Arrivals in 1997/98 and 1987/88

Nationality	Year Ending March		
	2007/08	1997/98	1987/88
UK/Ireland	13,223	6,530	6,647
India	5,105	1,840	267
Australia	4,797	4,306	3,978
China (PRC)	4,145	3,310	315
Philippines	3,638	676	373
Fiji	2,767	1,229	1,919
Germany	2,456	508	399
South Africa	2,355	2,313	343
USA	2,340	1,226	1,152
Japan	2,158	4,148	734
Malaysia	1,411	1,327	1,009
Samoa	1,178	1,086	1,526
Korea (ROK)	1,092	1,129	304
Canada	1,013	674	608

Source: Unpublished arrival/departure data, Statistics New Zealand.

the major reasons for movement across the Tasman into a country where they have the automatic right of residence anyway.

The other major sources of people of European ethnic origin in 2007/08 are Germany, Canada, the United States of America, and South Africa. It is often again lifestyle reasons, and sometimes the ability to purchase prime real estate in scenic areas, that attract European migrants to New Zealand (which has a real per capita income in between that of Spain and Portugal). The attractions of New Zealand's physical environment and the reputation the country has for being a "safe" place to live—with high-quality education and medical services—are sufficient to encourage migrants from high-income countries to seek a place of residence in the "Switzerland of the South Pacific."

One traditional source of immigrants from Europe, which does not reach the 1,000 PLT arrival threshold in the three years listed in Table 17-3, is the Netherlands. After World War II, the Dutch government promoted and subsidized settlement in "New World" countries such as New Zealand, and a sizable Dutch population emerged in rural and urban New Zealand between the early 1950s and the 1970s, when the sponsored settlement scheme ceased. Some 41,000 migrated from the Netherlands to New Zealand between 1947 and 1997, but with subsequent remigration of 13,000 (Hartog and Winkelmann 2003). Although the Netherlands-born population in New Zealand is now only a little over 20,000 and heavily skewed toward the older ages, estimates of the Dutch descent population are up to 150,000.

The Canadian and United States flows are also long-established and have their roots in somewhat similar colonial heritages (especially Canada), and the attraction of the New Zealand lifestyle. In common with the Australian flow, there is also some migration from North America linked to transfers of staff within multinational companies. American business interests gained a more significant stake in New Zealand's economy during the late 1980s and early 1990s, when deregulation of much of the government-owned infrastructural services (telecommunications, transport, and later power generation and transmission) opened up opportunities for external investors.

Another post–World War II migration flow that has remained significant in New Zealand's international migration system is the movement of peoples from islands in the eastern Pacific (Polynesia). There are essentially three groups involved in this flow, with different levels of access to residence in New Zealand. The first group comprises the Cook Islanders, Niueans and Tokelauans (who do not appear in Table 17-3). They are all New Zealand citizens by virtue of the former status of their islands as colonies of New Zealand and have the right to reside in New Zealand at will. The great majority of people of Cook Islands Maori, Niueans, and Tokelauans now live in New Zealand. They moved initially for economic reasons—there are limited wage employment opportunities in their island homes—as well as to take advantage of education opportunities in New Zealand. However, by the 1990s a considerable amount of the movement between the Cook Islands and New Zealand was essentially movement within transnational societies of Cook Islanders, Niueans, and Tokelauans—members of extended families conducting their economic and social activities in both the islands and New Zealand. The Polynesian "transnational corporation of kin" was discussed extensively in the context of what became known as MIRAB societies in the islands in the 1980s: societies dependent for their economic survival on migration, the transfer of remittances, aid, and employment in the local bureaucracy (e.g., Bertram and Karagedikli 2004).

The second group is the Samoans, whose islands were also formerly administered by New Zealand as a League of Nations (later United Nations) mandated territory from 1918. Samoans were not granted New Zealand citizenship when they obtained independence in 1962, but the Treaty of Friendship signed at the time made allowance for a quota of up to 1,100 Samoans per annum to become New Zealand residents subject to having a job. Over the subsequent 40 years a very sizable Samoan community has evolved in New Zealand; it is by far the largest Pacific Island community in the country. Again, the attraction of employment and education opportunities in New Zealand stimulated the initial migration flows in the 1950s and

1960s, but from the late 1970s use of family connections in New Zealand was by far the most important route into the country for prospective residents (Macpherson 1997), especially for those seeking access under the quota. Auckland, New Zealand's largest city, became the major urban center for Polynesia through the 1980s and 1990s, and is now home to communities from most parts of the eastern Pacific.

The third group of Pacific migrants to New Zealand is the Tongans and citizens of Fiji (indigenous Fijians as well as Indo-Fijians, who owe their origins in the Pacific to British indentured labor policies in the late nineteenth century). Neither of these countries had formal colonial connections with New Zealand, but from the 1950s both were sources of rural labor for New Zealand's agricultural and forestry industries (Gibson 1983). New Zealand has a much closer connection with peoples from the eastern Pacific through migration than Australia, and this is very much a function of the different policies governments in the two countries have had with regard to immigration from the Pacific (Bedford 1992, 2004a; Bedford et al. 2007).

The most important sources of immigrants since the early 1990s have been countries in Asia, especially northeast Asia (China, Japan, Korea, and in the 1990s, Hong Kong and Taiwan). The reasons for movement from these countries to New Zealand vary somewhat by source. In the case of Japan, the flows are associated with the development of Japanese business interests in New Zealand to service the Japanese tourist market. Japanese migration to New Zealand is much more associated with cycles of circulation of contract employees, students, and visitors, rather than the migration of Japanese seeking permanent residence in the country (except for spouses of returning New Zealanders who have been employed as contract teachers of English in Japan).

The Asianization of immigration to New Zealand is due to three major factors: active recruitment from New Zealand of business and skilled migrants in northeast Asia under the country's more liberal immigration policy after 1986, the unsettled nature of the societies and economies of Hong Kong and Taiwan in the lead-up to the return of Hong Kong to China in 1997, and the rapid growth in international student recruitment by New Zealand schools and tertiary institutions, especially from the late 1990s.

New Zealand has never been the preferred Western or Pacific Rim destination for Chinese, Koreans, or Japanese—the United States, Canada, and Australia, often in that order, are ahead of New Zealand as preferred destinations for work and study. However, during the 1990s New Zealand did manage to attract tens of thousands of immigrants from northeast Asia who were not able to get into their country of first choice. New Zealand's green and spacious environment, high-quality recreation facilities, good education system, and generally safe cities attracted many Asian families—especially those with school-aged children. Employment was not always easy to obtain, and at the time of the 1996 and 2001 censuses Chinese and Korean immigrants had the highest levels of unemployment despite meeting the criteria for entry under the points system.

Immigration to New Zealand from southeast and south Asia is also a response to different pull and push factors. In the case of Malaysia, the flow is mainly of Chinese, and has a history going back to the 1950s. There is a strong link with education in this flow, especially following the introduction of quotas for Chinese students entering into Malaysian tertiary institutions. Many of Malaysia's Chinese immigrants came to New Zealand to further the education of their children. In the case of India, the situation is different again—the flow in recent years is predominantly of skilled migrants seeking work and/or residence. New Zealand is a minor player among the modern Indian "diaspora," but the country is one of several destinations in the industrialized world that Indians are targeting for skilled work, especially in the information technology industries.

South Africa is the only source country in Africa which has regularly supplied more than 1,000 PLT arrivals per year since the early 1990s. The reasons for migration from South Africa have more to do with dissatisfaction with security and safety, social change, and the political scene in that country rather than with major attractions in New Zealand.

Finally, we note that PLT arrivals from the Philippines increased significantly in recent years to 3,638 in 2007/08. New Zealand has not been among the traditional destinations of Filipino migrants (such as North America, Australia, Japan, Malaysia, and the Middle East), but the Philippines is one of 30 countries in which prior work experience gained by skilled people is since 2004 recognized as gained in a "comparable labor market." The flows have also increased in response to active recruitment (Statistics New Zealand, 2007).

Acceptance in New Zealand

As a "country of immigration" New Zealand is something of an enigma. Until recently there has been no government-sponsored settlement policy for immigrants, except for the small number of refugees (750 per annum) accepted under the quota arrangements with UNHCR. These refugees are entitled to six weeks of support at the Mangere Refugee Centre in Auckland, where they receive medical treatment, instruction in the use of English language, and a rapid induction into life in New Zealand: the society, economy, political system, and their rights and obligations. Aside from this arrangement for refugees, successive New Zealand governments have seen their responsibility with regard to immigration as being limited to ensuring that selection policies admit people who may be expected to settle relatively easily. No support was provided other than information, on request, about social services and employment conditions. However, following the election of the Labour Government in November 1999, a focus on settlement outcomes for migrants was made more explicit in policy (Bedford 2004b).

While all migrants approved for residence in New Zealand have the same rights and privileges as citizens, especially after living in the country for two years or more (there is an initial two-year noneligibility period for many social security benefits for new migrants), there are some obvious differences in the extent to which immigrants from English speaking and non-English speaking backgrounds fare in terms of economic and social integration (Spoonley 2001).

The extent to which there are variations in migrant settlement outcomes by source of migrant is being assessed for the first time in a systematic way in New Zealand through a longitudinal survey of immigrants (*LisNZ*). Using

data from the first wave of this survey (with a sample of over 7,000 recent immigrants) Statistics New Zealand (2008) found only 6.5 percent of migrants claimed they experienced discrimination when seeking work because they were immigrants. There was very little difference in the proportions claiming discrimination by visa category, but information on the experiences of different ethnic groups, which has yet to be released, may show that discrimination is a problem among migrants from non-Western backgrounds. Data from the 2002/03 New Zealand Health Survey showed that about one quarter of Asian and Pacific peoples in New Zealand experienced racial discrimination, although that is about 10 percentage points less than among the indigenous Maori population (see Harris et al. 2006), who account for about 14 percent of the population.

Migration for residence is only one component of New Zealand's immigration flows. Movement for the purposes of study and work actually generates larger numbers of visa/permit approvals than movement for residence. In the year ended June 2007, for example, 20.5 percent of the total of 229,568 approvals were approved for residence, 50.3 percent for work for fixed periods, and 29.2 percent for study in New Zealand (see Table 17-4). The numbers entering (or renewing permits) for work and study increased rapidly from the late 1990s, partly in response to shortages of skilled (and unskilled) labor in particular industries, partly in response to rapid growth in the "export education" industry which, by 2003, was earning the country around $2.2 billion, making education the fourth largest export earner (Butcher 2004). While numbers of people on temporary work permits have continued to increase for the past decade, international student numbers peaked in 2004. The foreign demand for education in New Zealand is very sensitive to exchange rate fluctuations. A high value of the New Zealand dollar dampened demand since 2004 but a much lower dollar value is making the country again more attractive since 2008. China and Korea are the two major source countries of foreign students.

Migrants from the major source countries identified in the previous section enter with quite different mixes of permits and visas. Within the broad residence category there are

Table 17-4. Immigrants to New Zealand by Major Source Country/Region, Year Ending June 2007

Nationality	Residence approvals				Temporary approvals			Total
	Skill/ Business	Family Sponsored	Internat./ Humanitarian	Total Residence	Work	Student	Total Temporary	Approvals
	%	%	%	%	%	%	%	No.
Europe/N. America/S. Africa								
United Kingdom/ Ireland	27.6	7.2	0.2	35.0	58.9	6.1	65.0	36,140
Germany	4.7	2.1	0.0	6.9	68.6	24.5	93.1	10,643
Netherlands	16.6	4.7	0.1	21.4	70.2	8.4	78.6	2,121
Canada	6.6	5.2	0.2	11.9	75.0	13.0	88.1	4,019
United States of America	8.2	4.4	0.2	12.8	63.1	24.0	87.2	11,378
South Africa	34.6	5.5	0.6	40.6	43.0	16.3	59.4	9,262
Subtotal	20.7	5.7	0.2	26.5	60.2	13.3	73.5	73,563
Pacific								
Fiji	13.9	9.2	5.2	28.3	48.7	23.0	71.7	9,092
Samoa	0.6	19.8	31.0	51.4	38.7	9.9	48.6	3,558
Tonga	0.7	14.9	21.8	37.4	47.5	15.1	62.6	2,617
Subtotal	8.5	12.7	14.0	35.2	46.2	18.6	64.8	15,267
Asia								
Japan	2.2	3.2	0.0	5.4	58.0	36.7	94.6	10,011
China (PRC)	8.1	6.0	0.2	14.3	36.3	49.4	85.7	40,962
South Korea	4.2	2.2	0.1	6.5	28.1	65.4	93.5	17,048
India	12.7	18.7	0.2	31.6	44.3	24.1	68.4	12,783
Subtotal	7.3	6.9	0.1	14.3	38.5	47.2	85.7	80,804
Total all countries (%)	12.3	6.4	1.8	20.5	50.3	29.2	79.5	100.0
Total all countries (number)	28,140	14,705	4,119	46,964	115,457	67,147	182,604	229,568

Source: New Zealand Immigration Service.

three major streams: skilled/business, family sponsored, and international obligations/ humanitarian. These comprise the New Zealand Immigration Programme (NZIP), and within the major streams there are several more specific categories.

In Table 17-4 some of the mixes of residence, work, and study approvals are shown for a range of major migrant source countries in the year ended June 2007. Australia is not included in this table because Australians do not need visas/permits to reside, work, or study in New Zealand.

New Zealand, as a host country for immigrants seeking residence, work, and study, is welcoming at the level of government policy, but rather more ambivalent at the level of public opinion. Ward and Masgoret (2008) found that New Zealanders have generally positive attitudes toward immigrants and a multicultural society, but also note that there are marked differences between Maori and others, with the former having less positive attitudes toward immigration because they are more likely to see immigrants as a source of threat or competition.

Level of Immigrant Adjustment

Due to the relative homogeneity of the migrant inflow up to the 1980s and conformity of immigrants to the dominant culture there had been little concern for immigrant adjustment in policy circles. New Zealand was blessed in any case with full employment until the energy crises of the 1970s and unemployment among immigrants was not considered to be an issue. Pacific Island migrants—like Maori who migrated in large numbers from their rural tribal lands–readily found jobs in the large cities.

The situation changed dramatically since the early 1990s. Because of the high immigration and emigration rates, it is important to complement the flow data discussed earlier with data on the stock of migrants, as measured by the population census. In 1986, 14.9 percent of the population was foreign born and three quarters of these came from the United Kingdom, Ireland, continental Europe, North America, and Australia (see Table 17-5). Subsequently the overseas born population increased by one-quarter over the 1986–1996 decade and then by almost half over the following decade, while the New Zealand born population grew by less than 4 percent per decade. Consequently, the immigrant share of the population increased rapidly to 17.5 percent in 1996 and 22.9 percent in 2006. By that time, the traditional birthplaces accounted for less than half of the foreign born population.

Considering the continuum of immigrant adjustment from acculturation and assimilation through to marginalization and rejection elaborated in chapter 1 of this book, is it reasonable to argue that for English-speaking migrants and for Dutch and other continental Europeans, integration into mainstream predominantly English culture was almost complete. One simple indicator of integration relates to the (dis)similarities

in geographic distribution of the immigrant populations on the one hand, and the locally born population on the other (see also Johnston et al. 2003). Table 17-6 shows the 2006 geographical distribution of the New Zealand and foreign born populations across the regions.

Close to three quarters of the New Zealand population lives on the smaller but more densely populated North Island. Migrants are even more concentrated in the North Island. The largest metropolitan area, Auckland, is the main attractor of migrants. More than one half of the foreign born live in Auckland, compared with just over one quarter of the New Zealand born. Immigrants from non-English speaking backgrounds tend to concentrate even more in Auckland. While, once in New Zealand, migrants are more geographically mobile than the New Zealand born population, their spatial clustering is reinforced by new migrants continuing to cluster where their birthplace group is already highly concentrated (Maré et al, 2007).

Among migrants from Pacific Islands, Asia, and "Other" birthplaces, respectively 73.5 percent, 66.1 percent, and 55.8 percent reside in the Auckland region. Their presence in the schools, the labor force, on the streets, in business, and in specific residential neighborhoods is much more obvious there than in other parts of the country. Aucklanders tend to have more

Table 17-5. Population by Birthplace, New Zealand Census 1986, 1996, and 2006

Birthplace	Census year			% shares			% change	
	1986	1996	2006	1986	1996	2006	1986–96	1996–06
New Zealand	2,759,178	2,848,209	2,960,217	85.1	82.5	77.1	−3.2	−3.9
Overseas								
Australia[2]	47,208	54,711	62,742	1.5	1.6	1.6	15.9	14.7
Pacific Islands[3]	72,963	99,261	135,852	2.3	2.9	3.5	36.0	36.9
United Kingdom and Ireland	255,756	230,049	251,688	7.9	6.7	6.6	−10.1	9.4
Europe (excl. United Kingdom and Ireland)	46,461	55,599	68,070	1.4	1.6	1.8	19.7	22.4
North America	13,773	19,230	26,940	0.4	0.6	0.7	39.6	40.1
Asia	32,910	117,918	251,133	1.0	3.4	6.5	258.3	113.0
Other	13,413	28,293	83,124	0.4	0.8	2.2	110.9	193.8
Total Overseas	482,484	605,061	879,543	14.9	17.5	22.9	25.4	45.4
Total Population (specified birthplaces)	3,241,662	3,453,270	3,839,766	100.0	100.0	100.0	6.5	11.2

Source: New Zealand Census of Population and Dwellings, 1986, 1996, and 2006—Statistics New Zealand.

Table 17-6. Geographical Distribution of the Population by Birthplace, 2006 Census

	Distribution of NZ born population	Deviation from the distribution of the NZ born population by foreign birthplace							
		Australia	Pacific Islands	United Kingdom and Ireland	Europe (excl. United Kingdom and Ireland)	North America	Asia	Other	Total Overseas
North Island									
Northland	4.0	0.2	−3.2	−0.4	−0.5	0.2	−3.3	−2.0	−1.8
Auckland	26.2	6.0	47.3	8.9	11.6	7.8	39.9	29.6	25.6
Waikato, Bay of Plenty	17.3	−1.3	−12.2	−2.7	−3.7	−4.4	−10.1	−5.4	−6.6
Gisborne, Hawke's Bay, Taranaki, Manawatu, Wanganui	14.7	−3.9	−10.9	−4.7	−6.9	−6.3	−10.9	−8.3	−7.9
Wellington	11.2	−0.2	0.0	2.3	2.5	2.8	−2.1	−1.0	0.2
South Island									
Tasman, Nelson, Marlborough, West Coast	4.5	0.2	−3.9	−0.2	0.0	0.9	−3.7	−2.5	−1.9
Canterbury	14.0	−0.4	−10.2	−0.6	−0.6	−0.5	−4.5	−5.9	−3.7
Otago	5.3	0.5	−4.3	−0.9	−1.0	1.3	−2.9	−2.5	−2.0
Southland	2.7	−1.0	−2.4	−1.6	−1.5	−1.7	−2.5	−2.2	−2.0
Total	100.0	0.0	0.0	0.0	0.0	0.0	0.0	0.0	0.0

Source: New Zealand Census of Population and Dwellings, 2006—Statistics New Zealand.

polarized views about immigration, and there is an emerging debate about the need for subnational immigration policies that recognize the uneven impact of immigration on the host society (Spoonley and Bedford, 2008).

Migrant adaptation is judged against the length of stay in the host country. A common, or at least anticipated, pattern is one whereby a migrant initially experiences some disadvantage in terms of economic outcomes such as earnings and employment and then gradually catches up to comparable locally born. There are many reasons for an initial disadvantage, such as nontransferability of skills, limited English language ability, a bad job/worker match in initial employment, nonrecognition of qualifications, discrimination, and so forth. Convergence to the position of comparable persons in the host society may then be due to further investment in education and training, the gaining of local experience, the building up of useful networks of contacts, and so on.

With the increasing diversity of immigrant flows since the late 1980s there has been growing interest in the postsettlement outcomes of migrants. Migrants in the 1990s started to experience more difficulties in settling and less certainty of economic convergence. This can be partly explained by changing admission criteria that favored formal qualifications rather than practical experience, quotas that possibly exceeded the absorption capacity at the time, and a lack of postsettlement services to assist the migrants.

Formal methodologies for testing whether migrants integrate successfully in the host economy, such as summarized in, for example, Borjas (1999), have had limited application in New Zealand due to a lack of access to the necessary micro level data until the mid-1990s. Pioneering work on economic adaptation using cohort data confirmed that the very selective migration until the late 1980s led to generally favorable economic adaptation (Poot, 1993). The situation changed radically in the 1990s. Using 1996 unit record census data and comparing these data with those of 1986 and 1981, Winkelmann and Winkelmann (1998) detected that Asian and Pacific Island immigrants of the early 1990s came with a much larger entry disadvantage than other groups of immigrants or earlier arrivals from Asia and the Pacific, even after controlling for factors that affect relative incomes, such as age, education, and the level of economic activity.

Winkelmann and Winkelmann (1998) argued that structural changes in the New Zealand economy (with a decline in manufacturing and growth in business and personal services) favored migrants from traditional source countries. The introduction of the points system in 1991, that for a time virtually guaranteed entry with a high level of formal education, but without experience or a job offer, could have contributed to the greater entry disadvantage. Boyd (2003), also using 2001 Census data, found that the large initial economic disadvantage of certain groups of recent migrants in 1996 did reduce by 2001. In recent years public funding has been made available to update and expand research on immigrant integration, using new data sources such as the 2006 Census, the Longitudinal Immigration Survey (*LisNZ*), and the Household Labour Force Survey. We mention the *Integration of Immigrants Programme* (see http://newsettlers.massey.ac.nz/) and research commissioned by the Department of Labour (see http://www.dol.govt.nz/). However, these projects are still in progress, and results are not yet publicly available at the time of writing.

Immigrant Contribution to the Country

The contribution of immigrants to a country has many dimensions. These include the contributions of the immigrants to the host economy, the labor market, tax revenue, the political processes, social cohesion and cultural diversity, the environment, and so forth. The most fundamental impact, however, is demographic: immigrants affect the size, composition and distribution of the population.

Immigration is sometimes considered as a means to overcome population aging. The New Zealand population aged 65 and over is expected to increase from 12.5 percent in 1997 to one-quarter of the total by the middle of this century. While immigration may slow population aging slightly, it will not have a major impact unless immigrant fertility is much higher than that of the host population, which is unlikely (e.g., Bryant 2003). Nonetheless, it is clear from Tables 17-5 and 17-6 that New Zealand immigration has major impacts in terms of population size, birthplace/ethnic composition, and distribution.

What is the impact of this growth in the foreign born population on the New Zealand economy? An in-depth analysis of macroeconomic, labor market, public, and sectoral effects of immigration was conducted in the 1980s (Poot et al. 1988). Given major changes in the New Zealand economy and in immigration since then, a reassessment of the economic impact is essential, and a series of publicly funded projects (the *Economic Impacts of Immigration* research) was initiated in 2005 and coordinated by the Department of Labour. Much of this research has not yet been published at the time of writing (but see, for example, Stillman and Maré [2008] regarding a relatively benign impact on local housing markets).

A broad consensus based on research in the United States, Europe, and Australia is that immigration has generally been to the benefit of the host economy (see, e.g., Borjas 1999 and Poot and Cochrane 2005 for reviews). In simple terms, immigrants generate an increase in both the supply side of the economy—through their involvement in the labor market—and the demand side of the economy—through their expenditure patterns. In the short-run the effects either match, or the demand effect somewhat outweighs the supply effect, leading to additional buoyancy in the economy but also possibly inflationary pressures. In the long run, the net effect of immigration depends on its impact on technological change, economies of scale, investment and trade patterns, innovation and entrepreneurship, and related factors that may lead to higher productivity in the economy. Unfortunately, the evidence on the potentially beneficial effects of immigration on productivity is rather incomplete and further research is needed in New Zealand and elsewhere (see for recent U.S.-based research: Peri 2008; Hunt and Gauthier-Loiselle 2008).

Immigrant Drain on the Country

The extent to which immigrants are a drain on the country is usually assessed in terms of their demand for social services and housing, and the impact they may have on urban infrastructure. The standard question is whether immigrants supply more funds to the government in terms of direct and indirect taxes than they take by means of the additional cost of government services and social security payments. The assessment of the fiscal impact of immigration in the international literature consists of combining a demographic profile of the population before and after an immigration influx with the cost per capita of providing public consumption and transfer payments. Similarly, tax revenues are estimated based on the incomes and consumption patterns of different demographic groups. This literature suggests, by and large, that the fiscal impact of immigration is positive: immigrants add more to tax revenue than to government consumption or social security payments (e.g., Smith and Edmonston 1997; Coppel et al. 2001). The positive impact increases over time (at least up to the time of retirement).

New Zealand research on the fiscal impact confirms that migrants are net contributors to government finance. An economic consultancy, Business and Economic Research Ltd (BERL), calculated that the overseas born contributed in June year 2006 $8.1 billion in income tax, the Goods and Services Tax (GST), and petrol, alcohol, and tobacco excises (Slack et al. 2007). On the expenditure side, the foreign born accounted for $4.8 billion of government spending (including education, health, social security benefits, and student allowances). The net revenue is therefore $3.3 billion. The fiscal effect depends on region of birth, location in New Zealand, and duration of residence, but is positive for all subgroups of the migrant population analyzed by Slack et al. (2007). They also found that the net fiscal impact generally rises

with increasing duration of residence, although this is not the case for all migrant groups. For example, the net fiscal impact of those born in the United Kingdom and Ireland usually resident in New Zealand for 15 years or more is less than that of more recent arrivals.

There is nonetheless a caveat with this type of research in that the results take a "snapshot" perspective and do not take the life course of migrants and their offspring into account. Thus, migrants not arriving until age 45 or older may in present value terms be a net drain on the fiscal accounts when taking public superannuation and health expenditures into account. This could be partly offset by the net contributions of their descendants. Thus, Lee and Miller (2000: 351) note that "the only meaningful calculation is longitudinal, tracing the consequences of an immigrant's arrival through subsequent years, and taking full account of all the immigrant's descendants." Such a life course perspective has yet to be taken in New Zealand.

With respect to public infrastructure, a key New Zealand issue is that of urban motorways in the Auckland region, which have become severely congested in recent years. Congestion is also increasing in adjacent regions with rapid population growth such as the Waikato and Western Bay of Plenty. Congestion, however, is a symptom of inadequate infrastructural investment. A growing concentration of economic growth to large metropolitan areas is the result of the increasing importance of agglomeration advantages in knowledge-driven service economies, which is reinforced by the spatial concentration of immigrants of these agglomerations (e.g., Poot et al. 2008). The right question to ask, but difficult to answer, is what the potential return of further infrastructural investment might then be in a proper cost-benefit framework that takes externalities such as environmental costs into account also. Grimes and Liang (2008) found, using changes in land values as a revealed preference indicator, that the benefit-cost ratio of a recent northern motorway extension in Auckland was at least 6:1. Increasing congestion is therefore not a symptom of high levels of net immigration in the region but of public investment being less than economically desirable.

Effect of Immigration on the Functioning of the Host Country

Besides the impact on the economy and on the public sector there are many other effects of immigration on the host country. Just one aspect can be briefly touched upon here. There is a growing concern that immigration may be detrimental to social cohesion. In New Zealand, as in many other countries, the development of explicit measures of social cohesion is in its infancy and in many ways remains mired in definitional issues. If New Zealand is to be a socially inclusive society, policies for migrants need to be assessed in terms of providing the following elements of social cohesion: a sense of belonging, inclusion, participation, recognition, and legitimacy (see Spoonley et al. 2005). This assessment requires a range of quantitative and qualitative indicators that have yet to be developed. While economic adaptation in the form of convergence of economic indicators of migrants and the host population is desirable, with respect to broader well-being and culture the issue of integration is less clear cut. The full absorption of the dominant culture by the migrants was traditionally seen as desirable, but recent research on social cohesion has made clear that besides some cultural adaptation and predisposition to the value system of the host society, maintenance of the migrants' own cultural and social capital, and interaction with cultures and networks of other groups are preconditions for a socially cohesive society (Spoonley et al. 2005).

Economic and cultural assimilation in New Zealand was traditionally seen as a given and the notion of multiculturalism in any case did not sit easily with the push, since the 1980s, for a bicultural society that gives greater recognition and economic power to the Maori population who are the *tangata whenua*, the original settlers, of the land, but who continue to experience socioeconomic disadvantage. The contrast between bicultural and multicultural perspectives on integration and the development of social capital will remain an important issue.

Effect of Global Security Concerns

Heightened concern about security since the destruction of the twin towers of the World Trade Center in New York on September 11, 2001, the subsequent U.S.-led military operations in Afghanistan and Iraq, and acts of terrorism in many countries since then have had an impact on immigration policy and patterns of movement to New Zealand. Shortly after the 9/11 terrorist attacks, the New Zealand government introduced stricter controls over asylum-seekers and extended the powers of the security intelligence agency to detain people suspected of terrorist activity or connections. More recently, a Bill is being considered by Parliament to replace the Immigration Act of 1987. This Bill has greater effectiveness of immigration procedures with respect to security risks as a major objective.

One of the consequences of an increased sense of global insecurity and disillusionment with American policy in the Middle East has been an escalation in movement of Americans and others to New Zealand in search of a safe haven that provides investment opportunities (especially in prime real estate) as well as residence. For many the objective is to have a base in a relatively safe developed country in which everyday life is very affordable for high income foreign visitors, and which is known internationally for its attractive environment and outdoor living. The *Lord of the Rings* movie trilogy, which was set in New Zealand, has done a great deal to stimulate interest in New Zealand as a possible alternative place of residence for part of the year, if not on a full-time basis. New Zealand, like many parts of rural and coastal Europe, is beginning to attract long-stay multicountry residents.

Additional Issues for New Zealand

New Zealand's special relationships with Australia and selected Pacific Island countries provide a distinctive context for some dimensions of the country's immigration policy. The Trans-Tasman Travel Arrangement (TTTA), under which New Zealanders and Australians have access to each other's country without restriction as long as they are operating within the law, has made it possible for large numbers of New Zealanders especially to move to Australia and take up residence there. More than 10 percent of New Zealand's population now lives in Australia, as compared with a mere

0.3 percent of Australians living in New Zealand.

In the case of the special relationships with Pacific peoples in the Cook Islands, Niue, Tokelau, and Samoa, which were referred to earlier, international migration between the islands and New Zealand has resulted in the emergence of transnational communities. These communities play a very major role in the development of the island "homes" as well as the cultural maintenance of indigenous island societies in New Zealand (see Macpherson et al. 2003). The recently established Recognized Seasonal Employer policy, which is designed to provide seasonal labor for the horticulture and viticulture industries of up to 5,000 workers at any point in time, is drawing people from a range of Pacific countries, including countries in Micronesia (Kiribati) and Melanesia (Vanuatu, Solomons).

Conclusion

This review of New Zealand's immigration in recent decades has highlighted that this country represents a rather unusual and interesting case in the mosaic of global population movements. The combination of high levels of immigration from an increasingly diverse range of sources, extensive international movement of its own citizens, and growing short-term movements of students, professionals, and lifestyle seekers have led to a degree of population churning that is, given the small population base, the highest among developed countries. This is remarkable given the country's remote location in the South Pacific and provides evidence that growing global economic integration and the real decline in the costs of communication and air travel are irreversibly changing New Zealand society. It is clear that New Zealand's natural attractions and high quality of life are major assets used in strategies to benefit from globalization through immigration, international education, and tourism.

Given a two-century history of recruitment of people from a narrow range of Anglo-Celtic backgrounds, it is even more remarkable that the drastic changes in immigration numbers and composition since the late 1980s have led to less political resistance than might be expected. Immigration remains, however, tightly controlled, and there is not the mass influx of unskilled workers that are such a dominant feature of immigration to other high income countries. Nonetheless, it appears that New Zealanders accept that the forces of globalization, although not without problems, must be embraced by necessity in order for the country to maintain a high standard of living, despite its small size and peripheral location.

References

Bedford, R.D. (1992) "International migration in the South Pacific region." In M.M. Kritz, L.L. Lim, and H. Zlotnik (eds.) *International Migration Systems: A Global Approach.* Clarendon Press, Oxford, 41–62.

Bedford, R.D. (2004a) "International migration, identity, and development in Oceania: A synthesis of ideas." In D.S. Massey and J.E. Taylor (eds.) *International Migration: Prospects and Policies in a Global Market.* Oxford University Press, Oxford, 230–258.

Bedford, R.D. (2004b) "The quiet revolution: Transformation in migration policies, flows, and outcomes, 1999–2004," *New Zealand Geographer* 60(2): 50–54.

Bedford, R.D., and Lidgard, J.M. (1997) "Arrivals, departures and net migration, 1984/85–1995/96." In A.D. Trlin and P. Spoonley (eds.) *New Zealand and International Migration: A Digest and Bibliography, No. 4.* Department of Sociology, Massey University, Palmerston North, 28–41.

Bedford, R.D., Ho, E.S., and Lidgard, J.M. (2002) "International migration in New Zealand: Context, components, and policy issues." In G.A. Carmichael and A. Dharmalingam (eds.) *Populations of New Zealand and Australia at the Millennium: A Joint Special Issue of the Journal of Population Research and the New Zealand Population Review,* September 2002, Australian National University, Canberra, 39–66.

Bedford, R.D., Ho, E.S., Krishnan, V., and Hong, B. (2007) "The neighbourhood effect: The Pacific in Aotearoa and Australia." *Asian and Pacific Migration Journal* 16(2): 251–269.

Bedford, R.D., Lidgard, J.M., and Ho, E.S. (2005) "Arrivals, departures, and net migration, 1996/97–2002/03." In A.D. Trlin and P. Spoonley (eds.) *New Zealand and International Migration. A Digest and Bibliography, No. 5.* Department of Sociology, Massey University, Palmerston North.

Bertram, G., and Karagedikli, Ö. (2004) "Core-periphery linkages and income in small Pacific island economies." In J. Poot (ed.) *On the Edge of* the Global Economy. Edward Elgar, Cheltenham, UK, and Northampton, MA, 106–122.

Borjas, G.J. (1999) "The economic analysis of immigration." In O. Ashenfelter and D. Card (eds.) Handbook of Labor Economics, North Holland, 1697–1760.

Boyd, C. (2003) "Migrants in New Zealand: An analysis of labour market outcomes for working aged migrants using 1996 and 2001 Census data." Department of Labour, Wellington.

Bryant, J. (2003) "The ageing of the New Zealand population, 1851–2051." The Treasury, Wellington.

Butcher, A. (2004) "Educate, consolidate, immigrate: educational immigration in Auckland, New Zealand." Asia Pacific Viewpoint 45(2): 255–278.

Coppel, J., Dumont, J.-C., and Visco, I. (2001) Trends in Immigration and Economic Consequences. OECD Economics Department, Paris.

Evans, L., Grimes, A., and Wilkinson, B. (1996), "Economic reform in New Zealand 1984–1995: The pursuit of efficiency." Journal of Economic Literature 33: 1856–1902.

Farmer, R.S.J. (1985) "International migration." In ESCAP Population of New Zealand (Vol. 1). Country Monograph Series, No. 12, United Nations, New York, 54–89.

Gibson, K. (1983) "'Political economy and international labour migration': The case of Polynesians in New Zealand." New Zealand Geographer 39(1): 29–42.

Grimes, A., and Liang, Y. (2008) "Bridge to somewhere: The value of Auckland's northern motorway extensions." Motu Working Paper 08–07, Motu Economic and Public Policy Research, Wellington.

Harris, R., Tobias, M., Jeffreys, M., Waldegrave, K., Karlsen, S., and Nazroo, J. (2006) "Racism and health: The relationship between experience of racial discrimination and health in New Zealand." Social Science & Medicine 63: 1428–1441.

Hartog, J., and Winkelmann, R. (2003) "Comparing migrants to non-migrants: The case of Dutch migration to New Zealand." Journal of Population Economics 16: 683–705.

Hunt, J., and Gauthier-Loiselle, M. (2008) "How much does immigration boost innovation?" NBER Working Paper, National Bureau of Economic Research, Cambridge MA.

Ip, M. (ed.) (2003) Unfolding History, Evolving Identity: The Chinese in New Zealand. Auckland University Press, Auckland.

Johnston, R.J., Poulsen, M.F., and Forrest, J. (2003) "The ethnic geography of New Zealand: A decade of growth and change, 1991–2001." Asia Pacific Viewpoint 44(2): 109–130.

Kelsey, J. (1995) The New Zealand Experiment: A World Model for Structural Adjustment? Auckland University Press and Bridget Williams Books, Auckland.

Le Heron, R., and Pawson, E. (1996) Changing Places: New Zealand in the Nineties. Longman Paul, Auckland.

Lee, R.D., and Miller, T. (2000) "Immigration, social security, and broader fiscal impacts." American Economic Review 90: 350–354.

Macpherson, C. (1997) "The Polynesian diaspora: new communities and new questions." In K. Sudo and S. Yoshida (eds.) Contemporary Migration in Oceania: Diaspora and Network. Japan Centre for Area Studies, Osaka, 77–100.

Macpherson, C., Spoonley, P., and Anae, M. (eds.) (2003) Tangata o Te Moana Nui: The Evolving Identities of Pacific Peoples in Aotearoa/New Zealand. Dunmore Press, Palmerston North.

Maré, D.C., Stillman, S., and Morten, M. (2007) "Settlement patterns and the geographic mobility of recent migrants to New Zealand." Motu Working Paper 07–11, Motu Economic and Public Policy Research, Wellington.

McKinnon, M. (1996) Immigrants and Citizens: New Zealanders and Asian Immigration in Historical Context. Institute of Policy Studies, Victoria University of Wellington, Wellington.

Merwood, P. (2008) Migration Trends 2006/07. Department of Labour, Wellington.

Peri, G. (2008) "Immigration accounting: U.S. States 1960–2006." CReAM Discussion Paper 05/08, Centre for Research and Analysis of Migration, London.

Poot, J. (1993) "Adaptation of migrants in the New Zealand labour market." International Migration Review 27(1): 121–139.

Poot, J. (1995) "Do borders matter? A model of interregional migration in Australasia." Australasian Journal of Regional Studies 1(2): 159–182.

Poot, J., and Cochrane, B. (2005) "Measuring the economic impact of immigration: A scoping paper." PSC Discussion Paper 48, Population Studies Centre, University of Waikato.

Poot, J., Nana, G., and Philpott, B. (1988) International Migration and the New Zealand Economy. Victoria University Press for Institute of Policy Studies, Wellington.

Poot, J., Waldorf, B., and van Wissen, L. (2008) Migration and Human Capital. Edward Elgar, Cheltenham UK.

Slack, A., Wu, J., and Nana, G. (2007) Fiscal Impacts of Immigration 2005/06. Department of Labour, Wellington.

Smith, J.P., and Edmonston, B. (1997). *The New Americans: Economic, Demographic, and Fiscal Effects of Immigration.* National Academy Press, Washington, DC.

Spoonley, P. (2001) "Aliens and citizens in New Zealand." In A. Kondo (ed.) *Citizenship in a Global World: Comparing Citizenship for Aliens.* Palgrave, Houndsmill, 158–175.

Spoonley, P., and Bedford, R. (2008) "Responding to regional labour demand: International migration and labour markets in New Zealand's regions." *International Journal of Migration and Integration* 9: 203–223.

Spoonley, P., Peace, R., Butcher, A., and O'Neill, D. (2005) "Social cohesion: A policy and indicator framework for assessing immigrant and host outcomes." *Social Policy Journal of New Zealand* 24: 85–110.

Statistics New Zealand (2007) *Permanent and Long-Term Migration from the Philippines.* Statistics New Zealand, Wellington.

Statistics New Zealand (2008, 19 May) *Longitudinal Immigration Survey: New Zealand (LisNZ): Wave 1. Hot off the Press.* Statistics New Zealand, Wellington.

Stillman, S., and Maré, D.C. (2008) "Housing markets and migration: Evidence from New Zealand." Economic Impacts of Immigration Working Paper, Department of Labour, Wellington.

Ward, C., and Masgoret, A. (2008) "Attitudes toward immigrants, immigration, and multiculturalism in New Zealand: A social psycho-logical analysis." *International Migration Review* 42: 227–248.

Winkelmann, L., and Winnkelmann, R. (1998) *Immigrants in New Zealand: A Study of Their Labour Market Outcomes.* Department of Labour, Wellington.

18

Portugal

Immigration to Portugal

João Casqueira Cardoso

This chapter should be seen as a provisional analysis of the situation of immigrants in Portugal for three main reasons. First, the landscape of immigration in Portugal has changed radically over the past six years. A traditional country of emigration since at least the beginning of the twentieth century, Portugal has become without adaptation delay nor difficulty, a country of immigration. Second, the study's main source of reference for statistical data is the Census issued in 2001. As a matter of fact, this census collected information prior to the years 2000–2007, prior to the last and most relevant wave of immigration. Third, on the basis of the two reasons mentioned previously, it is easy to understand that the analysis will not depict with entire correctness the current state of things in Portugal. Actually, the study had to focus on the *major immigration movements* at the time of the census (2000–2001), and in the following years, using many provisional data (for the years 2006 and 2007), and leaving apart minor groups of immigrants that will certainly grow quickly in the future, as recent developments show. For these reasons, the study is an attempt to describe the reality in evolution, trends that are at work and, where possible, conclusions that may already be drawn from recent experience.

Major Immigration Movements into Portugal since 1990

Focus is placed primarily on groups that have entered the country since 1990, although immigrant flows that began earlier and continue into the present should be addressed. Immigration to Portugal witnessed a drastic change in the late 1990s and beginning of the 2000s. This change is seen in the quantitative flow of immigrants, but also in the national profile of these immigrants. Put simply, immigration to Portugal was, until the mid-1990s, an inheritance of the postcolonial period. Most immigrants, and indeed the largest immigrant group, from Cape Verde, originated from former colonial Portuguese territories. Since the late 1990s, with a peak registered at the beginning of the 2000s, new flows of immigration from Eastern Europe have been registered. Between 2000 and 2004, the number of foreign residents from other European Union countries increased 31.1%, and the number of foreign residents from other European countries increased 148.5% (Machado, 2006). This increase was confirmed in the following years.

Figure 18-1 shows the evolution of immigration in Portugal from 1980 to 2007. What is

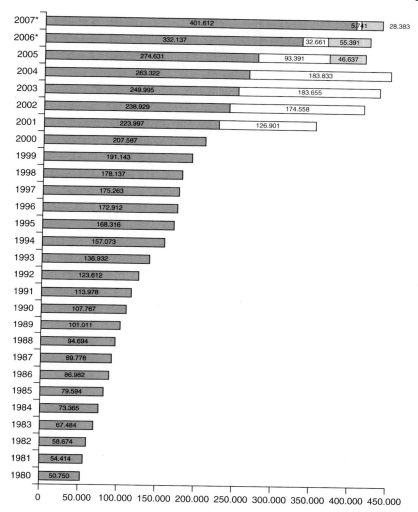

Figure 18-1. Foreign Nationals in Portugal
Source: SEF (2008)(Provisional data for 2006 and 2007).

striking is the constant and considerable increase in the flux of foreigners with residence in Portugal. Since 2001, a distinction is made between Authorization of Residence (indicated in blue on Figure 18-1), Authorizations of Stay[1] (indicated in grey on Figure 18-1), and Long-duration visas (normally one year, renewable) (indicated in orange on Figure 18-1). The subsequent withdrawal of the Authorization of Stay mechanism generated a decrease of the overall number of immigrants in 2005—but an exponential increase of the number of Authorizations of Residence.

Demographic Information Regarding Immigrants

Primary Sending Countries

In 2007, the primary sending countries of emigration to Portugal were: Brazil (66,354 nationals), Cape Verde (63,925 nationals), Ukraine (39,480 nationals), Angola (32,788 nationals), and Guinea Bissau (23,733 nationals).

The number of foreigners from Romania (19,155 nationals) is inferior to the number of foreigners from the UK (23,608 nationals), but superior to the number of nationals from Spain (18,030), Germany (15,498), Moldova (14,053 nationals) and China (10,448 nationals). All the other sending countries sent fewer than 10,000 persons.

Size of the Immigrant Population

The size of the immigrant population in Portugal assessed by the National Statistical Institute—INE (*Instituto Nacional de Estatística*) amounted, in 2008, to 401,612 persons.[2] This number may be divided into regional area of origin, according to the Service for Border Control and Aliens—SEF (*Serviço de Estrangeiros e Fronteiras*),[3] and is as follows: The most important regional area to provide immigrants is Africa, with a total number of 147,959 nationals; second is Europe, with a total number of 179,040 nationals; then comes Central and South America (73,146 nationals), Asia (24,269 nationals), North America (10,446 nationals), and Oceania (586 nationals).

The population in Portugal was 10,617,575 persons in May 2008 (www.ine.pt). The estimated immigrant population in Portugal represented, in 2008, 3.78% of the overall population. The data of the SEF allow for making a distinction on the basis of sex, so that the overall number of respective male and female immigrants is known (see Table 18-1).

Status (Legal or Undocumented Immigrants, Refugees)

Statistical data on immigrants only make a distinction between three categories of immigrants: first, foreigners resident in Portugal under common legal regime; second, immigrants having the status of refugees; third, a residual number of immigrants may have the status of stateless persons.

Under the first category, it is important to state that the SEF, as well as Portuguese

Table 18-1. Number of Foreign Nationals in Portugal (2007)

Total	**435,736***
Male	240,096
Female	195,640

Source: SEF (2008) (Provisional data for 2007).

embassies and consulates, may issue various types of visas, granting for a definite period of time temporary stay in the country. The following types of visa exist: (1) stopover visa (not registered as immigrant); (2) transit visa (not registered as immigrant); (3) short-stay visa (not registered as immigrant); (4) residence visa (registered as immigrant); (5) study visa (registered as immigrant); (6) work visa (registered as immigrant); and (7) temporary stay visa (registered as immigrant). Yet, it is impossible to know, from statistical data available, which type of visa is possessed by each immigrant. It is important to note that the number of undocumented immigrants in Portugal, as far as it can be estimated, is high. For instance, in a recent study Ferreira, Rato, and Mortágua (2004) estimated that the actual number of nationals from Ukraine resident in Portugal is double the number of legal residents, although this number might be slightly over-estimated.

The second category includes persons who were granted the status of refugee under the Asylum Law (Law No. 15/98 of 26 March 1998): this legal provision makes it possible for a person to be get an authorization to reside in Portugal as a refugee in the sense of Public International Law. The number of requests for asylum that were accepted in 2007 was 84, which represents a reduction when compared with previous years—namely 1999 (307 requests accepted) and 2004 (120 requests accepted).[4] The third category, stateless persons, amounted to 273 persons in Portugal in 2007. In 2007, there was also a residual number of persons whose nationality was unknown (17 persons).

Demographic Profile

The demographic profile of the immigrant population in Portugal shows clearly that it is a young population, concentrated in the peak activity ages (Rosa, 2004), as the data available from the SEF for year 2005 shows (Table 18-2). This data can be compared with the profile of the overall resident population (both immigrants and nonimmigrants)—available for year 2007 (Table 18-3). It shows that among the class of the age from 15 to 64, the immigrant population

Table 18-2. Foreign Residents by Sex and Age (Life Cycles) in 2005

Male/Female		
	Total	274,631
	0–14	44,785
	15–24	47,514
	25–64	166,851
	65 and more	15,481
Male		
	Total	154,211
	0–14	30,130
	15–24	24,468
	25–64	92,240
	65 and more	7373
Female		
	Total	126,651
	0–14	20,886
	15–24	23,046
	25–64	74,611
	65 and more	8,108

Source: SEF (2005).

Table 18-3. Resident Population by Sex and Age (Life Cycles) in 2007

Male/Female		
	Total	10,617,575
	0–14	1,628,852
	15–24	1,236,004
	25–64	5,902,888
	65 and more	1,849,831
Male		
	Total	5,138,807
	0–14	835,491
	15–24	630,723
	25–64	2,900,188
	65 and more	772,405
Female		
	Total	5,478,768
	0–14	793,361
	15–24	605,281
	25–64	3,002,700
	65 and more	1,077,426

Source: INE (2008). Estimated data, 2007.

is mostly in the group 25 to 64 (60.75% of the immigrants), which is a higher proportion than the overall population in the same group (55.59%). This difference in the population profile is even clearer in the class of age from 15 to 24 (17.30% of the immigrants, against 11.64% of the overall population). This information confirms the specificity of the immigrant population among the Portuguese population.

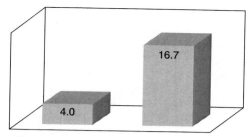

Portuguese nationals   Foreign residents

Figure 18-2. Indicator of Sustainable Renewal in 2001.
Source: INE, 2002.

In addition, and based on the last available census (2001), official data analysis underlined that the immigrant population has a higher indicator of sustainable renewal than the national population (Figure 18-2).

Human Capital

The immigrant population in Portugal forms a clear-cut dual manpower panorama: the global landscape is that of two main immigrant groups segmented into two employment markets and two types of human capital.

On the one hand, a first group is composed of immigrants from Western Europe; nationals from the UK make up the largest group (23,608 persons), followed by Spaniards (18,030 persons) and German nationals (15,498). Other minor groups are French (10,556 persons) and U.S. nationals (8,264 persons)—a large number of them binationals. This group itself is divided into three major subgroups: Spaniards are clearly residents in search of employment or employed—especially in the service, trade, and health sectors. This is reflected by the fact that the Spanish nationals concentrate in the Lisbon area (9,132 persons), the main job provider area. The second subgroup is composed of European immigrants who are mostly retired persons. This is the case of German citizens who concentrate in the Madeira Island region (where they represent the highest number of European immigrants). This is also the case of British citizens retiring in the Algarve region, where they represent the largest group of all categories of immigrants in that region of the country (more than 13,767 persons). As for the third and last subgroup, it is composed of U.S. and French nationals, who may be found all over the country and/or in atypical areas, such as the Aveiro region or the Açores (U.S. citizens). This may be explained by the high level of binationals among the French and U.S. citizens in Portugal. This last group of immigrants may not clearly be distinguished from Portuguese nationals from the point of view of labor aspects.

On the other hand, a second main group of immigrants is composed of immigrants from Cape Verde, Angola, and Guinea Bissau. In 2007 these groups of nationals represented more than 120,000 persons, with most coming from Cape Verde (63,925 persons). Another group, from Latin America, is composed of nationals from Brazil (66,354 persons). This African and Latin American immigration is rather dispersed, but tends to concentrate in the main cities (Lisbon and peripheral area of Setúbal, Porto, and Faro). This is the core of labor immigration. The last three years have acknowledged a rapid increase in the number of Brazilian immigrants—the figures show that this presence tripled between 2004 and 2007 (from less than 20,000 to more than 60,000). This new brand of Brazilian immigration differs from all the other immigration groups in one aspect: it is mostly feminine (the overall number of Brazilian nationals in Portugal included 34,520 women, against 31,834 men). They are employed in the service sectors, either domestic services or restaurants. The SEF, as well as other services (namely the police) have also reported an increase in prostitution among the Brazilian population. Despite the affirmation of new civil rights reserved to Brazilian citizens (see below), this evolution negatively alters the image of the Brazilian immigrant — especially female immigrants — socially if not symbolically (Machado, 2006).

This global picture of a twofold immigration universe is slowly changing, with the arrival of immigrants from Eastern Europe. A study by Carvalho (2004) of several businesses in Portugal shows that this new wave of immigrants started by concentrating in economic niches where there was a great need for labor (especially in the agricultural sector). According to the last available data (www.sef.pt), the Eastern European immigrants are at present a mainly masculine population,[5] and is mainly occupied in the construction sector (ACIME, 2004). In addition, the Eastern European immigrants are characterized by two specific features, as concerns labor: first, the geographical distribution of the workforce. Albeit dominant in the main cities, the number of immigrants from Ukraine, for example, is much more diffuse, with a presence in small or medium cities with no tradition of immigration (such as in the district of Santarém, in the center of Portugal, where their number exceeds the number of other immigrant groups). Second, a specific aspect of this labor pool is its high level of education (if not rare technical skills), which is being positively exploited by Portuguese small and medium-sized businesses. For example, 30.6% and 27.3% of all Ukrainians immigrants completed, respectively, upper secondary and tertiary education (this level is even higher for Moldovians, with respectively 33.9% and 28%). This figure is in clear contrast not only to the Portuguese nationals[6] but also to other immigrants—especially those from the African countries, but also the Brazilian immigrants. For example, only 7.1% and 1.4% of immigrants from Cape Verde had upper secondary and tertiary education, respectively. The Brazilian immigrants' education *ratio* is slightly below that of the Eastern Europeans (26.7% of Brazilian with upper secondary education and 14% with tertiary education).[7] This aspect also highlights the intermediate and increasingly uncomfortable situation of the Brazilian immigrants in the Portuguese society.

Reasons for Leaving the Home Country

Economic, Social, and Political Climate of the Home Country during the Migration Period

Following the typology presented earlier, it is possible to identify three main socioeconomic and sociopolitical climates in the home countries during the migration period (since the 1990s). As regards the Western European immigrants group, the socioeconomic and sociopolitical climate is related to the development of the

European Communities process after the adhesion of Portugal and Spain (January 1, 1986), although the relationship with the UK and the migration flux were, in this particular case, much older. The noticeable increase of Spanish immigrants is indeed due to the new socioeconomic climate and to the elimination of the quantitative and qualitative restrictions in the field of services and employment. The possibility for persons to circulate freely, and to retire in a state of their choice has also played a role in the case of German nationals.

As regards the second main group of immigrants (Cape Verde, Angola, Guinea Bissau), the political climate of instability in these home countries has been patent in the years following the collapse of the Soviet Union, seen as a provider of help in many nonaligned African countries. The accession of Cape Verde to independence in 1975 left the country with scarce resources, and emigration became a way of life (not only to Portugal, but also to other European countries, such as the UK). In other cases, the transition to democracy was slow (in the cases of Angola and Guinea Bissau, for instance); this factor worked as an incentive to a migration to the former center of the colonial authority, Portugal being seen as a provider of job and welfare opportunities. As for Brazil, not only the positive image of Europe, but also family bonds have played a decisive role in the structuring of migration movements to Portugal (as well as from Portugal to Brazil).

In the 1990s, Ukraine, Romania, and Moldova (and also Russia, to a minor extent) were transitioning to liberal democracies. Many saw this new political context as an opportunity to move, and to realize the dream of the previous generation: living in a Western European country.

General Reasons for Leaving the Home Country (Push-Pull Factors)

The immigrants from Western European countries have two main and almost entirely separate reasons for leaving their home country: on the one hand, the migration of Spaniards may be explained by economic factors, namely the increase of the Portuguese market demand in the service sectors, especially in the banking sector and in the sector of health services. This may also be explained by several other reasons, in particular, the high rate of unemployment in Spain—especially in the case of female unemployment rates. As a rule, Spaniards maintain strong links with their home country, and even with their home *tout court* by keeping their sole residence in Spain. As far as the German and UK nationals are concerned it must be said that, at least in the case of the UK, there have been strong, long-term relationships with Portugal since the nineteenth century. This is also applicable, to a more limited extent (see below), to French nationals. This tradition, together with the interest for developing trade and services in a new member state of the European Communities (since 1993, European Union) has played a decisive role motivating the exit from their home country. But economic development is not sufficient to explain the migration of UK and German citizens. A great part of the push-pull factors is highly individualistic. What happens is that the Britons and Germans have seen in Portugal an excellent opportunity to elevate their life standards, buying mansions or lifetime hotel resort services in Algarve or in Madeira, due to the fact that Sterling Pound or a German pension subsidy in Euro allowed them to do so.

The pull-push factors influencing nationals from Cape Verde, Angola, and Guinea Bissau include socioeconomic low standards in the home countries and political instability. It is also important to underline that the creation of the *Portuguese-Speaking Commonwealth*—the CPLP (*Communidade dos Povos de Língua Portuguesa*)[8]—in 1994 created a favorable climate for designating Portugal as the elder son of, if not the door to, the European Union. The same conclusions may be drawn in the case of Brazil, where the slow but certain economic progress in the home country did not eliminate the trends toward a greater emigration. On the contrary, the image of Portugal in Brazil grew positively since the early 1990s, together with the knowledge of the European Union advantages for immigrants.

The last wave of immigration, from Eastern Europe, is much harder to explain. One possible explanation lies in the difficulty gaining access to the labor market and society in general in more traditional immigration destinations in Western Europe (UK, France, Germany, and Italy, to quote the main labor receptors). The comparatively soft image transmitted by the Iberian peninsula, together with the great need for manpower in the field of construction in the late 1990s (especially with the organization of the 1998 Lisbon World Exposition), attracted new immigrants from the recently free countries of Central and Eastern Europe after 1989 (Russo and Soeiro, 2007).

Process of Emigrating/Immigrating

On one side, the geographic location of Portugal as a peripheral Southwestern European nation explains why the processes of immigration have so far been direct. This means that immigrants reach Portugal as the main destination directly, without any previous stay in other countries. It is important to pinpoint that even the continental territory of Portugal is mainly accessed by air. The number of immigrants from neighbor countries is—with the exception of Spain—extremely limited. As an example, the number of immigrants from Morocco was only 1,871 in 2007.

On the other side, the emigrating process is also mainly direct, due to the characteristics of the main immigrant groups described above. There is, however, very little evidence of the actual provenience of the groups of immigrants, especially the African group of immigrants, as a result of the lack of transparency and detail in the information provided by the SEF. In fact, immigrants are only registered on the basis of their nationality, and the circuits that they may have traveled before they reach Portugal are not disclosed, if ever investigated (except in the case of illegal immigration routes).

Readiness of Host Country to Accept Immigrants

There is a great deal of ignorance and lack of interest among the Portuguese nationals about the question of immigration. This is in part due to the fairly recent relevance of the issue, and also from the lack of political approach of the question—rarely discussed in public debates, except in the context of the European Union (Santos, 2004).

A field study by Lages and Policarpo (2003)[9] identifies a traditional preference among Portuguese nationals for Brazilian immigrants over other categories of immigrants, and for Eastern European immigrants over African immigrants. At the same time, the study shows that a large proportion (23.4%) of Portuguese nationals see immigrants from Eastern Europe as a threat to their employment, whereas only 16% and 13.2% see, respectively, Brazilians and Africans as a threat to their job. This data seems to indicate a *latent racism* of the Portuguese society—in line with, but at the same time different from, that of other Western European countries.

At the institutional level, both public and private institutions have recently emerged to facilitate—not always in a harmonious way—the integration process of immigrants. All of them share two main perspectives: first, a *voluntarist* perspective, with an emphasis on social aid, cultural dialogue, and education programs;[10] second, a focus on *legal rights and freedoms*, which potentially makes Portugal one of the most friendly countries for immigrants. For example, a recent change in the Law of Nationality allows for immigrants with at least six years of "legal residence" in Portugal (either with an Authorization of Residence or with any other valid title, such as a visa) to request Portuguese nationality.[11] These perspectives are coherent with a rather peculiar aspect of Portugal immigration policy: This policy is inspired by an idea of responsibility rooted in a sense or feeling of reciprocity. It is common to hear political speeches referring to the fact that many Portuguese (about 4 million) were and are themselves immigrants abroad.

This may explain the fact that the immigration policy, albeit recent, has proved to be constant, despite changes in political right- or left-wing options. To implement this policy, the Portuguese government is assisted by at least two main administrative bodies. The first is an organ created at the level of the Prime Minister's Office, the High Commission for Immigration and Intercultural Dialogue—ACIDI (*Alto Comissariado para a Imigração e Diálogo Intercultural*).[12] The second body is the already mentioned SEF (National Service for Border Control and Aliens), with specific authority to deliver Authorizations of Residence. The SEF is also competent for the prevention and repression of illegal immigration, together with the police and the Judicial Police.

The ACIDI, created in 2007, succeeded to the High Commission for Immigration and Ethnic Minorities—ACIME (*Alto Comissariado para a Imigração e Minorias Étnicas*), created in 2002—following the first creation of a High Commissioner for Immigration and Ethnic Minorities in 1996). The ACIDI has comparable powers to the former ACIME, namely the power to contribute to the elaboration of immigration policy in Portugal. In practice, the new body appears as an attempt to aggregate various experiences, programs, and somehow heteroclites organisms[13] into one line of action, with a special focus on the interaction with the civil society and immigrant associations.

The ACIDI is completed by a "Social and Cultural Ombudperson," which is a service of personalized assistance aimed at supporting and resolving immigrants' problems in one of the twelve languages available. The Social and Cultural Ombudspersons also replies to requests for explanations via e-mail or by post. The ACIDI has offices in the two main cities of Portugal, Lisbon and Porto. In Lisbon, its main office, the National Immigrant Support Center—CNAI (*Centro Nacional de Apoio ao Imigrante*) attended 1,136,807 persons between 2004 and 2008. Despite this impressive result, the creation of policy structures at local level over the territory still depends on the good will and resources of the municipalities.

Level of Immigrant Adjustment

Regarding the level of immigrant adjustment to Portugal, it would be artificial to use the common category assimilation/integration in the Portuguese case. Indeed, the background of immigration in Portugal is too recent and undefined to make a clear-cut distinction of this type, even in relation to the post-1970s first wave of immigrants from the former colonies. The Portuguese model of immigration is in a way a "no-model" (Casqueira Cardoso, 2003), or rather a model hesitating between an assimilation, French type model and an integration model similar to the UK. However, it is possible to describe three phenomena as the main lines of adjustment of immigration in Portugal:

First, a phenomenon of integration-separation. The group of immigrants composed of nationals from Western European countries do not acculturate, but remain instead relatively separated from the Portuguese nationals. In a way, the formula "equal but different" could apply to that group: "equal" because they enjoy the same status as European Union citizens, that Portuguese nationals do, especially in virtually all social benefits and also from the point of view of basic political rights (namely, the right to participate in local elections in their country of residence, as well as to the European Parliament elections). But these immigrants are also seen, and see themselves, as different, because they are strongly linked to their national culture in a peculiar way observable in Portugal: in effect, the Portuguese culture overvalues foreign cultures, especially foreign cultures from European Western countries. To that extent, the group of immigrants composed of nationals from Western European countries are encouraged to retain their own characteristics as an implicit strategy of power among the various minorities. This phenomenon does not apply to the most recent group of immigrants composed of nationals from Eastern European countries, due mainly to the ignorance and prejudice shared by the Portuguese population concerning Eastern European countries, generally seen as "the immigrant from the East" (Machado, 2006).

Second, a phenomenon of relative integration-accommodation. This phenomenon applies to the group of immigrants composed of nationals from Cape Verde, Angola and Guinea Bissau. This group is integrated but at the same time accommodated and not assimilated. This is the result of, broadly speaking, phenotypes and prejudice of race and also of sex (especially in the case of the Brazilians) commonly shared by Portuguese nationals.

Third, a phenomenon of integration-assimilation, applicable in the case of nationals from Brazil. This penetration of the Brazilian culture in Portugal, especially through TV programs and soap operas, has played a role in the relative knowledge, if not valorization, of the Brazilian way of life and of the Brazilian nationals as such. This has contributed, together with the reasonable level of education shared by the average Brazilian national in Portugal, to a phenomenon of mixed integration-assimilation in the Portuguese society. However, the recent trends in Brazilian immigration acknowledges the start of a process of prejudice—not only on the basis of race—but also specifically on the basis of sex. Due to the increase in women trafficking reaching Portugal,[14] the Brazilian women are more and more often depicted as belonging potentially to the world of prostitution. The official discourse (from the SEF and the Police) is that sexual exploitation must be eradicated. But prostitution as such is not defined as a crime in Portugal, the Brazilian nationals are not illegal immigrants, and the field civil servants are ready to admit that the prostitution phenomenon is specific in the case of Brazilians, and "softer" than in the case of Easter Europeans.

Immigrant Contribution to the Country—Economic, Political, Social, Cultural

From an specific economic perspective, a study published in May 2003 by the Immigration Observatory, a body associated to the former ACIME, assessed that 16.5 % of the costs of the Special Program for Rehousing (*Programa Especial de Realojamento*) made available by the state was spent for immigrants (Correa D'Almeida, 2003). However, the study also considered that such an expense may be spent only in part for immigrants, as a house may have a new owner (nonimmigrant) in the future. Moreover, the study found that, based on the budget of the Portuguese State in 2001, the overall expenses for immigrants are half the size of the gain (income) (namely expenses of 66,968,520 € against 131,845,678 € income).

On a broader basis, and taking into account a comprehensive analysis of the Portuguese labor market, Ferreira et al. (2004) show a high rate of activity among the immigrant population from Eastern Europe and Brazil (77%). This figure contrasts with the activity rate of the overall population (48.2%, according to the 2001 census). Moreover, the rate of unemployment is lower among these two groups of immigrants (4%) than among the overall population residing in Portugal (6.8%).

The situation of African immigrants is not as optimistic: In 2004, of the immigrant beneficiaries of the Social Aid Income (*Rendimento Social de Inserção*), 74% were nationals of the African countries sharing Portuguese as their official language (the abovementioned members of the CPLP) (ACIME, 2004). This situation contributes to the frustration and the social tensions among this historical group of immigrants—a high proportion of whom are willing to leave the country[15]—and to an increase in racial prejudice, already deeply rooted in the Portuguese society.

Immigrant Drain on the Country—Economic, Political, Social, Cultural

From a projection made on the basis of the study by Ferreira et al. (2004), and despite the fact that there is no nationwide study on this specific issue, it is estimated that immigrants may drain from 500 million up to a maximum of 750 million euros yearly from income earned in Portugal. Ferreira et al. (2004) noted that 66,000 immigrants from Ukraine legally resident in Portugal in 2004 send 200 million euros annually to their home country.

This projection may not apply to the group of immigrants from Western Europe, who do not send money on a systematic basis. It is however traditionally significant in the case of some historic immigrants, such as the immigrants from Cape Verde. It is also important to pinpoint that, from the point of view of human resources, immigrants who intend to return to their home country gained training skills in Portugal. A study by Lages and Policarpo (2003) showed that 78.6% of the immigrants surveyed planned to return to their home country within the period of 3 years (for 60% of them) to 6 years time (for 82% of them).

Implications of Immigrant Populations for the Functioning of the Host Country

The main implications of immigrant populations for the functioning of Portugal as a host country of immigrants are at least two: first, in the field of public policy and law, and second, in provision of services to immigrants.

On the one hand, as regards its legal compromises and public policy options, the Portuguese government is divided between the will to give preference to the integration of "historic" immigrants from its former colonies (integrated into the CPLP), the challenges of the EU integration policies, and the wish to adapt to questions posed by the new wave of immigrants from Eastern Europe (Withol de Wenden, 1999).

On the other hand, the renewal of the immigration groups from Eastern Europe has obliged the Portuguese government to consider new concerns of public policy in the field of access to services, to education and vocational training, and to health and safety at work. So far, the government has dealt with these issues by sharing or delegating either implicitly or explicitly its powers to private associations, foundations, or religious groups (such as the Jesuit Secretary for Refugees or other private bodies) that have the means and availability to help immigrants. In the field of education, for instance, the ACIDI (and the former ACIME, indeed) worked with an association linked to the Ministry for Education (*Secretariado Enterculturas*) to produce a brochure for immigrant parents who have school-age children.

Effects of September 11, 2001, Terror Attacks on Immigration to the Host Country

The September 11, 2001, terror attacks on the United States had no relevant effect on immigration in Portugal as such. Indeed, the border controls have been reinforced, especially regarding air transportation with connection to the United States. However, there is no evidence that this has substantially disturbed or even interfered with the population flux between the United States and Portugal, or even between the traditional areas of connection with the United States, such as the Portuguese Region of the Açores.

Additional Issues and Concerns for Portugal

One main additional concern for Portugal in the future years will be the level of tension between immigrants. In fact, whereas in the past the historic immigrants group from African Portuguese-speaking countries might have (and rightly so) considered itself as the core immigrant group, and the main focus of public policies (if any) in that field, the situation has changed since 2001.

Since 2001, the flux of immigrants from Eastern Europe and the higher sensitivity to immigration issues, in part due to the European Union debate and challenges in that area, have contributed to create and canalize state intervention, resources, and projects in the area of Eastern European immigrants. A latent but real competition between immigrant groups is emerging, already underlined in the field of employment (Carvalho, 2004).

Moreover, another group of immigrants—the Brazilians—acquired in 2003 specific and reserved civil rights.[16] Brazilian immigrants with at least three years of legal residence in Portugal may request the "status of equality," which includes either plain civil rights and duties, or "political rights." This version of the status of equality not only confers the same social and economic rights, but also imply a *full and exclusive*[17] political participation of Brazilians in Portuguese political life (with the exception of the election to the European Parliament). This includes the possibility to enjoy the same identity card as Portuguese nationals (with the indication of a different nationality), access to careers of the civil service, and the right to vote and to be elected at all election levels.[18] In 2007, at least 296 Brazilian effectively used the status of equality.[19] It is too early to assess the consequence of such a step, but it presents similar characteristics to the British Commonwealth system and represents an important precedent for other CPLP member states.

Conclusion

The Portuguese society suffered profound changes since the mid-1980s, when Portugal joined the European Communities. The public administration had to modernize quickly, and is still adapting, as the creation of the ACIDI in 2007 shows. In addition, its decision-making processes still lack transparency: We observe neither a real widespread habit of assessment nor an actual influence of its bodies in the decision- and law-making process. The social and economic sectors have drastically changed, and the opening to new habits of consumerism in the space of one generation has led to new problems that are still at stake. The education system has responded incompletely to these changes.

In this context, the immigration appears as a new element of crisis: a crisis seen as a transition and a separation from the past, from the postcolonial relationship and in particular from the African and Brazilian links that Portugal maintains, and a crisis also seen as a change of perspective of today's Portuguese society opening to a wider Europe. Immigrants from Eastern Europe put into question the "southern" European model developed in Portugal, much more than historical immigrants from Africa or Brazil, and also more than Western European immigrants in search of sun (such as Britons and Germans) or belonging to the same cultural model (such as Spaniards).

In sum, the immigration situation in Portugal highlights a serious identity crisis. It is also part of a wider crisis—that of European identity after the fall of the Berlin wall.

Notes

1. The Authorization of Stay (*Autorização de Permanência*, or AP) was created under Law No. 27/2000 of September 8, 2000, and entered into force in 2001. It could be granted for one year (renewable until a maximum of five years) to foreign nationals with or without visas, but with at least a formal offer of employment in Portugal. The AP could be replaced, after the fifth year, by an Authorization of Residence.

2. This number is somewhat higher (435,736 persons, in 2007) if we include the nonresident population, that is the immigrants either with an Authorization of Stay or with a visa that may be valid for a maximum of one year—and may be renewed (www.ine.pt).

3. www.sef.pt

4. The Decree Law 218 of August 4, 2001, regulates the implementation regime of the European Fund for Refugees in Portugal (according to the European Union Council Directive 2000/596/CE of September 28, 2000).

5. In the case of Ukrainians, the figures are: 24,243 men against 15,237 women (www.sef.pt). In 2002, the figures were much more equal in terms of gender.

6. According to the OECD data for 2002, only 11% and 9% of overall population in Portugal between the ages of 25 and 64 completed upper secondary and tertiary education, respectively (www.oecd.org).

7. Also see Baganha et al. (2004) on this educational gap between Portuguese nationals and immigrants from developing countries, on the one hand, and immigrants from Eastern Europe, on the other.

8. www.cplp.org

9. The study collected the opinion of 1,400 Portuguese nationals.

10. The main tone seems to be essentially cultural and probably orientated in the sense of a Christian culture, with a dominant influence of the Catholic Church structures and personalities as main actors. For instance, the president of the European Anti-Poverty Network (EAPN) in Portugal—REAPN (*Rede Europeia Anti Pobreza / Portugal*)—is a Catholic priest. The first High Commissioner for Immigration and Ethnic Minorities was a Jesuit priest. The current High Commissioner is not a clergyperson, but she is the former director of the Jesuit Refugee Service.

11. Organic Law No. 2/2006 of April 17, 2006 (amending the Law No. 37/81 of October 3, 1981, also known as the Law of Nationality).

12. www.acidi.gov.pt

13. The structure was created by Decree Law 167/2007 of May 3, 2007. Apart from the ACIME, the ACIDI also includes an administrative structure coordinating an educational program called "Escolhas," the Mission for Dialogue with Religions, and the *Secretariado Enterculturas*—a former division of the Ministry for Education on Intercultural Dialogue.

14. "Portugal, Brazil to Take Steps against Human Trafficking," *BBC Monitoring International Reports*, May 25, 2003 (http://www.protectionproject.org/human_rights_ reports/report_ documents/ portugal.doc).

15. Bruto da Costa and Pimenta (1991), as well as Pereira Bastos and Pereira Bastos (1999), already documented, in the city of Lisbon, the low self-esteem and will to leave the country from the African immigrants.

16. After the entry into force of the Decree Law No. 154/2003 of July 15, 2003, regulating the implementation of the Treaty for Friendship, Co-operation and Consultation between the Portuguese Republic and the Federal Republic of Brazil, signed in Porto Seguro (Brazil) on 22 April 2000.

17. Indeed, by opting for this status, the political rights of Brazilian nationals in Brazil are suspended.

18. The status of equality is based and depends on reciprocity. It contains a few exceptions, regarding access to the function of President of the Republic, Prime Minister, Presidents of the Supreme Courts, Army and Diplomatic Corp.
19. http://www.agenciabrasil.gov.br/noticias/2007/ 03/19/materia.2007-03-19.2889613864/view (consulted on October 15, 2008).

References

ACIME (2004). *Estatísticas da imigração.* Lisbon: Presidência do Conselho de Ministros/ACIME.

Baganha, M. I.,et al. (2004). The Unforeseen Wave: Migration from Eastern Europe to Portugal. *In*: Baganha, M. I., & Fonseca, M. L. (Eds.) *New Waves: Migration from Eastern to Southern Europe.* Lisbon: Fundação Luso-Americana.

Bruto da Costa, A., & Pimenta, M. (Coord.) (1991). *Minorias Étnicas Pobres em Lisboa.* Lisboa: Centro de Reflexão Cristã.

Carvalho, L. X. (2004). *Impacto e Reflexos do Trabalho Imigrante nas Empresas Portuguesas: Uma Visão Qualitativa Observatório da Imigração.* Lisbon: Immigration Observatory (ACIME).

Casqueira Cardoso, J. (2003). *Que Modelo de Integração das Minorias Etnicas em Portugal?* Actas do I Congresso Internacional de Investigação e Desenvolvimento Sócio-Cultural, Cabeceiras de Basto, AGIR [CD rom].

Correa D'Almeida, A. (2003). *Impacto da Imigração em Portugal nas Contas do Estado.* Lisbon: Immigration Observatory (ACIME).

Ferreira, E., Rato, H., & Mortágua, M. (2004). *Viagens de Ulisses: Efeitos da Imigração na Economia Portuguesa; Relatório Preliminar.* Lisbon: Immigration Observatory (ACIME).

Lages, M., & Policarpo, V. (2003). *Atitudes e Valores Perante e Imigração.* Lisbon: Immigration Observatory (ACIME).

Machado, I. J. de Renó (2006). Imigração em Portugal. *Estudos Avançados,* May/August, vol. 20, no. 57, p. 119–135.

Pereira Bastos, J., & Pereira Bastos, S. (1999). *Portugal Multicultural.* Lisbon: Fim de Século.

Rosa, M. J. V. (coord.) (2004). *Contributos dos Imigrantes na Demografia Portuguesa.* Lisbon: Immigration Observatory (ACIME).

Russo, H., & Soeiro, A. (2007). *Imigrantes de Leste: Vivências diferentes num espaço comum.* Azeitão, autonomia 27.

Santos, V. (2004). *O discurso oficial do Estado sobre a emigração dos anos 60 e 80 e imigração dos anos 90 à actualidade.* Porto: Immigration Observatory (ACIME).

Withol de Wenden, C. (1999). *L'immigration en Europe.* Paris: La Documentation française.

Websites

"Portugal, Brazil to Take Steps against Human Trafficking." (2003, 25 May). *BBC Monitoring International Reports* (http://www. protectionproject. org/ human_rights_reports/report_documents/ portugal. doc) (Consulted on 12 October 2008).

www.acidi.gov.pt [High Commission for Immigration and Intercultural Dialogue—ACIDI (*Alto Comissariado para a Imigração e Diálogo Intercultural*] (Consulted on 10 October 2008).

www.cplp.org [Portuguese-Speaking Commonwealth— CPLP (*Comunidade dos Povos de Língua Portuguesa*)] (Consulted on 5 October 2008).

www.ine.pt [National Statistical Institute—INE (*Instituto Nacional de Estatística*)] (Consulted on 12 October 2008).

www.sef.pt [Service for Border Control and Aliens—SEF (*Serviço de Estrangeiros e Fronteiras*)] (Consulted on 12 October 2008).

19

Sweden

The Immigration and Integration Experience:
The Case of Sweden

Pieter Bevelander

From the middle of the 1980s, increasing numbers of asylum seekers have been looking for protection in numerous European countries. Like many of its neighboring states, Sweden has been affected by this dramatic increase in refugee movement worldwide. The large inflow of people seeking refuge during the 1980s, 1990s, and continuing into the first years of the new millennium, together with a huge increase of unemployment and a low employment integration of immigrants, has provoked a debate about adjusting immigration and integration policies in Sweden. The deep economic recession of the early nineties obviously fueled this attention and directed it particularly toward the economic integration of immigrants and refugees. The continuing weak labor market integration of immigrants and refugees in the first half the new millennium led to a shift of focus in the public and political debate and evoked discussion of other integration arenas like education, politics, associations, and law. For more insight into this discussion see the following Swedish Official Publications (SOU) (SOU, 1996:55, 1997:118, 1997:152, 1997:174, 1998:25, 1999:8, 1999:34, 2004:21, 2004:33, 2004:48, 2004:49, 2005:3, 2005:12).

Historically, Sweden has received a substantial number of immigrants. In this sense, immigration is not new to Sweden. From the World War II up until the mid-1970s, the larger part of this migration was attributable to the high demand for foreign labor in the growing industries and service sectors. Only a minor part of the total migration was composed of refugees from non-European countries. As a result, immigration to Sweden has previously consisted almost entirely of European labor immigrants. However, since the seventies the decline in economic and industrial growth has removed the need for foreign labor. This has changed the composition of the immigrant population. Sweden has recently seen a large increase of refugees from Eastern Europe and from non-European countries. In turn, this new immigration has generated an increase of "tied movers" (relatives to earlier immigrants). In the year 2005, the foreign born part of the Swedish population numbered over one million, which amounts to 12.4 percent of the total population.

One of the central goals of the social-economic and citizenship policies of the welfare system in Sweden has been to ensure full employment for all Swedish residents, immigrants included, and to increase the political participation of immigrants, citizens as well as noncitizens. Linked to the equality aims of the integration policies of the Swedish governments since the mid-1970s, it is interesting to study the participation and possible nonparticipation of immigrants, and especially refugees, in the Swedish arenas of the labor market and democracy.

Immigration History

A simplified view of immigration to Sweden divides the postwar period into two distinct periods; the first primarily characterized by labor-force immigration, and the second by a shift toward refugee and "tied" immigration. This first period is usually said to have begun in 1945 and ended in the first half of the 1970s (Figure 19.1). During this time, Sweden's economy expanded rapidly, partly due to the reconstruction of her neighboring countries after World War II. Accordingly, labor shortages were solved in the 1950s through the import of skilled labor, which complemented the native labor force. This skilled labor was mainly recruited from Northwestern Europe, with the majority coming from Western Germany and the Nordic countries.

But the 1960s saw the beginnings of a rationalization phase in the Swedish economy. Now, the type of labur sought after shifted toward unskilled or low-skilled workers. In contrast to their counterparts a decade earlier, these workers were used more as a substitute for the native workforce than as a complement. While earlier immigrants allowed the economy to grow in size, the immigrants of the 1960s facilitated a widening of the economy. As they arrived, these new immigrants found employment in jobs vacated by Swedes during the expansion of the service sector. The fact that these newly vacated jobs could be filled by unskilled workers was a result of massive industrial investment aimed at increasing international competitiveness and reducing costs (Lundh & Ohlsson, 1999). Labor force immigrants during this decade came largely from Nordic countries but also from Mediterranean countries such as Greece, Yugoslavia, and Turkey.

By the end of the 1960s, however, the situation began to change for immigrants. The trade unions began to view immigration as producing a number of negative side effects. One such side effect was the delaying of industrial transformation through the steady supply of workers to replace Swedes who had moved into the service sector. This supply of labor also served to depress wage increases within industry, which would otherwise have occurred due to the scarcity of labor. In this

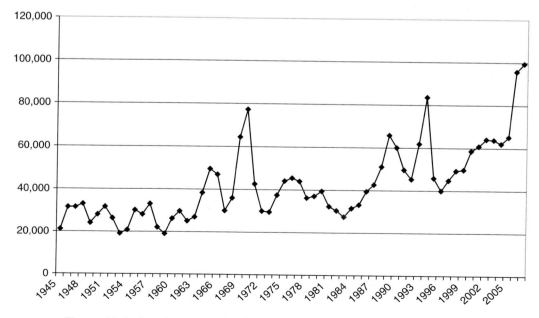

Figure 19-1. Immigration to Sweden 1946–2007. (Absolute Numbers)
Source: Sweden Statistics, Population Statistics. Available: http//www.scb.se/(2008–10–13).

way, immigration was criticized for preserving the traditional industrial structure at a time when it would otherwise have been forced to undergo significant transformation. The government responded to these criticisms through a change in the rules governing entrance into Sweden. The new rules began to apply in 1968, and meant that future applicants for work and residence permits from non-Nordic countries had to apply before they entered the country, and at the same arrange for both a job and a place to live. This dramatically cut down the labor immigration of non-Nordic countries during the next decades.

As stated earlier, Swedish economic growth dropped to a lower level following the crisis of the early 1970s. Simultaneously, the economy passed through a period of structural change with a decreasing industrial sector and an increasing service sector. Nordic labor migration—especially Finnish—gradually declined, mainly because of a diminishing gap in the standard of living between Sweden and Finland, and an increasing demand for labor in Finland. While labor migration dwindled during the 1970s, and more significantly in the 1980s and 1990s, other types of migration started to increase. These new groups were predominantly tied movers and various categories of

refugees, with a greater share of non-European immigrants having other motives than work for their migration. This also led to a major shift in the country of origin-mix among the immigrant population. In the 1970s, the major contributors to the immigrant population in Sweden were primarily refugees from Chile, Poland, and Turkey. In the 1980s, the lion's share of this new immigration came from Chile, Ethiopia, Iran, and other Middle Eastern countries. Individuals from Iraq, former Yugoslavia, and Eastern Europe countries dominated the 1990s. These countries dominated immigration to Sweden as well in the first five years of the new millennium. Especially Iraqi refugees but also immigrants from Poland and Denmark have come in increasing numbers. Relatively liberal asylum rules could explain the comparatively high number of Iraqis seeking asylum in Sweden. The entry of Poland to the EU is the main reason for their increasing numbers. The increase of Danes in Sweden is more locally explained and is mainly due to lower real estate prices in the Malmoe region (Sweden) compared to Copenhagen (Denmark) and the possibility to commute more easily since the bridge connecting Malmoe and Copenhagen was established in the year 2000.

Table 19-1. Stock of Native Born and Selected Groups of Immigrants (Foreign Born) 1960–2005 (Absolute Numbers)

Country/Year	1960	1970	1980	1990	2000	2005
Sweden	7,195,250	7,539,318	7,690,282	7,800,185	7,878,994	7,921,890
Denmark	35,112	39,152	43,501	43,931	38,190	42,598
Finland	101,307	235,453	251,342	217,636	195,447	183,675
Norway	37,253	44,681	42,863	52,744	42,464	44,852
Germany	37,580	41,793	38,696	36,558	38,155	41,578
Greece	266	11,835	15,153	13,171	10,851	10,744
USA	10,874	12,646	11,980	13,001	14,413	15,518
Italy	4,904	7,268	6,062	5,989	6,337	6,596
F.Yugoslavia	1,532	33,779	37,982	43,346	131,772	74,023
Bosnia-Herzegovina[a]	–	–	–	–	–	54,800
Turkey	202	3,768	14,357	25,528	31,894	35,844
Chile	69	181	8,256	27,635	26,842	27,811
Poland	6,347	10,851	19,967	35,631	40,123	46,177
Czechoslovakia	3,562	7,392	7,529	8,432	7,304	6,608
Ethiopia	59	346	1,797	10,027	11,907	11,214
Vietnam	1	195	1,602	6,265	10,898	12,352
Iran	115	411	3,348	40,084	51,101	54,417
Iraq	16	108	631	9,818	49,372	72,531

[a] Bosnia-Herzegovina is included in Former Yugoslavia up to the year 2000 in these statistics.
Source: Statistics Sweden, 1960, 1970, 1980 and 1990, Total Population part 1 (Folkmangd) and for the year 2000 Population statistics part 3, (Befolkningsstatistik), register data 2005.

Asylum and Admission

Like many other countries, Swedish refugee policy is based on the UN Geneva Convention of 1951 (which Sweden signed in 1954), and established in the Swedish Aliens Act of 1989 (1989:529). According to this Act (which has been amended and reinterpreted considerably), Sweden may give asylum to one category of refugees only, so-called *convention refugees*. These are individuals who are either stateless or outside the country of their nationality or former habitual residence, and who have a well-grounded fear of persecution in that country due to their race, nationality, membership of a particular social group, religious beliefs, or political opinion. These refugees have entered Sweden individually, applied for asylum, and subsequently obtained a residence permit. Outside this Act, Sweden obviously cooperates with the UN High Commissioner for Refugees, UNHCR, and admits its share of *quota refugees*. In contrast to convention refugees, the quota refugees are asylum-seekers who often come directly from a refugee camp and who have not individually entered the country. The size of the quota is decided yearly by the Swedish government and in agreement with UNHCR.

Also since that time, the Swedish Aliens Act of 1954 has been interpreted in a wider sense than the Geneva Convention, creating an established practice that has enabled other refugees than convention and quota refugees to obtain permanent residence in Sweden. If not being granted asylum according the restricted interpretation of the Geneva Convention, asylum-seekers could be granted refuge as so called *de facto refugees* or as *war-rejecters*. De facto refugees are individuals that can refer to political conditions or other circumstances in their country of origin that weight heavily in support for claiming asylum. War-rejecters are individuals that have fled war or impending military service. Both these categories were codified in 1976. Since 1997 a new category has been created called "refugees in need of sanctuary," including individuals with "refugee like" reasons, such as mass flight situations due to environmental catastrophes or civil war, and individuals who fear risk of persecution due to their gender or sexuality, which mainly includes the earlier de facto refugees. Individuals can also obtain a permanent residence for *humanitarian reasons,* for example, a state of war in their home country. In addition, the Swedish government has also the possibility to grant *temporary protection* to individuals.

More specific data on the admission status of refugees and the number of asylum seekers in Sweden is available first from the early 1980s. This was the time when countries in Western Europe started to observe the increase in asylum-seekers, and at the same time were faced with few and mainly unreliable statistical sources about the actual numbers. In Figure 19-2, the relation between asylum-seekers, refugees, and other types of admission status (tied movers, labor migrants, guest students, EU/EES nationals, and adoptees) from non-Nordic immigration is shown. From the figure, a clear connection between the number of asylum-seekers and the number that are granted refugee status can be established with a lag of one to two years. Like other European countries, Sweden has seen an increase in the number of asylum-seekers during the second half of the 1980s. However, if it were not for the civil war in former Yugoslavia and the subsequent increase in asylum-seekers all over Europe during 1992 and 1993 (see also Tables 19-2 and 19-3), the number of refugees would have decreased up until 1996, after which the number increased again from 1997 to 2002. A drop is visible for the years 2003 to 2005, after which an increase occurred again in 2006 and 2007. In connection to Figure 19-2, Table 19-2 shows that approximately one-third of all immigrants since 1980 are refugees and that over 50 percent of all asylum-seekers that are accepted are accepted for humanitarian reasons. The table also suggests that the number of convention refugees is rather stable over time. Moreover, the number that gained asylum as de facto refugees decreased in real numbers and was taken over by the number in need of protection in the analyzed period.

Figure 19-2 also indicates that over time other immigration than refugee immigration increased. This was mainly family reunification. Almost 50 percent of all non-Nordic immigrants that gained a residence permit in Sweden between 1980 and 2007 (see also Table 19-2) were of this category. To some extent, this increase could be due to the entrance of Sweden into the EES/EU in 1994/1995

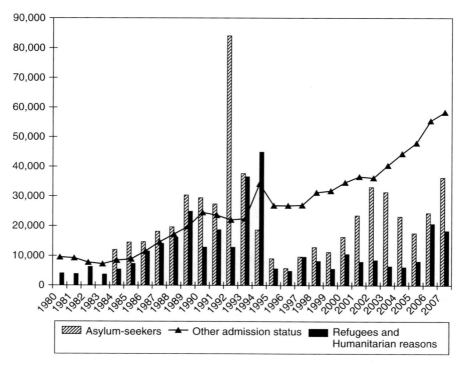

Figure 19-2. Asylum-Seekers, Refugees, and Humanitarian Reasons, and Immigrants with Other Admission Status, 1980–2007. (Absolute Numbers)
Source: The Swedish Migration Board, http://www.migrationsverket.se/pdffiler/statistik/.

Table 19-2. Residence Permits by Admission Category, 1980–2007 (Absolute Numbers)

Year	1980–1990	1991–1995	1996–2001	2002–2007	1980–2007
Total	248,855	247,466	234,707	350,752	1,081,780
Refugees	109,951	118,453	46,705	68,122	343,231
– by category					
– UN quota	5,947*	15,458	7,072	8,540	37,017
– UN convention	11,270*	3,977	4,002	4,541	23,790
– war-rejecters	2999*	49	–□	–	3,036
– de facto refugees	21,351*	14,724	1,651□	–	37,726
– in need of protection	–	–	4,496	17,340	21,836
– human. grounds	30,213	84,257	29,484	23,464	167,418
– Other~	–	–	–	14,237	14,237
Tied movers	119,218	106,370	128,444	146,787	500,819
Labor migrants	4,896	965	2,288	2,116	10,291
Guest students	7,005	6,403	16,676	39,203	69,287
Adoption	7,785	4,560	4,818	4,444	21,607
EU/EES	–	10,689#	35,776	90,080	136,545

* Since 1987.
□ Since 1997 in category *in need of protection*.
Since 1994.
~ Deportation impediments (2007) and Amnesty for children and families (2005–2007).
Source: The Swedish Migration Board, http://www.migrationsverket.se/pdffiler/statistik/.

Table 19-3. Asylum Seekers by Country of Citizenship, 1984–2007 (Absolute Numbers)

Country of citizenship	1984–1990	1991–1995	1996–2001	2002–2007	1984–2007	Percentage
Bulgaria	5,422	494	553	3,447	9,916	0.02
F. Yugoslavia	6,393	124,386*	24,444*	30,908	186,131	0.33
Bosnia-Herzegovina	–	38,476	9,840	5,905	54,221	
Serbia-Montenegro	–	66,452	13,166	22,624	102,242	
Poland	4,161	1,738	324	73	6,347	0.01
Romania	5,900	1,637	247	1,808	9,652	0.02
Russia	–	1,174	2,543	6,739	10,456	0.02
Ethiopia	8,184	824	392	667	10,061	0.02
Somalia	3,365	6,595	2,100	9,918	21,978	0.04
Uganda	645	1,290	54	137	2,126	0.00
Togo	53	547	12	82	684	0.00
Cuba	15	1,846	99	138	2,098	0.00
Chile	11,707	282	167	386	12,602	0.02
Peru	621	2,444	449	326	3,840	0.01
Afghanistan	422	867	1,972	3,879	7,140	0.01
Bangladesh	1,270	846	471	739	3,326	0.01
China	198	204	213	721	1,396	0.00
India	561	337	197	572	1,727	0.00
Iran	31,924	3,191	3,743	3,770	42,628	0.08
Iraq	8,347	11,230	21,738	39,442	80,757	0.14
Lebanon	11,139	898	740	2,481	15,258	0.03
Pakistan	1,073	311	737	416	2,537	0.00
Sri Lanka	316	1,104	360	130	1,910	0.00
Syria	3,327	951	1,542	2,883	8,703	0.02
Turkey	6,203	1,576	1,581	2,892	12,252	0.02
Stateless	8,707	1,850	2,024	7,655	20,236	0.04
Other countries	14,532	10,014	12,412	45,322	82,280	0.15
Total	138,564	176,637	79,308	165,591	560,100	

* Including asylum seekers from Bosnia-Herzegovina and Yugoslavia.
Source: The Swedish Migration Board, http://www.migrationsverket.se/pdffiler/statistik/.

(see also Table 19-2). Guest students increased as well in the studied period.

Almost 400,000 individuals sought asylum in Sweden between 1984 and 2007 (Table 19-3). Of these, 33 percent originated from former Yugoslavia. Together with Iran and Iraq, who stand for 8 and 14 percent each, these countries are the main contributors to the total numbers of asylum seekers during the years 1984–2007. Asylum seekers from Chile, Iran, Lebanon, and Ethiopia dominated in the period 1984–1990. Individuals from former Yugoslavia and Iraq have the highest percentage among asylum-seekers in the subsequent periods, 1991–1995 and 1996–2001. Iraq, Bosnia-Herzegovina, and Somalia are the countries that have high number of asylum seekers in Sweden in 2002–2007. For the year 2007 almost half of the total number of asylum seekers, 48 percent, obtained a residence permit. For the period 1991–2007 this is 55 percent.

Integration and Settlement Policy

Earlier, it was claimed that immigrants were warmly welcomed up until the middle of the 1960s, when Sweden still advocated a liberal integration policy due to its labor shortage. However, there was no clear political objective as to how immigrants and refugees should be integrated until the middle of the 1970s. According to Lundh & Ohlsson (1999), the main goal of the policy to assimilate the immigrants as quickly as possible and to authorize residence permits, often permanent, were heavily related to existing labor demands. A more distinct integration policy is discernible in the late 1960s, when a more restrictive immigration policy was implemented simultaneously. In 1965, the first steps were taken to facilitate the adaptation of immigrants to the Swedish society. These measures were taken through an initiative by LO (the Swedish Trade Union Confederation) and SAF (the Swedish Employers Confederation), and consisted mainly of education in the Swedish language, but also of general information about Sweden in several foreign languages, and the establishment of immigrant offices. In the early 1970s, further initiatives were taken to alleviate the increasing need of education in the Swedish language for immigrants. This led to legislation, in 1972, in which immigrants had the right to paid leave of absence by the employer in order to study Swedish for a minimum of 240 hours.

Since the middle of the 1970s, a policy of ethnic or cultural pluralism was implemented based on three pillars: equality, freedom of choice, and partnership (Hammar, 1993; Westin, 2000). Equality reflects a fundamental principle of the Swedish welfare state, and in the context of immigration it rejected the guest worker system. Immigrants were to enjoy the same social and economic rights and standards as native Swedes. Freedom of choice reflects the idea that individuals determine their personal and cultural affiliations and identities to the Swedish society. Partnership can be seen as the need for mutual tolerance and solidarity between immigrants and native Swedes. In 1998, the immigration policy was replaced by an integration policy aimed at the whole population, and a new central government agency, the Integration Board (*Integrationsverket*), was established with the special task to oversee integration efforts throughout the Swedish society. The focus of this new organization is to monitor and evaluate trends in integration, promote equal rights and opportunities for everyone, and combat xenophobia, racism, and discrimination (Jederlund, 1998).

Another watershed can be dated to the middle of the 1980s, when Sweden reorganized its refugee reception program. Before this reform, a majority of refugees traveled directly to a municipality and applied for asylum there. A vast majority arrived in the regions of Stockholm, Gothenburg, and Malmoe. The National Immigration Board (*SIV-Statens Invandrarverk*) took over primary responsibility from the National Labor Market Board (*AMS-Arbetsmarknadsstyrelsen*). This reorganization had the following principles:

Refugees should enjoy the benefits of Sweden's integration policy in the same way as other immigrants. The National Immigration Board should be responsible for this.

Asylum-seekers and refugees should be placed in a municipality as soon as possible and obtain education in the Swedish language and society as well as housing and social benefits according to "general" Swedish standards.

Around twenty percent of all municipalities (they are 280 in total) should be selected and made suitable to integrate refugees. Large municipalities should be avoided because they had already taken a disproportionate annual number of asylum-seekers and refugees. The Board should negotiate with the selected municipalities, and the state should pay for the costs of the integration program as well as the fixed costs for the asylum-seeker or refugee, including housing costs and social benefits during the first three years (see also Hammar, 1993).

In practice, this policy meant that depending on the circumstances, an individual could seek asylum or a residence permit directly at the border, or later at the local police station in the municipality where they chose to stay. The police, who forwarded the matter to the Swedish Immigration Board for further investigation, did the first hearing. The Board was further responsible for the reception of the asylum-seeker, who at first was placed at one of the clearance centers. In 1992 there were four of these centers located in Malmoe, Mölndal, Flen, and Upplands Väsby. Due to the waiting time for a residence permit, the asylum-seeker could be placed in a more permanent refugee camp facility as well as staying with relatives waiting on a residence permit. The latter had to be approved by the municipality and the Immigration Board. Nonapproval by these authorities could lead to the loss of financial support for the asylum-seeker. Up to 1990, the only activity for refugees in the refugee camps was language education and courses on the Swedish society. During 1991, more compulsory activities were allowed, encompassing at least four hours a day. In 1992, it was decided to allow asylum-seekers to work if the waiting time on a residence permit was estimated to take at least four months (SOU, 1992:69). The main idea with these organized activities was to counteract passivity and to increase the possibilities of integration after a resident permit was obtained. In the end, the focus of the activities became more a sort of "contribute to your own support" than an actual effort toward integration into Swedish society (Swedish Immigration Board, 1997). These activities could be anything from cleaning the camp, being an assistant in a day-care center, and holding information meetings for new asylum-seekers, to organizing theater groups, producing newspapers, and taking different kind of courses, such as language, computer knowledge, civics, and so forth. Work outside the refugee camp has been less than 20 percent of the total supply of activities. The main activity here has been internships, which are strongly influenced by the economic situation in the local labor market. Increasing competition for trainee places by the indigenous population during this period could explain this low percentage for asylum-seekers.

The Swedish Immigration board was responsible for the transfer of the refugee to the municipalities once a residence permit was obtained. The board also had the responsibility to negotiate with municipalities for the settlement of refugees. The municipality involved could reapply for social grants from the state during the refugees' first three years in the municipality and also receive a once only compensation for each refugee received to cover extra costs. The integration responsibilities of the municipality include housing, language courses, and an introduction plan with the focus on how to reach self-sufficiency. During 1985–1990, the municipalities were reimbursed for their actual expenditures. From 1991, however, the municipalities are given a standard reimbursement per received refugee.

This reform never functioned in its original form mainly due to the sharp increase of refugees granted a residence permit in Sweden during the period (see Figure 19-2, Tables 19-2 and 19-3). The waiting time for a resident permit and the following settlement in the municipality, as well as the amount of municipalities involved in settlement, increased over the years, from 137 municipalities in 1985 to the double of 273 municipalities in 1994 (Swedish Migration Board). The reform became known as the "Sweden-wide strategy" or "The Whole of Sweden Strategy." More and more municipalities,

even the less suitable ones with net out-migration because of a depressed local economy, became involved and were persuaded to rent their surplus housing to refugees. This also led to a new strategy of a temporary, three-year integration into these municipalities, and a subsequent, compulsory dispersal with little consideration given to the individual's interests. Basically, refugees were sent to municipalities with fellow countrymen. Secondary migration of refugees to other municipalities can be seen in different ways. Some advocate a failure of the local integration policies while others see this as an indication of individuals having the ability to act as agents (Hammar, 1993). Soininen (1999) suggests that the implementation of this reform became a conflict between the social services in the municipalities having their ideas about the care of clients and the ideas of the integration policy, which tried to meet every individual in a spirit of cooperation, equality, and freedom of choice. Also, little incentive was given to local governments to pursue a policy of labor market integration during the first period of the reform. Together, it could be claimed that this reform shifted the focus away from labor market integration.

The effect of the compulsory dispersal policy was also subject to economic analysis. Comparing immigrants arriving before and during the reform, Edin et al. (2000) suggests that eight years after arrival, earnings were 25 percent lower because of the new policy. Idleness had also increased by about six percent for those groups that came during the reform (from 1985), relative to those that came between 1982 and 1983. Franzén (1997) discusses the same problems but refers to how refugees were treated by local labor market authorities. In a follow-up study, she finds that the employment offices' integration strategy did not have the expected results. Seeing the refugees as a homogenous group instead of a diverse population, the various authorities' lack of interest in scrutinizing earlier labor market experience, together with a generally negative attitude toward the skills of the immigrants, led to a destructive pattern of clientization of refugees to the social security system.

Since 1994 the dispersal policy was abolished and replaced by a system in which asylum-seekers could opt for living with family, relatives, or friends during the time they waited for approval. The Migration Board however was still responsible for housing the asylum-seekers that did opt for this, and had still agreements with municipalities to resettle asylum-seekers during the time of investigation. The change in the system was a reaction to the huge numbers of asylum-seekers in this period and increased flexibility in finding appropriate housing. Since then, approximately 50 percent of all asylum-seekers have taken the option of living with family, relatives, and friends during the waiting time for a residence permit.

Economic Integration

Studies on the economic integration of immigrants in Sweden show a very high labor market attachment during the 1950s and 1960s. In this period, incomes and employment rates were relatively high, with consequently low unemployment rates (Ekberg, 1983). During the 1970s and 1980s, the unemployment rate was quite low in Sweden compared to most other OECD countries. Nevertheless, dating back to 1977, when unemployment began to be reported separately for different nationalities,

the unemployment rate for foreign citizens was at least double that of Swedish citizens. In the first half of the 1990s, however, the unemployment rates of both Swedish and foreign citizens increased dramatically, mainly because of the deep crisis in the Swedish economy. From 1993 to 1995, unemployment among foreign citizens was three times higher than for Swedish citizens. Since 1997, however, there has been a sharp decline in the unemployment rate for both natives and foreign citizens (Lundh et al., 2002).

Current research into the employment situation of the last decades, shows a different picture. Gradually, there has been a decline in immigrant employment rates for both men and women compared to natives. In Figure 19-3, age-standardized employment rates over time are shown for natives and immigrant men and women. Age-standardization here means that the age distribution is held constant when calculating the employment rates for the several groups, that is, we account for differences in age structures between groups when comparing employment rates. From the figures a negative trend can be observed in the employment rates for immigrants, which starts in the 1970s. After 1970, the

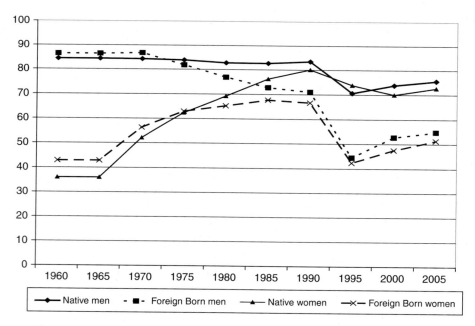

Figure 19-3. Age Standardized Employment Rate for Foreign Born and Native Born Men and Women Aged 16–64, 1960–2005 (Percent)
Source: Bevelander 2000, own calculations based on register data 2000 and 2005.

employment rate for foreign born men decreased gradually compared to native born men. Foreign born women showed an increase in employment over time but the increase was not in parity with the increase of native born women. It seems clear that the deep economic recession of the early 1990s widened the gap between natives and immigrants even more, whereas the economic recovery of the late nineties and early 2000s seems to have reversed the negative development to some extent. This general trend for both immigrant men and women was also observed in studies focusing on metropolitan areas of Sweden (Bevelander et al., 1997).

Table 19-4 shows the development in employment integration for selected groups of foreign born men and women 1970, 1990, and 2005. In general, it shows that nonnative men had a decline of roughly 15 to 20 percentage points in employment during this period. Foreign born men from Finland, Germany, Poland, Bosnia-Herzegovina, and Chile still had an employment rate of over 60 percent in 2005, while foreign born men from the Nordic countries, Norway and Denmark,[1] former Yugoslavia, and Middle Eastern countries like Turkey, Iran, and Iraq were below this level. Irrespective of admission status, almost all of the groups show a gradually decreasing employment rate after the 1970 census.

The development of the employment rate for native and foreign born women showed a different pattern when compared to men. With the exceptions of women from former Yugoslavia and from Turkey, most groups of foreign born women show an increase in employment attachment between 1970 and 1990. The decline in employment rates between 1990 and 2005 is for some groups almost 10 percent, for some groups its less, including women born in Bosnia-Herzegovina, Poland, Iran, and Chile.

The difference in employment integration is to some extent due to the fact that Nordic immigrants dominated the immigration cohorts of the 1950s and 1960s. These immigrants came as labor migrants and adjusted fast to the growing industrial labor market. A look at Table 19-5 shows that immigrant cohorts with a generally shorter "time in the country" have lower employment rates. Refugees from Asia, Africa, and Southeast Europe dominate the cohorts that entered the country since the beginning of the 1980s. Variations in employment adjustment are thus partly explained by "time of residence" and partly by the motivation for migration. The change in country of origin mix, however, cannot by itself explain the lower employment adjustment for immigrants in general. Nor can it account for the differences in employment integration between immigrant groups.

Table 19-4. Age Standardized Employment Rate for Selected Groups Foreign Born, 1970, 1990, and 2005 (Percent)

	Men			Women		
	1970	1990	2005	1970	1990	2005
Denmark	88	80	53	52	75	55
Norway	85	78	58	49	73	62
Finland	88	75	67	58	76	68
Germany	88	80	64	54	74	60
F.Yugoslavia	87	67	55	59	58	46
Bosnia-Hercegovina	–	–	63	–	–	56
Poland	74	70	62	48	64	59
Iran	–	46	53	–	32	46
Iraq	–	48	38	–	32	24
Turkey	80	55	55	59	41	39
Chile	74	75	63	47	64	60
Somalia	–	–	27	–	–	20
Etiopia	–	–	55	–	–	58

Source: Bevelander, 2000, p. 81; own calculations based on register data 2005.

Table 19-5. Age Standardized Employment Rates for Foreign Born by Immigration Cohort, 2005 (Percent)

		Men	Women
Natives		76	73
Foreign Born		55	51
Cohorts	–1975	67	65
	1976–1980	68	68
	1981–1085	64	64
	1986–1990	59	58
	1991–1995	57	54
	1996–2000	53	46
	2001–2005	39	30

Source: Own calculations based on register data 2005.

The majority of studies dealing with the economic integration of immigrants use human capital theory as their approach, in which different demographic and human capital characteristics are expected to explain the labor market integration of immigrants. In this framework, education is seen as an investment by the individual made in order to increase his or her productivity, which later supposedly results in improved labor market careers. Differences in the level of education could therefore explain variations in the employment integration of immigrants. However, aggregated data shows that this is not the case. Instead, we see how immigrants basically have the same educational level as natives. Figure 19-4 shows the share of natives and foreign born by educational level. It can clearly be seen that even if we control for age structure, the differences are marginal, although immigrant men and women are somewhat overrepresented in the category of primary education. Besides, immigrant women do have a higher share in university education than native and foreign born males.

Consequently, the difference in educational level could be the main explanatory variable for differences in the employment integration of immigrants groups in the Swedish labor market. Several studies based on individual data basically point toward the same conclusion; namely that a higher educational level increases the probability to obtain employment for both immigrants and

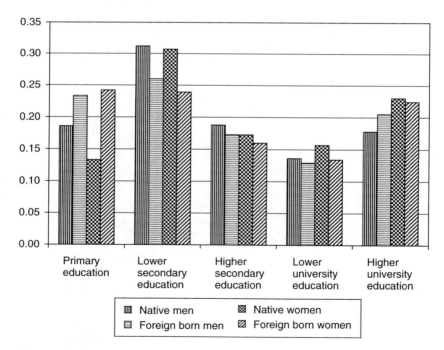

Figure 19-4. Age Standardized Educational Levels Native and Foreign Born Men and Women, Age 25–64, 2005 (Percentage)
Source: Own calculations based on register data 2005.

natives between 1970 and 1990. Having a Swedish degree also implies advantages compared to having a foreign degree. But variations in educational level do not explain the differences in the chances to obtain employment for individuals, neither by itself nor together with other individual characteristics (Schröder & Wilhelmsson, 1998; Bevelander & Skyt Nielsen, 2001; Rooth, 1999).

Indeed, other studies suggest that institutional and demand-side factors, and not only supply-side factors, may help to explain the varying labor market attachment, which for some immigrant groups may be characterized as very weak. Firstly, a lower level of economic growth was experienced during the last two decades compared to the earlier period, entailing a decreasing demand for "extra" labor. Secondly, on the aggregate level, there has been a structural change of the economy, where a declining industry sector has given way to an increasing service sector requiring higher education and language proficiency. This means that the number of low-skilled industry jobs has been decreasing steadily in recent years, jobs which traditionally have been filled by immigrants. Thirdly, the policies pertaining to immigration, integration, and the labor market, as mentioned earlier, have influenced the labor market integration of immigrants on entry and long afterward (Bevelander et al., 1997; Blos et al., 1997; Edin et al., 2000). Fourthly, more information- and communication-intensive working processes were introduced in both the industrial and the service sectors of the economy. This development increased the demand for employees with a higher general competence, while unskilled labor was made redundant by efficiency improvements. One effect of this increased demand for general competence has been to upgrade the importance of informal skills without reducing the importance of formal education and skills. Such informal skills include country-specific skills, for instance language skills, and the understanding of different behavior in teamwork and in relations with authorities and labor market organizations worldwide (see Chiswick & Miller, 1996, for a discussion of the importance of language skills). This structural change made it more difficult for immigrants with the same general formal human capital stock as natives

Swedes to obtain employment and earnings on the level as natives, see Scott (1999) and Bevelander (2000; 2001; 2005). Together with the shift in immigration toward what is perceived as culturally more distant from the Swedish society (Lange & Westin, 1993), this structural change may have entailed more discrimination by authorities, employers, and employees toward the new immigrants and refugees (Bevelander & Lundh, 2007; Schierup & Paulsson, 1994; Carlsson & Rooth, 2006). Quantitative multivariate analysis (Bevelander, 2000; 2005) and qualitative analysis (Knocke, 1994) show that these changes also affected employment integration for immigrant women.

Concluding this section, it is obvious that the employment integration of immigrants in Sweden has deteriorated in recent years. This lack of integration has in turn had negative effects on the relative income of the various immigrant groups (Scott, 1999). Due to the fact that unemployment benefits, parental leave, and various pensions are based on earlier income, immigrants have also a weaker welfare inclusion (for overview see Gustafsson, 2002; Ekonomisk Debatt, 2007:3). Self-employment among some groups has partially counteracted the situation (Bevelander et al., 1997), but the social security payments directed toward certain immigrant groups show a harsh reality and a strong exclusion from the labor market.

Political Integration

Voting in free elections is often viewed as the most basic and important form of political participation. As such, the level of participation can be seen as an indicator of how well democracy is faring. On this yardstick, electoral participation in Sweden is high compared to other democratic countries. Over 80 percent of eligible voters exercised their franchise in the 2006 national, provincial, and local elections.[2]

Linked to the issue of political participation is that of immigration and citizenship. Sweden was one of the first countries to extend local and provincial voting rights to immigrants with resident status, arguing that it would increase political influence, interest, and self-esteem among foreign citizens. In the following the voting participation of immigrants is discussed.

Citizenship in Sweden is based on the *jus sanguinis* principle. People whose parents are Swedish citizens are automatically granted citizenship. However, unlike the case of Canada, the children of non-Swedish citizens who are born in Sweden are not automatically entitled to Swedish citizenship. That aside, Swedish legislation on naturalization is one of the most liberal in Europe. In 2006, 77 percent of eligible foreign born residents with non-Swedish parents had obtained Swedish citizenship.

Since the 1970s, foreign citizens from most countries over the age of 18 without a criminal record have been able to acquire Swedish citizenship after five years of residency (four years for refugees). Foreign citizens from other Nordic countries can obtain citizenship after only two years of residence.[3] Gaining citizenship by notification is also possible. This is basically a simplified juridical naturalization procedure used mainly by Nordic citizens. Acquiring Swedish citizenship by notification is possible if the applicant is eighteen years of age or older, has lived in Sweden for five years and has not been sentenced to prison during this time.

While entrance to Swedish citizenship has become successively easier, there has existed one formal deterrent. Dual citizenship was forbidden in Sweden until July 1, 2001, except in cases where countries did not allow renunciation of citizenship. While many individuals may see uptake of a citizenship as a fairly casual act, renunciation of a citizenship is much more serious. After 2001, no such demands were placed on applicants.

General elections based on universal suffrage were introduced in Sweden in 1921, when the population voted for the second chamber of the Swedish parliament. It is in this election that women gained the right to vote, thereby doubling the electorate. Since then, the electorate has expanded through gradually lowering the voting age. In 1976, foreign citizens obtained the right to vote in municipal and provincial elections after three years of registered residency. The stated goal of this change was to increase the political influence, interest, and self-esteem of foreign citizens (SOU,

1975:15). In 1998, the three-year waiting period for foreign citizens from EU countries, Iceland, and Norway was removed. However, voting in national elections still requires Swedish citizenship.

According to Öhrvall (2006), a distinct increasing trend in electoral participation is visible up to the middle of the 1970s. In 1976, 91.8 percent of the electorate voted in the national election. This represents the highest level of electoral participation measured in Sweden. Of foreign citizens, 60 percent exercised their franchise and voted in municipal and provincial elections in 1976 (see Figure 19-5).

Electoral participation gradually decreased until the election of 2006, which saw a slight upsurge in participation (SCB, 2006).

Statistics Sweden does not consistently collect information on foreign born electoral participation. However, they have published electoral participation rates of foreign born citizens since 1988. Their data suggest that participation rose between 1988 and 1991 and then fell substantially in the 1998 elections. However, Öhrvall (2006) notes that while foreign born citizens are on average about 8 percent less likely to vote, the decline in voter participation by foreign born citizens is lower than for native born citizens.

Tracking voting probabilities of foreign citizens is more difficult, in part because a substantial number of foreign citizens leave the country without telling anyone (Öhrvall, 2006). Thus, at least part of the issue may be one of measurement—it is difficult to determine the denominator. Nonetheless, some work has been done which suggests that while initially assessed as high in 1976 (see Hammar, 1979), participation rates have decreased substantially since then. In 2002, it was down to 35 percent.

The 2006 elections are of particular interest since they showed an increase in voting participation by native born Swedes and immigrants, citizens and noncitizens (Bevelander and Pendakur 2008). Table 19-6 shows turnout rates by place of birth, generation, and citizenship, based on an electoral participation survey. While over 80 percent of the population voted in these elections, there are substantial differences in terms of place of birth and generation. Moreover, noncitizens voted at much lower rates

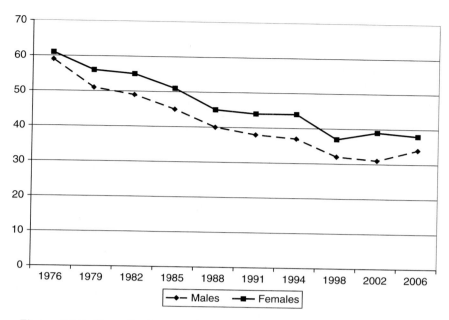

Figure 19-5. Voter Participation by Sex for Noncitizens, 1976–2006
Source: Sweden statistics.

Table 19-6. Voter Turnout Rates for Citizens and Noncitizens, 2006

Place of birth	Municipal citizens	Municipal including non citizens	Provincial citizens	Provincial including noncitizens	National
Sweden	84	47	83	48	85
Nordic not Swedish	72	55	71	56	74
EU not Nordic	70	62	70	62	71
Other Europe	59	62	59	62	60
African	58	71	57	71	58
North America & Oceania	81	67	81	67	80
South America	72	62	72	62	73
Asia	63	58	63	59	64
2 Immigrant parents	73	69	72	69	75
1 Immigrant parent	80	64	79	64	82
Total	82	64	81	65	83

Source: Bevelander and Pendakur, 2008.

than citizens. Only about 36 percent of noncitizens voted in the 2006 municipal and provincial elections. Non-Swedes, with the exception of those born in North America and Oceania, or those with only one immigrant parent, were also less likely to vote.

In a multivariate analysis controlling for demographic, socioeconomic, and contextual factors, Bevelander and Pendakur (2008) find that age, schooling, generation, place of birth, type of housing, city size, and especially (higher) income and citizenship acquisition are important factors for voting in the 2006 elections in Sweden. Indeed, citizenship has an enormous impact, increasing the odds of voting by over 80 percent.

Conclusion

Studying the immigration experience to Sweden diachronically shows that migration, as well as integration into the labor market, and participation in the political arena by newly arrived immigrants, have changed character over time. A majority of the immigrants arriving to Sweden in the first decades after World War II were labor migrants from mainly Nordic and other European countries. For the most part, they were driven by economic factors. On recommendation from the Labor Organization of Sweden (LO), a change in the admission legislation took place at the end of the 1960s, where a relatively liberal policy was replaced by a more restrictive one mainly toward non-Nordic labor migrants.

Internal conflicts, warfare, and various geopolitical developments have led to a general increase in the number of asylum-seekers in the world. Unaffected by the change in admission policy, and based on a relatively greater willingness to grant asylum, together with a liberal family reunification policy, most immigrants who arrived during the 1970s and the following decades were refugees from East European and non-European countries and tied movers from both labor migrants and refugees. Statistics reveal that tied movers and refugees both make up for almost 85 percent of those granted a residence permit in the last decades. The economic crisis of the early 1990s and the dramatic increase of asylum seekers during the same period paved the way for adjusting the refugee policy toward a more restrictive attitude, where temporary protection of asylum seekers replaced what formerly would have been the authorization of permanent residence permits.

Assimilation policy toward immigrants also changed, and since the middle of the 1970s the integration policy of Sweden is based on cultural pluralism and the slogans of equality, freedom of choice, and partnership. Integration into the labor market and political participation have been important goals of the policy. The settlement policy implemented since the middle of the 1980s, spreading refugees who gained a residence permit to a number of municipalities, and especially those with a favorable local labor market, can be seen as a way to attain these goals.

Whereas the labor migrants adjusted relatively well into the labor market and the concentration in settlement of various immigrant groups were seen as a way of retaining certain cultural elements of these groups in a new environment, the economic integration of immigrants in general declined gradually and for some groups deteriorated dramatically for some immigrant groups. The relatively liberal citizenship policy, as well as granting noncitizens the right to vote in local and provincial elections initially showed good results, but just like the labor market integration, showed over time a lower voting participation by immigrants.

Human capital and personal skills, occupational transferability, structural changes in the labor market, various types of discrimination, integration policies toward immigrants and labor market policies in general are all factors that can be seen as increasing the transaction costs for immigrants relative to natives to adjust in the labor market. Especially the structural change of the Swedish labor market into a service society demanding higher general skills and stressing language skills are likely to increase the cost for new immigrants to acquire these skills. Potential employers are placed in a position of increasing hiring costs and this affects the discrimination toward certain groups of immigrants.

Moreover, weak labor market integration of the individual indirectly has consequences for an individual's feeling of belonging to the host country and participation in the political sphere, namely, lower voting participation.

In this sense, integration policies in Sweden have not been effective during the last decades. The "multicultural" society does exist in Sweden only if we look at the number of foreign born relative to native born. However, when it comes to the two prominent measures of integration, employment integration and voting participation, it becomes clear that large groups of immigrants are marginalized by the Swedish society.

Notes

1. Both Norway and Denmark have large populations living in border municipalities in Sweden but working in their home country, which explains the relatively low employment rates of these immigrant groups.
2. The elections of 2006 are particularly interesting because it represents a reversal in the downward trend in electoral participation in Sweden.
3. If the foreign citizen is either under 18 or with a criminal record, there is a waiting period before the applicant can apply for Swedish citizenship.

References

Bevelander, P. (2000). *Immigrant Employment Integration and Structural Change in Sweden, 1970–1995.* Stockholm: Almqvist & Wiksell International.

Bevelander, P. (2001). "Getting a Foothold, Male Immigrant Employment Integration and Structural Change in Sweden, 1970–1995." *Journal of Migration and Integration,* 2(4): 531–559.

Bevelander, P. (2005). "The Emplyment Status of Immigrant Women: The Case of Sweden." *International Migration Review,* 39(1): 173–202.

Bevelander, P., Carlsson, B., & Rojas, M. (1997). *I Krusbärslandets Storstäder, om invandrare i Stockholm, Göteborg och Malmö.* Stockholm: SNS-förlag.

Bevelander, P., & Lundh, C. (2007). "Employment Integration of Refugees, the Influence of Local Factors on Refugee Job Opportunities in Sweden," Discussion paper 2551, IZA, Bonn.

Bevelander, P., & Pendakur, R. (2008). "Electoral Participation as a Measure of Social Inclusion for Natives, Immigrants, and Descendants in Sweden." Discussion paper 3764, IZA, Bonn.

Bevelander, P., & Skyt Nielsen, H. (2001). "Declining Employment Success of Immigrant Males in Sweden: Observed or Unobserved Characteristics?" *Journal of Population Economics,* 14(3): 455–471.

Blos, M., Fischer, P. A., & Straubhaar, T. (1997). "The Impact of Migration Policy on the Labour Market Performance of Migrants: A Comparative Case Study." *New Community,* 23(4): 511–535.

Carlsson, M., & Rooth, D-O. (2006). "Evidence of Ethnic Discrimination in the Swedish Labor Market Using Experimental Data." Discussion paper 2281, IZA, Bonn.

Chiswick, B. R., & Miller, P. W. (1996). "Ethnic Networks and Language Proficiency among Immigrants." *Journal of Population Economics,* 9(1): 19–35.

Edin, P-A., Fredriksson, P., & Åslund, O. (2000). "Settlement Policies and the Economic Success of Immigrants." In O. Åslund, *Health, Immigration, and Settlement Policies Economic Studies 53.* Uppsala: Department of Economics.

Ekonomisk Debatt (2007). "Invandrares integration på arbetsmarknaden." *Temanummer:* 3.

Ekberg, J. (1983). *Inkomsteffekter av invandring.* Växjö: Acta Wexionensia. Serie 2 Economy & Politics 1.

"Electoral Participation as a Measure of Social Inclusion for Natives, Immigrants and Descendants in Sweden." Discussion Paper No. 3764, IZA, Bonn.

Franzén, E. (1997). *Invandring och arbetslöshet.* Lund: Studentlitteratur.

Gustafsson, B. (2002). "Sweden's Recent Experience of International Migration: Issues and Studies." In R. Rotte & P. Stein (Eds.), *Migration Policy and the Economy: International Experiences.* München: Hanns Seidel Stiftung.

Hammar, T. (1979). *Det första invandrarvalet.* Stockholm: Liber förlag.

Hammar, T. (1993). "The 'Sweden-wide Strategy' of Refugee Dispersal." In R. Black & V. Robinson (Eds.), *Geography and Refugees, Patterns and Processes of Change.* London & New York: Belhaven Press.

Jederlund, L. (1998, December). *Current Sweden: From Immigration Policy to Integration Policy.* Swedish Institute, No. 422 [Online]. Available: http://www.si.se/infoSweden/594.cs.

Knocke, W. (1994). "Kön, etnicitet och teknisk utveckling." In C. U. Schierup & S. Paulson, (Eds.), *Arbetets etniska delning.* Carlssons: Stockholm.

Lange, A., & Westin, A, (1993). *Den mångtydiga toleransen: Förhållningssätt till invandring och invandrare 1993.* Stockholm: Ceifo.

Lundh, C., & Ohlsson, R. (1999). *Från arbetskraftimport till flyktinginvandring.* Stockholm: SNS-Förlag, Second edition.

Lundh, C., Bennich-Björkman, L., Ohlsson, R., Pedersen, P. J., & Rooth, D. (2002). *Arbete? Var god dröj!, Invandrare i välfärdsamhället.* Stockholm: SNS-förlag.

Öhrvall, R. (2006). "Invandrade och valdeltagande." In H. Bäck & M. Gilljam (Eds.), *Valets Mekanismer.* Malmö: Liber förlag.

Rooth, D-O. (1999). *Refugee Immigrants in Sweden, Educational Investments, and Labour Market Integration.* Lund: Lund Economic Studies.

SCB (Statistics Sweden) (2006). *Allmänna valen 2006 Del 4.* Stockholm: Statistics Sweden.

Schierup, C. U., & Paulson, S. (Eds.) (1994). *Arbetets etniska delning.* Stockholm: Carlssons förlag.

Schröder, L., & Wilhelmsson, R. (1998). " 'Sverigespecifikt' human kapital och ungdomars etablering på arbetsmarknaden." *Ekonomisk Debatt, 8.*

Scott, K. (1999). *The Immigrant Experience: Changing Employment and Income Patterns in Sweden, 1970–1993.* Lund Studies in Economic History 9. Lund: Lund University Press.

Soininen, M. (1999). "Refugee Care in Sweden: The Problems of Unemployment and Anti-Discrmination Policies." In J. Wrench, A. Rea, & N. Ouali (Eds.), *Migrants, Ethnic Minorities, and the Labour Market: Integration and Exclusion in Europe.* London: Macmillan Press.

Swedish Aliens act 1989.

Swedish Official Report (SOU), (1975: 15).
Swedish Official Report (SOU), (1992: 69).
Swedish Official Report (SOU), (1996: 55).
Swedish Official Report (SOU), (1997: 118).
Swedish Official Report (SOU), (1997: 152).
Swedish Official Report (SOU), (1997: 174).
Swedish Official Report (SOU), (1998: 25).
Swedish Official Report (SOU), (1999: 8).
Swedish Official Report (SOU), (1999: 34).
Swedish Official Report (SOU), (2004: 21).
Swedish Official Report (SOU), (2004: 33).
Swedish Official Report (SOU), (2004: 48).
Swedish Official Report (SOU), (2004: 49).
Swedish Official Report (SOU), (2005: 3).
Swedish Official Report (SOU), (2005: 12).

Swedish Immigration Board (Statens Invandrarverk) (1997). *Individuell Mångfald, Invandraverkets utvädering och analys av det samordnade flyktingmottagandet 1991–1996.*

Westin, C. (2000). "The Effectiveness of Settlement and Integration Policies towards Immigrants and their Descendants in Sweden." *International Migration Papers 34.* Geneva: ILO.

Statistical Sources

Statistics Sweden, Population, part 1 (Folkmangd del 1), 1960, 1970, 1980, & 1990.

Statistics Sweden, Population statistics, part 3 (Befolkningsstatistik del 3), 1995, & 2000.

Websites

Swedish Migration Board. Available: http://www.migrationsverket.se/pdffiler/statistik/ (2008–10–13).

Sweden Statistics, Population statistics. Available: http://www.scb.se (2008–10–13).

20

Thailand

Immigration to Thailand: The Case of Migrant Workers from Myanmar, Laos, and Cambodia

Supang Chantavanich and Ratchada Jayagupta

Since 1990, Thailand has experienced two major types of immigration into its territory: one being immigrant workers from neighboring countries; the other political refugees from Myanmar. Although these two groups were not the first migrants to enter Thailand, their characteristics and the root causes of their movements are quite distinct, thereby making them good cases for both academic and policy analysis in order to understand movements of international migration in a globalized world, and specifically in the region of Southeast Asia, and the national context of Thailand.

Historically, Thailand witnessed the massive arrival of overseas Chinese immigrants from Southern China who migrated to Thailand because of natural disasters like famine, drought, and floods as well as economic deprivation and ideological differences in the nineteenth and twentieth centuries (Chantavanich, 1997, p. 232–259; Chantavanich and Rabe, 1990, p. 66–67). The Chinese immigrants settled and assimilated into the Thai society. Currently, the third generation of the Chinese immigrants becomes Thai citizens and they are politically and socially well integrated, they only keep some Chinese cultural practices to identify their Chinese Thai identity. Thailand also received

millions of political refugees from Laos, Cambodia, and Vietnam in the decades 1970–1980. However, in contrast to the Chinese immigrants, the politically displaced persons from the Indochinese states were either resettled in third countries like the United States, Canada, France, and Australia or repatriated to their country of origin.

Major Immigration Movements into Thailand since 1990

During the decade 1980–1990, Thailand became one of the fastest growing economies in Southeast Asia. Its economy was transformed from agricultural oriented to industrial and services based. Consequently, Thailand adopted an export-led economic policy in the mid–1980s, and reached 10% a year economic growth, resulting in the employment of many female rural-urban and foreign migrants in manufacturing industries, especially in clothing and textiles businesses (Archavanitkul, 1998, p. 12). In addition, male migrants were hired in fisheries, construction, and agricultural work (Asian Research Center for migration 2000, p. 16).

The Asian financial crisis of 1997 was expected to increase unemployment among Thais, as well as encourage unemployed Thais to replace migrant workers. As a result, some immigrant workers left Thailand during 1997 to 1998 (the Ministry of Labour and Social Welfare [MOLSW], currently called the Ministry of Labour [MOL]). MOL indicated that a number of migrant workers fell from almost a million in 1998 to 664,000 in 1999. Later, the estimated number of migrant workers rebounded, as seen in September 2001, when the MOL estimated there were 816,000 unskilled migrant workers in Thailand (Ministry of Labour, 2004).

Immigrant Workers in Thailand

The rapid two-digit economic growth in Thailand at the end of the 1980s changed the status of Thailand from a sending country of migrant laborers into a receiving country of migrant workers from neighboring countries. The labor shortage was caused by better job opportunities for local young people and the national education policy to expand the number of years for basic education to nine years. Moreover, there were certain kinds of employment that were shunned by local workers. As a result, some workers from outside the country started to work in border areas. The first to employ migrant workers were the fishery and fishing-related industries (seafood processing, frozen seafood, dry seafood, etc). Some agricultural producers also required seasonal workers to help in the harvesting or cutting of rice, sugar cane, and rubber at certain periods of the year. Migrant workers from Myanmar, Cambodia, and Laos started to come to Thailand to work in the 3D jobs, i.e., dirty, dangerous, and difficult, in the early 1990s (Chantavanich, 2003b, p. 16).

From the beginning of 1990s, the number of migrant workers increased steadily and the government started to be aware of the immigration situation. In 1992, the government announced the first policy to allow migrant workers to be employed only in four border provinces, namely Chiang Rai, Tak, Kanchanaburi, and Ranong, which are all Myanmar border provinces (See Figure 20-1). In 1996, recognizing the rapid increase of workers, the government announced the second policy, offering amnesty to workers who come for registration. There were approx-

imately 300,000 migrant workers who came to register in 7 kinds of jobs in 43 provinces in Thailand. This number of registered workers was estimated as 50% of the overall number of migrant workers at the time. Of the total registered number, 87% were Burmese, 9% were Cambodian, and only 4% were Lao (Chintayananda et al., 1997). In 1998, the third policy to allow workers to be employed in 47 kinds of jobs in 54 provinces was announced. But this time, only around 100,000 workers showed up. Many employers thought that they could employ migrant workers without proper registration as long as they could bribe officials in charge of registering and monitoring the employment (Chantavanich et al., 1999; Chantavanich, 2003b).

A short-term policy for migrant workers was the 1999–2000 decision to allow 106,684 workers to be employed in 18 jobs in 34 provinces. The 18 jobs were mainly fishery and agricultural work, plus construction and other manual labor work (Chantavanich et al., 2000b; Chantavanich, 2003b). It is estimated that there were one million migrant workers in Thailand, employed in all provinces at the time. The Immigration Bureau had repatriated 200,000 persons in 1999 but many of them reentered the borders. Due to the lack of a clear policy and poor legal enforcement, the control of migrant worker numbers failed. Some officials were involved in smuggling those workers. Thus the government founded a new agency to be responsible for policy development, administration ,and coordination of labor migration in 2000 as recommended by consulted academics (Chantavanich et al., 2000b, Chantavanich, 2003b). As of 2003, the number of migrant workers who came for registration was 288,780. The most recent policy was the registration in 2006. There were 460,014 migrant workers who were granted work permits. Distribution by sector of employment is shown in Table 20-1.

The prevalence of migrant workers in Thailand was not only an economic issue. It also raised social, legal, cultural, political, and security concerns to the Thai society. Socially, the number of migrant children born in Thailand had increased, resulting in the needs for legal status, education, and health care

Thailand - Burma/Myanmar Border Area

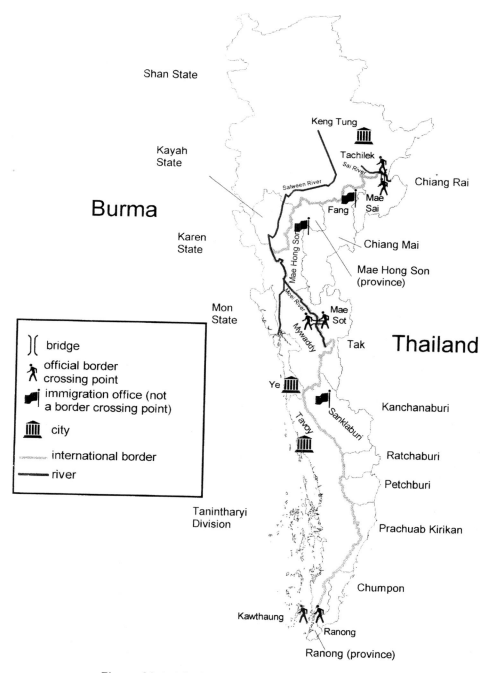

Figure 20-1. Thailand-Burma/Myanmar Border Area.
Source: Stern and Crissman, ARCM., 1998, p. 28.

Table 20-1. Summary of Migrant Workers' Work Permit Extension Approved by Cabinet Resolution of 2006

Sector of Employment	Registration for Work permit				
	Employer	Total	Myanmar	Laos	Cambodia
Total	**138,736**	**460,014**	**405,379**	**29,683**	**24,952**
1. Fishery	3,129	14,514	10,592	661	3,261
1.1 Sea fishery	2,130	11,543	8,384	394	2,765
1.2 Inland fishery	999	2,971	2,208	267	496
2. Fishery related	2,645	49,771	48,393	259	1,119
3. Agriculture and Livestock	30,035	94,708	83,896	5,580	5,232
3.1 Agriculture	26,672	82,628	73,712	4,653	4,263
3.2 Livestock	3,363	12,080	10,184	927	969
4. Rice mill	687	4,206	4,040	88	78
5. Brick factory	628	2,948	2,781	131	36
6. Ice factory	676	3,253	2,903	159	191
7. Marine transportation	203	1,715	1,042	93	580
8. Construction	11,054	71,423	64,020	2,542	4,861
9. Mining	163	864	847	2	15
10. Household servant	53,223	66,863	55,297	9,254	2,312
11. Others (including manufacturing)	36,293	149,749	131,568	10,924	7,267

Source: Office of Foreign Workers Administration, Department of Employment, Ministry of Labor.

services for them. Since Thailand had ratified the Convention on the Rights of the Child (CRC) and had lifted its reservation on education services for all children born and living in Thailand, the government had to assure that it was offering the services properly. There were also intermarriages between migrants and local Thais, resulting in problems of legal status and nationality of children born from such intermarriage and those born in Thailand from migrant parents. Politically, the push back of a huge number of migrants was done without consultation with the governments of major countries of origin. Diplomatic negotiation on the repatriation was not successful, even causing a sour relationship between two countries. The Cambodian government was more cooperative in receiving their nationals back. The negative response from other sending countries could be explained by the fact that many workers are of ethnic minorities who opposed the government. As for those who were citizens, they had left their country illegally. Therefore, the government was not ready to process an orderly repatriation for them.

Health and the reemergence of communicable diseases were another major concern with regard to migrant workers. Some diseases that had been almost eradicated from Thailand, like

polio, meningitis, and filariasis reemerged with transborder movement of migrants. Some other diseases like malaria, HIV/AIDS, anthrax, and TB became more difficult to control because of the mobile nature of the infected migrant workers and the high vulnerability of migrant people (Chantavanich et al., 2000a, Chantavanich et al., 2000b, Chantavanich, 2003b). The Thai Ministry of Public Health has recently adopted a unique policy on the prevention of communicable diseases and provision of health care services to migrant people, including child immunization, family planning, primary health care, and the establishment of a database on migrant population for heath care services and control. It also sought cooperation from health authorities in countries of origin of migrants, in which some memoranda of understanding were signed and some joint border committees were established.

The remarkably high number of migrant workers (circa 2 million) and their involvement in some criminal activities were security concerns for the Thai government. Since the control of migrants was hardly possible due to the lack of adequate personal data on each worker, security concerns were of top priority for the Thai police. There were no workable solutions to this concern for the time being.

Demographic Information Regarding Burmese, Lao, and Cambodian Migrant Workers

Primary Sending Countries

Cambodia, Laos, and Myanmar are countries in the Greater Mekong Subregion (GMS) in Southeast Asia. They are new members of the Association of Southeast Asian Nations (ASEAN) and are economically developing countries. Table 20-2 illustrates the economic status of these countries in the year 2003. Cambodia, with a 13.36 million population, has US$ 1555.83 GDP per capita, US$ 260 GNP per capita, and the poorest 20% earn only 6.9% of all income. The unemployment rate in Cambodia was 2.5% in 2003. For Laos, with only a population of 6 million and US$ 320 GNP per capita, the unemployment rate was as high as 5.7%. Myanmar had the highest population (42.7 million) with a 5.1% unemployment rate. With Thailand's economy growing at a two-digit rate before 2000, the three sending countries were struggling with their less advanced economic growth. As a result, tens of thousands of migrants emigrated from Laos, Cambodia, and Myanmar into Thailand.

Fleisher (1963) indicated that differentials in unemployment and wages were significant in determining the volume of migration between Puerto Rico and United States. As Puerto Rican unemployment increased, the volume of out-migration rose significantly. This was also the case of Thailand as related to Cambodia, Laos, and Myanmar, as can be seen in Table 20-2. Unemployment rates in the three countries of origin were higher than in Thailand during

1997–2003. Migration is also related to the Gross National Product (GNP) of the sending and receiving country: immigration is positively related to GNP of the receiving country and emigration is negatively related to GNP of the sending country. This was confirmed in the case of Thailand as receiving country since Thailand's GNP per capita was as high as US$ 2160 in 2003, nine times higher than Cambodia and seven times higher than Laos.

Size of the Immigrant Population and Its Status

With reference to the Ministry of Labour (MOL) estimation in year 2004, immigrant population in Thailand was 2,204,795. The number could be divided into six groups, namely, overstay immigrants, skilled migrant workers with work permit (professional), unskilled workers with work permit, undocumented migrant workers, asylum-seekers from conflict situations along border areas, and aliens who are in the process of applying for Thai citizenship. The distribution of each group is shown in Figure 20-2.

Demographic Profile

The majority of migrant workers in Thailand are from Myanmar, followed by Laos and Cambodia. Gender proportion was female:male 1:4 in the 1990s. Both single and married workers migrated to Thailand, bringing along with them their dependents. Most migrants were Buddhists. As for those from Myanmar, a sizable number were from ethnic Karen, Mon, and

Table 20–2. GNP, GDP, Minimum Wage, Income of the Poorest, Unemployment Rate, and Population of Cambodia, Loas, Myanmar, and Thailand (2003)

Country	GNP (per capita) (US$)	GDP (per capita) (US$)	Minimum Wage (per month) (US$)	Income Distribution (Poorest 20%) (%)	Unemployment Rate (%)	Population
Cambodia	260	1555.83	40	6.9	2.5	13,363,421
Loas	320	1756.29	41.7	7.6	5.7	6,068,117
Myanmar	N/A	1733.45	30	NA	5.1	42,720,196
Thailand	2,160	6936.87	126.6	6.4	2.2	64,265,276

Sources: www.nationmaster.com, www.worldbank.org, www.boi.go.th, www.Phiengch.free.fr, www.aworldconnected.org.

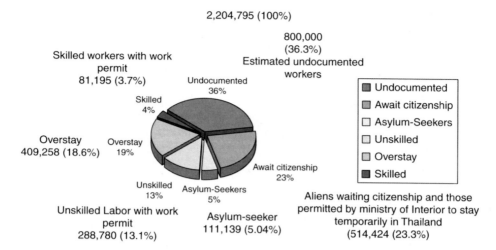

Figure 20-2. Immigrant Population in Thailand.

Shan. As for Laos and Cambodia, most of them were Lao and Khmer ethnicity respectively.

Human Capital

Most immigrant workers from Cambodia, Laos, and Myanmar have only primary education. As for Myanmar, a survey conducted by Asian Research Center for Migration in 2000 and 2003 indicated that 43.5% of workers received 5–8 years of education, 23.2% received between 1–4 years while 26% received more than 9 years and 7.4% have no education. (Chantavanich et al., 2003, p. 55) For Lao migrant workers, a survey result in 2003 showed that 70% of them graduated from primary school (Chantavanich and Prachason, 2004, p. 4). Cambodian migrants had the same educational profile. Overall migrant workers had low or no education. This confirmed Piore and Doeringer's finding (as cited in Hodson and Kaufman, 1981) that migrant workers with low or no education were recruited into secondary sector jobs rejected by natives. They also made lower returns to human capital in the secondary sector (Massey et al., 1994, pp. 715–716).

Apart from educational level, we can examine the human capital of these workers through their skills. Since most workers were from agriculture backgrounds, their skills were mainly

in farming, which became less useful when they entered the manufacturing or service sector.

Reasons for Leaving the Home Country and Process of Immigration

Migrant Workers from Myanmar

Unskilled migrant workers in Thailand left their home country because of economic rather than political reasons. The Burmese migrant workers had been forced by unemployment, low wages, family's poverty, lack of sufficient jobs, and lack of relevant qualification for available jobs. The problem of lacking sufficient job qualification played a significant role in motivating those migrants seeking unskilled jobs in Thailand. There were also some political and cultural reasons for their departure. Some escaped from forced labor in Myanmar. Others were influenced by consumerism values as earlier migrant workers who returned from Thailand brought back luxurious goods with them. A small number of migrants wanted to escape from family problems in Myanmar (Chantavanich and Prachason, 2004). In addition to the aforementioned factors pushing those migrants to seek employment in Thailand, family problems such as starvation, debt bondage, lack of land ownership, and forced labor also played important roles for these migrants to enter Thailand.

Research done in collaboration between the Asian Research Center for Migration and World Vision (Thailand) (Chantavanich et al., 2003), indicated that those Burmese migrants who entered Thailand at Mae-Sai district, Chiang Rai Province, tended to seek unskilled jobs in Thailand with the hope of improving their earnings and standard of living.

Most of the migrants entering Thailand through Mae-Sai area were passing the legal process either by car or bus with their families or friends. The majority of them were Burmese farmers and were informed about job opportunities in Thailand by their friends and relatives, with only a few migrants using the brokerage service for seeking jobs in Thailand. They worked in Thailand as factory laborers, domestic workers, entertainers, carpenters, fishermen, and sellers of goods.

Migrant Workers from Lao PDR

The Lao People's Democratic Republic shares a border with Thailand that stretches more than one thousand kilometers; the Mekong River functions as a natural divider for these two countries. It is connected with Thai border areas in many provinces, namely Chiang Rai, Nan, Nongkai, Nakorn Phanom, Mukdahan, and Ubon Ratchathani (See Figure 20-3). According to the registration of migrant workers over the past three years, the number of Lao workers ranked second. They tended to work in the bordering provinces with Laos. The main reason to seek jobs in Thailand is to earn more income.

According to the Asian Research Center for Migration (2004a), the details of the Lao immigration process were as follows:

Those Lao workers who entered Thailand through Chiang Rai were from Bokeo province.

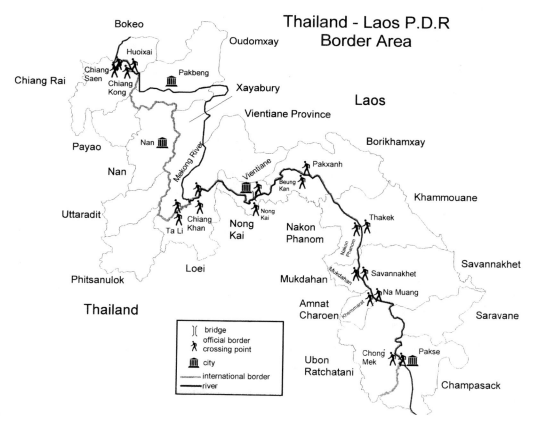

Figure 20-3. Thailand-Laos P.D.R. Border Area.
Source: Stern and Crissman, ARCM, 1998, p. 6.

Those who entered through Nan were from Xaignabouri province. Some entered Thailand legally with border passes by land, while some entered illegally by boat. Once they reached Thailand they spread out to work in the nearby provinces, where they tended to work as laborers, agricultural workers, service workers, and sex workers.

Lao workers came from Vientianne Municipality, and Borikhamxai province, entering Thailand at Nongkai. They would work in Nongkai for 1–2 years, then move and continue to work in a nearby city or even in Bangkok. Major reasons for Lao migrants to immigrate to Thailand were also economic. They came to look for jobs that offered higher wages, mainly in agriculture and service works, as most of them were employed in such jobs. Those who were persuaded by agents would move to Bangkok or other more distant big cities.

Migrants who entered Thailand legally would cross the Mekong River by car at a permanent immigration checkpoint at Thai-Lao Friendship Bridge in Nongkai, while illegal migrants tended to cross the river by boat. Sometimes those who passed the checkpoint gave false information to immigration offices or overstayed the border pass limitation, or went out of the allowed area. They held positions as agricultural workers, laborers, and factory workers.

Migrant Workers from Cambodia

Most Cambodian migrant workers found in Thailand were children, some of them came to Thailand with friends or relatives who had already settled here. There were various reasons for entering Thailand: some for political reasons, and some for economic reasons. The Thai-Cambodia Border was the focus of many years of war and civil unrest and was laden with thousands of landmines (Chantavanich, 2000). This unrest was a push factor for many migrants. Others expected Thailand to be a more civilized, more modernized country, as influenced by mass media reports (See Figure 20-4). The two major border crossings between Cambodia and Thailand are at Poipet-Aranyaprathet and Kohkong-Klongyai. The Poipet-Aranyaprathet area is the main crossing point where thousands of Cambodians cross the border every day. At the same time, several hundred Thais cross into Cambodia to work in the casinos at the border. And, in spite of the deterioration of the roads from Poipet to the rest of the country, trade and business remain brisk. Thousands of people have been involved in transportation, day laboring, portering, trading, services, and the entertainment business. From Poipet in Cambodia to Aranyaprathet in Thailand alone, there were 2,500 to 5,000 daily commuters who crossed over for nonagricultural work, while another 500–1,000 took up temporary jobs in agriculture (Chantavanich et al., 1999; Chantavanich, 2000).

Koh Kong-Khlong Yai was the other important border crossing accessible by both sea and land. Fishing and logging were the two main economic activities, although the latter has slowed down in recent years due to bans on cross-border logging. Many migrant fishermen from all over the country converged here either to work in Koh Kong, or to work in Thailand. There was a casino here, and, like Poipet, it was known for its sex industry, frequented by Cambodians and Thais from across the border (Angsuthanasombat et al., 2003).

Around 2,360 migrant workers in the Klong Yai district of Trad Province work in fisheries in Trad and Chantaburi, and thousands of others work in agriculture and day laboring, including commuters in Sra keaw, Trad, and Chantaburi. (Chantavanich, 2000).

Cambodian Children in Thailand

Seventy percent of Cambodian children arrested in Thailand came from Poipet, which is located in the northwest of the country, at the main border crossing between Cambodia and Thailand. Cambodians had been coming to Poipet from all over the country, with the hope of making a living from cross-border trade, either through self-employment in small business, as day laborers, or in the hope of getting a job in nearby Thailand. Many were former refugees or internally displaced people who were victims of the 1979 to 1990 armed conflicts, whose reintegration failed. Many children were poor, unskilled, and landless, did not attend school, and worked as day laborers carrying heavy loads of goods across the border.

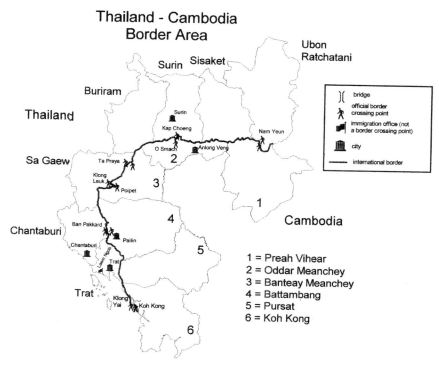

Figure 20-4. Thailand-Cambodia Border Area.
Source: Stern and Crissman, ARCM, 1998, p. 16.

Some children lived in the streets and had become addicted to glue sniffing or metamphetamine. While many women and children headed to Bangkok or Pattaya, or begged on the street, or sold flowers and candies in bars at night, young men often worked in construction, on plantations, or on deep-sea fishing boats.

To conclude, those Cambodian children had entered Thailand beginning in 1992. The main reason for migration was the unbalanced development between the urban and rural areas, and unallocated resources, which caused poverty. They tended to work mainly in agricultural and service sectors while they were in Cambodia. Once they reached Thailand, they were in the market and service sectors, employed as goods carriers, umbrella carriers, clothes sellers, and sex workers. Some were employed in fisheries and agricultural work. The vulnerability to human trafficking was also a concern for those children who were forced to work by their parents.

Readiness of Thailand to Accept Immigrants

Immigration Policies

To administer immigrants who come to Thailand, the Thai state has used two main laws as guidelines. One was the Immigration Act of 1979; the other was the Foreign Employment Act of 1978. Under the Foreign Employment Act, some occupations were preserved exclusively for Thai citizens. Any foreigners in the reserved jobs are in violation of the Foreign Employment Act, and also the Immigration Act because their entry for work was illegal as soon as they crossed the border and looked for a job in a prohibited category.

From the 1970s onward, some factories started to hire a few migrant workers, although, it was only in 1992 that the Thai government addressed the issue for the first time. This was due to recognition of an increasing gap between demand and supply of labor. Economic prosperity had boosted demand for workers in many economic sectors. In addition, the decreasing international comparative advantage in labor-intensive products required businesses to initiate cost-cutting. However, due to a higher education and a decline in birth rate of the Thai population, fewer Thai workers entered the unskilled labor market. As the economy developed, many Thai people became reluctant to do some occupations such as agriculture, fishing and fish-related, domestic work, and 3D work (dirty, dangerous and difficult). We can divide the immigration policy into four periods as explained below.

The First Period: Area-Based, Non-Quota System (1992–1998)

In 1992, some business groups put pressure on the government to relax the legislation prohibiting unskilled migrant workers because there was a labor shortage in Thailand. In order to solve the immediate problem, the government used a loophole in the legislation announcing the first registration through a cabinet resolution. The registration was to allow registered migrant workers to work for a period of time before they were deported back to their countries. It was limited to Burmese workers in four border provinces. Later, the areas were expanded to nine provinces. Thai employers would pay for bail out and work-permit fees. Eventually, only 704 Burmese workers were registered.

After 1992, the government made efforts to set a framework for the prospective policy by assigning the Ministry of Interior and the National Security Council (NSC) to be the two key policy makers for the country's development and security. Later came an agreement on the principle of migrant worker employment on necessity basis and an impact assessment from hiring migrant workers. The business groups requested the government to address an imbalance in the economy. They claimed that one million migrant workers were needed to fill the gap (Business Day 1995, cited in Chalamwong and Sevilla, 1996) and their wage could be reduced by 35–40% in border provinces if allowed (Nopporn, 1995, cited in Chalamwong and Sevilla, 1996). In 1996, therefore, another registration was announced via a cabinet resolution.

As the policy was not yet clear, this registration like the previous one was designed to systemize and control illegal workers. It was expanded to cover Lao and Cambodian citizens, in addition to Burmese workers, in labor work and domestic helpers in 43 provinces for 2 years. Of 323,123 migrant workers coming for the registration, 239,652 were eligible to get work permits. The surplus of workers and those found not registered would be deported.

In 1997 a committee headed by the NSC was set up and the policy makers reached an agreement to establish a central organization to supervise the migrant worker policy at the national level. The financial crisis in 1997 hit Thailand's economy severely and led to an unemployment rate of 4.37% in 1998 compared with 1.15% before the crisis (http://unpan1.un.org/intradoc/groups/public/Documents/APCITY/UNPAN001686.pdf, cited in Chantavanich and Prachason, 2004). Trying to open up more jobs on the labor market for Thai citizens, the government pushed 300,000 migrant workers back to their countries but the Ministry of Labour (MOL) could provide too few Thai workers to replace the deportees. As a result, a cabinet resolution launched another registration of migrant workers in 1998 for migrant workers in labor jobs in 54 provinces. Work permits were issued to 90, 911 workers out of 230, 617.

The Second Period: Area- and Quota-Based System (1999–2000)

Prior to 1999, a number of academics started to realize the shortcomings of the registration program, which was considered no more than a yearly relaxation of the immigration law. They argued that to formulate a better policy, concepts of management and protection must be in place (Archavanitkul, cited in Chantavanich and Prachason, 2004). Moreover, principles of migrants' well-being, social equity between Thai and migrant workers, and social inclusion of all concerned parties should be fundamental to the policy process (Asian Research Center for Migration, 2000). Unfortunately, the practice did not come easily. During 1999–2000, another two registrations for illegal workers were launched for those who were Burmese, Lao, and Cambodian, with the difference that a quota was imposed to limit numbers of the registered.

There were many policy discussions over the estimated needed number of workers, resulting in the government's following a recommendation from academics who suggested 106,684 people for registration; 99,974 out of 355,050 migrant applicants in 1999 and 99,656 out of 117,379 in 2000 successfully received their work permits. In the meantime, the NSC reinforced the idea of setting up a national organization to bundle the matter. Moreover, there was a discussion on actual need of migrant workers and how to replace migrant workers by Thai workers, disease prevention and control, public awareness toward the problem of illegal workers, effective immigration control, and people's attitudes toward living with the migrants (Buraphat, 2001, cited in Chantavanich and Prachason, 2004).

The Third Period: Short-Lived Expansionist Policy (2001–2003)

It was clear that the past policy was mainly built around an approach of registration, accompanied by border control and deportation. Such policy had proved unsuccessful in reducing the number of illegal migrant workers and bringing these people into the registration system. Realizing the limitation of the policy, the NSC urgently suggested abolishing the registration program and its yearly relaxation of the law and legalization of migrant workers. Nevertheless, in 2001 the new government took a reverse step toward fully opening the registration for migrant workers in all occupations, whether they had employers or were self-employed, throughout the country without imposing any quotas. The assumption was that this approach would bring all illegal and undocumented migrant workers to light, so that the government had an accurate number for future policy input. The highest number ever registered, 568,000 led some people to conclude the success of the registration. But for others such as academics, the registration has widened the scale of the problem into all areas and deepened the level of migrant dependency in many sectors. In late 2002, another renewal of registration was announced and the number had dropped from 568,000 to 409,339. In the meantime, the government started to negotiate with the Lao government, seeking cooperation in legalizing Lao workers.

The Fourth Period: The Implication of Pagan Declaration and Transitional Period (2003–2006)

In 2003, Thailand successfully signed a Memorandum of Understanding regarding migrant worker legalization with the other three sending countries of the migrants: Cambodia, Laos, and Myanmar. The Memorandum of Understanding with Laos, Cambodia, and Myanmar focuses on the government-to-government recruitment of migrant workers for specific periods of employment in Thailand, including conditions to motivate the workers to return home after the completion of employment, labor protection and dispute settlement, and measures against illegal employment. In November 2003, all the four governments had a conference on Economic Cooperation Strategy, and as a result of the conference the Pagan Declaration was signed. It stated the importance of partnership among the four countries to enhance economic growth, facilitate production, create employment and reduce income gaps, and advocate sustainable peace, stability and wealth in all the four countries (Ministry of Foreign Affairs, 2003). Although this was very much a trade and investment oriented approach, there was an implication of tackling some root causes of migration, poverty, and economic disparity.

The government's efforts at the international level were praised by many concerned parties. Nevertheless, as the process took time and the issues got more complicated as time passed, the practice had not yet been implemented. With the presence of millions of illegal migrant workers already in the country, the government was more likely to give priority to these workers than to recruiting new ones. But it needed the counterpart countries to guarantee their people's citizenship as most of them were without any identification. Certainly, this condition would not make an easy task especially in the case of Myanmar, where ethnic conflict was ongoing. At the same time, the number of those renewing their third registration in 2003 declined to 288,780 migrant workers; this worried the government, as it implied that a larger migrant population remained unidentified by the authority. In 2004 another registration was announced to bring as many migrant workers as possible to register with their employers and accommodators on home registrars before the government specified quotas for some specific industries that allowed migrant employment.

A comparison of the four period policies is presented in Table 20-3.

To conclude, Thailand began a registration process to identify unauthorized migrant workers in 1992. It gradually expanded the number of business sectors and provinces where employers could register migrants and employ them legally for one to two years. Reregistrations were

Table 20-3. Thai Cabinet Decisions on Registration of Migrant Workers: 1992–2001

Date	Where	Fees	Note
March 17, 1992	10 border provinces	5,000-Baht bond; 1,000-Baht fee	Burmese only; 706 migrants registered.
June 22, 1993	22 coastal provinces; fisheries		Not implemented in fisheries until 1939 law amended
June 25, 1996	39 (later 43) provinces; 7 (later 11) industries	1,000-Baht bond; 1,000-Baht fee 500-Baht health fee	Two-year permits for those who registered between September 1 and November 29, 1996–34 types of jobs open to migrants; 372,000 registered; and 303,988 permits granted
July 29, 1997 January 19, 1998	Step up border and interior enforcement; remove 300,000 migrants in 1997; another 300,000 in 1998		Provincial committees to deal with migrants; encourage factories in Thai border areas
April 28, 1998 May 8, 1998	Max 158,000, but 90,911 migrants registered; permit border commuters	1,000-Baht bond; 700-Baht medical exam fee; 500–1,200-Baht provincial health fee	54 provinces, 47 types of jobs; Extend permits expiring in August 1998 to August 1999
August 3, 1999 November 2, 1999	37 provinces; 18 sectors in 5 industries	1,000-Baht bond; 700-Baht medical exam fee,1,000-Baht health card	Maximum 106,000 permits good for one year, to expire August 31, 2000; 99, 974 migrants registered
August 29, 2000	37 provinces 18 sectors		Allowed 106,684 migrants in 18 sectors and 37 provinces to work until August 31, 2001
August 28, 2001	All industries and all jobs	3,250 Baht ($ 74) 1,200 Baht for six-month renewal	Six-month permits renewable for another six months until September–October 2002
September 24–October 25, 2002	All employers, provinces, and jobs	Same	568,000 migrants registered for six months; 409,339 reregistered in February–March 2002
November 2003–June 2006	–	–	288,780 migrants registered in 2003
April 2004–June 2005	All provinces, all jobs, employers also registered	3,800 Baht (1,800 Baht for one-year work permit, 1,300 for health insurance, 600 for medical exam, and 100 for registration fee)	1,284,920 migrants and dependents showed up; 838,943 went through complete registration for one year. In 2005 reregistration, the number dropped to 343,777 persons in June.

Source: Chantavanich, S., Vungsiriphisal, P., and Laodumrongchai, S., 2007, pp 46–47.

permitted in 1998, 1999, and 2000. In 2001, the cabinet resolution allowed migrants to register in all industries and all jobs with a requirement to reregister in 2002. In 2004 registration would allow Burmese, Lao, and Cambodian migrants to register with their employers for a one-year work permit.

Programs and Services Available to Immigrants

Thailand has depended on foreign workers for over a decade, which implies that some migrants have settled in Thailand with their families. Many of the migrants were young families with children. As a result, Thailand has had to deal with education for children born to and living with migrant parents, as well as health and other integration issues. (Martin, 2004).

Health Service. The expenditure on health care for migrants was divided into two parts: one was for health awareness and the other was for disease prevention. According to the migrants' health examination results, major illnesses for those who came for hospital services were malariaand diarrhea, as well as other diseases that had long ago been eradicated from Thailand, such as filariasis, meningitis, and TB If the Thai government ignored these diseases, it might cause epidemics in Thailand.

The second part of medical expenses was spent for child health care and family planning. Female migrants tended to face unexpected pregnancy, resulting in a sharp increase of newborn migrants, which also affected the number of immigrants in Thailand. Lack of family planning and efficient birth control could be seen among this population. Migrants used unclean and inefficient childbirth processes, which led to tetanus in infants. All children born in Thailand to migrant parents need to receive the same medical treatment as Thai children. The Thai Ministry of Public Health established an immunization program for migrant children. However, the program did not fully achieve its goal due to the mobility of the immigrant children, which made it difficult to deliver complete vaccinations. For women, unexpected pregnancy also led to unsafe abortion, which caused serious illness. Moreover, another health factor was male migrants had high risk from accidents, caused mainly by riding motorcycles.

Education. Children in the migrants' family could receive two forms of education: one was informal education provided in the migrants' community, the other was to join the formal Thai education system (Asian Research Center for Migration, 2000).

The Thai Ministry of Education issued a regulation in 1992 that allowed the children of registered migrants to attend Thai schools through the compulsory level (Amaraphibal and Worasaen, 2001). Many Burmese parents reportedly did not value education, and thus did not send their children to school. Others were deterred by the cost of school uniforms and materials. In some cases, migrant parents had organized Burmese schools designed for their children and contributed 100–150 Baht (equivalent to 2.5–4 dollars) a month to pay for teachers to educate their children up to the age of 9 years old. Ending school at this early age contributed to the reported tendency of many Burmese children to take up work (Martin, 2004). In 2005, the Ministry of Education adopted a new policy that all migrant and stateless children in Thailand could attend schools and be offered basic education. It also provided a budget of 2,000 Baht (70 dollars) per attending student to subsidize a child at school. As of 2003, there were 13,359 migrant children attending Thai schools.

Adjustment to the Host Country

Integration

In terms of migrant worker integration, Thailand as an old immigration country had no xenophobic attitude toward new migrants. For example, at Mae-sod, Tak province, Thai and Burmese had a long historical relationship before the construction of Moey River Bridge in the 1990s. Currently the relationship between migrants and Thai community at Mae-sod is still positive. The amount of migrants who were staying in Mae-sod were close to the number of Thai population in that area. In terms of the cultural context, those Thai families whose children were looked after by migrant workers may absorb different cultural aspects, and become more dependent on migrant workers (Chantavanich, 2003a.).

However, integration had an effect on the Thai community as to threats to security of their lives and properties, because the high number of migrant laborers in Mae-sod area, and the unemployment of migrant workers, caused high robbery rates in migrants' community as well as in Thai community. As a result, Thais started to feel afraid and unsafe. Many migrants did not speak Thai language, creating communication gaps with natives. Lao workers are the most integrated into Thailand due to language and cultural proximities between the two countries.

The insecure feeling of the Thai community toward living with migrants might be caused by the negative portrayal or stereotyping of migrants as exaggerated by the media. However, many Thais who had direct contact with migrants did not have negative feelings toward migrants, rather, some Thais were concerned about the migrants' status. If they did not register, they did not occupy legal status, causing difficulties in migrant management. NGOs and academics were also concerned about the migrants' vulnerability to exploitation and to their illegal status.

Immigrant Contribution to/Drain on the Country and Implications

Economic and Labor Market

In 2003, the ARCM interviewed policy makers in the 50 provinces about their perceptions of the need for migrants. They thought that in fisheries, agriculture, and rice milling migrant workers played significant roles in production. Those sectors needed to hire migrants because; (1) Thais did not want to fill these jobs, (2) It was a hard and dirty job, and (3) the wages of migrants were cheaper than those of Thais.

The increased number of immigrants could maintain the level of the country's competitiveness especially in the manufacturing sector, which had high demand for unskilled labor. The industrial processing that used Thai labor would also benefit.

The long-term effect on Thailand will be revealed in its public finance status. Looking at the expenditure side, the government might have more burdens for providing health, education, and legal protection services to those migrants. At present, this expenditure is hidden in the services expenditure provided to the Thais (Asian Research Center for Migration, 2000).

Health and Social Services

One significant burden caused by migrants in Thailand was the public health expense, which was relatively high in each year. Those migrants who registered for work permits were less burdensome to Thailand since they had legal status and health insurance cards. Those who were not registered had a significant effect, since they had no health insurance, lacked adequate health information, and also faced difficulties in getting health services In addition, Weerasuksawat (2002) indicated that the health service providers lacked proactive work strategies to solve health service problems such as lack of interpreters at hospitals and lack of protection and prevention strategies to alleviate the sickness of all migrants. During 2000–2003, the Thai Ministry of Public Health spent US$ 7.5 million each year for health care services to migrant workers and their dependents living in the country.

Education and Vocational Training

Children from migrant families were eligible for two types of education in Thailand. One was to attend informal classes organized by migrants themselves. Another was to join the formal classes in Thai schools. According to the Ministry of Education survey in year 2001, the number of children from migrant families who studied in Thai schools was 11,360 students. It was the Thai government policy that compulsory education (nine years) was free for all children, regardless of their nationality. The education budget was allocated throughout all schools in Thailand. If the number of migrant pupils increases without future efficient management, the high burden of education expense for migrant children would fall on the Thai government and society.

In the Thai parliament, the Chairman of the Standing Committee on Women, Youth, and Elderly Affairs noted that increasing numbers of children had no right to education due to the lack of Thai identification documents. This denial of education should no longer exist, because those regulations had been canceled in 1992. In addition, the National Security Council also agreed to provide education to stateless children. It was expected that as the children learn more about Thai culture and customs, they would become more integrated into society ("Birth Certificate and the Nation Security," 2004, p. 15).

Housing and Urban Issues

Migrants who stayed in border areas usually lived in Thai communities. They either rented rooms or stayed with employers. In Mae Sod, there was a Muslim migrant enclave in a downtown area. Some natives would refuse to walk through this area; a sense of social segregation could be felt there. In big cities and in the capital, Bangkok, there were many migrants' ethnic enclaves unknown to most people but known by neighbors. Although migrants lived together with natives, there was an atmosphere of social exclusion as in other countries (Castles and Miller, 2003).

The government tried to exercise control over the existence and mobility of migrants. Starting in year 2004, the management of hotels, guest houses, rented houses, apartments, mansions, and dormitories who sheltered immigrants were required to fill out the foreign travelers' information form provided by the Thai government, then to submit it to the immigration office within 24 hours in order to screen for wanted persons or transnational organized criminals. In the past, there had not been good coordination for such management; hence the immigration office requested that Thai people submit those details via e-mail within 24 hours. If someone failed to do so, he/she would pay a penalty between THB 1,600–20,000, which was equivalent to up to US$ 500 ("Illegal Employment," 2002, p. 2).

Additional Issues and Concerns for Thailand

The high influx of migrant workers into Thailand caused major concerns. After several attempts, the government decided to adopt the policy of signing a memorandum of understanding with countries of origin in collaboration for labor employment. The memorandum of understanding signed with Laos in 2002 in Vientiane concentrated on labor employment cooperation between Thailand and Lao PDR (Administrative Commission on Irregular Migrant Workers, 2002).

In 2003, Thailand successfully signed a memorandum of understanding (MOU) with the other two home countries of the migrants, Cambodia and Myanmar, in relation to migrant worker legalization. The memoranda with Laos, Cambodia, and Myanmar focused on the government-to-government recruitment of migrant workers for a specific period of employment in Thailand, incentives which motivated the workers after the completion of employment to return home, labor protection and dispute settlement, and measures against illegal employment. In November 2003, all the four governments had a conference on Economic Cooperation Strategy. As a result of the conference the Pagan Declaration was launched. The declaration stated the importance of partnership among the four countries to enhance economic growth, facilitate production, create employment, and reduce income gaps, and advocate sustainable peace, stability, and wealth in all the four countries. Although this was very much trade and investment oriented, there was an implication in tackling some root causes of migration, poverty, and economic disparity (Chantavanich and Prachason, 2004).

By the end of 2006, Thailand had implemented a new policy on proof of nationality for formal recruitment of migrant workers. This implementation was according to the MOU on the Cooperation for the Employment of Workers. Migrant workers from Cambodia and Laos went through a process of nationality proof and received a temporary passport from their respective embassies and a work permit from the Thai MOL to work legally in Thailand. Concurrently, Thailand started to import migrant workers

Table 20-4. Number of Migrant Workers from Laos, Cambodia, and Myanmar Who Were Registered for Work Permits in 2005–2006

Migrant Workers	2005	2006
who renewed work permits	705,293	460,014
who applied for a new permit	Not Allowed	208,562
went through nationality proof	Not Started Yet	49,214
Formal Recruitment	Not Started Yet	7,205
Total	**705,293**	**724,995**

Note: The number covers only registered workers and does not include undocumented ones.

Sources:

1. Ministry of Labour, *Labour Situation 2006*, p. 23 (only in Thai) http://www. mol.go.th/labour_situation.html.

2. Ministry of Labour, *Labour Situation 2006*, p. 23 (only in Thai) http://www.mol.go.th/labour_situation.html.

from the two countries of origin through a formal recruitment, which was a cooperation between the ministries of labor of the three countries. As of 2006, there were 49,214 Lao and Cambodian workers who had nationality proof. A number of the 7,205 Lao and Cambodian formal workers were also recruited through the new channel (see Table 20-4).

The government's efforts were praised by many concerned parties. Nevertheless, as the process took time and the problem got more complicated as time passed, the practice had not yet been implemented. With 1.2 million migrant workers already in the country, the government was likely to give priority to existing workers. But it needed the counterpart countries to guarantee their people's citizenship, as most of them were without any identification. Also, as the existing number of immigrant workers might exceed the number required, the repatriation of surplus workers will also be a burden on the Thai government and might cause problems with the countries of origin.

Other concerns for immigrant workers in Thailand were the protection of workers' rights and their integration into the Thai society. Because employment registration usually allowed workers to be hired only for one year, there were periods that some migrants were not under a registration period and were vulnerable to rights abuses by employers and officials in charge of migrant labor regulation (Illegal Employment, p. 12; *Bangkok Post*, July 14, 2002). The last concern, about the lack of integration of migrant workers into the Thai society, will be discussed in the next section.

Conclusion

As Thailand will continue to hire immigrant workers to contribute to its economic development, the prevalence of those people in the country will continue to be an issue of concern. The government has been torn between the needs to accept workers for economic reasons and the concerns for national security for political reasons. This dilemma put workers into disadvantageous situations. Employers were allowed to employ workers in their production, but the government was not ready to provide workers with full protection. It was also reluctant to accept the existence of workers' families. For example, children born from migrant parents were given birth certificates in some places but not everywhere. Some officials were worried that those children with a birth certificate would use it as a stepping stone to apply for Thai nationality in the future. Although foreign children born in Thailand were entitled to Thai nationality, it was with the condition that their parents must have a legal status during their stay in the country. As most parents of these children violated Thai immigration law, their children would not be eligible for citizenship.

With an estimate of more than 40,000 stateless migrant children in the country (Archavanitkul, 1998) and the 1.2 million migrant workers living in Thailand, the country was not prepared to integrate them into its society, despite the fact that the world had become more or less borderless. Those people were marginalized in their access to major social welfare (Chantavanich S,

2003b.). Migrant workers became the new urban poor disadvantaged group; local people came to consider them undesirable. In the future, it may turn out that neither Thailand nor migrants can win from this partnership, unless Thailand obtains wisdom in the regulation and protection of these people.

References

Administrative Commission on Irregular Migrant Workers (ACIRW). (2002). *Statistical Data of Irregular Migrant Workers Registration under the Resolution of the Cabinet, 1996–2001.*

Amaraphibal, A., & Worrasaen, J. (2001). *Needs Assessment for Migrant Children in Thailand: A Case Study of Burmese Children in Ranong.* Bangkok: Chulalongkorn University Press.

Angsuthanasombat, K., Petchote, J., Vanna, N., & Sokunthea, V. (2003). *Rapid Assessment on Child Labour Employment the Border Area between Thailand and Cambodia: Srakaew, Chantaburi, and Trad Province.* United Nation Children's Fund.

Archavanitkul, K. (1998). *Undocumented Migration from Myanmar to Thailand and Its Impact on Thai Society.* Paper presented at the seminar Migrant Workers from Myanmar: Impacts on Thai Society and International Relations, March 12, 1998.

Asian Research Center for migration (2000). *An Analysis of Labour Shortage in Thailand in 2000.* Report Submitted to the Department of Employment, Ministry of Labour. Institute of Asian Studies, Chulalongkorn University.

Asian Research Center for Migration, Family Health International (Asian Regional Office) and National Committee for the Control of AIDS (NCCA), Lao Peole's Democratic Republic. (2004a). *Cross Border Migration between Thailand and Lao PDR: A Qualitative Assessment of Lao Migration and Its Contribution to HIV Vulnerability.* Asian Research Center for Migration, Institute of Asian Studies: Chulalongkorn University.

Asian Research Center for Migration and World Vision (Thailand) (2004b). *Response to Trafficking of Persons, Especially Women, Youth, and Children along the Thai-Burmese Border.* Asian Research Center for Migration, Institute of Asian Studies: Chulalongkorn University.

Birth Certificate and the National Security. (2004, June 17). *Matichon*, p. 15.

Caouette, T., Archavanitkul, K., & Pyne, H. (2000). *Sexuality, Reproductive Health, and Violence: Experiences of Migrants from Burma in Thailand.*

Nakhonprathom, Thailand: Institute for Population and Social Research: Mahidol University.

Castles, S., & Miller, M. (2003). *The Age of Migration: International Population Movements in the Modern World* (3rd ed.). New York: Guilford Press.

Chalamwong, Y., & Sevilla, R. C. (1996). Dilemmas of Rapid Growth: A Preliminary Evaluation of the Policy Implications of Illegal Migration in Thailand. *TDRI Quarterly Review, 11(2).*

Chantavanich, S. (1997). Siamese-Chinese to Chinese Thai: Political Conditions and Identity Shifts among the Chinese in Thailand. In *Ethnic Chinese as Southeast Asian*, L. Suryadinata (ed.). Institute of Southeast Asian Studies: National University of Singapore.

Chantavanich, S. (2000). *Mobility and HIV/AIDS in the Greater Mekong Subregion.* Asian Research Center for Migration, Institute of Asian Studies: Chulalongkorn University.

Chantavanich, S. (2003a). *Culture of Peace and Migration: Integrating Migration Education into Secondary School Social Science Curriculum in Thailand.* Asian Research Center for Migration, Institute of Asian Studies: Chulalongkorn University.

Chantavanich, S. (2003b). Human Security Issues on Migration. In Wan'gaeo, S. (Ed.), *Challenges to Human Security in a Borderless World* (p. 89–150). Bangkok, Thailand. Chantavanich, S., et al. (2007). *Mitigating Exploitative Situations of Migrant Workers in Thailand.* The Asian Research Center for Migration, Institute of Asian Studies: Chulalongkorn University.

Chantavanich, S., Beesey, A., Amaraphibal, A., Suwannachot, P., Wangsiripaisal, P., & Paul, S. (2000a). *Cross-Border Migration and HIV/AIDS Vulnerability at the Thai-Cambodia Border: Aranyaprathet and Khlong Yai.* Asian Research Center for Migration, Institute of Asian Studies: Chulalongkorn University.

Chantavanich, S., Beesey, A., Amaraphibal, A., Suwannachot, P., Wangsiripaisal, P., & Paul, S. (2000b). *Cross-Border Migration and HIV/AIDS Vulnerability at the Thai-Myanmar Border: Sangkhlaburi and Ranong.* Asian Research Center for Migration, Institute of Asian Studies: Chulalongkorn University.

Chantavanich, S., Nittayananta, S., Ratanaolan-Mix, P., Ruenkaew, P., & Khemkrut, A. (1999). *The Migration of Thai Women to Germany: Cause, Living Conditions and Impacts for Thailand and Germany.* Bangkok: Chulalongkorn University Press.

Chantavanich, S., & Prachason, S. (2004). *Migration without Borders: A Conflict between National*

Security and Human Security in Thai Migrant Worker Policy. Asian Research Center for Migration, Institute of Asian Studies: Chulalongkorn University.

Chantavanich, S., and Rabe, P. (1990). Thailand and the Indochinese Refugees: Fifteen Years of Compromise and Uncertainty. *Southeast Asian Journal of Social Science, 18(1),* 66–80.

Chintayananda, S., Risser, G., & Chantavanich, S. (1997). *Report on the Monitoring of the Registration of Immigrant Workers from Myanmar, Cambodia, and Laos in Thailand.* Asian Research Center for Migration, Institute of Asian Studies: Chulalongkorn University.

Chantavanich, S. with P. Vungsiriphisal and S. Laodumrongchai (2003). *Research Report on Migration and Deception of Migrant Workers in Thailand.* World Vision Foundation of Thailand and the Asian Research Center for Migration, Chulalongkorn University.

Chantavanich, S., Vungsiriphisal, P., and Laodumrongchai, S. (2007). *Thailand Policies towards Migrant Workers from Myanmar.* Asian Research Center for Migration, Institute of Asian Studies: Chulalongkorn University.

Fleisher, B. M. (1963). Some Economic Aspects of Puerto Rican Migration to the United States. *Review of Economics and Statistics, 45,* 301–312.

Hodson, R., and Kaufman, R. L. (1981, January). Circularity in the Dual Economy: A Comment on Tolbert, Horan, and Beck. *American Journal of Sociology, 86,* 881–887.

Huguet, J. W., & Punpuing, S. (2005). *International Migration in Thailand.* Bangkok: International Organization for Migration.

Illegal Employment. (2002, July 14). *Bangkok Post,* p. 2.

Immigration to Thailand. (2004, June 17). *Matichon,* p. 13.

Insitute of Population and Social Research and Thailand Development Research Institute (2003). *Final Report on Needs Assessment for the Employment of Immigrant Workers in Thailand 2003-2005.* Institute of Asian Studies: Chulalongkorn University.

International Organization for Migration (IOM) (2002). *Improving Migration Policy Management with special Focus on Irregular Labour Migration: Case Study of Fisheries and Fish Processing Industry in Samut Sakorn, Thailand.* Asian Research Center for Migration, Institute of Asian Studies: Chulalongkorn University.

Martin, P. (2004). *Thailand: Improving the Management of Foreign Workers.* Asian Research Center for Migration (ARCM), International Labour Organization (ILO), and International Organization for Migration (IOM).

Massey, D., Arango, J., Hugo, G., Kouaouci, A., Pellegrino, A., & Taylor, J. E. (1994). An Evaluation of International Migration Theory: The North American Case. *Population and Development Review, 20(4).*

Ministry of Foreign Affairs (2003). *Theme of Pagan Declaration: Economic Cooperation Strategy among 4 Countries.* Retrieved December 16, 2003, from http://www.mfa.go.th.

Ministry of Labour (2004). Annual Labour Statistics.

Ministry of Public Health (MOPH). (2003). http://www.moph.go.th.

Ministry of Interior (2003). *Report of the Seminar on Illegal Migrant Workers.*

Ministry of Labor and Social Welfare (MOLSW) (2000). *Yearbook of Employment Statistics.*

Muntarbhorn, Vitit. (2005). *The Mekong Challenge: Employment and Protection of Migrant Workers in Thailand; National Laws/Practices versus International Labour Standards?* Bangkok: International Programme on the Elimination of Child Labour.

Paul, S. R., Amaraphibal, A., & Chantavanich, S. (2002). *Cross-Border Transportation Infrastructure Development and HIV/AIDS Vulnerability at NongKhai-Vientiane Bridge.* Asian Research Center for Migration, Institute of Asian Studies: Chulalongkorn University.

Rabe, P. (1990). *Voluntary Repatriation the Case of Hmong in Ban Vinai.* Bangkok: Pim Suay Press.

Sontisakyothin, S. (2000). *Major Factors Affecting Policy Changes on Illegal Migrant Workers in Thailand.* Unpublished doctoral dissertation, National Institute of Development Administration.

Stern, A., and Crissman, L. W. (1998). *Maps of International Borders between Mainland Southeast Asian Countries and Background Information Concerning Population Movements at These Borders: Cambodia, China, Lao PDR, Malaysia, Myanmar, Thailand, and Vietnam.* Asian Research Center for Migration, Institute of Asian Studies: Chulalongkorn University.

Thailand Development Research Institute (TDRI). (2003). http://www.info.tdri.or.th.

Weerasuksawat, P. (2002). *Access to Healthcare Services among Migrant Workers in Thailand: Case Study of Samut Sakorn Province.* Paper presented at the meeting on the Research of Thailand about the Immigration in Globalization.

PART IV

Nations with Low or Declining Immigrant Populations

21

Egypt

Immigration to Egypt

Ayman Zohry

Historically, Egypt was a land of immigrants. Egypt has been an area of international migration (migration from the eastern and the northeastern Mediterranean countries to Egypt). In the past, foreigners were coming to Egypt while Egyptians rarely migrated abroad till the mid-1950s. The ancestors of the Egyptian people include many races and ethnic groups, including Africans, Arabs, Berbers, Greeks, Persians, Romans, and Turks. This paper surveys Egyptian immigration with emphasis on emigration to complete the picture. The study is migrant-focused, though some elements of Egyptian government policy are also included. Sections on migration to Egypt focus mainly on refugees, using as examples the largest populations from Palestine, Sudan, Ethiopia, and Somalia, because they form the majority of new migrants to Egypt. These sections are primarily concerned with the policies of the Egyptian government and the United Nations High Commissioner for Refugees (UNHCR), which decides refugee status in Egypt. To take a migrant-focused approach to immigrants—mainly refugees—who come from at least 30 different countries, would require political and economic analyses of their countries of origin, and this is beyond the scope of this study.

The dominant geographical feature of Egypt is the River Nile. The Nile represents the main source of water for agriculture, and consequently is a major determinant of the spatial distribution of population and economic life. Rapid population growth is one of the crucial problems that hinder development efforts in Egypt. While the doubling of Egypt's population between 1897 and 1947, from 9.7 million to 19 million, took fifty years, the next doubling took less than thirty years, from 1947 to 1976. Today, Egypt's population approaches 70 million. The annual population growth rate is around 2%. About 95% of the population is crowded into the 5% of the total land area that is formed by the narrow ribbon of dense population and agriculture that follows the course of the Nile. The remaining 95% of the land is desert. Although it can be seen as a kind of "natural response" to the geography of economic opportunity, migration to large cities has further imbalanced Egypt's population distribution.

Associated with rapid population growth is a high level of unemployment. Official estimates placed unemployment at about 8.4% in 2000/2001 down from 9.2% in 1991/1992. Independent estimates push the number to 14% (Zohry 2002). However, to control unemployment, Egypt will need to achieve a sustained real GDP growth rate of at least 6% per year. The economy has to generate between 600,000 and 800,000 new jobs each year in order to absorb new entrants onto the labor force. Between 1990 and 1997, however, only about 370,000 new jobs were created each year. The size of the informal sector and the level of overemployment in the public sector add to the complexity of the problem.

Egypt's International Migration (Emigration)

Historical Development

Different migration phases can be distinguished in the Egyptian migration evolution, determined and defined by changing international conditions, events, and labor market needs, particularly in the Arab region, and different economic factors and policy decisions at the national level. These phases overlap and the beginning and end points of each phase are not discrete. There are no standard phases in the Egyptian migration literature that are agreed on by all researchers (Zohry 2006), but one can identify the main phases as follows:

Phase 1: The early phase of migration (before 1974)
Phase 2: The expansion phase (1974–1984)
Phase 3: The contraction phase (1984–1987)
Phase 4: The deterioration phase (1988–1992)
Phase 5: The immigration phase (1992–current)

In the first phase, prior to 1974, the government of Egypt was motivated to bear the burden of providing job opportunities in the public sector. However, increasing population growth, along with the lack of growth in the economic and technological sectors, diminished the state's ability to provide jobs. The state authorized permanent and temporary migration in 1971 and lifted restrictions on labor migration in 1974. Large numbers of temporary migrants began to work in the Arab Gulf countries, where oil revenues had quadrupled in 1973 due to the oil embargo. Graduate students' permanent migration had commenced after the end of the war of 1967. Between 1970 and 1974, an estimated 300,000 people migrated, compared to a migrant stock of 70,000 in 1970.[1]

Due to the rise of Egyptian nationalism led by Nasser in the 1950s and the expansion of the slogan "Egypt for Egyptians," considerable number of Greeks, Italians, Maltese, and other Mediterranean basin nationals made up a large part of the emigration at that time. In addition, a considerable number of Egyptians who were affected by the nationalization of the economy and the spread of socialism participated in another migration stream from Egypt, mainly to the West.

The expansion phase started in 1974. The increased oil prices fueled ambitious development programs in the Arab oil-producing countries, in turn increasing demand for foreign labor. To resolve unemployment problems and use remittances to supply payment deficits and finance private projects, the government further eased migration procedures and created the Ministry of State for Emigration Affairs (1981), which sponsored Egyptian migrants and drew up an overall migration strategy[2]. The strategy is based on encouraging emigration and protecting migrants' rights in addition to linking Egyptians abroad to development efforts in Egypt by providing incentives for them to invest in Egypt. The number of Egyptian emigrants increased to about two million by 1980, with an increasing demand for teachers in Arab countries.

The contraction phase (1984–1987) began after the start of the Iran-Iraq War, which depressed oil revenues and temporarily pushed down the number of Egyptian emigrants to about 1.4 million (1985). In addition, Egyptian migrant labor had to face a number of new problems since the second half of the 1980s, such as the end of the Iran-Iraq War in 1988, falling oil prices, declining demand for construction workers in Arab countries, and the policy of replacing foreign with national labor in the Arab Gulf States. The Egyptian government promulgated the Emigration and Sponsoring Egyptians Abroad Law in 1983, while skilled migrants progressively replaced unskilled workers.

The following phase (1988–1992) was characterized by stagnation in the number of Egyptian emigrants, with a significant flow of return migrants from the Gulf area to Egypt and a considerable decline in the number of contracts granted to new emigrants.

The 1990 Gulf War in particular forced about one million Egyptian migrants in Iraq and Kuwait to return home. By 1992 however, the number of Egyptian migrants exceeded 2.2 million (Zohry 2003). In 2006, number of Egyptian migrants abroad, as estimated by the Egyptian Central Agency for Public Mobilization and Statistics, was about 3.9 million (CAPMAS 2008). The immigration phase (1992–current) witnessed massive migration flows to Egypt from neighboring African countries due to conflict and political instability in the Sudan and some other parts of sub-Saharan Africa.

Volume of Egyptian Emigration

"Egyptians have the reputation of preferring their own soil. Few ever leave except to study or travel; and they always return. . . . Egyptians do not emigrate" (Cleland 1936: 36, 52). This was the case until the middle of the twentieth century with few exceptions. Only small numbers of Egyptians, primarily professionals, had emigrated before 1974. Then, in 1974, the government lifted all restrictions on labur migration. The move came at a time when Arab Gulf states and Libya were implementing major development programs with funds generated by the quadrupling of oil revenues in 1973. The number of Egyptians working abroad in the Arab region around 1975 reached about 370,000 as part of about 655,000 total migrants (Brinks and Sinclair 1980). By 1980 more than one million Egyptians were working abroad. This number more than doubled by 1986 with an estimated 2.25 million Egyptians abroad (CAPMAS 1989). The emergence of foreign job opportunities alleviated some of the pressure on domestic employment. Many of these workers sent a significant portion of their earnings to their families in Egypt. As early as 1979, these remittances amounted to $2 billion, a sum equivalent to the country's combined earnings from cotton exports, Suez Canal transit fees, and tourism.

The foreign demand for Egyptian labor peaked in 1983, when an estimated 3.28 million Egyptians workers were employed abroad. After that year, political and economic developments in the Arab oil-producing countries caused a reduction in employment opportunities. The decline in oil prices during the Iran-Iraq War forced the Arab Gulf oil industry into a recession, which cost some Egyptians their jobs. Most of the expatriate workforce remained abroad but new labor migration from Egypt slowed considerably. But in the early 1990s, the number of Egyptian workers abroad still exceeded 2.2 million.

The majority of Egyptian labor migrants are expected to return home eventually, but thousands left their country each year with the intention of permanently resettling in various Arab countries, Europe, or North America. These emigrants tended to be highly educated professionals, mostly doctors, engineers, and teachers. Iraq was the Arab country most likely to accept skilled Egyptians as permanent residents. Iraq, which sought agricultural professionals trained in irrigation techniques, encouraged Egyptian farmers to move to the sparsely populated but fertile lands in the south. Outside of the Arab countries, the United States was a preferred destination.

Temporary Migration

"Egypt is now experiencing what is called *the permanence of temporary migration*" (Farrag 1999: 55). In the last three decades, flows of temporary migrants to neighboring Arab countries exceeded permanent migration to Europe and North America. Official secondment through governmental authorities on the basis of bilateral contracts is one of the main forms of temporary migration. Travel through official channels increased in the last two decades as an alternative form of migration. Working in branches of Egyptian companies, especially in the construction sector, was one of the channels of temporary migration.

According to the official estimates of the Central Agency for Public Mobilization and Statistics (CAPMAS), the total number of Egyptian temporary migrant laborers is about 1.9 million. Most of the demand for Egyptian labor comes from Saudi Arabia, Libya, Jordan, and Kuwait. Migrants to these countries comprise 87.6% of the total number of Egyptian migrant laborers. In the most recent years, and after the end of its civil war, Lebanon became a

Table 21-1. Temporary Egyptian Migration by Receiving Country (2000)

Receiving Country	Number of migrants	Percentage
Saudi Arabia	923,600	48.3
Libya	332,600	17.4
Jordan	226,850	11.9
Kuwait	190,550	10.0
UAE	95,000	5.0
Iraq	65,629	3.4
Qatar	25,000	1.3
Yemen	22,000	1.2
Oman	15,000	0.8
Lebanon	12,500	0.7
Bahrain	4,000	0.2
Total	**1,912,729**	**100**

Source: CAPMAS (2001).

Table 21-2. Estimated Number of Permanent Egyptian Migrants by Country of Destination (2000)

Country of Destination	Number in Thousands	Percent
USA	318	38.6
Canada	110	13.3
Italy	90	10.9
Australia	70	8.5
Greece	60	7.3
Holland	40	4.9
France	36	4.4
England	35	4.2
Germany	25	3.0
Switzerland	14	1.7
Austria	14	1.7
Spain	12	1.5
Total	**824**	**100**

Source: CAPMAS 2000—"The United Evaluation 2000".

new destination for unskilled Egyptian migrants who work mainly in construction (See Table 21-1).

Toward the end of the 1980s, Egyptians in Saudi Arabia and other Gulf countries comprised a much smaller proportion of the foreign workforce than in the late 1970s before major construction projects were completed. In the 1980s, Egyptian workers represented 40% of the total foreign labor in Saudi Arabia. A smaller workforce was in Bahrain, Kuwait, Oman, Qatar, and the UAE. The fluctuation of the number of migrant laborers to Iraq and Libya in the last three decades was affected by political tensions including the Iran-Iraq War, the Gulf War, and the political and economic sanctions on Libya.

Permanent Migration

From the beginning of the 1960s, political, economic, and social developments led some Egyptians to migrate permanently to America and European countries. According to the estimates of CAPMAS, the total number of permanent Egyptian migrants in non-Arab countries is slightly more than 0.8 million (824,000). About 80% of them are concentrated in five countries: United States (318,000 or 38.6%), Canada (110,000 or 13.3%), Italy (90,000), Australia (70,000), and Greece (60,000). The other 20% are mainly in Western Europe countries, such as Holland, France, England, Germany, Switzerland, Austria, and Spain (See Table 21-2).

The statistics given by CAPMAS are just estimates, which are drawn from the reports of Egyptian embassies abroad, records of cross-border flows from the Ministry of Interior, emigration permits from the Ministry of Manpower, and some other sources. The receiving countries make different estimates than CAPMAS. For example, the Italian government estimates there are around 35,000 Egyptians in Italy whereas CAPMAS gives a figure of 90,000. Estimates by CAPMAS may need to be revised whenever reliable data are available.

Migration to Egypt (Immigration)

Voluntary Migration

According to the latest Egyptian Census of 1996 (CAPMAS, 1999), the number of foreigners living in Egypt reached 250 thousand. They represented only about 0.3% of the total population of Egypt in the 2006 Census. In light of this information, one may think there is no reason to include a chapter on Egypt in this volume, however, the 2006 census underestimates foreigners. For example, independent estimates of the Sudanese population in Egypt range between 500 thousand and five million.

In recent years, Egypt has become a major immigration country. In 2005 the Ministry of Manpower and Emigration issued 17,456 work permits for foreigners to work in Egypt; 40% of

Table 21-3. Number of Work Permits Issued for Foreigners in Egypt by Type of Permit and Main Nationality Groups (2002)

Nationality Groups	Type of Permit			Percent
	First Time	Renewals	Total	
Arab Countries	1487	7395	8882	49.6
African Countries	57	91	148	0.8
Asian Countries	923	1574	2497	14.0
European Countries	1919	2795	4714	26.3
Americas and Australia	520	900	1420	7.9
Other Nationalities	99	137	236	1.3
Total	**5005**	**12,892**	**17,897**	**100**

Source: Ministry of Manpower and Emigration.

them come from Arab countries. This voluntary migration of usually highly skilled people is negligible compared to the forced migration of refugees and asylum seekers to Egypt, for which it is impossible to give precise numbers. "Guesstimates" vary from 500,000 to 5 million (Zohry 2007). The main refugee communities in Egypt are Sudanese, Palestinians, Somalis, Ethiopians, Eritreans, and some other African nationalities.

According to the Egyptian labor regulations, the number of non-Egyptian employees in any establishment must not exceed 10% of the total work force for unskilled or semiskilled workers. For skilled workers the limit of foreigner labor is 25%. The Egyptian labor market is regulated by the Labor Law No.137 for 1981. However, a new "Unified Labor Law" has been drafted and is currently under parliamentary discussions. The proposed law comprises 270 articles that address all the legal aspects regulating the Egyptian labor market. The new law aims at increasing the private sector involvement and at the same time achieving a balance between employees' and employers' rights.

Foreigners interested in employment in Egypt have to obtain work permits and follow the corresponding regulations issued by the Ministry of Manpower and Migration in this regard. After a work permit is obtained, the foreign national's visa (whether tourist or temporary) is converted into a work visa, with the same duration as the work permit.

Work permits are easier to obtain for technical staff than for unskilled or semiskilled workers. Work permits are usually granted to foreigners for a period of ten months, after which they are usually easily renewed.

Forced Migration (Refugees)

The term "refugee" as used in this study includes Palestinian refugees who began arriving from the mid-1930s, with mass arrivals in 1948, 1967, and 1990–1991 (El Abed 2003). It also includes those of other nationalities who have been determined to be refugees by the United Nations High Commissioner for Refugees (UNHCR). In Egypt, UNHCR determines refugee status, not the Egyptian government. Thousands of refugees denied recognition by UNHCR also continue to live in Egypt (Kagan 2002; 2003). Wars and massive human rights violations in Africa and the Middle East have been the main source of refugees. Of the thirty nationalities of refugees known in Egypt, Palestinians form the largest group, followed by people from Sudan, Somalia, Ethiopia, and Eritrea. Other nationalities come in smaller numbers, but groups of significant size come from Afghanistan, Liberia, Sierra Leone, Yemen, and Burundi. UNHCR also has responsibility for stateless people in Egypt (Zohry 2003).

Today, Egypt's capital Cairo "accommodates one of the five largest refugee populations living in urban areas" in the world (Ismail 2002). This assessment is based on the number of asylum-seekers received by UNHCR. It is impossible to give precise numbers of refugees in Egypt, and "guesstimates" vary from 500,000 to 5 million. Although all refugees in Egypt face similar hardships and most rank among the poorest of the poor, each community in Cairo has its different cultural and religious background that makes it unique.

Refugees in Egypt: Policies and Groups

Article 53 of the Egyptian Constitution guarantees asylum for political refugees. This article states that "Egypt is obliged to grant the right of political asylum to any foreigner who has been persecuted for his defense of the interests of people, or of human rights, peace or justice." The Office of the President is in charge of granting asylum to political refugees. However, little is known about the procedures for qualifying as a "political refugee" (No Author 2002). It seems mainly reserved for certain high-profile cases such as the Shah of Iran, Jaafar Nimeri of Sudan, or the wife of the last king of Libya. The Palestinian refugees are regulated by a separate office. When they apply for residence permits, their cases are treated separately by the interior ministry.

Article 151 of the Constitution states that international treaties ratified by Egypt have the force of law and in all cases supersede domestic law. In 1951, Egypt was, with Turkey, the only non-Western member of the drafting committee of the UN Convention on Refugees. UNHCR established its office in the country in 1954.

In 1980, Egypt ratified the Organization of African Unity Convention Governing the Specific Aspects of Refugee Problems and the 1951 UN Convention. In 1981, it ratified the 1967 Protocol. In 1984, it ratified the African Charter on Human and Peoples' Rights, which also provides for the right to seek and obtain asylum. The Arab Declaration in 1992 also urged Arab States to adopt a broad concept of "refugee" and "displaced person" as well as a minimum standard for their treatment, guided by the provisions of the United Nations instruments relating to human rights and refugees as well as relevant regional instruments, and to also guard against *refoulement* (Grindell 2003).

At the time of ratifying the 1951 Convention, Egypt entered reservations to the following articles, making them inapplicable in Egypt: Articles 12.1; 20; 23; and 24. These cover personal status,

unequal treatment of refugees compared to nationals if there is a rationing system in Egypt; and access to public relief, but the two articles having the greatest impact on refugee populations living in Egypt are Article 22 on free primary education and Article 24 on employment. For these reasons alone refugees in Egypt have no chance for "integration," one of UNHCR's three "durable solutions."

Egypt is a signatory of the 1989 UN Convention on the Rights of the Child, which stipulates that children have the right to free access to education and support for psychological recovery after war. Nevertheless primary and secondary education for most refugees is not allowed in Egyptian public schools. (Until 1978, Palestinians were an exception to this prohibition.) Refugees who want a university education must pay foreigners' fees in foreign currency.

With the restriction on the right to work, refugees are forced to rely on the informal sector and are thus easily exploited. However, a policy issue open to exploration is Article 17(1), (2), and (3) of the 1951 Convention, to which Egypt did not enter reservations. Article 1 states, "the Contracting States shall accord to refugees lawfully staying in their territory the most favorable treatment accorded to nationals of a foreign country in the same circumstances, as regards the right to engage in wage-earning employment.

Despite constitutional provisions concerning refugees, the maintenance of Egypt's reservations to the Convention, the lack of national laws on refugees, and the unwritten nonintegration policy of the Egyptian government have all contributed to the hardships of refugees in Egypt. The government has allowed UNHCR to assume the responsibility for refugee status determination. But when UNHCR functions as the decision maker (or judge) in the decision process, it cannot effectively fulfill its primary mandate of refugee protection. Moreover, there is no judicial review of the status determination procedures and no independent appeal process to which rejected refugees have recourse (Kagan 2002; 2003).

Since 1997 there have been 63,243 registered asylum-seekers, but only 18,537 have been recognized (of which 12,251 have been resettled). In the past six years over 32,000 claims have been rejected and their files closed by UNHCR. This latter group, who fear to return home, earn a meager living in the informal economy, and live under the constant threat of detention and deportation (Grindell 2003). The acceptance rate for asylum-seekers has varied widely, ranging from 24% in 1997, to 38% in 1998 and 1999, back down to 31% in 2000, up to 42% in 2001, down again to 27% in 2002.

Before November 2002, asylum seekers eighteen and older who sought refugee status from UNHCR were given a minute slip of paper that only showed the date of the interview and passport number. It was not stamped by UNHCR and offered no other information. The holder of such a paper is supposed to be regarded as "under the protection of UNHCR," but police and security do not recognize it. Since most asylum seekers must wait for more than a year for a decision on their case, they continue to be at serious risk of detention or deportation. Since November 2002, new asylum seekers are issued yellow cards. This new card, valid for six months and renewable three times, provides refugees with residency from the Ministry of Interior through the Ministry of Foreign Affairs. Those who are recognized as refugees by UNHCR are issued a blue card that allows them to reside in Egypt. Most recently, the stamp "work prohibited" has been removed from the residence permit, a significant positive step by the Government of Egypt.

UNHCR has a special relationship with Palestinian refugees. Article 1D of the 1951 Convention excludes any group of refugees who receive protection or assistance from another UN agency. This provision was intended to exclude most Palestinian refugees from UNHCR's mandate, because they had been assisted by UNRWA (see above) since 1948, and it was included at the behest of Arab governments. However UNRWA has never been allowed to operate in Egypt, so Palestinians in Egypt do fall under UNHCR's mandate. Arab countries continue to advocate the exclusion of Palestinians from the mandate of UNHCR and from the 1951 Convention. They are primarily concerned that Palestinians continue to receive special United Nations attention. The Arab governments fear that Palestinian refugees "would become submerged [with other categories of refugees] and would be relegated to a position of minor importance" (Takkenberg 1998:66). The fear is that Palestinian refugees would effectively forfeit their right to return if UNHCR's "durable solutions," which include resettlement and integration as well as repatriation, were offered to them. The Palestinian refugee problem, Arab governments argued, was to be resolved with a special formula of repatriation and compensation rather than resettlement to a third state.

Because of Egypt's reservations to the 1951 Convention do not permit refugees to enjoy their basic rights; Egypt is viewed by most refugees as a transit country. There are significant resettlement programs to such countries as Australia, Canada, Finland, and the United States. From 1997 to May 2003, UNHCR resettled 12,051 refugees to western countries. This does not include refugees who have managed to get "sponsorship" to Australia and Canada through special programs. It also does not include refugees who have left Egypt for Libya in order to attempt to reach Italy using traffickers. Somalis are known to take this route, but other groups may also do so. Other refugees use traffickers to reach Israel.

Palestinian Refugees

The Palestinians have been subjected to changing policies which have become increasingly restrictive, largely due to the shifts in political relations among the government of Egypt, the Palestine Liberation Organization (PLO), and Israel. The Egyptian media promote a general stereotype of Palestinians as wealthy, though the actual number of the "wealthy" is very small. Another common and negative media image of Palestinians is that they have brought their troubles on their own heads, having sold their land to the Israelis. It is often speculated that Egypt's restrictive policies toward all refugees in general are a product of its policies toward the Palestinians.

No official figures on the Palestinians are available from the government. In 2003, according to unofficial sources, there were said to be 50,000 to 70,000 Palestinians in Egypt. According to the Palestinian ambassador there were 53,000 Palestinians living in Egypt in 2001.

The Arab League and the Egyptian Foreign Ministry continue to set the figure at 70,000. Yassin (1996) states that 256,973 Palestinians held Egyptian travel documents in 1994.

Today, most Palestinians live dispersed in many villages and towns across Egypt, existing below (or even far below) the poverty line. Due to the severe restrictions on education, Palestinians in Egypt are probably the least educated of all the diaspora Palestinians. Egypt has not heeded repeated Arab League resolutions advising governments to treat them on a par with nationals. In 1948, the UN Relief and Works Agency (UNRWA) was established to provide assistance (not protection) to Palestinian refugees in the following host states: Jordan, Lebanon, Syria, the West Bank, and Gaza. But UNRWA was never invited to work in Egypt.

In 1948, with the great numbers of Palestinians entering the country through land and maritime borders, an immense camp, Qantara Sharaq, was created in the northeast part of Egypt near the Suez Canal. Another camp, Azarita, was created in the north near Alexandria. Palestinians who desired to leave the camps were required to have an Egyptian guarantor. Subsequent people arrived as individuals or families and found their way to relatives across the country.

In 1950, Egypt's King Farouk signed an agreement with UNRWA to assist Palestinian refugees in Gaza but did not permit them to operate in Egypt. He wished to discourage Palestinians from staying in Egypt on the grounds that Egypt was already "too crowded with its own people and [could not] receive the refugees on their territories" (El Abed 2003).

When Nasser came to power in 1952 he addressed the Palestinian issue more favorably. Nasser set up "employment projects" for the 50,000 Palestinians residing in the Sinai in order to improve their situation. Nevertheless, Palestinian refugees were not allowed to work (except for the British army), open their own businesses, or hold Egyptian passports. In 1954, Nasser allowed Palestinians to work as teachers, and in 1962 he passed Law 66, which permitted Palestinians to work in the public sector and "to be treated as nationals of the United Arab Republic" (El Abed 2003). In addition to this law, Egypt ratified the Casablanca Protocol in 1965, which pledged to treat Palestinians on par with citizens and to work to preserve the Palestinian identity.

By the late 1970s, these favorable policies toward Palestinians in Egypt were withdrawn. In 1973 President Sadat succeeded in regaining control of the Sinai from Israel, after which he sought to make peace in exchange for economic and military aid from the United States. Palestinians saw Sadat's peace negotiations with Israel as unacceptable, and this strained relations between Egypt and the PLO. The assassination of the Egyptian Minister of Culture by a PLO faction further soured ties.

Later that year, two administrative regulations, Nos. 47 and 48, were issued, rescinding all regulations that gave Palestinians the same rights as nationals. With these special privileges taken away, Palestinians had no more rights than other foreigners. From 1978 until today, they have been prohibited from work in the public and private sectors, they need a permit for any work, they must pay foreigners' fees in hard currency for university education, their rights to travel are severely restricted, and those who overstay travel permits are subjected to deportation or detention.

Sudanese Refugees

"Sudanese in Egypt have for long enjoyed a status close to nationals on account of a number of bilateral agreements, the most recent being the Nile Valley Agreement of 1976 which inter alia allowed for free movement of goods and people across the common border" (Sperl 2001:20). During the civil war from 1955 to 1972, the first wave of Sudanese asylum-seekers came to Egypt. The second wave of Sudanese began arriving as a result of the current civil war that began in 1983. Most of the recent asylum seekers in Egypt are from Southern Sudan, South Kordofan, and South Blue Nile regions of Sudan. A significant number of Sudanese from the Muslim north have also sought refuge from persecution since 1983. Besides civil war and fear of persecution, some Sudanese have come to Egypt because of famine and the impossibility of sustaining life in the displaced camps around Khartoum (Cooper 1993:2).

Until 1995, it was not necessary for Sudanese refugees to seek asylum; they were usually referred to as "displaced people." However, the 1995 assassination attempt on President Mubarak in Ethiopia, allegedly by members of Egypt's Islamic fundamentalists supported by the Sudanese government, changed Egypt's open-door policy toward their southern neighbor. Since then, every Sudanese must have a visa to enter Egypt and, if a refugee, must proceed through the refugee status determination process at UNHCR.

In 2001 there were only 2,960 recognized refugees from Sudan. Their recognition rate in 2000 was only 30% and does not come near to reflecting the true number of Sudanese who have fled their country because of war and persecution.

As with most refugee populations, the Sudanese see education for their children as the only way out of poverty, but they have been barred from the free Egyptian public school system. Christian churches and refugee-run NGOs are the only source of education for refugees in Cairo. Only one of these primary school programs teaches the Egyptian curriculum. There are not nearly enough facilities and resources to educate the tens of thousands of refugee children living in Egypt, and there are no secondary schools.

In December 2000 the minister of education announced a plan to address the lack of public primary education for Sudanese children and in 2001 a ministerial decree was issued (Peterson 2001). The decree is problematic in two ways. Families are required "to present extensive documentation, including a birth certificate, last schooling level certificate, identity document with legal residence permit, and letter from the Embassy of Sudan" (Peterson 2001). A second obstacle is the resistance of the Sudanese refugees to the idea of local integration, preferring English-language teaching no matter how few opportunities are available, as preparation for their hoped-for resettlement to English-speaking countries in the West. Their resistance to Arabic teaching is also related to their deep-seated aspirations for an independent Southern Sudan where, as one Sudanese man put it, "Arabic is not going to be the main language" (Peterson 2001).

Somali Refugees

Prior to the Somali civil war that began in 1991; Somalis residing in Cairo consisted of three main groups: (1) diplomats and their families, (2) university students on scholarships, and (3) female-headed families who came to Egypt for the education of their children while their husbands worked in the Gulf (Al-Sharmani 2003). According to UNHCR, in 2003 there were 1,832 recognized Somali refugees, 952 rejected applicants, and 1,544 asylum-seekers. The Somali community maintains that there are at least 5,000 in Cairo.

Somalis who came to Egypt before the war or shortly thereafter differ from those who came to Egypt in the late 1990s. The first Somalis to settle in Cairo came mainly from urban areas, were highly educated, had held professional or administrative jobs, and fled Somalia via Kenya or the Gulf. The more recent Somali refugees have both urban and rural origins, and are more likely to be unskilled and young. Many are illiterate, and a number of them fled first to the Gulf before coming to Cairo.

Somalis are concentrated in two districts of Cairo, Ard El-Liwa and Nasr City. Because the Somali community in Cairo is "an integral part of well-connected communities of the transnational Somali Diaspora that have very strong economic and social ties," many Somalis receive remittances from relatives in western countries and Saudi Arabia, in addition to their income from the informal sector in Cairo (Al-Sharmani 2003).

Somalis suffer from the restrictions on attendance of public schools and very few, if any, benefit from the church-based educational programs on offer in Cairo. Self-help schools organized by the Somali Refugee Committee of Egypt (SRCOE), and other small NGO initiatives, provide an alternative for a few children. Also, some Somali households who have resisted resettlement out of fear of cultural assimilation in the West are said to receive more assistance from Caritas, UNHCR's implementing partner for humanitarian assistance to refugees in Egypt. This differential treatment understandably creates tensions within the group.

Ethiopian and Eritrean Refugees

From 1977 to 1979, Ethiopian refugees came to Egypt in order to escape the Mengistu regime's "Red Terror" (Cooper 1992). Another influx of refugees came in 1991–1992 when the Mengistu regime fell. Some were members of the military. The recent border conflict between Ethiopia and Eritrea (1998–2000), the suppression of civil liberties in both countries, and the downturn in the economy are all reasons why Eritreans and Ethiopians have continued to flee to Egypt. Eritrean refugees living in Sudan began coming to Egypt after UNHCR and the Eritrean government invoked the cessation clause (Article 1C(5)) of the 1951 Convention in 2000 because they feared forced return.

The majority of Ethiopians and Eritreans in Cairo during the early 1990s were educated and skilled single young men from urban areas, from both Muslim and Christian backgrounds (Cooper 1992). More than half came to Cairo directly by plane while others came by foot or train after having spent some time in other African countries and the Gulf countries. Financial support mainly stemmed from relatives in the West and local churches.

More recent data on the make-up of the Ethiopian and Eritrean refugee population in Egypt are not available. However, if trends from the early 1990s hold true, the profile of refugees from Ethiopia and Eritrea will have greatly changed. Before 1990, men coming from these two countries made up the majority but by 1992 more women than men were fleeing to Cairo.

UNHCR statistics show that as of March 2001, there were only 18 Eritrean and 59 Ethiopian recognized refugees living in Cairo. The recognition rate was 13% for Eritreans and 14% for Ethiopians in 2000. Nevertheless, the actual Eritrean and Ethiopian community is around 5,000. Most of their files have been closed by UNHCR, and they are vulnerable to detention and deportation, and still unable to return home.

The Economic Situation of Refugees in Egypt

Egypt's unemployment is estimated at around 20% (Sperl 2001). African refugees frequently experience racism on the streets and the media have been known to make xenophobic statements about refugees, who are seen as competing with Egyptians for work. However, "the thousands of refugees living in Cairo are irrelevant to the explanation of the pressing economic and social problems found in Cairo" (SUDIA 2003). They are "irrelevant" because they are consumers from the moment of their arrival, they receive remittances from abroad, they work in jobs not filled by Egyptians, and they receive very little assistance from UNHCR or the NGOs, which, in any case, represents income to Egypt in foreign currency. They, unlike many poor Egyptians, depend on the private sector for housing where rents are high. Refugees must pay school fees (when they can afford them). This expenditure directly benefits the local economy. And, unlike poor Egyptians, refugees have lost the social networks upon which they, like everyone everywhere, depend for support.

Assistance by NGOs is concentrated in Cairo and "discourage[s] the dispersal of refugees throughout the country" (Ismail 2002). Alexandria is the only other city in Egypt in which refugees receive (limited) assistance from UNHCR and churches. These services, which benefit at most a few hundred people, include education, health, food, and vocational training to help refugees obtain employment (as domestic workers, for example).

UNHCR gives monthly stipends to a limited number of refugees through its implementing partner, Caritas. However, while the number of refugees in need has been increasing each year, funds have been decreasing. From 1997–2002, this money has declined from $2,928,129 to $1,677,088. If every recognized refugee (the only ones eligible for assistance) was given these funds on a per capita basis, they would have received only $186.34 in 2002. That amount would not even pay the average household's rent for three months. UNHCR attempts to "target" the most "vulnerable" (the aged, the infirm, minor children). In doing so it has arbitrarily cut off assistance to certain categories who may also be "vulnerable," such as single men, *all* Sierra Leoneans, and *all* Liberians.

To conclude, the main sources of income for refugees are as follows:

UNHCR and NGOs assistance (to eligible refugees only);

Work in the informal sector; and
Remittances from relatives and friend abroad.

One can confidently say that refugees in Egypt belong to the poorest of the urban poor. Egypt calculates its poverty line on the basis of the cost of a diet sufficient to yield the daily minimum of 2,200 calories. The annual cost of the minimum diet was estimated at LE 4,439 for urban areas. "This is considered as the food-based poverty line. Those who are below this line are referred to as ultra poor" (UNDP 2003:115–6).

Conclusion

Cairo hosts one of the largest urban refugee communities in the world. Voluntary migration to Egypt is negligible if compared to the massive number of refugees who arrived in Egypt in the last few decades to escape wars, tribal and political conflict, and poverty. While voluntary migrants represented about 0.3% of the total population of Egypt in the last population census of 2006, estimates of forced migrants and refugees vary between 500 thousand and five million. Both voluntary and forced migrants in Egypt are considered temporary migrants. However, voluntary migrants enjoy decent lives in Egypt since most of them are international employees, investors, and highly skilled workers, while the lives of refugees are miserable.

Acknowledgments

I would like to thank Professor Barbara Harrell-Bond, Distinguished Adjunct Professor and Mr. Randy Chrisler, Forced Migration and Refugee Studies Program, The American University in Cairo for information on refugees and their comments on an early version of this chapter.

Notes

1. Source: estimations of the Central Agency for Public Mobilization and Statistics (CAPMAS)
2. The "overall migration strategy" was not translated to any kind of a written document.

References

Afifi, W. (2003) Research Report on Education for Refugees in Cairo. Unpublished Document: Forced Migration and Refugee Studies Library, American University in Cairo.

Al-Sharmani, M. (2003) Livelihood and Identity Constructions of Somali Refugees in Cairo. Forced Migration and Refugee Studies Working Paper 2, American University in Cairo. http://www.aucegypt.edu/academic/fmrs/Reports/final.pdf

Brinks, J.S., and Sinclair, C.A. (1980) *International Migration and Development in the Arab Region.* ILO, Geneva.

CAPMAS (1989) *Housing and Population Census, 1986.* Cairo.

CAPMAS (2008) *Arab Republic of Egypt: Housing and Population Census, 2006.* CAPMAS, Cairo.

Choucri, N. (1977) The New Migration in the Middle East: A Problem for Whom? *International Migration Review* 11(4), pp. 421–43.

Choucri, N. (1999) New Perspectives on Political Economy of Migration in the Middle East. In Appleyard, R. (ed.) *Emigration Dynamics in Developing Countries.* Volume 4: *The Arab Region,* pp. 19–43. Ashgate, Aldershot, UK.

Cleland, W. (1936) *The Population Problem in Egypt: A Study of Population Trends and Conditions in Modern Egypt.* Science Press Printing Company: Lancaster, Pennsylvania.

Cooper, D. (1992) Urban Refugees: Ethiopians and Eritreans in Cairo. *Cairo Papers in Social Science.* Volume 15, Monograph 2.

Cooper, D. (1993) A Needs Assessment of the Ethiopian and Eritrean Refugee Population. RSC Documentation Centre, Oxford University.

Corsellis, J. (1993) Yugoslav Refugees in Camps in Egypt and Austria 1944–47. *North Dakota Quarterly* 61(1) Winter, pp. 40–54.

Dingemans, E. (2002) Educational Needs and Priorities for South Sudanese Refugees in Cairo. Unpublished Report: Forced Migration and Refugee Studies, American University in Cairo, Egypt. http://www.aucegypt.edu/academic/fmrs/Research/Estherreport.pdf

El Abed, O. (2003) The Unprotected Palestinians of Egypt: An Investigation of Livelihoods and Coping Strategies. Unpublished Report: Forced Migration and Refugee Studies, American University in Cairo, Egypt.

Farrag, M. (1999) Emigration Dynamics in Egypt. In Appleyard, R. (ed.) *Emigration Dynamics in Developing Countries.* Volume 4: *The Arab Region,* pp. 44–88. Ashgate, Aldershot, UK.

Grindell, R. (2003) A Study: Refugees' Experiences of Detention in Egypt. Unpublished Paper: Forced Migration and Refugee Studies, American University in Cairo, Egypt.

Ismail, I. (2002, June) Co-ordinating 'Humanitarian Aid' for Refuges in Egypt. Unpublished Report: Forced Migration and Refugee Studies, The American University in Cairo, Egypt. http://www.aucegypt.edu/academic/fmrs/Reports/iman.pdf

Kagan, M. (2002) Assessment of Refugee Status Determination Procedure at UNHCR's Cairo Office 2001–2002. Forced Migration and Refugee Studies Working Paper No. 1, American University in Cairo, Egypt. http://www.aucegypt.edu/academic/fmrs/Reports/final.pdf

Kagan, M. (2003) Is the Truth in the Eye of the Beholder? Credibility Assessment in Refugee Status Determination. *Georgetown Immigration Law Journal* 17(3).

Library of Congress (2003, 6 June) Egypt: A Country Study. http://memory.loc.gov/frd/cs/egtoc.html

No Author (2002) Withdrawal of Egyptian Reservations to the 1951 Convention Relating to the Status of Refugees' Prepared by Lawyers from the EOHR Refugee Legal Aid Project. American University in Cairo, Egypt.

Peterson, N. (2001, 30 August–5 September) School's Out. *Cairo Times* 25(5).

Roudi, N. (2001) Population Trends and Challenges in the Middle East and North Africa. *Population Reference Bureau (PRB)*.

Yassin, A. (1996) Palestinians in Egypt. *SAMED Al-Iqtisadi* 18(106), In Arabic

Sperl, S. (2001) Evaluation of UNHCR's Policy on Refugees in Urban Areas: A Case Study Review of Cairo. EPAU 2001/07.

SUDIA (2003) Developing Pathways into Work for Sudanese Refugees: Labour Markets. Cairo.

Takkenberg, L. (1998) *The Status of Palestinian Refugees in International Law*. Clarendon Press: Oxford.

UNDP (2003). Human development Report 2003. Millennium Development Goals. A compact among nations to end human poverty. UNDP.

Zohry, A. (2002) Rural-to-Urban Labor Migration: A Study of Upper Egyptian Laborers in Cairo. Ph.D. dissertation, University of Sussex.

Zohry, A. (2003) The Place of Egypt in the Regional Migration System as a Receiving Country. *Revue Européenne des Migrations Internationales* 19(3), pp. 129–149.

Zohry, A. (2006) Immigration to Egypt. *Journal of Immigrant and Refugee Studies* 4(3), pp. 33–54.

Zohry, A. (2007) *Migration and Development in Egypt*. Paper Prepared for Project on Migration as a Potential and Risk, Robert Bosch Foundation and Institute for Migration and Cultural Studies (IMIS), Osnabruck University, Berlin, Germany, 16–17 December.

22

Taiwan

Immigration to Taiwan

Joseph S. Lee

There has been a rapid, global rise in the international migration of labor over the past two decades, with millions of men and women each year leaving their homes and crossing national borders in search of greater physical security and higher income for themselves and for their families (OECD 2008; ILO 2004; Skeldon 2000). Some countries accept considerable numbers of immigrants from abroad, including the United States, Canada, Australia, New Zealand and Singapore (Table 22-1). These highly developed Western and Asian countries utilize immigration policy as a tool to resolve the shortage of low-skilled workers and certain highly skilled workers, notably in information technology (IT), health, and education (Constant and Zimmermann 2005).

Asian countries in general are not so open to immigration; in 2008 the net immigration rates for Japan and South Korea were zero, and for Taiwan 0.04% (Table 22-1). However, the shortage of low-skilled workers since the late 1980s has forced the governments of these Asian countries to liberalize their immigration policy, at least for temporary immigrants. Although Korea and Taiwan have shortages of certain highly skilled workers, especially in science and technology, thus far they have depended on the

return of their own scientists, engineers, and managers who went to the United States, Canada, and other advanced countries for graduate studies and later on remained in those countries and became permanent residents. Hence they do not see the need for using immigration policy to resolve the problems associated with shortages of highly skilled workers.

During the early stage of development Taiwan adopted a very restrictive immigration policy because the government wanted to restrict mainland Chinese from entering Taiwan for fear of communist infiltration. Taiwan also adopted a very restrictive immigration policy because of its high population density rate; for example, in 2007, Taiwan's population density rate was 635 persons per square kilometer (CEDP 2008, p. 25). As Taiwan's relationship with Mainland China has improved and as Taiwan has become more and more globalized, its restrictive immigration policy has become more relaxed (Table 22-2). However most of these new immigrants are temporary low-skilled workers who are permitted to work in Taiwan, for a maximum of six years, and now extended to nine years, under an employment contract, and who must then return home as soon as these employment contracts expire. In 2008 there were 373,336 of these low-skilled

Table 22-1. Net Immigration Rates, by Selected Countries[*]

Country	1999	2001	2003	2008
Taiwan	0.3	−0.2	−0.5	0.04
Philippines	−1.0	−1.0	−1.5	−1.5
Thailand	0.0	0.0	0.0	0.0
Malaysia	0.0	0.0	0.0	0.0
India	−0.3	−0.1	−0.1	−0.05
Singapore	2.8	26.5	25.8	6.9
Japan	−0.1	0.3	0.0	0.0
South Korea	−0.3	0.0	0.0	0.0
China	−0.4	−0.4	−0.2	−0.4
United States	3.5	3.1	3.5	2.9
Canada	4.2	6.7	6.0	5.6
United Kingdom	2.8	3.1	2.2	2.2
Germany	2.5	3.3	2.2	2.2
France	0.8	1.1	0.7	1.5
Netherlands	2.8	3.5	2.4	2.5
Australia	6.3	5.7	4.1	3.7
New Zealand	3.0	4.7	4.3	2.6

[*] The net migration rate comprises net migrants per 1,000 of the mid-year population.

Source: CIA World Fact Book January 2008.

Table 22-2. Immigration in Taiwan (Unit: Persons)

Year	Emigration	Immigration	First time establishing household registration (permanent residence) in Taiwan	Number of immigrants
1991	41,062	27,723	190	−13,149
1992	47,151	30,553	146	−16,452
1993	48,495	38,059	82	−10,354
1994	41,743	41,113	131	−499
1995	78,420	51,855	314	−26,251
1996	119,144	67,089	307	−51,748
1997	66,644	73,583	4,137	11,076
1998	10,776	36,812	10,942	36,978
1999	34,258	28,395	12,438	6,575
2000	38,674	27,361	16,941	5,628
2001	44,086	25,522	14,957	−3,607
2002	45,846	27,582	14,729	−3,535
2003	49,560	25,500	11,805	−12,255
2004	47,185	36,061	14,715	3,591
2005	37,140	33,704	18,816	15,380
2006	42,247	56,279	23,960	37,992
2007	63,150	56,863	25,565	19,278

Source: Ministry of Interior: http://www.moi.gov.tw/state.

foreign workers in Taiwan. Another group of temporary immigrants are the highly skilled and professional workers. As Taiwan's economy becomes more mature, its demand for high-level professionals increases and therefore an increasing number of these foreign professionals have been admitted into Taiwan, but so far the absolute number is still very small.

As for permanent immigrants, most of them are foreign female spouses from Southeast Asian countries and Mainland China who have married Taiwanese men and have immigrated into Taiwan to join their husbands.

Taiwan not only has a very restrictive immigration policy, but also a very restrictive emigration policy. Of those who emigrated abroad between 1991 to 2006, most of them went to the United States (45%), Canada (31%), New Zealand (10%), and Australia (7%), and the remaining 7% went to other countries, such as Japan, Singapore, France, and various Southeast Asian countries (MOI 2005).

It is the purpose of this chapter to investigate the causes leading to the changes in the immigration policy in Taiwan, as well as the changing composition of immigrants, both "temporary" and "permanent." It is hoped that the following analysis can shed some light on the current debate on the effectiveness and consequences of different immigration policies.

Immigration Policy

Prior to 1980, the government of Taiwan had maintained a very restrictive immigration policy for fear of the infiltration of communists onto the island. It was not until after 1987, with the lifting of martial law and the liberalization of the Taiwanese economy, that the government revised its immigration policy, making it easier for foreigners to immigrate into Taiwan. The island's current policy on immigration can be divided into temporary and permanent immigration. For the first group, the policy has become much more liberalized since 1990, and especially since 2008. For the latter group, although the government enacted a special law in 1993, namely, the "Statute Governing the Relations between Peoples of the Taiwan Area and the Mainland Area" to relax the restrictive policy with regard to admitting mainland Chinese into Taiwan, and the law has been amended several times, the last time being in 2003, the immigration policy is nevertheless still very restrictive toward mainland Chinese. One can, however, expect this restrictive policy to be liberalized in the near future because Taiwan's newly elected President Ma Ying-jeou is seeking to improve relations between Taiwan and

Mainland China and to get the Taiwan economy moving again.

In Taiwan, permanent immigration is regulated by the Immigration Act and the Law of Nationality. According to Article 23 of the Immigration Act, an alien who has legally and continuously resided in Taiwan for seven years, or an alien who is the spouse or a child of a Taiwanese person with permanent residence rights in Taiwan, and who has legally and continuously resided in Taiwan for more than ten years, may apply to the government for permanent resident status. In all cases, applicants must be over 21 years of age, have a decent character, and have considerable properties, skills, or talent that will enable them to earn a living on their own. However Article 23 also states that those aliens who cannot satisfy the above conditions, but who have made exceptional contributions to Taiwan, or who possess the high technology skills needed by the island, may also apply for permanent residence in Taiwan. In 2007, the government established a National Immigration Agency (NIA) under the Executive Yuan to handle all matters related to immigration, except for temporary immigration, which is under the jurisdiction of the Council of Labor Affairs.

Temporary immigrants can be divided into professionals and low-skilled immigrants. The former group includes investment immigrants, professional immigrants, and religious workers as well as the spouses and family members of these highly skilled and professional workers. There is no quota and no restriction on the duration of their stay. Temporary low-skilled immigration, by contrast, is governed by the Labor Employment Services Act of 1992. According to this law, the admission of foreign workers is strictly for the purpose of alleviating the shortage of low-skilled workers in Taiwan. This is because, as Taiwan has become more industrialized, it has raised both the educational attainments and per capita income of its citizens, which has ultimately led to native Taiwanese being no longer willing to engage in low-skilled work or tasks involving arduous labor. Therefore, since the late 1980s, the island has been transformed into an economy with an acute shortage of low-skilled labor. As a result, employers in Taiwan have realized that they have had to import low-skilled foreign workers onto the island, even though such activities at least initially have been in violation of the existing immigration laws.

In 1992, in order to deal with the rapid increase in the number of illegal immigrants, the government enacted the Employment Services Act, which made the importation of foreign workers both open and legal. The fundamental rationale behind the admission of these foreign workers was to alleviate the acute labor shortage in the construction and labor-intensive industries, and for those "dirty, dangerous and difficult" (3D) jobs that were shunned by native Taiwanese workers.

Within the Employment Services Act, the main principles behind the admission of foreign workers were: (1) Foreign workers may be admitted only to supplement native workers and not to replace them; based upon this principle, the Taiwanese government sets quotas restricting the admission of foreign workers to designated industries and occupations. Any employers wishing to hire foreign workers must clearly show that a labor shortage exists within their industry or occupations, and that the shortage is hindering their operations, their expansion, or the upgrading of their production facilities. (2) Foreign workers may only be admitted on a temporary basis and cannot become permanent immigrants; thus, all foreign workers are allowed to stay in Taiwan for only two years. If their continued presence is proved to be necessary, they may apply for an extension of one year, giving a maximum of three years in Taiwan. However, many employers complained that a three-year period was too short, since it ultimately meant that employers in Taiwan must constantly train new workers. To respond to the employers' demands, the government changed this regulation twice, first by permitting foreign workers to work in Taiwan for a maximum of six years and in 2007 further extending this to a maximum of nine years. (3) The admission of foreign workers must not have any impact on the upgrading of Taiwan's industrial structure, or must not cause any delay in the speed of such upgrading. (4) The admission of foreign workers should result in minimal social costs; therefore, these workers cannot be allowed to bring their families into Taiwan. Furthermore, any female foreign worker who was previously found to have become pregnant was immediately deported; however, this policy was changed in 2002. Today it is permissible for a foreign worker to become pregnant and still remain in Taiwan.

Initially, the government's intention was that once the labor-intensive industries had completed their structural readjustment, the demand for foreign workers within these industries would be substantially reduced, or even eliminated; however, as the figures in Tables 22-3 and 22-4 show, the original purpose behind the admission of foreign workers into Taiwan had already been achieved by the late 1990s. Since then, the main purpose in admitting low-skilled foreign workers was changed to assist the rapid expansion of major export industries and high-tech industries. It was the government's hope that more jobs for native workers could be generated and the speed of upgrading of Taiwan's economic structure enhanced due to the rapid expansion of these two types of industries.

By the late 1990s, the government had also started to admit large numbers of foreign workers into the area of household work and health-care services. The main purpose behind this policy was to release the better-educated native Taiwanese women from their household duties, and thereby raise their labor force participation rate and thus their labor supply, while simultaneously alleviating the problem of a growing shortage of child care and health care service workers.

Since the admission of foreign health care workers has been determined by need and not by quotas, the number of these workers has increased rapidly and by 2007 its share among all foreign workers had quickly risen to 45%. Up to that time, the government had an informal agreement with trade unions and the public in general that it would not admit more than 300,000 foreign workers into Taiwan because it was deemed that at that level native workers' jobs would not be displaced by the presence of foreign workers. Thus a larger number of foreign healthcare workers in Taiwan meant a smaller number of foreign production workers. This caused problems for employers in the manufacturing industries and they therefore urged the government to separate foreign workers into two different categories of production and health care workers so that the increase in the number of foreign health care workers would not be at the expense of a reduction in foreign production

Table 22-3. Distribution of Foreign Workers, by Industry

Industry Sector	1992		1995		1997		1999		2001		2003		2005		2007		Aug. 2008	
	N	%	N	%	N	%	N	%	N	%	N	%	N	%	N	%	N	%
1. Manufacturing																		
Food	287	0.56	3,366	2.04	4,402	1.79	4,305	1.54	4,511	1.48	4,680	1.56	4,970	1.52	5,697	1.59	6,780	1.82
Textiles	4,369	8.54	23,435	14.21	32,956	13.41	33,113	11.87	28,026	9.20	26,911	8.97	23,995	7.33	22,816	6.37	22,021	5.90
Apparel	635	1.24	3,331	2.02	3,577	1.46	3,023	1.08	2,575	0.85	2,318	0.77	1,748	0.53	1,551	0.43	1,683	0.45
Leather & fur products	158	0.31	2,639	1.60	2,663	1.08	2,189	0.78	1,613	0.53	1,441	0.48	1,320	0.4	1,426	0.4	1,473	0.39
Wood & bamboo products	961	1.88	2,024	1.23	2,233	0.91	1,724	0.62	1,285	0.42	906	0.30	872	0.27	936	0.26	938	0.25
Furniture & fixtures	–		226	0.14	209	0.09	211	0.08	214	0.07	218	0.07	257	0.08	401	0.11	676	0.18
Pulp & paper	452	0.88	3,587	2.17	3,824	1.56	3,490	1.25	3,455	1.13	3,339	1.11	3,316	1.01	3,856	1.08	4,033	1.08
Printing	–		–		–		205	0.07	243	0.08	303	0.10	326	0.10	496	0.14	858	0.23
Chemicals	51	0.10	1,289	0.78	1,401	0.57	1,497	0.54	1,892	0.62	1,716	0.57	1,867	0.57	1,986	0.55	1,992	0.53
Chemical products	–		1,572	0.95	2,170	0.88	1,722	0.62	1,607	0.53	1,570	0.52	1,635	0.5	1,806	0.50	1,945	0.52
Rubber products	30	0.06	4,678	2.84	4,463	1.82	4,763	1.71	4,251	1.4	4,475	1.49	4,475	1.37	4,991	1.39	4,981	1.33
Plastic products	2,184	4.27	11,566	7.01	11,211	4.56	10,582	3.79	10,184	3.34	9,880	3.29	10,052	3.07	11,856	3.31	12,947	3.47
Nonmetallic minerals	–		8,042	4.87	9,688	3.94	7,460	2.68	6,141	2.02	6,177	2.06	6,195	1.89	6,879	1.92	7,167	1.92
Basic metal products	1,704	3.33	15,363	9.31	14,885	6.06	12,128	4.35	10,315	3.39	9,717	3.24	9,853	3.01	11,342	3.17	11,255	3.01
Metal products	3,520	6.88	14,758	8.95	18,994	7.73	17,304	6.20	16,413	5.39	17,175	5.72	17,895	5.47	22,909	6.40	25,756	6.90
Machinery & equipment	1,247	2.44	3,876	2.35	4,195	1.71	6,300	2.26	6,643	2.18	7,120	2.37	7,455	2.28	10,358	2.89	13,319	3.57
Electrical & Electronic machinery	1,492	2.92	21,230	12.87	35,825	14.58	42,105	15.10	44,135	14.49	51,135	17.04	57,057	17.43	59,420	16.60	60,455	16.19

(Continued)

Table 22-3. (Continued)

Industry Sector	1992 N	1992 %	1995 N	1995 %	1997 N	1997 %	1999 N	1999 %	2001 N	2001 %	2003 N	2003 %	2005 N	2005 %	2007 N	2007 %	Aug. 2008 N	Aug. 2008 %
Transportation	748	1.46	4,616	2.80	6,844	2.79	6,881	2.47	6,949	2.28	7,253	2.42	8,260	2.52	9,289	2.60	10,470	2.80
Precision instruments	14	0.03	536	0.32	624	0.25	704	0.25	752	0.25	695	0.23	840	0.26	1143	0.32	1436	0.38
Miscellaneous	86	0.17	–	–	237	0.10	4,550	1.63	5,851	1.92	5,010	1.67	4,540	1.39	4,170	1.17	4,020	1.08
Others	–	–	269	–	–	–	–	–	–	–	–	–	–	–	1	0.00	16	0.00
Subtotal	17,938	35.07	126,403	76.62	160,401	65.28	164,256	58.90	157,055	51.56	162,039	53.99	166,928	50.99	183,329	51.22	194,221	52.02
2. Construction	33,217	64.93	38,570	23.38	48,786	19.86	51,894	18.61	33,367	10.95	14,117	4.70	13,306	4.06	8,594	2.40	6,939	1.86
3. Maids and healthcare workers	–	–	–	–	35,245	14.34	61,723	22.13	112,934	37.08	120,598	40.18	144,015	43.99	162,228	45.32	167,679	44.91
4. Fishing Boat Crew	–	–	–	–	1,265	0.51	999	0.36	1,249	0.41	3,396	1.13	3,147	0.96	3,786	1.06	4,497	1.20
Total	51,155	100	164,973	100	245,697	100	278,872	100	304,605	100	300,150	100	327,396	100	357,937	100	373,336	100

Sources: 1. Survey of Utilization and Administration of Foreign Workers in Taiwan, Council of Labor Affairs, Various years.
2. Monthly Report of Salary and Productivity Statistics, DGBAS, Various years.

Table 22-4. Number and Missing Rate* of Undocumented Foreign Workers, by Country, 1998–2007

Year	Indonesia		Philippines		Thailand		Vietnam		Mongolia		Malaysia		Total	
	Total No	Missing Rate	Total No	Missing Rate	Total No	Missing Rate	Total No	Missing Rate	Total No	Missing Rate	Total No	Missing Rate	Total No	Missing Rate
1998	493	2.8	2,450	2.3	1,728	1.3	–	–	–	–	6	0.9	4,679	1.8
1999	760	2.5	1,882	1.6	1,403	1.0	–	–	–	–	12	2.2	4,057	1.4
2000	1,680	2.9	1,303	1.2	1,234	0.9	35	0.7	–	–	16	12.4	4,288	1.4
2001	2,804	3.2	1,048	1.2	942	0.7	293	2.8	–	–	2	2.5	5,089	1.6
2002	3,809	4.0	643	0.9	1,042	0.9	1,584	7.8	–	–	1	2.8	7,079	2.3
2003	3,411	4.6	873	1.2	1,171	1.1	4,233	9.6	–	–	–	–	9,688	3.2
2004	1,978	4.9	1,177	1.4	1,369	1.3	7,536	10.2	2	5.5	–	–	12,062	4.0
2005	1,973	6.7	1,543	1.7	2,040	2.1	7,363	8.2	19	24.0	–	–	12,937	4.2
2006	4,232	6.0	1,023	1.1	1,239	1.3	4,422	5.8	2	3.9	–	–	10,918	3.3
2007	4,870	4.7	867	1.0	959	1.1	4,529	6.5	1	6.5	–	–	11,226	3.2

* Missing Rate = number of undocumented workers divided by the total number of foreign workers of that particular country x 100.

Source: Council of Labor Affairs.

workers. In 2007 the government accepted such a recommendation and indeed separated foreign workers into production and service workers where "service workers" referred solely to health care workers. The government also abolished its previous admission standards for admitting foreign production workers to designated industries on a quota basis and replaced it with a new standard referred to as "3D3S" or the "special production process or special working hours" standard. According to this new standard, only jobs in dirty, dangerous, and difficult categories and jobs on the third shift of a three-shift work process (the night shift) are eligible for applications from foreign workers.

To preserve jobs for native workers, the government also established a 3:2 employment ratio, which means that for every two foreign workers hired the employer must hire three native workers. In addition, the total number of foreign workers employed by a firm may not exceed 15% of its total employment.

In October 2007 the government refined the 3D3S standards, so that 3D now refers to jobs that are exposed to excessive heat, dust, or poisonous gases, or involve chemical processes, non-automatic work or other jobs that are designated by the government; 3S refers to jobs that start after 10 p.m. and end at 6 a.m. the next morning.

Temporary Immigrants

Low-Skilled Foreign Workers

During the early 1990s, the admission of low-skilled foreign workers was concentrated in the construction and manufacturing industries. However, in later years there has been a continuous decline in the number of low-skilled foreign workers within the construction industry. The number of foreign workers in the construction industry reached its peak in 1999 when 51,894 workers or 18.6% of all foreign workers were employed in Taiwan and then this number gradually declined to 12,184 workers in 2004 or 3.88% of all foreign workers, and to 7,094 in July 2008 or 1.9% of all foreign workers in Taiwan. The decline in the number of foreign workers in the construction industry has been mainly due to the completion of the government's major

infrastructure projects and the subsequent slowdown within the construction industry in recent years.

Since the late 1990s, the share of foreign workers in the manufacturing industry has also begun to shrink while the share of foreign workers in the healthcare services area has begun to expand. Within the manufacturing industry the share of foreign workers has been shifting from the traditional labor-intensive industries to major exporting industries and high-tech industries. As the figures in Table 22-3 show, in 1997 the share of foreign workers in the labor-intensive industries accounted for 23% of all foreign workers in Taiwan (in the food, textiles, apparel, leather and fur products, wood and bamboo products, furniture and fixtures, pulp and paper, printing, rubber, and plastic products industries). However, by 2004, this share had fallen to 17.19% and by August 2008 to 15.1 percent of all foreign workers in Taiwan. Conversely, the share of foreign workers within the machinery and equipment, electrical and electronic machinery industries, and other capital and technological intensive industries had grown rapidly within the same period (Table 22-4).

Thus the foreign workers policy for low-skilled workers has changed three times since 1992. Prior to mid-1997 the policy was to provide labor supply to labor-intensive industries and to major construction projects. Subsequently, from 1997 to 2007, Taiwan's foreign workers policy was to provide labor supply to major exporting industries and to high-tech industries. It was the government's hope that such a policy could generate employment opportunities for native workers in these export and high-tech industries, where pay is higher and the upgrading of Taiwan's economic structure can be hastened. By 2007 the government foreign workers policy had switched to providing labor supply to 3D3S jobs, which are shunned by native workers.

Illegal Low-Skilled Foreign Workers

In order to receive permission to employ foreign workers, an employer must submit a formal application to the government, in accordance with the 1992 Employment Service Act. Only upon receiving permission from the government can the employer then start to recruit foreign workers. Furthermore, when these foreign workers arrive in Taiwan, they must remain with this particular employer for the duration of their employment contract; they are not allowed to change employers unless they do so under special circumstances, such as the closure of the factory or the death of the employer.

Nevertheless, some foreign workers do change their jobs or their employers without receiving permission from the Council of Labor Affairs (CLA) and they subsequently become classified by the CLA as "undocumented workers." If they are found, they are deported immediately.

There are several reasons why these workers would want to change their current employers and to go and work illegally for other employers. The most often cited reason is "to remain in close contact with other workers from their own country," which is hardly surprising since these foreign workers do not speak Chinese when they first arrive in Taiwan and they may not be accustomed either to the Taiwanese lifestyle or working conditions. Their aim is to find workplaces that have coworkers from their own country so that they can consult with them in their own language, and in confidentiality; they can also arrange to stay in the same dormitories and provide comfort for each other in cases of homesickness or loneliness.

The second most often cited reason is "contract expiry." Since many foreign workers pay large amounts in brokerage fees before coming to Taiwan, in order to recover such major expenses and to meet their main goal of making a certain amount of money while working in Taiwan, some of them may decide to take the risk of running away from their current employers once their employment contracts expire. "Searching for higher wage rates or better working conditions," "homesickness," "the inability to make necessary adjustments to the working environment" and "difficulties working with native coworkers" were other more often cited reasons that caused foreign workers to run away from their current employers.

As the figures in Table 22-4 show, the undocumented rates are rising every year, with the highest rate being among Indonesian and Vietnamese workers. Their undocumented rates are higher because a larger proportion of them are health care workers who work in private homes and institutions. Loveband (2003) and Young (2004) showed in their recent studies that these health care workers usually work very long hours, the work is stressful, both physically and mentally, and they are often denied any periods of vacation. Therefore, there is a greater tendency for them to run away in search of jobs in areas where more foreign workers, particularly foreign workers from their home countries can be found.

In order to reduce the number of "undocumented workers," the government has imposed fines of between NT$30,000 and NT$150,000 on offenders who are apprehended; the government has also established special programs to deal with foreign workers' personal or job-related problems. These include direct phone lines through which foreign workers can make known their complaints regarding difficulties at work and other job-related issues with their employers. These phone lines are available in four different languages, Filipino, Thai, Vietnamese, and Indonesian. With these types of arrangements and facilities, the problems faced by foreign workers can be dealt with in a timely manner and without any language barriers. Thus the undocumented rate can be more effectively reduced.

Highly Skilled and Professional Foreign Workers

McLaughlan and Salt (2002) show that most of the highly developed Western countries have experienced shortages of certain types of highly skilled workers, notably in IT and health and medical areas, and they have formulated special immigration policies in order to attract these workers from other countries. Taiwan also has a shortage of labor in certain areas of science and technology. However, in the past Taiwan has not relied on foreign professionals to resolve its shortage of certain types of highly skilled workers, but has instead relied on the return of its citizens who have studied or emigrated abroad, mostly from the United States and Canada. In recent years, the number of students studying abroad has been declining due to the narrowing of the wage gap between Taiwan and these high income countries, and there is therefore a need for Taiwan to hire foreign professionals to fill the gap caused by its shortage of professionals. As the figures in Table 22-5 reveal, there has in fact been an increase in the number of foreign professionals in Taiwan. In 1992, there were only 9,314 foreign professionals (businessmen, engineers, teachers and religious workers, and other professional workers) in Taiwan. This figure however rose to 28,804 in 2001 and to 37,578 in 2007. Along with the rising number of foreign professionals, there is a change in the composition of these foreign professionals. In the early 1990s the largest group of foreign professionals in Taiwan was that of businessmen, there being 2,394 foreign businessmen in Taiwan in 1992 which subsequently rose to 4,053 in 2001. Since then, however, this number has been gradually declining and by 2007 had fallen to 3,752 persons. In terms of its share among all foreign professionals it declined from 25.7% in 1992 to 14.1 percent in 2001 and then declined further to 10.0% in 2007. The decline in the number of foreign businessmen in Taiwan is mainly due to the opening up of Mainland China's economy, which has attracted many foreign companies that previously had their headquarters in Taiwan and have now relocated them to Mainland China.

While the number of foreign businessmen in Taiwan is declining, the number of foreign language teachers has been increasing rapidly. In 1992 there were only 1,527 foreign language teachers in Taiwan but by 2007 this figure had risen to 6,009. The increase in the number of foreign language teachers in Taiwan has been mainly due to the internationalization of the Taiwan economy, which makes foreign languages, especially English, an important communication tool. The demand for English teachers has therefore risen rapidly.

The Impact of Short-Term Immigrants on the Taiwan Economy

Very little research work has been undertaken on the impact of highly skilled foreign technicians and professionals, largely because their numbers are so small. Conversely, a considerable amount of research has been undertaken on the impact of low-skilled immigrant workers on the Taiwan economy. Most studies have looked into the issue of whether foreign workers have replaced native workers. Jiang, Liu and Tung (2003), Hsu (1997), San (1996), and Wu (2001) have pointed out that foreign workers have replaced native workers and in fact this is one of the main reasons for the

increase in the unemployment rate among less educated workers in Taiwan. However, other studies have argued that, prior to 1997, migrant workers and native workers worked in segregated labor markets, since they were allowed to work only in industries with serious labor shortages and in jobs that were shunned by native workers. Therefore, foreign workers and native workers were not substitutes for each other. However, with the rapid increase since 1997 in the number of undocumented foreign workers and illegal immigrants from Mainland China and Southeast Asian countries, the demarcation between the foreign and native labor markets has been blurred and thus foreign workers do substitute for native workers in certain ways (Lee 2004). The installation of the 3D3S criteria might be able to restore the separation of the foreign worker and the native worker markets and thereby prevent the substitution of foreign workers for native workers.

Other studies have argued that the crime rate is higher among migrant workers than among native workers. However, thus far, there has been no convincing evidence to support this argument. Crimes committed by migrants, regardless of whether they are major or minor crimes, will invariably be reported to the police and, in most cases, will lead to deportation. By contrast, minor crimes committed by native workers are not usually reported to the police; and therefore there is no record of these crimes.

In a recent study, Lin (2001) found that migrants had a negative effect on the migration of natives; in other words, native workers tended to stay away from those areas where there were large numbers of migrant workers, such as Taipei and Taoyuan counties. Other studies have found a negative effect of migrant workers on R&D work and technological upgrading. Lin and Lo (2004), for example, found that the rate of R&D and technological change in firms that were using large numbers of short-term migrants were lower than in those firms that were using fewer short-term migrants (or no migrant workers at all) since there was less pressure to upgrade products due to the comparatively lower labor costs.

Illegal Aliens

As Taiwan has become more liberalized and globalized, its borders have necessarily become much more open and, as a result, there has been a steady increase in the number of illegal immigrants. These illegal aliens can be classified into three specific groups: (1) those who entered Taiwan legally, but upon the expiry of their visas subsequently became illegal aliens; although they are not engaged in any form of employment, they are included within the category of "overstaying"; (2) those who entered Taiwan legally (for example, on a tourist visa) but subsequently began working illegally; and (3) those who entered and worked in Taiwan legally, but following the expiry of their visas/ work permits, became both illegal aliens and illegal workers.

During the early 1990s, the largest share of illegal workers was among those who had entered Taiwan legally with a visa, but subsequently overstayed and began working illegally; indeed, in 1992, this particular group accounted for 65.3% of all illegal aliens in Taiwan. However, since Taiwan decided to open its doors to foreign workers, this figure has dropped significantly. In fact, by 2007, its share among all illegal aliens had dropped to 39.6%, while the share of illegal aliens overstaying their visas was on the rise, increasing from 31.7% in 1992 to 51.0% in 2007 (Table 22-5).

It should be noted that the number of illegal immigrants listed in Table 22-5 does not include

Table 22-5. Legal Foreign Residents and Illegal Aliens in Taiwan, 1992–2007

	1992	1995	1997	1999	2001	2003	2005	2007
Legal Foreign Residents aged 15 years or over								
Business	2,394	3,080	3,034	3,834	4,053	4,034	3,878	3,752
Engineers	1,002	1,025	1,093	1,890	2,269	3,145	3,117	2,407
Teachers	1,527	1,781	2,169	2,876	4,435	5,958	6,630	6,009
Religious Workers	1,832	1,562	1,741	1,848	1,925	2,048	1,800	1,775
Other Occupations	2,559	6,270	5,784	11,042	16,140	13,563	16,533	23,635
Craftsmen	601	861	437	488	491	277	424	1,142
Low-skilled foreign workers	11,264	179,192	222,951	280,160	287,337	283,239	297,287	321,804
Unemployed	1,058	1,887	1,987	2,303	3,022	3,976	3,957	2,917
Not in the Labor Force	16,551	18,690	22,992	28,730	59,376	79,126	86,900	69,728
Subtotal	**38,788**	**214,348**	**262,188**	**333,171**	**379,048**	**395,366**	**420,526**	**433,169**
Legal Foreign Residents under 15 years of age	5,653	6,189	6,482	6,015	4,615	9,918	9,177	8,059
Total Males	29,134	149,796	168,518	185,806	167,094	157,046	156,370	163,575
Total Females	15,307	70,741	100,152	153,380	216,569	248,238	273,333	269,594
Total Legal Foreign Residents	**44,441**	**220,537**	**268,670**	**339,186**	**383,663**	**405,284**	**429,703**	**433,169**
Illegal Foreign Residents								
Illegally overstayed only	5,312	6,633	7,782	9,054	10,614	8,868	12,348	9,319
Working illegally only	488	4,731	2,513	2,258	2,869	1,193	1,283	1,699
Illegally overstayed and working illegally	10,933	8,055	9,192	6,245	4,794	7,099	10,685	7,246
Total Illegal Foreign Residents	**16,733**	**19,419**	**19,487**	**17,557**	**18,277**	**17,160**	**24,316**	**18,264**

Source: National Police Agency, MOI (2008).

those from Mainland China; since such immigrants are Chinese, just as all Taiwanese citizens are, they are not therefore regarded as aliens but as illegal "mainlanders." There are no official figures or estimates of the number of such illegal immigrants in Taiwan; thus, it may well be that the figures in Table 22-5 grossly underestimate the actual number of all categories of illegal immigrants in Taiwan.

Permanent Immigration and Naturalization

Prior to 1995, few foreigners were permanent immigrants in Taiwan, but as the island has become more affluent and globalized, there has been a corresponding rise in the number of such cases. According to Article 3 of the Law of Nationality, an alien who meets one of the following requirements may apply for naturalization: (1) Having legally stayed in Taiwan for more than 183 days each year for more than five years without interruption. (2) Who is 20 years old or above. (3) Has good character and no record of criminal conviction. (4) Possesses sufficient property or professional skills that enable him to make a self-reliant living or a living without worry. However, according to Article 4 of the same Law, if this person is a child, or a spouse of a Taiwanese and if he/she resides in Taiwan for more than 183 days continuously for more than 3 years, he/she may apply for nationalization. According to Article 10 of the nationalization law, an alien who is naturalized shall not be eligible for any high ranking public offices; however, this restriction shall be removed 10 years after naturalization.

The figures in Table 22-6 reveal that, even as late as 1995, only slightly more than 100 foreigners had been naturalized as Taiwan citizens, but by 1998, this figure had risen to 3,684, and by 2000, it had reached 5,198. The economic recession during 2001 and 2002 disrupted this upward trend of naturalization, but as the economy picked up in 2004 the trend resumed. As the figures in Table 22-6 show, by 2007, close to 11,000 people from various countries had been naturalized as Taiwanese citizens.

Although historically women have accounted for the largest share of naturalized citizens, the gap has become wider in recent years. As the figures in Table 22-7 show, in 1990, two-thirds of all naturalized Taiwanese citizens were women; however, by 2007, they accounted for 99% of all naturalized citizens. The largest groups of foreigners who have become naturalized Taiwanese citizens are those from Vietnam, Indonesia, and the Philippines. The question therefore arises as to why such large numbers of women from these various countries would want to become Taiwanese citizens. Marrying a Taiwanese man and joining his family in Taiwan is the major reason.

This picture is even clearer if we look at permanent immigration. In Taiwan, the most important source of permanent immigrants is spouses from Southeast Asian countries and from Mainland China. In 1998, for every 6.4 newly married couples one spouse was from abroad, but this ratio had fallen to 5.5 to 1 in 2007. As Table 22-8 shows, for all these nonnative spouses Mainland China is the most important source. For example, in 2004 60.87% of the 336,483 non-Taiwanese spouses were from Mainland China, and in 2008 this ratio was 63.27%. Vietnam was the second most important source since it accounted for one-fifth of all spouses from abroad.

This rapid rise in spouses from abroad is not simply a social phenomenon, but it is also a form of economic behavior, since many of these spouses from abroad do not actually meet their grooms either in Taiwan or in their home countries. Many of them never meet their future husbands until a matchmaker from Taiwan arranges a visit into one of the major cities of these Southeast Asian countries or Mainland China. If the potential husband is happy with the match, he pays the matchmaker between US$8,000 and US$10,000 for all the expenses involved in getting his bride into Taiwan; the parents of the bride will also receive around US$1,000 to US$3,000 from the matchmaker. When the bride arrives in Taiwan she does not only play the role of wife—in terms of taking care of her own children and the household chores—but in many cases will be required to take care of her disabled, or even slightly mentally retarded, husband and may even need to go out of the house and find a job to provide financial support for the family.

Table 22-6. Naturalized Taiwanese Citizens, by Gender, and Country of Origin (Unit: Persons)

Year	Total	Gender		Japan		Korea		Malaysia		Indonesia		Thailand		Vietnam		Cambodia		Myanmar		Philippines		Others		Unknown	
		M	F	M	F	M	F	M	F	M	F	M	F	M	F	M	F	M	F	M	F	M	F	M	F
1990	95	32	63	–	–	1	21	2	2	–	12	–	–	20	18	–	–	–	–	1	8	3	–	5	2
1991	130	52	78	–	–	3	26	3	3	–	–	–	2	34	32	–	1	–	–	1	2	2	2	9	10
1992	86	30	56	–	–	8	23	–	2	–	1	–	1	15	12	–	–	–	–	–	7	–	2	6	8
1993	127	65	62	–	–	26	26	–	–	–	3	–	1	17	3	–	–	–	–	9	15	5	6	8	7
1994	137	31	106	1	–	10	31	–	4	2	14	3	14	1	–	–	–	–	1	4	28	3	4	7	10
1995	129	27	102	–	1	6	25	2	11	–	11	–	13	–	1	–	–	–	1	3	22	2	4	13	13
1996	318	35	283	2	1	8	25	1	5	–	184	–	20	8	2	–	1	–	8	4	23	3	7	9	7
1997	2,243	27	2,216	–	–	1	19	1	3	6	1,997	1	27	5	51	–	–	–	49	8	56	1	6	4	8
1998	3,684	35	3,649	–	–	7	26	–	24	6	3,058	–	53	5	171	–	11	–	114	6	175	2	8	9	9
1999	4,627	47	4,580	–	–	11	31	3	23	6	2,727	–	37	–	907	–	183	3	352	8	303	9	6	7	11
2000	5,198	63	5,135	3	–	6	8	1	11	12	2,052	–	86	4	2,200	1	325	8	165	9	273	17	12	2	3
2001	2,204	104	2,100	3	5	2	8	–	14	13	320	2	77	1	1,279	–	96	16	49	15	205	11	9	41	38
2002	1,533	117	1,416	3	7	4	4	1	11	22	238	2	137	1	514	1	151	47	146	6	160	16	9	14	39
2003	1,465	54	1,411	1	6	2	3	1	11	3	261	1	92	1	407	–	317	21	114	6	187	14	2	4	11
2004	6,552	111	6,441	1	11	1	3	2	5	28	2,863	3	60	2	2,349	–	690	9	116	14	309	35	13	16	22
2005	11,302	112	11,190	5	7	1	–	2	5	34	2,197	–	33	9	8,197	–	350	4	14	15	374	37	7	5	6
2006	11,973	72	11,901	2	3	–	5	1	4	21	1,255	1	72	5	10,168	–	–	4	23	17	364	12	4	10	3
2007	10,764	94	10,670	2	3	–	2	1	7	20	1,273	2	116	13	8,213	1	830	1	26	11	187	34	9	9	4

Source: Department of Household Registration Affairs, Ministry of the Interior, ROC.

Table 22-7. Reasons for Naturalization, 1990–2007 (Unit: Persons)

Year	Naturalized Nationals			Naturalized on their own account		Naturalized because they are spouses of Taiwanese citizen		Naturalized because one of their parents is a Taiwanese citizen		Others	
	Total	Male	Female	Male	Female	Male	Female	Male	Female	Male	Female
1990	95	32	63	28	19	–	35	–	–	4	9
1991	130	52	78	46	40	–	25	–	–	6	13
1992	86	30	56	26	26	–	25	–	–	4	5
1993	127	65	62	59	23	–	37	–	–	6	2
1994	137	31	106	23	17	–	83	–	–	8	6
1995	129	27	102	17	17	–	78	–	–	10	7
1996	318	35	283	32	22	–	252	–	–	3	9
1997	2,243	27	2,216	20	15	–	2,191	–	–	7	10
1998	3,684	35	3,649	25	22	–	3,617	–	–	10	10
1999	4,627	47	4,580	41	32	–	4,537	–	–	6	11
2000	5,198	63	5,135	32	18	17	5,113	–	–	14	4
2001	2,204	104	2,100	62	86	24	1,995	4	2	14	17
2002	1,533	117	1,416	65	143	27	1,245	6	4	19	24
2003	1,465	54	1,411	26	59	20	1,340	2	3	6	9
2004	6,552	111	6,441	25	26	67	6,371	3	7	16	37
2005	11,302	112	11,190	6	24	75	11,145	4	2	27	19
2006	11,973	72	11,901	11	62	56	11,823	–	2	5	14
2007	10,764	94	10,670	18	128	67	10,533	2	0	7	9

Source: Department of Household Registration Affairs, Ministry of Interior, ROC.

Table 22-8. Numbers and Percentages of Nonnative Spouses

	Total	Vietnam		Indonesia		Thailand		Philippines		Cambodia	
		N	%	N	%	N	%	N	%	N	%
2004	336,463	68,181	20.26	24,446	7.27	8,888	2.64	5,590	1.66	4,336	1.29
2005	364,596	74,015	20.3	25,457	6.98	9,675	2.65	5,899	1.62	4,541	1.25
2006	383,204	75,873	19.8	26,068	6.8	9,426	2.46	6,081	1.59	4,514	1.18
2007	399,038	77,980	19.54	26,124	6.55	8,962	2.25	6,140	1.54	4,502	1.13
2008	408,547	80,031	19.59	26,079	6.38	8,517	2.08	6,260	1.53	4,439	1.09

	Japan		Korea		Others		Mainland China		HK	
	N	%	N	%	N	%	N	%	N	%
2004	2,163	0.64	751	0.22	7,429	2.21	204,805	60.87	9,874	2.93
2005	2,339	0.64	762	0.21	8,211	2.25	223,210	61.22	10,487	2.88
2006	2,467	0.64	797	0.21	8,860	2.31	238,185	62.16	10,933	2.85
2007	2,640	0.66	838	0.21	9,431	2.36	251,198	62.95	11,223	2.81
2008	2,727	0.67	849	0.21	9,774	2.39	258,480	63.27	11,391	2.79

Source: Office of Household Registration, 2008.

Such importation of large numbers of foreign spouses into Taiwan has led to a number of social problems. First of all, these marriages between native workers and their foreign spouses are formed as an arrangement, and not out of love or affection. Native males who marry these foreign spouses are usually poorly educated and old or physically disabled or slightly mentally retarded and therefore unable to find native women to marry them. It has been reported that many of these foreign spouses have experienced abuse by their husbands or other family members. To make matters worse, many of these foreign spouses do not speak any Chinese, nor do they have any knowledge of their legal rights, so they do not know where to get help when they are subjected to such abuse or violence. Some studies have concluded that the low educational attainment of these foreign spouses has also put their children's education in jeopardy, because they are unable to provide their children with any preschool education. As a result their children become slow learners or "troublesome" students at school (in 2007 for every 10.23 newly born children, one had a mother who was a non-Taiwanese).

In recognition of these problems, the government has recently allocated large sums of money to establish language classes; legal, health care, and cultural education classes; and other types of programs for these spouses from Southeast Asian countries and Mainland China. The children of these foreign spouses are now also given priority with regard to admission into the low cost publicly owned kindergartens, so that they are provided with proper preschool education.

Conclusion

The evolution of Taiwan's immigration policy is an interesting case for scholars and policy makers because at each different stage of economic development there has been a different policy to match the needs at that time. During its early stage of development, the Taiwanese government staunchly maintained a very restrictive immigration policy for a considerable period of time, partly as a means of deterring the immigration of people from Mainland China into Taiwan, since the two governments were not on good terms, and also because Taiwan already had a very high population density. However, as Taiwan's successful economic development over the last fifty years raised both the educational attainments and per capita income of its citizens to levels at which they no longer wished to engage in low-skilled work, or tasks involving arduous labor,

this led to a serious shortage of low-skilled labor in Taiwan. Alongside this labor shortage, the globalization and internationalization of the Taiwanese economy caused the government to respond with a more liberalized immigration policy and to permit limited numbers of foreign workers to come to Taiwan.

While many countries used an immigration policy to lure highly skilled workers from abroad to make up for the shortages of certain types of highly skilled workers and professionals, Taiwan relied on the return of its students studying abroad as well as scientists and engineers who had emigrated to the United States and other advanced countries. However, as Taiwan moved toward a knowledge-based economy, the demand for highly skilled workers and professionals increased quickly, and scientists and engineers returning from abroad could no longer meet the high demand. To respond to these changes, the government revised its immigration policy by permitting more foreign professionals to enter the island. However, on this occasion the changes were not sufficient for Taiwan to compete with other countries for certain types of scientists and engineers in the international market. New mechanisms have therefore had to be developed to accomplish this goal.

With the rapid improvements in educational attainment and employment opportunities during the last few decades, Taiwanese women have become more economically independent and more selective in their marriage partners. As a consequence, many poorly educated or physically handicapped Taiwanese men have recently experienced difficulties in finding marriage partners and many of them have turned to cross-border marriages as an alternative. With increasing numbers of spouses from abroad, the Taiwan government has been forced to amend its immigration policy by making it easier for these foreign spouses to immigrate into Taiwan and become permanent immigrants and naturalized citizens.

All of these developments are positive indications that Taiwan is moving toward a much more open society. There is, however, also a negative side to the recent developments in international migration. Taiwan is increasingly using cross-border marriages as one of the ways to deal with its domestic labor shortage, as well as the marriage problems of the poorly educated and physically- or mentally-disadvantaged males. Increasing numbers of older and low-income males, who cannot afford foreign household maids, are using cross-border marriages as substitutes for foreign household maids, to take care of them and their aging parents.

These developments have given rise to two social problems; the first one being the emergence of an increasing number of disadvantaged children in Taiwan, in terms of both their education and socialization with other citizens. This is because most of the foreign spouses are themselves poorly educated and have language difficulties. They can neither speak nor write Chinese, nor can they provide proper preschool education for their children, with the result that these children cannot communicate with their teachers when attending school. Secondly, many of the cross-border marriages are not based upon love and affection, but instead stem from the "commodification" of international marriages. There are many cases of the husbands and family members treating these foreign spouses badly, and without dignity; therefore, the issue of the violation of human rights is involved here. The Taiwan government is aware of both of these emerging social problems and, in fact, has established several programs aimed at dealing with them. However, they continue to need careful attention if the government is to prevent the emergence of a new disadvantaged social class in Taiwan.

References

Chen, C.K., C.S. Ku, Y.D. Lee, and C.H. Yu (2003), "Developing a Cross-Cultural Aspect Management System for Foreign Labor: A Study of Thai Labor in the Plastics and Fiber Industries," *Journal of Manpower Resource Management*, 3(2): 57–74.

CLA (2003), *Survey of Utilization and Administration of Foreign Workers in Taiwan, 1992–2003*, Taipei: Council of Labor Affairs.

CLA (2004), *Monthly Bulletin of Manpower Statistics, Taiwan Area*, Taipei: Council of Labor Affairs.

Constant, A., and K. Zimmermann (2005), "Immigrant Performance and Selective Immigration Policy: A European Perspective," IZA Working paper No. 1715.

CEPD (2008), *Taiwan Statistical Data Book*, Council for Economic Planning and Development, Executive Yuan, ROC.

DGBAS (2004), *Monthly Report of Salary and Productivity Statistics, 1992–2004*, Taipei: Directorate-General of Budget, Accounting and Statistics.

Jiang, F.F., K.C. Liu, and A.C. Tung (2003), An Inquiry into the Causes of Rising Unemployment in Taiwan, *Taiwan Economic Review*, 1(8): 15–71.

Hsu, M. (1997), "Substitution between Foreign Workers and Domestic Production Factors: The Case of Taiwan's Manufacturing Industries," in *Proceedings of the Annual Meeting of the Taiwan Economic Association*, pp. 65–91.

ILO (2004), "A Fair Deal for Migrant Workers in the Global Economy," ILO Conference Report VI.

Lee, J.S. (1996), "Recruiting and Managing Foreign Workers in Taiwan," *Asian and Pacific Migration Journal*, 5: 281–99.

Lee, J.S. (2002), "Foreign Workers in Taiwan," in R. Skeldon (ed.), *Migration and the Labor Market in Asia: Recent Trends and Policies*, OECD, pp. 225–250.

Lee, J.S. (2004), "The Role of Foreign Workers in Taiwan's Process of Economic Development," in C.C. Lo (ed.), *Policy on Foreign Workers*, Institute of Economics, Academic Sinica, Republic of China, pp. 1–21.

Lin, J.P. (2001), "Impacts of Foreign Labor on the International Migration of Domestic Labor: The Case of Taiwan," *Taiwan Economic Association Annual Conference Proceedings*, Taipei Taiwan, pp. 329–363.

Lin, Z.F., and C-C. Lo (2004), "The Impact of Foreign Workers on Production Technology in the Manufacturing Industries in Taiwan," in C.C. Lo (ed.), *Policy on Foreign Workers*, Institute of Economics, Academic Sinica, Republic of China, pp. 39–66.

Loveband, A. (2003), "Positioning the Product: Indonesian Women Workers in Contemporary Taiwan," paper presented to the SEARC-CAPSTRANS Workshop on Migration, Ethnicity, and Workforce Segmentation in the Asia-Pacific, held at the University of Wollongong, Australia, August 11–12, 2003.

McLaughlan, G., and J. Salt (2002), "Migration Policies towards Highly Skilled Foreign Workers," Migration Research Unit, Geography Department, University College London.

MOEA (2003), *Quarterly National Economic Trends, Taiwan Area, 1987–2003*, Taipei: Ministry of Economic Affairs.

MOI (2005), *Distribution of Foreign Professionals, by Occupation, 2001–2004*, Taipei: National Police Administration, Ministry of the Interior.

OECD (2002), *Migration and the Labor Market in Asia: Recent Trends and Policies*, Paris: OECD.

OECD (2008), *International Migration Outlook, Annual Report 2008 edition*, Paris: OECD.

San, G. (1996), "Substitutions among foreign workers, Technology, non-technical workers and Capital", in C.N. Chen, K.C. Liu and F.F. Jiang (eds.), *Population, Employment and Welfare*, Institute of Economics, Academic Sinica, Taipei, Taiwan, pp. 39–71.

Skeldon, R. (2000), "Trends in International Migration in the Asian and Pacific Region," *International Social Science Journal*, 52(165): 369–82.

Wang, H.Z., and S.M. Chang (2003), "The Commodification of International Marriages: Cross-border Marriage Business in Taiwan and Vietnam," *International Migration*, 40(6): 93–116.

Wang, H.Z. (2001), "Social Stratification, Vietnamese Partners, Migration and the Taiwan Labor Market," *Quarterly Social Studies*, 41(March): 99–127.

Wu, H.L. (2001), "The Trends of Foreign workers and Its Policies in Taiwan", *Journal of Population*, 22: 49–70.

Young, K. (2004), "Southeast Asian Migrant Workers in East Asian Households: Globalization, Social Change and the Double Burden of Market and Patriarchal Disciplines," Working Papers Series No. 58, Hong Kong: City University.

23

China

A New Pole for Immigration

Kim-wah Chung, Ji Qi, and Wenruo Hou

China has long been a country of emigrants. Since the mid-eighteenth century, when the West opened the door gate of the Central Kingdom with guns and wars, the Chinese began a steady stream of exodus while several Westerners entered for business but few settled here. In fact, poor economic conditions and political and social instability not only did not attract immigration to China, but resulted in departures, both legally and illegally.

Following the takeover by the Chinese Communist Party in 1949, Western anticommunism and tense international relationships resulted in doubts about the iron-curtained China. The nation became insular, and few migrated to Mainland China between 1949 and the mid-1980s. Since 1978, China's economic reform and open door policy improved international perceptions, and economic development has gradually opened up both tangible and intangible boundaries between China and the overseas. After three decades, the world's most populous country is ranked third in overall economic strength, and China is once again evidencing vigor and vitality, attracting increasing attention from the outside. Though still not an immigration hotspot, more people from overseas are entering China, and these entrants are no longer merely from the developing world and unstable neighboring societies. Increasingly more foreigners or *laowai*, are attracted by ancient mysteries, the ever opening social atmosphere, as well as the seemingly unstoppable economic engine of modern China. These *laowai* are staying longer as tourists, as immigrants, and even as retirees. This paper is going to describe and analyze recent changes and to discuss China's potential as a hotspot for international immigration.

Immigration to China from 1949 to the Mid-1980s

After the founding of the People's Republic of China (PRC), there were two major sources of immigration into China: the "Overseas Chinese" and people from the brotherhood nations of the developing world. The most significant group was the "Overseas Chinese." For some, it was a "home-coming," while others were "new immigrants" as they were neither born in China nor had ever lived there.

In the early years after 1949, the government of China issued political signals as well as explicit encouragement to attract the Overseas Chinese back to their homeland. Preferential treatment was offered as enticements for those envisioning contributions to the development of the New China. Although the number of "homecoming Overseas Chinese" is unclear, it is widely believed that several million may have done so after 1949.

Overseas Chinese also returned for more distressing reasons. In late 1950s and early 1960s, when the political crisis in Indonesia resulted in the exclusion of Chinese natives, the government of China welcomed their return. Furthermore, the long lasting civil wars in several countries of the Asian subcontinent instigated both legal and illegal immigration of the Overseas Chinese to Mainland China. The territorial conflicts between China and Vietnam beginning in the mid-1970s witnessed another wave of cross-border movement to the Mainland. This peaked in 1978 and 1979, when large outflows of people with Chinese ethnicity, some 160,000 to 250,000, fled Vietnam for southern China (Zhang, 2007). Many of these refugees were reportedly settled in state farms on Hainan Island in the South China Sea. Some arrived as "boat people," following the currents of the big oceans; some were offered asylum in Europe and the United States; some eventually settled in the regions where their boats landed, and some were admitted to China as immigrants.

The second source of immigration to Mainland China is from the brotherhood nations of the developing world, or the Third World. After the 1955 Asian-African Conference in Bandung and the Non-Aligned Movement in early 1960, China assumed the role of the most important, or leading, member of the Third World. To facilitate bilateral relationship between China and each developing country, the PRC government continuously offered financial and technical assistance, particularly to those from Africa. Many from these Third World countries came to China for academic exchanges, education, and training, and as workers, commercial and trade representatives, employees, or as diplomats. Many chose to stay for extended periods or even eventually settled in China.

Furthermore, it was also not uncommon for people to enter either legally or illegally along the lengthy borders of China. This was particularly apparent at the borders with North Korea and some areas of the former Soviet Union.

In September 1982, China became a signatory to the United Nations 1951 "Convention Relating to the Status of Refugees" and its 1967 Protocol, agreeing to assume international obligations and provide asylum for those with refugee status. Since then, it is estimated that China has become home to 400,000 refugees, mainly ethnic Chinese from the Indochina, but also significant numbers of ethnic Koreans from the border with North Korea (Kim, 2003).

Barring these groups, immigration into China has not been popular until this recent decade. The political atmosphere following World War II, and the long-term confrontation or cold war between the East and West, was not conducive to immigration to the "iron-curtained" China. Internal political movements also kept foreigners away from the country.

Until the early 1980s, since foreigners were not expected to migrate, no strict and formal policy was established to provide clear govern for the entry of people into China. This began to change when China opened up, and starting to evolve drastically from the mid-1980s until recent years.

Immigration to China since the Mid-1980s

A New Pole for Immigration

According to *People's Daily*, in 2005, there were already nearly 100,000 foreigners enjoying work and life on the Chinese mainland (People's Daily Online, 2005) The number of registered foreigners working in China jumped to 180,000 at the end of 2006, which doubled the number of three years earlier. When family members are included, the actual number is much greater, indicating that more foreigners are coming to China and staying longer. According to official statistics, in 2005, more than 40 million foreigners had entered and exited China, and 380,000 foreigners had been granted residence permission (Zheng, 2007). Foreign immigrants can now be found throughout China's territories, however, the majority of foreign immigrants live in major cities such as Beijing, Shanghai, Guangzhou, and Shenzhen, while others reside in areas and regions where the economy is thriving.

With China's increasing involvement with the outside world, more foreigners are likely to pour in and settle in China. Many factors contribute to this change. The first is the continued high level of economic growth of China that has become a very strong incentive for foreign venture capitalists. Second, improved living standards have made living in China no less attractive than in other countries. Particularly in the major cities and metropolitan areas, the infrastructure is well developed and commercial and residential premises are well integrated for a convenient lifestyle. Transportation and other basic amenities have also been developed efficiently. Education, health care, and other communal facilities are well available to urban dwellers, particularly to internationals who are usually able to afford quality services, yet the cost of living is low when compared to other major cities in the world. These endow China with a better competitive edge in attracting expertise and capital from around the globe. Thirdly, with ideological debates becoming secondary to economic development, the country has been politically stable since early 1990s. This offers both an environment conducive to economic development and stability to attract outsiders as residents. As China is now striving to integrate into the global village both economically and politically, it has put into the forefront international diplomacy. The result is a cooperative approach toward foreigners in China; preferential treatment also attracts more foreign talent. Finally, with more people entering and staying longer, interconnections between locals and outsiders become more substantive and substantial. Social networks are increasing and becoming more stable and intimate; more outsiders have been living in China long enough to develop their own families and establishing their career rooted in the country.

Policy Change Required for the New Realities

With the progress of the open door policy and economic reform, players in the economy of China, including state-owned enterprises, turned to overseas experts for guidance. Initially, overseas experts were those with special skills and knowledge essential for the reform or development of different economic sectors while others came with advanced capabilities in the management of modern economic operations. Under particular circumstances, employing foreigners was viewed as a symbol of progress and openness; it also became fashionable as a good selling point for some services and entertainment industries.

At first, most foreigners came to China temporarily, not necessarily with the intention of staying. To acquire a permit of residence, which is equivalent to a job visa, these expatriates had to go through complicated procedures each year in the offices of public security. Even if they did get the job visa, they still faced inconveniences in accessing entry and exit visas. To ease their difficulties, some form of permanent residency certification would be helpful. Furthermore, with time, as these expatriates established their careers and started families in China, particularly after the mid-1980s, it became essential that China accommodate these foreigners.

On the other hand, since the mid-1980s, the phenomenon of "foreign laborers" has drawn the attention of the administration. With booming foreign investment and an open-door policy, it was inevitable that more foreigners would live in China. However, other issues arose also, for example, some people entered China illegally, becoming engaged in an underground or grey economy and finding occupations as performers in night clubs and other entertainment enterprises to attract local residents. This phenomenon was particularly acute in the Heilongjiang Province and gradually spread to other regions. As there were mutual agreements between China and the former Soviet Union to facilitate border trade, it was not difficult for Russians to get travel permits into China. Given the changing economic situations on both sides of the border, many Russians entered China illegally, moving from Heilongjiang to the southern portion of the country. It became common for the entertainment industry to employ Russian girls as new attraction, and in that atmosphere, additional illegal and socially inappropriate activities became evident.

Moreover, the booming of the economy, although a benefit to China, becomes problematic when foreigners come to compete for jobs in which China itself has no labor shortage.

Local governments had to deal with this occurrence individually when no central policy was in place; some placed strict limitations on foreigners without residency permits that permitted employment. But the variations in handling this issue in different areas constituted a grey area that provoked discussion.

With this new phenomenon—China becoming a popular pole for migration, both long-term and short-term migration, and both legal and illegal residence—it may become necessary for the government to revise its original policy and practices to cope with new demands, handle emerging problems, and address discrepancies. The legal framework and policy for immigration management in China have been changing since the mid-1980s and continue to evolve.

Recent Changes in Immigration Policy in China

According to the "Law of the People's Republic of China on Control of the Entry and Exit of Aliens" adopted by the Standing Committee of the People's Congress in November 1985, and the related "Rules Governing the Implementation of the Law of the PRC on the Entry and Exit of Aliens," as well as the 1994 revised "Enforcement Regulations on Law of the People's Republic of China on Control of the Entry and Exit of Aliens," those foreigners who do not receive permission for residency and those who enter China to study are not allowed employment without authorization from the administration. Before 1996, the public security department could make reference to these legal statements when handling related issues.

With the increasing complexity of the economic environment of China after years of reform, many situations became "grey" and were beyond the realm of this legislation. Moreover, as China had not expected that the presence of foreigners could possibly become a major problem, the penalties were far from being deterrents. For example, according to a related regulation, "Regulations on Management on Employment of Foreigners and Overseas Students Who are without Residence Permit," the fine for illegal foreign employees and employers were just 1,000 *yuan* (RMB dollars) and 5,000 *yuan* respectively. Obviously, these punishment

terms were not sufficient to stop people from risking illegal employment.

Though China had experienced continual double-digit economic growth for more than a decade at that time, the ongoing reform of State enterprises and Collective Enterprises had laid off millions of laborers who were once living under the "iron bowl" system. On the other hand, surplus labors from the rural areas were also pouring into the cities seeking job opportunities. All these phenomena added pressures to the employment structures, making it necessary for the administration to place limits on the hiring of foreign workers.

The 1996 "Rules for the Administration of Employment of Foreigners in China"

In 1987, the Ministry of Labor, the Ministry of Public Security, and the Ministry of Foreign Affairs developed a set of administrative regulations against foreign employees and overseas students who were being employed illegally in China, but this still failed to halt the spreading illegal employment of foreigners. It was becoming obvious that a set of more comprehensive rules, regulations, or even legislation would be needed to address the changing situation, and this provided the backdrop to the "Rules for the Administration of Employment of Foreigners in China."

The rules were drafted jointly by the Ministry of Labour, the Ministry of Public Security, the Ministry of Foreign Affairs, the Office of External Affairs of the State Council, the Ministry for Foreign Trade and Commerce, and the Council on Foreign Experts. This profile is high enough to signify its strategic importance. It was formally announced in 1996 jointly by the Ministry of Labor, the Ministry of Public Security, the Ministry of Foreign Affairs, and the Ministry for Foreign Trade and Commerce.

On the practical side, this set of rules concretely stipulated the terms for regulating employment for foreigners, it required a foreign employee's card of legal employment, and it established procedures for employing bodies to apply for approval. Therefore, it was more practical and timely than were the earlier set of rules. Stipulations were that employing bodies should employ only foreigners with special skills and knowledge and whose expertise is lacking in China. The fundamental aim of the rules is to strictly control the potential influx of laborers seeking employment in China, and they set out formulated procedures for application to employ foreigners, the assessment principles for granting an "Employment Permit," and the punishment for failing to comply with the regulation. The regulations also explicitly set out the requirements for social insurance provisions, work hour control, labor protection, and procedures for labor dispute settlement for foreign employees.

The document could be perceived as a form of protection against the immigration of laborers who can compete for limited jobs with local citizens. While it is not a regulation on immigration control, it is, indeed, a very significant move by China to develop legal and administratively sound procedures to allow foreigners to live and work in China under prescribed conditions. It is, therefore, a significant step and a recourse for foreigners to establish their legal status in the country and is a worthy and effective outcome, granting legal permanent residency for those who have stayed and worked for several years in China.

Granting Permanent Residence for Foreigners in China

The need for formulating effective policy and procedures for granting permanent residency for foreigners in China was in fact not started after the 1996 "Rules for the Administration of Employment of Foreigners in China." In the mid-1980s, the Government of PRC had already proposed the idea of a "Green Card System" for foreigners to settle in China. According to clause no. 9 of the "Law of the People's Republic of China on Control of the Entry and Exit of Aliens" in 1985, foreigners would be allowed to get permanent residency after going through relevant procedures. In 1986, a set of regulations to match this law was put forward, however, stipulations in the regulation tended to be ambiguous and imprecise. Some required conditions for applications were unclear and subject to discretion; people often felt unable to access and complete the

documents required for them to apply for residency. Therefore, the "Green Card System" was, in fact, not at all functional in developing a practical system for immigration.

With China's application to reenter the World Trade Organization (WTO) in the late 1990s, the situation was no longer bearable and some major improvement became necessary. In 2002, the Xinhua (New China) News Agency, which is the official news agency of China, announced the "Summary of Planning for National Manpower Team Building 2002–2005," which is a document issued jointly by the Central Office of the Chinese Communist Party and the National Council Central Office. The document stated that the country has to "implement long-term stays or a permanent residency system for those senior experts who are let in" (Central Office of the Chinese Communist Party and the National Council Central Office, 2002). According to the elaboration of the Xinhua News Agency, the official news media of the PRC Government, "China is going to study and formulate laws on investment immigration and skilled immigration, so as to attract and encourage more overseas experts with advanced skills to come and work in China" (Xinhua News Agency, 2002).

According to statistics, after the implementation of the "Law of the People's Republic of China on Control of the Entry and Exit of Aliens" in 1985, the Chinese government had, until 2004, approved permanent residence for just over 3,000 foreigners (*China Daily*, 2004).

In December 2003, the State Council of the Central Government endorsed and enacted some administrative guidelines on immigration that were formally issued by the Ministry of Public Security and Ministry of Foreign Affairs in August 2004 as *Regulations on Examination and Approval of Permanent Residence of Aliens in China.*" The issuance of these regulations marked the official commencement of China's green card system, which allows foreigners to apply for permanent residence in China. The 29 articles of the regulations include explicit provisions on the prerequisites for foreigners to apply for permanent residence permits in China. Required supporting documents, steps to be followed, limits of authority, and cancellation of eligibility, and so forth, were all clearly stated. According to the regulations, eligibility for permanent residence mainly applies to high-level foreign personnel holding posts in businesses that promote China's economic, scientific, and technological development or social progress; foreign citizens who make relatively large direct investment in China; foreigners who have made outstanding contributions or are of special importance to China; and foreigners who come to China to be with their families.

The regulations set no limitation on the period of stay of aliens with permanent resident status in China, and they need not obtain visas and can enter and leave the country with valid passports and Alien Permanent Residence Permits, which are valid for five or ten years. Certificates with five-years' validity are granted to minors, while certificates with ten-years' validity are granted to adults.

This document spelled out some general principles for foreigners to stay in China with the Foreigner Permanent Residence Card. It also allowed multiple entry into China without the complicated procedures required to apply for a permit for every entry. Foreigners who are employed by public and registered private bodies, investors setting up business in China at the amount as stipulated for different parts of the country, or individuals fulfilling some other requirement are all eligible to apply. The document also established guidelines to cancel residency should people violate rules.

According to the 2004 "Method on Assessment and Approval for Foreigners to Permanent Residence in China," criteria for different categories of immigrants, including skilled migration, investment migration, and family reunion migration, were clearly identified as were the practical steps required of relevant departments or ministries. For those who could successfully get the "Card for Permanent Residence for Foreigner," residency limitation would no longer apply.

This "Method" may be the most important administrative measure in China's progress in handling immigration and is the materialization of the concept of the 1985 Green Card System. Moreover, it signified a milestone indicating that China has begun to address the global flow of populations, skills, and expertise and to integrate with the world economy. According to official announcements, by the end of September 2005, there were 260,000 foreigners staying in China with stable employment, and 649 people had already been granted Permanent Residency, and another 1,835 applications were being processed (Public Security Bureau of Government of PRC, 2005).

Although the implementation of this "Green Card System" is undoubtedly a significant progress, the orientation of the 2004 "Method on Assessment and Approval for Foreigners to Permanent Residence in China" is still just an attempt to control and monitor the inflow of foreigners and to prevent competition for the local labor market. It is still inadequate in that it does not offer incentives to attract foreign talents and expertise nor to facilitate investment immigration. While not further extending and opening the scope for foreigners to immigrate into China, it seems that the government is aware of limitations and understands the need for China to recruit more foreigners to enhance economic reform and further integration into the world economy.

Sources of Current Immigrants

There has long been an assumption that people who go to work in China usually come from Third World countries. While it was true, this is now changing. A variety of people now constitute the current immigrants to China.

Foreign Investors and Their Families

First and most important of all, despite the absence of governmental incentives, China's booming economy is a magnet to foreign investors who, along with their families, compose a large proportion of the total immigrants to China. According to People's Daily, there were nearly 100,000 foreigners enjoying their work and life on the Chinese mainland in 2005 (People's Daily Online, 2005). The number of registered foreigners working in China increased to 180,000 by the end of 2006 (YangChing Evening News, 2007). When family numbers are added, the total is much higher. Since most foreigners living in China prior to the late 1970s were from the developing world, many still wrongly assume that people who migrate to work in China continue to be from the less developed areas. In reality, this has been changing consistently since the mid-1980s and now a significant proportion of the people traveling to China for better opportunities and jobs are, in fact, those from the developed countries. Investors in China mostly come from Japan, the Republic of Korea, Singapore, the United States of America, and Europe, and most of them work in technological and management businesses in relatively prosperous regions such as Shanghai, Beijing, Guangdong, Jiangsu, and Zhejiang (YangChing Evening News, 2007). On one hand, staying long enough in China is important for foreign businessmen as they need to understand the Chinese culture and market, on the other hand, their high income and the relatively cheaper cost of living in China can guarantee them a high quality of life.

Foreign Students Staying Behind

Second to the foreign investors are the large numbers of foreigners studying in China. Since 1949, the government of China had devoted efforts to strengthen its ties with the developing world, and one of the strategies was to offer scholarships for students coming to China. This program was founded soon after 1949 and was maintained even during the time when China was facing difficulties in its economy and political stability. It has been grown aggressively in recent years. In 1996, China offered about 4,200 scholarships, in 2006, the number was 8,500 (Cha, 2007).

In recent years, as China's economy is booming and more people are interested in the country, it is increasingly being realized that Chinese is an important language not only because of the sheer number of Chinese people but also as the key skill required of people to hitch their futures to China's economic rise. As a result, thousands of foreigners are flocking to China to learn Mandarin. Many believe the country's economic boom will continue and indicate that knowing Chinese is not only interesting in and of itself, but will help them find interesting and lucrative jobs. According to the statistics of 2002, there were about 25 million people around the world learning Chinese. Some 60,000 of them had come to China to learn the language better. In 2004, a record of 110,844 students from 178 countries had enrolled at Chinese universities, which was a 43% increase on 2003 (Leavey, 2006). The Haidian District of Beijing, where most universities are located, has approximately 40,000 South Koreans, primarily students studying Chinese (Johnson, 2006).

According to the figures released by the Ministry of Education between 1995 and 2005, there were in total 880,000 foreigners who studied in China. Most of them majored in Mandarin, medicine, and economics. According to official statistics, the year 2005 is one with the highest record of foreign students staying in China since 1949. Not only was the number of foreign students at its highest, the number of their countries of origin, as well as the number of institutions/schools at which they were studying, also reached their heights. In all, 141,000 foreign students studied in China in 2005, a 27.28% upsurge from the preceding year (China Daily, 2006)

Among these foreign students, there are also children who come to China with their working parents. These children usually attend local public schools or expensive international schools. How long they spend in Chinese schools depends on their age and on the duration of parental posting. Children who came to China at a relatively young age are able to speak excellent Chinese, and although they are foreign in appearance, they are well versed in and have internalized the culture and values of the Chinese people.

One can never be certain how many of these overseas students will become immigrants into China. However, it is quite apparent that quite a number will eventually be involved in occupations linked to China's economy, and it would be quite natural that many will be staying in China for a period long enough to qualify them for a Permanent Residency, or a "Green Card." It would not only be practical and convenient for them to do so, it may also be a natural outcome of long-term residence and acclimatization to the lifestyle in China, acculturation to the local societies, and development of social networks and personal linkages with local people.

Cross Border Marriage and Immigration

There is an increasing number of foreign immigrants who stay in China with their Chinese spouses. Though concrete figures are unavailable, there is sufficient indirect evidence. Tianjin, a city just a half-hour's drive from Beijing, is an example that manifests recent changes. From 1980 to 1989, the average annual figure for cross border marriage was just 13 cases; from 1990 to 1998, the average annual rose rapidly to 86; then from 1999 to 2006, the figure further rose up to 224 couples. In 2006 alone, 327 cross-border marriages were registered. There are also hints that those cross-border marriages involve people of a higher socio-economic status. In 1999, 11% people in cross-border marriage had higher educational levels and 57% had only primary education or less; in 2002, 35% possessed higher education qualifications and only 22% involved people with primary level education. In terms of occupation, 33% among those in cross-border marriages in 1997 were jobless, but it was only 15% in 2002. More cross-border marriage involved people from managerial posts, people with senior technical skills, and people involved in commerce and trade. In 1997 they constituted only 26%, while it was 40% in 2002. Before 1995, most cross-border marriages in Tianjin were local women marrying foreign men; it was rare for local men to marry foreign women, and in the 17 years prior to 1995, only 56 cases were recorded, which was only 0.3% of the total number. This gender distribution suggested that in the early cross-border marriages, since the local partner was female, the marriage was an "outbound marriage" and the woman would eventually emigrate. However, from 1996 to 2000, the percentage of local males marrying foreign women rose to 12%, and in 2002 there was another 10% rise (Tinjian Daily, 2007). This change indicates that cross-border marriages are becoming more local and it is highly likely that female foreign partners will reside with their husbands' families.

Homecoming of Overseas Chinese

In recent years, quite a number of "Overseas Chinese" have returned to work in China. Many are students who once studied abroad after China implemented its opening and reform policy. Though they legally migrated to other countries and assumed citizenship elsewhere, many found that opportunities there for them to develop their careers were not as abundant as in China, where they still have links and where the growing economy keeps providing new opportunities that attract them home. Particularly at a time when economic globalization tends to be irreversible, industry pioneers in high technology are frequently traveling around the world to find commercial opportunities to expand business. Consequently, many in this new generation who had migrated earlier, have opted for another migration back to China.

Illegal Immigrants

The number of illegal immigrants into China has been rising in recent years. When compared with neighboring countries such as North Korea, Russia, and others from the Indo-China regions, which often experience political uncertainty, social unrest, or economic turbulence, China's economic growth is particularly enviable. This is also attractive for those seeking to improve the quality of their lives even when legal pathways are unavailable. In recent years, increasing numbers of foreigners with illegal status have been found in China. With China's traditional ties with developing Third World countries, people from such geographically distant areas as Africa, the Middle East, and Southeast Asia are entering China. Several have used China as a springboard to access other countries.

Some illegal immigrants enter China without relevant visas, some are employed illegally without relevant permits, some are found staying in the country without the appropriate permission. According to data from official sources, from 2000 to 2005, public security bureaus around the country handled over 120,000 cases of these three types, also called "Three Foreign-illegals," and 40,000 of them had already been repatriated. In 2005, 31,735 "Three Foreign-illegals" cases were identified, and 7,163 were sent back to their homelands. The 2005 figures were respectively 58% and 80% higher then the 2004 figures (*Global*

Times, 2006). Many of these "foreign-illegals" from the neighboring countries are those reattempting entry, some come and go repeatedly, and some even stay in China for the long term. Of these "foreign-illegals," some are engaged in a variety of petty crimes, smuggling, illegal drug and heroin trafficking, as well as other criminal activities. In addition, there is evidence that foreign women cohabit illegally with locals and then arrange for other relatives to enter China, also illegally (Global Times, 2006).

According to a featured report on illegal immigration to China (International Herald Leader, 2007), with more illegal immigration activities, counterfeit visas to China are sought in many African, East Asian, and West Asian countries. Many individuals from Africa are able to get links to international transportation routes that were opened decades ago with their home countries. While these are more readily traceable, the long borders between China and several neighboring countries pose a greater problem for the immigration and public security units. Many who cross these borders are strong, young males from rural areas. They take the risk associated with illegal entry primarily for one simple reason—to earn money for their families. Most are unconnected to anyone in China, having no trace of social networks, so when they enter the territory successfully, they are difficult to track and identify. As China has already developed comprehensive trade and economic, as well as social and cultural networks with most of the bordering countries, many illegal immigrants can be harbored by organizations that have roots in their countries of origin. Some local residents also benefit from their presence and employ illegal immigrants for cheap labor who do not request payments into pension funds or overhead costs. Their illegal status also makes them vulnerable to manipulation by their employers, with some employers even "trading" illegal laborers among themselves. According to the investigation of the press, this phenomenon is common in Guangdong, where there are agglomerations of foreign traders, particularly merchants from Africa; it is also popular in Zhejiang Yuyao and Yiwu, where many African merchants use the ports for goods transit.

It may be surmised that the changes beginning in the mid-1980s pose many problems regarding illegal immigration. The administration of China is facing new and unanticipated challenges related to this population of migrants and its activities.

Conclusion

There is no doubt that China is still a country with relatively low levels of immigration. The population of China is already large enough to make the recent upsurge in immigrants still only a negligible portion of its total numbers. It is also a fact that although more people have chosen to immigrate to China in recent years, and the pace of the increase is also impressive, China's attractiveness for immigrants is still low when compared to the United States of America, Canada, Australia, and most other European countries. However, it is most apparent and undeniable that push factors for individuals from less affluent countries and pull for those interested in investment are being strengthened and drawing foreigners. On the other hand, the pull that has drawn the Chinese people away from their home is less and less forceful.

China possesses several important attributes to make it a destination country. Its rapid economic growth and booming economy, improving standards of living, better social and physical infrastructures, a competitively low cost of living, a stabilized political atmosphere, the harmonization of international relationships, and the fair or even preferential treatment toward foreigners, will all remain as positive factors instrumental in attracting more people. China is the largest single market in the world, yet it is also a virginal territory for many professional and social services that are essential for it if it is to catch up, and keep pace, with international standards of social and economic development. Unlike many other immigration target countries, China is one of the most recent countries to evidence several prospering growth poles for potential immigrants. The North China Economic Region with Beijing and Tianjin as major cities, the Yangtze Delta Economic Region with Shanghai and Hangzhou as major cities, and the Zhujiang Delta Economic Region with Guangzhou and Shenzhen as major cities are now the most enticing options. Each is with its own assets and special attributes and opportunities for migrants with a variety of talents. It is expected that with strategic plans to develop the northwest, southwest, and the northeast better, additional growth poles will emerge in the next few decades. This is an advantage difficult to envision in the economically developed countries, where unexploited opportunities are not as plentiful or possible.

It should not be denied, however, that China still has quite a number of obvious disincentives for migrants. The political system is still frequently challenged by the international community, the administration still tends to be authoritative and there is widespread corruption, the legal framework still has much room for improvement, the civil society is still in its infancy of development, and the social and cultural quality of the population is also lagging. With twenty years of rapid growth and with economic development overshadowing all other considerations, the quality of the environment is also deteriorating too rapidly, scaring people away. In the experience of many societies, the early rapid growth from low standards always comes with a price, when the social order is jeopardized. Consistent with this, several cities in China are facing a worsening social order, rising crime rates, and weakening social controls, while the modernization of the legal framework is falling behind.

To improve the infrastructure of China for its own huge population, and to make it a destination for global citizens, the government of China has to make efforts for overall enhancement. Of the utmost importance is, of course, the country's ability to stay on the course, taking every effort to preserve the favorable conditions it now possesses. Apart from this, breakthrough has to be sought to overcome existing limitations and emerging problems. While it would be unrealistic to expect all problems be solved overnight, China must focus on keeping its competitive edge and become increasingly integrated into the global village where the world recognizes it as a highly prized destination. This will require the valuing of a more transparent government, openness in policies, a more responsible and accountable administration, and a legal system consistent with international standards that accompany economic development. More efforts must also focus on social problems such as corruption, crime and environmental pollution.

Foreign immigrants are essential for the further development of China. Many advanced skills in management, technology, and professional expertise are still lacking and are needed for China's ongoing progress. Conversely, the country also offers invaluable opportunities for several people from overseas to develop their talents, to actualize their dreams, and to achieve something not necessarily offered by other places. The global flow of talent is now both a reality as well as a necessary ingredient for balanced growth and common well-being. Foreigners coming to live in China, while developing their own abilities and taking advantage of new opportunities, are also bringing new skills, knowledge, ideas, insights, and styles of living and coping. These all interact and combine to foster the development of local civil society, uplifting living quality, and widening the vision of a nation. As such, immigrants should be recognized as contributive and beneficial to the ongoing development of China, for while they are utilizing the opportunities offered by China, they and the nation are uniting in enhancing the well-being of humankind.

References

Central Office of the Chinese Communist Party and the National Council Central Office, PRC Government. (2002). *Summary of Planning for National Manpower Team Building 2002–2005* (Chinese Version Only), announced on June 11, 2002, issued by the Xinhua News Agency. Retrieved from http://www.people.com.cn/GB/shizheng/3586/20020611/750475.html.

Cha, A.E. (2007, October 21). Chasing the Chinese dream. *Washington Post.* Accessed February 20, 2009, from http://www.china-embassy.org/eng/zt/mgryzdzg/t374521.htm.

China Daily. (2004, October 5). Foreigners welcome "green card." Retrieved from http://english.people daily.com.cn/200410/05/eng20041005_159117.html.

China Daily. (2006, June 17). China popular student destination. Retrieved from http://www.chinadaily.com.cn/bizchina/2006-06/17/content_619338.htm.

Global Times. (2006, August 21). 380,000 foreigners staying permanently in China. (In Chinese). Retrieved from the People Web at http://world.people.com.cn/GB/14549/4721714.html.

International Herald Leader. (2007, October 28). A report on the study on foreigners entering China illegally (In Chinese). Retrieved from http://qzone.qq.com/blog/622006595-1196246189.

Johnson, T. (2006). Foreigners in China. *China rises.* Accessed February 20, 2009, from http://washingtonbureau.typepad.com/china/2006/09/foreigners_in_c.html.

Kim, S. S. (2003). China and North Korea in a changing world. *Asia Program Special Report, 115,* 11–17.

Leavey, H. (2006, January 9). Foreigners flock to learn Chinese. *BBC News Online.* Retrieved February 20, 2009, from http://news.bbc.co.uk/2/hi/asia-pacific/4594698.stm.

People's Daily. (2005, July 25). "Foreign workers" find favor in China. Retrieved July 25, 2005, from http://english.peopledaily.com.cn/200507/25/eng20050725_198103.html.

People's Daily Online. (2005, July 25). 100,000 foreigners enjoy life in China. Retrieved from http://english.peopledaily.com.cn/200507/25/eng20050725_198118.html.

Public Security Bureau of Government of PRC. (2005, November 22). Press release on "20 years achievement on Entry and Exit Control." Retrieved from www.gov.cn/xwfb/2005-11/22/

Tinjian Daily. (2007, September 14). More marriage involving foreigners in Tinjian, in-laws from all over the six continents (In Chinese). Retrieved from *Sohu News* at http://news.sohu.com/20070914/n252148504.shtml.

Xinhua News Agency (2002, June 12). Our country is going to implement investment immigration and skill immigration law to attract overseas experts. (Chinese version only, English version deleted). Retrieved from http://www.chinaembassycanada.org/chn/xwdt/t28674.htm.

Yangching Evening News. (2007, May 31). Statistics show that 180,000 foreigners are working in China (Chinese version only). Retrieved from *Sina News* at http://news.sina.com.cn/c/2007-05-31/151713122427.shtml.

Zhang, C. (2007). *Jindai Xifang Qiaomin Laihua Yuanyin Pouxi* [The analysis of the motives of the modern Western residents coming to China]. *Tianjin Shifan Daxue Xuebao (Shehui Kexue Ban)* [*Journal of Tianjin Normal University (Social Science)*], Vol. 194, No. 5: 53–58.

Zheng, N. (2007). Chinese green card system continues to evolve. *China.org.cn.* Retrieved February 20, 2009, from http://www.china.org.cn/english/LivinginChina/221738.htm.

24

South Africa

Immigration to Post-Apartheid South Africa: Critical Reflections

Brij Maharaj

Internationally, cross-border movements are widely viewed as a consequence of globalization. However, cross-border migration in the developing world is a result of increasing economic and social inequalities. In spite of "a widespread strengthening of control measures," the cross-border movements are "a self-sustaining process destined to grow in the future, unless major changes in the distribution of wealth between rich and poor countries are implemented" (Balbo and Marconi, 2005:2).

In southern Africa, South Africa continues, as in the past, to attract migrants from nearly all neighboring countries. However, as the new South Africa seeks integration and greater participation in the global economy and in world politics, there is a contradictory trend toward exclusivity in respect to its immigration policy. There have been long delays in developing a new progressive immigration policy in South Africa, and this has been attributed to "national politics, bureaucratic bungling, and the very real dilemma of formulating democratic, rights-based migration in what is a highly xenophobic society" (Dodson, 2002:1).

In this chapter it will be argued that the South African government has two options: continue with the law-and-order approach and ineffective policing that contributes to high levels of xenophobia, or adopt a more sensitive human rights approach that recognizes the creative ways in which migrants contribute to the local economy. This chapter draws generously from the South African census, Department of Labour, surveys conducted by the South African Migration Project (SAMP), reports of the International Organization for Migration (IOM), reports of the South African Human Rights Commission (SAHRC), reports of Human Rights Watch, and reports of the United Nations High Commissioner for Refugees (UNHCR).

Historical Context

The migration of workers from other parts of Africa to South Africa has a long history Davies and Head, 1995). Historically, the mining and agriculture sectors in South Africa have been dependent on contract male migrant labor from southern African countries who were denied citizenship rights (Jeeves, 1985; Murray, 1995). Census data reveals that in 1911 there were 229,207 non–South Africans from the region in the country (Table 24-1). The

Table 24-1. Foreign Born Africans in South Africa, 1911–1985

	1911	1921	1936	1946	1951	1970	1980	1985
Angola			28	6,716	6,322	3,859	589	392
Botswana	5,020	11,959	4,048	38,559	51,017	49,469	33,366	26,015
Lesotho	75,132	111,733	163,838	199,327	219,065	157,499	172,879	135,563
Malawi	4,573	22,122	17,657	61,005	63,655	110,777	36,087	28,712
Mozambique	114,976	110,245	98,031	141,417	161,240	142,512	64,813	63,561
Namibia	2,230	2,926	1,879	4,990	4,129	2,518	10,342	9,210
Swaziland	21,662	29,177	31,092	33,738	42,914	29,167	31,981	30,722
Tanzania	n/a	n/a	118	2,937	7,127	288	145	887
Zambia	2,158	n/a	12,189	13,515	13,544	2,194	1,495	926
Zimbabwe	2,526	n/a	2,167	32,034	32,697	13,392	20,552	7,019
Other	930	5,146	2,730	22,569	4,282	4,369	4,234	14,003
Total	229,207	279,819	333,777	556,807	605,992	516,044	376,483	317,010

Source: Labor Market Survey, 2007, p. 5.

main foreign laborers in South African mines were recruited from Angola, Botswana, Lesotho Malawi, Mozambique, Swaziland, Tanzania, Zambia, and Zimbabwe.[1]

This increased progressively and in 1951 there were 605,992 migrants. Between 1951 and 1985 there was a decrease in migrants in South Africa (Table 24-1). This decline was associated with apartheid restrictions imposed after 1948 on African migrants. Many laborers were deported and others left voluntarily. Also, by the late 1980s "the South African gold mining industry entered a long period of restructuring and down-sizing as a result of declining ore reserves, rising costs and a stagnant gold price" (Labour Market Review, 2007:10).

However, there were also irregular migrants entering the country in the apartheid era. The apartheid government subtly encouraged or turned a blind eye to clandestine migration in order to ensure an abundant supply of cheap labor, especially in the agricultural sector, but was opposed to black migrants' applying for citizenship. This dispels the myth that "illegal immigration began after the end of apartheid" (Vigneswaran, 2008:141).

The racist orientation of South African immigration policy became very evident when the government welcomed whites from neighboring states in southern Africa who felt threatened by black majority rule (Crush, 2000). Between 1960 and 1980, skilled and semiskilled white migrants from Zambia, Kenya and Zimbabwe were given citizenship to boost the local population (Peberdy,

1997). In the post-apartheid era, undocumented migration has become a huge challenge.

Immigration Challenges in the Post-Apartheid Era

In the 1990s immigration to post-apartheid South Africa became a potentially explosive issue. The reasons for this are steeped in a variety of social, political, and economic situations not only in countries of origin but in destination areas as well. The patterns, nature, and socio-cultural and economic implications are extremely complicated. Immigration policy and controls have become very restrictive as emigration has increased. Legal immigration numbers are very low and there has also been a decline in temporary work permits. According to Mattes, Crush, and Richmond (2002:1–3) "immigration is not viewed as a public policy tool that could benefit South Africa." There has been an increase in irregular migration and at least three categories can be identified: (1) undocumented migrants; (2) refugees and asylum-seekers; and (3) victims of human trafficking.

Undocumented Migrants

It is possible to differentiate between two categories of undocumented migrants. The first category refers to those who enter the country without valid documents. The second refers to migrants who enter the country legitimately with visas or work permits. Once their permits lapse they remain in the country and join the ranks of the undocumented migrants (Lorgat, 1998). The primary focus of the rest of this chapter is on undocumented migrants. However, there is a need to elaborate on the other two categories, which are forms of forced migration.

Refugees and Asylum-Seekers

Generally, there has been little attempt to differentiate between refugees and undocumented migrants in South Africa. Refugees, as forced migrants, have suffered displacement under conditions not of their own choosing. When refugees abandon their own home, community, and country, they do so because there is a probability of their losing all rights and face being murdered, tortured, raped, imprisoned, enslaved, robbed, or starved (Worth, 2006).

During the apartheid era South Africa did not abide by the United Nations refugee conventions and it "exported" asylum-seekers (political activists) who received refuge in many African countries. The Refugees Act was passed in 1998 and was operational in the year 2000, and incorporated international conventions, including the 1951 United Nations Refugee Convention. Hence, in theory, the Consortium for Refugees and Migrants in South Africa (CRMSA) contended that asylum seekers and refugees were guaranteed "physical security, access to critical social services, and access to courts and due process of the law" (CRMSA, 2007:14). However, the country's legal and moral obligations have not been "supported by the necessary human and financial resources needed to offer basic protections to asylum seekers and refugees" (CRMSA, 2007:14). There appeared to be a lack of political will to address the needs of refugees.

There have been serious delays and backlogs in processing refugee and asylum applications, and delays of up to five years have been experienced in processing claims. In the first democratic decade South Africa received about 150,000 applications for asylum, of which 26,900 were granted refugee status (Labour Market Review, 2007:17). The UNHCR (2008:193) has suggested some economic migrants were attempting to use the asylum route to remain in the country because of "stringent immigration regulations."

Victims of Human Trafficking

According to research conducted by the IOM, South Africa is a destination, source, and transit point for human trafficking. Poverty-stricken people from the African continent, Asia, and Eastern Europe have become victims of traffickers who exploit this vulnerable group in the sex industry and labor-intensive agricultural and industrial activities. Most victims of human trafficking come from refugee-producing countries (Martens, Pieczkowski, and Vuuren-Smyth, 2003).

Internationally, human trafficking is a highly lucrative criminal activity, generating between $7 billion and $10 billion annually, with only the drug dealing and the weapons trade generating higher profits. However, it is not possible to estimate the profits generated from trafficking in South Africa (Martens, Pieczkowski, and Vuuren-Smyth, 2003:11). By its very nature human trafficking is clandestine and invisible, hence it is difficult to assess the scale and extent of the problem. However, the IOM, for example, has estimated that about 1,000 women from Mozambique are trafficked into South Africa annually (Martens, Pieczkowski, and Vuuren-Smyth, 2003:39). Preliminary research has revealed the following trends in human trafficking in South Africa:

South Africa is one of the central points for trafficking of women and children in southern Africa.
South Africans are trafficked to Hong Kong and Macau (China)
Women from other African countries are trafficked via South Africa to Europe.
Men and boys are trafficked from neighboring countries for forced agricultural labor.
Thai, Chinese, and Eastern European women are trafficked to South Africa for debt-bonded sexual exploitation.
Victims are recruited by deception, coercion, and force (Goliath, 2008:5).

South Africa is in the process of developing anti-trafficking laws. There has been considerable controversy about the number of undocumented migrants in the country.

Do the Numbers Add Up?

In the migration debate in South Africa there has been a focus on two key questions: "How many foreigners and how many of these are illegal?" (Wa Kabwe-Segatt and Landau, 2008:214). Estimates of the number of undocumented immigrants in South Africa varied widely. This was because the majority entered the country covertly. It was therefore not possible for the government or researchers to give a reasonable estimate of the number of migrants in the country (Hough, 1995). However, "in the vacuum, cavalier and exaggerated numbers predominate" (Crush and Williams, 2001:3).

In 1990 the South African Yearbook indicated that there were about 1.2 million illegal immigrants in the country, in 1991 the estimate was 2 million, in 1992 it was 2.5 million, 3 million in 1993, and 5 million in 1994 (Minnaar et al., 1995:33). The accuracy of these figures, however, has been questioned, and it subsequently emerged that these inflated statistics were based on a methodologically flawed survey conducted by the Human Science Research Council (HSRC). The HSRC acknowledged the flaws and withdrew the exaggerated projections (Wa Kabwe-Segatt and Landau, 2008).

South African census data dispelled the notion that the country was being flooded by foreigners. The 2001 census suggested that there were 1,025,072 foreign born people in South Africa, comprising 2.3 percent of the country's total population. In 2006 the census recorded 958,186 foreigners in South Africa (2.4 percent of the country's total population) (Labour Market Review, 2007:7).

A more realistic assessment is also presented by deportation figures. In 1988, 44,225 migrants were deported, and by 1993 the figure had increased to 96,515 (*Natal Witness*, January 1, 1995). In 1996 deportation reached a peak of 180,000 (Wa Kabwe-Segatt and Landau, 2008:214). The majority came from southern African countries, especially Mozambique and Zimbabwe (*Natal Witness*, January 1, 1995). However, the discredited and inflated figures of the number of immigrants have been routinely quoted by politicians and public policy makers, promoting an antiforeigner discourse.

Demographic Profile

The South African Migration Survey (SAMP) has been conducting numerous surveys focusing on immigration issues in the 1990s. One such survey was conducted in Durban in 1999. The Durban survey revealed that the average age of migrants was 34 years. A national survey revealed that the average age of migrants was 32 years (McDonald, Mashike, and Golden, 1999). In Durban most of the migrants (70 percent) were in their economic prime, between 25 and 44 years. Only 15 percent were younger than 24 years, and 4 percent were older than 55 years. The majority (74 percent) of the migrants were males (Maharaj and Moodley, 1999).

The migrants had a fairly good educational background. This is reflected by the fact that a significant number had secondary (45 percent) and tertiary (29 percent) education. Sixteen percent had some form of primary education, and only a few (10 percent) had no formal education. Over fifty percent of the migrants were single (never married). A significant proportion (32 percent) were married. Almost equal proportions who were married left their spouses in the country of origin or brought them to South Africa. Presently, 49 percent of the migrants were living with a partner, 27 percent were married, and 24 percent were single. It was interesting to note that many spouses/partners of migrants were South African (78 percent) (Maharaj and Moodley, 1999).

Gender imbalance among African immigrants to South Africa was clearly evident. African immigrants are composed of significantly more males than females (Dodson, 1998). This gender-related migration pattern may be due to the dangers of travel, the cost, and the fact that numerous obstacles have to be overcome on the long journey overland. These reasons could also be attributed to most married immigrants' leaving their children at places of origin. Women were subjected to greater levels of trauma and indignity in the migration process, and this was emphasized by Deputy Minister of Home Affairs, Nosiviwe Mapisa-Nqakula, who had been in exile during the apartheid era:

Television and newspaper images of millions of women with sick and malnourished babies strapped to their backs is evidence of how women are affected by the migration cycle. Women not only suffer the emotional trauma of helplessly watching their children die during these long journeys, but they also become victims of abuse and undignified treatment along the way. I have learnt first hand that women immigrants suffer a great deal more than their male counterparts. The trauma of being separated from their families and the indignity of having someone else taking decisions that affect your life without your involvement are just some of the added frustrations for women refugees. (*City Press*, September 29, 2002)

Given the number of years that they have been living in South Africa, many of them have established homes and families in this country. Some of the migrants have families back home, so returning would not be a problem, although they faced the specter of unemployment and poverty. The majority of immigrants were not enthusiastic about returning home (country of origin), and if they had a choice, they would remain in South Africa. A few of them stated that they would not return to South Africa again because it did not meet their expectations. Others maintained that regardless of the number of times they might be deported, they would return to South Africa (Maharaj and Moodley, 1999).

The migration process described above concurs with that experienced in most Third World countries. In regions where there are widespread social and economic inequalities, rapid migration would be expected between countries. Although there are internal institutional restrictions on movements between countries, many people are likely to take great risks to enter countries that are perceived to have better economic opportunities. Given their illegal status, they are subject to exploitation by employers and their "presence may also engender considerable resentment from other citizens, fearful of the effects of illegal workers on their own jobs and rates of pay" (Parnwell, 1993:53).

Reasons for Leaving Home Country

Most migrants came to South Africa to escape the poverty and destitution in their own countries, as well as civil wars and political instability. Harris (1995:189) contends that the "persistence of the idea that poverty drives out unskilled migrants from developing to developed

countries is extraordinary. They are, it seems, really refugees, expelled by economic processes." According to the World Bank the countries surrounding South Africa, with the exception of Namibia and Botswana, are among the poorest in the world (World Bank, 1999).

Many of these migrants trek to South Africa due to the changed political climate. It was assumed that since President Nelson Mandela's government had taken over, the country was overflowing with economic opportunities. Surveys conducted by SAMP have suggested that the majority of migrants have no intention of settling permanently in South Africa (Mattes et al., 1999). Reitzes (1997) has similarly argued that migrants were transient and wanted to commute across borders rather than to live permanently in South Africa.

Immigrants often have to depend on social networks. Various studies have revealed (e.g., Maharaj and Moodley, 1999; Muanamoha, Maharaj, and Preston-Whyte, 2008), that the majority of the illegal immigrants coming to South Africa had some sort of "contact" in this country, either a relative or friend. These contacts in South Africa provided housing and food and even organized some form of employment for the migrants. The majority of immigrants had some skills and training, and had been engaged in productive employment in South Africa.

Many migrants maintain links back home, still own houses, and have bank accounts and investments. Depending on resources and distance, most migrants return home on an "irregular basis." According to Mattes, Crush, and Richmond (2002:2) "in a transnational world many contemporary immigrants maintain strong and active backward linkages. This does not mean that they are uncommitted to their country of new residence."

Reception in Host Country

Often viewed as a source of cheap labor by some employers, the migrants have been accused of being parasites and stealing the jobs of South Africans, in an economy which had a high unemployment rate (up to about 40 percent). Such perceptions influenced the development of xenophobia, and the migrants increasingly became the targets of violence. Xenophobia is rife in the townships, where the migrants are referred to as *kwerekwere* (disparaging word for African immigrant. Crush (2008:44–55) presents a detailed chronology of xenophobic violence against foreign migrants between 1994 and 2008. The most serious was the outbreak of violence in May 2008, which started in the township of Alexandra in Johannesburg and subsequently spread to major informal settlements in the country for almost two weeks. At least 62 people lost their lives and about 43,000 foreigners were displaced.

Many reasons have been advanced for violence against foreigners. It has been argued that xenophobia thrives when there is competition for employment and social problems increase. Migrants are seen as tempting "scapegoats" for the "country's ills":

> With a black government in power and apartheid gone, many black South Africans have realised that they can no longer blame the system. Most are turning on the most visible scapegoat—immigrants. The new government would do well on its promise of a better life for all before discontented South Africans turn on foreigners and blame them for the country's ills. (*Sunday Times*, August 28, 1994)

A study conducted by the Human Science Research Council (HSRC, 2008:6) advanced four reasons for the outbreak and spread of xenophobic violence:

Frustration over the insufficient pace of service delivery and consultation in general, and over housing provision and administration in particular;

Ineffective communication and/or engagement with local citizenry around the violence and its underlying causes;

Perceived corruption and impropriety of government officials, especially in the police service and the Department of Home Affairs; and

Foreign nationals perceived to arrive in the country with cash, skills, and tolerance of low wages and hard work.

Moving beyond economic and material explanations, Bouillon (1998:23–24) has suggested that

"immigrants tend to interpret a culturally driven hostility among black South Africans . . . driven by the sight of the foreign and the culturally unknown." This point was emphasized in a recent article celebrating the adoption of the African Charter on Human Rights and People's Rights in the weekly newspaper, the *Mail and Guardian*, October 22–28, 1999, which suggested that "South Africa is regarded by its neighbours as rapacious, imperialist and xenophobic" (pp. 12–13).

The rising tide of xenophobia leads to demands for the immediate deportation and repatriation of migrants. However, given the social and political instability, and economic deprivation in Africa, South Africa will continue to be a haven for people who are desperate to improve their lives.

National surveys have revealed that most South Africans believed immigrants have a negative impact on the country (Crush, 2008). Also, there was very little differentiation between illegal immigrants and refugees. Almost 60 percent stated that immigrants weakened the economy and undermined South African resources, respectively. There was greater prejudice against migrants from Africa, and a preference for immigrants from Europe and North America. These perceptions were "widespread and cut across indicators of age, education, gender, economic status and race" (Crush, 2001:6). A national survey on South African attitudes toward migration revealed that 25 percent wanted a total ban on immigration, and 45 percent wanted this process to be rigidly controlled. Only 17 percent were in favor of a liberal, flexible approach related to the availability of jobs (Mattes, 1999:1). Yet only 4 percent of South African respondents actually had regular direct contact with migrants, "suggesting that these stereotypes may be the product of second-hand (mis)information" (Mattes, et al., 1999:2).

Exploitation of migrant workers was also quite common. In addition to lower wages, they were also deprived of benefits like pensions and medical aid. They did not belong to trade unions, hence they received no protection from exploitation and were often summarily dismissed. Reitzes (1994:9) describes the aliens as a "marginalised underclass who are easily open to abuse"

Devoid of state protection, and denied any rights and entitlements, aliens look for jobs to survive. Because of their illegal status they are forced to accept employment whatever the payment, risk, physical demand or working hours involved. Exploitation of migrant labour carries the risk of social decay, with decreasing wages and deteriorating working conditions.... The creation of such a rightless class also pushes many of them into the criminal underworld, either as a more attractive option or a means of survival.

Migrants and Crime

Migrants have been criminalized as a result of not having official travel documents as well as by media stereotyping that they were associated with illegal activities. In 1999, 606 foreigners were convicted of crimes in South Africa, and this increased to 1,586 in 2002 (Vigneswaran, 2008). Omar Osman, chairperson of the International Refugee Service argued that statistics from the police indicated refugees were responsible for less than 2 percent of crime in the country (Leeman, 2001).

However, the police and politicians often associated migrants with criminal activities without providing evidence to support this contention. In November 1997 Defense Minister Joe Modise argued that unauthorized migrants had contributed to the increase in crime in South Africa: "As for crime, the army is helping the police get rid of crime and violence in the country. However, what can we do? We have one million illegal immigrants in our country who commit crimes and who are mistaken by some people for South African citizens" (quoted in Human Rights Watch, 1998:1).

If the undocumented immigrant issue was viewed as matter of law and order, then the problem was likely to be aggravated in the long term. It would increase xenophobia, contribute to the development of a "criminal underclass," and adversely affect relations with neighboring countries. This would go against the "ANC's stated commitment to human rights, in terms of which the moral responsibility of the state is assumed to transcend territorial boundaries" (Reitzes, 1994:11).

A report by the South African Human Rights Commission (SAHRC) on the arrest and detention of migrants revealed that in many instances those arrested were subjected to violations of their basic rights. In most instances the police had no grounds to believe that a person was a foreigner. A significant proportion of those arrested had legal identification documents. Quite often those who were arrested were not given reasons for being apprehended. Corruption was rife among arresting officers, who accepted bribes from those in custody (SAHRC, 1999:3–4).

Given the high levels of prejudice, there was a failure to recognize that migrants have also been victims of crime. National surveys have suggested that "migrants are disproportionately the victims of crime, made worse by inadequate redress in law and lack of protection by the police" (McDonald, Mashike, and Golden, 1999:19). A persistent refrain has been that migrants increase the pressure on social and welfare services, and that they were carriers of disease.

Welfare, Health, and Disease

There has been a great deal of debate about the rights of noncitizens in South Africa. A major concern is that decades of institutionalized socio-economic inequalities will not be eliminated overnight. This has been compounded by increasing levels of poverty since 1994, a consequence of neoliberal macroeconomic strategies. Against this background, there are serious moral questions about whether social services like health and welfare should be extended to migrants when a large proportion of South Africans do not have such access. However, South African exiles had been granted asylum and social benefits by many African governments in support of the anti-apartheid struggle. Therefore, can a post-apartheid, ANC-dominated government deny such benefits to migrants from other parts of Africa? (McDonald, Mashike, and Golden, 1999:24).

Politicians in South Africa have expressed concern about the increased pressure that migrants will exert on basic services, and social and welfare resources (McDonald, Mashike, and Golden, 1999). The majority of South Africans believed that social services should not be extended to migrants (Taylor, et al., 1999). It has been argued that illegal immigrants increased the pressure and burden on health, welfare, and other social services; safety and security; and correctional services and justice. However, surveys have revealed that migrants do not expect their basic services to be subsidized, and are prepared to pay for any services that they obtain (McDonald, Mashike, and Golden, 1999). The international and South African experience suggests that migrants contribute to the economy and make low levels of demand for state welfare resources compared to locals (Centre for Development Enterprise, 1997).

Migrants also faced enormous difficulties in getting access to housing. This was not surprising, given that there was a national shortage of 3 million houses in South Africa. In 1997 the Minister of Housing, Sankie Mthembu-Mahanyele, attributed the escalating housing shortage to the increasing number of foreigners: "We can't keep immigrants out. Somehow our borders are porous" (*Business Report*, January 31, 1997). Although in theory the South African government is committed to providing reasonable access to housing for all who live in the country, in practice there are many contradictions, inconsistencies, and exclusions:

There are no clear policies on access to housing for non-citizens in South Africa. There are policy documents, constitutional clauses and international agreements which commit the South African government in various ways to "ensuring access to adequate housing for all persons living in the country," but these commitments are often inconsistent with one another and even contradictory when it comes to defining who is entitled to housing (McDonald, 1998:1).

Another area of concern is the link between migration and the spread of disease. There have been few well-documented and structured studies that have investigated the links between migration and the spread of infectious diseases (Williams et al., 2002). Since the migrants entered the country illegally, not much was known about the diseases they might have carried. However, when they were arrested and imprisoned the state of their health was assessed and the diseases they carried were identified. Many diseases with epidemic potential, for example, yellow fever, cholera, and other subtropical diseases, were

being brought into the country by the illegal immigrants. Some migrants were diagnosed as being HIV positive.

About 13,000 migrant mine workers from Malawi were repatriated from South Africa between 1988 and 1992 because 200 had tested HIV/AIDS positive (Chirwa, 1998). The relationship between migration and HIV/AIDS is very important in a southern African context because of the movement of migrant labor. In fact a "key neglected factor in explaining the rapid spread and prevalence of HIV/AIDS in Southern Africa over the last decade is human mobility" (Williams, et al., 2002:1). Migration influences the spread of HIV in several ways, including:

Mobility per se can encourage or make people vulnerable to high risk sexual behavior;

Mobility makes people more difficult to reach, whether for prevention education, condom provision, HIV testing, or postinfection treament and care;

Migrants' multilocal social networks create opportunities for sexual networking; and

There is a higher rate of HIV infection in "communities of the mobile," which often include socially, economically, and politically marginalized people (IOM, 2005:22).

It has been argued that "unless the issues of migration and disease are understood and dealt with effectively, it is unlikely that the greater struggle to control and manage AIDS can be won" (Williams, et al., 2002:32).

Immigrant Contribution

There has been some controversy about the economic impact of migrants. Some argue that migrants take away jobs from locals and work for lower wages. Others suggest that unskilled migrants accept jobs that locals would reject. Also, skilled migrants bring savings as well as add entrepreneurial creativity into the economy (Walker, Ellis, and Barf, 1992:235).

International experience suggests that immigrants contribute more to the economic development of their host countries than is acknowledged in South Africa (Harris, 1995;

Bouillon, 1998). Far from being parasites, studies have suggested that immigrants contribute generatively to the economy. On average, migrants tend to be more talented, healthier, and ambitious than the local population. They make fewer demands on social welfare services, and contribute as taxpayers (Meintjies, 1998:20).

One area in which immigrants had an indirect impact on the economy was in the area of formal and informal businesses such as hair saloons, supermarkets, African crafts, taxis, and upholstery. These businesses were established with funds from home countries, loans from friends, and earnings in South Africa. Direct revenue to the state did not accrue because of the nonregistration of most businesses and hence nonpayment of taxes. Those that did contribute to taxation paid an average of R805 per year. Indirectly, however they do contribute to value added tax (VAT) via their purchasing of goods (Maharaj and Moodley, 1999).

However, an area of direct conflict and confrontation between the locals and foreigners has been in the informal sector, particularly hawking. Given their vulnerable status, most migrants start off in the informal sector, often selling similar goods as locals. Migrants in the informal sector generally believed that South African engaged in similar economic activities were hostile toward them due to competition. Hunter and Skinner (2003:307) have argued that in Durban "the main competition between local and foreign traders is over space to operate . . . foreign traders involved in service activities seem to be doing work that South African traders are not carrying out, and even those in retail activities, such as those selling clothes, are servicing different market segments." The study of street traders in Durban revealed that the majority also sourced their goods from local suppliers and thereby created job opportunities for South Africans, in addition to employing South Africans in their enterprises. The major obstacles identified by foreign street traders in Durban include lack of economic recognition, harassment by the police, and inadequate infrastructure (Hunter and Skinner, 2003).

Perception of the failure of the state to stem the tide of migrants has led to the development of organizations such as Micro Business against Crime and Illegal Foreigners Action Group,

which have advocated a boycott of foreign street traders as well as firms employing migrants. More disturbingly, an organization called the Unemployed People of South Africa "threatened to take the law into its own hands and physically remove migrants from South Africa if the government fails to deport them" (Human Rights Watch, 1998:3).

Since 1994 the African Chamber of Hawkers and Independent Businessmen (ACHIB) has vociferously campaigned for the expulsion of migrant hawkers, and arranged a number of meetings and marches to rouse antiforeigner sentiment. Many of these marches turned violent, and foreign hawkers were assaulted, and received little or no protection from the police. In Durban and Johannesburg foreign hawkers complained that local authorities were trying to exclude them from applying for trading licenses. The situation was aggravated when the Deputy Minister of Home Affairs, Ms Lindiwe Sisulu, contended that the migrants were trading illegally and that South Africans should receive preference in the allocation of hawking licenses:

South Africa's immigration policy is premised upon the notion that no immigrant should be employed at the detriment of a South African citizen . . . As the Department of Home Affairs does not issue immigration or work permits to foreigners permitting them to become informal traders, those foreigners with immigration or work permits issued to them for employment other than hawking, have in fact illegally entered the hawking business. (Human Rights Watch, 1998:4)

Immigrant-owned businesses have become an important part of small, medium, and microenterprise sector in Johannesburg and have changed the socioeconomic structure of the inner city. Despite hostility from locals, the immigrant entrepreneurs were positive and intended to expand their enterprises. Significantly, such foreign owned enterprises were creating jobs for South Africans (Rogerson, 1997).

If the stigma of illegality were removed, it is possible that such migrants could contribute significantly to the local economy through the creation of employment opportunities as well as the training of local people. Further, the majority would then be compelled to pay taxes and this would increase the resource base of the government for reconstruction and development. Migrants can also compensate for the immigration or "brain drain."

Brain Drain Emigration

While there has been a tendency to overestimate the number of undocumented immigrants in South Africa, there has also been an inclination to underestimate the extent of emigration or the "brain drain." Between 1989 and 1997 about 233,000 South Africans emigrated to the UK, USA, Canada, Australia and New Zealand (Crush, et al., 2000:1). However, official statistics revealed that 82,811 people had left during this period (Centre for Development Enterprise, 2000). This loss of skills was not offset by a proactive, aggressive recruiting immigration policy.

The flight of skills has serious social, economic, and political consequences. There is also a clear gender dimension, with men being more likely to leave permanently then women (Dodson, 2002). The main reasons for the exodus are "unacceptable levels of crime and violence, economic stagnation, and perceptions of declining standards in the quality of public sector services, most notably education and health" (Rogerson and Rogerson, 2000:64).

Throughout the 1990s there has been a steady decline in the number of immigrants. In 1993 there were 9,824 immigrants and this declined to 4103 in 1997 (Table 24-2). The net migrant gain/loss for the period 1970–1999 is reflected in Table 24-2. The implications of these trends are very clear. There will continue to be a shortage of skills as well as an oversupply of unskilled labor.

Table 24-2. Immigrants and Emigrants: 1970–1997

Year	Total		Net	Gross
	Immigrants	Emigrants	Migration	Migration
1970	41,523	9,278	32,369	50,677
1971	35,845	8,407	27,554	44,136
1972	32,776	7,884	−1,232	14,536
1973	24,016	6,401	−1,040	11,762
1974	35,910	7,428	935	15,791
1975	50,464	10,225	1,573	22,023
1976	46,239	15,641	30,598	61,880
1977	24,822	26,000	−1,178	50,822
1978	18,669	20,686	−2,017	39,355
1979	18,680	15,694	2,986	34,374
1980	29,365	11,363	18,002	40,728
1981	41,542	8,791	32,751	50,333
1982	45,784	6,832	38,952	52,616
1983	30,483	8,247	22,236	38,730
1984	28,793	8,550	20,243	37,343
1985	17,284	11,401	5,883	28,685
1986	6,994	13,711	−6,717	20,705
1987	7,953	11,174	−3,221	19,127
1988	10,400	7,767	2,633	18,167
1989	11,270	4,911	6,359	16,181
1990	14,499	4,722	9,777	19,221
1991	12,379	4,256	8,123	16,635
1992	8,686	4,289	4,397	12,975
1993	9,824	2,013	7,811	17,902
1994	6,398	10,235	−3,837	16,633
1995	5,064	8,725	−3,661	13,789
1996	5,407	9,708	−4,301	15,115
1997	4,103	8,946	−4,843	13,049
Total	625,172	273,285	351,887	898,457

Source: Simelane, 1999, pp. 6–7.

The negative implications will reverberate throughout the South African economy and impact on the country's global competitiveness as "skilled workers generally create jobs for unskilled workers and the level of skills in the labour force is an attraction for foreign investment" (Wocke and Klein, 2002:441).

Changing Policy Perspectives

As Croucher (1998:654) emphasizes, "immigration in South Africa and elsewhere, is a complex social, political and economic issue that poses numerous policy challenges for even the most stable democratic states." Official policy toward the illegal immigrants has also sometimes been confusing, incoherent, and contradictory because the government had "been caught unawares by the enormity, complexity and seeming intractability of dealing with large scale black immigration" (*Mercury*, October 26, 1995). Various policy options have been advocated to resolve the illegal immigrant issue, ranging from tighter border controls and implementation of law and order, to those that attempt to understand the problem in its regional and historical context.

"Control, Exclusion and Expulsion"

In 1994 official government policy toward undocumented migrants was embodied in the Aliens Control Act (1991), which provided for the deportation of culprits as well as the prosecution of those who employed them, and was "a piece of legislation premised on principles of control, exclusion and expulsion" (Crush, 1999:2). The Aliens Control Act was described by the Human Rights Watch (1998:4) organization as an obsolete relic of the apartheid era, which conflicted with "internationally accepted human rights norms and the South African constitution."

Crush (1996) has presented compelling evidence that suggests that the Aliens Control Act (1991) had been implemented in a racially discriminatory manner in the post-apartheid era. In the first quarter of 1996 about 130,000 visitors to South Africa remained in the country after their visas had expired, and this included 12,000 from the UK, 11,000 from Germany, 3,000 from

the United States, and about 1,000 from Australia, Belgium, Switzerland, and Taiwan. A very small proportion of these people were arrested and deported—23 from the UK, 13 from Germany, 8 from the United States, 4 from Australia, 2 from Belgium, and 1 from Switzerland. In 1995, 98 percent of deportations were to southern African countries. Further more, in the first decade of democracy about one million illegal migrants were deported to countries in Africa (Crush and Williams, 2005:12–13).

In late 1996 the government appointed a Green Paper task group to develop a new framework for revising migration legislation. In pointing out that many aspects of the Aliens Control Act "would probably not withstand the test of constitutionality," the task group argued that the "challenge facing South Africa is to transform a racially motivated immigration/migration system into a non-racial and rational policy response to the objective needs of the country" (Republic of South Africa, 1997:19).

A Rights-Based Approach

The Draft Green Paper on International Migration, released in May 1997, argued for a migration policy that was humane, contributed to economic development, took cognizance of global realities, and was consistent with the new Constitution and Bill of Rights. The Green Paper emphasised the need to admit people with skills and resources, and was "in favour of more open and effectively managed rules of entry driven by labour-market need" (Republic of South Africa, 1997:19).

The Draft Paper acknowledged South Africa's historical and political linkages with other countries in the region. It maintained that as long as there was widespread inequalities and polarized economic growth in the region, South Africa would continue to attract large numbers of migrants. The Green Paper suggested that the "problem of unauthorised migration should in part be dealt with by giving bona fide economic migrants from other SADC countries, who have no intention of settling here permanently, increased opportunities for legal participation in our labour market" (Republic of South Africa, 1997:11). It was pointed out that South African jurisprudence on immigration is not well developed and focused on "arrest, detention and removals," a hangover from the apartheid era.

Big Brother Is Watching

Compared to the progressive recommendations of the Green Paper, the White Paper was actually retrogressive. The White Paper echoed the popular xenophobic view that migrants were linked to crime, competed with citizens for jobs, increased pressure on social services, and contributed to corruption. It did not provide any evidence to support these claims, and ignored research that suggested that this was not so (Republic of South Africa, 1999). There would heavy penalties for employers of illegal immigrants.

The intention was to cultivate an "environment which does not offer them (migrants) opportunities of employment and free available public services which they cannot find in their countries of origin" (Republic of South Africa, 1999:31). The focus was on enforcement, and in the White Paper there was a shift in emphasis from regulating borders to community and workplace monitoring of migrants. According to the White Paper the government expected civil society to play a critical watchdog role in enforcing immigration laws by ensuring that the community was not sheltering noncitizens (Republic of South Africa, 1999:16).

This was similar to Proposition 187 introduced by Californian Governor Pete Wilson to deny social services to undocumented migrants, and in terms of which service providers were required by law to report the presence of such individuals to the authorities (Diamond, 1996). However, such a policy shift was extremely distressing given the high levels of xenophobia and negative attitudes toward foreigners from Africa. There was enormous potential for witch hunts, "vigilantism and grievous human rights abuses" which would well "outweigh any potential benefit from community participation" (Mattes et al., 2000:216).

The sea of change between the Green and White papers reflects the tensions in the ruling alliance in government of National Unity, which up to 2004 comprised the majority ANC and the minority Inkatha Freedom Party (IFP). The Minister of Home Affairs, Chief Mangosuthu Buthelezi, who was also President of the IFP, consistently advocated a conservative, regulatory migration policy. Clearly, many with the ANC also supported his views. The Parliamentary Portfolio Committee on Home Affairs identified numerous problems with the White Paper. In spite of this, the Draft Immigration Bill to implement the White Paper on International Immigration was released on February 15, 2000, by the minister.

In terms of the bill, it appeared that the primary function of the Department of Home Affairs would be enforcement. For example, the Bill allowed for the creation of an inspectorate or special agency within the Department of Home Affairs to implement immigration law. The inspectorate would be empowered to conduct raids in communities and workplaces in search of illegal immigrants without warrants. If individuals were unable to provide proof of their legal status in South Africa they could be arrested and detained for up to 48 hours without review. Such draconian powers were compared with the repressive influx control legislation of the apartheid era, and were likely to conflict with the new South African constitution. Notwithstanding the many flaws, the bill was passed to avert a constitutional crisis (there was a June 2, 2002, Constitutional Court deadline for a new immigration law to replace the Aliens Control Act), and the South African Immigration Act was signed in 2002.

After the April 2004 general elections, Nosiviwe Mapisa-Nqakula became the new Minister of Home Affairs. She immediately tabled a number of amendments to the Immigration Act. The intention was to attract people with skills as well as those who wanted to invest in South Africa. Her ultimate goal was to have South Africa's immigration legislation totally rewritten (Quintal, 2004). However, this has yet to happen.

Conclusion

In South Africa illegal immigrants have been accused of taking away the jobs of locals, lowering wages, increasing crime and spreading diseases. The massive escalation in the number of illegal migrants in South Africa since 1990 can be attributed to political changes that have taken place in the country. A democratic majority government was expected to be sympathetic to immigrants from neighboring countries.

Policy relating to migrants has developed in a vacuum, especially in terms of the numbers involved and their role in the economy. The policy focus was initially the law-and-order approach. There was need for a more sympathetic and sensitive approach that would recognize the circumstances that contributed to the escalation in migration. The migrants were not necessarily parasitic, but rather contributed productively to the economy. Exploitation of these workers was quite common.

South African immigration policy is characterized by an understanding of immigration as the consequence of immigrants' individual actions and of the government as a passive agent not implicated in the process. In other words the South African state blamed foreigners for the immigration flow without recognizing how its past and present policies contribute to this process. If one adopts Sassen's (1996) perspective, then older pattern of relations between South Africa and its neighbors and its integration to the global political economy is responsible for the flow. Therefore the responsibility for immigration may not be exclusively the immigrants'.

It is true that despite the numerous problems that face the majority of blacks in South Africa, for Africans from other parts of the continent, the country is perceived as being the land of increased economic opportunities and hope, especially after the 1994 elections. In addition to these perceptions, the structure, character, and state of the South African economy, compared to those of other African countries have been the driving mechanisms behind most illegal migrations. Hence, as long as the widespread poverty and high levels of inequality prevail on the continent, South Africa will continue to attract migrants.

Note

1. These countries, with the inclusion of the Democratic Republic of Congo, Madagascar, Mauritius, Namibia, and South Africa are part of the Southern African Development Commnity (SADC), which was established in 1992.

References

Balbo, M., & Marconi, G. (2005). Governing international migration in the city of the south. GCIM Global Migration Perspectives No. 38.

Bouillon, A. (1998). *"New" African Immigration to South Africa.* Cape Town: CASAS.

Business Report. National Daily Newspaper. Johannesburg.

Centre for Development Enterprise (1997). People on the move: A new approach to cross-border migration in South Africa. Johannesburg.

Centre for Development Enterprise (2000). Becoming "the world's most promising emerging market": Is the government's White Paper on International Migration good enough? Johannesburg.

Chirwa, W.C. (1998). Aliens and AIDS in Southern Africa: The Malawi-South Africa debate. *African Affairs,* 97:53–79.

City Press. Weekly National Newspaper. Johannesburg.

CRMSA (2007). Protecting refugees and asylum seekers in South Africa. Johannesburg.

Croucher, S. (1998). South Africa's illegal aliens: Constructing national boundaries in a post-apartheid state. *Ethnic and Racial Studies,* 21: 639–660.

Crush, J. (1996). Migrancy: The colour of alien-nation. *Democracy in Action,* 10 (November 15).

Crush, J. (1999). Fortress South Africa and the deconstruction of Apartheid's migration regime. *Geoforum,* 30:1–11.

Crush, J. (2000). Migrations past: An historical overview of cross-border movement in southern Africa. In D.A. McDonald (ed.), *On Borders: Perspectives on International Migration in Southern Africa.* New York: St. Martin's Press, pp. 12–24.

Crush, J. (2001). Immigration, xenophobia, and human rights in South Africa. SAMP Migration Policy Series No. 22.

Crush, J. (2008). The perfect storm: The realities of xenophobia in contemporary South Africa. SAMP Migration Policy Series, No. 50.

Crush, J., et al. (2000). Losing our minds: Skills migration and the South African brain drain. SAMP Migration Policy Series No. 18.

Crush, J., and Williams, V. (2001). Making up the numbers: Measuring "illegal immigration" to South Africa. South African Migration Project, Migration Policy Brief No. 3.

Crush, J., and Williams, V. (2005). International migration and development: Dynamics and challenges in South and Southern Africa. Paper presented at United Nations Expert Group Meeting on International Migration and Development, 6–8 July.

Davies, R., and Head, J. (1995). The future of mine migrancy in the context of broader trends in migration in Southern Africa. *Journal of Southern African Studies*, 21:439–450.

Diamond, R. (1996). Right-wing politics and the anti-immigration cause. *Social Justice*, 23:154–168.

Dodson, B. (1998). Women on the move: Gender and cross-border migration to South Africa. SAMP Migration Policy Series, No. 19.

Dodson, B. (2002). Gender and the brain drain. SAMP Migration Policy Series, No. 23.

Goliath, P. (2008). Human trafficking: Southern African perspective. Paper presented at the 9th Biennial Conference of the International Association of Women Judges, 25–28 March.

Harris, N. (1995). *The New Untouchables: Immigration and the New World Order*. London: Penguin.

Hough, M. (1995). Illegal aliens in Africa with specific reference to migration to South Africa. Institute for Strategic Studies, University of Pretoria.

HSRC (2008). Citizenship, violence, and xenophobia in South Africa: Perceptions from South African communities. Pretoria: Human Science Research Council.

Human Rights Watch (1998). "Prohibited persons": Abuse of undocumented migrants, asylum seekers, and refugees in South Africa (www.hrw.org/hrw/reports98/sareport).

Hunter, N., and Skinner, C. (2003). Foreign street traders working in inner city Durban: Local government policy challenges. *Urban Forum*, 14:301–319.

IOM (2005). HIV/AIDS, population mobility, and migration in Southern Africa: Defining a research and policy agenda. Geneva: IOM.

Jeeves, A. (1985). *Migrant Labour in South Africa's Mining Economy*. Kingston: McGill-Queens Press.

Labour Market Review (2007). Labour migration and South Africa: Towards a fairer deal for migrants in the South African economy. Department of Labour, Republic of South Africa.

Leeman, P. (2001, May 22). Durban unicity accused of xenophobia. *Mercury*, p. 4.

Lorgat, H. (1998, December 6). Rising tide of xenophobia is sweeping away our rationality: And humanity. *The Sunday Independent* (www.queensu.ca/samp).

Martens, J., Pieczkowski, M., and Vuuren-Smyth, B. (2003). Seduction, sale, and slavery: Trafficking in women and children for sexual exploitation in southern Africa. Pretoria: IOM.

Maharaj, B., and Moodley, V. (1999). Socio-economic analysis of immigrants in the Durban Region. Paper prepared for the South African Migration Project.

Mail and Guardian, Weekly National Newspaper. Johannesburg.

Mattes, R., et al. (1999). Still waiting for the barbarians: SA attitudes to immigrants and immigration. SAMP Migration Policy Series No. 14.

Mattes, R., Taylor, D.M., McDonald, D.A., Poore, A., and Richmond, W. (2000). South African attitudes to immigrants and immigration. In D.A. McDonald (ed.), *On Borders: Perspectives on International Migration in Southern Africa*. New York: St. Martin's Press, pp. 196–218.

Mattes, R., Crush, J., and Richmond, W. (2002). The brain gain: Skilled migrants and immigration policy in post-apartheid South Africa. South African Migration Project, Migration Policy Series No. 20.

McDonald. D. (1998). Left out in the cold? Housing and immigration in the new South Africa. SAMP Migration Policy Series No. 5.

McDonald, D., Mashike, L. and Golden, C. (1999). The lives and time of African migrants in post-apartheid South Africa. SAMP Migration Policy Series No. 13.

Meintjies, F. (1998, September 20). Immigrants are people like us. *Sunday Times Business Times*, p. 20.

Mercury, Daily Newspaper. Durban.

Minnaar, A., Pretorius, S., and Wentzel, M. (1995). Who goes there? Illegals in South Africa. *Indicator SA*, 12 (Winter):33–40.

Muanamoha, R., Maharaj, B., and Preston-Whyte, E. (2008). Social networks and undocumented Mozambican migration to South Africa. Paper presented at the 31st International Geographical Congress, Tunis, 12–15 August 2008.

Murray, J.M. (1995). "Blackbirding" at "Crooks' Corner": Illicit labour recruiting in the northeastern Transvaal, 1910–1940. *Journal of Southern African Studies*, 21:373–397.

Natal Witness, Daily Newspaper. Pietermaritzburg.

Parnwell, M. (1993). *Population Movements and the Third World*. London: Routledge.

Peberdy, S. (1997, June 22). Ignoring the history of undocumented migration is akin to ignoring those who have helped build South Africa. *The Sunday Independent*(www.queensu.ca/samp/).

Quintal, A. (2004, June 29). Immigration law changes. *Mercury*, p. 2.

Reitzes, M. (1994). Alien issues. *Indicator SA*, 12 (Summer):7–11.

Reitzes, M. (1997). Undocumented migration: Dimensions and dilemmas. Paper prepared for the Green Paper Task Group on International Migration (www.polity.org.za/govdocs/gerrn_papers/migration/taskt.html).

Rogerson, C.M. (1997). International migration, immigrant entrepreneurs and South Africa's small enterprise economy. SAMP Migration Policy Series No. 3.

Rogerson, C.M., and Rogerson, J.M. (2000). Dealing in scarce skills: Employer responses to the brain drain. In J. Crush (ed.), *Losing Our Minds: Skills Migration and the South African Brain Drain.* SAMP Migration Policy Series No. 18, pp.43–59.

Republic of South Africa (1997). Draft green paper on international migration. Pretoria: Government Printer.

Republic of South Africa (1999). White paper on international migration (www.gov.za/whitepaper/1999/migrate.htm).

SAHRC (1999). Illegal? Report on the arrest and detention of persons in terms of the Aliens Control Act (www.niza.nl/Ihr/refugee/hrcreport.htm).

Sassen, S. (1996). *Losing Control? Sovereignty in an Age of Globalisation.* New York: Columbia University Press.

Simelane, S. (1999). Trend in international migration: Migration among professionals, semi-professionals and miners in South Africa, 1970–1997. Paper presented at the Annual Conference of the Demographic Association of Southern Africa, Saldanha Bay, 5–7 July.

Sunday Times, Weekly National Newspaper. Johannesburg.

Taylor, D.M., Mattes, R., McDonald, D.A., Poore, A. and Richmond, W. (1999) *Still waiting for the barbarians: SA attitudes to immigrants and immigration.* Southern African Migration Project, Migration Policy Series 14. Cape Town: IDASA and Kingston, Ontario: Queen's University.

UNHCR (2008). UNHCR global appeal 2008–2009. United Nations.

Vigneswaran, D. (2008). Undocumented migration: Risks and myths (1998–2005). In Wa Kabwe-Segatti and Landau (eds.), *Migration to Post-Apartheid South Africa: Challenges and Questions to Policy-Makers.* Paris: Agence Francaise de Developpement, pp. 135–162.

Wa Kabwe-Segatti, A., and Landau, L. (eds) (2008). *Migration to Post-Apartheid South Africa: Challenges and Questions to Policy-Makers.* Paris: Agence Francaise de Developpement.

Walker, R., Ellis, M., and Barff, R. (1992). Linked migration systems: Immigration and internal labour flows in the United States. *Economic Geography*, 68:234–248.

Williams, B., Gouws, E., Lurie, M., and Crush, J. (2002). Spaces of vulnerability: Migration and HIV/AIDS in South Africa. South African Migration Project.

Wocke, A., and Klein, S. (2002). The implications of South Africa's skills migration policy for country competitveness. *Development Southern Africa*, 19:441–454.

Wood, W.B. (1994). Forced migration: Local conflicts and international dilemmas. *Annals of the Association of American Geographers*, 84:607–634.

World Bank (1999). *World Development Report 1999–2000.* Washington.

Worth, H. (2006). Unconditional hospitality: HIV, ethics, and the refugee problem. *Bioethics*, 20(5):223–232.

25

Ghana

Immigration to Ghana

A. Essuman-Johnson

Major Immigration Movements into Ghana since 1990

Castles and Miller (1993) have noted that population movements have been with the world since time immemorial. International migration has become part of a transnational revolution that is reshaping societies and politics around the world. This has affected the regions of the world in different ways. Some areas like the United States, New Zealand, Canada, and Australia, have become classical countries of immigration. They point out that many countries have experienced immigration. Europe has been affected by labor migration between 1945 and the early 1970s and is now considered an immigration area. Even countries in southern Europe like Greece, Italy, and Spain, which were zones of emigration, have now become immigration areas, and several Central and Eastern European countries like Poland, Hungary, and the Czech Republic are becoming immigration countries. Richmond (1994) relates labor migration to globalization. He argues that the globalization of international labor migration is manifest in two ways:

Firstly, all countries now engage in migration systems growing in size and complexity and producing an increasing diversity of flows. Second, many of the processes that create and drive these systems operate on a worldwide basis, the consequence of economic globalization, capital mobility, the activities of international business corporations, and widespread realization by governments that human resources can be traded for profit like any other resource (Salt 1992, 1080 quoted in Richmond 1994: 32)

He argues further that "remittances from overseas workers are an important source of foreign currency for many developing countries. In terms of trade and commerce, transnational exchanges of goods have always occurred. Beginning from the Mediterranean and Asia Minor, the world system gradually spread to the rest of the world with the incorporation of the New World into a system of exploitation and colonization. An international division of labor, with substantial inequalities in the distribution of wealth and in the level of technological and economic development, persists despite the relative integration of the world economic system. In turn this gives rise to mass migrations of labor from the less to the more developed regions" (Richmond 1994: 32).

Inequalities in the level and pace of development within the Third World have also been seen as a cause of movement of workers from poorer to richer Third World countries (Parnwell 1993: 62–63). Parnwell notes that the majority of such movements naturally take place between neighboring countries and over relatively short distances. The influence of uneven development on patterns of labor migration is evident throughout the Third World. Parnwell points out that in Africa several countries encourage the export of labor as a way of alleviating unemployment and boosting foreign exchange earnings. In Western Africa he points to the Ivory Coast as a major recipient of temporary migrant workers, from Mali, Togo, and Burkina Faso, who migrate to work on the plantations and other fields of employment that are shunned by nationals. Parnwell points out however that in reflecting the way that economic fortunes may change, Ghana, once a major destination of migrants from elsewhere in West Africa, became a source of large-scale emigration during the 1980s as a result of a sharp economic downturn. A major stream of migration developed between Ghana and Nigeria until, with declining oil prices in the 1980s, large numbers of Ghanaian workers were expelled from Nigeria.

In his introduction to a seminar on migrations in West Africa, Samir Amin (1974: 66) argues that history and legends of creation indicates that many people of contemporary West Africa came from regions sometimes far removed from those they are presently occupying. Modern migrations in West Africa have seen periodical migration of labor. The migrants come to a society and acquire a generally inferior status as workers or share croppers. Prior to colonialism, Africa was the scene of mass movements of people. But since then it has been the movements of labor. The pattern of migration of labor across West Africa is that after a certain period of time of movement into the host country, the migrant ceases to be a migrant. This is when the migrant acquires a nationality, which provides protection from the perpetual threat of expulsion that has always haunted immigrants. Nationality gives them rights, which accelerates the process of assimilation. Most of the urban population of West Africa is made up of immigrants because they maintain strong ties with their rural origins.

Migrations in West Africa have not been hindered too much by national frontiers and are predominantly of unqualified and unskilled labor. The migration of merchants, office workers, skilled workers, and professionals is of secondary importance. There has been a general movement of unskilled labor from the interior to the coast in the francophone countries and Ghana. Many of such immigrants have been assimilated. In Ghana such migrants have settled in stranger quarters called zongos and are predominantly of unskilled labor from northern Ghana and the francophone countries to the north including Burkina Faso, Mali, and Niger. Looking at migrations in the 1960s Zachariah and Conde (1981: 5–8) point out that the principal recipients of migration in West Africa were Ghana and Cote d'Ivoire. They note that Ghana started attracting immigrants early in the twentieth century. Togo nationals in Ghana during 1925–1929 were estimated to be 75,000 reaching a peak of 280,000 in 1960. In 1969 Ghana expelled a large number of aliens under the Aliens Compliance Order and by 1970 the number of Togo nationals in Ghana had declined to 245,000. Burkina Faso was the second major exporter of emigrant labor to Ghana. In 1928, the British estimated that 60,000 Burkinabes entered Ghana. By 1960 the number had reached 195,000.

Groups That Have Entered Ghana since 1990

Ghana has been receiving immigrants from across West Africa, the Middle East, and Asia. From West Africa the immigrants have come mainly from Mali, Burkina Faso, Nigeria, Niger, Togo, and Liberia. From the Middle East the immigrants are mainly from Lebanon and from Asia the immigrants are mainly from India and Pakistan. Other immigrants have come from South Africa, China, and South Korea. Of course there are British and Americans. Prior to 1990, these same groups dominated immigration to Ghana (Affrifa 2004).

Demographic Information

The primary sending countries of immigrants to Ghana since 1990 include Lebanon, India, China, South Korea, Mali, Niger, Burkina Faso, Togo, Liberia, Nigeria, and Pakistan. The population of the immigrant population is estimated by the

Ghana Immigration Service (GIS) to be in excess of two hundred thousand, of which 59,367 are classified as legally resident, 45,695 are refugees, and the rest are undocumented (GIS Annual Report 2004). The majority of the undocumented immigrants are from the West African subregion and come from Nigeria, Burkina Faso, Togo, and Mali. Most of the Nigerians are traders who commute between Ghana and Nigeria and have taken advantage of the ECOWAS protocol on free movement of goods and persons, which allows them stay for three months without the need for visa, provided they have valid traveling documents. The traders however usually travel without much regard to the borders as they pay their way across the borders in lieu of traveling documents. The traders resort to this age-old practice due to the hassle involved with officialdom when they have to apply for valid traveling documents. Similarly the undocumented immigrants from Mali and Niger are mainly traders who are engaged in the trade in cereals. Migrants from Burkina Faso are both laborers in the gold mines and on cocoa farms and traders in cereals.

The immigrants have given various reasons for coming to Ghana. The legal residents are mainly merchants, office workers, skilled workers, and professionals. The interesting aspect of immigration to Ghana is the paradox that most Ghanaians look to leaving the country. There is thus the need to look at the push-pull factors that influence immigration to Ghana. The major push factor that has brought immigrants to Ghana has been the issue of refugees who were forced by circumstances to seek refuge in Ghana. The refugees are mainly from Liberia and Sierra Leone (Personal Interview with Tepe-Mensah 2004). Prior to the end of apartheid Ghana was a favorite destination for refugees from southern Africa, namely from South Africa, Namibia, and Zimbabwe. The refugees from southern Africa were forced to seek refuge following the racist and apartheid policies in southern Africa. In South Africa, the struggle of the ANC had led the apartheid state to embark on a policy of repressing the black population and most of them were forced to seek refuge outside South Africa. Similar policies in Namibia and racism in Zimbabwe also forced many citizens of these two countries to seek refuge, and some of them found refuge in Ghana. In the case of Liberia and Sierra Leone, they were forced to

come to Ghana following the civil wars in these two countries. In Liberia the civil war was touched off by the attempt to remove the government of President Samuel Doe by rebels led by Charles Taylor in December 1990. This touched off a civil war, which forced some twenty thousand refugees from Liberia to take refuge in Ghana (Essuman-Johnson 1992: 34). A similar civil war in Sierra Leone was touched off by the attempt of the Revolutionary United Front (RUF) to overthrow the government of President Tejan Kaba in 1998. The civil war forced many Sierra Leoneans to take refuge in Ghana.

The immigrants from other West African countries like Niger and Mali have come to Ghana as a result of pull factors. Malians and Nigerians have come to Ghana following the Sahel drought, which affected their countries in the mid-1980s. Most of these Malians and Nigeriennes were herders who lost their herds to the drought (Essuman-Johnson 1992).The Burkinabes have long traveled to Ghana to work on cocoa farms and to engage in the trade in grains. From the early 1990s one major pull factor has been the attractive vegetation for cattle herders from the Sahel region of Burkina Faso. Fulani cattle herders have driven their animals across the Burkina Faso border to Ghana to graze their herds, for which they have been in conflict with local farmers on whose farms the cattle graze. Togolese immigrants are mainly farmers and fishermen. Togolese farmers and especially fishermen have been prominent on the coastal towns where they have set up many fishing settlements. The immigrants from India, Pakistan, and Lebanon are mainly merchants and traders. They dominate the trade in fabrics, supermarkets, and electronic merchandise (Affrifa 2004). The attraction of Ghana to the immigrants is the opportunities provided by the cocoa industry and the environment for peaceful trade and economic activities.

Ghana's Immigration Policy

Ghana's immigration policy is geared toward using immigration to attract critical foreign investment, transfer of technology and human resource capital/skills for socioeconomic development. Running concurrently is the policy to prevent illegal immigration, transnational crime, economic exploitation, and social corruption. The policy is given effect in the following legislation: (1) Immigration Act, 2000, Act 573; (2) Immigration regulations; (3) GIPC Act, 1994, Act 478; (4) Free Zone Act, 1995 Act 504; (5) Citizenship Act, 2000, Act 591; and (6) Citizenship Regulations, 2001. These statutes set the conditions for legal immigration into Ghana. The conditions of entry into Ghana are very liberal as spelled out in the Immigration Act (Immigration Act 2000). The immigrant has to acquire a visa at any of Ghana's missions outside. The visa application procedure requires the applicant to show financial sufficiency. In countries where Ghana has no missions, the facility exists for people traveling to Ghana to acquire a visa on arrival, with the prior approval of the Director of Immigration. The Immigration Act also sets the conditions for residence and employment for foreign nationals in Ghana. On application to the Director of Immigration, foreign nationals may be issued a residence permit.

The Investment Laws, the Free Zone Act, and the Ghana Investment Promotion Centre (GIPC) (GIPC Act 1994) provide incentives for investment in the country. The investment law requires a foreigner to have a minimum of US$10,000 to invest. These go along with automatic immigrant quotas. Tax holidays are granted as well as the opportunity to employ expatriates. Under the Free Zone Act, Act 504 (1995), there is no limit to immigrant quotas for employment purposes. All expatriates employed under the Investment Laws have access to residence permits. The Immigration Act was reviewed in 2000. The revision made provision for long-term residence options, that is, Indefinite Stay and Right of Abode, which were absent in the repealed Aliens Act, Act 160 (1960). The Citizenship Act, Act 591 (2000), has also given effect to dual citizenship. These provisions are geared toward attracting long-term foreign investment to Ghana.

The Ghana Immigration Service (GIS) is one of the agencies implementing the Ghana Gateway Project. The project aims at attracting foreign investments to Ghana by making the country attractive to investments. The role of the GIS is to initiate and implement policies that will attract and facilitate the location of foreign investors and tourist to Ghana. In this regard the GIS is undergoing institutional restructuring. Among the key policy initiatives is the further review of the Immigration Act and standard procedures to ensure quick delivery of services. Operations which hitherto have been manually been done are now being automated.

Opportunities and Obstacles

Immigrants have access to Ghana's education facilities without any problems. The laws do not bar foreigners from investing in any aspect of the economy. Foreigners are thus engaged in retail trade, import, export, mining, timber, petroleum retail, education, and so forth. Qualified professionals, technocrats, and all manner of skilled labor required by companies and institutions can be employed if the statutory requirements are satisfied. Education is one area in which Ghana offers lots of opportunities for immigrants. Increasingly (though the statistics are not available) students from the Francophone countries of West and Central Africa are moving to Ghana to study English and information technology (Affrifa 2004). A number of private schools and hostels have sprung up in Accra to cater to these interests. Data from the GIS indicates that in 2003, 280 foreign students were documented. The majority of foreign students are undocumented. The majority of the foreign students are Nigerians, followed by Ivorians, and increasing numbers of students are coming from the Congo, Cameroon, Equatorial Guinea, and Gabon (GIS Annual Report 2004).

The obstacles to immigrants to Ghana would include, among others, the following: (1) visa requirements; (2) immigrants quotas on employment of expatriates and foreigners; (3) requirements of work and residence permit; and (4) requirement of minimum equity, namely, US$10,000 for investment. The requirement of US$10,000 as the minimum equity for investment is especially a drawback to West African immigrants, who constitute the majority of foreigners in Ghana who might want to invest. However the granting of residence is tied directly to investment, employment, education, or dependency on any of the principals. Most West African immigrants do not meet these requirements. Immigrants therefore engage in business and reside in Ghana without resident status and in so doing avoid the US$10,000 financial obligations. The ECOWAS Protocol on the Free Movement of Goods and Persons complicates this state of affairs, as it allows free entry and a 90-day stay for all members of ECOWAS. As a member of ECOWAS, Ghana is under treaty obligation to allow for the free movement of goods and persons and a 90-day stay of ECOWAS citizens in spite of Ghana's immigration laws. The problem this is posing is that ECOWAS citizens enter the country on the free movement protocol and stay on to conduct their business without informing the authorities. If they plan to stay beyond 90 days to carry on their business, they need to regularize their stay under the work and residence permit requirement of the Immigration Laws and satisfy the financial obligations requirement of minimum equity of US$10,000 for investment. ECOWAS citizens are thus able to get around the immigration laws of the country (Affrifa 2004).

When immigrants settle in the country, the GIS provide certain services to the immigrant community. The GIS provides them with residence permits, immigrant quotas, work permits, and the extension of visitor permits. According to Ghana's Immigration Laws (Act 573, 13) (1) persons who have been lawfully admitted entry into Ghana, may upon application to the Director of Immigration, be issued with a residence permit. The director may grant a residence permit for up to a period not exceeding eight years. The director may also, with the approval of the Minister of Interior, grant an indefinite residence status to a person who satisfies the director that he is qualified under section 15 of the Immigration Act. A person qualifying for the indefinite residence status should satisfy following conditions:

has resided in Ghana throughout the period of twelve months immediately preceding the date of the application;

has during the seven years immediately preceding the period of the twelve months, resided in Ghana for a period amounting in the aggregate to not less than five years;

is of good character as attested to in writing by two Ghanaians who are notaries public, lawyers, senior public officers, or any other class of persons approved of by the minister;

has not been sentenced to a period of imprisonment of twelve months or more;

has made, or is in the opinion of the minister capable of making, a substantial contribution to the development of Ghana;

intends to reside permanently in Ghana upon the grant of the status; and

possesses a valid residence permit on the date of the application.

Foreign nationals cannot work except by a permit granted by the Immigrant Quota Committee. The committee is composed of the following: (1) the Deputy Minister of Interior, who is the chairman; (2) the Director of Immigration; and (3) a representative of each of the following: (a) Ministry of the Interior, (b) Ministry of Employment and Social Welfare, (c) Ministry of Trade and Industry, (d) Registrar-General's Department, (e) Ghana Investments Promotion Centre, (f) Bank of Ghana, (g) Statistical Service, and (h) Ghana Employers Association. The Immigrant Quota Committee is responsible for the consideration of all applications for immigrant quotas and work permits and make recommendations to the minister for the issue of an immigrant quota and work permit (Personal Interview with Gyamfi 2004).

Immigrant Contribution to the Country

The contributions of immigrants to Ghana's economy would be examined from the point of view of the GIPC and the Free Zones Board. From the point of view of the Free Zones Board, the contributions of immigrants to the country are various. On the economic front, the immigrants inject new capital into the economy through the investments they bring into the country. This generates employment for Ghanaians. They also impart skills through the technology they transfer. The payment of fees for the issuance of work/residence permits, entry visas, and the payment of income tax are all sources of substantial revenue.

Data from GIPC (2004) indicates that the center developed a five-year corporate plan, which was implemented between 1995 and 2004. The main objective of the plan was to stimulate increased investment through various programs both at home and abroad. At the end of the plan period the center had registered 1,084 FDI projects in the service (314), manufacturing (300), tourism (129), building and construction (92), and agriculture (87) sectors of the economy. The projects were made up of 763 joint foreign-Ghanaian-owned and 321 wholly foreign-owned projects, which were initially estimated to cost US $1,209.64 billion and US$398.88 million respectively. The second medium term plan, 2000–2004, was a program designed to transform the center's promotional strategy targeted to firms and sectors predetermined in a FDI Demand Study. The results of the program have been considered by the center to be modest due partly to insufficiency in funding and the prevailing downturn in the world investment trend since September 11. Despite these issues the center recorded 165, 171, 138, 152, and 183 projects in 2000, 2001, 2002, 2003, and 2004 respectively, making a total of 809 projects valued at an initial cost of US$ 599.13 million. As at the end of year 2004, projects with foreign participation registered by the center totaled 183, with a total value of US$186.26 million. The number of projects registered during the year showed a 20% increase over the same period in 2003. The projects showed a positive and increasing pattern from 2002, during which year performance went down due to the combined effects of September 11, U.S. terror attacks and corporate meltdowns. At the end of 2004 the projects and liaison offices registered by the GIPC since 2001 totaled 771. The agricultural sector topped the list with 50 projects, building and construction 40, export trade 22, general trade 89, manufacturing 181, service 183, and tourism 79 projects. The remaining 27 were liaison offices (GIPC 2004). In 2007 the center registered 305 projects during the year, indicating a 28% increase in the number of projects if compared to 2006, when 238 projects were recorded. (Table 25-1)

The FDI component for 2007 was GH¢ 5.18 billion (US$5.56 billion) and a local currency component of GH¢92.93 million (US$99.9

Table 25-1. Sectoral Composition of Projects

Sectors	2007	2006	2005	2004
Manufacturing	96	63	78	52
Service	54	68	41	48
Tourism	31	19	15	24
Build. & Const.	32	20	19	11
Export Trade	12	13	8	6
Agriculture	15	6	9	9
Gen. Trading	65	49	42	33
Total	305	238	212	183

Source: The GIPC *Quarterly Report*, Vol. 3, No. 4.

million). In 2006 the FDI component of the registered projects was GH¢2.15billion (US$2.31 billion) with a local component of GH¢46.86 million (US$50.38 million) The expected employment to be generated from the 305 projects registered during the year was 25,367, which was almost double that of the same period in 2006, when 12,044 jobs were expected to be generated (Table 25-2). Of the initial capital transfers during the year, 2007 amounted to GH¢144.06 million (US$154.9 million) as against that of the same period of 2006, which amounted to GH¢ 50.0 million. (US$53.7) The Chinese and Indians were the leading countries from where a greater number of projects originated during the period. Others included Lebanon, the UK, the United States, Germany, the Netherlands, Nigeria, France, South Africa, Korea, the Ivory Coast, Benin, Austria, Bahrain, Sweden, and Cyprus. On foreign direct investments, out of the 75 projects with foreign participation registered during this period, 46, (61.33%) were wholly owned foreign companies, as against 29 (38.66) joint ventures with Ghanaians. In terms of the estimated cost, the joint venture projects were valued at Gh¢ 634.35 million (12.7%) (US$682 million), while the 100% foreign-owned enterprises accounted for Gh¢4.36 billion (US$4.68bn) (87.3%). This was made up of an FDI component of Gh¢4.92billion (US$5.29bn) (98.56%) and a local currency component of Gh¢70.95 million (US$76.2million) (1.46 %.). The initial capital transfers in respect of the projects with foreign participation was Gh¢114.81 million (US$123.45 million); this was much higher than the legally expected minimum equity requirement of Gh¢ 25.92 million (US$27.87 million). The total of initial transfers made for 2007 was thus Gh¢

Table 25-2. Expected Employment Creation by Projects

Sector	Cumulative January 2001 to March 2007			January 2007 to March 2007		2006		2005		2004		September 1994 to December 2000	
	Total	G*	F*	G	F	G	F	G	F	G	F	G	F
Manufacturing	16,788	15,542	1,246	313	68	3,508	226	4,055	281	2,513	281	20,680	1,122
Service	15,835	14,853	982	425	67	1,246	153	5,508	159	2,358	72	12,392	1,064
Build. & Constr.	7,603	6,968	635	181	40	1,896	115	1,906	230	1,413	52	10,357	470
Agriculture	5,170	4,897	273	254	37	216	17	748	41	1,406	32	10,313	346
Tourism	4,338	3,989	349	344	21	587	48	415	44	917	59	3,122	294
Gen. Trade	7,265	6,558	707	265	27	1,802	175	1,085	174	931	147	2,885	253
Export Trade	1,556	1,393	163	36	4	330	61	439	19	116	11	1,276	144
Total	58,555	54,200	4,355	1,818	264	11,088	956	9,894	942	12,804	741	61,025	3,693
	100%	92.56%	7.44%	87.32%	12.68%	92.06%	7.94%	91.31%	8.69%	94.53%	5.47%	94.29%	5.71%
				2,082	100%	12,044	100%	10,836	100%	13,545	100%	64,718	100%

*G = Ghanaian, F = Foreign

Source: GIPC: First Quarter 2007 Investment Report.

114.81 million (US$123.45 million), as against Gh¢50 million (US$53.7 million) in 2006. By the third quarter (July 1–September 30) of 2008, the total of new investments was Gh¢1.38 billion (US$1.38 billion), made up of Gh¢407.41 million worth of investments (capital goods imported) and Gh¢972.10 million equity transfers for new projects registered during the quarter and existing investments. Eighty-two new projects were registered over the period. For the corresponding quarter of 2007, the total of new investments was Gh¢851 million with 80 projects registered (GIPC 2008).

These investments were estimated to generate employment opportunities for some 61,025 Ghanaians and 3,693 non-Ghanaians in the first plan period and 20,719 Ghanaians and 1,515 non-Ghanaians in the second plan period from 1994 to 2000 (Table 25-3). Total foreign capital transfers in respect of the minimum required by the law amounted to US$202.0 million. The major sources of foreign investments into the country are Great Britain (146 projects), India (131 projects), China (128 projects), the United States (107 projects), Lebanon (102 projects), and Germany (90 projects). Others countries with investments are Korea (58 projects), Italy (55 projects), the Netherlands (51 projects), Switzerland (48 projects), Canada (30 projects), and France (29 projects). From the developing countries investments have come from Nigeria (39 projects), South Africa (26 projects), and Malaysia (12 projects) (GIPC 2004). Over the period from 2000 to 2004, Britain, India, China, Germany, and the United States have been the main sources of FDI inflow into Ghana. India for the period under review has overtaken Britain as the country with the most registered projects. India registered 183 projects, Britain 177, China 161, Lebanon 135, the United States 126, and Germany 104. Nigeria and South Africa continue to be the leading African countries investing in the country. With 53 and 33 projects respectively registered from Nigeria and South Africa respectively. Other developing countries that have made inroads have been Malaysia, with 12, and the Ivory Coast, with 11 (GIPC 2004).

About 13,545 jobs were expected to be generated from 183 projects registered between January and December 2004. The number is made up of 12,804 Ghanaians (94.53%) and 741 foreigners (5.47%). In line with growth in the service sector, 5,667 people were employed in that sector. This is made up of 5,508 Ghanaians and 159 expatriates. The manufacturing sector was also expected to employ as many as 2,794 people. The remaining sectors were expected to employ 1,456 for the building and construction sector; 1,438 for agriculture sector; 976 for tourism; 1,078 for general trade; and 127 for the export sector (GIPC 2004) (Table 25-2). From the number of projects registered in the third quarter of 2008 it was expected that 4,631 jobs will be created. Of these, 89.64% (4,151) will be for Ghanaians and the remaining 480 (10.36%) will be for expatriates. The total number of jobs created by the third quarter of 2008 is 19,262. Data from the GIPC Quarterly Update for the third Quarter of 2008 (Table 25-3) indicates that India and Nigeria topped the list of countries

Table 25-3. Top Ten Investor Countries (September, 2008)

Country	Registered Projects	Country	Value of Projects (US$Mil)
1. India	13	Netherlands	1,287.56
2. Nigeria	10	Nigeria	257.12
3. China	9	Luxembourg/Germany/USA	8.85
4. France	7	Britain	7.79
5. Britain	6	France	3.23
6. Lebanon	6	Singapore	2.99
7. South Africa	5	India	2.84
8. USA	4	South Africa	2.32
9. Netherlands	2	USA	1.14
10. Norway	2	China	1.02

Source: GIPC: Quarterly Update 3rd Quarter July 1–September 30, 2008.

with the highest number of projects registered during the period with 13 and 10 projects respectively. The Netherlands led in the value in of investments, with US$1,287.56 million, followed by Nigeria, with projects valued US$257.12 million.

Data from the records of the GIS indicate that the immigrant contribution to the economy is substantial. These can be gleaned from the number of foreign companies registered and applications for various permits applied for on behalf of foreigners. In 2002, 19,397 permits, excluding visa-on-arrival permits were issued to foreigners. In 2004, 15,394 residence permits were issued, as against 11,997 in 2003. On visas, 4,667 emergency entry visas were issued as against 3,370 in 2003. On foreign residents, 381,166 entered the country as against 276,624 in 2003. These indicators show a progressive increase over the years (*GIS Annual Report* 2004). The contributions of immigrants are various but prominent in the following areas: (1) employment of Ghanaians, (2) foreign investments, and (3) transfer of skills. Foreign elements also have a strong presence in some economic sectors. These include (1) mining, (2) construction, (3) timber, (4) industry, (5) retail, (6) hotels and restaurants (The Chinese are very prominent in the restaurant industry), (7) fishing (the South Koreans are very prominent in this industry), and (8) Airlines. Statistics on foreign owned companies (fully owned, partnered, or employing foreigners) include the following: (1) mineral companies 63, (2) construction 140, (3) timber 156, (4) hotel/restaurants 125, (5) fishing 41, and (6) airlines 31.

It is clear from the GIPC report (Table 25-4) for 2004 that considerable amounts of funds have been harnessed by the State Investment Agency. The cumulative equity from foreign sources, namely, foreign direct investment (FDI) from January 2001 to December 2004 was US$218.18 million compared to US$61.93 million from local sources and the equity from September 1994 to December 2000 was US$409.36 million compared to US$199.57 million from local sources. For loans, foreign sources provided US$223.79 million, compared to US$25.14 million from local sources for January 2000 to December 2004 (Table 25-5). What this indicates is that Ghana is using her

immigration policy also to attract foreign direct investment by making her investment laws attractive to foreigners.

Under Ghana's Immigration Laws, companies are permitted to employ foreigners, especially professionals and other skilled labor. From 2001 the Ghana Free Zones Board (GFZB) recommended visas for 10,112 foreign employees for companies that set up in Ghana's Free Zones through the Ghana Immigration Service. The numbers of foreigners granted visas through the Free Zones Board have increased through the years and by 2007 the GFZB had recommended visas for 60,920 foreigners. (Table 25-6)

On the political, social, and cultural fronts, the activities of immigrants in areas like religion, education, and health has been noteworthy. Prominent among them are the activities of (1) the Catholic Secretariat, which as a religious organization provides humanitarian assistance to the needy and refugees; and (2) USAID, the agency of the U.S. government that provides bilateral assistance in various aspects of Ghanaian national and economic life. Similarly the USIS provides cultural and educational assistance to Ghanaians. The British Council also provides cultural and educational services to Ghanaians. Similarly the French provides language training to Ghanaians and in so doing provides French cultural teachings to Ghanaians. The Goethe Institute also provides German cultural teachings to Ghanaians.

Immigrant Drain on Economy

Competition for employment from immigrants is not a big problem in the country. In this regard the Ghana Free Zones Board keeps a tight reign on the employment requirements of the firms that set up in the Free Zones. To the extent that some competition for employment may exist it is from ECOWAS citizens, who cross the borders easily under the terms of ECOWAS protocol on free movement of goods and persons. Most of the ECOWAS citizens mainly engage in trading in the local markets. This is especially so for immigrants from the Sahel region of West Africa, mainly Mali, Burkina Faso, and Niger, who engage in the trade in grains which they stock up for sale in the lean season. Others who

Table 25-4. Financing Plan of Projects (US$Mil)

Financing Plan	Cumulative 2001–2004	%	2004	%	2003	%	2002	%	2001	%	September 1994–December 2004	%
Equity												
Local	61.93	13.3	27.91	15.0	24.31	20.5	3.04	4.7	6.67	6.85	199.57	12.4
Foreign	156.25	33.5	47.63	25.6	56.55	47.8	19.49	29.9	32.58	33.49	409.36	25.4
Total	218.18	46.7	75.54	40.6	80.86	68.3	22.53	34.6	39.25	40.30	608.93	37.9
Loan												
Local	25.14	5.4	14.64	7.9	6.01	5.1	3.17	4.9	1.32	1.36	88.58	5.5
Foreign	223.79	47.9	96.10	51.6	31.51	26.6	39.44	60.5	56.73	58.31	911.00	56.6
Total	248.93	53.3	110.74	59.4	37.52	31.7	42.61	65.4	58.05	59.70	999.59	62.1
Grand Total	467.11	100.0	186.28	100.0	118.38	100.0	65.14	100.0	97.30	100.00	1608.52	100.0
FDI inflow												
Foreign Equity	156.25	41.1	47.63	25.6	56.55	47.8	19.49	29.9	32.58	33.49	409.36	25.4
Foreign Loan	223.79	58.9	96.10	51.6	31.51	26.6	39.44	60.5	56.73	58.31	911.00	56.6
Total	380.04	81.4	143.73	77.2	88.06	74.4	58.93	90.5	89.32	91.8	1320.36	82.1
Local Participation												
Local Equity	61.93	13.3	27.91	15	24.31	20.5	3.04	4.7	6.67	6.85	199.57	12.4
Local Loan	25.14	5.4	14.64	7.90	6.01	5.10	3.17	4.90	1.32	1.36	88.58	5.50
Total	87.07	18.6	42.55	22.8	30.32	25.6	6.21	9.5	7.99	8.2	288.16	17.9

Source: GIPC: Statistics on Registered Projects 4th Quarter 2004.

Table 25-5. Financing Plan of Projects (US$Mil)

Financing Plan	Cumulative 2001–March 2007 %		2007 %		2006 %		2005 %		September 1994–December 2004 %	
Equity										
Local	90.33	2.9	3.96	11.0	16.89	0.7	7.55	3.7	199.57	12.4
Foreign	2,060.86	67.1	14.40	39.2	1,782.70	75.3	107.77	53.4	409.36	25.4
Total	2,151.19	70.0	18.10	50.3	1,799.59	76.0	115.32	57.1	608.93	37.9
Loan										
Local	105.76	3.4	8.49	23.6	33.5	1.4	38.65	19.1	88.58	5.5
Foreign	815.96	26.6	9.44	26.2	534.76	22.6	47.97	23.8	911.00	56.6
Total	921.73	30.0	17.92	49.7	568.26	24.0	86.63	42.9	999.59	62.1
Grand Total	3,072.92	100.0	36.02	100.0	2,367.85	100.0	201.96	100.0	1608.52	100.0
FDI inflow										
Foreign Equity	2,060.86	71.6	14.14	39.2	1,782.70	75.3	107.77	53.4	409.36	25.4
Foreign Loan	815.96	26.6	9.44	26.2	534.76	22.6	47.97	23.6	911.00	56.6
Total	2,876.81	93.6	23.57	65.4	2,317.46	97.9	155.76	77.1	1,320.36	82.1
Local Participation										
Local Equity A4 Local	90.33	2.9	3.96	11.0	16.89	0.7	7.55	3.7	199.57	12.4
Loan	105.78	3.4	8.49	23.60	33.50	1.40	38.65	19.10	88.58	5.50
Total	196.11	6.4	12.45	34.6	50.39	2.1	46.2	22.9	288.16	17.9

Source: GIPC: First Quarter 2007 Investment Report.

Table 25-6. GFZB's Share of Immigration/Visa

Year	2001	2002	2003	2004	2005	2006	2007
Immigrant Visa	10,112	15,164	22,581	49,158	59,496	44,582	60,920

Source: Ghana Free Zones Board.

are not in the grains trade find work as farm hands especially on cocoa farms (Affrifa 2004).

This is exploited to the detriment of Ghanaians. By the Immigrant Quota System, foreigners who employ such labor are to do so for a three-year period and within that period a Ghanaian is to understudy him and then take over. This is hardly ever adhered to, as the proper monitoring is not done. Some foreigners however do not register their companies yet they engage in business. Others divert from what they were authorized to do. Other foreign companies also illegally employ foreign nationals. At the end of the day the country is deprived of critical income. The GIS also believe that some foreign companies have been set to engage in fraud. Some of these companies have been known to engage in socially negative activities like drug and child abuse. Some immigrants have also been known to engage in crime such as armed robbery and fraud known as 419. The 419-fraud scheme is named after a Nigerian Decree No. 419, which deals with the eradication of fraud. Fraudsters from Nigeria have used various means to defraud people such that many Ghanaians have fallen victim to the ploy and it is generally felt that Nigerian fraudsters have been operating across the West African subregion, including Ghana. A typical 419 fraud would involve an e-mail sent to an unsuspecting victim. The e-mail would relate a story to the effect that the person sending the mail has some fortune sitting in a named bank and they need to claim the fortune by transferring it through a bank account. The fraudster asks for the bank account of the recipient with a promise of some amount in U.S. dollars. If the account number is sent, the fraudsters manage to transfer monies from the bank account. Immigrants from certain West African countries like Nigeria have been said to be prominent in this type of fraud. Immigrant communities have also organized the use of Ghana as a transit point for smuggling and trafficking of their nationals to Western countries. For this reason some immigrants have been jailed and others have been repatriated or deported (Affrifa 2004).

Trafficking in Ghana

Migrant trafficking has been part of Ghana's emigration flow for sometime. Trafficking started with Ghanaians emigrating to the Ivory Coast in the early 1970s, when the country's economy began to experience a downturn. This was especially so in the case of women and young girls who were sent into the prostitution business hired or lured as house keepers (Ghana Statistical Services 1995: 7–8). Neighboring Togo and Burkina Faso were not exceptions. The pattern was diverted to Nigeria when Ghanaians started began emigrating there on a large scale from the mid-1970s to the mid-1980s. This time in addition to women and young girls, men were trafficked. However with the expulsion of aliens in 1982 and 1985 from Nigeria coupled with the economy downturn, Ghanaians found their way to Europe and North America. By the late 1990s the presence of large numbers of Ghanaians were noted in London, Amsterdam, Hamburg, New York, and other world cities (Peil 1998: 205). This phase of migration from Ghana was accelerated by the accumulation of migration culture, including bridgeheads and networks already established (Van Hear 1998: 209). These established communities have become influential in the network for emigration of their kinsmen from Ghana to join them.

However the traditional areas of attraction are particularly closing their doors. Restrictive immigration laws have been put in place and are being tightened. In November 1986, Ghanaians who had hitherto traveled to the United Kingdom without a visa were required

to hold a visa prior to entry. The adoption of a common immigration policy by the members of the European Union and also the Schengen agreement has turned Europe into a "fortress." The concept of "Fortress Europe" has made legal migration by a large section of Ghanaians impossible as they can never to satisfy the visa requirements. The UK, Italy, the Netherlands, and Germany, the major destinations of Ghanaians, are all members of the EU. With the exception of the UK, the other three are all Schengen states. The United States operates a similar tight visa regime.

Given the tight visa application procedures of the various embassies, the only option left for prospective migrants is clandestine immigration (EU: 41–42). This is where traffickers provide the avenues for entry. This situation conforms to the assumption that trafficking occurs because the possibilities for regular migration have declined as more stringent entry controls force migrants into using illegal channels (Salt 2000: 32). Ghanaians have thus graduated from trafficking to the Ivory Coast and Nigeria to the north-south trail. Here, self-styled individuals or syndicates emerged, collecting large sums of money from ignorant and unsuspecting persons wishing to travel abroad, with the aim of helping them to gain illegal entry into countries of their destination (Aboah 1994: 2). Evidence suggests that trafficking to the North started in the late 1970s and was in full flight in the early 1980s. By the early 1980s, Ghanaian returnees from Germany and other European countries, popularly called "Burgers" (shortened form of "Hamburgers"), had begun to arrive home. They had been abroad for sometime and had probably lived elsewhere for at least five years.

The trafficking business is mainly in the hands of Ghanaians. There are traces of the involvement of foreigners but they operate in collaboration with Ghanaian counterparts. Different categories of traffickers operate in Ghana depending on the need of the prospective migrant. The first category is made up of individual traffickers known as "connection men" or "visa contractors," who operate from their homes and small businesses, mostly shops, and operate with a small staff or assistants who run errands and perform administrative duties. This category is further divided into two: those permanently in Ghana with no travel experience and those who are returnees and are able to travel to and from North America and Europe. The second group often accompanies their "passengers" on the travels. Within the first group, there are the established "connection men," who have been in the trafficking business for years. It is estimated that over twenty of such traffickers operate in Accra alone. There are those who move in and out of the business, operating for short periods. Such people enter the trafficking business, make losses or encounter some form of problem or make some profit and get out. This category tends to deal in fraudulent travel documents. A second category is made up of travel and tour agencies. These organize tour trips for prospective migrants. These trips are organized most easily to east European states, from where the "tourists" are smuggled to Western Europe (Affrifa 2004).

The trafficking is done in phases. The first phase involves the recruitment of people. Would be migrants usually seek out the traffickers. The reputation of the traffickers is known and word gets round. For those who travel to and from the destination countries, the relatives of prospective migrants based there contract them, and all financial arrangements are concluded there. The would-be migrants then contact them back home. There is also evidence of the active recruitment of women to be employed abroad. The scale of such women trafficking cannot be determined, but considering the fact that many Ghanaian women are reputed to be in the prostitution business in Europe, this mode of recruitment cannot be underestimated. The women are tempted by false promises and prospects. They are promised among other things, free accommodation, free meals, employment, and guaranteed salaries. The second phase involves transportation to the destinations, with false travel documents, false business identities, and other guises. For most Ghanaians trafficked this would be the final phase. For those who are actively recruited, the third and final phase would be integration into the black economy of the destination. The nationality of those trafficked can be determined from the statistics of those arrested (Table 25-7).

The table reveals that Ghanaians are the most trafficked, followed by Nigerians and other ECOWAS nationals. In 2000 and 2001, 75.7% and

Table 25-7. Trafficked Nationals in Ghana**

Nationality	2000	2001
Ghanaians	347	412
Nigerians	57	103
Other ECOWAS Nationals	24	
Indians	11	14
Sri Lankans	8	1
Pakistanis	4	-
Bangladeshis		5
Lebanese		1
Palestinians		1
Malaysians		1
Jordanians		1
Ethiopians		1
Congolese		2
Ukrainians		1
Chinese	2	6
Total	**458**	**570**

**Data could not be secured for 2001–2008

Source: Ghana Immigration Service Fraud Office Records.

72.2% of all persons arrested were Ghanaians. These figures and the diversity of the other nationals, confirm Ghana's status both as a point of origin and transit in the trafficking process. Ghana plays a significant role in the rather clandestine human trafficking business.

Effects of September 11, 2001 Terrorist Attacks

Immigration authorities worldwide have had to review security measures following the terrorist attacks on the United States on September 11, 2001. Ghana has adopted similar measures. Even though the statutes have not been altered or regulations tightened, the monitoring of people of Arab extraction and countries with strong Islamic presence has been increased. Security at Ghana's only international airport, Kotoka International Airport, has been tightened, and physical checking of luggage has been increased. The United States has increased its cooperation with and support for Ghana immigration. The United States has provided funds, training, and equipment for the computerization of immigration processes at the Kotoka International Airport and Aflao Border, the country's two leading air and land entry points. Computers have now been installed to do passenger clearance and information storage. Paga and Elubo border posts, the other two major entry points are similarly being equipped (Affrifa 2004).

Conclusion

Immigration is one of the sensitive issues for most countries due to the tensions it can create between host and immigrant communities. Immigration to a large extent is influenced by the economic situation of the migrant's country as it relates to the destination country. When the economic situation of a country is good it attracts a lot of migrants. Increasing rates of immigration also tend to provide a convenient scapegoat for governments when economic difficulties set in and rising levels of unemployment begin to exert pressure on governments to restrict the scale of immigration. In West Africa this has manifested in the expulsion of immigrants or aliens. In 1969, Ghana expelled many West Africans, many of whom were Nigerians. Similarly in 1983 Nigeria expelled many Ghanaians who had migrated to Nigeria during the oil boom. In the early 1960s Ghana's buoyant economic situation made the country a favored destination for many migrants from the West African subregion. Following the Ghana example, the economic success of Cote d'Ivoire, the country became the destination of many migrants especially from Mali and Burkina Faso. Similarly when Nigeria hit the oil boom in the mid-1970s, it became the destination for many West African migrants. In the situation of Ghana economic difficulties still persist and many Ghanaians do emigrate to find greener pastures in other countries. Formerly Nigeria was a favored destination in West Africa, but with the end of the Nigerian oil boom Ghanaians have gone to South Africa and elsewhere in Europe and North America. The irony though is that while the economic situation of Ghana has pushed Ghanaians to move out to other countries, other West Africans prefer to migrate to Ghana. When Ghana's economic situation was good in the early 1960s, the country's immigration policy under the Aliens Act was pretty open and the government did not bother much about immigrants. The government has however reviewed the Aliens Act and replaced it with the Citizenship Act 2000 and the Immigration Act 2000. Ghana's immigration policy seeks to use immigration to attract critical foreign investment and transfer of technology and human resource capital/skills for the socioeconomic development of the country. Foreign direct investments also generate jobs for Ghanaians. At the same time the policy seeks to prevent illegal immigration, transnational exploitation and social corruption. Ghana is currently not an economic success story as it used to be in the postindependence era and even though Ghanaians seek to emigrate to other countries the political stability of the country over the period of 1992–2008 does attract other West Africans and non-Africans and it is affording the country the opportunity to streamline its immigration and citizenship laws. This chapter has highlighted Ghana's immigration and the efforts on the part of the government to review and streamline the set of laws that govern immigration policy.

References

Aboah W.K. (1994). "International Response to Trafficking in Migrants and the Safeguarding of Migrants Rights." Paper presented at the 11th IOM Seminar on International Response to Trafficking Migrants and the Safeguarding of Migrants Rights Geneva, October 26–28.

Affrifa Laud, K.O. (2004). *Ghana and the Problem of Migrant Trafficking.* Unpublished M.A. Dissertation, Legon Centre for International Affairs (LECIA), University of Ghana, Legon.

Amin, S. (1974). "Introduction." In Amin, S. (ed.), *Modern Migrations in Western Africa.* London, Oxford University Press.

Castles, S., & Miller, M.J. (1993). *The Age of Migration London.* London, Macmillan Press.

European Commission (2000, March). "Push and Pull Factors in International Migration." Country Report: Ghana No. 10 Compiled by J.K. Anarfi, K. Awusabo-Asare, & N.N.N. Nsowah-Nuamah.

Essuman-Johnson, A. (1992). "The Liberian Refugee Problem and Ghana's Response to It." In *LECIA Bulletin* Vol. 2, No. 1, March. GIPC: Statistics on Registered Projects 2004–2008.

Ghana Statistical Service (1995). *Migration Research Study in Ghana.* Vol. 2.

GIPC (2007). First Quarter 2007 Investment Report.

GIPC. *Quarterly Report.* Vol. 3, No. 4.

GIPC (2008). Quarterly Update, 3rd Quarter July 1–September 30, 2008.

GIPC (2004). Statistics on Registered Projects 4th Quarter 2004.

GIS Annual Report (2004).

Immigration Act (2000). Act 573.

Parnwell, M. (1993). *Population Movements and the Third World*. London, Routledge.

Peil, M. (1998). Quoted in Van Hear, H., *New Diaspora*. London, UCL Press p. 205.

Personal Interview (2004, July 20). Mr. Laud Affrifa, Comptroller of Immigration, Ghana Immigration Service.

Personal Interview (2004, August 14). Mr. Gyamfi M.K., Assistant Director of Immigration, Ghana Immigration Service.

Richmond, A. H. (1994). *Global Apartheid*. Toronto, Oxford University Press.

Salt J. (2000). "Trafficking and Human Smuggling: A European Perspective." *International Migration* Vol. 38, No. 3.

Personal Interview (2004, August 22). F. Tepe-Mensah, Social Services Officer, UNHCR Branch Office Accra.

GIPC Act (1994). Act 478.

Free Zone Act (1995). Act 504.

Citizenship Act (2000). Act 591.

Van Hear, N. (1998). *New Diaspora*. London, UCL Press.

Zachariah, K.C., & Conde, J. (1981). *Migration in West Africa*. London, Oxford University Press.

26

Nigeria

Experiences of Immigrants in Nigeria

Adejumoke Alice Afolayan

The experiences of immigrants in Nigeria are best seen in respect of the three main categories of immigrants: the voluntary, the conventional, and the nonconventional. It is expected that such a perspective would give an adequate picture of the varieties in the experiences of immigrants in Nigeria. The voluntary immigrants moved out of their own volition, while the involuntary were displaced from their country against their wish by ecological disasters, or by social, economic, or political conflicts. The involuntary class subdivides into conventional and nonconventional refugees. The conventional refugees comprise those persons that fulfill the United Nations 1951 Convention Declaration on Status of a Refugee, while the nonconventional refugees do not so qualify. Thus, a look at the three resultant classes would enable us to appreciate the experiences of immigrants in Nigeria. Understandably, such experiences are determined by not only the varied reasons and conditions under which they came into Nigeria, but also the circumstances of their living in the country. Surely, those circumstances would subsume the manner of their adaptation, integration, or even assimilation into the fabric of Nigerian society. Also, cases of disagreements, harassments, and even

expulsions should qualify to be included among other experiences of immigrants in the country.

However, in analyzing the experiences of immigrants in Nigeria, it is important to note the currency of the data in respect of their movements into and actual living in the country. The bane of such a study as this is the problem of availability of current data. This is resolved in two ways: obtaining information from secondary sources and application of the information in relevant sections to augment the information from the primary source, which is relatively recent.

Experiences of immigrants in Nigeria are, therefore, examined in the chapter in four main sections for each of the three categories of immigrants: the perspectives for examining experiences of voluntary and involuntary immigrants, the dynamics of their immigration flows, their conditions of entry, and circumstances under which they live in Nigeria.

A Psychosocial Perspective for Examining Experiences of Voluntary Immigrants

A psychosocial perspective is considered applicable to an examination of experiences of voluntary immigrants in Nigeria, in terms of the dynamics of the volume and directions of the flows, the conditions of entry and of stay of immigrants in the host country. These are based on the facts that human experiences take place at the individual and or group level. Broadly, experiences are either psychological or sociocultural. More elaborately, such experiences are physical, psychological, social, cultural, economic, religious, and political. The social, economic, and political conditions of the countries of origin and destination are causes or stimuli to which individuals react in their decision on whether or not to move. The individuals' responses are based on differences in their level of needs, perception, and evaluation. Consequently, what attracts one individual may be repulsive to another (Afolayan, 1972). The country that presents the highest and most preferred stimuli tends to be selected as the major destination, while others follow in descending order of preference.

Furthermore, the adoption of a psychosocial perspective is based on the reasoning that immigrants' interactions with people in the host community crystallize into stereotypes. Two major group behaviors result, the in-group and out-group behaviors. The in-group behavior of the immigrants may be contradictory to that of the host's out-group, in particular on socioeconomic matters. For example, the relationship between the two groups could be hostile when the economic activities of immigrants are seen to threaten the interests of their host population. In such a case, the strangers (immigrants) might be socially, economically, and politically excluded from the host community. Moreover, the experiences of immigrants would vary depending on their level of integration with the host. A change in the relationship between immigrants and the host could, therefore, be one of adjustment, a withdrawal/shrinking back to the group, or outright expulsion from the host community (Albert, 2003).

In addition, from the psychosocial perspective, experiences of both voluntary and involuntary immigrants in the host country can be considered as links/interconnectivities in the host's employment conditions and the socioeconomic characteristics of the immigrants. These could be with reference to the number and types of vacancies available, policies on recruitment/employment, immigrants' socioeconomic characteristics, and the ethnic and racial characteristics of the host country (Model, 1997). The psychosocial perspective, therefore, enables us to examine immigrants' experiences within the host country as they are shaped mostly by the social, economic, and political environment provided by the community.

Dynamics of the Volumes and Directions of Voluntary Immigration into Nigeria

The dynamics of the volumes and directions of voluntary immigration into Nigeria in 1963, 1991 (both the 1991 Census and Post Census Enumeration Survey), and 2004 are examined as a way of appreciating experiences of immigration in Nigeria. Tables 26-1 and 26-2 show that immigrants formed very small percentages of the total population, which increased slightly from 0.2 to 0.5 percent respectively in 1963 and 1991, resulting in a percentage growth rate of 5.5.

Furthermore, Tables 26-2 to 26-6 indicate varied and changing sources of the immigrants over the years. Africa was the base for 53.72 and 84.38 percent of the immigrants respectively in 1963 and 1991, while the non-African countries contributed a lower and decreasing proportion of total foreign population in the country at the two time periods (National Population Commission, 1998). Cameroon was in the lead in 1963, followed by Niger, Ghana, Togo, Benin, Sierra Leone, Chad, Liberia, and other African countries. In 1991 the four states to the west of Nigeria, which are Benin, Ghana, Togo, and the Ivory Coast contributed the most, while Niger, and Mali, and Burkina Faso to the north were the next major sources. Other neighboring countries, Chad and Cameroon, came next in importance. Immigrants from other African countries (Egypt, Equatorial Guinea) formed a lower percentage. The remaining percentage (non-Africans) indicates that immigrants from the United States of America topped the list; followed by those from Europe, Asia, other countries and not stated, and Australia (National Population Commission, 1998).

The drastic change in direction became obvious with the implementation of the Protocol of Free Movement of Persons, Residence, and Establishment of the Economic

Table 26-1. Population Distribution by Nationality in 1963–1991 Censuses

Countries	1963 Census		1991 Census		Percentage Growth
	Number	Percentage	Number	Percentage	RATE
Benin	5,214	5.14	100,939	21.16	10.6
Ghana	7,563	7.45	78,706	16.50	8.4
Liberia	712	0.70	8,175	1.71	8.
Níger	8,807	8.68	37,035	7.76	5.1
Sierra Leone	1,984	1.96	1,623	0.3	−0.7
Togo	7,392	7.29	48,993	10.27	23.7
Cameroon	18,434	18.17	10,703	2.24	−1.9
Chad	1,626	1.60	11,611	2.43	7.0
Africans	54,499	53.72	402,601	84.38	7.1
Other Africans	2,767	2.73	104,816	21.97	13.0
Non-Africans	46,951	46.28	74,534	15.62	1.7
Foreigners	101,450	100.0	477,135	100.0	5.5

Source: National Population Commission (1998).

Table 26-2. Population Distribution by Nationality and Sex, 1991 Census and PES

Nationality	Census			PES		
	Male	Female	Total	Male	Female	Total
Total	44,529,608	44,462,612	88,992,220	2,064,259	2,067,992	4,132,251
Nigerians	44,263,269	44,251,816	88,515,085	2,059,322	2,063,817	4,123,139
Foreigners	266,339	210,796	477,135	4,937	4,175	9,112
West Africans	198,769	157,369	356,138	3,793	3,214	7,007
Africans (Other)	25,05221,411	46,463	397	360	757	1,117
Americans	15,380	12,769	28,149	87	73	160
Asian	9,113	6,152	15,268	305	253	558
Australia	246	214	460	1	2	3
Europeans	13,764	9,995	23,759	205	139	344
Others & Not Stated	4,015	2,886	6,901	149	134	283
Percentage						
Total	100.0	100.0	100.0	100.0	100.0	100.0
Nigerians	99.4	99.5	99.4	99.7	99.7	99.7
Foreigners	0.5	0.4	0.5	0.2	0.2	0.2
West Africans	0.4	0.3	0.4	0.1	0.1	0.1
Africans (Other)	0.0	0.0	0.0	0.0	0.0	0.2
Americans	0.0	0.0	0.0	0.0	0.0	0.1
Asian	0.0	0.0	0.0	0.0	0.0	0.0
Australia	0.0	0.0	0.0	0.0	0.0	0.0
Europeans	0.0	0.0	0.0	0.0	0.0	0.0
Others & Not Stated	0.0	0.0	0.0	0.0	0.0	0.0

Sources: Nigeria, 1991, *Population Census & Post Enumeration Survey.*

Community of West African States (ECOWAS) in 1978. This manifests in the pull of Nigeria on immigrants mostly from member states, though at varying proportions, as shown in Table 26-1, on the situation between the two censuses (Afolayan, 1988).

Tables 26-5 and 26-6 are presented to show the current situation in 2004 in two of the states in the federation, for which reliable data are available. The two states can also be regarded representative of the whole nation. The available data for Oyo State buttress the notion of varied

Table 26-3. Population Distribution by Nationality and Sex

Country	1991 Census Population			Percentage Sex			
	Male	Female	Total	Male	Female	Total	Ratio
Benin[1]	54,347	46,592	100,939	24.28	26.06	25.071	16.64
Burkina Faso	2,019	1,496	3,515	0.9	0.84	0.87	134.96
Cape Verde	1,030	772	1,802	0.46	0.43	0.45	133.42
Cote d'Ivoire	1,043	802	1,845	0.47	0.45	0.46	130.05
Gambia	1,575	1,179	2,754	0.7	0.66	0.68	133.59
Ghana	49,214	29,492	78,706	21.99	16.5	19.55	166.87
Guinea	1,572	1,049	2,621	0.7	0.59	0.65	149.86
Guinea Bissau	1,115	936	2,051	0.5	0.52	0.51	119.12
Liberia	4,326	3,849	8,175	1.93	2.15	2.03	112.39
Mali	28,711	27,760	56,471	12.83	15.53	14.03	103.43
Mauritania	3,662	3,937	7,599	1.64	2.2	1.89	93.01
Niger[1]	23,290	13,745	37,035	10.41	7.69	9.2	169.44
Senegal	1,225	784	2,009	0.55	0.44	0.5	156.25
Sierra Leone	860	763	1,623	0.38	0.43	0.4	112.71
Togo	4,780	24,213	48,993	11.07	13.54	12.17	102.34
West Africa	198,769	157,369	356,138	88.81	88.02	88.46	126.31
Cameroon[1]	6,014	4,689	10,703	2.69	2.62	2.66	128.26
Chad[1]	6,966	4,645	11,611	3.11	2.6	2.88	149.97
Egypt	2,081	1,977	4,058	0.93	1.11	1.01	105.26
Equatorial Guinea	967	1,052	2,019	0.43	0.59	0.5	91.92
Africa (Others)	9,024	9,048	18,072	4.03	5.06	4.49	99.73
Africans	223,821	178,780	402,601	100	100	100	125.19
Neighboring Countries [1]	90,617	69,671	160,288	40.49	38.97	39.81	564.31

[1] Neighboring Countries.

Source: Nigeria, 1991, *Population Census & Post Enumeration Survey.*

Table 26-4. Arrival of ECOWAS Citizens into Nigeria through Recognized Routes (1979–1982)

Country	Year			
	1979	1980	1981	1982
Benin	11,255	49,814	27,724	25,49
Cape Verde Island–	–	2	4	–
Guinea	2,856	2,378	2,196	2,640
Gambia	2,755	944	3,355	2,800
Ghana	38,229	80,583	80,686	86,366
Guinea Bissau	–	–	3	–
Ivory Coast	1,763	4,052	3,486	2,091
Liberia	2,574	2,001	1,871	1,589
Mali	3,983	10,989	5,608	2,364
Mauritania	266	5	566	597
Niger	1,334	17,474	14,894	26,249
Togo	4,845	25,970	9,101	13,258
Senegal	3,275	6,488	1,208	2,740
Sierra Leone	2,118	1,873	1,498	2,636
Upper Volta	989	676	955	442
Total	76,202	203,258	153,155	169,267

Source: Statistics Section, Immigration Department Alagbon Close Ikoyi.

Table 26-5. Expatriates by Nationality Working in Oyo State, October 31, 2004

Nationality	No.	Nationality	No.
Algerian	1	Lebanese	138
American	10	Mexican	2
Belgian	2	Myanmar(Burma)	1
Brazilian	2	Pakistan	2
Swiss	2	Peruvian	1
British	23	Philippines (Filipino)	6
Bulgarian	2	Polish	2
Cameroonian	2	Romanian	1
Chinese	4	Rwandese	2
Congolese	1	South African	3
Danish	4	Sudanese	1
Egyptian	10	Sri Lankan	5
Ethiopian	1	Syrian	24
French	2	Sudanese	2
		Tanzanian	1
German	3	Yemeni	1
Indian	68	Total	350
Irish	12	Sri Lankan	5
Italian	10	Syrian	24

Source: Nigerian Immigration Service, Oyo State, Nigeria.

Table 26-6. No. of Holders of Aliens Green Card, Lagos State, Nigeria, January–June 2004

Month	No. of Holders
January	1,235
February	1,063
March	1,457
April	1,086
May	1,017
June	768
Total	6,626

Source: Nigeria Immigration Service, Zone "A" CERPAC Center, Ikoyi, Lagos. Mid-Year Report, 2004

sources of foreigners or non-ECOWAS aliens in the country. ECOWAS immigrants in recent time can be accepted as numerous and would possibly be close to the same proportions as revealed by the 1991 Census. The foreigners, revealed by Table 26.5 are the Lebanese, Indians, Syrians, and British, in that order of importance. Others are Irish, Americans, Italians, and Egyptians, to mention but a few. In addition, Table 26.6 reveals that even though

the record is just up to mid-2004, Lagos State has higher numbers of registered, working aliens, plus Commonwealth citizens, than the figure for Oyo State. This reveals the dominant position of Lagos State as an absorbing center of aliens. Other known states of the federation, almost in descending order, are Rivers and Delta states (the oil producing states), and Ogun and Kano states, to mention but a few. Other pockets of aliens' concentration are the nation's major ports, for example Lagos, Warri, Port Harcourt, and the Export Processing Zone of Calabar, where aliens are known as shoppers.

Entry Requirements as Explanatory Factor

The enactments of immigration laws and indigenization exercises have been not only the main instruments for promoting and defending national interests, but also a determinant of immigration flows. Such laws include the Immigration Act, 1969; the Immigration (Amendment) Decree No. 8, 1972; and the Immigration Act, 1990 (Federal Government of Nigeria, 1990). The salient requirements are that immigrants fulfill certain conditions before they are allowed in and during their stay in Nigeria. One such condition is the issuance of a visa or entry permit as appropriate to an immigrant applicant (defined as: any person other than a citizen of Nigeria or person accorded immunity by reason of diplomatic status, who enters or seeks to enter Nigeria). This is subject to the satisfaction of the director of Nigeria Immigration Services.

There are, therefore, significant differences in the conditions of entry for aliens as against those for ECOWAS citizens. The holding of a Nigerian visa is required for entry into the country for aliens, but not for immigrants from member states of ECOWAS. This is because the Protocol for the Free Mobility of Persons of the Community supersedes the holding of a visa. Immigrants' identity card and (or) ECOWAS passport are (is), therefore, required for citizens of ECOWAS to enter Nigeria. Evasion is, however, rampant among the majority of immigrants from ECOWAS countries that enter through unofficial inlets.

The entry of the non-ECOWAS immigrants is based on their holding any of the three main types of visa (ordinary, diplomatic, and gratis courtesy visa) and abiding by its stipulated conditions of entry and stay in Nigeria. The ordinary visa is further differentiated as transit, single journey, and multiple journeys visa. The federal government, through its Nigeria Immigration Service, lays the conditions for applying for any of the visa, thus: "In order to successfully obtain a visa to visit Nigeria, you should ensure that you meet the requirements of the country's mission in your country" (Bureau of Public Enterprises, 2003).

For the avoidance of doubt, Section 51, 4(a) of the Federal Government of Nigeria, Immigration Act, 1990, states: "A person seeking entry shall be treated as in Nigeria after he has complied with all formalities prescribed for inspection by immigration, health and of customs authorities, and whether the compliance is subject to conditions or otherwise."

Also, there are certain regulations applied to the entry and movement of the category of those referred to in the Act as "aliens." An alien refers to any person not a Commonwealth citizen or a citizen of Ireland. Aliens are to register their presence at the immigration offices closest to their places of residence or occupation. These are stated under the Immigration (Control of Aliens) Regulations, as follows:

The Director of Immigration may, by notice in writing addressed to any alien, require him to:

a) Report to a Senior Immigration Officer or the Aliens Officer or to any Police Officer at a time and place stated and to provide such Officer with any information regarding his movement. . .
b) Report to the Senior Immigration Officer or the Aliens Officer. . ., his intention to absent himself from his place of residence for any period exceeding 24 hours. . .
c) Obtain from the Senior Immigration Officer or the Aliens Officer of any State. . ., in which he resides, a permit to travel in respect of any journey which he intends to undertake exceeding a distance of 30 miles from the place in which he is resident. (Federal Government of Nigeria, 1990)

In addition, the paper-based residence permit was replaced with the Combined Expatriate Residence and Aliens Card (CERPAC) in August 2002. Applicants for the card include employees (foreigners) and their dependents, missionaries, students, and non-ECOWAS Africans. Also, immigrants' subsequent stay still depends on their ability to abide by the laws of the land, which are in conformity with the principles of international laws (Cchangani, 1983; Afolayan, 1999).

However, Nigeria had not signed nor ratified the International Convention on the Rights of All Migrant Workers and Their Families, and had not provided official explanations for this. The legal implications of the Convention are being studied to ensure that conflicts with existing provisions on the rights of migrant workers and their families are not generated, if ratified (Adedokun, 2003). *(As a postscript, The Convention was ratified in January 2009).*

Geographic and Psychosocial Factors as Explanatory Factor

The physical, geographic, and psychosocial factors are discussed in more depth. The geographic factor is in terms of physical contiguity. Even this is moderated by socio-cultural factors, of artificiality of boundaries, and difficulties of separating related people by boundaries. The psychological factors cover poor Nigerian image, adverse publicity/travel warnings, and unmanned or poorly manned control posts.

Geographic factors stand out prominently among factors responsible for the volumes and patterns of the voluntary immigration. The directions of the flows have been from neighboring countries in the West African region, and immigration into Nigeria is mostly by land. These geographic features are moderated by the socio-cultural affinities that the country has with its neighboring countries. The artificiality of the Nigerian borders is evident in the contradiction in the use of the term "border," in the place of "boundary." What borders are supposed to be, limits of spatial movement are, therefore, not operative because of the presence of families and friends across borders. Instead, the consistent, trans-border mobility of people across Nigerian boundaries is only possible within its maximal borderlands, and not across borders (Afolayan, 2000).

In addition, the perception of the affinity of people in the borderlands of Nigeria is aptly summed up in what a local chief in the Benin

Republic, the Alaketu of Ketu (1937–1963), said of his people and the generality of the Yoruba people that are on both sides of the border between the two countries: "We regard the boundary as dividing the British and the French, not the Yoruba" (quoted in Prescott, 1971).

Immigrant-host similarities have, therefore, developed. Asiwaju (1989), Adejuyigbe (1989), Labo (2000), and Afolayan (2000), for example, have attested to the artificiality of the Nigerian borders that divide contiguous, similar ethnic groups but fail to arrest their consistent, on-going socio-cultural, economic and political interactions. Labo (2000) buttressed the statement for immigrants from Niger in the northwestern border of Nigeria, as: "The cohesion and solidarity among the people across these boundaries and the movements are still going on in spite of the arbitrary international borders."

Swings in the Political Economy of Nigeria and Membership in ECOWAS

The ease of movement of persons that the Protocol of Free Mobility of Persons of the ECOWAS afforded, and the almost overriding importance of petroleum in the country's economy beginning in the mid-1970s accounted for the trooping in of West African immigrants on a relatively large scale, at least up to the eve of the first expulsion exercise in 1983. The relatively high thrust of immigration into Nigeria, up to the first two stages of implementation of the Protocol, has been adduced to economic buoyancy of the country relative to that of other Member States. Addo (1982), for example, tried to capture this when he stated that: "Nigeria, enjoying a booming economy, thanks to oil, is able to receive foreign workers and so far tolerated a large number, but appears to be wavering as to what final official policy she should adopt on foreign nationals."

Afolayan (1988) also buttressed the above: "The immigration of ECOWAS citizens into Nigeria gathered momentum after the Protocol was ratified in 1980. This period coincided with the era of oil-boom in the country."

Poor Nigerian Image and Adverse Publicity

Furthermore, other factors that dictated the volumes and directions of immigration in Nigeria in recent times are the poor image of the country abroad and the negative publicity about conditions in the country.

While violent crime, as in some other major cities of the world, constitutes a big headache to law enforcement agencies and the citizens alike, a serious crime issue for Nigeria has been the Advance Fee Scam, otherwise known as 419. This has drawn considerable adverse attention to the country, which has been making concerted efforts with foreign governments and agencies to expose the felons and their methods. The Advance Fee Scam seeks to take advantage of the greed or gullibility of foreigners, by usually promising them huge windfalls if they cooperate in bilking agencies of the Nigerian government of sums sometimes running into millions of dollars.

The Bureau of Public Enterprises (October 12, 2004) clarifies the operation of Advance Fee Scam and its practice to date, as:

The Advance Fee Fraud is perpetrated by enticing the victim with a bogus business proposal, which promises millions of U.S. dollars as a reward. The scam letter usually promises to transfer huge amounts of money, usually in U.S. dollars, purported to be part of certain contract to the addressees' bank account, to be shared in some proportion between the parties. A favorable response to the letter is followed by excuses why the funds cannot be remitted readily and subsequently by demands for proportionate sharing of payments for various taxes and fees supposedly to facilitate the processing and remittance of the alleged funds. The use of fake Government, Central Bank of Nigeria, Nigerian National Petroleum Corporation, etc, documents is a common practice.

The security implication of the above cannot but be noted by many people worldwide. Many sources of information have noted this and other areas of concern. For example, the U.S. Department of State on July 23, 2003, gave the following travel warnings to prospective U.S. citizens into Nigeria, as:

Conditions in Nigeria pose considerable risks to travelers. Violent crime, committed by ordinary criminals, as well as by persons in police and military uniforms, can occur throughout the country.... Religious tension between some Muslim and Christian communities results in occasional acts of isolated communal violence that erupt quickly and without warning. Nigerian-based business, charity, and other scams target foreigners worldwide and pose a risk of financial loss.

Circumstances of Voluntary Immigrants Living in Nigeria (1970s–1980s)

Level of Participation in Economic Activities and Government Policies

Circumstances of the voluntary immigrants' stay in the country indicated that they actively participated in the buoyant economy offered, so long as the situation permitted. In addition, the business promotion activities of the government are another form of the government policies that influenced the circumstances of immigrants in Nigeria. They are considered from the following documents: the Nigerian Enterprises Promotion Acts (Indigenization Acts) of 1972 and 1977; the Nigerian Enterprises Promotion Decree, 1989; and the Nigerian Investment Promotion Commission Decree, 1995. Many of these stipulate specific procedures for the employment of non-nationals, conditions for work permits, and for the establishment of and/or procurement of jobs and of business. Companies and organizations wishing to engage the services of expatriates for short-term assignments are required to apply directly to the Comptroller General in Abuja for visa/entry permit. For such expatriates, it is the temporary work permit visa. In addition, the 1995 Decree was to create an environment conducive for investment in Nigeria. Part 5 of the Decree, for example, permitted the registration of enterprises in which there is foreign participation. Such an enterprise must have been duly registered with the commission.

Also, a foreign enterprise may buy the shares of any Nigerian enterprise in any convertible foreign currency. Furthermore,

a foreign investor in an enterprise to which the Decree applies is guaranteed unconditional transferability of funds through an authorized dealer, in freely convertible currency, of

a) Dividends or profits (net of taxes) attributable to the investment.
b) Payment in respect of a loan servicing where a foreign loan has been obtained and
c) The remittance of proceeds (net of all taxes), and other obligations in the event of a sale or liquidation of the enterprise or any interest attributable to the investment. (Nigerian Investment Promotion Commission, 1995, p. A523)

Nevertheless, in the late 1970s and early 1980s, the economic spotlight of the entire West African region was undoubtedly on Nigeria, as reflected in the volume of immigration earlier presented and from what is known of the large volume of undocumented immigrants. The high immigration flows were because of relatively large openings in the economy of Nigeria. Afolayan (1988) described the circumstances of ECOWAS citizens during this period:

Most of the immigrants were willing to take up jobs that Nigerians regarded as mean or too tedious.... Moreover, their wages, especially in the private sector were comparatively low. Typically, they worked as carpenters, bricklayers, house-maids, night guards, factory workers, iron benders, and as laborers on farms.... a few of them were skilled workers, such as teachers, doctors, lawyers, accountants, engineers and pilots.... They were engaged mainly in the major employment center, that is, Lagos, which housed the majority of the ECOWAS citizens from countries to the south-west of Nigeria and Kano for aliens from the north.

Groups of immigrant businessmen in the country have, however, been changing and comprised other nationals. In the mid-1960s and up to the recent past, the Lebanese flooded the Lagos market. Also, the estimated number of Israeli in Nigeria is currently, that is, by mid-2008, put at 700–800, most of whom are employees of companies seeking to further business interests in the country. The Israelis handle major construction works in the country. The Chinese are also appearing in larger number. There are also other nationals in the oil sector. Each of these groups of immigrants has been faced with different challenges of living in Nigeria.

For instance, it is stated that the volume of trade between Nigeria and China has increased. This is because of improved business relationship between the two countries. However, the cordial relationship that the Chinese community enjoys in Nigeria is not reciprocated to Nigerians in China, as can be gleaned from the quote below:

There are thousands of Chinese living and doing business in Nigeria. They do not face discrimination. The number of Chinese in Nigeria surpasses the number of Nigerians in China by almost ratio of 10 to 1. If they are gaining so much in Nigeria why can't they respect us in their country and extend our visas. Today, many innocent Nigerians are being detained and are wasting away because of expired visas, and hundreds of others are in danger of being detained. (Biafranigeriaworld.com)

Differences in Interpretation of ECOWAS Protocols and Swings in Government Policies

Nonetheless, there have been conflicts of interest, in particular as the domestic laws of the country often conflicted with those of the regional body. Where such conflicts of interest surfaced, the solution has been in favor of nationals. A case in point was a Nigerian immigration policy that came into being barely a few weeks after the second phase of the Protocol took off in June 1986. This restricted the employment of non-indigenous workers to six categories, irrespective of their place of origin, and preference was for nationals. This policy became effective almost straight off and took precedence over the Community Protocols. The expulsion of May–June 1986 marked a change in relation to immigrants, based on a change in economic conditions. Afolayan (1988) sums up the changes in the experiences:

The workers did not appear to have been in the way of anybody; instead, their labor, in most cases was said to have been appreciated and desired.... Briefly stated, the precipitating factors leading to the expulsion of ECOWAS aliens from Nigeria are three-fold: the loopholes in the ECOWAS protocol, the situation of the ECOWAS itself, and the ailing socio-economic and political situations in Nigeria.

The subsequent trends of the political economy of Nigeria, particularly in the mid-1980s spelled a downward trend in voluntary immigration into Nigeria. Economic indicators can be used in validating the change in attitude of the Nigerian government toward uncontrolled immigration. For example, the country's Gross Domestic Product (GDP) dropped by 2 percent in 1982. This was as a result of a 16 percent decrease in the petroleum sector's contribution to national revenue (Nigerian Yearbook, 1983: 100; also quoted in Brown, 1989: 261–262). Between 1983 and 1985, the country was faced with declining oil prices. The importance of this was that the government implemented drastic policy issues on relations with other member states of ECOWAS, one of which was the expulsion of over 2 million illegal immigrants (Afolayan, 1988; Brown, 1989). However, not every illegal immigrant left, as some went into hiding, especially those who were in locations that were far removed from the full glare of the government. Even a few of the expelled made a roundabout turn when suitable occasions made it possible.

Furthermore, the Structural Adjustment Program (SAP) that was introduced by June 1986 was based on the premise of a dwindling economy. It failed, however, to achieve the expected turnaround condition for the country, as revealed by the socioeconomic indicators for Nigeria. These included a declining GNP, a negative growth in consumption both at the government and private levels, and a very high inflation rate. Other indicators were an increasing unemployment rate, an increasing annual retirement, dismissal from the Federal Civil Service, constricting white-collar job openings, and an acute shortage of foreign exchange to finance industrial inputs. These are based on indices from different tables of the Federal Office of Statistics, 1987–1992. This downward trend, of necessity, further limited opportunities for immigrants. It also added to their stresses of fewer jobs and lower purchasing power of the Nigeria naira.

Further evidence of these problems was the drop in Nigeria's Gross National Product (GNP) per capita, from $1,040 for 1980–1985 to $331.33 in 1987–1992. The awful gap in the level of economic performance of the country against other developed countries or even against other African countries with higher foreign currency exchange rates created its own scenario. For example, the per capita GNP for Nigeria and the United States of America were $290 and $22,560 respectively in 1992, and $800 and

$28,780 respectively by 2002 (Meyers, 2002). The CFA franc also became a higher and convertible currency, compared to the lower, inconvertible naira (West Africa Long Term Perspectives [WALTPS] 1990).

The implications of all these trends are many, one of which is the negative impact that they had on immigration into Nigeria (Adepoju, 1990; Afolayan, 1992). These were reflected in reversals of both the volume and directions of immigration, particularly from ECOWAS Member States. While a relatively large number of women traders shuttled between Lagos and Abidjan (Ivory Coast) and other coastal West African countries, fewer immigrants came in from those countries. The reversals occurred as the traders perceived the external markets outside the country more lucrative than markets within the country in trading off their Nigerian wares. Many of the traders, therefore, preferred carrying out their activities on a circulatory basis (Afolayan, 2000, 2002). For the self-employed professionals, such as artisans and traders, African countries that had stronger and convertible currencies were preferred (i.e., Gambia, Botswana, Zimbabwe, and South Africa, and countries outside Africa—Taiwan, Singapore, and China).

Reversals were, therefore, characteristic of immigration flows into Nigeria. Guyer and Idowu (1991), for example, reported that international sources of labor in many Nigerian rural areas and even in the urban centers were declining in importance. This was because the devalued naira hardly sufficed for any appreciable purchase outside Nigeria. Immigrants, therefore, found it less lucrative moving into Nigeria.

Dividends of Democracy

However, the relative increase in the number of immigrants recently is adduced to the rising economic and political conditions relative to the situations in the mid-1990s and to economic downturn in other countries south of the Sahara. Evidence of a gradual picking-up of the voluntary immigration in the recent past is hard to substantiate with comprehensive data for the whole nation, as stated earlier. Nonetheless, if available, the incipient increase cannot be separated from the relatively positive changes in the social, economic, and political events in the

country and in other countries in Africa recently. For example, the movement of immigrants of European and Asian origin can be traced to the relative peace that prevails in the country since democracy was installed in 1999 (Bureau of Democracy, Human Rights, and Labor, 1998).

Also, even though the value of the country's currency, the naira, is very low compared to currencies of other nations, the relatively cheap labor in Nigeria encourages the immigration of foreigners who own businesses in Nigeria. Most of the immigrants came in with mixed expectations, depending on where they were coming from. While some came with high hopes, others came with caution, following the negative image Nigeria has acquired over time. Citizens of ECOWAS often perceive life in Nigeria to be better than what they were used to in their own countries. The European/Asian immigrants, however, evaluate it otherwise. But even if the foreigners do not rate conditions in Nigeria higher, they continue to stay in the country because it represents a land of opportunity, where little investments yield plenty of returns.

Recent Positive Economic Factors

Immigrants from within the West African region consist of unskilled labor, artisans, and farmers, in contrast to foreigners, who are mostly skilled. Also, the former group of immigrants tends to stay in rural areas more than the latter. The unskilled immigrants are mostly miners, artisans, traders, fashion designers, hairdressers, and sex workers, as against the skilled immigrants, who are company owners, workers in the oil sector, and missionaries. Moreover, the gains that immigrants could reckon on are in terms of the amount of money they are able to remit home periodically (Nigeria Immigration Service, 2004).

Moreover, foreigners are known to be in relatively large number in the oil producing Rivers and Delta states. It is estimated that Shell Oil Company has between 4,000 and 5,000 foreigners employed as oil drillers and other professionals; and Chevron has about 3,000 foreign workers. Also, aliens show up as workers in the pharmaceuticals, food and beverage, textile and distillery industries in the industrial estates of Agbara and Ota in Ogun State. In addition, they have their community pockets, for example in the "Chinese City" of Ikeja, Lagos State, where they are known for their commercial enterprises of very cheap materials.

Evidence of Default as Unsatisfactory Circumstance

There have, however, been reports of unsatisfactory living conditions of some of the immigrants in the host country, Nigeria. For example, the *Post Express* (1996) revealed that Indian business moguls forged and issued Nigerian resident permits to not fewer than 25 young Indian and Pakistani girls, who were recruited to come and work in the country, as a result of hardship in their home countries. The loophole has been adduced to faulty logistics in the issuance of the residence permit. It is hoped that a tightening up of the system by restricting the issuance to eight states and by implementing a computerized system, would curb the abuse (*The Guardian*, 2003).

Also, there have been reports of multinationals abusing the expatriate quota, and through that means transferring money to their home bases (*Vanguard*, 2004). In this case, the named oil servicing firm has no less than 327 expatriate welders, electricians, and other technicians, contrary to the law that stipulates that only where there are no qualified Nigerians should expatriates brought in. The investigations also revealed that besides Indians and Italians, Filipino, Portuguese, Colombian, Turkish, and Romanian nationals have large numbers of expatriates for jobs that thousands of qualified Nigerians could do.

Examples of Mixed/Undecided Weight of Circumstances of Living in Nigeria

The experiences of some other individual foreign immigrants reveal fears, which make the few that come do so with mixed feelings. The experience of a Briton in a rural setting of the country, Offatedo, in southwestern Nigeria, is quoted below from (Expat e-mail. 20 January, 2003):

Nigeria is a country that has a very poor image in the West. I find it diverse, vibrant, fascinating—and frightening.... It's not unusual to pass 10 armed police check points in a 100 kilometers' journey. To

travel at night is to run the gauntlet of all too frequent armed robberies.... Corruption is endemic and political, religious and ethnic tensions are not too far below the surface in a country where immense wealth and extreme poverty are every day sights.... basic facilities are erratic at best.... Clean running water is a luxury... but collecting water from the well is a great way to learn village gossip.... After 11 months here, the hardships and joys will stay with me forever: sharing a taxi with six people, two children, a basket of chickens and a goat; the immense delight when a parcel of chocolate gets through from the UK; picking mangoes straight from the tree; the stranger who takes my hand, asks my name and bids me welcome.... But after you get used to all these deprivations—and you very quickly do—it's the immediate kindness, humor and generosity that keep you going a long way from home. And being an ex-pat has given me a new perspective on my home country. A Nigerian will certainly have access to facilities (in the UK)—but would they enjoy the overwhelming welcome I've received here?

Generally, it can be said that the circumstances of living in Nigeria are relative, depending on which of the positive or negative evaluations overrides the other. The information provided by the Nigeria Immigration Service (2004), for example, illustrates this:

The Europeans/Asians, while not seeing Nigeria as better than their countries of origin, it represents for them a land of opportunities where little investments yield plenty. This can be said to account for the reason why most of them refuse to return after expiration of their permits and or contracts.

Furthermore, some other recent dynamics dictate other experiences of immigrants in Nigeria. For example, Haarez.com (August 28, 2008) reported the following:

There are an estimated 700–800 Israelis currently in Nigeria, most of whom are employees of companies seeking to further business interests in the country.... Nigeria has suffered from a recent spate of kidnappings of foreigners, with over 200 having been reported over the past year.... "Nigeria is a blessed country, with oil, gas and other natural resources that bring a lot of money to the government," says an Israeli businessman who has lived and worked in the country for several years and prefers to remain anonymous.... There is no need to use your own money since the government pays 30% of the contract sum up front in addition to a monthly payment according to the work that has been completed. The basic salary of an Israeli employee in Nigeria is around

$7,000 plus a yearly bonus of two to three salaries.... Government money is not reaching the common citizen in Nigeria and millions are living in poverty, which creates a huge security threat as people are forced to steal and rob foreigners.... MEND has been linked to attacks on foreign-owned petroleum companies in Nigeria and abductions of foreign citizens.... Most of the Israelis working in the Niger Delta area are taking security precautions in order to protect them ... Foreigners, including Israelis, must always remain alert.

The UK Foreign and Commonwealth Office extended its warning on travel to Nigeria after another kidnapping in mid July 2007 (UKP&I Club, 2007). It advised against all travel to the Niger Delta and to riverine areas of Cross River State because of the very high risk of kidnapping, armed robbery and other armed attacks in these areas. The militia forces, some armed by international arms dealers, in the Niger Delta of recent, are targeted at international oil companies, as they destroy oil infrastructure and kidnap expatriate staff. Many of the expatriate oil workers have, therefore, left the country and if at all they were to work in the country would prefer the off-shore activities or work in the far-away administrative centers.

The above sections are, therefore, for the purposes of examining experiences of immigration worldwide as relative, Nigeria inclusive, as it depends on individuals' perspectives of the situation and setting. For those who are lucky or chanced to experience the good aspects of a destination, the report would be favorable and vice versa. No doubt, the socio-cultural and economic settings vary locally and worldwide.

Push-Pull Perspective for Examining Involuntary Immigration

While the psychosocial perspective explains the movement of voluntary immigration, the push-pull account fits the involuntary immigrants, whose movement is unpremeditated. The push-pull account is mechanical, as it describes immigrants moving away from places of repulsion to places of attraction, with no allowance made for weighing situations or for evaluating conditions in the source as against possible destinations (Mitchell, 1959; Lee, 1966). The causal factors

for the conventional and non-conventional immigrants reflect, therefore, the compelling, repulsive conditions of conflict and wars for some of the cases, and ecological disasters for some other cases. In addition, activities of the United Nations Humanitarian Commissioner for Refugees (UNHCR) and of the National Commission for Refugees (NCFR) indicate some of causes of involuntary moves, especially those of the Commission that was assigned the responsibilities of concern for refugees and Internally Displaced Persons (IDPs) in Nigeria by the Federal Government in 1989.

Experiences of involuntary immigration are defined by the reasons for their flight, that is, to secure refuge. Consequently, their experiences prior to moving into Nigeria can be expected to be different from those of the voluntary immigrants, in particular, their conditions prior to arrival and the entry requirements. The latter is mainly a question of which country would offer them asylum and the form of assistance the conventional refugees would receive. Many of the refugees arrived in poor health; had been traumatized, and invariably were fleeing from threatening situations to a safer host country.

Dynamics of Involuntary Immigration into Nigeria

On one hand, a sizable number of immigrants from ECOWAS qualify as non-conventional, economic refugees, as they escaped into Nigeria where conditions were better. Ecological disasters, such as the Sahelian drought of the mid-1980s are largely responsible for the sizable number of non-conventional refugees from Chad and Niger during the period. These refugees claimed that the continued ecological problems in their countries made their survival difficult; thus, pushing them southward into Nigeria.

On the other hand, conflict-ridden countries to the west of Nigeria have been largely responsible for the spate of conventional refugees that Nigeria had in the last one and a half decades. It is estimated that Nigeria has hosted between 5,000 and 9,000 conventional refugees since the wars started in many of the countries beyond its western border. Also, some political refugees have taken asylum in Nigeria, such as Mohammed Siad Barre, former Somali

President, groups of other individuals from Ghana, Chad, and recently from Liberia, including the controversial Charles Taylor, the former Liberian President.

Another category of non-conventional immigrants is the trafficked. Daily Sun Thursday, October 28, 2003, for example, reports the gory tales of how children, between ages 5 and 14, had been abducted from neighboring countries and ferried into Nigeria on different kinds of vehicles. They were kidnapped either on the street, at school, or in their neighborhoods and transported usually through bush paths across the border. Some of the kids were rescued later by the Nigerian police, following the smashing of the syndicate behind the kidnapping and other forms of child abuse in September 2003.

In addition, the most used route for both voluntary and involuntary immigrations, in particular the latter, is the least effectively policed, in comparison to the other routes. All points of entry by land are known as Immigration Control Posts, but not all are fully manned. As a result, the transition of smugglers and of trafficked women and children, for example, is indirect. The barons that recruit the trafficked get fake passports and visas for them and bribe their way through recognized borders. In addition, the porosity of the borders has allowed for the influx of immigrants of dubious character, who have been known to foment and escalate religious riots in parts of northern Nigeria.

Circumstances of Living in Nigeria: Conventional Refugees within Camp.

Circumstances of refugees' livelihood in the country are conditioned by the reality of the country's economic situation and the level of assistance offered by both the host country and any other humanitarian bodies after the initial relief might have been given.

According to the 2003 Global Refugee Trends (UNHCR Statistical yearbook, 2003), the population of Oru Camp, the only designated, official camp in Nigeria, was 7,292. The camp was established in 1990 by the Federal Military Government in response to the flow of refugees that were generated by the political crisis and civil war in Liberia. Experiences of the refugees in Oru camp can be gathered from reports on inadequacies of facilities in the camp. Over 7,000 refugees were accommodated as of 2003, which exceeded the ideal number for the camp of 1,200.

This implies congestion and its attendant problems (Longe, 2003; Eyetsemitan, 2004).

One of the dailies, the *Nigerian Tribune* of December 6, 2002, gives more vivid descriptions on experiences/conditions in the camp:

While the refugees may be said to be enjoying relative peace when considering the situation in their home countries, they are finding it difficult to cope with the situation in the camp. The provision of basic amenities—food, clothing and shelter, which initially was adequate, has been stretched by the increasing number of refugees to the camp, due to hostilities in other countries, like Sierra Leone, Congo and Cote d'Ivoire, as well as the renewed fighting in Liberia. The recent crisis in Cote d'Ivoire has also forced many more Ivorian into the camp, while the persistent, on-going crisis of Liberia still makes Liberians and Sierra Leonean run there for safety, that is, flee to Nigeria.

The report continues the review of Oru Camp, as follows:

an average of three refugees arrives in Oru camp daily.... new entrants and most Liberians as well as Sierra Leonean are having life difficult there.... Securing employment has been one major problem for the refugees, because the camp is located far from the commercial cities in the country. Also, because the major occupation of the indigenes is farming, many of them have resorted to farming, but are restricted due to their inability to secure large farm lands. Their farm product (gari) is often under-priced by the indigenes, being aware of the refugees' desperation to survive. The provision of food at the camp has been precarious, as several families cannot afford a single meal for their children.... the Liberians had not received food in the camp for years. For about eight months now, the food aid to Sierra Leonean too has been cut off. The change in policy on refugees from Liberia and Sierra Leone... was due to the short-lived peace that reigned in the countries before the renewed fighting. Health care delivery has also become a pressing problem in the camp. Most youths in the camp do not have the opportunity to go to school.... The situation has pushed many of the female refugees into a vulnerable position. Many have ended up using their bodies to get what they need, meaning engaging in prostitution to sustain themselves.

Non-conventional Immigrants Implicated in Riots and Criminal Offenses

Yet another angle to appreciating experiences of immigrants in Nigeria, in particular non-conventional immigrants, is from the perception of the host. For example, many times immigrants are associated with rising levels of insecurity in the country. The expulsions of illegal aliens in January–March 1983 and in May–July 1985 were partly due to illegal aliens being implicated in the religious riots in the northern part of the country, as the then Internal Affairs Minister stated, "the recent Kano, Maiduguri and Kaduna disturbances were traceable to this influx and the whole nation witnessed with dismay the wanton destruction of property and lives" (African Research Bulletin, 1983).

Such accusations of immigrants being responsible for many religious riots have continued to be levied, although not all cases have been proven. While they have not been proven in many cases, they cannot be ignored. The *Nigeria Tribune* of Thursday, March 11, 2004, for instance, reported, "The Federal Government on Tuesday attributed increase in crime wave, armed robbery and killings in Nigeria to the infiltration of trans-Saharan refugees (illegal aliens) from neighboring countries. Government specifically mentioned Chad, Niger, Cameroon and the Benin Republic."

In addition, many of the aliens are said to have come into the country during elections to vote. People are still apprehensive of immigrants. Part of the premise for this is the close resemblance of some non-Nigerians with Hausa people in the northern part of the country and their active participation in the local and even national political affairs, as if they were full-fledged Nigerians. This is associated with religious and social affinity of that part of the country with the neighboring countries, among many others. Also, after main events such as elections, "salah," and return of pilgrimage from holy lands are over, a large number of the illegal immigrants, including the non-conventional immigrants, go into hiding, while the relatively elderly or unproductive ones, especially the women and the little children, take to the streets begging. This usually constitutes unsightly social malaise, especially in southern states of Nigeria.

Conclusion

This chapter has shown that the experiences of immigrants depend on the conditions under which they came in, the manner in which those conditions continued to affect them, the places where they stayed and worked, and the political economy of the country at any particular time. The experiences of the three categories of immigrants, voluntary, conventional, and non-conventional immigrants, therefore, differ from one another. The multidimensional and dynamic experiences of most immigrants, that is, the voluntary immigrants in Nigeria, have therefore been brought out in the chapter more by the psychosocial perspective rather than by the push-pull perspective. The analyses revealed the varied historical, social, economic, and political factors that have characterized the immigration flows over the years.

The experiences of immigrants prior to their arrival are captured by the category of immigrants under discussion. For voluntary, economic immigrants, the political economy of the country is of interest in gauging the volume and direction of their immigration and in appreciating how much of their expectations were realized when they moved in. For the non-conventional refugees, it was mainly the security succor that the country afforded that accounted for their forced movement, but after they came, shortfalls in their expectations were revealed and what they would have wished for in a more conducive atmosphere was not forthcoming. For the three categories of immigrants, experiences at points of entry and within the country also depended on the conditions of their entry and the social and economic transactions they were able to make. Cases of default resulted in the massive expulsions and accusations levied against illegal immigrants and their actions. On the other hand, cases of conformity with the dictates of the social and economic conditions in the host community made their stay in the country beneficial to them.

Moreover, a lot of the illegal, voluntary immigrants of ECOWAS origin have had varied experiences. These include easy integration into the religious culture of the north and less so in the south where they constitute an unacceptable nuisance. They face expulsion where they have been suspected or proven to contribute to religious riots, social unrest in political seasons and other nuisance factors.

Deriving from all these, even though it is almost impossible to generalize experiences of immigrants, the determining conditions need be addressed so that sojourn in another country could be advantageous to both immigrants and the host community. Immigrants in Nigeria need to be seen as unavoidable intra- or interregional visitors. The right attitude will be to make their presence mutually beneficial. There is, therefore, the need for more formal or organized monitoring of their stay. This will ensure checks and balances through activities such as assessment of their continued relevance to the community where they settle and renewal or revocation of their permits.

References

Addo, N.O. 1982. Government-induced transfers of foreign nationals. In: Kosinski, L.A., and Clarke, J.I. (eds.) *Redistribution of population in Africa.* Heinemann, London, pp. 31–38.

Adejuyigbe, O. 1989. Identification and characteristics of borderlands in Africa. In: Asiwaju, A.I., and Adeniyi, P.O. (eds.) *Borderlands in Africa.* University of Lagos Press, Lagos, Nigeria, pp. 27–36.

Adepoju, A. 1990. State of the art: Review of migration in Africa. In: *Spontaneous Papers.* UAPS Conference on the Role of Migration in African Development: Issues and Policies for the 90s. Nairobi, February 19–24. Union for African Population Studies, Dakar, pp. 3–41.

Adedokun, O.A. 2003, October 13. The rights of migrant workers and members of their families: Nigeria, international migration, and multicultural policies. Section UNESCO Series of Country Reports on the Ratification of the UN Convention on Migrants.

Afolayan, A.A. 1972. Behavioural approach to the study of migration into and mobility within the metropolitan Lagos. Unpublished PhD thesis, University of Ibadan.

Afolayan, A.A. 1988. Immigration and expulsion of ECOWAS aliens in Nigeria. *International Migration Review* 22 (1), pp. 4–27.

Afolayan, A.A. 1992. Female migration in Nigeria and national development. In Olowu, T.A., and Akinwunmi, J.A. (eds.) *Proceedings of the National Conference of the Ibadan Socio-Economic Group.* African Economic Research Consortium, Ibadan, pp. 245–259.

Afolayan, A.A. 1999. Official and illegal migrations in Africa. In: Union for African Population Studies. Dakar, Senegal, 3rd African Population Conference Durban, South Africa. "The African Population in the 21st Century," pp. 519–542.

Afolayan, A. A. 2000. Trans-border mobility and trading: A case study of south-western border of Nigeria. IFRA Occasional Paper, No. 13. African BookBuilders Ltd., Ibadan, pp. 33–91.

Afolayan, A.A. 2002. Circulatory migration in West Africa: A case study of Ejigbo in south western Nigeria. Laboratoire SEDET, University of Paris, International Migration Unit (40 pages).

African Research Bulletin. 1983. January 1–31; January 15–February 14.

Albert, I.O. 2003. Host-stranger conflicts in the context of international migrations in Africa: An explanation and three case-studies. In: Coquery-Vidrovitch, C., Goerg, O., Mande, I., and Rajaonah, F. (eds.) *Être étranger et migrant en Afrique au XXe siècle : Enjeux identitaires et modes d'insertion*, L'Harmattan, Paris, (Volume 1), pp. 143–166.

Asiwaju, A.I., and Adeniyi, P.O. (eds.). 1989. *Borderlands in Africa.* University of Lagos Press, Lagos, Nigeria.

Brown, M. 1989. Nigeria and the ECOWAS protocol on free movement and residence. *Journal of Modern African Studies* 27 (2) pp. 251–273.

Bureau of Democracy, Human Rights, and Labor. 1998, January 30. *1997 Human Rights Report: Nigeria.*

Bureau of Public Enterprises. 2004. http://www.bpeng.org/10/0317731656532b.asp?DocID=39 &MenuID=3.

Cchangani, R.C. 1983. *Illegal aliens under Nigerian law.* Associated Law Publications, Jodhpur, Raj., India.

Daily Sun Thursday, 2003. Woman held over "child trafficking". Tubosun Ogundare. p. 2.

Expat e-mail: Nigeria. 2003, 20 January. Justin Scully in Nigeria.

Eyetsemitan, K.O. 2004. Managing educational needs for refugees and internally displaced persons in Nigeria. Unpublished M.Sc. Research Project, Centre for Peace and Conflict Studies, University of Ibadan.

Federal Government of Nigeria. 1990. Immigration Act. In: *Federal Ministry of Justice: The Laws of the Federation of Nigeria*, Chapter 171. Federal Government of Nigeria Printers and Publishers, pp. 6755–6818.

Guyer, I., and Idowu, O. 1991. Women's agricultural work in a multi-modal rural economy: Ibarapa District, Oyo State, Nigeria. In: Gladwin, C.N. (ed.) *Structural adjustment and African women farmers.* University of Florida Press, Gainesville, pp. 257–280.

Haarez.com, 2008. Nigerian militants: We know where abducted Israeli is held. HYPERLINK "mailto:barakravid80@gmail.com" Barak Ravid, HYPERLINK "mailto:ymelman@haaretz.co.il" Yossi Melman, and HYPERLINK "mailto: assafu@haaretz.co.il" Assaf Uni, Haaretz (Correspondents and Reuters).

Labo, A. 2000. The motivation and integration of immigrants in the Nigeria-Niger border area: A study of Magama-Jibia. In: Occasional Publication No. 13. Intitut français de recherche en Afrique, University of Ibadan, Ibadan, Nigeria, pp. 1–32.

Lee, A. 1966. A theory of migration. *Demography* 3, pp. 47–57.

Levine, D.N. 1979. Simmel at a distance: On the history and systematics of the sociology of the stranger. In: Shack, W.A., and Skinner, E.P. (eds.) *Strangers in African societies.* University of California Press, Berkely, pp. 21–36.

Longe, A.G. 2003. Social reintegration of refugees for improved welfare: The case of Oru refugee camp, Ijebu Oru, Ogun State, Nigeria. Unpublished M.Sc. Research Project, Centre for Peace and Conflict Studies, University of Ibadan.

Magazine.biafranigeriaworld.com/Osita_chiagorom/ 2005/10/07.

McDougal, M., Lasswell, H., and Chen, L. 1976. The protection of aliens from discrimination and world public order: Responsibility of states conjoined with human rights. *American Journal of International Law* 70 (3) July.

Meyers, E. 2002, November. Multinational co-operation, integration, and regimes: The case of international labour mobility. The Center for Comparative Immigration Studies (CCIS) Working Paper No. 61, pp. 1–64.

Mitchell, J.C. 1959. The causes of labour migration. *Bulletin of the Inter-African Labour Institute* 6 (1), 12–46.

Model, S. 1997. An occupational tale of two cities: Minorities in London and New York. *Demography* 34 (4), pp. 539–550.

National Population Commission (NPC). 1998. Migration. In: *1991 Population Census of the Federal Republic of Nigeria: Analytical Report at the National Level.* NPC, Abuja, Nigeria, pp. 265–298.

Nigeria. 1991. *Population Census & Post Enumeration Survey.*

Nigeria Immigration Service. Oyo State Command Headquarters, Ibadan, 2004, September 7.

Nigeria Immigration Service. 2004. Zone "A" CERPAC Center, Ikoyi, Lagos. Mid-Year Report.

Nigerian Investment Promotion Commission, Decree No. 16. 1995, July 21. *Supplement to Official Gazette Extraordinary* 4 (82), pp. A517–A528

Nigerian Tribune. 2002, December 6. Refugees forced to sell their bodies. Pp. 18–19.

Nigerian Tribune. 2004, March 11. FG blames violence on refugees.

Nigerian Yearbook, 1983. 100, Federal Government of Nigeria, Lagos.

Post Express. 1996, December 7. Immigration smashes syndicate on fake resident permit.

Prescott, J.R.V. 1971. *The evolution of Nigeria's international and regional boundaries: 1861–1971.* Tantalus Research, Vancouver.

Statistics Section. Immigration Department, Alagbon Close, Ikoyi, as of the time of survey, 1987.

The Guardian. 2003, July 1. How foreign firms defraud Nigeria through expatriate quota, by minister.

UNHCR. Statistical Yearbook, 2003.

United Nations High Commissioner for Refugees (UNHCR). 2000. Refugees and others of concern to UNHCR. 1999 Statistical Overview. Geneva. http:/www.unhcr.ch

UKP&I Club. 2007, July 17. Local conditions in Port Harcourt, Nigeria. http://www.ukpandi.com/ UKPaneI/Infopool.nsf/html/index.

U.S. Department of State. 2003, July 23. Nigeria Travel Warning. http://www.expatexchange.com/trv.cfm.

Vanguard. 2004, February 4. Multinationals abuse expatriate quota. http://www.vanguardngr.com/articles/ 2002/business/b1040022004.html 9/15/2004.

West Africa Long Term Perspectives (WALTPS), CINERGIE, 1990.

27

Brazil

Immigration in Brazil: The Insertion of Different Groups

Zeila de Brito Fabri Demartini

Brazilian researchers are increasingly aware of the influence of immigration on the profile and experience of the Brazilian population. Clearly, immigration is a phenomenon that indelibly influences the both the society of origin and the society of adoption (Demartini, 2004). Sayad (2000) aptly captures the sentiment embodied in the changes associated with migration. In this article we focus on the strong migratory movements of indentured workers that had come to Brazil, especially for the state of São Paulo, from the second half of the nineteenth century up to 1970.

Migration Flows to Brazil

Any discussion of the Brazilian population must address the phenomenon of immigration. Internal dislocation and the immigration of thousands immigrants over the centuries are "defining characteristics of (the) population" (Sayad, 2000:10).

The indigenous population (Indians) had moved from the west to the east in the last centuries, influencing the composition of the Brazilian population (currently about 300 thousand Indians inhabit the country) (Betto, 2000:10). Also it was in the sixteenth century, during the colonial period, that black Africans were brought to work as slave labor in the farming of the sugar cane; this flow intensified itself in the seventeenth and eighteenth centuries with the exploration for gold and diamonds and, in the nineteenth century mainly for the farming of coffee; the blacks also carried out many other activities, beyond the agrarian ones. Blacks labored as slaves in many regions of Brazil—the Census of 1872 indicated the existence of 1.5 million slaves (Ianni, 1966:95). They must be distinguished from immigrants, who came as "free" labor to replace slave labor. The problems still faced today by the blacks in Brazil are rooted in the treatment they had received historically as slaves. While the immigrants experienced many difficulties and suffered discrimination in Brazil (Seyferth, 2005), their arrival and their social insertion were radically different fromthat of the blacks. While for the former immigration to Brazil represented a chance for a new life and also held the possibility of return, for the blacks it meant death. Their owners had total control over them—and Brazil refused to grant them either freedom or citizenship.

Data indicate that the most important recipients of immigrants were São Paulo, Rio de Janeiro, and the states of the southern region, respectively. It was into the southeast region that foreigners settled in higher proportions, which grew over time—68.2% in 1872 and 83.5% in 1980. In the south, they settled in much smaller proportions, oscillating in growth between 19% in 1900 and 9.5% in 1980. These regions, together, received 97% of the foreigners reflected in the 1900 Census and approximately 95% in the other census counts of the twentieth century (Bassanezi, 1996:13).

The largest groups of immigrants came from Portugal, Italy, Spain, Germany, and Japan, although there were also migratory flows from Russia, Lebanon, Austria, Poland, Hungary, Switzerland, and Lithuani,a among other countries, in the period 1872–1972 (Bassanezi, 1996: 8).

After the first half of the nineteenth century, European immigrants (other than the Portuguese) were especially attracted to the uninhabited areas of the country. Colonies with small plots of land were created for German immigrants in some Brazilian states. During the nineteenth century immigrants came either as free laborers to replace slave labor in agricultural work (large agricultural properties had economic-political-social power) or to live and work in the small properties of the colonies (Petrone, 1990). The large coffee farms located in the states of São Paulo and Minas Gerais attracted the majority of immigrants. A smaller number acquired small parcels of land in the colonies of the states of Santa Catarina, Rio Grande do Sul, Paraná, and Espírito Santo. There were also colonies in the urban areas of the state of São Paulo, where many immigrants preferred to settle.

Many Lebanese immigrants also came to Brazil; beyond the great number who came to São Paulo, they came to the Tríplice Border region (Brazil, Argentina, and Paraguay) in the south, which received many immigrants who developed commercial activities there, participating actively of the local society (Gattaz, 2005, 2007).

Despite the current decrease of immigration from Europe and Asia to Brazil, groups of immigrants, especially from Latin America (most prevalent are Bolivians) continue to arrive, particularly in São Paulo (Baeninger and Leoncy, 2001; Silva, S. A. 1997; 2006). In the 1970s an intense, though not officially registered, inflow of Africans (Portuguese and luso-Africans) occurred as a result of the independence movements of Angola and Mozambique (Demartini, Cunha,

and Doppenschmitt, 2005). Nowadays, it is estimated that 1,500 million unregistered foreigners reside in Brazil: 80% of them Bolivians, followed by Peruvians, Chinese, and Africans of many origins, but especially from Nigeria (Giannini, 2005:12–13). Internal migrations continue to be significant.

A more recent phenomenon, which involves new difficulties for the country, is the inversion of the migratory process; Brazil is now experiencing the emigration of Brazilian citizens to other countries. At the end of the 1990s it was estimated that 150,000 Brazilian immigrants lived in Japan, 100,000 in New York, and 150,000 in the Boston area (330,000 thousand in the United States). Approximately 1.25 million people (1% of the population) left Brazil permanently between 1985 and 1987 (Sales, 1996:89, 2006). This number may have since increased, despite restrictive policies of the developed countries, and there are many Brazilians living in Portugal, Germany, France, Italy, and so forth (Savoldi and Renk, 2006).

Factors That Favored Immigration to Brazil

Some factors appear to be essential in understanding migration flows to Brazil since its official "discovery" and colonization by Portugal in 1500. One major factor that attracted the Portuguese after that time and other Europeans after 1822, when the country became independent, was the large expanse of unoccupied land. A second important factor was the need for laborers to work in agriculture and mining. Large groups of Africans were brought as slaves during the seventeenth, eighteenth, and nineteenth centuries through "forced migration." That deeply marked the demographic composition of the population. The flows of free immigrants must be understood in the context of the transformations of the slave regime in the country. For example, when the slave trade was abolished in 1850, free workers of European origin were recruited to substitute for the slaves. However, even with the prohibition of the slave trade, ships continued to bring enslaved blacks from Africa. As new laws were approved aiming for the abolition of slavery itself—Lei do Ventre Livre (Law of the Free Womb) and Lei dos Sexagenários (Law of the Sexagenarians)—interest focused on replacing the "blacks" with immigrants, either in agriculture or in urban activities, considering that their number were insufficient to take care of the demand for manual labor. The elimination of slavery in the Brazilian society only occurred in 1888 with the enactment of the Lei Áurea; even so, before this date many slaves already been given their freedom (Ianni, 1967; Prado Jr., 1953).

Azevedo (1987) proposed that an immigration project was launched that aimed to ameliorate effects of the inferiority of the blacks and *mestizos* (who were the majority population in the nineteenth century) by introducing "ethnic virtues" of white workers. In fact, the immigration project was intended to build a white nation, and this became possible with the massive introduction of European workers. Furthermore, with the abolition of the slavery in Brazil in 1888 (Lei Áurea) came the concept of completely free work, emphasizing concern with the whitening of the population. This was linked with the policies that provided incentives to immigrate. The country had to face problems resulting from granting freedom to blacks and *mestizos* and had to define the limits of desirable migratory flows. In the beginning of the Republic (declared in 1889), the "Serviço de Introdução e Localização de Imigrantes") was enacted, and it stated in Article 1:

Entry is completely free, in the Republic's ports, to individuals capable of working, who are not subjected to their countries' criminal actions, excepting the Asian or African aborigines, who, only with the authorization of the national Congress, will be admitted according to the conditions to be stipulated (Decree No. 528 of June 28, 1890) (In Vainer, 1996:43).

However, because of the dire need for agricultural workers, particularly in São Paulo, Brazil accepted immigrants from all areas of the world, even those considered "undesirable."

The policy to attract immigrants for the agricultural work decreased during the 1920s, culminating in 1930 with the central government restricting and disciplining the entry of foreigners. The Constitutions of 1934 and 1937 established a system of quotas (limiting the number of immigrants to 2% of all immigrants that had entered into the country in the last 50 years) and also mandated that at least two-thirds of

the employees of all companies be native Brazilians (Petrone, 1990). In addition, emphasis was placed on the assimilation of immigrants, because "ethnic cysts" were seen as dangerous by the strong nationalist policy of that period. At this time, Japanese immigrants were already large in number, especially in São Paulo, and in many regions of the country, German "enclosures" were also considered a menace. Both groups were targeted by nationalist measures that simultaneously discriminated against them and tried to assimilate them. It is important to mention that political problems in several countries kept impelling new immigrants to the Brazilian territory.

During World War II, nationalist measures were intensified, as Brazil aligned itself against Germany, Italy, and Japan. Consequently, the immigrants who had come from these countries were closely monitored: their meetings and trips were forbidden, they were not allowed to speak in their mother languages, and they could not live in the coastal areas. After the war, the Brazilian government maintained its position that European immigrants were the most desirable ones as is reflected in Article 2 of the Decree below:

In the admission of immigrants consideration will be given to the need of preserving and developing, in the ethnic composition of the population, the most convenient characteristics of its European ascendance, as well as the defense of the national worker" (Decree-Law No. 7,967 of Sept. 18, 1945) (In Vainer, 1996:44).

Despite the eugenic intentions of the government, not only did European immigrants, especially Portuguese and Spanish, keep arriving, but so did the Japanese, who came to Brazil to escape a difficult postwar situation. In the 1970s and 1980s, new flows came from Africa, Korea, and other South American countries. At the same time, the government's attention had to turn to the growing number of Brazilians that emigrated to European, Asian, and North American countries (Castro, 2001).

In the twenty-first century, Brazil is a country with contradictory, ambiguous characteristics:

It is still receiving immigrants seeking better living conditions and economical success (after the Koreans, the entry of Bolivians, Argentines,

Chinese, and Africans). This demands continuous legislative and research discussion, regarding hazardous working conditions and the large number of immigrants without appropriate documents. Some legislation has been proposed to solve some serious problems experienced by most of these new immigrants, particularly those related to exploitation in the workplace and literacy. Children may attend school, but they do not get a certificate. Currently, Brazilian legislation allows entry to foreigners of any country, however, in order to work immigrants must have a two-year temporary visa or a permanent visa. Immigrants can also request definitive residency if they marry Brazilian citizens or have children with Brazilian citizens.

It has begun sending a growing number of people from different areas of the country (including those areas that are still receiving immigrants) to several nations in Europe, North America, and Asia. In this situation, the government's attention has focused on the clandestine departures of several Brazilian emigrants in this group. Frequent captures have occurred, especially in the United States. In Japan, many Brazilian "dekassegui" (one who goes far away to work) and their families are subjected to precarious working and educational conditions. In Portugal, discrimination in the work environment is one of many problems Brazilians experience.

Governmental policy regarding migratory flows must, of necessity, address the concerns and problems of both those who enter Brazil and those who leave to go elsewhere. The Brazilian government must seek to understand the reasons why so many Brazilians are leaving the country. It must also explore the numerous difficulties its citizens are experiencing in their respective countries of adoption and develop a mechanism to address them.

It is important to study the various experiences of immigrants. Consistent with our observations and those of authors such as Vainer (1996) and Bassanezi (1996), although they may have arrived in the same time period, immigrants from different countries of origin have experienced the same immigration policies and programs differently. This is well apparent in the experiences of several groups that have settled in São Paulo, and, as such, it will provide the backdrop to exemplify this occurrence.

Immigration in São Paulo: Several Groups—Different Experiences

This chapter focuses on the immigration phenomenon in São Paulo.

São Paulo has attracted the largest flows from other regions of the country and from abroad since the middle of the nineteenth century; those particularly from Portugal, Italy, Spain, Japan, and Germany arrived between 1888 and 1940 (Atlas da População do Estado de São Paulo, 1991).

Most arrived in this state primarily because of the dynamism of its economy and the associated opportunities. This state experienced great expansion of its agriculture (especially coffee), great development and diversification of industries, transformations of the villages and cities, a strong demographic growth, and intense urbanization, among other changes. (Camargo, 1952; Silva, S., 1960). Thus, immigration has been an intrinsic part of the history of São Paulo.

As many groups of immigrants from different countries arrived simultaneously in São Paulo, several of the problems associated with immigration become much more complex, both for the immigrants themselves as well as for the society of adoption (Demartini, 2004). Not only must immigrants face the sociocultural conflicts inherent in the bicultural experience, they must acclimatize themselves to other peoples from third countries with additional differences. This exacerbates the complexities for the society of adoption that must accommodate, or address, the range of problems and social differences. However, some groups have received more research attention than have others.

Most studied are the Italians and the Germans. The Italians constituted the largest group of foreigners who entered Brazil in the nineteenth century, deeply influencing the economic, social, and cultural development of some regions of the country. German immigration, likewise, started at the beginning of the nineteenth century, and its strong influence is still visible in the south and southeast regions of the country. Other immigration flows, although strong, such as those of the Portuguese, the Spanish, and the Japanese have only recently begun receiving research attention. The diversity of the populations migrating into São Paulo makes it clear that they cannot be viewed as a homogeneous group. In fact, the problems they experienced and the effects of immigration policy differed substantially. Of particular interest because of their numbers and influence on the state of São Paulo, four groups—the Germans, the Italians, the Japanese, and the Portuguese—will receive some focus here.

The Germans: Ancient Immigrants

Germans began entering Brazil and the state of São Paulo in the first decades of the nineteenth century, facilitated by the marriage of the Brazilian emperor to an Austrian princess. The Decree signed in 1808 by the king of Portugal D. João VI (who escaped from Portugal to Brazil) that allowed foreigners to own Brazilian lands and the Decree of 1820 facilitated German immigration to Brazil (Bassanezi, 1996). Some researchers speculate that in Germany some factors also stimulated the emigration to Brazil, particularly the lack of cultivable lands, the high demographic density in some areas, high taxes, resistance from craftsmen and workers to the industrialization process, and the advertisement of the Immigration Companies that propagated the advantages of coming to Brazil (Willems, 1946; Simson, 1997).

The German immigration to Brazil was constituted as colonization, that is, most of the immigrants established themselves as settlers, land owners in pioneer lands, constituting small centers where they tried to lead the same kind of life they had in Germany. This form of colonization, in homogeneous areas, where the German cultural characteristics were maintained, occurred more intensively in the states of Rio Grande do Sul and Santa Catarina; both are still very influenced by such an ancient immigration (Seyferth, 1988, 1990; Kreutz, 1998). In São Paulo the immigrants worked as settlers in a partnership system. Here, they did not own the lands they cultivated, they worked for the farmer instead, and shared with him the production's profits, usually coffee. There were also some German agricultural colonies in São Paulo, but there is not much research about them. One of the few researchers of the German immigration in São Paulo, Simson (1997), indicated that many Germans started to come to the state

beginning in 1846, when they had their trips subsidized by the coffee farmers. These farmers kept them connected to their farms through the partnership contracts signed by them and which involved family labor. Many Germans had trouble with the farmers because of these contracts that kept them bound to the properties through the debts they had accrued through the trip subsidies. Others, however, became landowners and were successful as farmers.

Many Germans came directly to the cities of the state of São Paulo, where they worked as teachers, doctors, joiners, clockmakers, businessmen, laborers, employees, and other urban activities. The German almanacs published in the city of São Paulo had advertisements of the companies and professionals that worked in the different regions of the state.

All these immigrants and their descendants were, usually, connected to associations created by them. Most of these associations were developed to sustain their culture and heritage. The numerous Protestant churches, where the Germans gathered, were also important. This group's religion created problems in the Brazilian context, where the population is predominantly Catholic.

Also important were the schools created by the Germans, possibly the first immigrants' schools of the state of São Paulo. According to surveys made by Simson (1993), there were several German schools in the city of São Paulo and in the cities of the countryside of the state.

The German institutions and schools in São Paulo suffered with the restrictions of the Brazilian nationalist policy, less than those in the south region of the country, but yet, they suffered, especially during World War II. They kept working, despite the threats and problems faced. Research about this subject is relatively limited, but interviews with German families in the city of São Paulo (Demartini, 1993), reveal that during the World War II period, this group suffered different pressures and had to develop strategies in order to face on the one hand, the Brazilian nationalist policy that wanted to eliminate any characteristic that identified their German origin and on the other hand, the Nazi government that not only exalted the "pure" German people, but also demanded that these families make their Brazilian children serve the German Army.

It is interesting to emphasize that before, during, and immediately after World War II, many Germans came to São Paulo. Some came to escape from the Nazis and others because they had joined the Nazi party. In the last decades, the descendants of this group have also emigrated to Europe, and especially to Germany (Baeninger and Leoncy, 2001).

The German immigration in São Paulo has yet to be better studied, however it appears that their experiences have been different from those of German immigrants who settled in other areas of the country.

The Italians: The Largest Number of Immigrants

The Italians constituted the largest number of immigrants who came to Brazil, most of them to the state of São Paulo. According to Alvim (1986:62), between 1876 and 1920 there were around 1,243,633 Italian immigrants in Brazil, 850,000 of them in the state of São Paulo, which was interested in replacing the slaves by free immigrant workers as the coffee culture was expanding. Italy, unable to address the needs of its rural population and small-scale producers, viewed emigration as a viable alternative for some of its problems. Italian mobility was the easiest solution in times of crisis in the nation. In the second half of the nineteenth century (especially after 1886), Brazil became the third entry option for the Italian immigrants, following the United States and Argentina (Bassanezi, 1996). They came, mostly, to work in the coffee culture, subsidized by the farmers and later many of them became landowners, however, they were very important to the development of many cities, once their migration to the urban regions, especially to those that developed quickly with the commercial and industrial activities such as the city of São Paulo, was also intense (Camargo, 1952; Petrone, 1990; Trento, 1989). Some Italian immigrants became renowned by making their fortune in the city of São Paulo as industrialists, bankers, businessmen, farmers, and so forth, and had great influence in the state's economic development, once they were present all over the state.

São Paulo became a city where the Italian language was spoken by most of the population, which was strongly influenced not only by the economic changes effected by Italian immigrants but also by their customs, music, religious activities, politics, and food. In 1900, the entrance of Italian immigrants decreased (as of 1902, Italy barred subsidized immigration), nevertheless, their influence is present today. The decrease of the Italian migratory flow coincided with the problems faced by the coffee culture and with the restrictions imposed by the Italian Fascist government. The Italian immigration to Brazil restarted after World War II, when a little over 100,000 immigrants came to the country; but this occurred only until the end of 1960 (Bassanezi, 1996:8). Since then, the flow has inverted: Brazilians, usually descendants of the former immigrants, started to emigrate to Italy, despite the economic stability of most of the families (Castro, 2001).

According to several studies of the Italian immigration, confirmed through our research, despite the resistance and discrimination of the national population against the Italian immigrants in the first periods of immigration, they were able to insert themselves into the society, and to some extent, the changes that the Brazilian economy and society then experienced, allowed them to achieve economic success and to integrate themselves in the society. As the data from the beginning of the twentieth century indicate, the largest number of foreign schools in the city of São Paulo was Italian: 63 between 1887 and 1907 (Demartini and Espósito, 1989; Annuário do Ensino, 1907–1908).

The schools they created were called "Italian-Brazilian" schools and had the objective to transmit and preserve, in Brazilian lands, the Italian culture and customs. The government restrictions to the Italian schools and institutions were also present with the strong nationalism in the 1930s and during World War II (Brazil declared itself against Germany and its allies). Even so, many schools kept on working, and some of them remain open until now. The most famous one is Colégio Dante Alighieri, in the city of São Paulo, considered one of the most important schools of the city, attended by students who come from families socially and economically well positioned.

The Japanese: Undesirable "Yellows" but Hard Workers

Japanese immigration to Brazil started in 1908, and according to many authors (Ando, 1976; Saito, 1980; Sakurai, 2002), the Japanese came in two stages: the first from 1908 to 1941, when 190 thousand immigrants entered into the country, and the second from 1952 to 1979, the postwar period, when 50 thousand Japanese arrived in Brazil. Most of these immigrants were concentrated in the state of São Paulo, for the reasons aforementioned: the needs of the coffee culture and the great urban-industrial development. In 1977 it is estimated that there were 727,605 Japanese in this state, 123,165 of them were Japanese people and 604,440 were *Nisei* (second generation Japanese), *Sansei* (third generation Japanese), and naturalized citizens. Most lived in the metropolitan area of São Paulo, representing 64.7% of the total of the Japanese-Brazilian population (Vários Autores, 1992:425).

Currently, it is estimated that there are 1.35 million Japanese living in Brazil (Freitas, 2002) and that over a million live in São Paulo. The city of São Paulo is considered the biggest Japanese city outside Japan, and traces of this immigration are spread throughout the city and are incorporated by the national population.

Although the Japanese are now valued and considered to be honest, hard-workers, and studious and good neighbors, it was not always so. In the early years of their migration history, they were considered the most undesirable of immigrants, because they were "yellow," not European, and not Catholic; in debates about the possibility of their entering Brazil, they were always considered "not assimilable." Immigration policy allowed them to enter only because they had a tradition in agricultural work and because of the pressure coffee farmers' were experiencing. The Japanese government, too, was interested in emigration from Japan to solve the crisis in its rural economy and decrease the excessive rural population. This immigration was first subsidized by the Brazilian government and later by the Japanese government. By 1920, Brazil sought to end the funds allocated for immigration but caved under the pressure of the Immigration Offices, and in 1921, restarted the planned immigration. The Japanese government then, authorized subsidized emigration and beginning in 1924, a heavy flow of immigrants came to Brazil, mostly constituted by family labor. This flow decrease in the 1930s, with the restrictive immigratory policy (Handa, 1987; Vainer, 1996; Demartini, 1997). Another flow began in Brazil after World War II, as many sought to escape the Japanese political situation of the time. Several already had established social and familial networks in Brazil, making it easier for them to adjust (Sakurai, 2002; Hastings, 1969).

In the twenty-first century, the Japanese in Brazil are experiencing an inverse movement that began in 1980: a strong emigration to Japan as "dekassegui" (those who go away to work). It is estimated that there are about 250 thousand Brazilians living in Japan as "dekassegui" (Ninomiya, 2002; Ishikawa, 2003).

It is impossible to detail here the myriad of ways that the Japanese immigrants integrated themselves into the state of São Paulo, where they were concentrated. The experiences of those who settled in the countryside, first as agricultural laborers and later as landowners, are substantially different from the experiences of those who settled in the metropolitan region of São Paulo. Japanese social-economic ascension was enhanced through the population's mobility toward the city, where the best schools (Japanese and Brazilian), the best job opportunities, and the economic investments were concentrated (Cardoso, 1972).

The Japanese invested heavily in their children's education, viewing this as a means of leveling the playing field in a society in which they were seen as being very alien. In a short time, the Japanese group becomes the most educated in the state of São Paulo; most of the young people achieve college education in the best universities and consequently, they are much more competitive in the work market. Furthermore, now, because of Japan's economical standing in the world and Brazilian emigration toward it, there has been an increased interest among Brazilians to learn the Japanese language. Nevertheless, now, as before, Japanese-Brazilians continue to integrate with other Brazilians. Communication among the children is predominantly in Portuguese, families read and subscribe to Brazilian newspapers, and interracial marriages increase with each generation (Sakurai, 2002).

The Portuguese: The Undesirable European Colonizer and the Hard Work in the Cities

If one is to ignore the primary relationship between the Portuguese and the Brazilians—that associated with issues of colonization—one can say the primary aim of the Portuguese in this country was not agriculture, but commerce (Serrão, 1971). Several economic activities resulted in wealth for the Portuguese, creating problems among the Brazilians, who developed strong anti-Portuguese attitudes (Ribeiro, 1990). Interestingly, however, the Portuguese were also divided between those who remained separate from the locals and those who integrated themselves to the Brazilian way of life to assure their "success." Although it has decreased in the beginning of this century, the anti-Portuguese sentiment remained latent throughout the twentieth century (M. Silva,1992). It was also one of the factors implicated in the restriction of Portuguese immigrants, who were not considered, by many nationals, to be the desirable "white Europeans."

While the Brazilian government sought agricultural workers, the Portuguese government was more interested in urban business and commerce. Consequently, numerous Portuguese Chambers of Commerce spread through Brazil and served to maintain bonds with the country of origin (Demartini, 2002). Many, who came to São Paulo, did not identify themselves as agricultural laborers. In the period of 1908 to 1936, of the total Portuguese immigrants who arrived in the Santos harbor, 131,545 stated they were agricultural laborers (47.79% of the total), 13,158 claimed to be artists, and 130,554 identified other skills (D.T.C.I., 1937:74). As it can be noticed, even on arrival, the percentage of nonagricultural works surpassed that of agricultural laborers.

In 1920, the foreigners owned most of the industrial establishments of the state of São Paulo (64.2%); the Italians were the most enterprising, comprising 75% of all the foreigners' owners, but they were followed by the Portuguese, Spanish, Syrians, and Germans. The Portuguese maintained the second position also in 1940 (Camargo, 1952).

It is interesting that the professions selected by the second and third generations, oftentimes, were similar to those of the first generation, either those which the immigrants engaged in before they left Portugal or those they engaged in once they settled in Brazil. Thus, these constituted "family professions" that were passed through the generations. In a few instances, some members of the second generation achieved college level education or attended technical courses in the city of São Paulo, resulting in a movement away from the profession of the parental generation.

Members of the third generation, in most families, completed college, even if they continued in the business of the first generation. Several, particularly the males, attended programs in Business Administration or Economy. Women did not have the same opportunities as the men, even when they helped in the family business. More frequently, however, the third generation chose different professions, electing to become doctors, economists, psychologists, analysts, and so forth.

Current Governmental Policies Regarding Immigrants

Since World War II, Brazilian immigration policy has moved to a focus on "qualified" immigrants to work in urban-industrial development. Lei de Estrangeiros (The Foreigners' Law), still in force in 2000, determined in the sole paragraph of Article 16, "Sole Paragraph: The immigration will intend, primarily, to propitiate specialized labor to the various sectors of the national economy, aiming at the Política Nacional de Desenvolvimento [National Development Policy] in all its aspects and specially at the increase of productivity, the assimilation of technology and the capitation of resources for specific sectors" (Barreto, 2001:67). The immigration of "nonqualified" laborers was only of interest in a few uninhabited areas to develop special projects. These days, although explicit racial selections are not permitted, there certainly are restrictions on immigration for people who are believed to be "less qualified" or considered "undesirable" (Sales and Salles, 2002).

In Brazil, current immigration control is held by three offices: the Ministry of Justice, the Ministry of Foreign Relations, and part of the Ministry of Labor and Employment. The Ministry of Justice's duty is, essentially, the control of the foreigners after their entrance in Brazil, as well as the application of the immigration policy (visa, residence, naturalization, extradition, etc.).

According to information of the Brazilian government, the international migration to Brazil is contemplated in the Plano Nacional de Direitos Humanos (National Plan of Human Rights) that in 1995–1996 emphasized three topics: Brazilians living abroad, foreign immigrants in Brazil, and, refugees. Immigration has been managed by the Conselho Nacional de Imigração (National Council of Immigration), which regulates the entry of foreign groups, facilitating (or impeding) the granting of visas and also the admission and rooting of immigrants. This office, subordinate to the Ministry of Labor and Employment, is composed of representatives from several ministries of the Brazilian government and also by representatives of Confederações da Indústria, do Comércio, da Agricultura, das Instituições Financeiras (Confederations of Industry, Commerce, Agriculture, Financial Institutions) and Sociedade Brasileira para o Progresso da Ciência (Brazilian Society for Science Progress). Currently, this council, through about 50 resolutions, supports immigration to enhance technology, foreign capital investment, family reunion, care activities, specialized work, and scientific, academic, and cultural development (Barreto, 2001:68–71).

To regulate immigration, the legislation establishes different types of visas: (1) transit visa; (2) tourist visa; (3) temporary visa: student, scientist, professor, technician, or other professional category visa—under contract or serving the Brazilian government—artist and sportsmen visa, cultural and business trip visa, religious visa, and newspaper correspondent visa; (4) permanent visa (favoring those who fulfill the requirements of the immigration policy); (5) courtesy visa; and (6) diplomatic visa. The immigration policy also counts on the work developed by the Comitê Nacional de Refugiados (National Committee of Refugees), an office of collective resolution linked to the Ministry of Justice. The Ministry of Foreign Relations, the Federal Police, the United Nations High Commissioner for Refugees (UNHCR) and the Cáritas Arquidiocesana do Rio de Janeiro e São Paulo (Archdiocesan Charities of Rio de Janeiro and São Paulo) are also part of the committee (Barreto, 2001:67–68).

Brazil is signatory of the Geneva Convention of 1951, concerning the regulation of refugees. The Brazilian Law no. 9.474/97 (of 1997) includes in its definition of refugee, every person persecuted for racial, religious, nationality, social group, or political reasons. The law also considers as a refugee the individual who, due to a serious and generalized violation of human rights, is forced to leave his/her country of nationality. As in many countries, Brazil only considers the first generation immigrants to be foreign citizens. Their children, born in Brazil, are Brazilian citizens, according to the "jus soli" (Barreto, 2001:71).

The Brazilian government has been working in four lines of action regarding Brazilian immigrants living abroad: (1) appreciation of the immigrant, such as the Law of 1993 that allows dual citizenship and Conselho de Cidadãos (Citizens' Council), that work in almost 40 cities, together with the Brazilian consulates; (2) measures leading to a better consular assistance, through the Manual de Serviço Consular (Consular Service Manual), which is available on the internet and the Consulados Itinerantes (Itinerant Consulates); (3) diplomatic protection actions, defending the rights of the Brazilian citizens abroad, and (4) actions of supplementary basic assistance in health and education, specially in the Consulates in Japan (Sales and Salles, 2002).

The growing departures of Brazilians to different countries have required the continuing and increasing of the government to focus on the multiple problems involved. Several Brazilians have been arrested and even killed along the borders of Mexico and the United States. There are numerous networks of trafficking women; racial discrimination against Brazilian immigrants in European countries is prevalent. Diplomas and documents of the qualified Brazilian professionals that would allow them to perform their activities in other countries are unrecognized. Particularly in Japan, Brazilian families live in vulnerable and dangerous conditions, and children are deprived of adequate education.

In 2003, Brazil participated in the creation, together with others eighteen countries, of the Global Commission on International Migration, with the purpose to debate the two axes that guide the current debate: migratory politics, anchored in human right,s and the balance of the flows of people of poor countries as a form of combatting poverty (Patarra, 2006:18).

Particular Issues Nation Faces Due to Immigration

The information on the number of foreigners in Brazil is divergent. According to the Departamento de Estrangeiros do Ministério da Justiça (Foreigners' Department of the Ministry of Justice) (Barreto, 2001:64), there were, in 2000, about one million foreigners in Brazil, less than the 1.5 million Brazilians living abroad. This number of immigrants represented between 0.6% and 0.7% of the Brazilian population, a small percentage if compared to that of Argentina (3%) (Sales and Salles, 2002). However, entities that deal directly with immigrants, like Pastoral do Migrante (Migrant's Pastoral) and Centro de Estudos Migratórios de São Paulo (Center of Migratory Studies of São Paulo), question these numbers and the idea that in ten years there was no significant increase in immigration. These offices state that the immigrant flow, especially to São Paulo, is still strong and that it has increased recently.

Most of the present-day immigrants come from the South American countries, especially Bolivia, Argentina, Paraguay, Chile, and Uruguay. There are limited studies about these newer immigrants. One conducted with Bolivians (Silva, S. A. 2001) revealed that although they immigrated in search for a better quality of life conditions, to survive, many were forced to work in unsafe environments. Frequent media reports discuss the exploitation to which they are subjected, particularly if they are in the country without documentation.

Recently, many young African men have also immigrated to Brazil. Many come as students and stay in the country (Vida, 2001; Kaly, 2001). The presence of African students is evident in São Paulo in both public and private universities. Based on interview data gathered, Demartini, Gusmão, and Campos (2003) have found that the immigration of Africans to Brazil has increased since the 1970s, precipitated by the revolutionary movements and internal conflicts in the new African nations. Most came from Angola, Mozambique, and Cape Verde (Demartini, Cunha, and Doppenschmitt, 2005). Although, conditions in these countries are improving, immigrants from Africa continue to enter Brazil as São Paulo and Rio de Janeiro especially are still believed to have better work and educational opportunities, despite the great prejudice the immigrants often have to face in these areas.

Specialists in human rights, who work with immigrants living in Brazil, have been calling attention to what they consider a contradiction in the Brazilian legislation: while the Brazilian Constitution in force emphasizes the human being's dignity and fundamental rights, legislation concerning foreigners is still corrupted by a repressive ideology, which was in force during the dictatorship between the 1960s and 1980s, and which viewed the foreigner (especially the Latin Americans) as subversive and dangerous to the political stability of the country. These days, they are perceived as being potential drug dealers. Discussion of drug trafficking is constantly permeated with discussion about the entrance of foreigners, particularly those coming from the South American countries, but also from some African countries. As a consequence, organizations that work with immigrants indicate several discriminatory practices in the application of the Foreigner's Regulations, such as arbitrary denial of a permanent visa, expulsion of children from schools, prejudicial application of the penal laws with foreigners, unconstitutional discrimination of naturalized citizens, slave labor regimes, human rights violations, administrative inefficiency, and delay in the delivery of foreigners' papers. Most of the recent immigrants have no documents, which creates difficult situations for both the adults and the children of these families.

Unique Experiences of Newer Immigrants

Some indicators suggest the integration of immigrants, not only to the local society, but also among the various groups that arrived in São Paulo's territory. The frequency of interracial marriages in São Paulo has increased among the second and third generations of immigrants, even in those groups considered "closed," such as the Japanese. This has resulted in a high rate of miscegenation involving the most ancient populations (native Indians, white Portuguese, and black Africans), the white immigrants that arrived since the end of the nineteenth century, and the most recent groups.

Children and young people from different origins attend public and private schools together. In fact, often the different ethnic groups in Brazil seek the schools established by the early immigrants because of the high quality of education provided and the opportunities open to their graduates in the world market. Language fluency (especially German, French, Japanese, Spanish, and English) attained in these schools is a great asset when working internationally. Interestingly, attraction to these schools is based more on the opportunities offered once students graduate than on aims to preserve the culture of the founding immigrant group.

The success of the second generation, above that of the first, is evident among both the early immigrant groups (German, Italian, Portuguese, Japanese, and Spanish) as well as among the most recent ones (Korean, Chinese, Bolivian, African, and Argentine). In all groups, the second generation has had better access to higher levels of education, which, in turn has allowed them greater access to higher paying and professional positions even when they kept the same professions as their families. This is particularly true in the state of São Paulo, which consequently is the greatest magnet for immigrants to Brazil, and perhaps in all of Latin America. Despite facing difficult working conditions, and sometimes even being exploited as slave laborers, even those who have arrived recently in São Paulo (Bolivians, Nigerians, and Koreans), are resistant to leaving Brazil. All wish to stay as they anticipate a future with greater opportunities for their children in Brazil than in their homelands.

Programs to Address the Unique Needs of Immigrants and their Families

In an effort to diminish the legal problems faced by illegal immigrants in the country, some measures were recently taken by the Brazilian government, particularly the amnesty laws of 1980 (Law 6.815) and of 1998 (Law 9.675). These laws sought to identify and regulate foreigners in Brazil without imposing fines or any other governmental penalty (excluding for those involved in criminal activity). There was extensive advertisement in the media, but only a small segment of the illegal immigrants (40,000 of the 100,000 expected) took advantage of this opportunity to regulate its situation in the country (Sales and Salles, 2002).

The government is, in a general way, interested in regulating immigrants who enter in the country, however, there is still a long way to go before immigrants can all benefit from the human rights protection of the Brazilian Constitution. The non-qualified, poor immigrants tend to integrate and assimilate into the poorer strata of Brazilian society, which itself is often deprived and unprotected. A large part of this population is also migrant, transplanting itself from distant rural parts of the country, to the more industrialized areas, such as São Paulo, in search of better living conditions. Furthermore, immigrants and migrants are often in competition for the same low paying occupations. Thus, because their needs are so similar, organizations that work with immigrants also provide services to the migrant workers. In addition, the metropolitan area of São Paulo has also attracted the native Indian population that has demanded special assistance in education and health.

Most nongovernmental organizations in Brazil that have assisted immigrants, defended their legal rights, and kept authorities and policy makers aware of the importance of updating laws, were established during the dictatorial regime. The majority are religious organizations such as the pastorals, the centers of the Scalabrini's brothers and sisters, and the Catholic and Protestant churches. The church assumed responsibility for working with Latin immigrants as an ongoing commitment. This was formally consolidated into the SPM (Migrants' Pastoral Service) and the Latin Pastoral in São Paulo. The Pastoral das Migrações (Migrations' Pastoral) was introduced in 1983 by the Conferência Nacional dos Bispos do Brasil (Brazil's Bishops National Conference).

Milesi, Bonassi, and Shimano (2001), in their study of religious organizations that work with foreigners in Brazil and with Brazilians living abroad, found that the first such organization appeared in 1826. These increased in number during the twentieth century, especially from the 1980s, coinciding with the increased movement of refugees and immigrants coming from the neighbor countries. A total of 30 organizations were researched. While they are distributed around the country, the city of São Paulo has seven, the largest concentration. These entities work, primarily, with Latin-American immigrants, African refugees, and Brazilian migrants from other areas of the country. According to the research, most of these entities' clientele are: non-documented (50%), unemployed (46.6%), newly arrived (40%) and homeless (40%) individuals. Similar observations were made of the religious organizations working with Brazilians living abroad. A large number of the clientele were living in irregular situations. According to these entities, the migrants need is for documentation, and also for employment, education, health, housing, and matrimonial/affective support. In addition, these organizations also served to provide their constituencies cultural and leisure activities. Much of the judicial assistance supports the immigrants in seeking and achieving permanent resident status and helping them get access to legal documentation (Ferretti, 2002).

Some other entities of the civil society are also present in Brazil, such as Instituto Brasileiro de Análises Sociais e Econômicas—IBASE—(Brazilian Institute of Social and Economical Analysis); Centro de Estudos de Cultura Contemporânea—CEDEC—(Center of Studies of the Contemporary Culture); Associação de Apoio aos Dekaseguis (Association of Support to the Dekaseguis); Centro Humanitário de Apoio à Mullher—CHAME—(Humanitarian Center of Support to Women). However, these Brazilian nongovernmental organizations are not directly concerned with the assistance to foreigners in Brazil, as the religious organizations have assumed primary responsibility for this population (Sprandel, 2001).

In addition, at least seven associations of recent immigrants are in existence in Brazil: five associations of Bolivians in the state of São Paulo, one in the state of Rondônia, and two associations of Paraguayans in the state of Mato Grosso do Sul. These serve to meet the needs of their respective immigrant groups. It appears that there are at least seventeen nongovernmental organizations and thirty-two associations of Brazilians outside

Brazil. This number appears to be low; others may not be well publicized. It is important to emphasize that these organizations' work (religious, university, etc.) should be integrated and connected. Some joint events have occurred, allowing a better discussion of the issues facing immigrants.

Conclusion

Most apparent in Brazil is the high rate of interracial interaction and exchange among the oldest Brazilian population groups and the immigrants, including the most recently arrived peoples. These interactions are visible in all fields—economic, social, political, religious, artistic, and others. This is an extremely relevant observation and the occurrence of such interactions is essential for the social integration of groups that are so different from each other. On the other hand, it troubles several immigrants who fear the loss of their "cultural roots" if they integrate with the larger community.

Conversely, in the state of São Paulo, the culture readily accepts variations and rapidly adopts and absorbs customs and habits of its immigrant groups. For example, words and expressions are incorporated into the Portuguese language and behavior is also modified. The cuisine is influenced by new dishes. Different religious practices are incorporated to Catholicism, and what may appear to be conflicting practices sometimes occur simultaneously (a person may be Catholic and also practice oriental rituals). Finally, artistic expression and products are frequently a mixture of different cultures and styles.

There are still numerous problems that must be overcome. Discrimination and prejudice toward the poor and illegal immigrants are frequent, especially because they compete directly with much of the Brazilian population, which is also poor. Competition is not only in the employment market but also for the limited resources offered by the government. The government's immigration policies still carry the characteristics of authoritarianism, and the economic and social policies concentrate on paying the incalculable national debt to the rich countries. Little remains to address the social issues faced by either migrants or immigrants. The Brazilian government and people are also disturbed about the rising interest and control other countries try exert on some groups of immigrants in some Brazilian areas, targeting them as participants in drug trafficking. Of concern, furthermore, is the increasing recruitment of some into the world of terrorism, particularly in the area of the triple border, in the south of Brazil—Paraguay, Argentina, and Uruguay—where several groups of Islamic origin have settled.

Focusing on immigrants in Brazil and on its immigration policy is essential. Although a poor country, Brazil has been attracting immigrants for over a century and it may be able to contribute to international discussions about the conditions of immigrant worldwide in the aim to develop an understanding of the human dimension involving those who migrate, those who stay, and those who receive foreigners.

It is impossible to deal, in this article, with the problems faced by the immigrants from many origins in their insertion in the Brazilian and São Paulo's society. It is necessary to write down that the studies carried through about many groups show the great difficulties faced especially by the first generation of them; most of them lived in the great agricultural areas, in precarious conditions of life and work (Pereira, 1986). In cities such as São Paulo, they inhabited tenement houses (slums). They also had to compete for jobs in the developing urban-industrial economy. So, by the characteristics of the economy and the characteristics of Brazilian society, in the periods of great migratory flow, we can affirm that the immigrants had a social ascension that could differentiate them from the composed national population (black, Indians, mestizos, "caboclos," "caipiras," etc.).

The acceptance in Brazil, and especially in the state of São Paulo, of thousands of European immigrants (and Asian), was, as we saw, was in part a response to the demand for labor in agriculture and in part a component of the governments' policy of whitening of the population. The perception of immigrants and their descendants as hard and enterprising workers—aspects that had been used to affirm their ethnic identities—strengthened the preconception against the "Brazilians," perceived in contrast, as people who dislike work (Seyferth, 1986). The abolition of slavery did not solve the problems for the blacks, thenceforth in competition in the labor market; racist practices hindered their access to economic participation (Munanga, 1990).

In summary, it should be noted that most immigrants who came to Brazil from the nineteenth century until the post-war period, managed to overcome their difficulties and integrate themselves into the Brazilian context, especially in São Paulo. They accomplished this through the development of social relations and by involving themselves in Brazil's economy and immersing themselves in academic achievement. To truly understand the immigrants in Brazil in the nineteenth and twentieth centuries it is necessary to analyze how and why these immigrants, who came from such different parts of the world and at different times, managed to integrate themselves into the Brazilian society and acclimatize themselves to the variety in Brazil (climate, vegetation, demographic composition, culture, etc.). This understanding is still elusive and Brazilian researchers are actively exploring, through different approaches (demographic, historical, sociologic, anthropologic, linguistic, etc.) means to develop a systematic and complete knowledge base about the several immigrant groups and the implications of their presence in Brazilian society.

References

Alvim, Z. (1986). *Brava gente*. São Paulo: Brasiliense.

Ando, Z. (1976). *Estudos sócio-históricos da imigração japonesa*. São Paulo: Centro de Estudos Nipo-Brasileiros.

Annuário do Ensino do Estado de São Paulo (1907–1908). São Paulo: Directoria Geral de Instrucção Pública.

Atlas da População do Estado de São Paulo (Governo do Estado de São Paulo). (1991). São Paulo: Fundação SEADE.

Azevedo, C. M. M. de. (1987). *Onda negra, mundo branco: O negro no imaginário das elites, século XIX*. Rio de Janeiro: Paz e Terra.

Barreto, L. P. T. F. (2001). Considerações sobre a imigração no Brasil contemporâneo. In: Castro, M. G. (Coord.) *Migrações internacionais: Contribuições para políticas brasileiras*. Brasília: CNPD, p. 63–71.

Bassanezi, M. S. B. (1996). Imigrações internacionais no Brasil: Um panorama histórico. In: Patarra, N. L. (Coord.) *Emigração e imigração internacionais no Brasil contemporâneo*. 2 ed. São Paulo: FNUAP, Vol. 1, p. 1–38.

Baeninger, R., & Leoncy, C. (2001). Perfil dos estrangeiros no Brasil segundo autorizações de trabalho (Ministério do Trabalho e Emprego) e registros de entradas e saídas da Polícia Federal (Ministério da Justiça). In: Castro, M. G. (Coord.) *Migrações internacionais: Contribuições para políticas brasileiras.* Brasília: CNPD, p. 187–242.

Betto, F. (2000). Índios e os 500 anos de Brasil. *Revista A. M.,* São Paulo, Vol. 101, abr.

Camargo, J. F. de. (1952). *Crescimento da população no estado de São Paulo e seus aspectos econômicos.* São Paulo: FFCL/USP (Boletim; 153).

Cardoso, R. (1972). *Estrutura familiar e mobilidade social: Estudo dos japoneses no Estado de São Paulo.* Tese (Doutorado)—Faculdade de Filosofia, Letras e Ciências Humanas, Universidade de São Paulo, São Paulo.

Castro, M. G. (Coord.) (2001). *Migrações internacionais: Contribuições para políticas brasileiras.* Brasília: CNPD, p. 187–242.

Demartini, Z. B. F. (2004). Imigração e educação: Discutindo algumas pistas de pesquisa. *Pró-Posições,* Campinas, v. 15, n. 3 (45), set./dez.

Demartini, Z. B. F. (2002). Imigrantes portugueses em São Paulo: Algumas questões sobre sua inserção no campo econômico. *Revista Convergência Lusíadas,* Rio de Janeiro, n. 19, n. Especial.

Demartini, Z. B. F. (1997). Viagens vividas, viagens sonhadas: Os japoneses em São Paulo na primeira metade deste século. In: Lang, A. B. S. G. (Org.) *Família em São Paulo: Vivências na diferença.* São Paulo: Humanitas (Coleção Textos, série 2, n. 7).

Demartini, Z. B. F. (1993). *Relatório de pesquisa: Famílias alemãs em São Paulo.* São Paulo: CERU/CNPq, mimeo.

Demartini, Z. B. F., & Espósito, Y. L. (1989). São Paulo no início do século e suas escolas diferenciadas. *Ciência e Cultura,* v. 41, n. 10, p. 981–995, out.

Demartini, Z. B. F., Cunha, D. O., & Doppenschmitt, E. (2005). Desafios da pesquisa com fluxos migratórios recentes: Portugueses e luso-africanos em São Paulo. *Cadernos CERU,* São Paulo, série 2, n. 16, p. 14–54.

Demartini, Z. B. F., Gusmão, N. M. M., Campos, M. C. S. S. (2003). *Imigrantes portugueses e luso-africanos no pós-guerra: trajetórias no contexto paulista.* São Paulo: CERU/CNPq. Pesquisa Integrada.

D.T.C.I. (1937). *Estatística de imigração.* São Paulo: Departamento de Imigração e Colonização/Secretaria da Agricultura do Estado de São Paulo.

Ferretti, M. (2002). Direitos humanos e imigrantes. In: Sales, T., & Salles, M. do R. (Orgs.) *Políticas migratórias: América Latina, Brasil e brasileiros no exterior.* São Paulo: EduFSCar/Sumaré, p. 7–19.

Freitas, S. M. (2002). Espírito Uchinanchu: Okinawanos em São Paulo. *Travessia: Revista do Migrante,* São Paulo, v. 15, n. 44, p. 11–17, set./dez.

Gattaz, A. C. (2005). *Do Líbano ao Brasil: História oral de imigrantes.* São Paulo: Gandalf.

Gattaz, A. C. (2007). Líbano uno e diverso: As múltiplas identidades entre imigrantes libaneses no Brasil. *História Oral: Revista da Associação Brasileira de História Oral,* Rio de Janeiro, v. 10, n. 1.

Giannini, D. (2005). Terra estrangeira. *Revista da Folha,* São Paulo, v. 13, n. 661, p. 12–18.

Handa, T. (1987). *O imigrante japonês: Histórias de sua vida no Brasil.* São Paulo: T. A. Queiroz/Centro de Estudos Nipo-Brasileiros.

Hastings, D. (1969). Japanese emigration and assimilation in Brazil. *International Migration Reviews,* New York, v. 3, n. 2.

Ianni, O. (1967). O progresso econômico e o trabalhador livre. In: Holanda, S. B. de. *História Geral da Civilização Brasileira.* São Paulo: Difel. Tomo 3. Vol. 3.

Ianni, O. (1966). *Raças e classes sociais no Brasil.* Rio de Janeiro: Civilização Brasileira. (Retratos do Brasil, v. 48).

Ishikawa, E. A. (2003). Migration movement from Brazil to Japan: The social adaptation of Japanese-Brazilian in Japan. *Regional Studies,* Japan, v. 30, n. 2.

Kaly, A. P. (2001). Os estudantes africanos no Brasil e o preconceito racial. In: Castro, M. G. (Coord.). *Migrações internacionais: Contribuições para políticas brasileiras.* Brasília: CNPD, p. 463–478.

Kreutz, L. (1998). Identidade étnica e processo escolar. In: *Encontro Anual Da Anpocs,* 22. Caxambu, 27 a 30 de outubro. Mimeo.

Milesi, R.; Bonassi, M.; & Shimano, M. L. (2001). Migrações internacionais e a sociedade civil organizada: Entidades confessionais que atuam com estrangeiros no Brasil e com brasileiros no exterior. In: Castro, M. G. (Coord.) *Migrações internacionais: Contribuições para políticas brasileiras.* Brasília: CNPD, p. 547–562.

Munanga, K. (1990). Negritude afro-brasileira: perspectivas e dificuldades. *Revista de Antropologia.* São Paulo, v. 33, p. 109–117.

Ninomiya, M. (2002). Imigrantes brasileiros frente às políticas migratórias: A presença dos brasileiros no Japão. In: Salles, T.S.M.R.R. *Políticas migratórias: América Latina, Brasil e brasileiros no exterior,* São Carlos: EdUFScar/Sumaré.

Patarra, N. L. (2006). Migrações internacionais: Teorias, políticas e movimentos sociais. *Estudos Avançados,* São Paulo, n. 57, p. 7–24, maio/ago.

Pereira, J. B. B. (1986). A morte nos estudos sociológicos e antropológicos sobre a imigração estrangeira no Brasil. *Revista de Antropologia*, São Paulo, v. 29, p. 85–97.

Petrone, M. T. S. (1990). Imigração. In: Pinheiro, P. S. et al. *História geral da civilização brasileira: O Brasil Republicano*. 4 ed. Rio de Janeiro: Bertrand Brasil, Vol. 2: Sociedade e Instruções: 1889–1930, p. 93–133.

Prado Jr., C. (1953). *História econômica do Brasil*. 3 ed. São Paulo: Brasiliense.

Ribeiro, G. S. (1990). *Mata galegos: Os portugueses e os conflitos de trabalho na República Velha*. São Paulo: Brasiliense.

Saito, H. (1980). *A presença japonesa no Brasil*. São Paulo: Edusp.

Sakurai, C. (2002). Mais estrangeiro que os outros?: Os japoneses no Brasil. *Travessia: Revista do Migrante*, São Paulo, v. 15, n. 44, p. 5–10, set./dez.

Sales, T. (2006). ONGs brasileiras em Boston. *Estudos Avançados*, São Paulo, n. 57, p. 75–92, maio/ago.

Sales, T. (1996). O trabalhador brasileiro no contexto das novas imigrações internacionais. In: Patarra, N. L. (Coord.). *Emigração e imigração internacionais no Brasil contemporâneo*. 2 ed. São Paulo: FNUAP, Vol. 1, p. 90–103.

Sales, T., & Salles, M. do R. R. (Orgs.) (2002). *Políticas migratórias: América Latina, Brasil e brasileiros no exterior*. São Paulo: EduFSCar/Sumaré.

Savoldi, A., & Renk, A. (2006). Traços da imigração européia ao Brasil e da emigração brasileira à Europa. *Revista Grifos*, Chapecó, n. 20–21, p. 125–148, jun./dez.

Sayad, A. (2000). O retorno: Elemento constitutivo da condição do imigrante. *Travessia: Revista do Migrante*, São Paulo, v. 13, n. Especial, jan.

Serrão, J. (1971). *A emigração portuguesa: Sondagem histórica*. Lisboa: Livros Horizonte.

Seyferth, G. (1988). Imigração e colonização alemã no Brasil: Uma revisão da bibliografia. *Revista BIB*, Rio de Janeiro, n. 25.

Seyferth, G. (1986). Imigração, colonização e identidade étnica: Notas sobre a emergência da etnicidade em grupos de origem européia no sul da Brasil. *Revista de Antropologia*, São Paulo, v. 29, p. 57–71.

Seyferth, G. (2005). Imigração, preconceitos e os enunciados subjetivos dos etnocentrismos. *Travessia: Revista do Migrante*, São Paulo, v. 18, n. 5, p. 5–15, jan./abr.

Silva, M. B. N. da. (1992). *Documentos para a história da imigração portuguesa no Brasil, 1850–1938*. Rio de Janeiro: Nórdica.

Silva, S. A. da. (2006). Bolivianos em São Paulo: Entre o sonho e a realidade. *Estudos Avançados*, São Paulo, n. 57, p. 157–170, maio/ago.

Silva, S. A. da. (2001). Hispano-Americanos no Brasil: Entre a cidadania sonhada e a concedida. In: Castro, M/ G. (Coord.). *Migrações internacionais: Contribuições para políticas brasileiras*. Brasília: CNPD, p. 489–501.

Silva, S. A. da. (1997). *Costurando sonhos: Trajetória de um grupo de imigrantes bolivianos que trabalham no ramo da costura em São Paulo*. São Paulo: Paulinas. (Estudos e Debates).

Silva, S. (1960). *Expansão cafeeira e origens da indústria no Brasil*. São Paulo: Alfa-Omega.

Simson, O. de M. von. (1997). Diversidade sócio-cultural, reconstituição da tradição e globalização: Os teuto-brasileiros de Friburgo-Campinas. In: Lang, A. B. S. G. (Org.) *Família em São Paulo: Vivências na diferença*. São Paulo. Humanitas/ CERU. p. 63–75 (Coleção Textos, série 2, n. 7).

Simson, O. de M. von. (1993). *Relatório de pesquisa: Famílias alemãs em Campinas*. São Paulo: CERU/ CNPq. Mimeo.

Sprandel, M. (2001). Migrações internacionais e a sociedade civil brasileira. In: Castro, M. G. (Coord.) *Migrações internacionais: Contribuições para políticas brasileira*. Brasília: CNPD, p. 547–562.

Trento, A. (1989). *Do outro lado do Atlântico*. São Paulo: Nobel.

Vainer, C. B. (1996). Estudo e migração internacional no Brasil: Da imigração à emigração. In: Patarra, N. (Coord.). *Emigração e imigração internacionais no Brasil contemporâneo*. 2 ed. São Paulo: FNUAP.

Vários Autores. (1992). *Uma epopéia moderna: 80 anos da imigração japonesa no Brasil*. São Paulo: Hucitec/Sociedade Brasileira de Cultura Japonesa.

Vida, S. S. (2001). Africanos no Brasil: uma ameaça ao paraíso racial. In: Castro, M. G. (Coord.) *Migrações internacionais: Contribuições para políticas brasileira*. Brasília: CNPD, p. 449–461.

Willems, E. (1946). *A aculturação dos alemães no Brasil*. São Paulo: Nacional.

PART V

Regional Movements

28

African Union

Return and Resettlement: A Survey of Refugee Law and Policy in Africa

Andrew Joseph Novak

Defining the Parameters of the African Refugee Crisis

Displaced populations are as old as conflict itself, but only in the last century or so have enormously destructive wars uprooted entire nations, changing the political and social position of refugees. Africa's position in the current global refugee crisis stems from the political upheavals surrounding decolonization, the Cold War, and the trauma of democratization and its failure in the 1990s. As Clapham (2000: 218) writes, Africa's high number of refugees is also related to its large number of states with permeable boundaries and the relative ease of the "exit" option in response to political oppression or disturbance. Elsewhere, he notes that, "in Africa . . . states are for the most part smaller, boundaries more artificial and more easily crossed" than in other regions of the world (Clapham, 1985:183). Many of Africa's current refugee crises have become endemic. Entire communities may fester in refugee camps with squalid conditions or live a transient, insecure life in rapidly urbanizing cities. The prospects for these refugees to return home depends in part on political calculations by government elites.

Many serious refugee crises remain unsolved because of the important political stakes certain actors hold. Indeed, many of the greatest successes of international humanitarian relief efforts depended heavily on the participation of key political, economic, and military interests. As colonial governments clung to power in Southern Africa in the 1960s and 1970s, refugees fleeing "white Africa" for "black Africa" against the backdrop of the glaring injustices of white minority rule were often welcomed in their new countries of asylum. With the end of Portuguese rule in Angola and Mozambique, the conversion of white-ruled Rhodesia to independent Zimbabwe, and finally South Africa's withdrawal from Namibia, the strategic value of refugee populations in the region drastically declined. Similarly, in the Horn of Africa, where Cold War tensions were particularly high, refugees were often political pawns in the shifting alliances among Ethiopia, Sudan, and Somalia, each of which were immersed in a series of intertwined civil wars backed by Soviet or American support and arms.

As Crisp (2005: 19–20) explains, a new political consensus developed in the mid-1980s that the most durable solution for refugees in Africa was to repatriate to their homelands, not to integrate into local communities or abroad in developed countries. Because of the destabilizing impact large refugee flows have on the peculiarly weak governments of sub-Saharan Africa, the international community has focused more on providing short-term humanitarian aid in camps rather than on various forms of economic assistance to help refugees create new lives in their countries of asylum. In this way, refugees are often segregated from local populations and dependent on aid from the outside world, with all the social disruptions this isolation causes such as xenophobia and antirefugee sentiment.

By the end of 2007, nearly 2.5 million refugees were displaced on the African continent (United Nations High Commissioner for Refugees [UNHCR], 2008). The conflict in Darfur, Sudan, has created the worst current refugee crisis. Darfur had long been an isolated province, subject to repeated famine in the twentieth century and conflict over land rights. A low-intensity civil war had waged in the province for years, but when the Darfur militias intensified their fight against the government in 2003, they sparked an annihilatory, even genocidal, response from government-backed troops (De Waal, 2005). Refugees crossed hundreds of miles of desert to flee the government-supported Janjaweed militia and were forced to travel in UNHCR convoys to camps across the Chadian border before the rainy season began. The inaccessibility of the region hampers relief efforts. However, the hundreds of thousands of refugees fleeing to Chad are dwarfed by the 1 to 4 million Darfurians who are uprooted from their homes but remain in Darfur (Lacey, 2004). The conflict also shows how internal conflict can easily become international conflict; the destabilizing presence of Darfurian refugees in Chad and the Central African Republic has sparked civil war in both countries and allegations that both are supporting the Darfur militias fighting the Janjaweed in Darfur (BBC News, 2006).

The major source countries of African refugees today besides Sudan include the Democratic Republic of the Congo, Somalia, and Angola. In 2007, the Democratic Republic of the Congo saw the displacement of 243,000 people during the year, while Somalia saw an additional 600,000 uprooted. However, in Uganda, nearly 600,000 displaced persons from elsewhere in the country and 43,000 refugees from Sudan returned home

in 2007 (UNHCR, 2008). The formerly displaced populations from Liberia, Sierra Leone, Angola, Rwanda, and Ethiopia that had crippled the continent in the 1990s diminished greatly as the political situations in each of the countries stabilized and protracted conflicts subsided.

Protection of African Refugees: The Legal Regime

The 1951 Refugee Convention, the foundational document of international law on which the current legal refugee regime is based, defines a refugee as a person with a "well-founded fear of being persecuted for reasons of race, religion, nationality, [or] membership of a particular social group or political opinion." Unlike other forms of migration, refugees are not "pulled" by the promise of more stable economic opportunities or political freedoms; rather, they are pushed by violence, human rights abuses, natural disaster, or conflict. The second part of the definition is just as salient: refugees must be "outside the country of his nationality" and be "unable . . . or unwilling to avail himself of the protection of that country" (1951 Refugee Convention, Art. I). In 1950, the United Nations General Assembly created the office of the High Commissioner for Refugees (UNHCR), with a mandate to assist qualifying refugees worldwide.

The definition of "refugee" as one who crosses an international boundary is today customary international law. Internally displaced persons (IDPs) do not have the same enforceable rights that refugees have. At the end of 2005, the number of IDPs worldwide reached nearly 24 million, more than double the number of refugees. More than half this total, 12.1 million in twenty countries, are on the African continent, two thirds of them in Uganda, Sudan, and the Democratic Republic of the Congo (Hollenbach, 2008: 178–79). Calling for the creation of a new UN High Commissioner for Forced Migrants, Martin, et al. (2005: 123) describe the protection regime for IDPs as "outmoded, overly fragmented, and in need of significant reform." Extending UNHCR's mandate to cover IDPs is practically and politically unrealistic given resource constraints and political opposition engendered by the possible infringement on national sovereignty.

All refugees enjoy the right of nonrefoulement under these conventions and customary international law. This means that refugees cannot be returned to their country of origin against their will. Refugee law, as implied above, also specifies the so-called durable solutions to refugee flows: permanent acceptance and integration in the country of first asylum, third-country resettlement, often in developed nations, and voluntary repatriation to the country of origin. Repatriation is the preferred solution in Africa, although the endemic nature of conflicts and disasters and lack of development and economic opportunity often hinder repatriation (Koehn 1994: 97). One of the most successful repatriations was the return of almost 2 million refugees in Mozambique between 1992 and 1994. Resettlement in a country of first asylum is problematic because the host nation often does not have the resources, arable land in particular, to feasibly absorb the population. Many developed nations also accept quotas of African refugees, with about half being accepted by the United States annually (Koehn 1994: 105–106).

The development of the legal refugee protection regime was strengthened early on the African continent. The Organization of African Unity (OAU), today known as the African Union, broadened the definition of refugee in 1969 as one not simply fleeing persecution, but also domestic political and social upheaval and struggles for national liberation (Bakwesegha, 1994: 7). Signed in Addis Ababa, Ethiopia, at the OAU headquarters, the OAU Refugee Convention extended refugee protection to those groups of people escaping external aggression, occupation, or foreign domination (Loescher, 1996: 81). In particular, the OAU Convention chose voluntary repatriation as the primary durable solution to a refugee crisis (Article V). In line with this provision, successful large-scale repatriations occurred following the colonial wars in the former Portuguese colonies and the war for the independence of Zimbabwe (Loescher, 1996: 82). The Convention also prohibits refugee involvement in subversive activities and requires governments to provide for refugee security by placing refugees a measured distance from the border (Articles II and III).

The institutional development of UNHCR as an international organization has made a profound difference in refugee protection. In 1950, UNHCR was founded against the backdrop of troubled League of Nations efforts to resettle displaced persons from the Bolshevik Revolution in the 1920s and the failure to protect the Jewish refugees fleeing central Europe in the 1930s. For much of its early history, its efforts focused on postwar Europe. In the 1960s, African refugees tended to be self-settled and widely dispersed, easing the burden on international actors. In 1967, the Protocol Relating to the Status of Refugees broadened UNHCR's mandate. While the 1951 Convention was originally drafted for the postwar refugee crisis in Europe, the Protocol made the Convention universal. In the 1970s, UNHCR took a more active role in humanitarian assistance, and the focus of its operations began to shift from Europe to Africa (Loescher, 1996: 83). UNHCR's experience in Bangladesh, Indochina, and Algeria prepared it to deal with refugees from Rhodesia, Western Sahara, Sudan, and Rwanda, among others, in the 1970s.

Because of the constrained mandates of intergovernmental organizations like UNHCR, much of the protection of refugees and IDPs is provided by nongovernmental organizations (NGOs). NGOs often have a certain expertise in an area, independence from political actors such as governments or rebel groups, capacity to collaborate with many other organizations, and mobility to reach conflict victims before governments or militaries can (Raper, 2003: 350). Prominent NGOs operating in Africa include Save the Children, the International Committee of the Red Cross, Oxfam, and the Catholic organization Caritas. NGOs have had particular success in the campaigns to ban landmines, oppose child soldier recruitment, and cancel the debt of developing nations, not to mention assisting in HIV/AIDS efforts (Raper, 2003: 355). For protection of refugees, NGOs play a particularly valuable role in monitoring human rights violations, publishing reports, and shaming governments. Many NGOs are professional, international organizations, while many others are local community-based organizations, often religiously based, assisting in such efforts as HIV/AIDS care.

The operations of NGOs are particularly important when humanitarian disasters fall outside the scope of the mandate of the United Nations and UNHCR. The civil war in Nigeria in the late 1960s over the rebellious province of Biafra sparked a famine in 1968. The Joint Church Aid airlift transported quantities of food only surpassed by the Berlin airlift (De Waal, 2002: 73). The conflict was remembered for political manipulation of humanitarian aid and threats to relief workers. Scholars have suggested that the large humanitarian response helped prolong the war (De Waal, 2002: 76–77). In many ways, the operations of humanitarian relief organizations may be morally ambiguous although their intentions may be pure.

Refugee protection and assistance are not only limited to the work of nongovernmental organizations and international agencies. Government structures as well have been designed to provide for refugees and asylum-seekers. Many African governments have ministries or departments that deal with immigration and refugee issues, often a ministry of interior or social welfare. The South African Department of Home Affairs is one of the most comprehensive (Jacobsen, 1996). South African entry channels are backlogged, however, as the country continues to be a safe haven for refugees from all over Southern Africa, and the waits for asylum requests and identity cards are severe. The political crisis and the devastating economic deterioration of Zimbabwe have led to waves of undocumented migrants crossing the border into South Africa, finding haven primarily in urban areas. More than 40,000 people applied for asylum in South Africa in 2007 (UNHCR, 2008).

While many refugees are clustered in camps in relatively rural areas, urban refugees face a different set of constraints. In Kenya, many refugees went to Nairobi because they possessed skills or professional backgrounds that allow them to take up employment in the city. The number of refugees living in urban Nairobi may be as high as 100,000. Urban refugees may be harassed by police or live in unsafe housing; they may not receive work permits; and they may be caught up in urban gang or factional violence (Wagacha and Guiney, 2008: 94). Urban refugees often have urban backgrounds and education and are disproportionately male (Landau, 2008: 106). Urban refugees are often blamed for high crime rates and prostitution, and they may be excluded from national health or HIV/AIDS policies.

The final legal constraint on the definition of "refugee" is that refugees must be civilians; combatants, whether state-supported troops or privately armed rebels, are excluded by definition. The definition also specifically excludes persons guilty of serious human rights abuses or international crimes. In practice, this distinction is hard to police, particularly with the legal complications of such groups as child soldiers, who fall outside the customary law definition of a "combatant." As Clapham (2000: 218) writes, even distinguishing refugee camps from insurgent bases can be difficult. In the late 1980s, many Sudanese refugee camps in southwest Ethiopia had high proportions of young men. This may be the result simply of the greater resources this population had to reach safety, or it may be that these were effectively rebel training camps. The aftermath of the Rwandan genocide is starker: enormous colonies of refugees developed in Zaire and Tanzania, where Hutu militiamen, many of them implicated in genocidal activity, seized control of internal social networks in the refugee camps to organize bases for their return. The African refugee crisis cannot be divorced from the reality of weak African states. While the refugee legal regime guarantees juridical equality for refugees in host states, including the right of access to the legal system, the right to documentation and identification, and the right to non-discrimination, the weakness of African legal systems and justice regimes may make many of these rights illusory.

Protection of African Refugees: Political Considerations

Refugees are no longer the by-products of popular wars of liberation against colonizers. As governments buckle under ethnic animosity, crumbling infrastructure, massive debt, and the crippling effects of HIV/AIDS, the ability of a ruler to maintain control over the entirety of the nation's territory becomes limited. As the numbers of collapsed or collapsing states increase, the potential for attempted coups, terrorist or rebel activity, or outside intervention increases as well. Today, refugees most often flee internal violence among factions with little ideological cohesiveness. The refugee flows in Africa are both byproducts and contributors to this instability. In their countries of asylum, refugees are often blamed for many societal ills, including high levels of crime, the spread of disease, food insecurity, or job competition, as are many migrants worldwide.

Refugees who fled unpopular regimes such as the white minority governments in Southern Africa or the wars of independence in Angola and Mozambique were generally welcomed in their new states. However, the spread of the Cold War to Africa dramatically changed this. Refugees became political pawns in the tension between East and West. After the Cold War, many African client regimes propped up by the United States or the Soviet Union collapsed or contracted. Refugees, like insurgents, traffickers in contraband, economic migrants, and other actors, have thrived at the expense of the porous boundaries between states (Clapham, 2000: 273). There is some indication that this situation is changing. The African refugee crisis peaked at nearly 7 million in 1994 (Veney, 2007: 4). Some of the most costly wars in postcolonial African memory came to a close in the late 1990s and early 2000s, resulting in durable peace treaties in Mozambique and Angola, the independence of Eritrea, the end of white minority rule in southern Africa, the conclusion of the conflicts in Liberia and Sierra Leone, and the restoration of at least some political authority in Somalia, Rwanda, northern Uganda, and Ivory Coast. Not all has been progress: Zimbabwe's economic collapse, continued instability in Darfur, and a political crisis in the Democratic Republic of the Congo have created waves of displacement in the first decade of the 2000s. The tumultuous 1990s, however, are over.

Cultural and social circumstances may affect how society treats the displaced. These may involve ethnic and kinship considerations. As a refugee host nation, Somalia was perceived as treating ethnic Somali Muslims from Ethiopia better than Amharic Christian Ethiopians, who were identified with the ruling regime in Ethiopia (see, e.g., Bariagabe, 2006: 45, 57). This is particularly common in countries where the same ethnic group lives on both sides of a border and refugees to the region share a common linguistic, cultural, or religious tie to the host community. On the other hand, refugees may be unwelcome if they are perceived to alter the ethnic makeup of a community. Burundi's Tutsi government considered the influx of Hutu refugees from Rwanda into Burundi as a security threat (Jacobsen, 1996).

Sympathies in the wars of neighboring countries help explain how the refugees from those countries are treated. For as long as the Eritrean conflict was seen as a Muslim versus Christian conflict, Eritrean refugees were well treated in Sudan, and they were able to receive supplies through Sudanese ports (Smock, 1982). However, upon Eritrea's independence in 1993 after rebels overthrew the Derg, the Marxist-inspired junta in Ethiopia, a diplomatic revolution of sorts occurred. Both Ethiopia and Eritrea grew hostile toward the increasingly repressive Islamist regime in Sudan, and Eritrea closed its border with Sudan in 1997. Though many Eritrean refugees had secure jobs and other vested interests and had so successfully integrated into their new life that they did not want to return home, their continued presence in Sudan created some diplomatic friction (Bascom, 1993).

Civil wars and population displacement may elicit foreign humanitarian intervention. This intervention has mixed success in managing refugee crises. Liberia was a major refugee producing country in the early 2000s, and the situation there highlights the dangers of peacekeeping. The Liberian crisis came shortly after a series of military coups and United Nations intervention in neighboring Sierra Leone fueled a civil war. The interconnectedness of the two wars, along with the current crisis in Ivory Coast, shows the spillover effects of internal civil turmoil. After the overthrow of President Charles Taylor, hundreds of thousands of IDPs rushed toward the capital city, Monrovia, seeking the protection of recently deployed peacekeeping troops. The huge crowds of people built shelters and awaited relief in the suburbs surrounding the city until they could settle into local IDP camps or return home (Wilkinson, 2003).

As in Liberia and Sierra Leone, Angola suffered from devastating conflict fueled by resource wealth such as diamonds and oil. More than one million people were killed over the nearly 30-year period, four million were internally displaced, and 500,000 were refugees in neighboring countries. After the peace agreement was signed in 2002, 1.6 million displaced persons spontaneously began to return home, with UNHCR organizing repatriation of refugees from neighboring countries. Most of the country's infrastructure was destroyed and the landscape retained scars of bullet-sprayed homes, shops, barracks, and churches (Del Mundo, 2003). This repatriation effort came at a cost. While mobility was extremely difficult during the civil war, Angola's HIV/AIDS rate was much lower than that of its neighbors, possibly as low as one-fourth the rate of a country like Botswana. As refugees began to return and infrastructure was rebuilt, the increased movement caused the relatively low HIV/AIDS rate to drastically increase (Spiegel, 2004).

Uganda exemplifies a nation that has both created and hosted large refugee populations. At Uganda's independence in 1962, the territory was already host to over 100,000 refugees from the Congo, Rwanda, and Sudan (Pirouet, 1988: 239). The disastrous reign of Idi Amin created tremendous economic and political dislocation, including the expulsion of 50,000 Ugandans of Asian descent in 1972. By the end of Amin's reign, as many as 130,000 Ugandans had fled to Southern Sudan or Kenya (Woodward, 1988: 234); Uganda hosted a similar number of refugees during the same time period (Pirouet, 1988: 242). The second reign of President Milton Obote in the early 1980s proved even more disastrous. The rise to power of Obote meant an upswing in rebel activity, the deterioration of discipline in the military and consequent human rights abuses, and the more general targeting of ethnic groups such as the Acholi rather than the individualized persecutions of the Amin era (247). Only with Obote's overthrow by Yoweri Museveni in early 1986 did the country begin to stabilize. Following the Rwandan genocide, second-generation Rwandan Tutsi refugees who had fled in the 1960s for Uganda played an important role in overthrowing the genocidal regime. As Ogata (2005: 173) writes, "six to seven hundred thousand Tutsis who fled Rwanda between 1959 and 1973 still considered themselves refugees in their host countries by the beginning of the Rwandan genocide, many of whom were hosted by Uganda."

Asylum or resettlement in a third country has helped a smaller number of people than either integration in the host country or repatriation. In addition to providing sanctuary to asylum-seekers who reach the borders of the West, about seventeen governments of Europe, North America, and Australia, and New Zealand resettle a certain number of refugees from around the world every year. The United States began its resettlement program in the 1970s, helping thousands of Vietnamese refugees and Jewish dissidents from the Soviet Union, and, with the help of a variety of organizations, began to expand the refugee resettlement program to include thousands of refugees from Somalia and Ethiopia. The Somali resettlement in the United States was the most ambitious resettlement program ever taken outside of Africa. Throughout the United States and Canada, communities of former refugees from the Horn of Africa began appearing in many major cities such as Minneapolis, contributing to the rich cultural diversity of urban life (Darboe, 2003: 460).

There are, however, limits to this protection. In some places, refugees do not want to be resettled or integrated into a new society, but political constraints prevent their return. This is the situation that confronts refugees from Western Sahara who have made their homes in the refugee camps on the Algerian border. Having fled more than three decades ago, it is increasingly less likely that they will return home in the foreseeable future; peace plans proposed by mediators from the African Union, the United Nations, or other governments are continually rejected by Morocco, the occupying power of Western Sahara since 1975. A string of refugee camps in the Algerian desert have become permanent settlements, similar to the camps in the occupied territories of Palestine. Since the refugees cannot be sent elsewhere against their will and most have hope of one day returning to their homes, UNHCR, under mandate by the UN General Assembly to assist the Saharawi refugees of Western Sahara, can do little else but continue dispensing humanitarian assistance and wait for the political stalemate to be resolved (Hopper, 2004).

Refugees may not only place local communities under stress due to competition for jobs and resources or ethnic tensions; they may also play important roles in national politics. In the 1990s, both Kenya and Tanzania experienced a very dramatic rise in refugee populations within their borders, coinciding with both countries' processes of democratization and economic liberalization. Both governments became, in the 1990s, more economically frugal and more responsive to their citizens (Veney, 2007: 9). As Veney adds, as a result of the refugee displacements from Rwanda, Somalia, and elsewhere, national legislation in Kenya and Tanzania "became more restrictive or ruthless[;] asylum was increasingly determined in terms of groups rather than individuals; camps that were virtually beyond the rule of law became the mainstay of refugee protection; and forced repatriation assumed prominence over local integration and third-country resettlement" (Veney, 2007: 9), with refugees occasionally deported and forced to carry color-coded identity documents.

Finally, the decision to classify displaced migrants as refugees may ultimately be a political one rather than a legal one. Often, characterizing the threat that refugees face is a political choice: are they fleeing for a "qualifying" reason? Many refugees flee with mixed motivations, and many crises have both economic and political consequences. The disintegration of the political and economic sphere in Zimbabwe after 2002 is a recent example. Because of the tendency for economic migrants from Zimbabwe to temporarily and repeatedly cross the long border with Botswana to engage in petty trade or make purchases, many economic migrants resist classification as refugees since this would likely mean limitations on the freedom of movement. The difference in treatment between Burundian refugees in Tanzania fleeing violence or political persecution at home and a properly documented migrant with a visa, passport, or residency permit is respect for the displaced person's freedom of movement. Refugees are obligated to live in refugee camps in which their freedom of movement is heavily restricted, while documented migrants can move about the country freely for the duration of their visa (Joint Commission for Refugees of the Burundi and Tanzania Episcopal Conference, 2008: 55).

Current Controversies in African Refugee Policy

Refugee flows are inevitably tied to illicit trade in arms and other contraband, as well as to the spread of disease. In the years following the Al-Qaeda bombings of the U.S. embassies in Kenya and Tanzania in 1998, and especially following the events of September 11, 2001, the question of whether refugees contribute to the spread of terrorist activity is particularly controversial. On the one hand, Sudan and Somalia, ravaged by years of war, are perceived to be havens and sponsors of terrorism; on the other hand, the East African nations of Kenya, Tanzania, and Uganda have been and may continue to be targets for terrorist activities (Juma and Kagwanja, 2003: 225). Refugee policy in East Africa and the Horn has long been intertwined with security concerns. These states often cannot control their long porous borders and ports from refugees, pirates, illicit arms or drug traders, or rebels. In addition, many of these countries have radicalized citizens with longstanding grievances, among them some Muslim communities in northeastern Kenya. The tendency to criminalize refugees and view them within the security prism is increasing (234–235).

Environmental refugees are another important source of controversy in the twenty-first century. These include both persons displaced by economic catastrophe such as desertification or flooding, or most controversially climate change, and persons displaced by conservation efforts, such as the large numbers of indigenous populations forced out of national parks and other conserved lands. The practice of moving indigenous persons out of protected areas has displaced thousands of people in countries as diverse as Cameroon, Gabon, the Republic of the Congo, and Botswana (Schmidt-Soltau, 2005: 284 [table]; Taylor, 2004: 152).

Finally, gender issues play an increasingly important role in addressing human vulnerability in refugee situations. Approximately 75 to 80 percent of displaced persons worldwide are women or children (Mertus, 2003: 257). The experience of flight is different for men and women since men often have the resources to travel further afield or seek asylum in the West; in addition, men tend to be combatants more often than women and thus are excluded from the definition of "refugee." Rural women may also be unable to continue their livelihoods farming or raising livestock when violence strikes. When detained, women may be at particular risk for violence in prisons or detention facilities (Veney, 2007: 201). Violence against refugees is often gendered; women are more vulnerable to sexual exploitation, domestic violence, and rape. In addition, the lack of maternal and reproductive health care in conflict settings falls most heavily on women.

Similar to the problem of women's rights, many conflict settings see a rise in unaccompanied minor refugees: separated or orphaned children who flee alone. These children can account for 2% to 5% of refugee camp populations and are often vulnerable to child trafficking schemes (Bhabha, 2004: 141). Elder refugees pose many of the same challenges as children; they may be separated from caregivers or in special need of social guidance, therapy, or health care. Humanitarian assistance agencies often engage in family reunification efforts during postconflict situations. The special problem of demobilizing and reintegrating child soldiers, particularly where the children were forced to fight among or against their own communities, is within the mandate of a number of NGOs and the United Nations Children's Fund (UNICEF).

Conclusion

Africa has suffered from some of the most destructive internal conflicts in the world in part because resource constraints and poorly established democratic systems have contributed to the weakness and ineffectiveness of many African states. Particularly in countries with long, often arbitrary boundaries and heterogenous populations, the "exit option" becomes attractive when the "voice option," including free and fair elections, a responsible media, and a strong civil society, is suppressed. Africa continues to host some of the highest refugee populations in the world in places as diverse as Darfur, Ivory Coast, the Congo basin, and Zimbabwe. The traditional wisdom concerning refugees is that they are "pushed" out of their countries by persecution, civil strife, or famine, while economic migrants are "pulled" in favor of better economic opportunities, education, or employment. This view is inevitably reductionist; the reality of migration patterns in Africa is much more complex. While the definition of refugee as an individual fleeing persecution or conflict across an international border is fairly stable as a matter of international customary law, the African reality problematizes this definition. Internally displaced persons, environmental refugees, child soldiers, and other groups who fall outside the traditional definition of "refugee" are often just as in need of assistance and often indistinguishable from traditional refugees. Nonetheless, the mandates of many NGOs, governmental agencies, and international institutions are based on this distinction.

Despite the crippling effects of mass migration movements, the refugee situation in Africa is considerably more positive than it was in the 1990s. With the end of major wars in Angola, Mozambique, Liberia, and Rwanda, and with decreases in violence in countries such as Uganda, Somalia, Southern Sudan, and elsewhere, millions of refugees on the continent have returned home. Repatriation continues to be the ideal solution to refugee crises in the developing world today. As a result, many refugee movements are designed to be temporary, and refugees remain aloof from the host populations among whom they dwell, despite the problems that this segregation may cause and the dangers of refugee camp life. While resettlement tends to be more politically controversial than repatriation, hundreds of thousands of refugees have migrated to urban areas or to third countries of asylum in an effort to escape the effects of conflict.

Refugees are a phenomenon as old as conflict, but the rapid advance of modern technology, including the proliferation of small arms, has turned conflict deadlier in postcolonial Africa. Refugee movements are often much more catastrophic than they once were, and human costs far more severe. But innovation has always been only one step behind: medical advances, legal developments, and the institution of relief strategies in complex emergencies have ultimately helped reduce the shocking numbers of displaced persons on the African continent.

References

Bakwesegha, C. 1994. "Forced Migration in Africa and the OAU Convention." *African Refugees: Development Aid and Repatriation*, H. Adelman and J. Sorenson (eds). Boulder: Westview Press.

Bariagabe, A. 2006. *Conflict and the Refugee Experience: Flight, Exile, and Repatriation in the Horn of Africa*. Aldershot, UK: Ashgate.

Bascom, J. 1993. "The Peasant Economy of Refugee Resettlement in Eastern Sudan." *Annals of the Association of American Geographers*, 83(2), p. 320.

BBC News. 2006. "Darfur Conflict Zones Map." December 6. Available at: http://news.bbc.co.uk/2/hi/africa/6213202.stm (last accessed October 12, 2008).

Bhabha, J. 2004. "Seeking Asylum Alone: Treatment of Separated and Trafficked Children in Need of Refugee Protection." *International Migration*, 42(1), p. 141.

Clapham, C. 2000. *Africa and the International System: The Politics of State Survival*. Cambridge, UK: Cambridge University Press.

Clapham, C. *Third World Politics: An Introduction*. Madison: University of Wisconsin Press, 1985.

Crisp, J. 2005. "No Solutions in Sight: The Problem of Protracted Refugee Situations in Africa." *Displacement Risks in Africa: Refugees, Resettlers, and Their Host Populations*, I. Ohta and Y. Gebre (eds). Victoria, Australia: Trans Pacific Press.

Darboe, K. 2003. "New Immigrants in Minnesota: The Somali Immigration and Assimilation." *Journal of Developing Societies*, 19(4), p. 458.

De Waal, A. 2002. *Famine Crimes: Politics and the Disaster Relief Industry in Africa*. Indianapolis: Indiana University Press.

De Waal, A. 2005. *Famine That Kills: Darfur, Sudan*. New York: Oxford University Press.

Del Mundo, F. 2003. "Angola: A New Beginning." *Refugees Magazine*, 3(132), p. 21.

Hollenbach, D. 2008. "Internally Displaced People, Sovereignty, and the Responsibility to Protect." *Refugee Rights: Ethics, Advocacy, and Africa*, D. Hollenbach (ed). Washington, DC: Georgetown University Press.

Hopper, S. 2004. "Western Sahara: Photo Essay." *Refugees Magazine*, 3(136), p. 23.

Jacobsen, K. 1996. "Factors Influencing the Policy Responses of Host Governments to Mass Refugee Influxes." *International Migration Review*, 30(3), p. 655.

Joint Commission for Refugees of the Burundi and Tanzania Episcopal Conference. 2008. "The Presence of Burundian Refugees in Western Tanzania: Ethical Responsibilities as a Framework for Advocacy." *Refugee Rights: Ethics, Advocacy, and Africa*, D. Hollenbach (ed). Washington, DC: Georgetown University Press.

Juma, M. K., and P. M. Kagwanja. 2003. "Securing Refuge from Terror: Refugee Protection in East Africa after September 11." *Problems of Protection: The UNHCR, Refugees, and Human Rights*, N. Steiner, M. Gibney, and G. Loescher (eds). New York: Routledge.

Koehn, P. 1994. "Refugee Settlement and Repatriation in Africa: Development Prospects and Constraints." *African Refugees: Development Aid and Repatriation*. Boulder: Westview Press.

Lacey, M. 2004. "In Sudan, Militiamen on Horses Uproot a Million." *The New York Times*. May 4, p. 1.

Landau, L. 2008. "Protection as Capability Expansion: Practical Ethics for Assisting Urban Refugees." *Refugee Rights: Ethics, Advocacy, and Africa*, D. Hollenbach (ed). Washington, DC: Georgetown University Press.

Loescher, G. 1996. *Beyond Charity: International Cooperation and the Global Refugee Crisis*. Oxford: Oxford University Press.

Martin, S., P. W. Fagen, K. Jorgensen, L. Mann-Bondat, and A. Schoenholtz. 2005. *The Uprooted: Improving Humanitarian Responses to Forced Migration*. Lanham, MD: Lexington Books.

Mertus, J. 2003. "The New Sovereignty and Refugee Women." *Refugees and Forced Displacement: International Security, Human Vulnerability, and the State*, E. Newman and J. van Selm (eds). New York: United Nations University Press.

Ogata, S. 2005. *The Turbulent Decade: Confronting the Refugee Crises of the 1990s*. New York: W.W. Norton.

Pirouet, L. 1988. "Refugees in and from Uganda in the Post-Independence Period." *Uganda Now: between Decay and Development*, H. B. Hansen and M. Twaddle (eds). Athens: Ohio University Press.

Raper, M. 2003. "Changing Roles of NGOs in Refugee Assistance." *Refugees and Forced Displacement: International Security, Human Vulnerability, and the State*, E. Newman and J. van Selm (eds). New York: United Nations University Press.

Schmidt-Soltau, K. 2005. "The Environmental Risks of Conservation Related Displacements in Central Africa." *Displacement Risks in Africa: Refugees, Resettlers, and Their Host Populations*, I. Ohta and Y. Gebre (eds). Victoria, Australia: Trans Pacific Press.

Smock, D.R. "Eritrean Refugees in the Sudan." *The Journal of Modern African Studies*, 20(3) 1982, p. 451.

Spiegel, P. 2004. "HIV/AIDS among Conflict-Affected and Displaced Populations: Dispelling Myths and Taking Action." Presentation before the Inter-Agency Advisory Group on AIDS. Feb. 9–10.

Taylor, M. 2004. "The Past and Future of San Land Rights in Botswana." *Indigenous Peoples' Rights in Southern Africa*, R. Hitchcock and D. Vinding (eds). Copenhagen: IWGIA.

United Nations High Commissioner for Refugees (UNHCR). *Global Report 2007*. June 2008. Available at: http://www.unhcr.org/publ/3b7b87e14.html (last accessed Oct. 12, 2008).

Veney, C. 2007. *Forced Migration in Eastern Africa: Democratization, Structural Adjustment, and Refugees*. New York: Palgrave Macmillan.

Wagacha, J. B., and J. Guiney. 2008. "The Plight of Urban Refugees in Nairobi, Kenya." *Refugee Rights: Ethics, Advocacy, and Africa*, D. Hollenbach (ed). Washington, DC: Georgetown University Press.

Wilkinson, R. 2003. "Africa on the Edge." *Refugees Magazine*, 2(131), p. 12.

Woodward, P. 1988. "Uganda and Southern Sudan: Peripheral Politics and Neighbor Relations." *Uganda Now: Between Decay and Development*, H. B. Hansen and M. Twaddle (eds). Athens: Ohio University Press.

29

European Union

Immigration and the European Union

Karen Lyons and Nathalie Huegler

In this chapter we examine some aspects of migration within a "regional" rather than a national context, and focus particularly on Europe. While "Europe" might be regarded as a geographical region encompassing a large number of countries, two groupings have been established since the end (in 1945) of World War II. Both the Council of Europe and the European Union were aimed, minimally, at promoting peaceful interchange between European countries and both have accrued additional roles and powers in the decades since the late 1940s. In fact, the European Union (EU), encompassing a smaller membership, has developed as a more significant actor in relation to national policies, not least in the field of migration, and it is with immigration and the EU that this chapter is concerned. In three major sections we shall be considering the characteristics of immigration into and within the EU; some of the major policies promoted by the EU in relation to immigration; and particular aspects of the immigrant experience within this (sub)region. However, first we shall say a bit more about the geography of Europe; the Council of Europe, and the membership of the EU itself.

Unlike a continent such as North America, the borders of Europe and its constituent countries are complex and contested: it is a region of great diversity, not least as demonstrated by the large number of languages spoken (over 50) with related variations between and within in national cultures. Geographically, it stretches from islands such as Greenland and Iceland in the northwest across the Nordic and Baltic countries to encompass part of the huge territories of Russia in the northeast. In the southwest it includes the Iberian Peninsula and off-shore islands related to Portugal and Spain, while in the southeast it extends to Turkey (or at least to the "European part" located West of the Bosphorus, the remainder having traditionally been viewed as part of Asia Minor). Fundamental to this conception of "Europe" is the notion of countries that historically were part of "Christendom," whether they were part of Catholic (and later Protestant) or Orthodox (Greek or Russian) traditions. While the Mediterranean Sea has for centuries provided a natural border separating European countries from those of North Africa, the Middle East, and Asia Minor, it also provided an important trade route and more recently it has assumed significance as a sea route for entry to the European Union (notably via Italy and Spain), for instance, by undocumented migrants.

Geographically, therefore, in 2007 Europe consisted of 48 countries, 47 of which (with a combined population of 800 million) are members of the Council of Europe (the exception being Belarus). This Council—which should not be confused with the European Union—was established in 1949 in Strasbourg, France (where it is still based), with the specific purpose of defending "human rights, parliamentary democracy and the rule of law." Accordingly, one of its first actions was to draft the European Convention on Human Rights (1950) which should be ratified by all countries in membership. It also established the European Court of Human Rights, to which individuals can bring cases which apparently contravene the Convention by national governments. Rulings of the court are not binding on member states but they have symbolic value in identifying legislation and executive actions which are at variance with human rights: findings have thus sometimes played a part in subsequent policy change in individual countries. Current aims of the Council of Europe include the promotion of Europe's cultural identity and diversity; and finding common solutions to current challenges (Council of Europe, 2008a). Although established earlier and having a much wider membership, the Council does not have the same range of powers or aspirations as the European Union, although there are clearly areas of overlap in their areas of concern, and some of the issues related to immigration to EU countries arise from conditions in other member states of the Council of Europe.

The European Union also grew out of an initiative taken in 1950 (the establishment of the European Coal and Steel Community), aimed at ensuring peaceful trade and use of resources between six countries which had previously been on opposing sides in World War II (Belgium, France, [W] Germany, Italy, Luxembourg, and the Netherlands). In 1957 the ECSC members agreed the Treaty of Rome, which established the European Economic Community (EEC, often referred to as the Common Market) and this body was joined by Denmark, Ireland, and the UK in 1973. Policy developments at the time were mainly concerned with economic and trading arrangements (for instance, establishing a common agricultural policy to address food shortages) although the EEC also became more involved in policy developments in the field of employment. 1979 marked a shift toward the democratization of the Community, giving all citizens of member states a chance to elect European Members of Parliament. The European Parliament joined the European Council of Ministers in approving laws drafted by staff employed by the European Commission (the executive arm of the EU) and complimenting the work of the European Court of Justice (which has responsibility for the interpretation of European law and any disputes concerning its application by member states).

Further states joined the EEC in the next two decades (Greece in 1981; Spain and Portugal in 1986; Austria, Finland, and Sweden in 1995), and 1993 saw the formal establishment of the European Union with the ratification of the Maastricht Treaty. This marked the completion of the "Single Market" allowing for the free movement of goods, services, capital, and people within the area of the EU. It also set out rules for a single currency (since adopted by 12 countries); joint foreign and security policy; and increased cooperation over justice and domestic policies, including in relation to immigration. 2004 saw a significant expansion of the EU membership with the inclusion of "the accession states" mainly from the former East European bloc (Czech Republic, Estonia, Hungary, Latvia, Lithuania, Poland, Slovakia, and Slovenia, as well as Cyprus and Malta) and these were joined by Romania and Bulgaria in 2007. Croatia, Macedonia, and Turkey are currently (2009) seeking membership. The number of countries within the EU has therefore nearly doubled since 2004 and now stands at 27, representing 495 million citizens (Europa, 2008).

As should be clear from the foregoing, the EU is not therefore a "region" in a geographical sense but it is a political entity whose members comprise a substantial part of the European continent. Its member states are for the most part wealthy—although there are significant variations between the GDPs of established members relative to those of some of the more recent members, as well as countries beyond its borders. Additionally, it should be noted that two of the wealthiest countries in Europe, Switzerland and Norway, are not members of the European

Union. Having identified the origins, countries, and main institutions of the EU, we shall say more about its policies as these relate to immigration, after we have looked at the scale and flows of immigration in this context. We shall finally discuss the experiences of immigrants in the EU context.

Migration to Europe

The history of Europe is inherently connected with migrations, involving not only people moving across borders, but also "borders [moving] over people" (Bade, 2003, p. x). While labor migration and itinerant trade played an important role in Europe at the time of transition from agrarian to industrialized societies, early examples of forced migration included French Protestant Huguenots seeking refuge in seventeenth-century Britain (Bade, 2003; Marfleet, 2006).

The large scale uprooting of people across Europe by the end of World War II brought about the United Nations Refugee Convention of 1951, which, through a protocol in 1967, subsequently became universally applicable to refugees throughout the world. While the immediate postwar years were predominantly a time of *emigration* from Western Europe (particularly to the Americas), millions of people also moved *into* the region. This included ethnic German minorities from Eastern European territories, which had come under Soviet control, and "returnees" from former British, French and Dutch colonies to the "mother countries." Despite the postwar devastation, economic growth and subsequent labor shortages from the mid-1950s onward led to migrant worker recruitment in most Western European countries. Some countries provided opportunities for long-term settlement of immigrants (e.g., Sweden, UK, France), while others, notably Germany and Switzerland, attempted to prevent settlement of temporary "guest workers" through systems of "rotating" recruitment. Typically young and male, migrant workers were recruited mainly from South European states, North Africa, and Turkey. At the same time, France and the UK attracted migrants from former colonies in Africa, the Caribbean, and the Indian subcontinent to fill labor shortages, often relying on "word-of-mouth" advertisement among potential immigrants rather than formal recruitment systems (Schierup et al.,

2006). By 1970, around 11 million migrants were living in Western Europe, accounting for 5% of the total population (Castles, 2000). Policies changed drastically with the oil crisis and economic downturn in the early 1970s, and "guest workers" were expected to return. Instead, the ending of this phase of recruitment led many migrants (particularly those from non-EU states such as Turkey or Yugoslavia) to stay on. In the following years, many were joined by family members.

Since the 1980s and 1990s, migration to Europe has changed significantly—in parallel with fundamental political, socioeconomic and demographic transformations affecting the region (as part of global processes of change). Several trends have been observed to characterize migration in recent decades, including globalization, flexibilization, "illegalization" and politicization (Schierup et al., 2006; Statham and Gray, 2005). Different migration patterns (and associated public discourses) are distinguished between EU members in the "north" (or "west") of the region (e.g., Germany, France, the UK, and Sweden), the "south" (e.g. Spain, Italy, or Greece), and "new" member states in Central and Eastern Europe (Statham and Gray, 2005). These differences concern the (changing) status of regions as predominantly "sending," "receiving," or "transit" areas, and, to some extent, the dominance of specific "categories" of migration—for example, asylum, undocumented/ irregular and (skilled) labor migration.

Asylum migration to North and West European countries increased from the mid-1970s onward. In the first decades after World War II, the "classical refugees of the Cold War" (Castles and Loughna, 2005, p. 40) had predominantly been dissidents from Eastern Bloc countries. These immigrants were relatively few in number and marginal in terms of "political" and economic costs to the countries providing protection. Meanwhile, conflicts in Southern Europe, Africa, and Asia had led to increasing refugee flows from the 1960s onward, with many of those fleeing able to reach EU countries as labur migrants. However, when recruitment schemes ceased, claiming asylum became the only available route to safety for many, including for migrants with "mixed motivations" of seeking escape from repressive regimes *and* following existing patterns of settlement (e.g., Turkish / Kurdish asylum applicants in Germany) (Castles and Loughna, 2005).

The number of asylum applications rose in the early 1990s, reaching a "peak" of over 670,000 in EU countries in 1992 (438,190 in Germany alone), mainly from Eastern Europe (particularly Romania and former Yugoslavian states), as well as Africa (e.g., Somalia and DR Congo), Asia (e.g., Afghanistan, Iran, and Sri Lanka), and the Middle East (Eurostat, 2007; Castles and Loughna, 2005). This was accompanied by politically fueled "panic" about migration and the introduction of increasingly restrictive systems of border control and deterrence (Schierup et al., 2006). Although the number of applications had fallen significantly by the mid-1990s, asylum migration continued (and continues) to dominate the public and political discourse on migration in North and West European countries.

Economic and demographic changes in Southern Europe from the 1980s onward meant that states such as Spain, Greece, and Italy were transformed into countries of immigration, and, through the process of European integration, gained significance as "border guards" of EU territory. Many migrants reaching Western Europe have since that time had to resort to increasingly sophisticated "illegal" means of crossing borders, frequently using the "services" of people smugglers. Such "undocumented" migration takes many different forms—including irregular entry with subsequent "regularization," and irregular stay following the expiry of "regular" statuses. For instance, estimates suggest that around 1 million undocumented migrants (mainly from Latin America, Eastern Europe, and North Africa) were living in Spain in 2003, at least 500,000 in Italy (2006), and similar numbers in Portugal (2004) and Greece (2006) (IOM, 2008). In addition to land routes from Eastern Europe and Asia, the Mediterranean functions as a main "border" crossed by migrants from North Africa (although the Canary Islands, part of Spain, have also recently become a significant "entry point" from West Africa). Various regularization initiatives have been launched to "legalize" the presence of undocumented migrants, particularly in Italy and Spain.

Although irregular migration is often debated from a perspective emphasizing migrants'

desired economic gains and the exact figures are unknown, at least several hundred thousand people are estimated to be victims of a subform of irregular migration, namely trafficking for (labor, sexual, and other forms of) exploitation (Council of Europe, 2008b). The links between irregular and forced migration are both longstanding and complex: not only have refugees often been faced with irregularity as the only route of escape, but states themselves have been identified as complicit beneficiaries of a cheap and "disposable," and arguably "unfree" workforce (Marfleet, 2006, p. 184).

The role of Central and Eastern European countries in relation to migration has shifted significantly in the past 20 years—moving from pre-1989 regimes (which allowed very little international mobility); through being countries of emigration and transit or "buffer zones" for irregular migration to western EU states; to gaining significance as destination countries particularly for asylum-seekers from the Russian Federation (Statham and Gray, 2005). In this process, there has been considerable pressure from "established" EU countries on new and potential Central and East European members to introduce measures of border enforcement and deterrence.

In 2005, the total number of international migrants in Europe (as a whole region) was estimated at over 64 million—8.8% of the overall population (UN, 2006), around 40 million of whom lived in the 27 states now constituting the EU (own calculations). From 2001 to 2006, the number of asylum applications to the European Union[1] decreased by over 50%, with a slight increase in 2007 (229,000), mainly attributed to a growing number of refugees fleeing the Iraq war (UNHCR, 2008). Notably, this increase has affected mainly Southern European countries, Sweden, and some "new" EU member states—whereas "traditional" destination countries (e.g., Germany, France, and Austria) recorded fewer applications. Main countries of origin in 2007 were Iraq (18.4% of all applications), the Russian Federation (8%), Pakistan (6.3%), Serbia (6.1%), Somalia (4.5%), and Afghanistan (3.7%) (UNHCR, 2008). Within this overall view, however, diverse patterns exist for individual countries, which no longer necessarily follow historical links.[2]

Despite ongoing public and political concerns about asylum migration in many European states, numbers are relatively small in the context of overall immigration, including movement within the EU itself. Eurostat (2008a), the EU statistics organization, suggests that around 3 million international migrants settled in the EU-27 area in 2006, around 1.8 million of whom were non-EU nationals.[3] However, in terms of nationality, the largest group came from Poland (290,000), followed by Romanians (230,000), and—only in third place—Moroccans (140,000). British and German nationals were also active in migration, and their numbers, at 100,000 and 90,000 migrants respectively, were over 3.5 times the total number of asylum applications made to the same countries in 2007. While Spain, Germany, and the UK reported the highest numbers of international immigrants (around 800,000; 560,000; and 450,000 respectively), only Spain had higher *per capita* immigration.

Given the comparative youth of new migrants, particularly from non-EU countries,[4] there have been both demographic and economic arguments in favor of continued net immigration into the EU, a region with falling birth rates and a projected 7-year increase in median age to 47.9 by 2060, with the population aged over 80 years expected to triple (Eurostat, 2008b). Several European countries have continued to experience labor shortages in certain industries in recent years, and have therefore been running (usually temporary) recruitment programs for both unskilled and highly skilled migrants from within the EU and beyond its borders. Immigrants form a significant part of the work force in sectors such as agriculture and construction, or in the fields of IT and health care (Martin, 2007; Schierup et al. 2006). The extent to which such new "guest worker" schemes will continue following the 2008 global economic downturn, and whether such employment will lead to new long-term settlement, will need further exploration. On the other hand, there are also indications that at least some of the contemporary patterns of migration to and mobility within the EU are *transnational*—involving networks and communities that exist across national boundaries and that follow circular patterns of "flux" and "flow" rather than linear paths of emigration, immigration, and settlement (Favell, 2008; Marfleet, 2006).

EU Frameworks and Policies

As identified above, the EU is a political entity with the ability to promote policies and legislation that should be agreed to by all member states and that should therefore inform national policy debates and actions of its members. Of course, the EU and member states should also observe international (United Nations) declarations (e.g., on Human Rights, 1948) and regional conventions (e.g., the European Convention on Human Rights, 1950), particularly those relating to refugees (e.g., the UN Convention on the Status of Refugees, 1951). Similarly, migrant labor should be protected by the provisions of the International Labour Organisation's (ILO) Declaration on Fundamental Principles and Rights at Work and the ILO's aim to promote the idea of "decent work." However, in reality, the experience of different categories of immigrants can vary significantly between EU member states, according to a range of factors including public attitudes and political initiatives as well as the economic resources either to "police borders" or to address the needs of immigrants on arrival or at the settlement stage.

As can be seen from the foregoing section, some EU countries, while often benefiting from their labor, have also felt under heavy pressure from immigrants from poorer neighboring states over the past decade or so. While wars and poverty in African countries have for several decades led to immigration mainly to former colonial countries, two particular events on the European continent itself led to greater movement from the former Eastern Bloc countries, namely, the fall of the Berlin Wall (1989) and the break up of Yugoslavia in the early nineties. Thus, by the 1990s the European Union was taking a more active role in the regulation of immigration, and individual countries have since also enacted more restrictive and even repressive legislation.

One of the issues facing the EU and member states concerns the conflation of debates and policy formation in relation to immigration with those related to a specific group of immigrants, that is, asylum-seekers. In addition, the attacks on the World Trade Center in the United States in 2001 and subsequent attacks in Spain (2004) and the UK (2005) have led to a conflation of immigration control policies with measures designed to support "the war on terror." In effect, immigrants have increasingly been seen as a threat to (national) security or, at very least, as people who are the perpetrators or victims of international criminal activities, such as drug smuggling or people trafficking. In this section we therefore consider ways in which the EU has sought to regulate immigration and to address some of the issues that have been identified as related to immigration.

Despite a recent "firming up" of EU policies and instruments in the area of immigration, this is not a new focus of concern for some of its member states—nor is the association with terrorism and criminality. In 1976 the Trevi group was established within the then EEC to counteract "terrorism, radicalism, extremism and violence" (Lyons, 1999, p. 120). Further moves were made toward harmonizing national immigration laws over the next decades, including the establishment of the Schengen Agreement on intergovernmental processes in relation to population movement in 1990. This agreement abolished border controls between signatory countries (initially, France, Germany, Belgium, Netherlands, Luxembourg, Italy, Spain, and Portugal); introduced common visa and "carrier liability" policies; detailed checks on non-EU nationals; a list of "undesirable aliens"; and a stipulation that asylum-seekers must apply in their first country of entry and, if refused, are not eligible to seek asylum elsewhere in the EU. With the enactment of the "free mobility of labor" provision under the Maastricht (Single Market) Treaty in 1993, most of these provisions (including the last) have since been adopted by all EU member states whether or not they were formerly part of the Schengen group. The role played by some EU countries in promoting restrictive immigration policies had earned it the title, "Fortress Europe" (Moraes, 2003).

However, it was not until 1999 that a general EU Asylum and Migration Policy was formulated at a meeting of Council Ministers in Tampere. The comprehensive nature of this spanned "the areas of Justice and Home Affairs, Development and Humanitarian Assistance and Common Foreign and Security policy...(and) has consolidated existing restrictive national asylum practices in an effort to curb unregulated migration into the Union" (Lindstrom, 2006, p. 29). In the ensuing period six directives or regulations were passed as follows:

Temporary Protection Directive (2001/55/EC) setting minimum standards for temporary provision for displaced persons;

Reception Directive (2003/9/EC) laying down the minimum standards for the reception of asylum-seekers;

Dublin 2 Regulation (EC No. 343/2003) identifying member state responsibility and procedures for examining an asylum application lodged by a third country national;

Family Reunification Directive (2003/86/EC) on the right to family reunification;

Qualification Directive (8043/04 Asile 23 (2004)) setting minimum standards for the qualification and status of refugees and others needing international protection and the content of the protection granted;

The Procedures Directive (14203/04, Asile 64 (2004)) setting minimum standards for granting and withdrawing refugee status (adapted from Lindstrom, 2006, p. 40).

In addition to developing this shared policy framework in relation to asylum-seekers and refugees, discussions are underway to explore the feasibility of establishing a Common European Asylum *system* (potentially to be adopted by the end of 2010) aimed at the joint processing of asylum applications within the EU. This is building on the work of the Hague Program, which, since 2005, has launched pilot refugee protection programs, including assistance to countries for improving local infrastructure; local integration of refugees; and cooperation on legal migration. In addition, attention has also been paid to the sustainable return of immigrants and "prevention" of future migration through EU programs aimed at addressing issues such as governance, citizenship rights, and human trafficking as well as the economic problems that are often contributory aspects of the "push factors" operating in the migration process. These include the AENEAS program (from 2004[5]) and the Migration, Asylum Refugees Regional Initiative (MARRI) with its focus on the Western Balkan region (Lindstrom, 2006).

A comprehensive approach, partly in relation to refugees but now also in relation to "illegal immigration," is very much the goal of the European Union, but coordinated actions are not without their tensions and setbacks (Moraes, 2003).

This links with the role of individual states in controlling immigration flows and also debates about the citizenship rights of immigrants, particularly in relation to welfare provisions. In relation to the first, there are indications that patterns of immigration in the EU are changing, assisted by national government policies. For instance, it seems that the British Government took advantage of the enlargement of the EU in 2005 and subsequent immigration from the accession states (notably Poland and the Baltic States) to restrict immigration from outside the EU. One example was the amendment of the list of "shortage occupations" (for which staff recruited from overseas could be given work permits) to exclude workers in the social care field. However, there is also anecdotal evidence that, as the economy of the UK has gone into recession, workers from other EU countries previously employed, for instance in the construction industry, have returned to their home countries (BBC, 2008).

In relation to the second point, Geddes (2003) has pointed out that there is no simple or consistent pattern of relationships between immigrants and welfare systems across the EU countries, but rather that account must be taken of the type of "welfare state" prevalent in individual member states and the identification of particular types of immigrants, as being "wanted" or "unwanted." These categories denote the contribution which particular types of immigrants are expected to make to national economies relative to the strain that others are perceived as placing on welfare systems. A significant aspect of recent public debates and political initiatives in most member states has been an ever tighter demarcation of "the community of legitimate receivers of welfare state benefits (relative to those) deemed bogus or abusive" (Geddes, 2003, p. 150). This reflects—or is reflected in—contradictory pressures to expand migration relative to policies aimed at closure and protection of national resources.

However, immigrants can be seen as the victims rather than the cause of policies aimed at curtailing expenditure on welfare states, which have been a common feature of EU countries over the past decade—or in Geddes' terms "international migration . . . possesses the capacity neither to save nor to destroy these welfare states" (2003, p. 151). Geddes (2003) goes on to summarize the welfare state model proposed by Esping-Andersen (1990) with the addition of a Southern rim type; and uses the examples of the UK (liberal type); Germany (conservative-corporatist type); Denmark (social democratic type), and Italy and Portugal (Southern rim) to illustrate the different positions that immigrants occupy relative to welfare states. These include the weakened position and isolation of asylum-seekers in relation to the British welfare system; labor market protection in Germany; increased marginalization of "unwanted immigrants" in Denmark; and the relatively greater "space" for immigrants in the informal economies of Southern Europe (where, in general, welfare states have been less developed).

However, while national policies might indicate increased marginalization and exclusion of (some types of) immigrants (accompanied by, or as a result of, the rise in popularity of center- or far right political parties (Saggar, 2003)), the EU, mindful of the human rights of all its "citizens"—or perhaps fearful of the social unrest that can result from social exclusion,[6] has advanced various policies aimed more broadly at promoting social inclusion (since the 1990s). More recently, policies have included reference to the notion of "valuing diversity" or, more specifically, a logo including the tag line, "For Diversity—Against Discrimination" used in a campaign launched in 2008. This shift might be seen as both an increased acknowledgment of the complex nature of diversity in all EU societies but also a loss of faith in the effectiveness of multicultural policies, as propounded for example, in the UK since the 1980s. The 2008 campaign "aims to inform people about their rights and obligations under EU wide anti-discrimination legislation": its remit clearly extends wider than simply to immigrants but, given the high degree of ethnic diversity in many EU member states, immigrants could be the beneficiaries of improved public attitudes and governmental policies aimed at addressing discrimination on the grounds of "racial or ethnic origin" and/or "religion and belief" (*For Diversity, Against Discrimination*, 2008). While this is primarily an information campaign aimed at influencing public opinion, the existence of EU-wide legislation in this field is also aimed at promoting policies in particular member states which are more consistent with human rights values and with legislation already implemented in many other European countries. This suggestion—that conditions are not the same for immigrants in all EU states, together with the earlier comments about immigrants and "the welfare state," leads us on to a discussion about ways in which experiences of immigrants might differ.

"The Immigrant Experience" in a European Perspective

The experiences of any migrant are likely to be shaped by a variety of factors and circumstances. These include the extent to which receiving countries provide or deny "newcomers" opportunities for inclusion and participation, public "discourses" about migration and the responses of "settled" (indigenous and existing ethnic minority) communities, as well as the ways in which migrants themselves deal with processes of displacement, exile and resettlement.

Migrants arriving in European countries in the postwar decades faced different conditions as far as states' attitudes toward the nature and duration of their stay was concerned. Subsequently, "guest workers" in Germany experienced what Schierup et al. (2006, p. 40–45) describe as "differential exclusion," meaning that they were given (partial) access to the labor market and some aspects of welfare provision—while being excluded from political participation and citizenship. De facto, a variety of circumstances (including employers wanting to retain trained workers) had led to long-term settlement, particularly of Turkish ethnic minorities. Nevertheless, the political and public denial of the multiethnic reality perpetuated the ongoing conceptualization of third- and fourth-generation immigrants[7] as "foreigners." This continued into the new millennium, when access to citizenship was gradually (and reluctantly) improved (Schierup et al., 2006). In other instances, models of "assimilation" or (varying forms of) multiculturalism dominated in countries' responses to immigration. The former involves a belief that immigrants, if granted full citizenship rights and encouraged to adopt social and cultural practices of the receiving country, will over time become indistinguishable from the indigenous population—a model which has impacted on the experiences of North African migrants to France, but which has been criticized for ignoring structural inequalities and racism (Schierup et al., 2006). Multiculturalism, on the other hand, has been applied in various ways in countries such as Sweden, the UK, and the Netherlands—with the general expectation that different ethnic groups will form distinct communities but have equal rights. Such approaches have been criticized by some for promoting separatism, and more recently, accused of encouraging fundamentalism. In many European countries, recent debate and rhetoric has focused on the need for immigrants to adhere to certain "core values" and on "social cohesion" (Zetter et al., 2006).

While different "legacies" continue to influence the experiences of settled immigrant and ethnic minority populations in "old" EU countries, many more recently arrived migrants are subjected to new, more pronounced forms of exclusion. For instance, asylum-seekers in particular have, in many countries, progressively been barred from accessing mainstream welfare provisions, denied access to the (regular) labor market, detained (during and after the determination of their claims) and compulsorily dispersed, preventing settlement in areas with existing community links (Schuster, 2006). For many undocumented migrant workers, particularly in South European countries, the (sometimes strategic) exploitation of their labor has contrasted with exclusion from social rights—while even periodic regularization programs, suggesting that some barriers to immigration are only "notional" (Marfleet, 2006, p. 170), have merely led to new temporary and precarious positions (Schierup et al., 2006). Zorn (2007) provides an example of the manifestations of "new" exclusions in Slovenia: in addition to barriers faced by refugees, asylum-seekers, and undocumented migrants, over 18,000 people who had entered Slovenia in the 1970s from fellow Yugoslavian republics became "erased" from the register of permanent residents in 1992, losing the social and political rights they had previously shared in preconflict Yugoslavia (an example of "borders moving over people," as mentioned earlier in this chapter).

Exclusionary policies toward migrants seem to be both influenced by and precipitating negative public attitudes. The sustained "othering" of Turkish and other migrant groups in Germany led to a series of racist attacks in the early 1990s, at the heart of national reunification (Marfleet, 2006). Those very incidents were, however, used as arguments for further restrictions of migrants' rights, purporting that "too lenient" migration control systems had fueled these violent acts. While there have been examples throughout history of migrants being vilified in the press of receiving societies, more recent media coverage in European countries draws explicit links between migration and threats to the security and very integrity (in cultural, social, and economic terns) of receiving societies (Marfleet, 2006; Solé, 2004). The Independent Asylum Commission (2008) in the UK found that a large proportion of the British public had negative associations with the term "asylum" and that most drew on national media in forming their views (with minimal direct contact with asylum-seekers themselves). Looking at Southern European states, Solé (2004) finds a paradoxical dynamic: although migrants fill vacancies rejected by indigenous workers, public perception is that "newcomers" are profiting more than the settled population—while on the other hand, the progressive socioeconomic marginalization of migrants contributes to sustained negative public attitudes toward them. In this context, recent debate has polarized "new" and "established" migration, portraying the former as a "threat" to social cohesion and community relations (Zetter et al., 2006). A pessimistic view in the current phase of economic downturn is that the negative rhetoric directed at "new" migrants will increase further.

In the face of dominant and powerful negative discourses on migration, there has rightfully been an increased emphasis, particularly in the field of forced migration studies, on perspectives that stem from "real-life" individual and group experiences of migrants. In respect of Europe's longer-standing immigrant and ethnic minority communities, the gap between expectations and lived experiences has often been a dominant feature. hile many immigrants from former colonies to the UK or France had been motivated by the notion of moving to the "mother country," upon arrival, this often contrasted with experiences of racism, discrimination in employment, and deplorable housing conditions (Castles, 2000). On the other hand, many "guest workers" in Germany or Switzerland held to the idea of eventual return, even after their grandchildren had been born and grown up in the "host" country. The resulting ambivalence continues to influence concepts of identity, particularly among Germany's large Turkish ethnic minority population.

For refugees, expectations of life in countries of asylum are likely to be variable—given that a significant proportion of those crossing borders with smugglers have limited knowledge about their exact final destination (e.g., Marfleet, 2006). Experiences before and during migration (such as war, violence, and the loss of freedom, rights, and familiar sociocultural environments), as well as upon arrival (including access to psychosocial and material support) have been found to have a significant influence on refugees' experiences of acculturation (e.g., Dona and Berry, 1999). The external and internal barriers of "Fortress Europe" lead refugees to undertake complex, risky journeys with considerable time spent "in orbit" (Marfleet, 2006, p. 221), while they continue to face adverse conditions in destination countries. This can include experiences of further violence and victimization—such as the (in one case, fatal) hostilities suffered by a group of asylum-seekers dispersed by the British government to a deprived council estate in Glasgow (Hickman et al., 2008). On the other hand, the many examples of refugees' extreme marginalization have been juxtaposed by movements, throughout Europe, of solidarity and even civil resistance from the settled population in support of "new arrivals" (Marfleet, 2006).

Some of the experiences of recent labor migrants reflect trends such as the flexibilization of work or the commodification of services in European societies. McGregor (2007), for example, provides accounts of Zimbabwean care workers in the UK, some of whom, coming from well-educated backgrounds, felt unable to admit to families "back home" that they had joined the ranks of the "BBC" (or "British

Bottom Cleaners")—many expressing their shock at Western approaches to care for elderly people. At the same time, a growing body of research highlights how changed patterns of migration, particularly circular and transnational migration within the enlarged EU, transform the very structures and practices of families—such as the "transnational" care, provided mainly by migrant women, for "left-behind" children or older people (e.g., Ryan et al., 2009).

The latter point links to the influence of factors such as gender, age, or disability on the migration experience. Children, for example, are, for various reasons, considered particularly vulnerable. Their involvement in migration to EU countries includes being trafficked, on the street, or being "unaccompanied" and "accompanied" asylum-seeking children. Perspectives on the experiences of children highlight, in a particular way, that migration policies and professional interventions (e.g., by social workers providing care and protection for children) need to be set in a context of human rights. On the other hand, such perspectives also remind us of the complex nexus between "vulnerability" and "agency" within which the experiences of many migrants are constructed.

Conclusion

In this chapter we have focused on the nature and scale of immigration into and within the European Union; with the particular policies and strategies that the EU has devised to address issues of migration and associated diversity; and with the differential experiences of immigrants within the EU. We have taken the EU as providing a framework for analysis and source of statistical data, while also indicating at various points the way in which individual member states demonstrate their own "autonomy" or illustrate (on the basis of their distinct national histories and cultures) different opportunities and constraints for immigrants.

Lindstrom (2006) has suggested that the EU faces three challenges "to manage population movements in a way that upholds basic human rights and the institution of asylum . . . to safeguard the legitimate interests of the states and communities affected by (immigration) . . . to invest the necessary political resources in preventing and

reversing the causes of involuntary migration" (p. 43). He was referring specifically to concerns about whether EU policies respect international legal standards, particularly in relation to refugees; whether sufficient recognition will be given to the needs of some countries and the EU as a whole for a reliable labor supply (given national and EU demographics); and whether policies and programs can be implemented that effectively improve conditions in "sending countries" (rather than simply aiming to prevent immigration or to return immigrants to their home countries).

One of the points made in this chapter concerns the association often made between immigration and crime, whether in the form of people trafficking or other forms of (international) criminal activity (including drug smuggling). Clearly, there are real issues in this area that need to be addressed through intergovernmental policies and cross-border cooperation between a range of agencies and professionals: some of this work can be carried out in the context of the EU and some must be on the basis of arrangements between European institutions and countries and their counterparts in other regions of the world. These are indeed significant challenges for the European Union in a context in which public opinion in many member states is suspicious if not downright hostile toward many immigrants, particularly those differentiated on the grounds of race or religion (actual or assumed).

However, in this climate, efforts to promote more positive attitudes to diversity and observance of antidiscriminatory legislation at EU and national levels also need to be supported as do debates about the nature of citizenship and the rights of various types of immigrants. A contribution to the latter has been made by Kymlicka (2003, p. 195) who identifies alternative views as follows: "in a world of migration . . . the whole notion of national citizenship is increasingly obsolete"—new ways of assigning rights and responsibilities need to be devised.

Alternatively, (he suggests) others believe that increasing levels of ethnic and religious diversity require greater effort (by governments) to "construct and sustain a sense of common national citizenship," that is, "a revaluation of citizenship." Either of these approaches might provide increased opportunities—or at least less negative conditions—for the development of more just immigration policies and more positive experiences of immigrants in the EU.

Notes

1. In 2001 around 400,000 applications were recorded—this figure decreased to just under 200,000 in 2006 (Eurostat, 2007).
2. For example, over 18,000 applications from Iraqi nationals were made in Sweden in 2007, but only 144 in France. Greece, on the other hand, which, overall, had more applications than Germany, received applications from over 9,000 Pakistani nationals—contrasting with only 61 such applications in Sweden (and, given historical links, a still comparatively low number of 1,765 in the UK) (UNHCR, 2008).
3. This includes migration of non-EU nationals from one EU country to another.
4. The median age among immigrants from non-EU countries was 27.7 in 2006, compared with a median age of the current EU population of 40.4 (Eurostat, 2008a and 2008b).
5. The ANEAS program has since been replaced by the Thematic Cooperation Programme with Third Countries in the Development Aspects of Migration and Asylum, set out between 2007 and 2013 (European Commission, 2008).
6. For instance, the rioting that took place in some of the poorer districts of Paris and other French towns densely inhabited by immigrant communities in 2007 and 2005 (CNN, 2007).
7. This was particularly the case for immigrants from non-EU countries, who were non-Christian, or were "non-White."

References

Bade, K. (2003) *Migration in European History*. Oxford: Blackwell Publishing.

BBC (2008, Oct. 28) *Homeward bound?* BBC Radio Five Live Breakfast.

Castles, S. (2000) *Ethnicity and Globalization*. London: Sage.

Castles, S., and Loughna, S. (2005) "Trends in asylum migration to industrialized countries, 1990–2001," in Borjas, G., and Crisp, J. (eds.) *Poverty, International Migration, and Asylum*. Basingstoke: Palgrave Macmillan.

CNN (2007, November 27) *French suburbs rocked by more riots*. http://edition.cnn.com/2007/WORLD/ europe/11/27/france.riots/index.html (accessed 12.12.08).

Council of Europe (2008a) *About the Council of Europe*. www.coe.int/T/E/Com/About_COE/ (accessed 08.11.08).

Council of Europe (2008b) *Trafficking in Human Beings: Slaves at the Heart of Europe*. www.coe.int/T/E/Com/ Files/Themes/trafficking/ (accessed 08.11.08).

Dona, G., and Berry, J. (1999) "Refugee acculturation and re-acculturation," in Ager, A. (ed.) *Refugees: Perspectives on the Experience of Forced Migration*. London: Pinter.

Esping-Anderson, G. (1990) *The Three Worlds of Welfare Capitalism*. Cambridge, Polity Press.

Europa (2008) *Gateway to the European Union*. www.europa.eu (accessed 08.11.08).

European Commission (2008) *Migration and Asylum Overview*. http://ec.europa.eu/europeaid/where/ worldwide/migration-asylum/index_en.htm (accessed 12.12.08).

Eurostat (2007) *Asylum Applications in the European Union*. Statistics in focus 110/2007.

Eurostat (2008a) *Recent Migration Trends: Citizens of EU–27 Member States Become ever more Mobile while EU Remains Attractive to non-EU Citizens*. Statistics in focus 98/2008.

Eurostat (2008b) *Aging Characterises the Demographic Perspectives of the European Societies*. Statistics in focus 72/2008.

Favell, A. (2008) "The new face of East-West migration in Europe," *Journal of Ethnic and Migration Studies*, 34(5): 701–716.

For Diversity, against Discrimination (2008). www.stop-discrimination.info (accessed 28.11.08).

Geddes, A. (2003) "Migration and the welfare state in Europe," in Spencer, S. (ed) *The Politics of Migration: Managing Opportunity, Conflict and Change*. Oxford, Blackwell Publishing.

Hickman, M., Crowley, H., and Mai, N. (2008) *Immigration and Social Cohesion in the UK: The Rhythms and Realities of Everyday Life*. York: Joseph Rowntree Foundation/London Metropolitan University.

Independent Asylum Commission (2008) *Saving Sanctuary: The Independent Asylum Commission's First Report of Conclusions and Recommendations*. www.independentasylumcommission.org.uk/files/ Saving%20Sanctuary.pdf (accessed 20.11.08).

IOM (International Organisation for Migration) (2008) *World Migration 2008: Managing Labour Mobility in the Evolving Global Economy*. Geneva: IOM.

Jones Finer, C. (ed.) (2006) *Migration, Immigration, and Social Policy*. Oxford: Blackwell Publishing.

Kymlicka, W. (2003) "Immigration, citizenship, multiculturalism: Exploring the links," in Spencer, S. (ed) *The Politics of Migration: Managing Opportunity, Conflict and Change*. Oxford, Blackwell Publishing.

Lindstrom, C. (2006) "European Union policy on asylum and immigration: Addressing the root causes of forced migration; A justice and home affairs policy of freedom, security and justice?" in Jones Finer, C. (ed) *Migration, Immigration, and Social Policy*. Oxford: Blackwell Publishing.

Lyons, K. (1999) *International Social Work: Themes and Perspectives*. Aldershot: Ashgate.

Martin, P. (2007) *Towards Effective Temporary Worker Programs: Issues and Challenges in Industrial Countries*. International Migration Papers No. 89. Geneva: ILO.

Marfleet, P. (2006) *Refugees in a Global Era*. Basingstoke, UK: Palgrave Macmillan.

McGregor, J. (2007) "Joining the BBC (British Bottom Cleaners): Zimbabwean Migrants and the UK Care Industry," *Journal of Ethnic and Migration Studies* 33(5): 801–824.

Moraes, C. (2003) "The politics of European Union migration policy," in Spencer, S. (ed.) *The Politics of Migration: Managing Opportunity, Conflict and Change*. Oxford, Blackwell Publishing.

Ryan, L., Sales, R., Tilki, M., and Siara, B. (2009) "Family strategies and transnational migration: Recent Polish migrants in London," *Journal of Ethnic and Migration Studies* 35(1): 61–77.

Saggar, S. (2003) "Immigration and the politics of public opinion," in Spencer, S. (ed.) *The Politics of Migration: Managing Opportunity, Conflict and Change*. Oxford, Blackwell Publishing.

Schierup, C.-U.; Hansen, P., and Castles, S. (2006) *Migration, Citizenship, and the European Welfare State: A European Dilemma*. Oxford: Oxford University Press.

Schuster, L. (2006) "A sledgehammer to crack a nut: Deportation, detention and dispersal in Europe." In: Jones Finer, C. (ed.) *Migration, Immigration, and Social Policy*. Oxford: Blackwell Publishers.

Solé, C. (2004) "Immigration policies in Southern Europe," *Journal of Ethnic and Migration Studies* 30(6): 1209–1221.

Spencer, S. (ed.) (2003) *The Politics of Migration: Managing Opportunity, Conflict and Change*. Oxford, Blackwell Publishing.

Statham, P., and Gray, E. (2005) *Briefing Paper: The Politics of Immigration and Asylum Policy in Western Europe*. European Political Communication Working Paper Series No. 12. Leeds: Centre for European Political Communications.

UN (2006) *World Migrant Stock: The 2005 Revision Population Database*. http://esa.un.org/migration/ (accessed 03.12.08).

UNHCR (2008) *Asylum Levels and Trends in Industrialized Countries 2007*. www.unhcr.org/statistics/STATISTICS/47daae862.pdf (accessed 29.09.08).

Zetter, R., Griffiths, D., Sigona, N., Flynn, D., Pasha, T., and Beynon, R. (2006) *Immigration, Social Cohesion, and Social Capital: What Are the Links?* York, UK: Joseph Rowntree Foundation.

Zorn, J. (2007) "Borders, exclusion, and resistance: The case of Slovenia," in Lavalette, M., and Ferguson, I. (eds.) *International Social Work and the Radical Tradition*. Birmingham, UK: Venture Press.

PART VI

Concluding Chapter

30

Immigration Worldwide: Themes and Issues

Doreen Elliott, Uma A. Segal, and Nazneen S. Mayadas

Chapter reviews indicate that countries with high immigrant flows may be suffering from compassion fatigue and both immigration and immigrant policies are beginning to become more stringent. Most countries with increasing immigration have traditionally been nations of emigration, but with declining native populations and increasing economic opportunities are attracting large numbers of migrants from countries other than Western Europe. This is a new phenomenon for several of the "increasing migration" nations and as the entry of immigrants corresponds to the labor needs of their growing economies, policies and programs of entry and integration are receptive and inclusive. However, as immigrant populations are rising rapidly in these nations, there is indication that some of the receptivity is being withdrawn as policies move slowly toward restriction, and evidence the beginnings of attitudes toward immigrants that may reflect those found in nations of high immigration. In countries where immigration is low or declining, policies are pro-immigration, actively seeking both skilled and unskilled labor, services are available, and there is an acceptance of foreigners, even the unauthorized, since the majority of refugees and asylees are from neighboring states. A few nations have

a two-tier system for refugees and for legal migrants and citizens.

Reviews of the chapters reveal that policies of several countries are directed toward exclusion, with the aim to keep out particular groups. An increasing recent concern with ethnic boundaries and global terrorism has contributed to this emphasis (Australia and the United States). Thus, the reception of immigrants by host countries can be viewed as being placed on a continuum from high to low receptivity. In some countries such as Taiwan, Nigeria, Ghana, and Canada skilled workers are likely to be preferred; whereas unskilled labor is needed in the United States, Sweden, and Russia. On the high end of receptivity are those countries that have significant labor force shortages due to demographic changes, where graying of the population occurs through lower birth rates and greater longevity. Immigration policies in these countries recognize the worth of human capital. The chapters on Canada, Sweden, and Ireland give examples of high receptivity with immigrant policies designed to facilitate the integration of newcomers. On the opposite end of the continuum, the theme of compassion fatigue is evidenced in low receptivity (France, the United Kingdom, Poland, the United States, Australia, Asia, and China). Low receptivity applies particularly to refugees, asylees, irregular (undocumented) migrants, and other marginalized populations who have fled their own land for economic or political reasons, and who are grudgingly, if at all, accepted by the wealthy industrialized countries, or even by nations that may be less developed, such as Nigeria, Ghana, and Brazil. This low receptivity is demonstrated, for example, by, unrealistic citizenship readiness tests, lack of government aid for integration demonstrated in early termination of welfare benefits, and no public education to combat xenophobia. The citizens of many rich countries are unaware that demographic trends have produced labor-force shortages and that their countries need immigrants to maintain productivity levels.

Changing Political Boundaries

The phenomenon of human migration is evident in cross-border movements as well as in internal migration. Just as individuals move to different countries in search of improved opportunities, they also relocate themselves and their families from one region of a country to another. However, when nations' political boundaries change, these movements are reclassified, and the policies that govern them are also affected. Thus, the imposition of new political boundaries or the removal of boundaries may put a different face on the picture, although established or commonly occurring migration patterns may not have changed.

The conflict between national political boundaries and long held religious, ethnic, and cultural bonds emerges as a theme in the chapters on Nigeria, Ghana, Pakistan, and Thailand, where political boundaries have been superimposed over historic ethnic and religious affiliations. Another theme prevalent in African countries is that political boundaries of newly established sovereign states are not recognized by nomadic tribesman and merchant traders who, for generations, have adhered only to cultural boundaries. Movement across nations is natural yet national boundaries have been drawn arbitrarily or according to political or economic rather than cultural needs. This is also evident in nations of the European Union where cross-border movement is substantially easier than it once was and labor migration is commonplace.

The dissolution of the Union of the Soviet Socialist Republic (USSR) resulted in the development of several independent states, and what was internal migration prior to its collapse has now become international migration. Likewise, internal migration in the Indian subcontinent became international migration after 1947, when Pakistan was created along its eastern and western borders. Migrants of the regions previously unified may believe they have the right to move as they did before the establishment of boundaries, and receiving nations, such as Russia and India, struggle with the moral obligation of denying entry to these individuals.

The Schengen agreements of 1985, 1990, and 1995, on the other hand, abolished border controls between most countries of the European Union (EU), allowing unrestricted travel and making previously international migration not dissimilar to internal migration. Entry for short term travel (3 months within any 6 month period) into one nation of the Schengen agreement countries of the EU authorizes unrestricted movement to any other Schengen signatory country. These agreements however, opened the way for labor migrants or undocumented immigrants to travel freely also once they had gained access to one country. Permanent settlement and internal migration are however still controlled by member countries' labor migration policies and visa policies and the EU does not have, at this time, a unified immigration policy. Therefore, migrants who seek to use a border EU nation, such as Spain, as a transit country find that legal access to permanency in Germany, for example, is not possible.

Regions such as Africa continue to have national boundaries, but these are political, not ethnic boundaries. Tribes and some ethnic groups have traditionally moved regularly across the continent, particularly if they are of nomadic culture, and the newly established political boundaries have not necessarily deterred this pattern. Chapters on Ghana and Africa discuss the problems arising from lack of congruence between political and ethnic boundaries.

Immigrant Integration

Most countries with large immigrant flows mention integration, but do not specify integration policies, methods, strategies, or processes, suggesting that although all may have integration efforts, emphasis on these may be relatively little in deliberations on immigration. These nations indicate three approaches regarding integration: (1) direct attempts to integrate immigrants through well-established integration policies; (2) assumptions that integration will occur over time, but is dependent on immigrant initiative; and (3) deliberate efforts that keep immigrants excluded through policies that marginalize them.

Canada reports that once people are legally admitted into the country, federal ethnosensitive resources are available to expedite integration efforts. This is evidenced by extensive language education programs, established mechanisms for the transferability of professional credentials from the home country, and equal access to welfare benefits. Sweden has equal and mandatory benefits to integrate into society. For example, employers are required to provide paid time out from work to immigrants to learn the language. France, likewise, has a policy of obligatory integration, and entrants must sign a contract to participate in language and civic integration efforts if they are to be given permanent residence. Nations such as Australia and the United States may believe that integration is necessary, but place no demand on a particular engagement by immigrants, assuming that integration will occur, either through immersion in the receiving country's culture or through immigrant efforts to access resources. Thus, for these nations, integration is dependent on immigrant choice and utilization of opportunities that may be available in the community. South Africa's view of immigration is that of individual choice that does not merit governmental support or involvement. They are deprived of benefits to which natives are entitled such as medical benefits and pensions. Other countries, such as the United Kingdom, implement policies that deliberately keep people marginalized and excluded through policies, controls, and differential support. Certain groups are perceived as "undesirable aliens," if they evidence that they are potential dependents of the state and unable to be self-supporting. The U.S. and France suggest some paradoxical splits, expecting integration, but making immigrants ineligible to receive welfare benefits for several years after their entry. Thus,

these countries' policies allow people to enter as permanent residents, yet they receive support unequal to that of citizens. Birth certificates for children of immigrant parents in Thailand are given at the discretion of the certification officer, reflecting a tendency to devalue immigrant children.

The other side of the integration coin is a nation's perception of cultural diversity. In this world of increasing cross-national mobility, multiculturalism is inevitable. Beliefs in the necessity for assimilation have changed, as is specified by the United States and France, and the thrust is toward integration, which allows people to maintain their own cultures while learning to function successfully in the majority culture. Australian policies view multiculturalism as an asset, and companies utilize employees of diverse cultural backgrounds to serve as mediators with other immigrants in the country as well as recognize their utility in the global market.

Several nations speak to the role of Diasporas in supporting newer immigrants. This is evident in the most extreme form by what the Russian chapter identifies as parallel communities, such as the Chinatowns of Russia and the United States, which have their own financial systems and employment patterns, while still benefiting from the economic opportunities of the host country. This is seen as a form of self-preservation by immigrants who may find it difficult to assimilate into the majority community.

Immigrant integration may be somewhat easier when there are ethnic and religious affiliations, for example in Pakistan and Israel. Pakistan is not affluent, but in the Islamic tradition, has hosted Afghan refugees on its northwest borders for the last twenty years, and many Afghans have since founded villages and settled in Pakistan. Similarly Israel opened its portals to Ethiopian and Russian Jews. At the end of apartheid, New Zealand was a welcoming host to white South Africans who could identify with New Zealand on the basis of language and a Caucasian heritage. However problems arise when, for example, radical immigrant Muslims in the United Kingdom call for an Islamic state based on the "Shari'a" within a Christian Democratic tradition of government, and where division between the radical and moderate Muslims, themselves, exacerbates the conflict.

Furthermore, clashes between a Muslim theocracy and a secular state are reflected in French legislation, such as forbidding the wearing of the "hijab" in schools and other public places. Ethnic, cultural, and religious differences present new challenges in immigrant integration policies in some host nations.

Immigrant Status

Immigration in general and immigrant status in particular are cause for discussion, debate, and concern in most countries of the world and in the chapters included here. Circumstances under which immigrants enter a country clearly differentiate the policies that apply to them, the host nation's perception of them, and their short- and long-term integration into the larger host society in most countries.

While country of origin and the migrants' human resources certainly do affect this, immigrant status greatly affects level of acceptance and integration efforts and possibilities offered by the host nation. All nations have differing categories of immigrant entry. Immigrants may enter legally as voluntary migrants, and most nations admit them for two significant reasons—either because the host country needs the labor/professional skills of the immigrant or because the immigrant is applying for reasons of family reunification. Immigrants may also be admitted for humanitarian reasons and because the nation has signed the UN Convention and is obliged to accept refugees and to process asylees' applications. Undocumented or unauthorized immigrants are found in significant numbers in all countries, and they appear to have mixed reception as most are workers that fulfill labor shortages in the host country.

George, in her chapter on Canada, aptly summarizes Castles' (1997) assertion that a fundamental dilemma in global migration is the contradiction nations evidence in their aims to include and exclude particular groups. These chapters indicate that even within one nation there are conflicting policies or programs about the value of a particular immigrant group. Even perceptions of documented workers are ambiguous as they bring not only their much needed practical skills but also their personal backgrounds, values, and cultures, and the nation is faced with the dilemma pithily voiced by the Swiss writer Max Frisch and quoted by many, "We wanted workers, but we got people."

Most authors have indicated that documented voluntary immigrants are generally perceived as bringing usable human capital. Immigration policies are relatively inclusive if applicants have skills required of the nation and if there are close family connections in the host nation. On the whole, these immigrants are viewed as potential contributors to the country and, at the very least, because of family networks, are less likely to be dependent on the state. However, even so, access to benefits may be limited if one is even a documented immigrant. The United States limits early access to Social Security and welfare benefits to immigrants, and the UK penalizes immigrants if they are deemed "unwanted aliens" by virtue of illness or disability. Interestingly, in the United States, the original governmental office responsible for processing immigration applications, the Immigration and Naturalization Service, in 2001 was moved to the newly created Office of Homeland Security, suggesting that the immigrant entry process is less focused on welcoming the newcomer and more focused on ensuring that the immigrant is not a terrorist threat. Furthermore, since a large segment of the immigrant population in most nations is increasingly sending remittances home, there is some concern that the benefits to the homeland are at the expense of the host country.

People without the requisite documents to live or work in a particular country pose particular dilemmas for host countries. These may be individuals who have come into the country illegally or those who have continued to remain once their legal papers have expired. Clearly they stay because their opportunities and options are greater in the host country than they were in the homeland. All countries in this volume mention struggles to control flows of undocumented immigrants, however, none seems to have captured the ability to do so. While there is some ambiguity about the entry and integration of voluntary documented immigrants, the discourse is substantial about the costs and benefits of the voluntary unauthorized/illegal/undocumented population in a country. All countries indicate estimates of substantial unauthorized workers who may have entered either legally or illegally, but who are working without the proper permits in the host country. These individuals are the focus of numerous debates regarding their necessity in the labor market, their perceived displacement of natives, their utilization of services and benefits, and perceptions that they are a drain on the country's resources. Policies regarding response to their presence vary in nations. The United States continues to debate the guest worker program and, in the meantime, has attempted to prevent entry, at least along the Mexican-U.S. border, penalize workers, and deport undocumented workers, but given the size of the population that is estimated to be at over 12 million, these are feeble attempts. Eight amnesty programs in the United States between 1986 and 2000 allowed over five million unauthorized workers to come out of the shadows, yet these programs are believed to have "failed" as they have not provided a satisfactory solution to the problem. Other nations, such as France and Spain, also write of "border controls," some suggest methods of deporting/repatriating illegal immigrants (Ireland, Israel, South Africa, United States), and yet others have a means to amnesty and citizenship (Greece and Thailand). Others merely speak of policies that "regulate" illegal immigration (China, Brazil, Spain). Several of these measures are short-term minimal resolutions to the dilemma of this population. France and the UK indicate stringent approaches and punitive policies for the control of illegal immigration and residence. Russia recognizes the presence of a large undocumented population and a shadow economy and is also aware that this group is often protected by criminal organizations as it receives no support from Russian law enforcement. In Russia, there is no discussion about a path to legalization. While deportation is the legitimate response to unauthorized immigrants, in reality this is not a satisfactory solution as their labor is necessary in many countries and deportation may violate humanitarian principles; besides, the size of this segment of the population defies deportation. Nigeria's undocumented population is seen as a nuisance and one that contributes to religious violence and social and political unrest, and it often faces expulsion. In Taiwan few people now enter the country illegally (although some overstay their visas), as foreign nationals can enter easily to work and businesses can readily find documented workers.

Unlike other migrants discussed above, refugees are involuntary migrants who have been forced out of their homes for a number of reasons. Countries accept these immigrants for humanitarian reasons and usually have programs and services in place to ease the initial resettlement process. Countries that have signed the 1951 UN Convention and its 1967 Protocol are obligated to accept and house refugees and to provide asylees a good-faith review of their applications for asylum. The translation of this obligation varies somewhat among nations. Most nations recognize that refugees will have substantial needs and will be dependent of the state for a period of time and settlement, or resettlement, policies and programs attempt to meet basic requirements and help refugees become self-sufficient.

All countries, barring Brazil, China, Taiwan, and Thailand indicate the presence of refugees. Of the remaining countries, all but India and Pakistan have signed the United Nations Convention on Refugees, nevertheless, both countries have large refugee populations. When natives of receiving countries, themselves, experience extreme poverty, as in Nigeria, India, and Pakistan, policies toward refugees are either ambivalent or vacillating. Expectations of refugees to Nigeria were high, but they found that both their reception and the opportunities available to them were meager. As it has not signed the United Nations Convention, Pakistan's immigration policy defines refugees as undocumented immigrants and repatriates them, however, large UN-run refugee camps in Pakistan house thousands of refugees. Despite its failure to sign the Convention, India maintains its history of providing asylum, providing shelter through its own resources, however, the ambivalence toward them and ambiguity in laws, politics, and ethical responsibility is also evident. Some nations may evidence the shades of a colonial model of a two-tier system of governance. The chapter on Egypt refers to the absence of benefits for refugees, no free education for refugees, and no free schooling for their children, while Egyptian children have free education through high school. The most dilapidated living quarters are provided for refugee families. The UK does not provide equal opportunity for education of children of refugees. In Sweden, there is a tendency to "clientize" refugees. However, most developed countries, for example Australia, the United States, and Canada, provide access to housing, health, language education, and skill development programs and include financial assistance for the family for a circumscribed period of time. They recognize that refugees, particularly in the early years, receive more in governmental subsidies than they offer the community.

Perceptions and treatment of asylees is much more restrained, and applications appear to be suspect, particularly if at the time of application the asylee does not have papers (such as a visitor's visa) to be in the country legally. Furthermore, national origins may significantly impact response to asylees as in Australia, when a disproportionate number of asylees in 2002 came from Afghanistan, Iran, and Iraq, nations that are portrayed as housing terrorists. Children were also held in detention centers reflecting suspicion about their presence. The Sangatte reception center, established by the Red Cross for refugees who cross the North Sea channel between France and the UK was closed in 2002, and the asylum law in France was reformed with the introduction of the concept of safe third countries to prevent applications for asylum in multiple nations. Asylum seekers are often kept in closed facilities until a decision is made regarding their adjudication. The UK, United States, and Australia indicate that they are closely scrutinized and measures used on them, including detention conditions, may be harsh and punitive.

Based on political discussions, labor needs, and ethical considerations, definitions of immigrants, legal labor migrants, and undocumented immigrants may become blurred or require redefinition. This is reflected in the chapters on France, Greece, Poland, Portugal, Spain, and Sweden. However, immigrant status in all countries is, at the same time, a source of the perception of the immigrant as well as reflective of those perceptions. Legal status, coupled with perceived and transferable human resources, is more likely to result in greater immigrant acceptance than is illegal status or dependency.

Migration Trends and Immigration Policies

A number of countries in the nineteenth and the first several decades of the twentieth century saw the migration predominantly of Europeans.

Among the countries to which they immigrated were Africa, as well as Australia, Brazil, Canada, France, and New Zealand. During this period, other countries such as Greece, India, Ireland, Poland, Spain, Sweden were sending countries, or countries of emigration. Historically, countries composed of immigrants include Egypt, Israel, Pakistan, and the United States, while some nations were so closed that there was relatively little cross-border movement. These included China and Taiwan. Among African nations, cross-national migration was commonplace, as was internal migration in the former Union of the Soviet Socialist Republic. All immigrant countries indicate that undocumented or irregular immigrants are numerous, while all, except China and Taiwan, speak to the presence of refugees. Almost all countries report the entry of migrant labor. While most of the developed countries indicate that individuals from other nations provide both high-skilled labor and unskilled or low-skill labor. Countries of the Global South, on the other hand, report a greater entry of unskilled laborers.

Underlying all chapter studies, the reasons for migration are regarded as being complex and reflecting the interplay of political and/or economic difficulties in the home country coupled with economic opportunities, family networks, and immigration policies in the destination country. All the chapters address immigration policies to regulate the inflow of migrants; all the countries studied recognize the inevitability of immigration, while several seek to actively recruit, but regulate the entry of, newcomers.

Nations with declining populations and those seeking foreign experts or unskilled migrant labor have immigration policies that attract immigrants but attempt to control the profile of entrants to meet their needs. Australia, Canada, and New Zealand have developed a "points system" that allocates points to particular entry criteria (i.e., skills needed in the host country, family network, education level, language competence, etc.) and those meeting the cutoff are eligible for admission (World Bank, 2006). Others have sought to actively recruit skilled (or unskilled labor) by providing temporary work visas (for periods of 3–6 years). China, Ireland, Poland, Sweden, Taiwan, the UK, and the United

States provide such visas, however, constraints require that immigrants arrive with a commitment for a particular job. While some nations may not strongly recruit workers, they have policies that facilitate the entry for particular jobs (i.e., Taiwan and Thailand). The "brain drain," long known as the occurrence when educated, trained, and skilled people, who could benefit their own countries, move to developed nations, is now recognized as the "brain gain" for the latter, dramatically benefiting receiving countries. However, sufficient evidence shows that in this global economy, with easy communication and interconnectedness, the high rates of remittances sent to the home country, the homeland can also benefit by the exodus of skilled workers. Increasingly, with improved economic conditions in traditionally sending countries (such as China, India, and Korea), nationals of developed countries are migrating to these nations, resulting in a "reverse brain drain."

Economic Implications

The impact of the assets newcomers bring to a country versus the drains they place on the infrastructure is a matter of debate in many countries, and countries in this collection of readings represent differing views of the costs and benefits of immigration in the twenty-first century.

In the chapter on Sweden, Bevelander posits that in regard to the negative economic impact of migration, economic crises in the Swedish economy in the 1990s, the decline of the industry sector in the economy and the rise of the service sector with lower paid jobs, and an increasing demand for entry of asylees, increased unemployment rates in Sweden, in which immigrants were represented at a higher rate than natives. In recent years, the total unemployment rate for both immigrants and natives has declined more than in other OECD countries. Michalowski writing on France reports a similar finding that the unemployment rate among immigrants is three times that of the native population. Such situations place a higher burden on unemployment benefits and the welfare system.

Many chapters in this collection, however, provide considerable evidence that the net result of immigration is a benefit to the receiving country. In the chapter on Australia, Gray, Agllias,

and Lee give a good summary of the benefits of immigration. They argue that with the typical demographics of a developed country, namely, lower birth rates and increasing longevity resulting in an older population, one of the benefits of immigration is that the population is increased without the need for investment in education as would be necessary if the birth rate increased. A further benefit in terms of the effect of immigrants on the demographics of countries with developed economies is that they balance the worker to retiree ratio in the population, thus contributing to the efficacy of state pension programs. In the case of undocumented immigrants, many contribute to programs from which they will never benefit because of more restrictive welfare policies for immigrants. Immigrants arrive in the host country at the most productive times in their lives and so there is immediate benefit to the labor force. Additionally, Gray, Agllias, and Lee in the Australia chapter indicate that overall there are tax benefits for the country in that taxes paid amount to more than welfare benefits claimed by immigrant populations. An additional benefit of immigration is that since most immigrants settle in urban areas, this pushes up the price of property and therefore establishes Australians benefit from capital gains. Several chapters (Ireland, Israel, France, Greece, Ireland, Israel, South Africa, Thailand, Spain, Taiwan) report that immigrant labor is cheap and immigrants are often exploited by unscrupulous employers. Immigrants are willing to do work that indigenous citizens do not wish to do because of the hard and dirty condition of the jobs. Although this may result in keeping down wage levels for everyone, it also has the benefit that prices are contained and thus the cost of living is contained also. Frequently, immigrant workers will undertake jobs below their qualification level, and sometimes these new roles involve a gender role reversal such as that observed in Israel, where many cleaners in private homes are immigrant males. These views are supported by a number of researchers, such as Borjas (2001), who suggests that net gains through immigration contribution may be significant, because many immigrants work for lower wages than natives, and thus immigration shifts several billions of dollars each year to employers.

Table 30-1. Immigration Policy Institute Studies

State	Research by:	Date of study	Fiscal impact of immigrant population***
Arizona	University of Arizona Udall Center for Studies in Public Policy	2007	+ $940 million
Arkansas	Urban Institute	2007	+ S2.9 billion
Florida	Florida International University	2007	+$10.99 billion
Nevada	Progressive Leadership Alliance of Nevada	2007	+$4.2 billion
New York	Fiscal Policy Institute	2007	+$229 billion
Washington, DC	Urban Institute	2006	+$9.8 billion
Studies of Undocumented Immigrants			
Iowa	Iowa Policy Project	2007	+$90–139.8 million
Oregon	Oregon Center for Public Policy	2007	+$ 134–$187 million
Texas	Texas State Comptroller	2006	+$17.7 billion
Chicago	University of Chicago Center for Urban Economic Development	2002	+$5.45 billion

***Fiscal impact is measured variously in these studies from measures of taxes paid to economic output.
Source: Adapted from *Assessing the Impact of Immigration at the State and Federal Level.* Immigration Policy Center, A Division of the American Law Foundation 2008. http://immigration.server263.com/images/File/factcheck/State%20and%20Local%20Study%20Survey%20FINAL%201-15-08.pdf.

The Immigration Policy Institute has reviewed studies relating to the fiscal impact of immigrants in the United States. While these studies are limited to the United States, the consistency of outcomes despite differing researchers and measures, illustrates that on balance there seems to be greater benefits for a host country than costs. This is a consistent message from numerous chapters in this collection and from research and has a far reaching impact on immigration policies. A United Nations (2003) study indicated that more than one-third of countries worldwide reported that they want to lower immigration levels, and less than five percent want to raise them. Table 30-1 summarizes the studies reviewed by the Immigration Policy Institute:

On the positive side for developed countries is the view that skilled labor arrives to enhance its own opportunities, bringing with it a variety of capabilities that can benefit the receiving country, particularly when those on student visas apply for permanent residence. International competition for skilled labor is evident in policy discussions on qualifications for admission to the United States, where currently the majority of immigrants enter for family reunification purposes. Countries such as the United Kingdom,

Canada, and Australia admit highly skilled immigrants according to a points system based on education, skills, and language proficiency (Murphy, 2006). The health systems of the developed world benefit from doctors trained in developing countries that fill more than one in five positions in developed nations.

One question that recently received heightened attention from lawmakers is whether or not immigrants should be admitted to the United States less on the basis of family ties and more on the basis of the skills they can contribute to the U.S. economy. Today, the most common way permanent immigrants enter the United States legally is through sponsorship by a family member already in the country. By contrast, nations such as Canada, Australia, and the United Kingdom admit immigrants primarily for employment reasons, based on a point system. Points are assigned on the basis of educational level, professional skills, proficiency in the host country's language, and other qualities that increase immigrants' likelihood of integrating into the host country's labor market.

What is clear from many of the chapters in this current collection of readings on different countries, is that information about the benefits of immigration is not widely publicized from an evidence based perspective, but that political positions are often framed and maintained by the media in inflammatory and discriminatory terms. It is clear that the level of public debate in many countries is not well informed, and therein lie objectives and goals for policy analysts and policy makers.

Host Country and Social Capital

Several immigrant policies are instrumental in determining how well human capital is nurtured and developed. The readiness of a receiving country to accept immigrants in general, or an immigrant group in particular is, itself, a complex matter. When immigration is viewed as inextricably bound to a nation's political, economic, and social well-being as well as its future security interests, it is likely to be welcomed. Nevertheless, immigration policies of many countries are temporal, reflecting what is believed to be of benefit at a particular moment. Nations also fulfill international agreements in the resettlement or provision of asylum to large numbers of refugees, to facilitate government action, and for humanitarian reasons. Policies that allow immigration are coupled with those that permit the expulsion or deportation of foreign nationals.

Social capital, "the internal social and cultural coherence of society, the norms and values that govern interactions among people and the institutions in which they are embedded" (Serageldin, 1999: i), is essential in ensuring that opportunities within a nation are strong and viable. It is a necessity in the creation of human capital (Coleman, 1988) and immigrants' adjustment is often linked to the social capital available to them. Social capital is a necessity for successful immigrant settlement.

Particularly for immigrants arriving with limited human capital, the implementation of sustainable development projects can ensure that immigrants receive the social and economic tools to succeed in their new countries. In addition to providing new arrivals with economic subsidies, housing and health care, community-based educational programs and training can provide the components for new immigrants to move away from dependency on society's support programs (Lobo & Mayadas, 1997). Hence, knowledge about prevention of disease, ability to

function through society's institutional structures, and earning capacity in the legitimate economy of the country will enhance the likelihood of self-sufficiency. Social and mental health services that recognize difficulties associated with the immigration experience can assist immigrants in their adjustment to the receiving country. Resistance, communication barriers, personal and family background, and ethnic community identity (Lum, 2004) are exacerbated by the experience of many immigrants and refugees, who closely guard information because of fear (perhaps unfounded) of exposure, past experience with oppression, and mistrust of authority.

Some nations indicate a purposeful process to integrate or accommodate newcomers, however, the process itself may differ depending on the immigration status of the newcomers or the region of their origins. Most nations that admit refugees have some resettlement services and programs (African countries, Australia, Canada, France, United States), yet the services may be different for them than it is for natives.

Australia provides social and economic services for new arrivals and, in France, legal newcomers receive a reception program. Further, in France, both legal and illegal immigrants receive the same educational benefits, while in the United States, children of irregular immigrants do not have access to higher education. In Ireland, Portugal, and Thailand, immigrants are integrated into the health, education, and welfare systems, while in South Africa, perceptions are that services should not be extended to migrants. The United States allows limited access to health and welfare benefits in the early years after voluntary migration and there are constraints on access for illegal immigrants.

What is recommended is a shift in the paradigm of immigration policies from the old residual approaches to an investment and asset based approach. If host countries could recognize the human capital potential of immigrants and invest in new arrivals in the early stages, immigrants' transition from recipient to creator of resources may be accelerated.

Conclusion

In a project such as this the expectation is that in the twenty-first century, receiving nations will capitalize on immigration and enhance its utility as a benefit, given the inevitability of human migration, the globalization of the world, and the natural progression of international and foreign policies. While any discussion of immigration will point to the costs as well as the gains, the net result of immigration for a nation should be positive. The case studies in this book emphasize not only the unavoidability of immigration but the tangible and intangible exchanges between countries, peoples, and cultures. A major issue emerging from this project is that of public attitudes to immigration in the developed world. Natives fear the dilution of the culture, race, and access to jobs. One may posit that with the increase of communication, ease of transportation, and the sharing of information, the world may be moving toward a global culture, and perhaps a global race. Thus, the fear of the dilution of culture and race could well be valid. On the other hand, the chapters in this book and the extant literature suggest that while immigrants do take jobs, the net result is, in general, not a replacement of natives. Frequently, the jobs they take are those that natives are unable or unwilling to fill.

Discriminatory policies and concerns that jobs of residents will be taken prevail in many receiving countries. However, there is a need for recognition that with the decline and/or limited growth of populations in developed nations, the consequent labor force shortage can be filled in the short term only by immigrant labor. Countries must view immigrants as social capital, rather than drains on the economy or as those who draw jobs away from native-born citizens. Overall, there is a need for greater awareness on the part of host nations, both in the developed and the emerging economies, that immigrants constitute essential social capital. The entry of immigrants results in a universally winning situation: (1) host countries benefit by filling their labor (both skilled and unskilled) shortages; (2) immigrants benefit by improving their opportunities and enhancing their quality of life; and (3) the sending nations' economies benefit from the substantial remittances sent home by their émigrés. There is a need for receiving countries and their residents to understand that immigration may be a necessity for their long-term survival. In tandem with the development of policies that allow the smooth

integration of immigrants, governmental programs should undertake public awareness programs that educate both policy makers and the general public not only of the benefits of immigration but its essential nature.

The chapters further suggest that, on balance, even if immigrants and refugees are dependent on governmental subsidies early in their residency they soon become self-sufficient contributors to the host country, oftentimes employing natives in their businesses. In recognition of this, aims of governmental and nonprofit organizations may be to provide the tools to expedite this independence. Hence, social policy may be changed to a human investment approach. This will enable less skilled immigrants to build sustainable lives with the help of investment to build assets in the early stages of the settlement process (Sherraden, 2005; McKernan & Sherraden, 2007).

All nations report the presence of undocumented or irregular immigrants. Their presence poses a tremendous dilemma for host countries: They are necessary for the functioning of the economy, yet they are in the country without the requisite authorization. Perhaps the more attempts there are to open and equalize opportunities to enter a country where jobs are plentiful, such as in Taiwan, the less likelihood there may be for illegal access. The most frequent illegal modes of entry, illegal border crossings and human trafficking, are often dangerous. Often human rights are violated as immigrants resort to a variety of means of entering a country more affluent than their own. Governments should make attempts to recognize the human rights of irregular migrants, and provisions may involve negotiations between the sending and the receiving countries. Increasing globalization may support the possibility of such practical investments in the sending country that they will benefit the host country while creating opportunities for those who may otherwise immigrate illegally.

If guidelines that drive immigration policies are based on the belief that immigration is a benefit, receiving nations may nurture the human capital of immigrants to enhance their contributions. Furthermore, social capital enhances human capital, so government should encourage family reunification and settlement where there are communities of people of similar origins. Furthermore, nations that accept large numbers of refugees, and/or those that provide amnesty or a path to citizenship for undocumented/irregular immigrants, are viewed as being humanitarian with altruistic reasons for accepting these newcomers. While this may, indeed, be true, it is not only altruism that underpins these policies; they have deep rooted and far reaching economic and sociopolitical implications. However, there are no easy answers, for immigration, as all other phenomena, must be regulated. Each nation has to assess its economic needs and its standing in the global sociopolitical arena.

Underlying difficulties in understanding immigrants and refugees is a far reaching xenophobia—both of the immigrants and by them. It is difficult to assess who should be responsible for crossing this bridge—is it the host or is it the self-invited newcomer? Should the host country accommodate immigrants and refugees or should immigrants and refugees adapt to the host country? Host countries have policies that allow the entry of several thousand immigrants annually and, often, several thousand more refugees. Therefore, should the country not attempt to accommodate them? Immigrants must make application to enter a country. Hence, they are here voluntarily. Should they not make attempts to adjust? With whom does the responsibility lie?

For any immigrant community, it is a long road from its country of origin. The physical distance may be great, but the social, psychological, and emotional distance of immigrant travel is always greater. Nevertheless, the human condition and its similarities bind peoples together to a much greater extent than one tends to accept, regardless of social norms, culture, religion, or language. With increasing international travel and communication, immigration will continue to grow. As these chapters reveal, immigrants are bringing a plurality of cultures to host countries. Delgado, Jones, & Rohani (2005) note that a common discussion in policies toward immigrants, whether they are immigration or immigrant policies, is either how to keep them out of the country (regulate them) or assimilate them into the prevailing structure of the host nation. Little consistent discourse revolves around developing a path to mutual learning or recognition that immigrants may be able to offer the host country more than their job-related skills.

As immigrants adapt to life in their new homeland, they bring with them a diversity of cultures and norms. As the host country influences these newcomers, it is influenced by their social norms, family patterns, art, music, dance, cuisine, and businesses. They expose native-born citizens to alternative modes of behavior and social relationships, differences in religions, perceptions and interpretations, and variations in experiences and observations. They may challenge traditional norms and require that natives reassess or defend them. It is clear, further, that immigrants affect the local economy; however, it is essential that one evaluate the larger impact immigrants have on host nations. The tendency of theoreticians to focus merely on immigrants' adaptation provides only a partial picture (Orum, 2005).

The Global Commission on International Migration (GCIM) was a body of the United Nations, appointed by the Secretary-General and sitting for two years from 2003 to 2005. It consisted of representatives from 19 countries and was given the mandate to provide a global policy response to the immediacy of problems arising out of global immigration. Among other outcomes of the Commission, its report, published in 2005, proposes six principles for action (GCIM, 2005). These principles are reported from Annex One of the GCIM report in Appendix I of this collection of readings. The GCIM in formulating its principles aimed to maintain a balance between the human rights of migrants, asylees, and refugees without violating the sovereign rights of governments to administer their own immigration policies. The Commission recognizes the right of all humans to achieve their potential in either country of origin or in the global labor market without fear of punitive consequences. It further recognizes the positive impact of an open labor market system on poverty reduction and development in both countries of origin and adoption. The GCIM proposes that international migration should be made an integral part of strategies for global development.

The recommendations of the GCIM are sensitive to the rights of sovereign states and expects government actions to be consistent with human rights whether working on integration or repatriation of migrants. The Commission further proposes that the diversity brought by immigrants into the sociocultural climate of a nation should be recognized and valued and that immigrants receive status equity with native citizens.

The Commission recommended interstate cooperation in handling cases of irregular migration. Finally the GCIM recommended that human migration in all its forms be recognized as a natural process in the interests of world wide development, (economic, political, sociocultural, and human), alongside the human rights of migrants and the sovereignty of nation-states.

While the principles expressed in this report serve as a good policy goal for nations involved in global migration, the report lacks sufficient detail about how to implement these values. The recognition of both human rights and sovereignty is good, but there is insufficient assistance for policy planners on the recognition that these are conflictual values.

Closing Thoughts

In his defense of the welfare state, Titmuss (1958), sometimes called the "Father of Social Policy," asked "should the costs of social progress be allowed to lie where they fall?" We may very well ask a similar question on a global scale in relation to human migration: should the privileges and economic advantages of the industrialized nations be available only by accident of birth? It may be argued further that the wealth of the Western world has been achieved through continuing exploitation of the resources of developing countries. Should there be open borders and freedom of movement on a global scale in the twenty-first century or will the rich nations become fortresses? The latter is not inconceivable: some already advocate building a new Berlin type wall on the Southwestern border of the United States. Would liberalizing immigration controls create a global redistribution of wealth? The way forward is yet by no means clear. However, the principles of the GCIM are a step toward that direction. How far these may be implemented by the receiving nations remains to be seen.

References

Asian Development Bank. (2005). *Brain drain versus brain gain: The study of remittances in Southeast Asia and promoting knowledge exchange through Diasporas.* Fourth Coordination Meeting on International Migration, New York: U.N. Secretariat. Retrieved March 9, 2008, from http://www.un.org/esa/population/meetings/fourthcoord2005/P13_ADB.pdf.

Borjas, G. (2001). *Heaven's door.* Princeton, NJ: Princeton University Press.

Castles, S. (1997, June 16). *Globalisation and migration. Some pressing contradictions.* Keynote address presented at the UNESCO-MOST Intergovernmental Council, Paris. Retrieved February 14, 2005, from http://www.unesco.org/most/igc97 cas.htm.

Cohen, R. (1995) Prologue, chapter one. In: Cohen, R., (ed.) *The Cambridge Survey of World Migration.* Cambridge, UK: Cambridge University Press.

Coleman, J. S. (1988). Social capital in the creation of human capital. *American Journal of Sociology,* 94(supplement), S95–S120.

Delgado, M., Jones, K., & Rohani, M. (2005). *Social work practice with refugee and immigrant youth in the United States.* Boston: Pearson.

DeTrani, J. R. (2005). The North Korean Human Rights Act: Issues and implementation; Statements to the House Committee on International Relations, Subcommittee on Asia and the Pacific and Subcommittee on Africa, Global Human Rights, and International Operations. Washington, DC. Retrieved March 9, 2008, from http://www.state.gov/g/prm/rls/45792.htm.

Dobelstein, A. W. (1990). *Social welfare: Policy and analysis.* Chicago: Nelson Hall.

Gil, D. G. (1992, 5th ed). *Unraveling social policy.* Rochester, NY: Schenkman Books.

GCIM (2005). *Migration in an interconnected world: New directions for action.* Report of the Global Commission on International Migration, Switzerland. Retrieved March 9, 2008, from: www.gcim.org.

Goldthorpe, J. H. (1997). Current issues in comparative macrosociology: A debate on methodological issues. *Comparative Social Research,* 16, pp. 1–26.

Hayter, T. (2004). *Open borders: The case against immigration controls.* Sidmouth, UK: Pluto Press.

Immigration Policy Center (2008). *Assessing the impact of immigration at the state and federal level.* Immigration Policy Center, a Division of the American Law Foundation. Washington, DC. Retrieved from http://immigration.server263.com/images/File/factcheck/State%20and%20Local%20Study%20Survey%20FINAL%201-15-08.pdf Downloaded 3/5/08 Contact Michele Waslin, mwaslin@ailf.org.

Leeming, M. (2005). *Sociological theory: A social science approach to the family.* Retrieved March 9, 2008, from http://www.stolaf.edu/people/leming/soc371res/theory.html.

Lobo, M., & Mayadas, N. S. (1997). International social work practice: A refugee perspective. In: Mayadas, N. S. , Watts, T. D. , & Elliott, D. (eds.) *International Handbook on Social Work Theory and Practice*. Westport, CT: Greenwood Press, pp. 411–428.

Lum, D. (2004). Cultural competence, practice stages, client intersectional systems, and case studies. In Lum, D. (ed.) *Cultural Competence, Practice Stages, and Client Systems*. Brooks/Cole, pp. 1–31.

Karger, H. J., & Stoesz, D. (2006). *American Social Welfare Policy: A Pluralist Approach*. Boston: Pearson.

Massey, D. S. (1999). Why does immigration occur? A theoretical synthesis. In: Hirschman, C., Kasinitz, P., & DeWind, J. *The Handbook of International Migration: The American Experience* (ch. 2). New York: Russell Sage Foundation.

Murphy, K. (2006). Attracting the best and the brightest: The promise and pitfalls of a skill-based immigration policy. *Immigration Policy in Focus, 10*(5). Immigration Policy Center. Washington, DC. Retrieved March 8, 2008, from http://immigration.server263.com/images/File/infocus/Best%20&%20Brightest%20v5i10%20PR.pdf.

Levi-Faur, D. (2005). Comparative methods in political and social research. Retrieved October 15, 2005, from http://poli.haifa.ac.il/~levi/method.html.

McKernan, S. M., & Sherraden, M. (eds.) (2007). *Poor finances: Asset accumulation in low-income households*. Washington, DC: Urban Institute Press.

Orum, A. (2005). Circles of influence and chains of command: The social processes whereby ethnic communities influence host societies. *Social Forces, 84*(2), 921–939.

Özden, C., & Schiff, M. (eds.) (2006). *International migration, remittances, and the brain drain*, Washington, DC: The World Bank & Palgrave Macmillan.

Pessar, P. R., (1999). The role of gender, households, and social networks in the migration process: A review and appraisal. In: Hirschman, C., Kasinitz, P., & DeWind, J., *The Handbook of International Migration: The American experience* (ch. 3). New York: Russell Sage Foundation.

Portes, A. (1999). Immigration theory for a new century: Some problems and opportunities. In: Hirschman, C., Kasinitz, P., & DeWind, J., *The Handbook of International Migration: The American Experience* (ch. 1). New York: Russell Sage Foundation.

Rempel, T. M. (2006). Who are Palestinian refugees? *Forced Migration Review, 26*, 5–8. Retrieved June 13, 2007, from http://www.fmreview.org/FMRpdfs/FMR26/FMR26full.pdf.

Rose, R. (1991). Comparing forms of comparative analysis. *Political Studies, 39*, 446–462.

Sanderson, S. K. (1995). *Sociological worlds*. Los Angeles: Roxbury Publishing.

Sandell, R. (2007). Immigration: World differences (ARI). Madrid: Fundación Real Instituto Elcano. Retrieved June 10, 2007, from http://www.real institutoelcano.org/analisis/1121.asp.

Schiff, M., & Özden., C. (eds.) (2007). *International migration, economic development, & policy*. World Bank and Palgrave Macmillan.

Schiller, N. G. (1999). Transmigrants and nation states: Something old and something new in the U.S. immigrant experience. In: Hirschman, C., Kasinitz, P., & DeWind, J., *The Handbook of International Migration: The American Experience* (ch. 5). New York: Russell Sage Foundation.

Serageldin, I. (1999). Foreword. In: Feldman, T. R., & Assaf, S. (eds.) *Social Capital: Conceptual Frameworks and Empirical Evidence* (working paper #5). Social Capital Initiative, The World Bank.

Segal, E. A., & Brzuzy, S. (1998). *Social welfare policy, programs, and practice*. Itasca, IL: Peacock.

Segal, U. A. (2002). *A framework for immigration: Asians in the United States*. New York: Columbia University Press.

Sherraden, M. (ed.) (2005). *Inclusion in the American dream: Assets, poverty, and public policy*. New York: Oxford University Press.

Suhrke, A. (1995). Refugees and asylum in the Muslim world. In Cohen, R., *The Cambridge Survey of World Migration*. Cambridge, UK: Cambridge University Press.

Tilly, C. (1998). *Durable inequality*. Berkeley: University of California Press.

Titmuss, R. M. (1958). *Essays on the welfare state*. London: Allen & Unwin.

United Nations (2000). *Replacement migration*. Population Division, Department of Economic and Social Affairs, United Nations Secretariat. Retrieved October 15, 2005, from http://www.un.org/esa/population/publications/migration/presseng.htm.

United Nations (2003). *International migration 2002*. Population Division. United Nations Publication (ST/ESA/SER.A/219). Retrieved March 9, 2008, from http://www.un.org/esa/population/publications/ittmig2002/Migration2002.pdf.

United Nations (2004). *World economic and social survey 2004: International migration*. The Department of Economic and Social Affairs of the United Nations Secretariat. New York: United Nations Publication Sales No. E.04.II.C.3. Retrieved March 9, 2008, from http://www.un.org/esa/policy/wess/wess2004files/part2web/preface.pdf.

United Nations (2005a). *2004 world survey on the role of women in development: Women and international migration.* Department of Economic and Social Affairs of the United Nations Secretariat, Division for the Advancement of Women. New York: United Nations Publication Sales No. E.04.IV.4.

United Nations (2005). International migration and development: Report of the Secretary-General. New York: United Nations. Agenda Item 54(c).

UNHCR (2005). *Basic facts: Refugees by numbers 2005.* United Nations High Commissioner for Refugees. Retrieved October 8, 2005, from http://www.unhcr.ch/cgi-bin/texis/vtx/basics/opendoc.htm?tbl=BASICS&id=3b028097c.

U.S. Bureau of the Census (2004). *Global population at a glance 2002 and beyond.* U.S. Department of Commerce, Economics, and Statistics Administration; U.S. Census Bureau. Retrieved October 7, 2005, from http://www.census.gov/ipc/prod/wp02/wp02-1.pdf.

Weber, A. M. (2004, February 23). Reverse brain drain threatens U.S. economy. *USA Today.* Retrieved October 7, 2006, from http://www.usatoday.com/news/opinion/editorials/2004-02-23-economy-edit_x.htm.

World Bank. 2006. *Global Economic Prospects 2006: Economic Implications of Remittances and Migration.* Washington, DC.

Yang, D. (2006). Mass migration: A worldwide phenomenon. *Analysis Online.* Retrieved June 9, 2007, from http://analysisonline.org/immigration/yang.html.

Zolberg, A. R. (1999). Matters of state: Theorizing immigration policy. In: Hirschman, C., Kasinitz, P., & DeWind, J., *The Handbook of International Migration: The American Experience* (ch. 4). New York: Russell Sage Foundation.

Appendix

Report of the Global Commission on International Migration

Principles for Action

I. Migrating out of choice: Migration and the global economy
Women, men and children should be able to realize their potential, meet their needs, exercise their human rights and fulfill their aspirations in their country of origin, and hence migrate out of choice, rather than necessity. Those women and men who migrate and enter the global labour market should be able to do so in a safe and authorized manner, and because they and their skills are valued and needed by the states and societies that receive them.

II. Reinforcing economic and developmental impact
The role that migrants play in promoting development and poverty reduction in countries of origin, as well as the contribution they make towards the prosperity of destination countries, should be recognized and reinforced. International migration should become an integral part of national, regional and global strategies for economic growth, in both the developing and developed world.

III. Addressing irregular migration
States, exercising their sovereign right to determine who enters and remains on their territory, should fulfill their responsibility and obligation to protect the rights of migrants and to re-admit those citizens who wish or who are obliged to return to their country of origin. In stemming irregular migration, states should actively cooperate with

one another, ensuring that their efforts do not jeopardize human rights, including the right of refugees to seek asylum. Governments should consult with employers, trade unions and civil society on this issue.

IV. Strengthening social cohesion through integration
Migrants and citizens of destination countries should respect their legal obligations and benefit from a mutual process of adaptation and integration that accommodates cultural diversity and fosters social cohesion. The integration process should be actively supported by local and national authorities, employers and members of civil society, and should be based on a commitment to non-discrimination and gender equity. It should also be informed by an objective public, political and media discourse on international migration.

V. Protecting the rights of migrants
The legal and normative framework affecting international migrants should be strengthened, implemented more effectively and applied in a non-discriminatory manner, so as to protect the human rights and labour standards that should be enjoyed by all migrant women and men. Respecting the provisions of this legal and normative framework, states and other stakeholders must address migration issues in a more consistent and coherent manner.

VI. Enhancing governance: Coherence, capacity and cooperation
The governance of international migration should be enhanced by improved coherence and strengthened capacity at the national level; greater consultation

and cooperation between states at the regional level, and more effective dialogue and cooperation among governments and between international organizations at the global level. Such efforts must be based on a better appreciation of the close linkages that exist between international migration and development and other key policy issues, including trade, aid, state security, human security and human rights.

Source: Report of the Global Commission on International Migration (GCIM 2005) Annex One, Page 4.

Index